ENCYCLOPEDIA OF

BUSINE$$
AND
FINANCE

Editorial Board

ENCYCLOPEDIA OF

BUSINE$$
AND
FINANCE

VOLUME 1

BURTON S. KALISKI,
Editor-in-Chief

Macmillan Reference USA
an imprint of the Gale Group
New York • Detroit • San Francisco • London • Boston • Woodbridge, CT

Encyclopedia of Business and Finance

Macmillan Reference USA
An imprint of the Gale Group
27500 Drake Rd.
Farmington Hills, MI 48331-3535

Macmillan Reference USA
An imprint of the Gale Group
1633 Broadway
New York, NY 10019

Library of Congress Catalog Card No.: 00-107932

Printing number
2   3   4   5   6   7   8   9   10

ISBN 0-02-865065-4 (set).—ISBN 0-02-865066-2 (v. 1).—ISBN 0-02-865067-0 (v. 2)

Printed in the United States of America by the Gale Group

Gale Group and Design is a trademark used herein under license.

Contents

Editorial and Production Staff

Preface

Business is the backbone of American society and is one of the keys to making our system work as well as it has for more than two hundred years. Yet as a body of knowledge, business is much younger. There has been, to this point, no organized work that has attempted to present the discipline of business in a single place. The major purpose of the *Encyclopedia of Business and Finance* is to summarize the body of knowledge that we know as business in a single place and in language accessible to the layperson.

This two-volume collection of more than three hundred entries presents a wealth of information about the major functional areas of business: accounting, economics, finance, information systems, law, management, and marketing. The articles vary in length and in depth, in bibliographic support, and in writing style. Thus, the reader will encounter a variety of approaches and discern a number of perspectives about business. Some articles are quantitative, since some aspects of business are numerically based. Other articles tend more toward the qualitative, to accommodate the more descriptive aspects of business. Some of the articles present a historical perspective, incorporating long-proven knowledge, while others focus more on current concepts and newer data. All entries have the same goal: to provide useful knowledge about the business and financial world.

Because of their importance, we have given special treatment to two topics: careers and ethics. In each case, a lead entry is followed by an article about that topic in each of the functional areas of business. Thus, there are articles about careers in accounting, economics, finance, information systems, law, management, and marketing, as well as a similar series of articles for ethics.

There is also a strong emphasis on organizations in the field of business and government. Wherever an organization is discussed, the article provides a Web site for further information. Relevant federal legislation is also featured in this work. All acts that have had a major impact on business are included in the Encyclopedia.

The entries are arranged in the usual alphabetical order, with extensive cross-referencing of three types. First, there are "See" references, referring the reader to an entry by another name. For example, under Bait and Switch Advertising one finds the line "See Advertising." The second type of cross-referencing is the "See Also" reference. At the conclusion of the article on Insurance, for example, one reads "See Also Personal Financial Planning." The third type of cross-referencing is the Related Articles listing. At the conclusion of most articles, there is a list of other articles that may shed more light on the topic just discussed.

Is the knowledge contained in this work the definitive and final word on each topic? The answer is "most certainly not." In this day and age of dynamic and rapidly growing knowledge, a positive answer would be quite inappropriate. However, this is not necessarily a negative. The information contained in this Encyclopedia is valid and reliable and enables readers to do further research by going easily accessible sources. Today's technological environment thus offers a unique opportunity that was not available to previous generations: to extend one's knowledge on every topic presented.

This work was designed for different types of users. The middle school student may be looking for a starting point for a paper on careers. The high school student may be seeking background on a major research topic, such as the corporate form of organization. The businessperson may be seeking a summary of antitrust laws. The business teacher may be preparing a lesson on the history of computers. The interested layperson may simply want to learn about something new, such as government accounting standards or matrix organization.

The *Encyclopedia of Business and Finance* can serve as a survey document for the many aspects of business or as a guide to those aspects. It can be the beginning point of lengthy secondary research, the background for primary research, or the ending point for research on a specific item covered within its pages. It can be used to help ask questions or to find answers. It can be used as a summary of existing knowledge or the basis for acquiring new knowledge.

A number of individuals deserve to be mentioned for their contributions to this project. First, I must thank the five associate editors on this project: Roger Luft, Dorothy Maxwell, Jim Maxwell, Mary Ellen Oliverio, and Allen Truell. Without their tireless efforts at securing contributors of quality, we would have a very small work. Second, great appreciation goes to Elly Dickason, Publisher of Macmillan Reference USA, for her inspiration in conceiving of this project and getting it off the ground. Third, I want to express my indebtedness to Allison Marion, Editor at the Gale Group, for her professional work in keeping this project running to its conclusion. Fourth, I must thank all the contributors for the best efforts that each put forth. Writing for an encyclopedia is not a financially rewarding activity; however, it is a contribution to posterity, so what each contributor has written is of great intangible value to knowledge and to future scholars. Finally, I speak for all of the people involved in what has been a lengthy project when I thank our families for their encouragement and support.

BURTON S. KALISKI

Acknowledgments

The editors wish to thank the copyright holders of the excerpted criticism included in this volume and the permissions managers of many book and magazine publishing companies for assisting us in securing reproduction rights. We are also grateful to the staffs of the Detroit Public Library, the Library of Congress, the University of Detroit Mercy Library, Wayne State University Purdy/Kresge Library Complex, and the University of Michigan Libraries for making their resources available to us. Following is a list of the copyright holders who have granted us permission to reproduce material in this volume of the Encyclopedia of Business and Finance Every effort has been made to trace copyright, but if omissions have been made, please let us know.

PHOTOGRAPHS AND ILLUSTRATIONS APPEARING IN THE ENCYCLOPEDIA OF BUSINESS AND FINANCE WERE RECEIVED FROM THE FOLLOWING SOURCES:

89th Annual Chicago Auto Show (workers put the final touches on displays), photograph. Associated Press/AP. Reproduced by permission.—Ace Hardware logo (displayed outside the St. Louis Convention Center) photograph. Associated Press/AP. Reproduced by permission.—Al Lundberg (left), with Terry Brewer (center) and Al Anderson (right)(talking about the tents that will be used for temporary housing for migrant farm workers), photograph. Associated Press/AP. Reproduced by permis-

sion.—Allen, Tim, photograph. Associated Press/AP. Reproduced by permission.—American Electric Power's Muskingum River Plant, photograph. Associated Press/AP. Reproduced by permission.—Andreas, Michael (standing, arms at sides), Chicago, Illinois, 1998, photograph. AP/Wide World Photos. Reproduced by permission. Associated Press/Ford Motor Company.—Berners-Lee, Tim, photograph. Associated Press/AP. Reproduced by permission.—Billboard displaying a Joe Camel advertisement(Vehicles passing by), photograph. Associated Press/AP. Reproduced by permission.—Billboards along the Palmetto expressway, photograph. Associated Press/AP. Reproduced by permission.—Bush, George (center) signing the Americans with Disabilities Act, Harold Wilke (rear left), Evan Kemp (left), Sandra Parrino, and Justin Dart (right), Jefferson Memorial in the background, photograph. Associated Press/AP. Reproduced by permission.—Bush, President George (standing, center), Mexican President Carlos Salinas Gortari (left), Canadian Prime Minister Brian Mulroney (right), Julie Puche (seated, left), Carla Hills (center), and Michael Wilson (right), photograph. Bettmann/Corbis. Reproduce—Businesswoman tele-commuting to her office (laptop on desk), photograph. Michael Pole/Corbis. Reproduced by permission.—Camdessus, Michel, photograph. AFP/Corbis. Reproduced by permission.—Carlson, Chester (standing with first Xerox copier), photograph. Corbis-Bettmann. Reproduced by permission.—Chicago Cubs logo, photograph. Sandy Felsenthal/Corbis. Reproduced by permission.—Clinton, William Jefferson (announcing a new equal pay initiative for women), photograph. Associated Press/AP. Reproduced by permission.—Clinton, William Jefferson (speaking at podium to America's corporate leaders), photograph. Associated Press/AP. Reproduced by permission.—Construction of the light rail line (connecting downtown Portland with Portland International Airport), photograph. Associated Press/AP. Reproduced by permission.—Consumer labor activists (protesting a meeting of the American Petroleum Institute), photograph. Bettmann/Corbis. Reproduced by permission.—Customers (entering a Target store), photograph. Associated Press/AP. Reproduced by permission.—Deming, Edward, photograph. Bettmann/Corbis. Reproduced by permission.—Demonstrators (carrying signs expressing concern over genetically modified foods), photograph. Associated Press/AP. Reproduced.—Dickman, Donald, photograph. Associated Press/AP. Reproduced by permission.—Dingell, Congressmen John, photograph. Associated Press/AP. Reproduced by permission.—Escalante, Roberto, photograph. Associated Press/AP. Reproduced by permission.—Facade of the New York Stock Exchange, photograph. Corbis Corporation. Reproduced by permission.—Federal Reserve Building, photograph. Lee Snider/Corbis. Reproduced by permission.—Four employees of McCellan's IGA Family Store (standing in an aisle of the supermarket), photograph. Philip Gould/Corbis. Reproduced by permission.—Francis, Robert, photograph. Associated Press/AP. Reproduced by permission.—Friedman, Milton, photograph. Archive Photos, Inc./Camera Press, Ltd. Reproduced by permission.—Gates, Bill, photograph. Associated Press/AP. Reproduced by permission.—Gates, Craig, photograph. Associated Press/AP. Reproduced by permission.—Gilbreth, Lillian Evelyn and Frank Gilbreth (standing together), photograph. Underwood & Underwood/Corbis. Reproduced by permission.—Greenspan, Alan, photograph. Associated Press/AP. Reproduced by

permission.—Group of inner city youths (holding signs and protesting outside Nike Town store, New York), photograph. Associated Press/AP. Reproduced by permission.—Group of people watching girl with hula hoop. Public Domain.—Hill, Anita (seated, testifying, wearing light dress), Washington D.C., 1991, photograph. AP/Wide World Photos. Reproduced by permission.—Hollerith, Herman, photograph. Bettmann/Corbis. Reproduced by permission.—Hollerith tabulator and sorter, photograph. Hulton-Deutsch Collection/Corbis. Reproduced by permission.—IBM Personal Computer AT, photograph. Bettmann/Corbis. Reproduced by permission.—Inslee, Jay, photograph. Associated Press/AP. Reproduced by permission.—Japanese businessman (pointing at an electronic stock board on which most of the share prices are blinking "plus" signals), photograph. Associated Press/AP. Reproduced by permission.—Japanese worker (taking inventory of Toyota trucks and minivans for export at the Yokohama port), photograph. Associated Press/AP. Reproduced by permission.—Johnson, Lyndon Baines, photograph. Bettmann/Corbis. Reproduced by permission.—Johnson, Lyndon Baines (seated, turned toward the people behind him), photograph. Bettmann/Corbis. Reproduced by permission.—Kennedy, Joseph P., photograph. Bettmann/Corbis. Reproduced by permission.—Keynes, John Maynard (seated), photograph. UPI/Corbis-Bettmann. Reproduced by permission.—Man (scooping rice out of a gigantic pan), photograph. James Marshall/Corbis. Reproduced by permission.—Marx, Karl, photograph. Archive Photos. Reproduced by permission.—Maslow, Abraham (wearing crew neck sweater over checked shirt), photograph. UPI/Corbis Bettmann. Reproduced by permission.—McCloy, John J. (1895-1989), photograph. Bettmann/Corbis. Reproduced by permission.—McDonald's employees, (serving customers at a in Moscow), photograph. Associated Press. Reproduced by permission.—McGregor, Douglas, photograph. Bettmann/Corbis. Reproduced by permission.—McLuhan, Marshall, photograph. Bettmann/Corbis. Reproduced by permission.—Men in line for jobs at E.F. Keating during the Depression, photograph. The Library of Congress.—Morgan, J. P., photograph. Archive Photos. Reproduced by permission.—Mundell, Robert, photograph. Reuters Newmedia Inc./Corbis. Reproduced by permission.—Nader, Ralph, photograph. Associated Press/AP. Reproduced by permission.—National Labor Relations Board supervising steel workers' vote on union representation, 1937, photograph. UPI/Corbis-Bettmann. Reproduced by permission.—New York City street (crowded with Christmas shoppers and traffic, in front of Macy's department store), photograph. Bettmann/Corbis. Reproduced by permission.—Nonprescription medicine labels (shown with warnings printed on them before and after the new labeling system, 1999), photograph. Associated Press/AP. Reproduced by permission.—Pacioli, Fra Luca, photograph. Achivo Iconografico, S.A./C. Reproduced by permission.—Pascal, Blaise, painting. The Library of Congress.—Patent certificates, photograph. Charles E. Rotkin/Corbis. Reproduced by permission.—People (seated in a circle, during the morning trade in the Japanese markets), photograph. Associated Press/AP. Reproduced by permission.—People stretching (during a corporate management training session), photograph. Layne Kennedy/Corbis. Reproduced by permission.—Pepsi television ad (showing a boy getting sucked into a Pepsi bottle), photograph. Associated Press/AP. Reproduced by permission.—President Roosevelt resurrecting the Sherman Anti-Trust Law, political cartoon by Bartholomew.—Proctor & Gamble Co. headquarters, photograph. Associated Press/AP. Reproduced by permission.—Prodi, Romano, photograph. Associated Press/AP. Reproduced by permission.—Raines, Franklin (standing at podium), 1996, photograph. AP/Wide World Photos. Reproduced by permission.—Safety Recall posters, photograph. Associated Press/CPSC. Reproduced by permission.—Sakic, Joe (Colorado Avalanche center), photograph. Associated Press/AP. Reproduced by permission.—Samaranch, Juan Antonio (back to camera)(listening to Michael Knight during the Sydney Organizing Committee for the Olympic Games by video conference, International Olympic Committee headquarters), photograph. AFP/Corbis. Reproduced by permission.—Schumpeter, Joseph (seated, wearing light-colored suit), photograph. Corbis-Bettmann. Reproduced by permission.—Sculley, John, Steve Jobs and Steve Wozniak, photograph. UPI/Corbis-Bettmann. Reproduced by permission.—Segregation sign (officer placing segregation sign), Jackson, Mississippi, 1956, photograph. AP/Wide World Photos. Reproduced by permission.—Socrates (marble bust), photograph. Gianni Dagli Orti/Corbis. Reproduced by permission.—Taylor, Frederick W. (1856-1915), photograph. Bettmann/Corbis. Reproduced by permission.—The New York Stock Exchange (trading floor), photograph. Associated Press/AP. Reproduced by permission.—Trains in CN Railyard, photograph. Paul A. Soulder/Corbis. Reproduced by permission.—Two men working a UNIVAC computer, photograph. Corbis-Bettmann. Reproduced by permission.—Vehicles parked in front of a WalMart store (on Hawaii's big island), photograph. James Marshall/Corbis. Reproduced by permission.—Walker, James (left) and Elena Kholodenko, photograph. Associated Press/AP. Reproduced by permission.—Warden, John (arriving at the federal court) Washington DC 1998, photograph by Tyler Mallory. AP/Wide World Photos. Reproduced by permission.—Weber, Max (wearing dark suit, greying beard, frowning), photograph. The Library of Congress.—West, Wade H., photograph. Corbis. Reproduced by permission.—White, Harry Dexter, photograph. Bettmann/Corbis. Reproduced by permission.—Wilson, Woodrow, photograph. The Library of Congress.—Woman at desk (with dictaphone and earphones), photograph. Bettmann/Corbis. Reproduced by permission.—Women operating machinery (in a munitions factory, Europe, ca. 1914-1918), photograph. Corbis. Reproduced by permission.—Workers in cubicles making calls, photograph. Associated Press/AP. Reproduced by permission.

List of Articles

List of Contributors

Mohammad Abdolmohammadi
  Bentley College
  AUDITING

Theo B. A. Addo
  San Diego State University
  INFORMATION SYSTEMS
  PROGRAMMING

Connie Anderson
  University of Nebraska
  PROFESSIONAL EDUCATION

Marcia Anderson
  Southern Illinois University,
  Carbondale
  BEHAVIORAL SCIENCE
    MOVEMENT
  EMPLOYEE DISCIPLINE
  SCIENTIFIC MANAGEMENT

Carolyn Ashe
  University of Houston
  OUTSOURCING
  RECORDS MANAGEMENT

Linda J. Austin
  Tomball, Texas
  CAREERS IN INFORMATION
    PROCESSING
  DOCUMENT PROCESSING
  OFFICE TECHNOLOGY

C. Richard Baker
  University of Massachusetts,
  Dartmouth
  INDEPENDENCE STANDARDS
    BOARD

William H. Baker
  Brigham Young University,
  Provo
  DESKTOP PUBLISHING
  WORD PROCESSING

Lloyd Bartholome
  Utah State University, Logan
  INTERNET
  MANAGEMENT INFORMATION
    SYSTEMS

Marsha Bayless
  Stephen A. Austin State
  University
  E-MAIL

Jean C. Bedard
  Northeastern University
  ANALYTICAL PROCEDURES

Dennis R. Beresford
  University of Georgia
  FINANCIAL ACCOUNTING
    STANDARDS BOARD

Robert G. Berns
  Bowling Green State University
  DECA
  ENTREPRENEURSHIP

Craig A. Bestwick
  San Francisco, California
  CAREERS IN LAW FOR
    BUSINESS

Keith Bice
  Indianapolis, Indiana
  CONTRACTS
  PARTNERSHIP

Lauren Block
  New York, New York
  CONSUMER BEHAVIOR

Winnifred Bolinsky
  Allentown, Pennsylvania
  SCHOOL TO CAREER
    MOVEMENT

Richard Bortz
  Southern Illinois University,
  Carbondale
  JOB ANALYSIS AND DESIGN

David Bowers
  Case Western Reserve
  University
  BUSINESS CYCLE

Louis Braiotta, Jr.
  SUNY, Binghamton
  AUDIT COMMITTEES

Clarice Brantley
  Pensacola, Florida
  SEXUAL HARASSMENT

Clifford Brown
  Bentley College
  ACTIVITY-BASED
    MANAGEMENT COSTING
  COST ALLOCATION

Michael Brun
  Illinois State University
  FACTORS OF PRODUCTION

Phyllis Bunn
  Delta State University
  CONSUMER PRODUCT SAFETY
    ACT OF 1972

FAIR PACKAGING AND
LABELING ACT OF 1966
FEDERAL TRADE COMMISSION
ACT OF 1914
FOOD, DRUG, AND COSMETIC
ACT
ROBINSON-PATMAN ACT OF
1936
SHERMAN ANTITRUST ACT OF
1890
STAGGERS RAIL AND MOTOR
CARRIER ACTS OF 1980

Charles H. Calhoun
Westport, Connecticut
CERTIFIED INTERNAL
AUDITORS (CIA)
FOREIGN CORRUPT PRACTICES
ACT OF 1977

Patrick Casabona
St. John's University
DERIVATIVES

Judith Chiri-Mulkey
Colorado Springs, Colorado
CAREERS OVERVIEW
INTEGRATED SOFTWARE

Frederick D. S. Choi
New York University
INTERNATIONAL FEDERATION
OF ACCOUNTANTS

Diane Clevesy
Bradford, Massachusetts
CORPORATE EDUCATION

B. Douglas Clinton
Central Missouri State
University
STATEMENTS ON
MANAGEMENT ACCOUNTING

John Conant
Indiana State University
SUPPLY AND DEMAND

Tena B. Crews
State University of West
Georgia
WORK GROUPS

Henry H. Davis
Eastern Illinois University
INTEREST RATE(S)

Ian Domowitz
Pennsylvania State University
STOCK EXCHANGES

Roger Doost
Clemson University
BUDGETS AND BUDGETING

Douglas R. Emery
University of Miami, Coral
Gables
CAPITAL INVESTMENTS

Samir B. Fahmy
St. John's University
SECURITIES ACTS:
REQUIREMENTS FOR
ACCOUNTING

Mary L. Fischer
University of Texas, Tyler
BENCHMARKING
GOVERNMENT ACCOUNTING

Marie Flatley
Del Mar, California
COMMUNICATIONS
CHANNELS
POLICY DEVELOPMENT

Carrie Foley
West Baldwin, Maine
TIME MANAGEMENT

Nashwa George
Jersey City, New Jersey
PUBLIC OVERSIGHT BOARD
WORK MEASUREMENT

Rosario Girasa
Pace University
BANKRUPTCY

Rajeev K. Goel
Illinois State University
OLIGOPOLY

Keith Goree
St. Petersburg, Florida
ETHICS OVERVIEW

Audrey A. Gramling
Wake Forest University
INTERNAL CONTROL SYSTEMS

Pat Graves
Eastern Illinois University
ERGONOMICS
MOTIVATION

Mary B. Greenawalt
The Citadel
ETHICS IN ACCOUNTING
FINANCIAL STATEMENT
ANALYSIS

Mary Alice Griffin
Valdosta State University
INFORMATION PROCESSING
TELECOMMUNICATIONS

Lisa E. Gueldenzoph
Bowling Green State University
PRIVACY AND SECURITY

Mahendra R. Gujarathi
Bentley College
INTERNATIONAL ACCOUNTING
STANDARDS

Louise Dratler Haberman
New York, New York
NATIONAL ASSOCIATION OF
STATE BOARDS OF
ACCOUNTANCY

Jewel Hairston
Bowling Green State University
BUSINESS PROFESSIONALS OF
AMERICA
ENTREPRENEURSHIP

Walter A. Hamilton
South Hadley, Massachusetts
COMPUTER GRAPHICS

Gary Hansen
Brigham Young University,
Provo
DATABASES

James Hansen
Brigham Young University,
Provo
ARTIFICIAL INTELLIGENCE

Jan Hargrave
Houston, Texas
LISTENING SKILLS IN BUSINESS
SPEAKING SKILLS IN BUSINESS

Jean E. Harris
Pennsylvania State University,
Harrisburg
CHIEF FINANCIAL OFFICERS
ACT
INCOME TAX, HISTORY OF
UNITED STATES GENERAL
ACCOUNTING OFFICE

Beth Haynes
Brigham Young University,
Hawaii
CONSUMER PRICE INDEX

Thomas Haynes
Illinois State University

ETHICS IN MANAGEMENT
MANAGEMENT/LEADERSHIP
STYLES
MANUFACTURING
SOCIAL RESPONSIBILITY

Harvey Hendrickson
Florida International University
ACCOUNTING

Margaret Hicks
Howard University
SINGLE-AUDIT ACT

Patrick Highland
Iowa City, Iowa
DIVERSITY IN THE
WORKPLACE
EMPLOYEE ASSISTANCE
PROGRAMS
HUMAN RELATIONS

Vicky B. Hoffman
University of Pittsburgh
COMPILATION AND REVIEW
SERVICES

Edward Hsieh
California State University, Los
Angeles
MONETARY POLICY

Lisa Huddlestun
Greenup, Illinois
BALANCE OF TRADE
MACROECONOMICS/MICROEC
ONOMICS

Jesse Hughes
Kingwood, Texas
GOVERNMENT ACCOUNTING
STANDARDS BOARD

David Hyslop
Bowling Green State University
TRAINING AND DEVELOPMENT

Christine Irvine
Nagodoches, Texas
VOICE MESSAGING

Jeffrey Jacobs
Quinnipiac College
TAXATION

Christine Jahn
Springfield, Illinois
HUMAN RESOURCE
MANAGEMENT
ORGANIZATIONAL STRUCTURE

Steven E. Jameson
Norwalk, Connecicut
INSTITUTE FOR INTERNAL
AUDITORS

Edmund L. Jenkins
Norwalk, Connecticut
GENERALLY ACCEPTED
ACCOUNTING PRINCIPLES

Jennifer Jennes
Hooksett, New Hampshire
FADS
PUBLICITY

Carol Jones
California State Polytechnic
University
TELECOMMUTING

Randy L. Joyner
Greenville, North Carolina
CAREERS IN MARKETING
COPYRIGHTS
PATENTS
RESEARCH IN BUSINESS
TRADEMARKS

Burton S. Kaliski
New Hampshire College
CREDIT/DEBIT/TRAVEL CARDS

Surendra Kaushik
Pace Univeristy
CAPITAL MARKETS
FINANCIAL INSTITUTIONS

Edward J. Keller, Jr.
Franklin Square, New York
INSURANCE

Donna McAlister Kizzier
University of Nebraska, Lincoln
DIVISION OF LABOR
NEGOTIATION

Masaaki Kotabe
Blue Bell, Pennsylvania
INTERNATIONAL INVESTMENT
TRADING BLOCS

Alan G. Krabbenhoft
Roosevelt University
SERVICE INDUSTRIES

Anthony T. Krzystofik
Hadley, Massachusetts
CERTIFIED PUBLIC
ACCOUNTANT (CPA)
UNIFORM CERTIFIED PUBLIC
ACCOUNTANT EXAMINATION

Janel Kupferschmid
Bloomington, Illinois
ANTITRUST LEGISLATION
OPERATIONS MANAGEMENT

Gerard A. Lange
St. John's University
FRAUDULENT FINANCIAL
REPORTING

Audrey Langill
Derry, New Hampshire
SHOPPING

Christine Latino
Atkinson, Connecticut
MARKET RESEARCH

Lee Wonsick Lee
Newington, Connecticut
EMPLOYEE COMPENSATION
LEADERSHIP
PERFORMANCE APPRAISAL

Mark Lefebvre
Bow, New Hampshire
INVENTORY CONTROL

Joel Lerner
Sullivan County Community
College
PERSONAL FINANCIAL
PLANNING
STOCK INDEXES
STOCKS

Paula Luft
Dahinda, Illinois
COLLECTIVE BARGAINING
ECONOMIC CYCLES
LABOR UNIONS

Roger Luft
Dahinda, Illinois
CIRCULAR FLOW
ECONOMICS
ECONOMICS: A HISTORICAL
PERSPECTIVE
ETHICS IN ECONOMICS
FORECASTING IN BUSINESS
MANAGEMENT
MANAGEMENT: HISTORICAL
PERSPECTIVES
QUALITY MANAGEMENT

Mary Jean Lush
Delta State University
AMERICAN MARKETING
ASSOCIATION
CONSUMER BILL OF RIGHTS
DEMOGRAPHICS

ENVIRONMENTAL
  PROTECTION AGENCY
FOOD AND DRUG
  ADMINISTRATION
INTERSTATE COMMERCE
  COMMISSION
NATIONAL RETAIL
  FEDERATION
NATIONAL TRANSPORTATION
  SAFETY BOARD
OCCUPATIONAL SAFETY AND
  HEALTH ADMINISTRATION
SECURITIES AND EXCHANGE
  COMMISSION
SMALL BUSINESS
  ADMINISTRATION
STANDARD METROPOLITAN
  STATISTICAL AREAS

Dorothy Maxwell
  Cornish, Maine
    FACSIMILE REPRODUCTION
    TELEPHONE SKILLS
    TEMPORARY EMPLOYMENT

G.W. Maxwell
  Cornish, Maine
    CORPORATION
    NATIONAL BUSINESS
      EDUCATION ASSOCIATION
    SOLE PROPRIETORSHIP
    WRITING SKILLS IN BUSINESS

Beryl McEwen
  Greensburough, North Carolina
    JOB SATISFACTION

Thaddeus McEwen
  Greensburough, North Carolina
    CAREERS IN MANAGEMENT

David McGrady
  Eastern Illinois University
    EUROPEAN UNION
    FISCAL POLICY

Robert Mednick
  Chicago, Illinois
    AMERICAN INSTITUTE OF
      CERTIFIED PUBLIC
      ACCOUNTANTS

Earl Meyer
  Lutz, Florida
    CONSUMER AND INDUSTRIAL
      GOODS
    DISCOUNT STORES
    GOODS AND SERVICES
    MARKET SEGMENTATION
    MARKETING CONCEPT
    MASS MARKETING
    TELEMARKETING
    TRADE SHOWS

Mary Michel
  Manhattan College
    COST-BENEFIT ANALYSIS
    NORTH AMERICAN INDUSTRY
      CLASSIFICATION SYSTEM

Michael Milbier
  St. Louis, Missouri
    PRODUCT LABELING
    PRODUCT LINES
    PRODUCT MIX

James Miles
  Pittsford, New York
    INFORMATION PROCESSING:
      HISTORICAL PERSPECTIVES
    STANDARDS-BASED WORK
      PERFORMANCE
    VIDEOCONFERENCING

Allie F. Miller
  Drexel University
    ACCOUNTING CYCLE
    BONDS

Theodore J. Mock
  University of Southern
    California
    ACCOUNTING INFORMATION
      SYSTEMS

Hassan Mohammadi
  Illinois State University
    MONEY SUPPLY

Melvin Morgenstein
  Plainview, New York
    FEDERAL RESERVE SYSTEM

George Mundrake
  Ball State University
    MULTIMEDIA SYSTEMS

Robert J. Muretta, Jr.
  Westbook, Maine
    GOVERNMENT FINANCIAL
      REPORTING

Michael Nelson
  Illinois State University
    TRANSFER PAYMENTS

Bernard H. Newman
  Pace University
    BUREAU OF LABOR STATISTICS
    CAREERS IN ACCOUNTING
    FINANCIAL FORECASTS AND
      PROJECTIONS
    GOVERNMENT AUDITING
      STANDARDS
    INTERNATIONAL MONETARY
      FUND

STANDARD COSTING

Cheryl Noll
  Eastern Illinois University
    CHANGE PROCESS
    MANAGEMENT: AUTHORITY
      AND RESPONSIBILITY
    ORGANIZATIONAL BEHAVIOR
      AND DEVELOPMENT

Mary Ellen Oliverio
  Pace University
    FINANCE: HISTORICAL
      PERSPECTIVES

Sharon Lund O'Neil
  Houston, Texas
    COMMUNICATION IN
      BUSINESS

Don Pallais
  Richmond, Virginia
    ASSURANCE SERVICES

Lou E. Pelton
  University of North Texas
    CHANNELS OF DISTRIBUTION

Nikole Pogeman
  Bartonvill, Illinois
    AMERICAN MANAGEMENT
      ASSOCIATION
    AMERICANS WITH
      DISABILITIES ACT
    CIVIL RIGHTS ACTS
    EQUAL EMPLOYMENT
      OPPORTUNITY ACT
    EQUAL PAY ACT

Karen Puglisi
  Hooksett, New Hampshire
    CLASSICS

Zane Quible
  Oklahoma State University
    OFFICE LAYOUT

Barry L. Reece
  Pittsboro, North Carolina
    CUSTOMER SERVICE

Brenda Reinsborough
  Yarmouth, Maine
    HEALTH ISSUES IN BUSINESS
    MEETING MANAGEMENT

Tod Rejholec
  Bridgeport, Illinois
    NATIONAL LABOR RELATIONS
      BOARD

James Rinehart
Francis Marion University
DEREGULATION

Wendy Rinholen
Galva, Illinois
CAREERS IN ECONOMICS

Jim Rucker
Fort Hays State University
STRESS, WORK-RELATED

Wanda Samson
Fremont, Nebraska
SOFTWARE

Marcy Satterwhite
Charleston, Illinois
COMPETITION
COOPERATIVE
DECISION MAKING
EMPLOYEE BENEFITS
JOB ENRICHMENT

B. June Schmidt
Virginia Polytechnic Institute
and State University
OFFICE TECHNOLOGY:
HISTORICAL PERSPECTIVES
READING SKILLS IN BUSINESS

Armand Sequin
Emporia State University
HARDWARE
INTRANET

Anand Shetty
Iona College
ETHICS IN FINANCE
MUTUAL FUNDS

Victoria Shoaf
St. John's University
FINANCIAL STATEMENTS

Kathleen A. Simons
Bryant College
STATE SOCIETIES OF CPAS

G. Stevenson Smith
West Virginia University
COST-VOLUME-PROFIT
ANALYSIS
NOT-FOR-PROFIT
ACCOUNTING

Michael Spahr
Nashua, New Hampshire
MONOPOLY

Patricia Spirou
Manchester, New Hampshire

CONSUMER ADVOCACY AND
PROTECTION
FRANCHISES
INTERSTATE COMMERCE
PRICE FIXING
RETAILERS
WHOLESALING

James E. Stoddard
Appalachian State University
MARKETING: HISTORICAL
PERSPECTIVES

John Swope
East Carolina University
ADVERTISING AGENCIES
ETHICS IN MARKETING

Ellen Szarleta
Indiana University, Northwest
ECONOMIC DEVELOPMENT

Philip D. Taylor
Wesleyan College
INTERACTIVE TECHNOLOGIES

Allen D. Truell
University of Missouri,
Columbia
ADVERTISING
CRIME AND FRAUD
GOVERNMENT ROLE IN
BUSINESS
INTERNATIONAL TRADE
MARKETING
MARKETING MIX
PRICING
PROMOTION

Tatum Turner
Manchester, New Hampshire
TARGET MARKETING

Gregory Valentine
University of Southern Indiana
GROSS DOMESTIC PRODUCT
INCOME

Carson Varner
Illinois State University
ETHICS IN LAW FOR BUSINESS
LAW IN BUSINESS

Miklos A. Vasarhelyi
Rutgers University, Newark
ELECTRONIC COMMERCE

Annette Vincent
University of Southwestern
Louisiana
ETHICS IN INFORMATION
PROCESSING

Michelle Voto
Londonberry, New Hampshire
LIFESTYLES

Julie Watkins
Brownfield, Maine
COTTAGE INDUSTRIES

Roman L. Weil
University of Chicago
TIME VALUE OF MONEY

Jill White
Pensacola, Florida
FUTURE BUSINESS LEADERS OF
AMERICA

Kathy Williams
Montvale, New Jersey
CERTIFIED MANAGEMENT
ACCOUNTANT (CMA)
INSTITUTE OF MANAGEMENT
ACCOUNTANTS

Mark Wilson
Columbus, Ohio
CAREERS IN FINANCE

Denise Woodbury
Brigham Young University,
Hawaii
CURRENCY EXCHANGE
ECONOMIC SYSTEMS
MONEY
OPPORTUNITY COST

Charles W. Wootton
Eastern Illinois University
ACCOUNTING: HISTORICAL
PERSPECTIVES

Ralph Wray
Bloomington, Indiana
ECONOMIC ANALYSIS

Norman Wright
Brigham Young University,
Hawaii
GLOBAL ECONOMY
STRATEGIC MANAGEMENT

Douglas E. Ziegenfuss
Virginia Beach, Virginia
PERFORMANCE AUDITS

A

ABSOLUTE AND COMPARATIVE ADVANTAGES

(SEE: *Marketing*)

ABSOLUTE AND RELATIVE PRICES

(SEE: *Pricing*)

ACCOUNTING

Accounting is a field of specialization critical to the functioning of all types of organizations. Accounting often is referred to as "the language of business" because of its role in maintaining and processing all relevant financial information that an entity requires for its managing and reporting purposes.

Accountants often have a specific sub-specialization and function at one of several levels. Preparation for the field is provided by secondary schools, postsecondary business schools, community colleges, and four-year colleges and universities.

WHAT IS ACCOUNTING?

Accounting is a body of principles and conventions as well as an established general process for capturing financial information related to an entity's resources and their use in meeting the entity's goals. Accounting is a service function that provides information of value to all operating units and to other service functions, such as the headquarters offices of a large corporation.

Origin of Accounting Modern accounting is traced to the work of an Italian monk, Luca Pacioli, whose publication in A.D. 1494 described the double-entry system, which continues to be the fundamental structure for contemporary accounting systems in all types of entities. When double-entry accounting is used, the balance sheet identifies both the resources controlled by the entity and those parties who have claims to those assets.

Early histories of business identify the book-keeper as a valuable staff member. As businesses became more complex, the need for more astute review and interpretation of financial information was met with the development of a new profession—public accounting. In the United States, public accounting began in the latter part of the nineteenth century. The first organization was established in 1887; the first professional examination was administered in December 1896.

In the early days of the twentieth century, numerous states established licensing requirements and began to administer examinations. During the first century of public accounting in the United States, the American Institute of Certified Public Accountants (and its predecessor organizations) provided strong leadership to meet the changing needs of business, not-for-profit, and governmental entities.

Fra Luca Pacioli's 1494 publication described the double-entry system.

Generally Accepted Accounting Principles (GAAP) No single source provides principles for handling all transactions and events. Over time, conventional rules have developed that continue to be relevant. Additionally, groups have been authorized to establish accounting standards. The Financial Accounting Standards Board (FASB) assumed responsibility for accounting standards and principles in 1973. It is authorized to amend existing rules and establish new ones. In 1992, the Auditing Standards Board established the GAAP hierarchy. At the highest level of the hierarchy are FASB statements and interpretations; APB opinions were issued from 1959 to 1973 by the Accounting Principles Board (APB), and Accounting Research Bulletins, issued until

1959 by the Committee on Accounting Procedure (CAP); both the APB and CAP were committees of the American Institute of Certified Public Accountants (AICPA).

What type of unit is served by accounting? Probably no concept or idea is more basic to accounting than the accounting unit or *entity*, a term used to identify the organization for which the accounting service is to be provided and whose accounting or other information is to be analyzed, accumulated, and reported. The entity can be any area, activity, responsibility, or function for which information would be useful. Thus, an entity is established to provide the needed focus of attention. The information about one entity can be consolidated with that of a part or all of another, and this combination process can be continued until the combined entity reaches the unit that is useful for the desired purpose.

Accounting activities may occur within or outside the organization. Although accounting is usually identified with privately owned, profit-seeking entities, its services also are provided to not-for-profit organizations such as universities or hospitals, to governmental organizations, and to other types of units. The organizations may be small, owner-operated enterprises offering a single product or service, or huge multi-enterprise, international conglomerates with thousands of different products and services. The not-for-profit, governmental, or other units may be local, national, or international; they may be small or very large; they may even be entire nations, as in national income accounting. Since not-for-profit and governmental accounting are covered elsewhere in this encyclopedia, the balance of this article will focus on accounting for privately owned, profit-seeking entities.

What is the work of accountants? Accountants help entities be successful, ethical, responsible participants in society. Their major activities include observation, measurement, and communication. These activities are analytical in nature and draw on several other disciplines (e.g., economics, mathematics, statistics, behavioral science, law, history, and language/communication).

Accountants identify, analyze, record, and accumulate facts, estimates, forecasts, and other data about the unit's activities; then they translate these data into information that can be useful for a specific purpose.

The data accumulation and recording phase traditionally has been largely clerical; typically and appropriately, this has been called bookkeeping, which is still a common and largely manual activity, especially in smaller firms that have not adopted state-of-the-art technology. But with advances in information technology and user-friendly software, the clerical aspect has become largely electronically performed, with internal checks and controls to assure that the input and output are factual and valid.

Accountants design and maintain accounting systems, an entity's central information system, to help control and provide a record of the entity's activities, resources, and obligations. Such systems also facilitate reporting on all or part of the entity's accomplishments for a period of time and on its status at a given point in time.

An organization's accounting system provides information that (1) helps managers make decisions about assembling resources, controlling, and organizing financing and operating activities; and (2) aids other users (employees, investors, creditors, and others—usually called stakeholders) in making investment, credit, and other decisions.

The accounting system must also provide internal controls to ensure that (1) laws and enterprise policies are properly implemented; (2) accounting records are accurate; (3) enterprise assets are used effectively (e.g., that idle cash balances are being invested to earn returns); and (4) steps be taken to reduce chances of losing assets or incurring liabilities from fraudulent or similar activities, such as the carelessness or dishonesty of employees, customers, or suppliers. Many of these controls are simple (e.g., the prenumbering of documents and accounting for all numbers); others require division of duties among employees to separate record keeping and custodial tasks in order to reduce opportunities for falsification of records and thefts or misappropriation of assets.

An enterprise's system of internal controls usually includes an internal auditing function and personnel to ensure that prescribed data handling and asset/liability protection procedures are being followed. The internal auditor uses a variety of approaches, including observation of current activities, examination of past transactions, and simulation—often using sample or fictitious transactions—to test the accuracy and reliability of the system.

Accountants may also be responsible for preparing several types of documents. Many of these (e.g., employees' salary and wage records) also serve as inputs for the accounting system, but many are needed to satisfy other reporting requirements (e.g., employee salary records may be needed to support employee claims for pensions). Accountants also provide data for completing income tax returns.

What is the accountant's role in decision making? Accountants have a major role in providing information for making economic and financial decisions. Rational decisions are usually based on analyses and comparisons of estimates, which in turn, are based on accounting and other data that project future results from alternative courses of action.

External or financial accounting, reporting, and auditing are directly involved in providing information for the decisions of investors and creditors that help the capital markets to efficiently and effectively allocate resources to enterprises; internal, managerial, or management accounting is responsible for providing information and input to help managers make decisions on the efficient and effective use of enterprise resources.

The accounting information used in making decisions within an enterprise is not subject to governmental or other external regulation, so any rules and constraints are largely self-imposed. As a result, in developing the data and information that are relevant for decisions within the enterprise, managerial accountants are constrained largely by cost-benefit considerations and their own ingenuity and ability to predict future conditions and events.

But accounting to external users (financial accounting, reporting, and auditing) has many regulatory constraints—especially if the enterprise is a "public" corporation whose securities are registered (under the United States Securities Acts of 1933 and 1934) with the Securities and Exchange Commission (SEC) and traded publicly over-the-counter or on a stock exchange. Public companies are subject to regulations and reporting requirements imposed and enforced by the SEC; to rules and standards established for its financial reports by the FASB and enforced by the SEC; to regulations of the organization where its securities are traded; and to the regulations of the AICPA, which establishes requirements and standards for its members (who may be either internal or external accountants or auditors).

If the entity is a state or local governmental unit, it is subject to the reporting standards and requirements of the Government Accounting Standards Board. If the entity is private and not a profit-seeking unit, it is subject to various reporting and other regulations, including those of the Internal Revenue Service, which approves its tax status and with which it must file reports.

Largely as a result of the governmental regulation of private profit-seeking businesses that began in 1933, an increasingly clear distinction has been made between managerial or internal accounting and financial accounting that is largely for external users. One important exception to this trend, however, was the change adopted in the 1970s in the objectives of financial reporting such that both managerial and financial accounting now have the same objective: to provide information that is useful for making economic decisions.

But it must be recognized that although the financial accounting information reported to stakeholders comes from the organization's accounting system, its usefulness for decision making is limited. This is because it is largely historical—it reflects events and activities that occurred in the past, not what is expected in the future.

Even estimated data such as budgets and standard costs must be examined regularly to determine whether these past estimates continue to be indicative of current conditions and expectations and thus are useful for making decisions. Thus historical accounting information must be examined carefully, modified, and supplemented to make certain that what is used is relevant to expectations about the future.

But it also must be recognized that accounting can and does provide information that is current and useful in making estimates about future events. For example, accounting provides current-value information about selected items, such as readily marketable investments in debt and equity securities and inventories, and it provides reports on what the organization plans to accomplish and its expectations about the future in budgets and earnings forecasts.

Who uses accounting information for decision making? The information developed by the accountant's information system can be useful to:

- Managers in planning, controlling, and evaluating their organization's activities
- Owners, directors, and others in evaluating the performance of the organization and determining operating, compensation, and other policies
- Union, governmental, regulatory, taxing, environmental, and other entities in evaluating whether the organization is conforming with applicable contracts, rules, laws, and public policies and/or whether changes are needed;
- Existing and potential owners, lenders, employees, customers, and suppliers in evaluating their current and future commitments to the organization
- Accounting researchers, security analysts, security brokers and dealers, mutual-fund managers, and others in their analyses and evaluations of enterprises, capital markets, and/or investors

The services that accounting and the accountant can provide have been enhanced in many ways since the 1970s by advances in computers and other information technology. The impact of these changes is revolutionizing accounting and the accounting profession. But the changes have yet to reach their ultimate potential. For example, accounting in the 1990s began to provide current-value information and estimates about the future that an investor or other user would find useful for decision making. The availability of computer software and the Internet greatly enhanced the potential for data and information services. Such changes create opportunities for accounting and accountants and also will require substantial modifications in the traditional financial accounting and reporting model.

What is the profession of accounting? At the core of the profession of accounting is the certified public accountant (CPA) who has passed the national CPA examination, been licensed in at least one state or territory, and engages in the practice of public accounting/auditing in a public accounting or CPA firm. The CPA firm provides some combination of two or more of four types of services: accounting, auditing, income tax planning and reporting, and management advising/consulting. Analysis of trends indicates that the demand for auditing services has peaked and that most of the growth experienced by public accounting firms is in the consulting area.

Accounting career paths, specializations, or subprofessions for CPAs who join profit-seeking enterprises include being controllers, chief financial officers, or internal auditors. Other career paths include being controllers or chief financial officers in not-for-profit or government organizations and teaching in colleges and universities. Students should note that non-CPAs also could enter these subprofessions and that certificates, but not licenses, could be earned by passing examinations in several areas, including internal auditing, management accounting, and bank auditing.

How do environmental changes impact the accounting profession? Numerous changes in the environment make the practice of accounting and auditing much different in the new century than it was in the 1970s. For example, professional accounting firms now actively compete for clients by advertising extensively in various media, a practice that at one time was forbidden by their code of professional conduct. Mergers of clients have led CPA firms into mergers as well, such that the Big Eight is now the Big Five and the second-tier group has been reduced from twelve firms to about five. Another result of competition and other changes has been that some of the largest employers of CPAs now include income tax and accounting services firms such as H&R Block and an American Express subsidiary.

Competition among CPAs also has led the SEC to expand its regulatory and enforcement activities to ensure that financial reports are relevant and reliable. From its inception, the SEC has had legal authority to prescribe the accounting principles and standards used in the financial reports of enterprises whose securities are publicly traded, but it has delegated this responsibility to the accounting profession. Since 1973, that organization has been the FASB, with which the SEC works closely. But since the FASB is limited to performing what is essentially a legislative function, the SEC has substantially increased its enforcement activities to ensure that the FASB's standards are appropriately applied in financial reports and that accountants/auditors act in the public interest in performing their independent audits—for which the Securities Acts have given the CPA profession a monopoly.

How does a student prepare for the accounting profession? Persons considering entering the accounting profession should begin by doing some self-analysis to determine whether they enjoy mathematical, problem- or puzzle-solving, or other analytical activities; by taking some aptitude tests; or by talking with accounting teachers or practitioners about their work.

Anyone interested in becoming an accounting professional should expect to enter a rigorous five-year education program and to earn a master's degree in order to qualify to enter the profession and to sit for the CPA examination. To build a base for rising to the top of the profession, students should select courses that help them learn how to think and to define and solve prob-

lems. The courses should help them to develop analytical (logical, mathematical, statistical), communication (oral, reading, writing), computer, and interpersonal skills. The early part of the program should emphasize arts and sciences courses in these skill-development areas.

The person should begin to develop word-processing, data-processing, and Internet skills long before entering college and should expect to maintain competence in them throughout his or her professional career. These skills greatly enhance and facilitate all phases and aspects of what accounting and accountants attempt to do. What can be done is limited only by technology and by the sophistication of the system, its operators, and users.

(SEE ALSO: *Accounting cycle; Careers in accounting; Financial Accounting Standards Board; Certified Management Accountant; Generally Accepted Accounting Principles; Government accounting; Institute for Internal Auditors; Institute of Management Accountants; International Accounting Standards; International Federation of Accountants; National Association of Boards of Accountancy; Public Oversight Board; Uniform Certified Public Accountant examination; United States General Accounting Office; Securities Acts: Requirements for accounting*)

BIBLIOGRAPHY

Hansen, Don R., and Mowen, Maryanne M. (2000). *Management Accounting*, 5th ed. Cincinnati, OH: Southwestern College Publishing.

Kimmel, Paul D., Weygandt, Jerry J., and Kieso, Donald E. (2000). *Financial Accounting*, 2d ed. New York: Wiley.

HARVEY S. HENDRICKSON

ACCOUNTING CYCLE

The primary objectives of the accounting function in an organization are to process financial information and to prepare financial statements at the end of the accounting period. Companies must systematically process financial information and must have staff who prepare financial statements on a monthly, quarterly, and/or annual basis. To meet these primary objectives, a series of steps is required. Collectively these steps are known as the *accounting cycle*. The steps, applicable to a manual accounting system, are described below. Later, there will be a brief discussion of a computerized processing system.

THE STEPS OF THE CYCLE

1. *Collect and analyze data from transactions and events:* As transactions and events related to financial resources occur, they are analyzed with respect to their effect on the financial position of the company. As an example, consider the sales for a day in a retail establishment that are collected on a cash register tape. These sales become inputs into the accounting system. Every organization establishes a chart of accounts that identifies the categories for recording transactions and events. The chart of accounts for the retail establishment mentioned earlier in this paragraph will include *Cash* and *Sales*.

2. *Journalize transactions:* After collecting and analyzing the information obtained in the first step, the information is entered in the *general journal*, which is called the *book of original entry*. Journalizing transactions may be done continually, but this step can de done in a batch at the end of the day if data from similar transactions are being sorted and collected, on a cash register tape, for example. At the end of the day, the sales of $4,000 for cash would be recorded in the general journal in this form:
Cash 4000
   Sales 4000

3. *Post to general ledger:* The general journal entries are posted to the general ledger, which is organized by *account*. All transactions for the same account are collected and summarized; for example, the account entitled "Sales" will accumulate the total value of the sales for the period. If posting were done daily, the "Sales" ac-

count in the ledger would show the total sales for each day as well as the cumulative sales for the period to date. Posting to ledger accounts may be less frequent, perhaps at the end of each day, at the end of the week, or possibly even at the end of the month.

4. *Prepare an unadjusted trial balance:* At the end of the period, double-entry accounting requires that debits and credits recorded in the general ledger be equal. *Debit* and *credit* merely signify position—left and right, respectively. Some accounts normally have debit balances (e.g., assets and expenses) and other accounts have credit balances (e.g., liabilities, owners' equity and revenues). As transactions are recorded in the general journal and subsequently posted to the ledger, all amounts recorded on the debit side of accounts (i.e., recorded on the left side) must equal all amounts recorded on the credit side of accounts (i.e., recorded on the right side). Preparing an unadjusted trial balance tests the equality of debits and credits as recorded in the general ledger. If unequal amounts of debits and credits are found in this step, the reason for the inequality is investigated and corrected before proceeding to the next step. Additionally, this unadjusted trial balance provides the balances of all the accounts that may require adjustment in the next step.

5. *Prepare adjustments:* Period-end adjustments are required to bring accounts to their proper balances after considering transactions and/or events not yet recorded. Under accrual accounting, revenue is recorded when earned and expenses when incurred. Thus, an entry may be required at the end of the period to record revenue that has been earned but not yet recorded on the books. Similarly, an adjustment may be required to record an expense that may have been incurred but not yet recorded.

6. *Prepare an adjusted trial balance:* As with an unadjusted trial balance, this step tests the equality of debits and credits. However, assets, liabilities, owners' equity, revenues, and expenses will now reflect the adjustments that have been made in the previous step. If there should be unequal amounts of debits and credits or if an account appears to be incorrect, the discrepancy or error is investigated and corrected.

7. *Prepare financial statements:* Financial statements are prepared using the corrected balances from the adjusted trial balance. These are one of the primary *outputs* of the financial accounting system.

8. *Close the accounts:* Revenues and expenses are accumulated and reported by period, either a monthly, quarterly, or yearly. To prevent their not being added to or comingled with revenues and expenses of another period, they need to be closed out—that is, given zero balances—at the end of each period. Their *net* balances, which represent the income or loss for the period, are transferred into owners' equity. Once revenue and expense accounts are closed, the only accounts that have balances are the asset, liability, and owners' equity accounts. Their balances are carried forward to the next period.

9. *Prepare a post-closing trial balance:* The purpose of this final step is two-fold: to determine that all revenue and expense accounts have been closed properly and to test the equality of debit and credit balances of all the balance sheet accounts, that is, assets, liabilities and owners' equity.

COMPUTERIZED ACCOUNTING SYSTEM

A computerized accounting system saves a great deal of time and effort, considerably reduces (if not *eliminates*) mathematical errors, and allows for much more timely information than does a manual system. In a real-time environment, accounts are accessed and updated immediately to reflect activity, thus combining steps 2 and 3 as discussed in the preceding section. The need to test for equality of debits and credits through trial balances is usually not required in a computerized system accounting since most systems test for equality of debit and credit amounts as they are entered. If someone were to attempt to input data containing an inequality, the system would not accept the input. Since the computer is programmed to post amounts to the various accounts and calculate the new balances as new entries are made, the possibility of mathematical error is markedly reduced.

Computers may also be programmed to record some adjustments automatically at the end of the period. Most software programs are also able to prepare the financial statement once it has been determined the account balances are correct. The closing process at the end of the period can also be done automatically by the computer.

Human judgment is still required to analyze the data for entry into the computer system correctly. Additionally, the accountant's knowledge and judgment are frequently required to determine the adjustments that are needed at the end of the reporting period. The mechanics of the system, however, can easily be handled by the computer.

(SEE ALSO: *Accounting; Accounting information systems*)

BIBLIOGRAPHY

Dansby, Robert, Kaliski, Burton, and Lawrence, Michael (1999). *College Accounting.* St. Paul, MN: EMC Paradigm.

Ingram, Robert W., and Baldwin, Bruce A. (1998). *Financial Accounting: A Bridge to Decision Making.* Cincinnati, OH: South-Western College Publishing.

Larson, Kermit D. (1997). *Essentials of Financial Accounting.* Boston: Irwin/McGraw-Hill.

Meigs, Robert F., Meigs, Mary A., Bettner, Mark, and Whittington, Ray. (1998). *Financial Accounting.* Boston: Irwin/McGraw Hill.

Needles, Belverd E., and Powers, Marian (1998). *Financial Accounting.* Boston: Houghton Mifflin.

Porter, Gary A., and Norton, Curtis L. (1998). *Financial Accounting*. Fort Worth, TX: Dryden Press.

ALLIE F. MILLER

ACCOUNTING: CONCEPTUAL FRAMEWORK

(SEE ALSO: *Accounting*)

ACCOUNTING: HISTORICAL PERSPECTIVES

With the establishment of the first English colonies in America, accounting or bookkeeping, as the discipline was referred to then, quickly assumed an important role in the development of American commerce. Two hundred years, however, would pass before accounting would separate from bookkeeping, and nearly three hundred years would pass before the profession of accounting, as it is now practiced, would emerge.

For individuals and businesses, accounting records in Colonial America often were very elementary. Most records of this period relied on the single-entry method or were simply narrative accounts of transactions. As rudimentary as they were, these records were important because the colonial economy was largely a barter and credit system with substantial time passing before payments were made. Accounting records were often the only reliable records of such historical transactions.

THE EMERGENCE OF ACCOUNTING

Prior to the late 1800s, the terms *bookkeeping* and *accounting* were often used interchangeably because the recording/posting process was central to both activities. There was little need for financial statements (e.g., income statements) because most owners had direct knowledge of their businesses and, therefore, could rely on elementary bookkeeping procedures for information.

Although corporations (e.g., banks, canal companies) were present in the United States prior to the early 1800s, their numbers were few.

Beginning in the late 1820s, however, the number of corporations rapidly increased with the creation and expansion of the railroads. To operate successfully, the railroads needed cost reports, production reports, financial statements, and operating ratios that were more complex than simple recording procedures could provide. Alfred D. Chandler, Jr. (1977), noted the impact of the railroads on the development of accounting in his classic work, *The Visible Hand*, when he stated "after 1850, the railroad was central in the development of the accounting profession in the United States" (p. 110).

With the increase in the number of corporations, there also arose a demand for additional financial information that A.C. Littleton (1933/ 1988) in his landmark book, *The Rise of the Accounting Profession*, called "figure" knowledge. With no direct knowledge of a business, investors had to rely on financial statements for information, and to create those statements, more complex accounting methods were required. The accountant's responsibility, therefore, expanded beyond simply recording entries to include the preparation, classification, and analysis of financial statements. As John L. Carey (1969) wrote in *The Rise of the Accounting Profession*, "the nineteenth century saw bookkeeping expanded into accounting" (p. 15).

Additionally, as the development of the corporation created a greater need for the services of accountants, the study of commerce and accounting became more important. Although there had been trade business schools and published texts on accounting/bookkeeping, traditional colleges had largely ignored the study of business and accounting. In 1881, however, the Wharton School of Finance and Economy was founded, and two years later, the school added accounting to its curriculum. As other major universities created schools of commerce, accounting secured a significant place in the curriculum.

With a separation of management and ownership in corporations, there also arose a need for an independent party to review the financial statements. Someone was needed to represent the owners' interest and to verify that the statements accurately presented the financial conditions of the company. Moreover, there was often an expectation that an independent review would discover whether managers were violating their fiduciary duties to the owners. Additionally, because the late nineteenth century was a period of major industrial mergers, someone was needed to verify the reported values of the companies. The independent public accountant, a person whose obligation was not to the managers of a company but to its shareholders and potential investors, provided the knowledge and skills to meet these needs.

In 1913, the responsibilities of and job opportunities for accountants again expanded with the ratification of the Sixteenth Amendment to the Constitution, which allowed a federal income tax. Accountants had become somewhat familiar with implementing a national tax with the earlier passage of the Corporation Excise Tax Law. Despite the earlier law, however, many companies had not set up proper systems to determine taxable income and few were familiar with concepts such as depreciation and accrual accounting.

As tax rates increased, tax services became even more important to accounting firms and often opened the door to providing other services to a client. Accounting firms, therefore, were often engaged to establish a proper accounting system and audit financial statements as well as prepare the required tax return.

Thus, in contrast to bookkeeping which often had been considered a trade, the responsibilities of accounting had expanded by the early twentieth century to such an extent that it now sought professional status. One foundation of the established professions (e.g., medicine, law) was professional certification, which accounting did not have. In 1896, with the support of several accounting organizations, New York State passed a law restricting the title certified public accountant (CPA) to those who had passed a state examination and had acquired at least three years of accounting experience. Similar laws were soon passed in several states.

PROFESSIONAL ORGANIZATIONS

Throughout the history of accounting, professional organizations have made major contributions to the development of the profession. For example, in 1882, the Institute of Accountants and Bookkeepers of New York (IABNY) was organized with the primary aim of increasing the level of educational resources available for accountants. In 1886, the IABNY became the Institute of Accounts, and it continued to be active in promoting accounting education for nearly twenty years. Meanwhile, the first national organization for accounting educators, the American Association of University Instructors in Accounting (AAUIP), was organized in 1916. In 1935, the AAUIP was reorganized as the American Accounting Association.

The national public accounting organization, the American Association of Public Accountants (AAPA), was incorporated in 1887. Reflecting the need of most professions for a code of ethics, the AAPA added a professional ethics section to its bylaws in 1907. The AAPA was reorganized as the American Institute of Accountants in the United States of America and then later as the American Institute of Accountants (AIA). In 1921, the American Society of Certified Public Accountants (ASCPA) was established and became a rival to the AIA for leadership in the public accounting area. The rivalry continued until 1937, when the ASCPA merged with the AIA. In 1957, the AIA became the American Institute of Certified Public Accountants (AICPA).

In contrast to the public accounting emphasis of the AIA and ASCPA, the National Association of Cost Accountants (NACA) was founded in 1919. The NACA placed an emphasis on the development of cost controls and proper reporting within companies. In 1957, the NACA changed its name to the National Association of Accountants (NAA) in recognition of the expansion of managerial accounting beyond traditional cost accounting. Then, in 1991, recognizing its emphasis on the managerial aspects of accounting, the NAA became the Institute of Management Accountants.

EXTERNAL AND INTERNAL REGULATION

During the nineteenth century, the federal government generally allowed accounting to regulate itself. Then, in 1913, Congress established the Federal Reserve System and, one year later, the Federal Trade Commission (FTC). From this date forward, federal agencies have had an increasing impact on the profession of accounting.

The government's first major attempt at the formalization of authoritative reporting standards was in 1917 with the Federal Reserve Board's publication of *Uniform Accounting*. In 1918, the bulletin was reissued as *Approved Methods for the Preparation of Balance Sheet Statements*. Although directed toward auditing the balance sheet, the report presented model income and balance sheet statements. Because the proposal was only a recommendation, however, its acceptance was limited.

The impetus for stricter financial reporting was provided by the collapse of the securities market in 1929 and the revelation of massive fraud in a company listed on the New York Stock Exchange (NYSE). In 1933, the NYSE announced that companies applying for a listing on the exchange must have their financial statements audited by an independent public accountant. The scope of these audits had to follow the revised guidelines set forth by the Federal Reserve in 1929.

Another major innovation in the regulation of accounting was the passage of the Securities Act of 1933 and the Securities and Exchange Act of 1934. The 1933 act conferred upon the FTC the authority to prescribe the accounting methods for companies to follow. Under this act, accountants could be held liable for losses that resulted from material omissions or misstatements in registration statements they had certified. The 1934 act transferred the authority to prescribe accounting methods to the newly established Securities and Exchange Commission (SEC) and required that financial statements filed with the SEC be certified by an independent public accountant.

With the creation of the SEC and the passage of new securities laws, the federal government assumed a central role in the establishment of basic requirements for the issuance and auditing of financial reports. Additionally, these acts increased the importance of accountants and enlarged the accountant's responsibility to the general public. Under these acts, not only did accountants have a responsibility to the public, they were now potentially liable for their actions.

In 1938, the SEC delegated much of its authority to prescribe accounting practices to the AIA and its Committee on Accounting Procedures (CAP). In 1939, CAP issued its first of fifty-one Accounting Research Bulletins. Responding to criticism of CAP, the AICPA (formerly the AIA) in 1959 replaced the CAP with the Accounting Principles Board (APB). The APB was designed to issue accounting opinions after it had considered previous research studies, and in 1962, the APB issued its first of thirty-one opinions. Although the SEC had delegated much of its standard-setting authority to the AICPA, the commission exercised its right to approve all standards when it declared that companies did not have to follow the rules set forth in APB No. 2, The Investment Credit.

Responding to criticism of the APB, a study group chaired by Francis M. Wheat was established to review the board structure and the rule-making process. The committee recommended that an independent, full time, more diverse standards board replace the APB. Following the recommendations, the Financial Accounting Standards Board (FASB) was established in 1973. This board is independent of the AICPA and issued its first statement in 1973.

THE CHANGING GENDERIZATION OF THE WORK FORCE

With the separation of bookkeeping from accounting, the demand for women bookkeepers dramatically increased, and by 1930, over 60 percent of all bookkeepers were women. A similar increase in the demand for women accountants, however, did not occur. Although World War II created some opportunities for women in accounting, at the start of the second half of the twentieth century, accounting still was not considered an appropriate career for most women. In fact, in 1950, only 15 percent of the more than 300,000 accountants in the United States were women. Moreover, less than 4 percent of college students majoring in accounting then were women.

In the 1960s, social and legal events began that ultimately provided opportunities for women in the profession of accounting. As these events occurred, the overall demand for accounting services and accountants also greatly increased. This demand became so large that the traditional labor pool of men was not sufficient to maintain the accounting work force. Concurrently, women majoring in accounting increased dramatically from less than 5 percent of all accounting majors in 1960 to over 50 percent in 1985.

Given the increase of women accounting majors and the inability of the traditional labor pool to meet the work force demand, accounting (especially public accounting) increased the hiring of women. By 1990, women comprised a majority of the accounting work force. It would be the turn of the twenty-first century, however, before women began to obtain a significant number of upper-level management positions in accounting.

THE TWENTY-FIRST CENTURY

The accountant, the accounting firm, and the accounting profession of the twenty-first century are quite different from what existed at the beginning of the twentieth century. In contrast to a bookkeeper manually recording entries in a large bound volume, an accountant is now responsible for information concerning all facets of a business and is dependent on the latest technology for processing that information. In contrast to small local firms, accounting firms now can be large international organizations with reported revenues of billions of dollars. In addition to the traditional audit/attest information, accounting firms provide their clients with tax services, financial planning, system analysis, consulting, and legal services. At the beginning of the twentieth century, the accounting profession was just

emerging. Today, the profession is comprised of thousands of men and women working in public and private firms as well as profit and nonprofit organizations as members of management teams or as valued consultants.

(SEE ALSO: *American Institute of CPAs; National Association of Boards of Accountancy*)

BIBLIOGRAPHY

Carey, John L. (1969). *The Rise of the Accounting Profession from Technician to Professional 1896-1936*. New York: American Institute of Certified Public Accountants.

Carey, John L. (1970). *The Rise of the Accounting Profession to Responsibility and Authority 1937-1969*. New York: American Institute of Certified Public Accountants.

Chandler, Alfred D. Jr., (1977). *The Visible Hand: The Managerial Revolution in American Business*. Cambridge, MA: Harvard University Press.

Chatfield, Michael, and Vangermeersch, Richard, eds. (1996). *The History of Accounting: An International Encyclopedia*. New York: Garland.

Edwards, James Don. (1978). *History of Public Accounting in the United States*. Tuscaloosa, AL: University of Alabama Press.

Hills, George H. (1982). *The Law of Accounting and Financial Statements*. New York: Garland. (Original work published 1957)

Johnson, H. Thomas, and Kaplan, Robert S. (1987). *Relevance Lost: The Rise and Fall of Management Accounting*. Boston: Harvard Business School Press.

Littleton, A.C. (1988). *Accounting Evolution to 1900*. New York: Garland. (Original work published 1933)

Lockwood, Jeremiah. (1938). "Early University Education in Accountancy." *Accounting Review* 38(2): 131-143.

Miranti, Paul J. Jr., (1990). *Accountancy Comes of Age: The Development of an American Profession*. Chapel Hill: University of North Carolina Press.

Previts, Gary John, and Merino, Barbara Dubis. (1998). *A History of Accountancy in the United States: The Cultural Significance of Accounting*. Columbus: Ohio State University Press.

Reid, Glenda E., Acken, Brenda T., and Jancura, Elise G. (1987). "An Historical Perspective on Women in Accounting." *The Journal of Accountancy* 163(5) (May): 338-355.

Study on Establishment of Accounting Principles. (1972) "Recommendation on the Study on Establishment of Accounting Principles." *The Journal of Accountancy* 133(5) (May): 66-71.

Wootton, Charles W., and Kemmerer, Barbara E. (1996). "The Changing Genderization of Bookkeeping in the United States, 1870-1930." *Business History Review* 70(4) (Winter): 541-586.

Wootton, Charles W., and Kemmerer, Barbara E. (2000). "The Changing Genderization of the Accounting Workforce in the US, 1930-1990." *Accounting, Business & Financial History* 10(2) (July): 303-324.

CHARLES W. WOOTTON
CAROL J. NORMAND

ACCOUNTING INFORMATION SYSTEMS

Accounting Information Systems (AISs) combine the study and practice of accounting with the design, implementation, and monitoring of information systems. Such systems use modern information technology resources together with traditional accounting controls and methods to provide users the financial information necessary to manage their organizations.

AIS TECHNOLOGY

Input The input devices commonly associated with AIS include: standard personal computers or workstations running applications; scanning devices for standardized data entry; electronic communication devices for electronic data interchange (EDI) and e-commerce. In addition, many financial systems come "Web-enabled" to allow devices to connect to the World Wide Web.

Process Basic processing is achieved through computer systems ranging from individual personal computers to large-scale enterprise servers. However, conceptually, the underlying processing model is still the "double-entry" accounting system initially introduced in the fifteenth century.

Output Output devices used include computer displays, impact and nonimpact printers, and electronic communication devices for EDI and e-commerce. The output content may encompass almost any type of financial reports from budgets and tax reports to multinational financial statements.

MANAGEMENT INFORMATION SYSTEMS (MIS)

MISs are interactive human/machine systems that support decision making for users both in and out of traditional organizational boundaries. These systems are used to support an organization's daily operational activities; current and future tactical decisions; and overall strategic direction. MISs are made up of several major applications including, but not limited to, the financial and human resources systems.

Financial applications make up the heart of an AIS in practice. Modules commonly implemented include: general ledger, payables, procurement/purchasing, receivables, billing, inventory, assets, projects, and budgeting.

Human resource applications make up another major part of modern information systems. Modules commonly integrated with the AIS include: human resources, benefits administration, pension administration, payroll, and time and labor reporting.

AIS—INFORMATION SYSTEMS IN CONTEXT

AISs cover all business functions from backbone accounting transaction processing systems to sophisticated financial management planning and processing systems.

Financial reporting starts at the operational levels of the organization, where the transaction processing systems capture important business events such as normal production, purchasing, and selling activities. These events (transactions) are classified and summarized for internal decision making and for external financial reporting.

Cost accounting systems are used in manufacturing and service environments. These allow organizations to track the costs associated with the production of goods and/or performance of services. In addition, the AIS can provide advanced analyses for improved resource allocation and performance tracking.

Management accounting systems are used to allow organizational planning, monitoring, and control for a variety of activities. This allows managerial-level employees to have access to advanced reporting and statistical analysis. The systems can be used to gather information, to develop various scenarios, and to choose an optimal answer among alternative scenarios.

DEVELOPMENT

The development of an AIS includes five basic phases: planning, analysis, design, implementation, and support. The time period associated with each of these phases can be as short as a few weeks or as long as several years.

Planning—project management objectives and techniques The first phase of systems development is the planning of the project. This entails determination of the scope and objectives of the project, the definition of project responsibilities, control requirements, project phases, project budgets, and project deliverables.

Analysis The analysis phase is used to both determine and document the accounting and business processes used by the organization. Such processes are redesigned to take advantage of best practices or of the operating characteristics of modern system solutions.

Data analysis is a thorough review of the accounting information that is currently being collected by an organization. Current data are then compared to the data that the organization should be using for managerial purposes. This method is used primarily when designing accounting transaction processing systems.

Decision analysis is a thorough review of the decisions a manager is responsible for making. The primary decisions that managers are responsible for are identified on an individual basis. Then models are created to support the manager in gathering financial and related information to develop and design alternatives, and to make actionable choices. This method is valuable when decision support is the system's primary objective.

Process analysis is a thorough review of the organization's business processes. Organizational processes are identified and segmented into a series of events that either add or change data. These processes can then be modified or reengineered to improve the organization's operations in terms of lowering cost, improving service, improving quality, or improving management information. This method is appropriate when automation or reengineering is the system's primary objective.

Design The design phase takes the conceptual results of the analysis phase and develops detailed, specific designs that can be implemented in subsequent phases. It involves the detailed design of all inputs, processing, storage, and outputs of the proposed accounting system. Inputs may be defined using screen layout tools and application generators. Processing can be shown through the use of flowcharts or business process maps that define the system logic, operations, and work flow. Logical data storage designs are identified by modeling the relationships among the organization's resources, events, and agents through diagrams. Also, entity relationship diagram (ERD) modeling is used to document large-scale database relationships. Output designs are documented through the use of a variety of reporting tools such as report writers, data extraction tools, query tools, and on-line analytical processing tools. In addition, all aspects of the design phase can be performed with software tool sets provided by specific software manufacturers.

Reporting is the driving force behind an AIS development. If the system analysis and design are successful, the reporting process provides the information that helps drive management decision making. Accounting systems make use of a variety of scheduled and on-demand reports. The reports can be tabular, showing data in a table or tables; graphic, using images to convey information in a picture format; or matrices, to show complex relationships in multiple dimensions.

There are numerous characteristics to consider when defining reporting requirements. The reports must be accessible through the system's interface. They should convey information in a proactive manner. They must be relevant. Accuracy must be maintained. Lastly, reports must meet the information processing (cognitive) style of the audience they are to inform.

Reports are of three basic types: A *filter report* that separates select data from a database, such as a monthly check register; a *responsibility report* to meet the needs of a specific user, such as a weekly sales report for a regional sales manager; a *comparative report* to show period differences, percentage breakdowns and variances between actual and budgeted expenditures. An example would be the financial statement analytics showing the expenses from the current year and prior year as a percentage of sales.

Screen designs and system interfaces are the primary *data capture devices* of AISs and are developed through a variety of tools. *Storage* is achieved through the use of normalized databases that assure functionality and flexibility.

Business process maps and *flowcharts* are used to document the operations of the systems. Modern AISs use specialized databases and processing designed specifically for accounting operations. This means that much of the base processing capabilities come delivered with the accounting or enterprise software.

Implementation The implementation phase consists of two primary parts: construction and delivery. Construction includes the selection of hardware, software and vendors for the implementation; building and testing the network communication systems; building and testing the databases; writing and testing the new program modifications; and installing and testing the total system from a technical standpoint. Delivery is the process of conducting final system and user acceptance testing; preparing the conversion plan; installing the production database; training the users; and converting all operations to the new system.

Tool sets are a variety of application development aids that are vendor-specific and used for customization of delivered systems. They allow the addition of fields and tables to the database, along with ability to create screen and other interfaces for data capture. In addition, they help set accessibility and security levels for adequate internal control within the accounting applications.

Security exists in several forms. Physical security of the system must be addressed. In typical AISs the equipment is located in a locked room with access granted only to technicians. Software access controls are set at several levels, depending on the size of the AIS. The first level of security occurs at the network level, which protects the organization's communication systems. Next is the operating system level security, which protects the computing environment. Then, database security is enabled to protect organizational data from theft, corruption, or other forms of damage. Lastly, application security is used to keep unauthorized persons from performing operations within the AIS.

Testing is performed at four levels. Stub or unit testing is used to insure the proper operation of individual modifications. Program testing involves the interaction between the individual modification and the program it enhances. System testing is used to determine that the program modifications work within the AIS as a whole. Acceptance testing ensures that the modifications meet user expectations and that the entire AIS performs as designed.

Conversion entails the method used to change from an old AIS to a new AIS. There are several methods for achieving this goal. One is to run the new and old systems in parallel for a specified period. A second method is to directly cut over to the new system at a specified point. A third is to phase in the system, either by location or system function. A fourth is to pilot the new system at a specific site before converting the rest of the organization.

Support The *support* phase has two objectives. The first is to update and maintain the AIS. This includes fixing problems and updating the system for business and environmental changes. For example, changes in generally accepted accounting principles (GAAP) or tax laws might necessitate changes to conversion or reference tables used for financial reporting. The second objective of support is to continue development by continuously improving the business through adjustments to the AIS caused by business and environmental changes. These changes might result in future problems, new opportunities, or management or governmental directives requiring additional system modifications.

ATTESTATION

AISs change the way internal controls are implemented and the type of audit trails that exist within a modern organization. The lack of traditional forensic evidence, such as paper, necessitates the involvement of accounting professionals in the design of such systems. Periodic involvement of public auditing firms can be used to make sure the AIS is in compliance with current internal control and financial reporting standards.

After implementation, the focus of attestation is the review and verification of system operation. This requires adherence to standards such as ISO 9000-3 for software design and development as well as standards for control of information technology.

Periodic functional business reviews should be conducted to be sure the AIS remains in compliance with the intended business functions. Quality standards dictate that this review should be done according to a periodic schedule.

ENTERPRISE RESOURCE PLANNING (ERP)

ERP systems are large-scale information systems that impact an organization's AIS. These systems permeate all aspects of the organization and require technologies such as client/server and relational databases. Other system types that currently impact AISs are supply chain management (SCM) and customer relationship management (CRM).

Traditional AISs recorded financial information and produced financial statements on a periodic basis according to GAAP pronouncements. Modern ERP systems provide a broader view of organizational information, enabling the use of advanced accounting techniques, such as activity-based costing (ABC) and improved managerial reporting using a variety of analytical techniques.

(SEE ALSO: *Accounting; Internal Control Systems*)

THEODORE J. MOCK
ROBERT M. KIDDOO

ACHIEVEMENT MOTIVATION THEORY

(SEE: *Motivation*)

ACTIVITY-BASED MANAGEMENT

Activity-based management (ABM) is an approach to management in which process managers are given the responsibility and authority to continuously improve the planning and control of operations by focusing on key operational activities. ABM strategically incorporates activity analysis, activity-based costing (ABC), activity-based budgeting, life-cycle and target costing, process value analysis, and value-chain analysis. Enhanced effectiveness and efficiencies are expected for both revenue generation and cost incurrences. Since the focus is on activities, improved cost management is achieved through better managing those activities that consume resources and drive costs. The focus for control is shifted away from the financial measurement of resources to activities that cause costs to be incurred.

As an overall framework, ABM relies on ABC information. ABC deals with the analysis and assignment of costs. In order to complete cost analyses, activities need to be identified and classified. An activity dictionary can be developed, listing and describing all activities within an organization, including information on each activity's location, performance measure(s), and key value-added and non-value-added attributes. (See "ABC/ABM Dictionary," which was used to help construct many of the definitions used in this entry.) ABC information is extremely helpful in the strategic analysis of areas such as process and plant layout redesign, pricing, customer values, sourcing, evaluation of competitive position, and product strategy.

ACTIVITY AND ACTIVITY ANALYSIS

An activity is a business task, or an aggregation of closely related purposeful actions, with clear beginning and ending points, that consumes resources and produces outputs. An activity could be a single task or a simple process. Resources are inputs, such as materials, labor, equipment, and other economic elements consumed by an activity in the production of an output. Outputs are products, services, and accompanying information flowing from an activity. In seeking continuous business improvement, an overall examination of variations in performances of key organizational activities and their causes is referred to as activity analysis. Performance is measured by a financial or nonfinancial indicator that is causally related to the performance (adding value to a product or service) of an activity and can be used to manage and improve the performance of that activity.

The level of an activity within an organization depends on that level of operations supported by that activity. For instance, a unit-level activity is one that is performed directly on each unit of output of an organizational process. A batch-level activity is one performed on a small group, or batch, of output units at the same time. For example, the setup activity to run a batch job in a production process and the associated cost for completing such a setup is a batch-level activity. A customer-sustaining activity supports an individual or a particular grouping of customers, such as mailings or customer service. A product-sustaining activity supports an individual product or product line, such as product (re)design or (re)engineering. These last two types of activities are sometimes referred to as service-sustaining activities. Lastly, a facility-sustaining activity supports an entire facility, such as the actions of the manager of an entire plant, with an associated cost equal to the manager's compensation package. Not every activity within an organization is significant enough to isolate in an activity analysis.

A process is a set of logically related activities performed in order to achieve a particular objective, such as the production of a unit of product or service. Identification of all such processes within an organization along with a specification of the relationships among them provides a value chain. Value chains are often presented in terms of functional areas (a function provides the organization with a particular type of service or product, such as finance, distribution, or purchasing). Within each of these key processes, activities can be classified as primary activities, secondary activities, and other activities. Primary activities contribute directly to the providing of the final product or service. Secondary activities directly support primary activities. The "other activities" category is comprised of those actions too far removed from the intended output to be individually noted. They should be examined to determine if they are necessary and should be continued.

VALUE-ADDED AND NON-VALUE-ADDED

Each of the key (primary and secondary) activities noted from our analysis must be categorized as either value-added or non-value-added. This analysis is referred to as value analysis. An activity is value-added to the extent that its performance contributes to the completion of the product or service for consumers. While value-added activities are necessary, the efficiency with which they are performed often can be improved through best practice analysis and benchmarking. This process of improvement is referred to as business process redesign or reengineering.

Because many activities may not fit neatly into a value-added/non-value-added dichotomy, weightings may be assigned to indicate the extent to which an activity is value-added, such as a scale ranging from one to eight, with an eight representing total value-additivity and a zero, none. A non-value-added activity transforms a product or service in a way that adds no usefulness to the product or service. Non-value-added activities should be minimized or eliminated. An overall value-chain analysis would examine all the activities and associated processes in an attempt to provide greater value at the same cost, the same value at less cost, or both.

ACTIVITY-BASED COSTING

Because costs are initially assigned from resource cost pools to activity cost pools and from there to final cost objects, activity-based costing is viewed as a two-stage allocation process. Once activities have been identified, an activity-based costing analysis can be completed. Activity-based costing is a form of cost refinement, designed to obtain greater accuracy than traditional allocations in cost assignments for product costing and decision-making purposes. Costs are assigned to activities from resource cost pools. Costs are first accumulated according to the type of resource, such as materials or labor, with which they are associated. Then resource (cost) drivers, which measure the consumption of a resource by an activity, are identified and used to assign the costs of resource consumptions to each activity. The result of this assignment is an activity cost pool for each activity.

From the activity cost pool, the focus shifts to one or more activity drivers. An activity driver measures the frequency or intensity with which a cost object requires the use of an activity, thereby relating the performance of an activity's tasks to the needs of one or more cost objects. A cost object is why activities are performed; it is a unit of product or service, an operating segment of the organization, or even another activity for which management desires an assignment of costs for unit costing or decision making purposes. The activity cost pools are then reassigned to the final cost objects according to the intensity with which each cost object used the respective activity drivers.

A cost driver may be defined to be "any factor that has the effect of changing the level of total cost for a cost object." (Blocher et al., 1999, p. 8) In general, four types of cost drivers can be identified: volume-based, activity-based, structural, and executional (Blocher, et al., 1999, p. 61). Activity-based management focuses on activity-based cost drivers. In investigating and specifying cost drivers, many methods are used,

such as cause-and-effect diagrams, cost simulations, and Pareto analysis.

Traditional cost assignment systems typically would assign directly to the cost objects the costs of those resource consumptions that can be economically traced directly to units of output requiring the resources. The remaining costs, referred to as indirect costs, would be accumulated into one or more cost pools, which would subsequently be allocated to the cost objects according to volume-related bases of allocation. When different products consume resources at rates that are not accurately reflected in their relative numbers (volumes), a traditional cost allocation approach will result in product cost cross-subsidization. That is, a high-volume, relatively simple product will end up overcosted and subsidizing a subsequently undercosted, low-volume, relatively complex product, resulting in inaccurate unit costing and suboptimal product-line pricing decisions and performance evaluations. Activity-based costing tries to take the nonuniformity of resource consumption across products into account in the assignment of costs.

(SEE ALSO: *Management*)

BIBLIOGRAPHY

"ABC/ABM Dictionary." http://www.saffm.hq.af.mil/SAFFM/FMC/ABC/dictionary.htm.

Blocher, Edward J., Chen, Jung H., and Lin, Thomas W. (1999). *Cost Management: A Strategic Emphasis.* New York: Irwin/McGraw-Hill.

Cooper, Robin, Kaplan, Robert S., Maisel, Lawrence S., Morrissey, Eileen, and Oehm, Ronald M. (1992). *Implementing Activity-Based Cost Management: Moving from Analysis to Action.* Montvale, NJ: Institute of Management Accountants.

Hilton, Ronald W., Maher, Michael W., and Selto, Frank H. (1999). *Cost Management: Strategies for Business Decisions.* New York: Irwin/McGraw-Hill.

CLIFFORD BROWN
LAWRENCE KLEIN

Billboards are a popular form of advertising.

ADVERTISING

Advertising is often thought of as the paid, non-personal promotion of a cause, idea, product, or service by an identified sponsor attempting to inform or persuade a particular target audience. Advertising has taken many different forms since the beginning of time. For instance, archaeologists have uncovered walls painted in Rome announcing gladiator fights as well as rock paintings along Phoenician trade routes used to advertise wares. From this early beginning, advertising has evolved to take a variety of forms and to permeate nearly every aspect of modern society. The various delivery mechanisms for advertising include banners at sporting events, billboards, Internet Web sites, logos on clothing, magazines, newspapers, radio spots, and television commercials. Advertising has so permeated everyday life that individuals can expect to be exposed to more than 1,200 different messages each day. While advertising may seem like the perfect way to get a message out, it does have several limitations, the most commonly noted ones being its inability to (1) focus on an individual consumer's specific needs, (2) provide in-depth information about a product, and (3) be cost-effective for small companies.

FORMS OF ADVERTISING

Advertising can take a number of forms, including advocacy, comparative, cooperative, direct-mail, informational, institutional, outdoor, persuasive, product, reminder, point-of-purchase, and specialty advertising.

Advocacy Advertising Advocacy advertising is normally thought of as any advertisement, message, or public communication regarding economic, political, or social issues. The advertising campaign is designed to persuade public opinion regarding a specific issue important in the public arena. The ultimate goal of advocacy advertising usually relates to the passage of pending state or federal legislation. Almost all nonprofit groups use some form of advocacy advertising to influence the public's attitude toward a particular issue. One of the largest and most powerful nonprofit advocacy groups is the American Association of Retired Persons (AARP). The AARP fights to protect social programs such as Medicare and Social Security for senior citizens by encouraging its members to write their legislators, using television advertisements to appeal to emotions, and publishing a monthly newsletter describing recent state and federal legislative action. Other major nonprofit advocacy groups include the environmental organization Greenpeace, Mothers Against Drunk Driving (MADD), and the National Rifle Association (NRA).

Comparative Advertising Comparative advertising compares one brand directly or indirectly with one or more competing brands. This advertising technique is very common and is used by nearly every major industry, including airlines and automobile manufacturers. One drawback of comparative advertising is that customers have become more skeptical about claims made by a company about its competitors because accurate information has not always been provided, thus making the effectiveness of comparison advertising questionable. In addition, companies that engage in comparative advertising must be careful not to misinform the public about a competitor's product. Incorrect or misleading information may trigger a lawsuit by the aggrieved company or regulatory action by a governmental agency such as the Federal Trade Commission (FTC).

Cooperative Advertising Cooperative advertising is a system that allows two parties to share advertising costs. Manufacturers and distributors, because of their shared interest in selling the product, usually use this cooperative advertising technique. An example might be when a soft-drink manufacturer and a local grocery store split the cost of advertising the manufacturer's soft drinks; both the manufacturer and the store benefit from increased store traffic and its associated sales. Cooperative advertising is especially appealing to small storeowners who, on their own,

could not afford to advertise the product adequately.

Direct-Mail Advertising Catalogues, flyers, letters, and postcards are just a few of the direct-mail advertising options. Direct-mail advertising has several advantages, including detail of information, personalization, selectivity, and speed. But while direct mail has advantages, it carries an expensive per-head price, is dependent on the appropriateness of the mailing list, and is resented by some customers, who consider it "junk mail."

Informational Advertising In informational advertising, which is used when a new product is first being introduced, the emphasis is on promoting the product name, benefits, and possible uses. Car manufacturers used this strategy when sport utility vehicles (SUVs) were first introduced.

Institutional Advertising Institutional advertising takes a much broader approach, concentrating on the benefits, concept, idea, or philosophy of a particular industry. Companies often use it to promote image-building activities, such an environmentally friendly business practices or new community-based programs that it sponsors. Institutional advertising is closely related to public relations, since both are interested in promoting a positive image of the company to the public. As an example, a large lumber company may develop an advertising theme around its practice of planting trees in areas where they have just been harvested. A theme of this nature keeps the company's name in a positive light with the general public because the replanting of trees is viewed positively by most people.

Outdoor Advertising Billboards and messages painted on the side of buildings are common forms of outdoor advertising, which is often used when quick, simple ideas are being promoted. Since repetition is the key to successful promotion, outdoor advertising is most effective when located along heavily traveled city streets and when the product being promoted can be purchased locally. Only about 1 percent of advertising is conducted in this manner.

Persuasive Advertising Persuasive advertising is used after a product has been introduced to customers. The primary goal is for a company to build selective demand for its product. For example, automobile manufacturers often produce special advertisements promoting the safety features of their vehicles. This type of advertisement could allow automobile manufactures to charge more for their products because of the perceived higher quality the safety features afford.

Product Advertising Product advertising pertains to nonpersonal selling of a specific product. An example is a regular television commercial promoting a soft drink. The primary purpose of the advertisement is to promote the specific soft drink, not the entire soft-drink line of a company.

Reminder Advertising Reminder advertising is used for products that have entered the mature stage of the product life cycle. The advertisements are simply designed to remind customers about the product and to maintain awareness. For example, detergent producers spend a considerable amount of money each year promoting their products to remind customers that their products are still available and for sale.

Point-of-Purchase Advertising Point-of-purchase advertising uses displays or other promotional items near the product that is being sold. The primary motivation is to attract customers to the display so that they will purchase the product. Stores are more likely to use point-of-purchase displays if they have help from the manufacturer in setting them up or if the manufacturer provides easy instructions on how to use the displays. Thus, promotional items from manufacturers who provide the best instructions or help are more likely to be used by the retail stores.

Specialty Advertising Specialty advertising is a form of sales promotion designed to increase public recognition of a company's name. A company can have its name put on a variety of items, such as caps, glassware, gym bags, jackets, key chains, and pens. The value of specialty advertising varies depending on how long the items used

in the effort last. Most companies are successful in achieving their goals for increasing public recognition and sales through these efforts.

ADVERTISING OBJECTIVES

Advertising objectives are the communication tasks to be accomplished with specific customers that a company is trying to reach during a particular time frame. A company that advertises usually strives to achieve one of four advertising objectives: trial, continuity, brand switching, and switchback. Which of the four advertising objectives is selected usually depends on where the product is in its life cycle.

Trial The purpose of the trial objective is to encourage customers to make an initial purchase of a new product. Companies will typically employ creative advertising strategies in order to cut through other competing advertisements. The reason is simple: Without that first trial of a product by customers, there will not be any repeat purchases.

Continuity Continuity advertising is a strategy to keep current customers using a particular product. Existing customers are targeted and are usually provided new and different information about a product that is designed to build consumer loyalty.

Brand Switching Companies adopt brand switching as an objective when they want customers to switch from competitors' brands to their brands. A common strategy is for a company to compare product price or quality in order to convince customers to switch to its product brand.

Switchback Companies subscribe to this advertising objective when they want to get back former users of their product brand. A company might highlight new product features, price reductions, or other important product information in order to get former customers of its product to switchback.

ADVERTISING BUDGET

Once an advertising objective has been selected, companies must then set an advertising budget for each product. Developing such a budget can be a difficult process because brand managers want to receive a large resource allocation to promote their products. Overall, the advertising budget should be established so as to be congruent with overall company objectives. Before establishing an advertising budget, companies must take into consideration other market factors, such as advertising frequency, competition and clutter, market share, product differentiation, and stage in the product life cycle.

Advertising Frequency Advertising frequency refers to the number of times an advertisement is repeated during a given time period to promote a product's name, message, and other important information. A larger advertising budget is required in order to achieve a high advertising frequency: Estimates have been put forward that a consumer needs to come in contact with an advertising message nine times before it will be remembered.

Competition and Clutter Highly competitive product markets, such as the soft-drink industry, require higher advertising budgets just to stay even with competitors. If a company wants to be a leader in an industry, then a substantial advertising budget must be earmarked every year. Examples abound of companies that spend millions of dollars on advertising in order to be key players in their respective industries (e.g., Coca Cola and General Motors).

Market Share Desired market share is also an important factor in establishing an advertising budget. Increasing market share normally requires a large advertising budget because a company's competitors counterattack with their own advertising blitz. Successfully increasing market share depends on advertisement quality, competitor responses, and product demand and quality.

Product Differentiation How customers perceive products is also important to the budget-setting process. Product differentiation is often necessary in competitive markets where customers have a hard time differentiating between products. For example, product differentiation might be necessary when a new laundry detergent is advertised: Since so many brands of detergent already exist, an aggressive advertising campaign would be required. Without this aggressive advertising, customers would not be aware of the product's availability and how it differs from other products on the market. The advertising budget is higher in order to pay for the additional advertising.

Stage in the Product Life Cycle New product offerings require considerably more advertising to make customers aware of their existence. As a product moves through the product life cycle, fewer and fewer advertising resources are needed because the product has become known and has developed an established buyer base. Advertising budgets are typically highest for a particular product during the introduction stage and gradually decline as the product matures.

SELECTING THE RIGHT ADVERTISING APPROACH

Once a company decides what type of specific advertising campaign it wants to use, it must decide what approach should carry the message. A company is interested in a number of areas regarding advertising, such as frequency, media impact, media timing, and reach.

Frequency Frequency refers to the average number of times that an average consumer is exposed to the advertising campaign. A company usually establishes frequency goals, which can vary for each advertising campaign. For example, a company might want to have the average consumer exposed to the message at least six times during the advertising campaign. This number might seem high, but in a crowded and competitive market repetition is one of the best methods to increase the product's visibility and to increase company sales. The more exposure a company desires for its product, the more expensive the advertising campaign. Thus, often only large companies can afford to have high-frequency advertisements during a campaign.

Media Impact Media impact generally refers to how effective advertising will be through the various media outlets (e.g., television, Internet, print). A company must decide, based on its product, the best method to maximize consumer interest and awareness. For example, a company promoting a new laundry detergent might fare better with television commercials rather than simple print ads because more consumers are likely to see the television commercial. Similarly, a company such as Mercedes-Benz, which markets expensive products, might advertise in specialty car magazines to reach a high percentage of its potential customers. Before any money is spent on any advertising media, a thorough analysis is done of each one's strengths and weaknesses in comparison to the cost. Once the analysis is done, the company will make the best decision possible and embark on its advertising campaign.

Media Timing Another major consideration for any company engaging in an advertising campaign is when to run the advertisements. For example, some companies run ads during the holidays to promote season-specific products. The other major consideration for a company is whether it wants to employ a continuous or pulsing pattern of advertisements. Continuous refers to advertisements that are run on a scheduled basis for a given time period. The advantage of this tactic is that an advertising campaign can run longer and might provide more exposure over time. For example, a company could run an advertising campaign for a particular product that lasts years with the hope of keeping the product in the minds of customers. Pulsing indicates that advertisements will be scheduled in a disproportionate manner within a given time frame. Thus, a company could run thirty-two television commercials over a three- or six-month period to promote the specific product is wants to sell. The advantage with the pulsing strategy is twofold. The company could spend less money on advertising over a shorter time period but still gain the same recognition because the advertising campaign is more intense.

Reach Reach refers to the percentage of customers in the target market who are exposed to the advertising campaign for a given time period. A company might have a goal of reaching at least 80 percent of its target audience during a given time frame. The goal is to be as close to 100 percent as possible, because the more the target audience is exposed to the message, the higher the chance of future sales.

ADVERTISING EVALUATION

Once the advertising campaign is over, companies normally evaluate it compared to the established goals. An effective tactic in measuring the usefulness of the advertising campaign is to measure the pre- and post-sales of the company's product. In order to make this more effective, some companies divide up the country into regions and run the advertising campaigns only in some areas. The different geographic areas are then compared (advertising versus nonadvertising), and a detailed analysis is performed to provide an evaluation of the campaign's effectiveness. Depending on the results, a company will modify future advertising efforts in order to maximize effectiveness.

SUMMARY

Advertising is the paid, nonpersonal promotion of a cause, idea, product, or service by an identified sponsor attempting to inform or persuade a particular target audience. Advertising has evolved to take a variety of forms and has permeated nearly every aspect of modern society. The various delivery mechanisms for advertising include banners at sporting events, billboards, Internet Web sites, logos on clothing, magazines, newspapers, radio spots, and television commercials. While advertising can be successful at getting the message out, it does have several limitations, including its inability to (1) focus on an individual consumer's specific needs, (2) provide in-depth information about a product, and (3) be cost-effective for small companies. Other factors, such as objectives, budgets, approaches, and evaluation methods must all be considered.

BIBLIOGRAPHY

Boone, L. E., and Kurtz, D. L. (1992). *Contemporary Marketing*, 7th ed. New York: Dryden.

Churchill, G. A., and Peter, P. J. (1995). *Marketing: Creating Value for Customers.* Boston: Irwin.

Farese, L., Kimbrell, G., and Woloszyk, C. (1991). *Marketing Essentials.* Mission Hills, CA: Glencoe/McGraw-Hill.

Kotler, P., and Armstrong, G. (1993). *Marketing: An Introduction*, 3d ed. Englewood Cliffs, NJ: Prentice-Hall.

Semenik, R. J., and Bamossy, G. J. (1995). *Principles of Marketing: A Global Perspective*, 2d ed. Cincinnati, OH: South-Western.

ALLEN D. TRUELL
MICHAEL MILBIER

ADVERTISING AGENCIES

Advertising agencies are independent businesses that evolved to develop, prepare, and place advertising in advertising media for sellers seeking to find customers for their goods, services, and ideas (American Association of Advertising Agencies, 2000). Advertisers use *agents* when they believe the agency will be more expert than they are at creating advertisements or at developing an advertising campaign. As businesses have become more complex and diversified, many of them have consulted agencies to help them carry out their marketing communication efforts.

The modern advertising agency provides a variety of important services to clients, including media planning and buying, research, market information, sales promotion assistance, campaign development and creation of advertisements, plus a range of services designed to help the advertiser achieve marketing objectives. The first documented advertising agency in the United States was the N. W. Ayer Agency, established in 1877 (Gilson, 1980). Prior to this time, advertising agents were *space brokers*—agents who solicited ads from businesses and then sold them to newspapers that had difficulty getting out-of-town advertising (Gilson, 1980; Russell and Lane, 1998).

EVOLUTION OF THE ADVERTISING AGENCY FROM THE 1870s TO THE EARLY 1900s

During the late nineteenth century, most advertising appeared in newspapers, on posters, and in handbills (Wells et al. 2000). Because it was difficult to reproduce illustrations, most of these ads were simple text-based items.

By 1900, the first specialized magazines had begun to appear in the United States. Magazines such as *Field & Stream* (in 1895) and *Good Housekeeping* (in 1900) established niche markets, which allowed for mass marketing to consumers with varied interests. Also, print technology had evolved considerably, making full-color illustrations possible. Advertising agencies began to use the new technology to create more attractive advertisements for the new niche markets, thus becoming creative centers rather than merely space brokerages.

The late nineteenth and early twentieth centuries were times of public concern about unethical business practices. Many professions formed their own organizations to create ethical standards of operation. The American Association for Advertising Agencies (AAAA) was founded in 1917, partially in response to these ethical concerns.

Newspapers also set their own ethical standards concerning rates charged for advertisements. By 1917, publishers had agreed to set a flat rate of 15 percent as the standard commission an advertising agency would receive—with the exception of local advertising, for which there was generally no predetermined commission (Russell and Lane, 1998).

In addition, two laws were passed to alleviate concerns about unethical advertising practices. The *Federal Trade Commission Act of* 1914 was originally designed to make all unfair methods of competition unlawful. It was not until 1922 that advertising was legally regulated under this act. The case that set this legal precedent was *FTC v. Winsted Hosiery Company* (1922) (Russell and Lane, 1998). The *Pure Food and Drug Act* of 1906 was the first act that limited the advertising of patent medicines—drugs that were advertised

A popular Pepsi-Cola television advertisement from the mid-1990s.

using exaggerated claims of effectiveness—for use by children.

EVOLUTION OF THE ADVERTISING AGENCY FROM 1920 TO THE EARLY 1950s

By the 1920s, the majority of advertising agencies had determined that most family purchasing decisions were either made by or influenced by women (Goodrum and Dalrymple, 1990). Thus, advertising agencies created full-color magazine advertisements for goods such as expensive automobiles, refrigerators, and radios. Newspapers continued to use simple advertisements.

Although Guglielmo Marconi had invented the first operating radio in 1895, radio became popular for home and family use only in the early

1920s. In that decade, as a result of radio's mass appeal, advertising agencies produced radio programs for the sole purpose of attracting consumers for popular national products. For example, soap operas were originally created for the purpose of advertising Procter & Gamble's soap products (Gilson, 1980).

The 1930s were a time of renewed public interest in legislation concerning unfair and deceptive business practices. The 1934 *Wheeler-Lea Amendment* to the *Federal Trade Commission Act* enabled the Federal Trade Commission (FTC) to protect consumers from deceptive advertising in the food, drug, therapeutic device, and cosmetic industries (Russell and Lane, 1998). The *Robinson-Patman Act* of 1936 prevented manufacturers from providing promotional allowances to a retail customer unless it also offered promotional allowances to that customer's competitors.

Although World War II suspended production of many peacetime goods and services, many advertising agents found employment working for the War Advertising Council, which was responsible for mobilizing public support for the war effort. This organization later became the Ad Council.

EVOLUTION OF THE ADVERTISING AGENCY FROM THE 1950s TO THE EARLY 1990s

The end of World War II saw a culmination of more than a decade of unsatisfied consumer demand as a result of the Great Depression and war. Most markets for goods and services found a willing consumer base for new products— including television sets. Due to the proliferation of television sales in the 1950s, advertising agencies began to combine the visual impact of print ads with the aural impact of radio to create a lifelike effect. This, in turn, created a change in the structure of advertising agencies. For example, prior to the 1950s, the main source of creativity was the person writing the advertising message—referred to as the *copywriter*. As television made more consumers comfortable with visual imagery, the art director and artist became more important (Goodrum and Dalrymple, 1990).

It was during the 1950s that large numbers of returning veterans began to marry and have children—the generation of children known as *baby-boomers*. For the first time in the United States, advertising agencies found it profitable to market certain goods and services directly to the youth market. Ads for blue jeans and stereo equipment appeared in newspaper inserts, in youth-oriented niche market magazines, and on television.

During the 1960s, large accounts from Fortune 500 companies migrated from the larger agencies to smaller, more responsive agencies (Goodrum and Dalrymple, 1990). The newer, more creative advertisements proved popular and profitable. The profits allowed agencies to spend more money on advertising research— often employing behavioral psychologists to design elaborate studies of consumer buying behavior (Goodrum and Dalrymple, 1990). It was the function of the behavioral psychologist to determine why consumers buy goods and services.

Advances in product design during the 1960s and 1970s resulted in few differences between most products—a problem known as product parity (Goodrum and Dalrymple, 1990)—and forced advertising agencies to become more creative in order to differentiate their client's product from competitors' equally good products. All of this creativity had a cost—it became very expensive to produce two-minute TV advertisements. Advertising agencies solved the cost dilemma by designing thirty-second television commercials with memorable *advertising slogans*—short phrases designed to keep a consumer's attention and maintain recognition of a particular brand of good or service.

Advertising agency clients began to demand results for increasingly expensive ads—in the form of research data from the end-consumer (Goodrum and Dalrymple, 1990). However, the cost of this research, including the employment of advertising researchers, was too great for small agencies, forcing smaller agencies to merge into larger ones during the 1980s (Goodrum and Dalrymple, 1990). During this decade, some advertising agencies moved from traditional radio and TV advertising toward *sales promotion* techniques (such as rebates, coupons, and sweepstakes) that offered measurable proof of increased sales (Wells et al., 2000).

EVOLUTION OF THE ADVERTISING AGENCY FROM 1991 TO THE PRESENT

Present-day advertising agencies employ many of the techniques that were popular in the early years of advertising. Newspapers continue to advertise primarily in text format, although color inserts are becoming popular. Advertising agencies continue to be able to advertise in smaller and smaller niche-market magazines. Radio remains a popular advertising medium in local markets. The widespread availability of cable TV and satellite transmission has fragmented television advertising into niche markets. However, some changes in the advertising industry continue to change how advertising agencies operate. These changes are discussed below.

Globalization. Advertising agencies are under increasing pressure to create ads for products in a global market, often advertising the same brand to different markets around the world. Agencies must often consider culture, language, and customs when designing an advertisement tailored to the international market. Today, in order to meet the demands of a global market, advertisers are forming large multinational agencies and continuing to debate whether to standardize advertising globally or to segment advertisements by culture or nationality (Wells et al., 2000).

The Internet. Although the Internet continues in be most accessible in developed countries, satellite transmission may soon make Internet access available to most people worldwide. The Internet allows advertising agencies to target consumers worldwide and to conduct market research inexpensively. The easy access to market research information may allow advertising agencies to continue developing ads to reach smaller and smaller niche markets worldwide. At the same time, certain forces are reducing the availability and use of information gathered over the Internet. For example, the Children's Online Protection Act (1998), or COPA, is a U.S. law

that affects business transactions by children using the Internet. COPA requires Web sites soliciting personal information from children under the age of 13 to prominently post a privacy policy and require parental consent for the release of personal information provided by those children before any business can be transacted. Many countries are developing laws similar to COPA, and it remains to be seen how COPA and other impending legislation will affect advertising agencies that conduct business globally.

The Role of Government in Advertising As of 2000, the Ad Council acts as an advertising agency that addresses social ills such as drunk driving, racial intolerance, and domestic violence (Russell and Lane, 1998; The Ad Council, 2000). The Ad Council will probably expand its role as an advertising agency that serves as a catalyst for social change.

Changing Incentives While the 15-percent commission on gross sales has been around for some time, it is now common to offer other incentives, such as box seats at sporting events and music concerts (Mayer, 1991).

EVOLVING CAREER FIELDS IN ADVERTISING

Today's advertising agencies include a vast array of specialists who work together to create a complete and thorough advertising campaign. Account managers allocate agency resources, including time, money, and personnel for individual projects. An account manager often assembles a team of individuals, each bringing a particular advertising specialty to the project. The team includes an art director, creative director, artist(s), copywriters, and designers. The team may also include other specialists such as media analysts, product testers, researchers, and public relations consultants.

BIBLIOGRAPHY

Ad Council, The. (2000). http://www.adcouncil.org.

American Association of Advertising Agencies. (2000). http://www.aaaa.org.

Balachandran, M.E., and Smith, M.O. (2000). "E-Commerce: The new frontier in marketing." *Business Education Forum* 54(4): 37-39.

Gilson, C.C. (1980). *Advertising Concepts and Strategies.* New York: Random House.

Goodrum, C. and Dalrymple, H. (1990). *Advertising in America: The First 200 Years.* New York: Harry N. Abrams.

Mayer, M. (1991). *Whatever Happened to Madison Avenue?* Boston: Little, Brown.

Norris, J.D. (1990). *Advertising and the Transformation of American Society: 1865-1920.* Westport, CT: Greenwood.

Russell, J.T., and Lane, W.R. (1998). *Kleppner's Advertising Procedure*, 10th ed. Upper Saddle River, NJ: Prentice-Hall.

Wells, W., Burnett, J., and Moriarty, S. (2000). *Advertising: Principles & Practice.* Upper Saddle River, NJ: Prentice-Hall.

SCOTT WILLIAMS
JOHN A. SWOPE

AGGREGATE INCOME

(SEE: *Income*)

AMERICAN INSTITUTE OF CERTIFIED PUBLIC ACCOUNTANTS

The American Institute of Certified Public Accountants (AICPA) is the premier national professional organization for the certified public accountant (CPA) profession in the United States. Its founding in 1887 was a milestone in establishing accountancy as a profession distinguished by rigorous educational requirements, high professional standards, a strict code of professional ethics, and a commitment to serving the public interest.

As of 2000, its membership numbers more than 336,000 certified public accountants from around the country employed in various types of environments. Approximately 45 percent work in business and industry, nearly 40 percent work in public accounting firms, and still others are on the staffs of government bodies and agencies or are employed by educational institutions. In ad-dition, some members work in the legal profession, offer consulting services, or have retired. Along with these membership segments, the AICPA has associates (those who have passed the Uniform CPA Exam and are in the midst of fulfilling the other requirements to become CPAs), as well as student and international affiliates. All together, the AICPA represents more than 350,000 people.

The AICPA's primary mission is to provide the resources, information, and leadership necessary to enable CPAs to perform services in the best professional manner to benefit the public as well as employers and clients. Activities include advocacy, certification and licensing, communications, recruiting and education, standards development, and performance monitoring. In carrying out its mission, the Institute works with local CPA societies in fifty-four accountancy jurisdictions (the fifty states plus Washington, D.C., Puerto Rico, the U.S. Virgin Islands, and Guam), giving priority to those areas where public reliance on CPA skills is greatest.

In light of its scope and resources, the AICPA is the national representative of CPAs before governments, regulatory bodies, and other organizations in protecting and promoting members' interests while preserving public confidence in the financial reporting system. It also promotes public awareness of and confidence in the integrity, objectivity, competence, and professionalism of CPAs. Most notably, to enhance key business decision makers' understanding of the skills and knowledge of CPAs, the AICPA launched the nation's first advertising campaign conducted on behalf of a profession. Having completed five consecutive successful years, the comprehensive ad campaign included television, radio, print, and Web site advertisements nationwide.

Through its volunteer member committees and professional staff, the AICPA also establishes, monitors, and enforces professional standards, as well as assisting members in continually improving their professional conduct, performance, and expertise. It also promotes and protects the CPA designation and encourages, among the states that license CPAs, the highest possible level of uniform certification and licensing standards. In fact, the AICPA develops the Uniform CPA Examination, which is administered to all candidates for the CPA designation in all states and U.S. licensing jurisdictions.

As the largest association for the accounting profession, the AICPA is also the primary information resource for CPAs and on the CPA profession. As such, the AICPA, as of 2000, is developing an Internet-based vertical portal that will provide CPAs with resources to better service small to medium-sized business clients and organizations. It will deliver information and services to the CPA more quickly, efficiently, and cost-effectively than is readily available today. The goal of the portal is to become the ultimate e-business destination for both the professional and business needs of CPAs, their clients, and employers. *AICPA Online*, the Institute's Web site (www.aicpa.org), offers the public the most comprehensive single source of information that exists on the CPA profession. For its members, the Institute houses the nation's most extensive accounting library and publishes numerous volumes of technical standards and topical publications.

Another mission of the AICPA is to encourage highly qualified individuals to become CPAs. Through member educators, recommendations for accounting curriculum, targeted recruitment, and promotional materials, the AICPA helps to ensure the continuous flow of qualified CPAs into the profession. Besides supporting the development of outstanding academic programs for students, the AICPA also is a major provider of educational courses and materials for continuing professional education, which is required by most jurisdictions for the continued licensing of CPAs and membership in the AICPA.

The AICPA's initiatives carried out on behalf of the CPA profession are numerous and always evolving to keep in step with the changing needs of a very diverse membership in a volatile business environment. As a major component of this goal, the AICPA in 1998 launched the ongoing *CPA Vision Project* (www.cpavision.org). Through this nationwide grassroots initiative, the CPA profession defined its own future, culling the views of CPAs in all segments of the profession throughout the nation. By consensus, the profession crafted a Core Purpose and Vision Statement and identified a new set of core values, services, and competencies that will characterize the work of CPAs in the future. The CPA Vision, a collective term for these findings, will extend the CPA's unique skills, expertise, and training to new services and products that bring unique added value on an ongoing basis to an ever-changing marketplace.

In an effort to identify areas where CPAs can market new services built on their special expertise and to drive markets to members, the Institute developed "assurance services," which are designed to improve the quality of information, or its context, for decision makers. Decision makers can be management, users of financial and nonfinancial information, or even consumers. The AICPA trains and licenses CPAs to offer an exclusive assurance service and seal for Web sites of companies engaging in electronic commerce over the Internet. Known as *CPA WebTrust*, the service indicates by means of a special *WebTrust* seal that appears on a company's Web site that a CPA has verified the company's business practices, transaction integrity, and privacy and security measures. The seal is intended to give consumers assurance in conducting e-commerce transactions on that Web site. Other assurance services include *CPA ElderCare Services* (providing financial and nonfinancial services to assist older clients), *CPA SysTrust* (increasing confidence in systems that support a business or activity), and *CPA Performance View* (facilitating an entity's development of a performance measurement system tailored to its unique mission and strategic plan).

For the increasing number of CPAs who are members of management in corporations of all sizes—referred to as members in "business and industry"—the AICPA established the *Center for Excellence in Financial Management* (CEFM). The CEFM is a virtual resource for the many AICPA programs, products, services, internal resources, and external partnerships that support the work of business and industry members. Those offerings include a broad benchmarking program, special conferences, group and self-study professional education courses, research on leading-edge management accounting topics, and new publications. The CEFM also aims to keep members current on the skills, knowledge, technologies, and management techniques required by CPAs to fill decision-making roles as key members of their companies' management teams.

Embracing the talent and multiple perspectives offered by America's many demographic groups, the AICPA has adopted a diversity statement that it hopes will serve as a model for the CPA profession as well as other professional organizations. In that statement, the AICPA vows to take the lead in encouraging, valuing, and fostering diversity in its membership and the work force by identifying, recognizing, and supporting strategies and efforts within the organization and the profession dedicated to achieving those diversity objectives.

In all its wide-ranging efforts on behalf of the CPA profession, the AICPA maintains the goal of becoming the best professional association in existence. In June 1998, it became the first professional membership organization in the United States to earn the *ISO 9001* certification, awarded by the International Organization of Standards using a certification system based on a series of international standards for quality management and assurance.

Organizationally, the AICPA is member-driven and -managed. It carries out its mission and objectives through the volunteer work of approximately 2,000 members who serve on a governing council, board of directors, boards, committees, subcommittees, and task forces. The governing council, the nearly 300-member governing body of the AICPA, meets twice a year and is responsible for establishing general policy. To ensure representation from all fifty-four accountancy jurisdictions, one AICPA member is designated by each CPA state society for a one-year term, and members from state societies with vacancies on the council are elected each year for a three-year term. In addition, the board of direc-

tors, past chairs, and twenty-one members-at-large serve on the council.

The board of directors, the executive committee of the council, advances the Institute's continuing objectives through leadership and management. Its twenty-three members consist of sixteen directors and three public (non-CPA) members who serve for three-year terms, as well as the chair, vice chair, immediate past chair, and the president, who is a member of the Institute staff.

With a staff of approximately seven hundred, the AICPA has four office locations. Its headquarters is located at 1211 Avenue of the Americas, New York, NY 10036-8775. The other sites are in Washington, D.C.; Jersey City, New Jersey; and Lewisville, Texas.

(SEE ALSO: *Accounting; Accounting: historical perspectives*)

BARRY C. MELANCON

AMERICAN MANAGEMENT ASSOCIATION

The American Management Association (AMA) is the world's leading membership-based management development organization. The business education and management development programs offered by the AMA provide its members and customers the opportunity to learn superior business skills and the best management practices available. The AMA fulfills this goal through a variety of seminars, conferences, assessments, customized learning solutions, books, and on-line resources. The range of programs offered by the AMA includes finance, human resources, sales and marketing, manufacturing, and international management, as well as numerous others.

The philosophy of the AMA is to be a non-profit, membership-based educational organization that assists individuals and enterprises in the development of organizational effectiveness, which is the primary sustainable competitive advantage in a global economy. A major goal of the

AMA is to identify the best management practices worldwide to provide assessment, design, development, self-development, and instruction services. The AMA meets this goal with an abundance of print and electronic media and learning methodologies, which are designed for the sole purpose of enhancing the growth of individuals and organizations.

The origins of the AMA can be traced back to 1913, when the National Association of Corporation Schools was founded. Around 1922, the National Association of Corporation Schools merged with the Industrial Relations Association of America, which had been founded in 1918. The result of the merger was the National Personnel Association. Shortly after the merger, in 1923, the National Personnel Association's board of directors chose the new name of the American Management Association. The modern AMA, as it is known today, began with a consolidation of five closely related national associations, which were all dedicated to management education. The consolidation of the organizations into one organization prompted the regents of the State University of New York to grant the AMA the title of an educational organization.

The AMA offers numerous beneficial programs aimed at a variety of people. In addition to its traditional programs, the AMA also provides programs for high school and college students and has special partnerships with local management training organizations. More information is available from the American Management Association at 1601 Broadway, New York, NY 10019; (212) 586-8100 (phone), (212) 903-8168 (fax), (800) 262-9699 (customer service); or www .amanet.org.

NIKOLE M. POGEMAN

AMERICAN MARKETING ASSOCIATION

During the mid-1930s, the American Marketing Society (organized in 1931) and the National Association of Teachers of Marketing (founded in 1915) arrived at two realizations: both organizations held common interests in marketing, and many of their publications and memberships overlapped. Following such realizations, the idea of merging the groups became a reality in 1937 with the inception of the American Marketing Association (AMA).

AMA is a professional, nonprofit organization for marketers with more than 500 North American professional chapters and worldwide membership (in ninety-two countries) in excess of 45,000. AMA also furthers students' professional development through approximately 400 collegiate chapters globally.

AMA was organized to advance marketing science and has always emphasized improving marketing management through marketing knowledge gained through researching, recording, and disseminating information. Today, AMA strives to encourage greater interest in and concern for education, to assist marketing professionals in their efforts toward personal and career development, and to promote integration of ethical considerations and general marketing practices.

In 1938, AMA agreed to work with the U.S. Bureau of the Census to unify government agency marketing definitions. The AMA board debated appropriate definitions and, in 1985, approved definitions for marketing ("The process of planning and executing the conception, pricing, promotion and distribution of ideas, goods and services to create exchanges that satisfy individual and organizational objectives)" and marketing research (the "function that links the consumer, customer, and public to the marketer through information.") (AMA, *Definitions*, 1999).

AMA disseminates information through four scholarly journals, which provide forums for sharing marketing research efforts; three business magazines, which provide discussions on emerging marketing issues for senior-level marketing executives; and one newsletter, which addresses all aspects of marketing, including insights on ethics, new products, and more. Online versions of these publications are available at www.ama .org/pub. More information is available from AMA at 250 South Wacker Dr., Suite 200, Chicago, Illinois 60606; (312) 648-0536 or (800) AMA-1150; or, http://www.ama.org.

BIBLIOGRAPHY

American Marketing Association (AMA). "AMA at a Glance." Archived at: http://www.ama.org/about/ama/atglance.asp. 1999.

AMA. "Contacts at AMA." Archived at: http://www.ana.org/contact/. 1999.

AMA. "Definitions." Archived at: http://www.ama.org/aboutama/marketdef.asp. 1999.

AMA "Six Decades of Leading and Learning American Marketing Association 1937 to 1997." Archived at: http://www.ama.org/about/ama/sixtieth/index.asp. 1999.

AMA. "About Us." Timeline. Archived at: http://www.ama.org/about/ama/sixtieth/timeline.asp. 1999.

MARY JEAN LUSH
VAL HINTON

AMERICANS WITH DISABILITIES ACT

The Americans with Disabilities Act of 1990 (ADA) is a comprehensive civil rights act for people with disabilities. On July 26, 1990, President George Bush signed the ADA into law as wide-ranging legislation intended to make American society more accessible to people with disabilities and to prohibit discrimination on the basis of disability. The act is divided into five titles:

1. Employment. Businesses must provide reasonable accommodations in all aspects of employment to protect the rights of individuals with disabilities.

2. Public services. People with disabilities cannot be denied participation in public service programs or activities that are available to people without disabilities.

3. Public accommodations. All new construction must be accessible to individuals with disabilities.

4. Telecommunications. Telecommunication companies must have a telephone relay service for individuals who use telecommunications devices for the deaf (TTYs) or similar devices.

5. Miscellaneous. This title includes a provision prohibiting coercing, threatening, or retaliating against individuals with disabilities or those assisting them in asserting their rights under the ADA.

The protection of the ADA applies primarily, but not exclusively, to individuals with physical and mental disabilities.

Built on a foundation of statutory, legal, and programmatic experience, the ADA was modeled after the Civil Rights Act of 1964 and the Rehabilitation Act of 1973. In order to understand the basis for the enactment of the ADA, one must look at certain historical events of the 1970s and the disability rights movement. First and foremost has been the desire of individuals with disabilities to work toward their goal of full participation in American society, which led to the Rehabilitation Act of 1973 and the Individuals with Disabilities Education Act of 1974 that so strongly influenced the ADA.

Effects the ADA may have on businesses include restructuring or altering the layout of a building, modifying equipment, and removing barriers. For example, in September 1999, Greyhound Bus Lines of Dallas, Texas, removed architectural barriers and began to provide assistance to passengers with disabilities by means of lift-equipped buses. Another example of the effects of the ADA occurred in February 1997, when Harrison County, Mississippi, gave people who are deaf or hard of hearing an equal opportunity to serve as jurors.

The Americans with Disabilities Act of 1990 has been regarded as the most sweeping piece of legislation since the Civil Rights Act of 1964. More information on the ADA is available at (800)514-0301 (voice) or (800)514-0383 (TDD).

BIBLIOGRAPHY

The Consumer Law Page; http://consumerlawpage.com

Department of Rehabilitation Web Site; http://www.rehab.cahwnet.gov/adaoview.htm#overview

President George Bush signed the Americans with Disabilities Act into law on July 26, 1990.

Indiana University/Purdue University Web Site; http://www
.iupui.edu/~aao/legis.html

Job Accomodation Network; http://janweb.icdi.wvu.edu/
kinder/overview/htm

U.S. Department of Justice Web Site; http://www.usdoj.gov/
crt/ada/adahom1.htm

NIKOLE M. POGEMAN

ANALYTICAL PROCEDURES

Analytical procedures have become increasingly important to audit firms and are now considered to be an integral part of the audit process. The importance of analytical procedures is demonstrated by the fact that the Auditing Standards Board, the board that establishes the standards for conducting financial statement audits, has required that analytical procedures be performed during all audits of financial statements. The Auditing Standards Board did so through the issuance of Statement on Auditing Standards (SAS) No. 56 in 1988, which requires that analytical procedures be used by auditors as they plan the audit and also in the final review of the financial statements. In addition, SAS No. 56 encourages auditors to use analytical procedures as one of the procedures they use to gather evidence related to account balances (referred to in auditing as a substantive test). The purpose of this article is to provide the reader with a general understanding of analytical procedures and to describe the process that auditors use in applying analytical procedures.

SAS No. 56 describes analytical procedures as the "evaluation of financial information made by a study of plausible relationships among both financial and nonfinancial data" (AICPA, 1998, 56 p. 1). Accounting researchers have helped to clarify the process that auditors use to perform analytical procedures by developing models that describe the various stages of the process. One such model developed by Hirst and Koonce (1996) describes the performance of analytical procedures as consisting of five components: expectation development, explanation generation, information search and explanation evaluation, decision making, and documentation. Due to the importance of each of these five components to understanding the analytical procedures process, each of them is described in more detail.

The first step in the analytical procedures process is the development of an expected account balance. SAS No. 56 and auditing textbooks (e.g., O'Reilly et al., 1998) provide some guidance as to the sources of information an auditor can use to develop these expectations. Examples of such sources include the following:

- Financial information from comparable prior periods adjusted for any changes expected to affect the current-period balances. For example, an expectation of sales revenues for the current year might be based on the prior year's sales, adjusted for factors such as price

increases or the known addition or loss of major customers.

- Expected results based on budgets or forecasts prepared by the client or projections of expected results prepared by the auditor from interim periods or prior comparable periods.

- Available information from the company's industry. For example, changes in sales revenue or gross margin percentages might be based on available data from industrywide statistics.

- Nonfinancial information. For example, sales revenue for a client from the hotel industry might be based on available data as to room occupancy rates.

After an auditor has developed an expectation for a particular account balance (e.g., sales revenue), the next step in the analytical procedures process is to compare the expected balance to the actual balance. If there is no significant difference (referred to by auditors as a material difference) between the expected and actual balance, this conclusion provides audit evidence in support of the account balance being examined. However, if there is a material difference between the expected and actual balance, the auditor will investigate this difference further. At this point the auditor will develop an explanation for the difference. Hirst and Koonce (1996) interviewed auditors from each of the six largest accounting firms and found that the source of the explanation usually depends on what types of analytical procedures are being performed. If analytical procedures are being performed during the planning phase of the audit, the auditor usually asks the client the reason for the unexpected difference. However, if the analytical procedures are being performed as a substantive test (method of obtaining corroborating evidence) or during the final review phase of the audit, in addition to asking the client, auditors will often generate their own explanation or ask other members of the audit team for an explanation.

When developing an explanation for an unexpected change in account balances, an auditor considers both error and nonerror explanations. Nonerror explanations are sometimes referred to as environmental explanations, since they refer to changes in the business environment in which the client operates. For example, an environmental explanation for an unexpected decline in gross profit (sales revenue less cost of sales) may be that the client faces increasing foreign competition and has been forced to reduce selling prices. An error explanation, on the other hand, might be that the client has failed to record a profitable sale to a major customer. If this mistake is unintentional, then auditors refer to the mistake as an "error." However, if this mistake was intentional (i.e., the client failed to record the sale on purpose), auditors refer to the mistake as a "fraud." Auditors are much more concerned about errors and fraud than changes resulting from environmental factors. In fact, auditors are most concerned about fraud, since this raises doubts about the integrity of the client as well as about the process of recording transactions affecting other account balances.

Once an auditor has a potential explanation, whether self-generated or obtained from the client, the next step in the analytical procedures process is to search for information that can be used to evaluate the adequacy of the explanation. Similar to the explanation generation phase of the process, the extent of information search and explanation evaluation depends on the type of analytical procedures being performed. Hirst and Koonce (1996) found that during the planning phase of analytical procedures, auditors do little if any follow-up work to evaluate an explanation. Instead, consistent with SAS No. 56, auditors typically use analytical procedures at the planning stage to improve their understanding of the client's business and to develop the audit plan for the engagement. For example, if analytical procedures performed on inventory during audit planning indicated the inventory balance was higher than expected, the auditor would most likely adjust the audit plan by increasing the number of audit tests performed on inventory or assigning more experienced personnel to the audit of inventory. Thus, if an error or fraud has occurred with inventory, the revised audit plan for obtaining corroborating evidence will lead to detection of the error or fraud.

If analytical procedures are being performed as a substantive test, the auditor will need to gather information to evaluate the explanation being considered, since the primary purpose of substantive analytical procedures is to provide evidence as to the validity of an account balance. The type and amount of corroboration for the explanation will vary based on factors such as the size of the unexpected difference, the significance of the difference to the overall financial statements, and the risks (e.g., internal control and inherent) associated with the account balance(s) affected. As any of these factors increase, the reliability of the information obtained in support of the explanation should also increase. SAS No. 56 provides guidance for auditors in the evaluation of the reliability of data. Some of the factors to be considered by the auditors include the following:

- Data obtained from independent sources outside the entity are more reliable than data obtained from sources within the entity.

- If data are obtained from within the entity, data obtained from sources independent from the amount being audited are more reliable.

- Data developed under a system with adequate controls are more reliable than data from a system with poor controls.

After an auditor gathers information for purposes of evaluating an analytical procedures explanation, it is a matter of professional judgment in determining whether the evidence adequately supports the explanation. This is one of the most important steps of the analytical procedures process and is referred to as the decision phase of the process. Factors the auditor should consider in evaluating the acceptability of an explanation include the materiality of the unexpected difference, reliability of the evidence obtained to support the explanation, and whether the explanation is sufficient to explain a material (significant) portion of the unexpected difference. If, after evaluating the evidence, the auditor finds that the explanation being considered does not adequately explain the unexpected difference, the auditor should return to the "explanation generation" phase of the process. If the auditor believes that the audit evidence obtained adequately supports the explanation, the auditor may proceed to the final step of the process, which is "documentation." While the extent of written documentation will vary depending on the materiality of the unexpected difference, the audit work papers will generally include a written description of material unexpected differences, an explanation for the difference, evidence that corroborates the explanation, and the judgment of the auditor as to the adequacy of the explanation.

The purpose of this article has been to provide the reader with a basic understanding of analytical procedures. Space limitations, however, preclude discussing in more detail some of the complexities associated with analytical procedures. Thus, the interested reader is referred to Statement on Auditing Standards No. 56 (AICPA, 1988) or to *Montgomery's Auditing* (O'Reilly et al., 1998) for a more in-depth discussion. Further, while the focus of this article has been on the use of analytical procedures during financial statement audits, portions of analytical procedures can also be helpful to both management and investors. For example, managers of a business may develop certain key ratios and statistics, which can be used to monitor the progress of the business. For example, a manager may use data such as the number of new customers, number of customer complaints, and other customer satisfaction measures to monitor the sales revenue and profitability of the company. An investor might also use analytical procedures to evaluate his or her investment portfolio. For example, an investor may try to forecast the future sales of a company based on knowledge of the industry in which the company operates and the prior sales history of the company. The sales forecast could then be used to develop an earnings forecast for that company, which is a critical component in developing an investment decision. Thus, while analytical procedures are an integral part of the audit process, they can also be a useful tool for managers and investors.

(SEE ALSO: *Financial statement analysis; Accounting; Auditing*)

BIBLIOGRAPHY

American Institute of Certified Public Accountants. (1988). *Statement on Auditing Standards No. 56: Analytical Procedures.* New York: Author.

Hirst, Eric D., and Koonce, Lisa. (Fall 1996). "Audit Analytical Procedures: A Field Investigation." *Contemporary Accounting Research*: 457-486.

O'Reilly, Vincent M., McDonnell, Patrick J., Winograd, Barry N., Gerson, James S., and Jaenicke, Henry R. (1998) *Montgomery's Auditing*, 12th ed. New York: Wiley.

JEAN C. BEDARD
JAMES J. MARONEY

ANTITRUST LEGISLATION

In the United States, toward the last part of the nineteenth century, widespread business combinations known as trust agreements existed. These agreements usually involved two or more companies that combined with the purpose of raising prices and lowering output, giving the trustees the power to control competition and maximize profits at the public's expense. These trust agreements would result in a monopoly. To combat this sort of business behavior, Congress passed antitrust legislation.

In 1890 Congress passed the Sherman Antitrust Act, which forbade all combinations or conspiracies in restraint of trade. The act contained two substantive provisions. Section 1 declared illegal contracts and conspiracies in restraint of trade, and Section 2 prohibited monopolization and attempts to monopolize. When an injured party or the government filed suits, the courts could order the guilty firms to stop their illegal behavior or the firms could be dissolved. The Sherman Antitrust Act pertained only to trade within the states, and monopolies still flourished as companies found ways around the law.

In 1914 Congress passed the Clayton Act as an amendment to the Sherman Act. The Clayton Act made certain practices illegal when their ef-

A cartoon illustrating antitrust legislation attacking monopolies.

fect was to lessen competition or to create a monopoly. The main provisions of this act included (1) forbidding discrimination in price, services, or facilities between customers; (2) determining that antitrust laws were not applicable to labor organizations; (3) prohibiting requirements that customers buy additional items in order to obtain products desired; and (4) making it illegal for one corporation to acquire the stock of another with intention of creating a monopoly. Because loopholes were also present in the Clayton Act, the Federal Trade Commission (FTC) was established to enforce the antitrust legislation.

Passed in 1914, the Federal Trade Commission Act provided that "unfair methods of competition in or affecting commerce are hereby declared unlawful." The FTC consists of five members appointed by the president and has the power to investigate persons, partnerships, or corporations in relation to antitrust acts. Examples of unlawful trade practices include misbranding goods quality, origin, or durability; using false advertising; mislabeling to mislead consumer about product size; and advertising or selling rebuilt goods as new. The act also gave the FTC the power to institute court proceedings against alleged violators and provided the penalties if found guilty.

The Robinson-Patman Act of 1936 strengthened the price discrimination provisions of the Clayton Act. One amendment involved the discrimination in rebates, discounts, or advertising service charges; underselling and penalties. Another provided for the exemption of non-profit institutions from price-discrimination provisions. The main purpose of this act was to justify the differences in product costs between customers and clarify the Robinson-Patman Act.

The Celler-Kefauver Antimerger Act, passed in 1950, extended the Clayton Act's injunction against mergers. Since the purpose of this act was to forbid mergers that prevented competition, corporations that were major competitors were prohibited from merging in any manner. This amendment extended the FTC's jurisdiction to all corporations. This act, however, was not intended to stop the merger of two smaller companies or the sale of one in a failing condition. Due to court decisions that had weakened the Clayton Act, the Celler-Kefauver Antimerger Act was necessary to restrict mergers.

Although antitrust laws have contributed enormously to improving the degree of competition in our system, they have not been a complete success. A sizable number of citizens would like to see these laws broadened to cover professional baseball teams, labor unions, and professional organizations. Without the antitrust legislation that now exists, however, our economy would be worse off in the end.

(SEE ALSO: *Sherman Antitrust Act of 1890*; *Robinson-Patman Act of 1936*; *Federal Trade Commission Act of 1914*)

BIBLIOGRAPHY

Antitrust statutes. http://www.stolaf.edu/people/becker/antitrust/statutes/shermann.html.

Boarman, Patrick M. (1993). "Antitrust Laws in Global Market. Challenge." Jan/Feb: 30-45.

Mueller, Charles E. (1997). "Antitrust Law and Economics Review." http://home.mpinet.net/cmueller/ii-03.html.

http://www.stolaf.edu/people/becker/antitrust/statutes/clayton.html.

http://www.stolaf.edu/people/becker/antitrust/statutes/ftc.html.

JANEL KUPFERSCHMID

ARTIFICIAL INTELLIGENCE

Computer systems are becoming commonplace; indeed, they are almost ubiquitous. We find them central to the functioning of most business, governmental, military, environmental, and health-care organizations. They are also a part of many educational and training programs. But these computer systems, while increasingly affecting our lives, are rigid, complex and incapable of rapid change. To help us and our organizations cope with the unpredictable eventualities of an ever-more volatile world, these systems need capabilities that will enable them to adapt readily to change. They need to be intelligent. Our national competitiveness depends increasingly on capacities for accessing, processing, and analyzing information. The computer systems used for such purposes must also be intelligent. Health-care providers require easy access to information systems so they can track health-care delivery and identify the most recent and effective medical treatments for their patients' conditions. Crisis management teams must be able to explore alternative courses of action and support decision making. Educators need systems that adapt to a student's individual needs and abilities. Businesses require flexible manufacturing and software design aids to maintain their leadership position in information technology, and to regain it in manufacturing. (Grosz and Davis, 1994)

The history of artificial intelligence (AI) predates the development of the first computing machines. On a general level, intelligence has been the subject of philosophical study for 2000 years. At the computational level, mathematician Alan Turing constructed a framework for AI during the era of analog computers.

While precise definitions are still the subject of debate, AI may be usefully thought of as *the branch of computer science that is concerned with the automation of intelligent behavior*. The intent of AI is to develop systems that have the ability to perceive and to learn, to accomplish physical tasks, and to emulate human decision making. AI seeks to design and develop intelligent agents as well as to understand them. Currently, the main fields of research and development include the following:

1. *Natural languages*: These studies focus on problems related to natural language interface, machine translation, understanding spoken language, and so forth.

2. *Expert systems*: No generalizable solutions are researched, but expertise is used to deal with ill-defined problems and relationships.

3. *Cognition and learning*: Investigations are being made into modes of thinking, learning, and problem solving.

4. *Computer vision*: Efforts are being made to develop principles and algorithms for machine vision and the interpretation of visual data.

5. *Automatic deduction*: This area deals with the resolution of problems, theorem proving, and logic programming.

FOUNDATIONS

The term "AI" was applied about 1956, giving a formal name to work that had been developing over the previous five or six years. Individuals and organizations have an abiding interest in AI for several important reasons, including the following:

1. To preserve expertise that might be lost when an acknowledged expert is unavailable.

2. To create organizational knowledge bases so that others may learn from past problem-solving successes.

3. To help decision makers be consistent in their evaluation of complex problems.

During its early years AI was dominated by reliance on logic as a means of representing knowledge and on logical inference as the primary mechanism for intelligent reasoning. In the 1990s other paradigms arrived on the scene, some of which had a dramatic impact. *Artificial neural networks* (ANNs) were motivated by assumptions about how the brain functions—particularly the ideas of massively parallel connections, each of which performs simple computational tasks. Taken together, they represent knowledge as a property of patterns of relationships. *Genetic algorithms* apply principles of biological evolution to the problems of searching complex solution spaces. The programs do not use logical reasoning either, but evolve toward better and better solutions to complex problems.

Multiagent systems have recently come to the fore of AI research. This emergence has been driven by a recognition that intelligence may be reflected by the collective behaviors of large numbers of very simple interacting members of a community of agents. These agents can be computers, software modules, or virtually any object that can perceive aspects of its environment and proceed in a rational way toward accomplishing a goal.

A variety of disciplines have influenced the development of AI. These include philosophy (logic), mathematics (intractibility, computability, algorithms), psychology (cognition), engineering (computer hardware and software), and linguistics (knowledge representation and natural-language processing).

Long before the development of computers, the notion that thinking was a form of computation motivated the formalization of logic. These efforts continue today. Graph theory provided the architecture for searching a solution space for a problem. Operations research, with its focus on optimization algorithms, used graph theory and other methods to solve complex decision-making problems.

In 1950, Alan Turing proposed what has become known as the Turing Test for defining intelligent behavior. The idea was to specify requirements that a computer would have to exhibit in order to demonstrate intelligence. Briefly, the Turing Test proposes that the computer should be interrogated via telecommunications by a human. Intelligence is exhibited by the computer if the interrogator cannot tell whether there is a human or a computer at the other end. In order to pass the test, a computer would need to have capabilities for natural-language processing, knowledge representation, automated reasoning, and machine learning.

AN EVOLUTION OF APPLICATIONS

While computer systems have become commonplace, they are generally rigid, complex, and incapable of rapid change. According to *A Report to ARPA on Twenty-First Century Intelligent Systems*, for us and our organizations to cope with the unpredictable eventualities of an ever-more volatile world, these systems need capabilities that will enable them to adapt readily to change. The report argues that our national competitiveness depends increasingly on capacities for accessing, processing, and analyzing information (Grosz and Davis, 1994).

One of the early milestones in AI was Newell and Simon's General Problem Solver (GPS). The program was designed to imitate human problem-solving methods. This and other developments such as Logic Theorist and the Geometry Theorem Prover generated enthusiasm for the future of AI. Simon went so far as to assert that in the near-term future the problems that computers could solve would be coextensive with the range of problems to which the human mind has been applied.

Soon difficulties in achieving this objective began to manifest themselves. In scaling up from earlier successes, problems of intractability were encountered. A search for alternative approaches led to attempts to solve typically occurring cases in narrow areas of expertise. This prompted the development of expert systems. A seminal model was MYCIN, developed to diagnose blood infections. Having about 450 rules, MYCIN was able to perform as well as many experts. This and other expert-systems research led to the first commercial expert system, R1, implemented at Digital Equipment Corporation (DEC) to help configure orders for new computer systems. Subsequent to R1's implementation, it was estimated to save DEC about $40 million a year.

Other classic systems include the PROSPECTOR program for determining the probable location and type of ore deposits and the INTERNIST program for performing medical diagnosis in internal medicine.

THE FUTURE

A Report to ARPA on Twenty-First Century Intelligent Systems identified four types of systems that will have a substantial impact on applications: intelligent simulation, intelligent information resources, intelligent project coaches, and robot teams (Grosz and Davis, 1994).

Intelligent simulations generate realistic simulated worlds that enable extensive affordable training and education that can be made available any time and anywhere. Examples may be hurricane crisis management, exploration of the impacts of different economic theories, tests of products on simulated customers, and technological design—testing features through simulation that would cost millions of dollars to test using an actual prototype.

Intelligent information resources systems (IRSS) will enable easy access to information related to a specific problem. For instance, a rural doctor whose patient presents with a rare condition might use IRSS to help assess different treatments or identify new ones. An educator might find relevant background materials, including information about similar courses taught elsewhere.

Intelligent project coaches (IPC) could function as co-workers, assisting and collaborating with design or operations teams for complex systems. Such systems could remember and recall the rationale of previous decisions and, in times of crisis, explain the methods and reasoning previously used to handle that situation. An IPC for aircraft design, for example, could enhance collaboration by keeping communication flowing among the large, distributed design staff, the program managers, the customer, and the subcontractors.

Robot teams could contribute to manufacturing by operating in a dynamic environment with minimal instrumentation, thus providing the benefits of economies of scale. They could also participate in automating sophisticated laboratory procedures that require sensing, manipulation, planning, and transport.

CONCLUSION

AI is a young field and faces many complexities. Nonetheless, the Spring 1998 issue of *AI Magazine* contained articles on the following innovative applications of AI: This is suggestive of the broad potential of AI in the future.

1. "Case- and Constraint-Based Project Planning for Apartment Construction"
2. "CREWS_NS: Scheduling Train Crews in The Netherlands"
3. "An Intelligent System for Case Review and Risk Assessment in Social Services"
4. "CHEMREG: Using Case-Based Reasoning to Support Health and Safety Compliance in the Chemical Industry"
5. "MITA: An Information-Extraction Approach to the Analysis of Free-Form Text in Life Insurance Applications"

BIBLIOGRAPHY

AI Magazine. (Spring 1998).

Grosz, Barbara, and Davis, Randall, eds. (1994). *A Report to ARPA on Twenty-First Century Intelligent Systems.*

Luger, George F., and Stubblefield, William A. (1998). *Artificial Intelligence: Structures and Strategies for Complex Problem Solving,* 3d ed. Reading, MA: Addison-Wesley.

Russell, Stuart J., and Norvig, Peter. (1995). *Artificial Intelligence: A Modern Approach.* Upper Saddle River, NJ: Prentice-Hall.

JAMES V. HANSEN

ASSURANCE SERVICES

Assurance services are a class of services provided by certified public accountants (CPAs) in public practice. While the term is sometimes used inconsistently among individual CPA firms, the American Institute of Certified Public Accountants (AICPA) Special Committee on Assurance Services defined assurance services as "independent professional services that improve the quality of information, or its context, for decision-makers."

Assurance services are rooted in the CPA's tradition of independent verification of data prepared by others. They differ from many services historically provided by CPAs in that they represent an expansion of the information and forms of reports provided. Indeed, they represent an evolution in the nature of services provided by CPAs, as CPAs have begun to provide services not just on accounting information but on many other types of information that people need in order to make decisions.

THE EVOLUTION OF CPA SERVICES

Since the early part of the twentieth century, CPAs have audited financial statements. The *audit* is the CPA's defining service and, aside from preparation of income taxes, the service most closely associated with the CPA profession. In an audit of financial statements, the CPA examines the transactions that underlie an entity's financial statements and reports whether the financial statements are fairly stated in conformity with generally accepted accounting principles. Such an opinion is required by the Securities and Exchange Commission (SEC) for companies whose stock is publicly traded and is often demanded by others, such as lenders, for entities that are not subject to the SEC.

Beginning in the 1970s, financial statement users requested that CPAs provide some of the benefits of audits at a lower cost. As a result, CPAs began providing a lower-level service, called a *review*, on financial statements. Reviews are based on inquiry and analytical procedures applied to financial statement amounts, rather than on the more rigorous procedures required in an audit, such as physical inspection and confirmation with third parties. The review culminates in a report that provides limited assurance, that is, that the CPA is not aware of any material modifications that should be made to the accompanying financial statements in order for them to be in conformity with generally accepted accounting principles. Reviews are used for quarterly financial statements of publicly held companies. Reviews are performed for privately owned companies when the financial statement user wants some assurance about the statements but do not require the level of assurance provided in an audit.

CPAs also provide a third level of service on financial statements, the *compilation*. This service, provided only to privately owned companies, is usually done in connection with helping the company record its transactions and transform its records into financial statements. The accountant does not do any tests of the underlying data, but helps put the data into financial statement form and reads the statements for material misstatements. The compilation report expresses no assurance, but if the accountant discovers material misstatements, they must be corrected or described in the CPA's report.

The 1980s brought additional expansion of the CPA's role. Users wanted CPAs to use the audit and review services to report on subjects in addition to financial statements, such as the effectiveness of internal control and the company's compliance with laws, regulations, or contracts. The profession's response was the creation of standards for *attestation* engagements. In an attestation engagement, the CPA applies the tools used in audits and reviews to provide assurance on whether the subject matter of the engagement (such as internal control or management's discussion and analysis of operations) complies with applicable criteria for measurement and disclosure. The result is a report much like an audit (reasonable assurance) or review (limited assurance) of financial statements. In addition, CPAs can apply procedures specifically designed by the expected users of the report to financial or nonfinancial items. This service is neither an audit nor a review. These engagements, called *agreed-upon procedures* engagements, result in a report in which the CPA describes the procedures applied and their results but provides no overall conclusion.

By the 1990s CPAs were being asked to expand still further into additional services, including those that involve subjects far removed from financial reporting and that do not involve an explicit report or conclusion. This area of service—assurance services—is an extension of the audit/attest tradition. It is generally distinct from common consulting services, which generally either provide advice to clients or create internal systems. Probably the most famous assurance service is that provided in controlling and counting the ballots for the annual Oscars ceremony. Another common assurance service involves CPAs observing the drawing of numbers in state lotteries.

Figure 1 is a pictorial depiction of the relationship among CPA services.

Assurance services might involve the type of reports provided in more traditional attestation engagements or they might provide less structured communications, such as reports without explicit conclusions or reports that are issued only when there are problems. Assurance services are often desired to be more customized to information needs of decision makers in specific circumstances. To be responsive to those needs, the form of CPA communication is expected to be more flexible. Thus, a significant difference between assurance and attestation engagements is that assurance engagements do not necessarily result in a standard form of report, whereas attestation engagements (and more familiar audits and reviews) do. Yet assurance services require adherence to key professional qualities by practitioners.

ELEMENTS OF AN ASSURANCE ENGAGEMENT

The important elements involved in assurance engagement are:

- Independence
- Professionalism

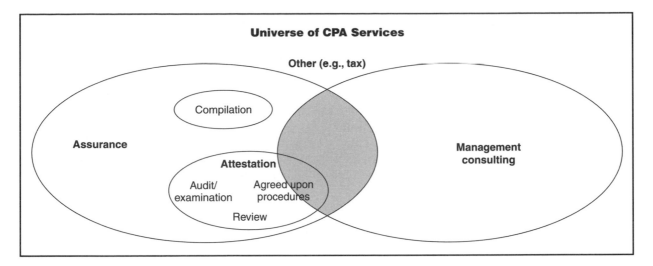

Figure 1

SOURCE: *Assurance Services: Definition and Interpretive Commentary.* AIPCA Committee on Assurance Services, Final Report.

- Information or context improvement
- Decision makers

The CPA should be independent in order to provide an assurance service; that is, he or she should have no vested interest in the information reported on. The CPA's only interest should be the accuracy of the information, not whether the information portrays results favorable or unfavorable to either the entity that prepares the information or the one that uses it.

An assurance service is a professional service, meaning it draws on the CPA's experience, expertise, and judgment. It is based on the skills brought to bear in more traditional services, such as measurement, analysis, testing, and reporting.

Information in an assurance service can be financial or nonfinancial, historical or forward-looking, discrete data or information about systems, internal or external to the decision maker. The information's context relates to how it is presented. An assurance service improves the information or its context by providing assurance about its reliability, increasing its relevance, or making it easier to use and understand.

Decision makers are the users of the information and immediate beneficiaries of the assurance service. They might be internal to an entity,

such as the board of directors, or a trading partner, such as a creditor or customer. The goal of an assurance service is to improve the information or its context so that decision makers can make more informed—and presumably better—decisions. The decision maker need not be the party engaging the CPA or paying for the service.

The needs of decision makers are evolving. For decades their needs were generally met by periodic cost-based financial statements. As information technology advances and needs become more decision-specific, decision makers are likely to:

Replace their need for . . .	With a need for . . .
periodic information	real-time or continuous data
historical data	forward-looking data
cost-based information	value-based information
financial information	comprehensive data that includes nonfinancial information
static statements	searchable databases

Assurance services, how they are delivered, and the types of information they deal with are evolving to meet these changing needs.

Although the needs of each decision maker are unique, in research done by the Special Committee on Assurance Services, decision makers expressed keen interest in better information about topics such as:

- Business risks
- Product quality
- Performance measures
- Quality of processes and systems
- Strategic plan execution
- Government performance

TYPES OF ASSURANCE SERVICES

The Special Committee on Assurance Services identified hundreds of assurance services that CPAs provide. It also identified several services that it believed would be of particular appeal to decision makers in the near future. They included the following.

Comprehensive risk assessments. The CPA identifies and assesses the various risks facing an organization, such as the operating environment, operating systems, or information systems. The risks might be internal, external, or regulatory. The CPA can help prioritize the risks and assess the entity's efforts to control or mitigate risks faced.

Business performance measurement. Many organizations use, or should use, data to run their businesses other than that emanating from the financial reporting system. The service deals with identifying or providing explicit assurance on the financial or nonfinancial measures used to evaluate the effectiveness or efficiency of the organization's activities. While CPAs have historically been involved in the development of financial statement information, their skills and knowledge can add similar value to the creation of other information that can monitor the organization's results and its effectiveness in implementing strategic plans.

Electronic commerce. As more business is conducted electronically (via the Internet or in business-to-business electronic data interchange systems) participants have concerns about the integrity and security of data transmitted in furtherance of those transactions. An assurance service can help to address the risks and promote the integrity and security of electronic transmissions, electronic documents, and the supporting systems. One such service, CPA WebTrust, provides explicit assurance about the disclosure of an entity's business policies and about the controls over privacy and information integrity in consumer purchases over the Internet.

Systems reliability. As information technology advances, it becomes increasingly common for critical information to be produced and acted on electronically. Accordingly, decision makers need confidence that the information is continuously reliable. There is an increased need for assurance that systems are designed and operated to produce reliable data in such areas as information about customers, suppliers, and employees, project costing, rights and obligations related to contractual agreements, and competitors and market conditions. In systems reliability engagements, CPAs provide assurance about the design and operation of such systems.

Elder care services. The CPA assists the increasing population of older adults with a wide range of services such as bill paying, providing assurance that health care providers are providing services in conformity with the client's criteria, and consulting on care alternatives and how to pay for them. The CPA provides independent, objective information to protect vulnerable clients from potentially unethical individuals and businesses as well as more traditional services (such as financial control) for nontraditional clients.

Policy compliance. The CPA provides assurance that a company complies with its own policies. The policies—such as ones involving treatment of women or minorities, conflicts of interest, animal testing, environmental matters, or customer service-might be based on internal concerns, calls for social accountability, or laws and regulations.

Trading partner accountability. The CPA provides assurance that the client's trading partners—such as suppliers, customers, or joint venture partners—have appropriately fulfilled their responsibilities. Common situations involve collecting rents or royalties based on sales made by another entity or agreements regarding use of lowest prices or specific billing practices.

Mergers and acquisitions. The CPA applies the types of services done on a client's records and practices to a potential acquisition. He or she can, for example, provide insights into the acquisition target's business risks, appropriateness of accounting methods, the value of its assets, or the adequacy of its systems and controls.

BIBLIOGRAPHY

AICPA Special Committee on Assurance Services, Final Report.http://www.aicpa.org/assurance.

Elliott, Robert K., and Pallais, Don M. (1997). "Are You Ready For New Assurance Services?" *Journal of Accountancy* June: 47-51.

Pallais, Don M., Spradling, L. Scott, and Ecklund, Kathy J. (1998). *Guide to Nontraditional Engagements.* Fort Worth, TX: Practitioners Publishing Company

DON M. PALLAIS

ATTESTATION

(SEE: *Assurance Services*)

AUDIT COMMITTEES

Audit committees are a key institution in the context of corporate governance because they help boards of directors fulfill their financial and fiduciary responsibilities to shareholders. Through their audit committees, boards of directors establish a direct line of communication between themselves and the internal and external auditors as well as the chief financial officer. Such an organizational structure and reporting re-

sponsibility in an environment of free and unrestricted access enables full boards of directors not only to gain assurance about the quality of financial reporting and audit processes, but also to approve of significant accounting policy decisions. Moreover, strong and effective audit committees, through their planning, review, and monitoring activities, can recognize problem areas and take corrective action before such problems impact the company's financial statements and investors. Thus, audit committees have an important role in helping boards of directors avoid litigation risk because such committees provide due diligence related to financial reporting.

REQUIREMENT FOR AUDIT COMMITTEES

Audit committees have long been seen as an important group in assuring greater corporate accountability in the United States. The value of such committees has been noted by the U.S. Congress, the U.S. Securities and Exchange Commission, the New York Stock Exchange, and the American Institute of Certified Public Accountants. Audit committees are required by the New York Stock Exchange, American Stock Exchange, and National Association of Securities Dealers (NASDAQ/NMS issuers).

Key recommendations and decisions in the evolution of audit committees in the United States include the following

1940 The Securities and Exchange Commission (SEC) recommended the establishment of audit committees (Accounting Series Release No. 19). Specifically, the SEC recommended that shareholders elect the auditors at annual meetings and a committee of nonofficer directors nominate the auditors. Also, the New York Stock Exchange Board of Governors issued a similar recommendation.

1967 The executive committee of the American Institute of Certified Public Accountants (AICPA) recommended that publicly held corporations establish audit committees to nominate the auditors and discuss the audit.

1972 The SEC issued Accounting Series Release No. 123, "Standing Audit Committees Composed of Outside Directors."

1973 The New York Stock Exchange (NYSE) issued a white paper, "Recommendations and Comme..s on Financial Reporting to Shareholders and Related Matters," strongly recommending that each listed company form an audit committee.

1974 The SEC amended Regulation 14A dealing with the proxy rules. Registrants are required to disclose in their proxy statements the existence of audit committees and the names of the committee members.

1977 A NYSE audit committee policy statement required each domestic corporation listed on the exchange to establish and maintain an audit committee of outside directors before July 1, 1978.

1987 The National Commission on Fraudulent Financial Reporting recommended that the SEC require that all public companies have audit committees.

1987 The National Association of Securities Dealers required each NASDAQ/NMS issuer to establish an audit committee.

1991 Congress passed the Federal Deposit Insurance Corporation Improvement Act. The law provided for the establishment of audit committees for insured depository institutions that have total assets of $150,000,000 or more.

1993 American Stock Exchange required its listed companies to establish audit committees.

1994 The American Law Institute issued *Principles of Corporate Governance: Analysis and Recommendations*. The Institute strongly supported and endorsed the concept of audit committees.

1999 The Independence Standards Board issued its first standard, "Independence Discussions with Audit Committees," which requires independent auditors to issue an annual independence confirmation to the audit committee of the company.

1999 The SEC approved changes to its rules to implement several of the recommendations by the Blue Ribbon Committee on Improving the Effectiveness of Corporate Audit Committees. Registrants are required to disclose information about audit committee composition and practices.

In addition to the presence of audit committees on U.S. stock exchanges, a number of stock exchanges in Canada, Europe, Africa, the Middle East, and the Asia/Pacific region have adopted audit committees. As worldwide financial markets expand and more companies are listed on major stock exchanges in different countries, the international investing public's demand for consistent and equal oversight protection through the use of audit committees will continue. In addition, international investors are concerned about the quality of corporate governance because of the impact of financial collapses and alleged frauds on securities markets.

In response, a number of stock exchanges have adopted audit committees to increase transparency and competence in the management of their listed member companies in order to deal effectively with attracting foreign equity investment.

ORGANIZATION AND STRUCTURE OF AUDIT COMMITTEES

Boards of directors form their audit committees by either passing a board resolution or amending corporate bylaws. Audit committees' responsibilities should be clearly defined and documented in their charter. Although the scope of the audit committees' responsibilities is predetermined by boards, the committees should be allowed to expand their charge with board approval and investigate significant matters that impact financial reporting disclosures.

Boards of directors should carefully give consideration to the following points with respect to their appointments of directors to audit committees:

1. *Number of directors*: The number of independent directors appointed to audit committees depends on the nature of the business and industry dynamics, the size of the company, and the size of the board of directors. The general consensus seems to be that three to five members are adequate.

2. *Composition*: Because members of audit committees have varied backgrounds and occupations, they provide a mix of skills and experience. Although the members have different levels of expertise, it is strongly advisable to have at least one individual who has a financial accounting background.

3. *Meetings*: Audit committees meet from one to four times each year, with three or four meetings being the most common schedules.

NATURE OF AUDIT COMMITTEES RESPONSIBILITIES

Boards of directors define the role and responsibilities of their audit committees. This jurisdictional charge is usually disclosed in the audit committees' written charter, which includes the terms of reference, such as mission statement, membership (size and composition), term of service, frequency of meetings, scope of responsibilities, and reporting responsibilities. Audit committees are primarily responsible for the quality related to such matters as:

- External auditing process
- Internal auditing process
- Internal controls
- Conflicts of interest (code of corporate conduct, fraud presentation)
- Financial reporting process
- Regulatory and legal matters
- Other matters (interim reporting, information technology, officers' expense accounts)

Although boards of directors have defined the responsibilities of audit committees, boards may expand the scope of the audit committees' charter; however, boards should avoid diluting the committees' charge with information overload. Recognizing that audit committees operate on a part-time basis and serve in an advisory capacity to boards, it is essential that boards place limitations on the scope of the committees' charge. Such a scope limitation enables boards to evaluate the committees' performance as well as protect the committees against legal claims for their inactions that are outside their charge. An illustration of the roles and responsibilities of audit committees is disclosed in the annual proxy statement of a company.

BLUE RIBBON COMMITTEE ON IMPROVING THE EFFECTIVENESS OF CORPORATE AUDIT COMMITTEES

On September 28, 1998, Arthur Levitt, chairman of the SEC, presented an address at the New York University Center for Law and Business entitled "The Numbers Game." He discussed matters related to the issues involving the quality of financial reporting (e.g., earnings management, reserves, audit adjustments, revenue recognition, creative acquisition accounting, in-process research and development, and restructuring charges). Because these issues impact a firm's quality of earnings and market capitalization (e.g., price-earnings ratios), Levitt requested a response from the entire financial community.

In response to Levitt's concerns, in October 1998, the New York Stock Exchange and the National Association of Securities Dealers created the Blue Ribbon Committee on Improving the Effectiveness of Corporate Audit Committees. In February 1999, the committee issued its report, which contains ten recommendations designed to (1) strengthen the independence of audit committees; (2) increase the effectiveness of audit committees; and (3) improve the relationship between boards and their audit committees the activities of auditors and management. In December 1999, the SEC approved changes to its rules to implement several of the Blue Ribbon Committee's recommendations with respect to audit committee composition and practices.

In view of the aforementioned recommendations of the Blue Ribbon Committee, it is clearly evident that the scope for the responsibilities of audit committees will significantly increase. Therefore, it is essential that audit committees engage in an active continuous educational improvement program to help their boards discharge their fiduciary responsibilities to shareholders.

The duties of the Audit Committee are (a) to recommend to the Board of Directors a firm of independent accountants to perform the examination of the annual financial statements of the Company; (b) to review with the independent accountants and with the Controller the proposed scope of the annual audit, past audit experience, the Company's internal audit program, recently completed internal audits and other matters bearing upon the scope of the audit; (c) to review with the independent accountants and with the Controller significant matters revealed in the course of the audit of the annual financial statements of the Company; (d) to review on a regular basis whether the Company's Standards of Business Conduct and Corporate Policies relating thereto has been communicated by the Company to all key employees of the Company and its subsidiaries throughout the world with a direction that all such key employees certify that they have read, understand and are not aware of any violation of the Standards of Business Conduct; (e) to review with the Controller any suggestions and recommendations of the independent accountants concerning the internal control standards and accounting procedures of the Company; (f) to meet on a regular basis with a representative or representatives of the Internal Audit Department of the Company and to review the Internal Audit Department's Reports of Op-

erations; and (g) to report its activities and actions to the Board at least once each fiscal year.

(SEE ALSO: *Auditing*; *Securities and Exchange Commission*)

BIBLIOGRAPHY

American Institute of Certified Public Accountants. (1978). *Audit Committees, Answers to Typical Questions About Their Organization and Operations.* New York: Author.

American Law Institute. (1994) *Principles of Corporate Governance: Analysis and Recommendations.* Philadelphia, PA: Author.

Blue Ribbon Committee on Improving the Effectiveness of Corporate Audit Committees. (1999). *Report and Recommendations of the Blue Ribbon Committee on Improving the Effectiveness of Corporate Audit Committees.* New York: New York Stock Exchange and Washington, DC: National Association of Securities Dealers.

Braiotta, L. (1986). "Audit Committees: An International Survey." *The Corporate Board* May/June: 18-23.

Braiotta, L. (1994). *The Audit Committee Handbook.* New York: Wiley.

Bristol-Myers Squibb Company. (1999). *Notice of 1999 Annual Meeting and Proxy Statement.* New York: Author.

National Commission on Fraudulent Financial Reporting. (1987). *Report of the National Commission on Fraudulent Reporting.* Washington, DC: Author.

New York Stock Exchange. (1983). "Corporate Responsibility: Audit Committee, Sec. 303.00." In *New York Stock Exchange Listed Company Manual.* New York: Author.

Securities and Exchange Commission. (1999). *Audit Committee Disclosure, Release No. 34-42266.* Washington, DC: Author.

LOUIS BRAIOTTA, JR.

AUDITING

The objective of an audit is to provide assurance that an assertion corresponds with some established criteria. An audit involves gathering and evaluating evidence to support the assertions and preparing a communication indicating the work done by the auditor and his or her opinion regarding the degree of correspondence between the assertions and established criteria.

TYPES OF AUDITS

Two primary types of audits are financial audits and compliance audits. In a financial audit, the management of a business asserts that the financial statements are prepared in accordance with generally accepted accounting principles (GAAP), which are the applicable criteria. The financial statement auditor attests to the degree of correspondence between those financial statements and GAAP. In a compliance audit, an individual or business asserts that it is complying with specific laws, regulations, policies or procedures. The compliance auditor provides assurance that the entity is, in fact, complying with those applicable criteria. More details are provided below.

Audits are related to a wide range of criteria. Operational, or performance, audits evaluate the effectiveness and/or efficiency of an organization. For example, an auditor may determine whether or not a recipient of government funds is performing the funded services in a cost-efficient manner. The term "attestation engagement" includes audits and other services in which an auditor is engaged to issue a written communication that expresses a conclusion about the reliability of a written assertion that is the responsibility of another party. For example, an auditor may attest to the reliability of awards programs. The key components are an assertion made by one party with the expectation that a third party will rely on it and an attestor providing a written report on the assertion. Assurance services are independent professional services, including attestation services, that improve the quality of information or its context for decision makers. Developing areas for assurance services include Webtrust, which provides assurance regarding controls related to electronic commerce.

TYPES OF AUDITORS

The three broad groups of auditors are external, internal, and governmental. Certified public accountants (CPAs) are external, independent auditors who are licensed by individual states to provide auditing services. The public accounting profession has played an active role in developing and providing attestation services. The American Institute of Certified Public Accountants (AICPA), a voluntary national professional organization, represents the accounting profession in the United States in general and the public accounting profession in particular. The AICPA publishes books, journals, and other materials, manages a Web site (www.aicpa.org), lobbies legislators, and sets professional standards. State professional societies, such as the New York State Society of CPAs, provide support on a local level. The United States Securities and Exchange Commission (SEC), in requiring publicly held companies to have annual audits, promoted the role of the CPA in providing services of this nature (i.e. independent, professional, external verification). SEC requirements are discussed below.

Internal auditors are employees of organizations. In publicly owned companies, internal auditors typically report to senior management and the board of directors, through its audit committee. Internal auditors are primarily involved in compliance and operational audits. The Institute of Internal Auditors (IIA), an international organization, is the professional organization representing the internal auditing profession. The IIA publishes materials, encourages local chapter activities, offers certification as a certified internal auditor (CIA), and provides general support for practicing internal auditors. (For more information, go to http://nan.shh.fi/raw/iia/.)

Government auditors evaluate their own agencies and those for which they are responsible, including recipients of funds. These auditors exist on the national, state, and local levels. Internal Revenue Service (IRS) auditors and General Accounting Office (GAO) auditors are the most visible government auditors. IRS auditors examine tax returns. (For more information, go to http://www.irs.gov/.) The GAO is responsible for oversight, review, and evaluation of federal agencies and recipients of federal funds. The GAO reports to the U.S. Congress. (For more information, go to http://www.gao.gov/index.htm.)

FINANCIAL AUDITS

The objective of a financial audit is to determine whether the financial statements are prepared in accordance with generally accepted accounting principles (GAAP). The management of an organization is responsible for preparing the financial statements. The auditor is responsible for rendering an opinion on the fairness of those financial statements based on his or her audit.

When preparing the financial statements, management must follow GAAP, which are the principles and practices that govern financial reporting. Formal Statements of Financial Accounting Standards are issued by the Financial Accounting Standards Board (FASB), an independent standards-setting organization in the United States. (For more information, go to www.rutgers.edu/Accounting/raw/fasb/.) The Audit Committee of the company's board of directors acts as a liaison with the auditors who are performing the financial statement audit.

SECURITIES AND EXCHANGE ACT OF 1934

The Securities and Exchange Act of 1934 requires publicly held companies to file Form 10-Ks with the Securities and Exchange Commission (SEC) within 90 days after the end of the fiscal year. This filing must include audited financial statements and an independent auditors report. The SEC was established to protect investors, and the requirement to publish audited annual financial statements plays a role in meeting that objective. (For more information, go to www.sec.gov.)

Nonpublic companies may have their financial statements audited for several reasons. The company may be planning to go public in the near future and will need audited financial statements for several years prior to an initial public offering. A bank or other creditor may require audited financial statements annually. A business may voluntarily hire an auditor to provide the owners with assurance that its financial statements are reliable.

CPA FIRMS

Audited financial statements that will be submitted to the SEC or to others are audited by CPAs. These CPAs practice in public accounting firms, many of which are referred to as professional services firms. The largest firms are commonly referred to as "The Big Five." These five firms are: Arthur Andersen & Co. (http://www.arthurandersen.com/), Deloitte & Touche (http://www.dttus.com/), Ernst & Young (http://www.ey.com), KPMG Peat Marwick (http://www.kpmgcampus.com/), and PricewaterhouseCooper (http://www.pwcglobal.com/). These companies, and many other public accounting firms, operate as limited liability partnerships (LLPs) and thus carry LLP designation in their names. In addition to accounting and auditing services, many CPA firms offer tax and consulting services. These consulting services include systems design, litigation support, pension and benefits consulting, and financial planning.

GENERALLY ACCEPTED AUDITING STANDARDS

The external, independent CPA must follow generally accepted auditing standards (GAAS) when performing the financial statement audit. These ten broad standards include three general requirements for the individual auditor, three standards for fieldwork, and four reporting standards. Authoritative guidance regarding the application of these ten general standards is provided in Statements on Auditing Standards (SASs), which are issued by the AICPA's Auditing Standards Board.

The general standards require the CPA to be proficient in accounting and auditing, to be independent from his or her client, and to exercise due professional care. Before accepting an audit client, the auditor must determine if he or she will be able to provide the necessary services on a timely basis and must have no financial or managerial relationship with the company whose financial statements are being audited.

The fieldwork standards address what is required when actually performing the audit work.

The auditor must plan the engagement and supervise assistants. The auditor must obtain an understanding of the company's internal controls. The auditor must obtain sufficient competent evidence to support the financial statement assertions.

The reporting standards set requirements for the auditor's report. The report must explicitly refer to GAAP and must state an opinion on the financial statements as a whole. If there has been a change in accounting principles used by the company or inadequate disclosure of significant information, the auditor's report should address those issues.

TYPES OF AUDITOR'S REPORTS

The auditor can issue five types of reports on financial statements: unqualified opinion, unqualified opinion with explanatory language, qualified opinion, adverse opinion, or disclaimer of opinion.

If the financial statements present fairly, in all material respects, an entity's financial position (i.e., the balance sheet), results of operations (i.e., the income statement), and cash flows (i.e., the statement of cash flows) in conformity with GAAP, and if the audit is performed in accordance with GAAS, then a standard unqualified report can be issued. The standard unqualified report is as follows:

Independent Auditor's Report

We have audited the accompanying balance sheets of X company as of December 31, 20X2 and 20X1, and the related statements of income, retained earnings, and cash flows for the years then ended. These financial statements are the responsibility of the Company's Management. Our responsibility is to express an opinion on these financial statements based on our audits.

We conducted our audits in accordance with generally accepted auditing standards. Those standards require that we plan and perform the audit to obtain reasonable assurance about whether the financial statements are free of material misstatement. An audit includes examining, on a test basis, evidence supporting the amounts and disclosures in the financial statements. An audit also includes assessing the accounting principles used and significant estimates

made by management, as well as evaluating the overall financial statement presentation. We believe that our audits provide a reasonable basis for our opinion.

In our opinion, the financial statements referred to above present fairly, in all material respects, the financial position of X Company as of [at] December 31, 20X2 and 20X1, and the results of its operations and its cash flows for the years then ended in conformity with generally accepted accounting principles.

Under certain circumstances, which are specified in the professional guidance, an auditor adds explanatory words or paragraph to a report in which an unqualified opinion is expressed. The unqualified opinion is not affected. There are nine situations in which such explanations are allowed. Among the most common are those instances in which there has been a change in accounting principle with which the auditor concurs. In such instances, the auditor adds a paragraph after the opinion paragraph. The additional paragraph identifies briefly the accounting change.

The auditor would issue a qualified opinion in situations where the auditor views a departure from GAAP as being material, but not pervasive or highly material relative to the entire set of financial statements; or when the auditor has not been able to obtain sufficient competent evidence pertaining to a material, but not pervasive or highly material, part of the financial statements. The auditor must add an explanatory paragraph before the opinion paragraph describing the reason for the qualification and then qualify the opinion paragraph. In the case of inadequate evidence, which is referred to as a scope limitation, the second paragraph of the report would also been modified.

If, in the auditor's judgment, pervasive or highly material deviation(s) from GAAP exist and the auditee cannot be persuaded to adjust the financial statements to the satisfaction of the auditor, then the auditor must express an adverse opinion. In this condition, the auditor expresses an opinion that the financial statements taken as a whole do not present fairly the financial position, results of operations, and cash flows of the company in accordance with GAAP.

A disclaimer of opinion, which basically means giving no opinion, is issued when the scope limitation (typically lack of evidence regarding financial statement assertions) is so pervasive or highly material that the auditor cannot draw conclusions as to the fairness of the financial statements, taken as a whole. A disclaimer is also issued when the auditor lacks independence from the auditee. Disclaiming an opinion is also permitted, but not required, in conditions of major uncertainty about the company's ability to continue as a going concern for a year following the date of the financial statements.

CODE OF PROFESSIONAL CONDUCT

The AICPA Code of Professional Conduct guides the CPA in the performance of professional services, including audits. The code consists of principles, rules, interpretations, and rulings, going from the very broad to the very specific.

The six ethical principles of professional conduct provide the basis for the rest of the code. CPAs are expected to exercise professional and moral judgments in all their activities. CPAs should act in the public interest. CPAs should perform all their work with the highest sense of integrity. CPAs should be free of conflicts of interest when performing professional services. CPAs should observe the profession's technical and ethical standards. CPAs in public practice should observe these principles of the Code of Professional Conduct in determining the scope and nature of services to be provided.

The rules address more specific ethical concerns. CPAs are required to be independent, to act with integrity and objectivity, and to follow and comply with applicable standards. When expressing an opinion on financial statements, the CPA must use GAAP as the criteria for evaluating fairness. Client information is confidential. Contingent fees, commissions, or referral fees are not acceptable when providing audit services. CPAs shall not commit discreditable acts, advertise in deceptive ways, or practice in a form of organization that is not permitted by state law.

The interpretations provide more detail regarding the rules. The independence rule has the most interpretations. Interpretations give guidance on issues such as financial and managerial relationships with the client, honorary directorships, loans, litigation, and firm and family relationships. Interpretations of other rules address issues such as conflicts of interest, competency, departures from promulgated GAAP, disclosure of confidential client information, sale of a practice, contingent fees in tax matters, client's records, governmental requirements in attest services, and CPAs operating a separate business.

Rulings are answers to specific questions. They provide guidance to CPAs regarding particular concerns that surface in providing professional services. Examples include whether or not a CPA can accept a gift from a client, when an individual can refer to him- or herself as a CPA, and the recruiting of personnel to fill a client position.

COMPLIANCE AUDITS

The objective of a compliance audit is to determine whether the auditee is following prescribed laws, regulations, policies, or procedures. These audits can be performed within a business organization for internal purposes or in response to requirements by outside groups, particularly government. Compliance audits can also be performed on individuals, for example, a compliance audit of an individual's tax return.

Typically, internal auditors are involved with compliance audits, within an organization, although independent CPAs perform this work as well. A compliance audit may focus on internal controls and whether or not the organization is following the internally prescribed policies and procedures. As part of the compliance audit, the auditor will obtain evidence supporting the assertion that the controls are being followed. Based on the auditor's evaluation of the evidence, he or she will usually write a report discussing the findings and making recommendations for improvement. A compliance audit could also look at external laws and regulations. The auditor would assess whether or not the organization, or the applicable part of the organization such as the marketing department, is adhering to specific laws and regulations, such as the Foreign Corrupt Practice Act of 1977. This law prohibits business entities from bribing officials of other governments in order to win business contracts.

Standards to be used when auditing federal government agencies and recipients of federal funds are found in "Government Auditing Standards," issued by the Comptroller General of the United States. This publication, which is referred to as the "Yellow Book," includes additional auditing standards that must be followed, in addition to GAAS. As part of any Yellow Book audit, the auditor must evaluate compliance with laws and regulations.

The auditor must perform several steps. First, the auditor must identify pertinent laws and regulations. Then, the auditor assesses the risks of material noncompliance; in so doing, the auditor must consider and assess internal controls. Next, the auditor designs steps and procedures to test compliance with laws and regulations to provide reasonable assurance that both

unintentional and intentional instances of material noncompliance are detected. The auditor must issue a report on the tests of compliance in which all instances of noncompliance or illegal acts must be reported.

(SEE ALSO: *Assurance services; Audit Committees; Government Auditing Standards*)

BIBLIOGRAPHY

Messier, William F. Jr., (1997). *Auditing: A Systematic Approach.* New York: Irwin McGraw-Hill.

MOHAMMAD J. ABDOLMOHAMMADI
ELLIOTT S. LEVY

AUDITOR REPORTS

(SEE: *Auditing*)

AUTHORITY

(SEE: *Management: Authority and Responsibility*)

B

BABY BOOMERS

(SEE: *Lifestyles*)

BAIT AND
SWITCH ADVERTISING

(SEE: *Advertising*)

BALANCE OF TRADE

Even though the United States has many natural resources and the ways and means to use them in manufacturing, it cannot provide its people with all that they want or need. For this reason, the United States participates in international trade, which is the exchange of goods and services with other nations. Without international trade, goods would either cost more or not be available.

Throughout the world, there are substantial differences in the natural resources available. For example, Canada, with its huge forests, is a major producer of lumber and paper products; the Middle East has rich oil reserves; and the coastal regions of the world are leaders in the fishing industry.

Without international trade, each country would have to be totally self-sufficient. Each would have to make do only with what it could produce on its own. This would be the same as an individual being totally self-sufficient, providing all goods and services, such as clothing and food,

that would fulfill all wants and needs. International trade allows each nation to specialize in the production of those goods it can produce most efficiently. Specialization, in turn, causes total production to be greater than it would be if each nation tried to be self-sufficient.

Goods and services sold to other countries are called exports; goods and services bought from other countries are called imports. The U.S. Bureau of the Census, Foreign Trade Division, indicates that U.S. exports include such goods as corn, wheat, soybeans, plastics, iron and steel products, chemicals, and machinery, while imports include such goods as chemicals, crude oil, machinery, diamonds, and coffee.

The balance of trade is the difference between the dollar amount of exports and the dollar amount of imports. The United States has many trade partners. Table 1 shows the U.S. balance of trade with three selected nations.

In order to have a trade surplus, a country must export (sell) more than it imports (buys). The opposite of a trade surplus is a trade deficit. This occurs when a country imports (buys) more than it exports (sells). As can be seen from Table 1, a country can have a trade surplus with one country and a trade deficit with another. The Bureau of the Census records indicate that for the month of November 1998 the United States had a trade surplus with such countries as Saudi Arabia, the Netherlands, Australia, and Brazil. During the same month, the United States had a

United States Trade with Selected Countries, 1998

Country	Goods Exported (In Millions)	minus	Good Imported (In Millions)	equals	Balance of Trade
Japan	58	–	122	=	–64
Canada	154	–	175	=	–21
Australia	12	–	5	=	+7
(exports – imports = balance of trade)					

Table 1

SOURCE: U.S. Bureau of the Census, Foreign Trade Division, 1998.

trade deficit with such countries as Japan, China, Canada, and Mexico.

The Bureau of the Census also reports that the United States experienced its first trade deficit (total of all exports minus total of all imports) of the twentieth century in 1971, with a trade deficit of approximately $1.5 billion. A record high trade deficit occurred in 1998, when imports exceeded exports by approximately $230 billion. Table 2 shows the U.S. balance of trade for the years 1960 through 1998. As can be easily seen in the table, the U.S. trade deficit continues to increase.

As stated earlier, total production increases when a nation specializes in the production of those goods it can produce most efficiently instead of attempting to be totally self-sufficient. Allen Smith (1986), states that "a country that can produce a product more efficiently than another country is said to have an absolute advantage in the production of that product" (p. 315). When a nation can use fewer resources to produce the same amount of a product, it has an absolute advantage in the production of that product. For example, Brazil has an absolute advantage over the United States in the production of coffee, and the Middle East has an absolute advantage over the United States in the production of crude oil. Because of its ideal climate, Ecuador can produce bananas more efficiently than the United States; therefore, Ecuador has an absolute advantage over the United States in the production of bananas. However, the United States has an absolute advantage over Ecuador in the production of most products. Both nations benefit by trading those products that each nation can produce more efficiently. Nations usually will not trade with other nations unless there are gains to be made by each nation. However, the gains made will not necessarily be equal.

Smith (1986) also states that "any time a nation has an absolute advantage in the production of two goods or services, the nation has a comparative advantage in the production of that good or service where the absolute advantage is greater" (p. 315). In other words, if a nation has a two-to-one absolute advantage in the production of one product and a three-to-one absolute advantage in the production of another product, the comparative advantage lies with the product with the larger ratio. Smith (1986) also states that "even though a nation has an absolute disadvantage in the production of two products, it has a comparative advantage in the production of that product in which the absolute disadvantage is less" (p. 316). For example, even though a nation has a disadvantage in the production of a certain product, if that disadvantage is small compared to its disadvantage in the production of other products, it still has a comparative advantage with the former product.

When the United States buys goods from another country, it usually pays for the goods in the currency of the exporting country. There are many transactions that involve the exchange of money between nations. The balance of payments is an accounting record of the difference

Trade Balance
Goods on a Census Basis

VALUE IN MILLIONS OF DOLLARS
1960 THRU 1998

Year	Balance	Total Exports	Total Imports
1960	4,609	19,626	15,018
1961	5,476	20,190	14,714
1962	4,583	20,973	16,390
1963	5,289	22,427	17,138
1964	7,006	25,690	18,684
1965	5,333	26,699	21,366
1966	3,830	29,372	25,542
1967	4,122	30,934	26,812
1968	837	34,063	33,226
1969	1,290	37,332	36,042
1970	3,225	43,176	39,951
1971	−1,476	44,087	45,563
1972	−5,729	49,854	55,583
1973	2,389	71,865	69,476
1974	−3,884	99,437	103,321
1975	9,551	108,856	99,305
1976	−7,820	116,794	124,614
1977	−28,353	123,182	151,534
1978	−30,205	145,847	176,052
1979	−23,922	186,363	210,285
1980	−19,696	225,566	245,262
1981	−22,267	238,715	260,982
1982	−27,510	216,442	243,952
1983	−52,409	205,639	258,048
1984	−106,702	223,976	330,678
1985	−117,711	218,815	336,526
1986	−138,280	227,159	365,438
1987	152,119	254,122	406,241
1988	−118,526	322,426	440,952
1989	−109,400	363,812	473,211
1990	−101,719	393,592	495,311
1991	−66,723	421,730	488,453
1992	−84,501	448,164	532,665
1993	−115,568	465,091	580,659
1994	−150,630	512,626	663,256
1995	−158,801	584,742	743,543
1996	−170,214	625,075	795,289
1997	−181,488	689,182	870,671
1998	−230,852	682,977	913,828

Table 2

NOTE: Balances are rounded.

SOURCE: U.S. Bureau of the Census, Foreign Trade Division, February 19, 1999.

between the amount of money that a country receives and the amount of money that it pays out during a year. A positive balance of payments means that a country receives more money in a year than it pays out. Likewise, a negative balance of payments occurs when a country pays out more money than it takes in. Any transaction that involves payments between countries is included in the balance of payments. The largest component of the balance of payments is the balance of trade, but many more financial transactions are included, such as foreign aid to other nations, government support of military personnel stationed in other nations, and money spent by tourists.

The importing and exporting of goods and services are controlled by the U.S. government. Three of the most common barriers to trade are tariffs, import quotas, and embargoes. A tariff is a tax imposed by the government on imported goods. An import quota places a limit on the amount of a product that may be imported or exported during a given period of time. An embargo occurs when the government halts the import or export of a certain product.

BIBLIOGRAPHY

Gottheil, Fred M., and Wishart, David. (1997). *Principles of Economics with Study Guide.* Cincinnati: South-Western College Publishing.

Smith, Allen W. (1986). *Understanding Economics.* New York: Random House.

U.S. Bureau of the Census, Foreign Trade Division. http://www.census.gov/foreign-trade/site1/1998.

LISA S. HUDDLESTUN

BANKRUPTCY

Bankruptcy law was created initially to enable persons inundated with debt to have a new beginning. It is also designed to permit individuals and business entities to have additional time to pay and compromise existing debts without liquidating all assets. The U.S. Constitution, Article 1, Section 8(4) grants the power exclusively to Congress "[T]o establish . . . uniform laws on the subject of bankruptcies throughout the United States." The current Code is based on the Bankruptcy Reform Act of 1978 as amended. Bankruptcy Courts, under the supervision of U.S. District Courts, administer petitions under the statute.

The Code is divided into a number of chapters, the most important of which are Chapter 7 ("Liquidation"), Chapter 11, ("Reorganization"), and Chapter 13, ("Adjustment of Debts of an Individual with Regular Income"). The remaining chapters concern definitions, case administration, a discussion of creditors' claims, debtors' duties, estate of the debtor, U.S. trustees, municipal indebtedness, and debts of farm families.

CHAPTER 7: LIQUIDATION

A Chapter 7 proceeding is "bankruptcy" as envisioned by most persons. The crux of such a proceeding is the collection and reduction to cash of all nonexempt assets owned by the debtor; the monies, to the extent available, are distributed to classes of creditors.

Petition. The proceeding is begun by the filing of a petition with the clerk of the Bankruptcy Court. The petition may be "voluntary" or "involuntary." A "voluntary" petition is one filed by the debtor individually or with the debtor's spouse. The filing of a voluntary petition operates automatically as an order of relief, which means that all nonexempt civil lawsuits and any other civil proceedings (e.g., foreclosures and sheriff's seizures) are suspended.

An involuntary proceeding may be begun by the filing of a petition as follows: (1) Where there are twelve or more creditors, then three or more creditors who are owed a minimum amount of $10,775 are required to file; or (2) if there are fewer than twelve claimants, then any one or more creditors with claims totaling at least $10,775 may file the petition. Farmers and nonprofit corporations are exempted from an involuntary filing. The court, after notice and hearing for cause, may require creditors filing an involuntary petition to post a bond to indemnify the debtor for damages in the event of a dismissal of the involuntary petition.

Creditor's meeting and appointment of a trustee. The debtor is required to file a list of creditors, a schedule of assets and liabilities, and a statement concerning details of the debtor's financial affairs. Within a reasonable time of filing of the petition, the court appoints an interim trustee and a first meeting of creditors is called. At such meeting, the debtor is required to undergo an examination under oath by the creditors. The creditors may then select a qualified person to act as trustee. If none is selected, then the interim trustee remains in such capacity. The duties of a trustee include collecting all assets owned by or owed to the debtor, examining and determining debts payable, accounting for all property received, instituting lawsuits if necessary to collect indebtedness due the estate, and reporting to the creditors at the final meeting of creditors.

Exemptions. The Bankruptcy Code is rather generous in its provisions concerning property the debtor may keep after filing for bankruptcy. The debtor is given the choice of choosing either exemptions provided by the laws of the state in which the debtor resides or exemptions permitted under the Code, whichever is more generous.

Under the Bankruptcy Act, a debtor may keep the following assets:

1. Debtor's interest up to $16,150 in realty used as a principal residence or as a burial plot
2. Debtor's interest in a motor vehicle up to $2,575 in value
3. Debtor's interest up to $425 in any one item or aggregate of $8,075 of unused exemption in household goods
4. Debtor's interest up to $1,075 in jewelry for personal, household, or family use
5. Debtor's interest in any other property up to $850 plus unused amount of the $8,075 exemption
6. Debtor's interest up to $1,625 in implements, professional books, or tools of the trade of the debtor or dependent
7. Unmatured life insurance contract owned by the debtor, except a credit life insurance contract

8. Debtor's interest up to $8,625 in unmatured life insurance

9. Professionally prescribed health aids for the debtor or dependent

10. Social Security, unemployment compensation, veteran's, disability, or illness benefits

11. Payments for losses payable under a crime victim's reparation statute; wrongful death benefits, life insurance proceeds; and award up to $16,150 arising from personal injury award.

Voidable transfers. In order to prevent certain creditors and insiders from gaining an unfair advantage over other creditors, the Code permits the trustee to set aside certain transfers of property made by the debtor that enabled the creditor to receive more than would otherwise have been received. A trustee, except for certain limited exceptions, may avoid the transfer of property of the debtor made to a creditor on account of an antecedent debt owed by the debtor made while the debtor was insolvent within 90 days before filing of the petition. If the transfer was made to an insider (to a relative, partner, or corporation with whom the debtor has a close relationship), then a transfer made within one year of filing may be avoided.

Fraudulent transfers. The trustee may avoid a transfer of assets made by the debtor to any transferee within one year of filing the petition where such transfer was made to defraud creditors or where the transfer was made for less than its fair market value. The trustee is empowered to invalidate such transfer after having returned the amount paid by a good-faith purchaser.

Exceptions to discharge. Although the debtor has the right to keep certain property, the debtor is not discharged from all debts. The following sums continue to be due and owing even after relief is granted:

1. Taxes due three years prior to filing

2. Payment for property obtained under false pretenses

3. Monies owed to creditors the debtor failed to list or schedule

4. Monies obtained through fraud, embezzlement, or larceny

5. Alimony, maintenance, and child support

6. Monies owed for willful and malicious injury by the debtor

7. Government fines, penalties, or forfeitures incurred within three years

8. Money due to a government unit or nonprofit institution of higher education for an educational loan within seven years unless payment would impose undue hardship upon the debtor or the debtor's dependents

9. Debts not dischargeable under a prior bankruptcy proceeding

10. Judgments arising due to driving while intoxicated

11. Credit card debts and cash advances exceeding $1,075 incurred within sixty days of filing and debt incurred within sixty days of filing for purchase of luxury goods over the sum of $1,075 to any one creditor

Priority of distribution. All creditors are not treated equally. There are several levels of priority in the distribution of assets. A creditor with a security lien on property (e.g., bank mortgage) has priority over other creditors.

In descending order, the following *unsecured* creditors are entitled to the expenses and claims:

1. Administrative expenses incurred by the trustee

2. Post-petition credit extended to debtors

3. Claims up to $4,300 for wages, salaries, or commissions earned by an individual within ninety days of filing of the petition

4. Claims for contributions to employee benefit plans up to $4,300 for services rendered up to 180 days before filing of petition

5. Claims up to $4,300 for a person operating a grain storage or fish produce storage or processing facility

6. Claims by consumers up to $1,950 for deposits made for purchase, lease, or rental of property or for the purchase or consumer goods or services

7. Claims for alimony, maintenance, or child support

8. Income and other taxes due to governmental units

9. The remaining unsecured creditors

CHAPTER 11: REORGANIZATION

One of the goals of the Bankruptcy Act is to allow a business to continue to operate, if possible, in order to prevent the inevitable discharge of employees from a bankrupt firm. Accordingly, Congress permits either a voluntary petition or involuntary petition under this Chapter. The proceedings may be commenced, with certain exceptions, by an individual or business entity, such as a partnership or corporation.

The debtor may file a voluntary petition within 120 days of the order of relief. An involuntary petition may be filed by the trustee, creditor's committee, creditor, and other interested parties if the debtor has not filed a plan within the said 120 days, or the plan filed by the debtor has not been accepted within 180 days.

The plan permits the debtor to remain in possession of the business unless there is fraud or gross mismanagement. The plan has to specify those claims or interests not impaired under the plan from those that will be so impaired. Each class of claims is to be treated equally unless the claimant otherwise consents. The plan may provide for the debtor to remain in possession; for certain assets to be transferred to other entities; for a consolidation or merger; for the sale of property subject to the rights of lienholders; for the satisfaction or modification of a lien; and other terms. The plan may impair a class of claims whether they are secured or unsecured.

The court must confirm the plan. Confirmation may be granted only if the plan complies with the statute, has been proposed in good faith, is not forbidden by law, is fair and equitable, has been accepted by at least one class of claimants, and confirmation of it is not likely to end in liquidation. A plan is fair and equitable as to secured claims if the holders thereof retain their lien on the secured property or receive equivalent value.

Collective bargaining agreements previously entered into by the debtor are subject to the plan. The plan must be offered by the debtor to the union and be discussed with the union; if there is no resolution, a hearing must be held by the court to determine whether a modification will be permitted.

CHAPTER 13: ADJUSTMENT OF DEBTS OF INDIVIDUAL WITH REGULAR INCOME

A gainfully employed person may be inundated with debts that cannot be paid in full but may be paid if that person were extended additional time to pay. Accordingly, Congress created a Chapter 13 filing that permits such a debtor with unsecured debts of less than $269,250 and secured debts of less than $807,750 to voluntarily file a plan that provides for the submission of earnings to a trustee, the payment in full of all allowable claims unless a creditor agrees otherwise, and the classification of claims with the same treatment of all claims within each class. The plan may modify the rights of holders of secured claims except holders of a security interest in real property used as a principal residence by the debtor.

The plan must be confirmed by the Bankruptcy Court. The court will do so if the plan was properly filed, fees were paid, the plan was made in good faith, and the value of property to be distributed allows holders of unsecured claims to receive no less than what they would have received under Chapter 7. As to secured claimants, the plan will be allowed where the holder of the claim has agreed to the plan, the plan provides that the holder retains the lien securing the property, and the value of property to be distributed is not less than the allowed amount of such claim. The debtor may, in the alternative, surrender the property securing the claim to the holder of the lien. Once the plan is confirmed and lived up to, the debtor will be discharged.

FUTURE TRENDS

Because of intense lobbying efforts by banks and other creditors' organizations, there have been proposals for significant changes in the law, such as the Bankruptcy Reform Act of 2000. This act would make all exemptions federal in nature, so that debtors in one state are not treated more advantageously than those in another. Debtors would be required to undergo credit counseling before filing a petition. Substantially enhanced requirements of proof of inability to pay within a five-year period would be necessary. Credit card debts would undergo much greater scrutiny. Resorting to Chapter 13 plans of payments would be made mandatory in some cases. Passage of such legislation appears to be dependent on the political party having control over both the Congress and the presidency.

BIBLIOGRAPHY

Bankruptcy Code, Rules and Official Forms. (annual). St. Paul, MN: West Publishing.

Cowans, David R. (1998). *Bankruptcy Law and Practice.* New York: Lexus Publishing.

Epstein, David G., Nickles, Steve H., and White, James J. (1993). *Bankruptcy.* St. Paul, MN: West Publishing.

ROY J. GIRASA

BANKS AND BANKING

(SEE: *Financial Institutions*)

BARBIE DOLLS

(SEE: *Classics*)

BARTER

(SEE: *Currency Exchange*)

BEHAVIORAL MANAGEMENT THOUGHTS

(SEE: *Management*)

BEHAVIORAL SCIENCE MOVEMENT

The exact date of when the behavioral science, or human relations, movement came into being is difficult to identify; however, it was not until the second half of the nineteenth century that much attention was paid to workers' needs, since there was little understanding of how those needs affect total worker productivity. Prior to that time, most managers viewed workers as a device that could be bought and sold like any other possession. Long hours, low wages, and miserable working conditions were the realities of the average worker's life.

Then, at the beginning of the twentieth century, Frederick Winslow Taylor, one of the most widely read theorists on management, introduced and developed the theory of scientific management. The basis for scientific management was technological in nature, emphasizing that the best way to increase output was to improve the methods used by workers. According to this perspective, the main focus of a leader should be on the needs of the organization, not the needs of the individual worker. Taylor and his followers were criticized on the grounds that scientific management tended to exploit workers more than it benefited them.

In the 1920s and early 1930s, the trend started by Taylor was gradually replaced by the behavioral science movement, initiated by Elton Mayo and his associates through the famous Hawthorne studies. Efficiency experts at the Hawthorne, Illinois, plant of Western Electric designed research to study the effects of illumination on worker productivity. At first, nothing about this research seemed exceptional enough to arouse any unusual interest, since efficiency experts had long tried to find the ideal mix of physical conditions, working hours, and working methods that would stimulate workers to pro-

Psychologist Abraham Maslow proposed a new motivation theory in 1943.

duce at maximum capacity. Yet by the time the Hawthorne studies were completed ten years later, there was little doubt that they were one of the most important organizational studies, causing the behavioral science movement to gather momentum. The major conclusion of the Hawthorne Studies was that attention to workers, not illumination, affected productivity. Essentially, then, the scientific management movement emphasized a concern for output, while the behavioral science movement stressed a concern for relationships among workers.

Various individuals have made important contributions to the behavioral science movement. In 1943 psychologist Abraham Maslow proposed a theory of motivation according to which workers' behavior is determined by a wide variety of needs. Motivation starts when an individual experiences a need; the individual then formulates a goal, which, upon achievement, will satisfy the need. Maslow identified these needs and arranged them in a hierarchy, positing that lower-level needs must be satisfied, at least in part, before an individual begins to strive to satisfy needs at a higher level (Maslow, 1954).

Douglas McGregor, Maslow's student, studied worker attitudes (McGregor, 1960). According to McGregor, traditional organizations are based on either of two sets of assumptions about human nature and human motivation, which he called Theory X and Theory Y. Theory X assumes that most people prefer to be directed; are not interested in assuming responsibility; and are motivated by money, fringe benefits, and the threat of punishment. Theory Y assumes that people are not, by nature, lazy and unreliable; it suggests that people can be basically self-directed and creative at work if properly motivated.

Management is often suspicious of strong informal work groups because of their potential power to control the behavior of their members, and as a result, the level of productivity. In 1950 George C. Homans developed a model of social systems that may be useful in identifying where these groups get their power to control behavior (Homans, 1950).

In the 1960s another psychologist, Frederick Herzberg, examined sources of worker satisfaction and dissatisfaction (Herzberg, 1959). Herzberg cited achievement, responsibility, advancement, and growth as job satisfiers—factors that motivate workers. He also proposed that other aspects of the job environment called job maintenance factors—company policy, supervision, working conditions, interpersonal relations, salary and benefits—contribute to the desired level of worker satisfaction, although these factors rarely motivate workers.

Also in the 1960s, another behavioral science researcher, Chris Argyris, presented his immaturity-maturity theory (Argyris, 1964). He said that keeping workers immature is built into the very nature of formal organizations. These concepts of formal organizations lead to assumptions about human nature that are incompatible with the proper development of maturity in the human personality. He saw a definite incongruity between the needs of a mature personality and the structure of formal organizations.

More and more leaders in both for-profit and nonprofit organizations recognize the importance of the goals of the behavioral science (human relations) movement. Those goals consist of fitting people into work situations in such a manner as to motivate them to work together harmoniously and to achieve a high level of productivity, while also providing economic, psychological, and social satisfaction.

BIBLIOGRAPHY

Argyris, Chris. (1964). *Integrating the Individual and the Organization.* New York: Wiley.

Benton, Douglas A. (1998). *Applied Human Relations.* Upper Saddle River, NJ: Prentice-Hall.

Greenberg, Jerald. (1999). *Managing Behavior in Organizations: Science in Service to Practice.* Upper Saddle River, NJ: Prentice-Hall.

Hersey, Paul, Blanchard, Kenneth H., and Johnson, Dewey E. (1996). *Management of Organizational Behavior.* Upper Saddle River, NJ: Prentice-Hall.

Herzberg, Frederick, Mausner, Bernard, and Snyderman, Barbara. (1959). *The Motivation to Work.* New York: Wiley.

Homans, George C. (1950). *The Human Group.* New York: Harcourt, Brace & World.

Maslow, Abraham H. (1954). *Motivation and Personality.* New York: Harper & Row.

McGregor, Douglas. (1960). *The Human Side of Enterprise.* New York: McGraw-Hill.

Rue, Leslie W., and Byars, Lloyd L. (1990). *Supervision: Key Link to Productivity.* Homewood, IL: Irwin.

Whetten, David A., and Cameron, Kim S. (1995). *Developing Management Skills.* New York: HarperCollins.

Wray, Ralph D., Luft, Roger L., and Highland, Patrick J. (1996). *Fundamentals of Human Relations.* Cincinnati, OH: South-Western Educational Publishing.

Yukl, Gary. (1994). *Leadership in Organizations.* Englewood Cliffs, NJ: Prentice-Hall.

MARCIA ANDERSON

BENCHMARKING

Benchmarking is a process of comparing an organization's or company's performance to that of other organizations or companies using objective and subjective criteria. The process compares programs and strategic positions of competitors or exemplary organizations to those in the company reviewing its status for use as reference points in the formation of organization decisions and objectives. Comparing how an organization or company performs a specific activity with the methods of a competitor or some other organization doing the same thing is a way to identify the best practice and to learn how to lower costs, reduce defects, increase quality, or improve outcomes linked to organization or company excellence.

Organizations and companies use benchmarking to determine where inputs, processes, outputs, systems, and functions are significantly different from those of competitors or others. The common question is, What is the best practice for a particular activity or process? Data obtained are then used by the organization or company to introduce change into its activities in an attempt to achieve the best practice standard if theirs is not best. Comparison with competitors and exemplary organizations is helpful in determining whether the organization's or company's capabilities or processes are strengths or weaknesses. Significant favorable input, process, and output benchmark variances become the basis for strategies, objectives, and goals. Often, a general idea that improvement is possible is the reason for undertaking benchmarking. Benchmarking, then, means looking for and finding organizations or companies that are doing something in the best possible way and learning how they do it in order to emulate them. Organizations or companies often attempt to benchmark against the best in the world rather than the best in their particular industry.

A problem with benchmarking is it may restrict the focus to what is already being done. By emulating current exemplary processes, benchmarking is a catch-up managerial tool or technique rather than a way for the organization or company to gain managerial dominance or marketing share. Benchmarking can foster new ideas or processes when management uses noncompetitive organizations or companies outside its own industry as the basis of benchmarking. What if new ideas are not generated? It is possible that no one in some other organization or company has had a great idea that is applicable to the input, process, or outcome that the organization is attempting to improve or change by benchmarking.

Benchmarking is not a competitive analysis. Benchmarking is the basis for change. It is about learning. The organization performing the benchmark analysis uses the information found in the process to establish priorities and target process improvements that can change business or manufacturing practices. Benchmarking commonly takes one of four forms.

Generic benchmarking investigates activities that are or can be used in most businesses. This type of benchmarking makes the broadest use of data collection. One difficulty is in understanding how processes translate across industries. Yet generic benchmarking can often result in an organization's drastically altering its ideas about its performance capability and in the reengineering of business processes.

Functional benchmarking looks at similar practices and processes in organizations or companies in other industries. This type of benchmarking is an opportunity for breakthrough improvements by analyzing high-performance processes across a variety of industries and organizations.

Competitive benchmarking compares the organization's processes to those of direct competitors. In competitive benchmarking, a consultant or other third party rather than the organization itself collects and analyzes the data because of its proprietary nature.

Internal benchmarking compares processes or practices within the organization or company over time in light of established goals. Advantages of internal benchmarking include the ease of data collection and the definition of areas for future external investigations. The primary disadvantage of internal benchmarking is a lower probability that it will yield significant process improvement breakthroughs.

Each form of benchmarking has advantages and disadvantages, and some are simpler to conduct that others. Each benchmarking approach can be important for process analysis and improvement. Breakthrough improvements are generally attributed to the functional and generic types of benchmarking.

Eight steps are typically employed in the benchmarking process.

1. Identify processes, activities, or factors to benchmark and their primary characteristics.
2. Determine what form is to be used: generic, functional, competitive, or internal.
3. Determine who or what the benchmark target is: company, organization, industry, or process.
4. Determine specific benchmark values by collecting and analyzing information from surveys, interviews, industry information, direct contacts, business or trade publications, technical journals, and other sources of information.
5. Determine the best practice for each benchmarked item.
6. Evaluate the process to which benchmarks apply and establish objectives and improvement goals.
7. Implement plans and monitor results.
8. Recalibrate internal base benchmarks.

A recurring problem that must be addressed during the eight steps is the determination of criteria to ensure that inaccuracies or inconsistencies do not occur that will make any comparison meaningless.

The eight steps of the benchmarking process can be summarized as an improvement analysis. That is, the organization investigates another organization to find out what it does and how it is done. During the investigation, what goes right and what goes wrong is determined. This information is then used for the improvement of activities or processes. When the activities and processes of the organization making the investigation are equal to or better than the measurements found during the investigation, no change is warranted because the investigating organization has the better practice.

Another view of benchmarking is as an organization gap analysis. The organization determines what it lacks in terms of what it knows and how it does things. The shortfalls that initiate the gap analysis can be activities and processes or they can be tactics and strategies. The organization must then determine what other organization is good at doing those things that can be improved or changed for the better. A very systematic investigation is made of the organization with the best practices to discover what is done, how it is done, how it is implemented, and how it fits into the organization's operations. The findings of the systematic investigation then become the basis of revision or modification for the organization doing the investigation.

Benchmarking efforts typically collect information on responsibilities, program design, operating facilities, technical know-how, brand images, levels or integration, managerial talent, and cost or financial performance. Financial or cost data are often the category of greatest concern because these are factors in the input, processing, and output activities of the organization or company.

Benchmarking is frequently referred to as a "wake-up call." Organizations and companies benchmark for many reasons: They want to determine where they spend their time and how much value they add, or they are curious about how they stack up against others. Through the knowledge gained by benchmarking, organizations and companies redefine their roles, add more value, reduce costs, and improve performances.

The electronics industry has a unique style of benchmarking. Here benchmarking involves running a set of standard tests on a system to compare its performance with that of others. That is, it is a tool for measuring the power and performance of hardware and software systems and applications as well as the capacity of a system. There are four categories of benchmarking in the electronics industry:

- An application-based benchmark runs real applications or parts of applications either in full or modified versions.

- A synthetic benchmark emulates applications activity.

- A playback test uses logs of one type of system call (e.g., disk calls) and plays the calls back in isolation.

- An inspection test exercises a system or component to emulate an application activity.

The synthetic and playback benchmarks are used to get a rough idea of how a system or component performs. If application-based benchmarks are available that match the application, they are used to refine the evaluation. The inspection benchmarks are used to determine whether a system or component is functioning properly. These benchmarks use a well-defined testing methodology based on real-world use of a computer system. They measure performance in a deterministic and reproducible manner that allows the system administrator to judge the performance and capacity of the system. Benchmarks provide a means of determining tuning parameters, reliability, bottlenecks, and system capacity that can provide marketing and buying information.

Although benchmarking in the electronics industry is a testing mechanism or process, it, too, is a technique for learning, change, and process improvement. Benchmarking is an effective way to ensure continuous improvement or progress toward strategic goals and organizational priorities. A real benefit of benchmarking comes from the understanding of processes and practices that permit a transfer of best practices or performances into the organization. At its best, benchmarking stresses not only processes, quality, and output but also the importance of identifying and understanding the drivers of the activities.

(SEE ALSO: *Activity-based management costing*; *Performance Appraisal*; *Work Measurement*)

BIBLIOGRAPHY

Blinn, James D. (1998). "Benchmarking Can Help Control Cost of Risk." *National Underwriter* October: 24-25.

Camp, Robert C. (1989). *Benchmarking: The Search for Industry Best Practices That Lead to Superior Performance.* Milwaukee, WI: ASQC Quality Press.

Camp, Robert C. (1995). *Business Process Benchmarking: Finding and Implementing Best Practices.* Milwaukee, WI: ASQC Quality Press.

Camp, Robert C., ed. (1998). *Global Cases in Benchmarking: Best Practices from Organizations Around the World.* Milwaukee, WI: ASQC Quality Press.

George, Steven. (1992). *The Baldrige Quality Ssystem: The Do-It-Yourself Way to Transform Your Business.* New York: Wiley.

Hammer, Michael, and Champy, James. (1993). *Reengineering the Corporation: A Manifesto for Business Revolution.* New York: HarperCollins.

Hurwicz, Michael. (1998). "Behind the Benchmarks," *Byte* April: 75-81.

MARY L. FISCHER

BENEFITS

(SEE: *Employee Benefits*)

BONDS

A *bond* is a type of interest-bearing security issued by an organization that needs funds. The issuer—a corporation, governmental agency, or municipality—compensates the bondholders by paying interest for the life of the bond. At maturity, the bondholder will be repaid for the funds lent. Maturity dates vary, but bonds are most commonly used for long-term debt. The discussion here will focus primarily on such long-term bonds. Corporate bonds and government bonds from the perspective of issuers will be introduced first. Investing in bonds from the point of view of individuals will be discussed later.

CORPORATE BONDS

Most corporate bonds are sold in $1,000 denominations. This $1,000 is the *par* (or *face*) value of the bond. When bonds are issued, the actual price paid by the bondholder may be the par value (face value) or an amount below (referred to as issued at a *discount*) or above (referred to as issued at a *premium*) par value. Regardless of the amount received when they are issued, at maturity the corporation will pay the par value (or $1,000 per bond) to the bondholders. While the bonds are held by the bondholders, the corporation will pay the holders interest at a rate specified on the bond. Interest payments are usually made semi-annually. As an example, a corporation issues fifteen-year, 6 percent $1,000 bonds with a total par value of $300,000,000 on November 1, Year 1. If the bonds sell at par, the corporation would receive $300,000,000 at issuance (less the cost of underwriting). Over the fifteen years, the corporation would pay its bondholders $9,000,000 ($300,000,000 × 6% × ½ year) every six months on May 1 and on November 1, for total interest of $270,000,000 over the fifteen years. At maturity on November 1, Year 16, it would also return the $300,000,000 par value to the bondholders.

When corporations issue bonds, they generally do not sell directly to the public; rather, they sell their entire issues to underwriters, which act as "middlemen" for the corporation and the bondholders. The underwriter, in turn, will sell the bonds to the bondholders. As compensation for its services, the underwriter sells the bonds to the bondholders for slightly more than what it paid the corporation. Once the bonds are sold, the underwriter is no longer involved with the bond issue.

The *stated* (also called the *coupon* or *nominal*) rate of interest relative to the *market* (sometimes referred to as the *real* or *effective*) rate determines whether a bond will sell for an amount equal to its par value, at a discount, or at a premium. When purchasing a corporate bond, the investor knows the *stated* rate of interest, the rate that determines the periodic interest payment. This stated rate is fixed during the life of the bond. The market rate of interest (i.e., the interest rate demanded by investors in the market), however, fluctuates, usually on a daily basis in the secondary market. This fluctuation is due to a number of factors, some of which are federal monetary policy, investors' perception of growth and strength of the economy, and investors' increasing or decreasing fear regarding inflation. When the stated rate equals the market rate, the bonds sell at par value. If, however, the stated rate is less than the market rate, investors are unwilling to pay the par value of the bonds; thus the bonds would sell at a discount. As an example, a bond has a stated rate of interest of 6 percent, but the current market rate of return for bonds of similar quality is 7 percent. In order to induce the investor to buy the bonds, the bonds will sell for an amount less than par that provides the investor a 7 percent return, the market rate. The opposite relationship can also exist: that is where the stated rate of the bonds is greater than the market rate. In that situation, the bonds would sell for a premium. When the bonds are sold, the issuer will "lock in" the market rate of interest that existed on that date. This will be the *real* interest rate for the issuer over the life of the bond. Similarly, an investor will "lock in" that same market rate and will earn that return for the time he or she holds the bonds, possibly until the bonds mature.

If bonds sell at par, they are said to sell for 100, meaning they are selling for 100 percent of their par value. If bonds sold for 98½, they would have sold at a discount, in this case for 98½ percent of their par value. Bonds sold at a premium sell at an amount greater than 100 such as 101¼. As bond prices fall—that is sell for less than par value—the rate of return rises for the reasons stated above. Conversely, as bond prices rise, rate of return falls.

Bonds are *registered* in the name of the person who purchased them. The registered owner receives the interest on the interest payment date. With the use of electronic processing, however, most bonds are *book entry*, meaning there is no certificate or document issued. The bondholder holds a "virtual" bond, and the corporation's computer files merely contain the names and addresses of those to whom interest checks will be sent on the appropriate dates. Additionally, with the ability to transfer funds electronically,

corporations are able to deposit interest payments directly into their bondholders' bank accounts.

Some corporate bonds are issued with a *call provision*. This allows the issuing corporation to "call" the bonds—that is, buy them back from the bondholders—before their maturity date. This call provision is likely to be exercised by the corporation if the market interest rates have fallen since the bonds were issued. This allows bonds with a high interest rate to be retired and replaced by lower-interest bonds.

Another feature of some bonds allows the bondholders to convert bonds into shares of common stock of the issuing company. These are referred to as *convertible bonds*. This is often an attractive feature to bondholders who want to switch from being a creditor of the corporation to an owner if the company's stock begins to appreciate in value. The conversion ratio (e.g., 40 shares of common stock for each $1000 bond) would be specified.

The bond market is dominated by institutional investors, such as insurance companies, mutual funds, and pension funds, but bonds can be purchased by individual investors as well. Bonds are traded in the both the *primary market* and the *secondary market*. The primary market refers to the initial sale of bonds by the underwriters. The secondary market refers to the sale of bonds subsequent to their original sale by issuer or underwriter.

Bonds are one of the primary ways corporations raise large amounts of capital. A corporation can sell previously unissued shares of stock (equity) to shareholders, or it can borrow the money by issuing bonds (debt). There are advantages and disadvantages to both.

By issuing equity, the corporation does not increase debt, thus avoiding paying interest to bondholders. This method of raising capital, however, causes a dilution of ownership to existing shareholders and, thus, may not be favored by the current owners. If the corporation issues bonds, it will be required to pay interest, but there will be no change in the ownership structure of the company. Furthermore, the corporation's management hopes—and expects—that they will earn a greater return than the interest they are paying on the bonds. As an example, if the cost of borrowing on bonds is 6 percent, but the corporation is able to earn 10 percent on the money it has borrowed from the bondholders, the 4 percent difference earned above the cost of borrowing accrues to the existing shareholders. Thus, shareholders earn a 4 percent return on funds borrowed from bondholders.

An important consideration for a corporation deciding whether to issue stocks or bonds is the tax deductibility of the bond interest. Interest paid on bonds is a tax-deductible expense on a corporation's income tax return, meaning their taxable income will be reduced by the amount of interest paid. Their *after-tax cost of borrowing* is, as a result, less than the interest paid on the bonds. As an example, if a corporation issues 6 percent bonds and has an average tax rate is 40 percent, the after-tax interest rate on the bonds is 3.6 percent [(6% × (1 − tax rate)].

GOVERNMENT BONDS

The U.S. federal government borrows large amounts of money. Since the late 1970s, the federal government has consistently spent more money than it has collected in taxes. (In the late 1990s, that trend began to reverse.) In order to have adequate money to pay for its expenditures, the United States borrows money. Bonds issued by the federal government have different names depending on their maturity date. Those which have a maturity date of less than a year are called "Treasury bills" (or "T-bills" for short). Debt instruments with maturities from one to ten years are called *notes*; those with maturities exceeding ten years are called *bonds*. Collectively all are referred to as *Treasuries*.

Federal bonds are auctioned according to a schedule, for example, thirteen-week T-bills are auctioned every Monday and two-year treasury notes on the last Wednesday of every month. The results of these auctions, including market interest rates, are reported in the financial press. These rates not only reflect the interest the bondholder will earn; they also influence interest rates for debts such as mortgages, car loans, and credit cards.

State and local governments also borrow money by selling municipal bonds (frequently referred to as "munis"). Municipal bonds are either *general obligation* or *revenue* bonds. General obligation bonds (also known as "GOs") will be paid off by money received from taxes and possibly by user fees. The costs of building schools and sewers are paid for through general obligation bonds. A revenue bond is one that is issued by an enterprise that serves a public function. Examples include airports, utility companies, toll roads, universities, and hospitals. The money to pay the bond interest and the bonds at maturity will be generated by these enterprises' revenue-generating activities.

While interest on corporate bonds is fully taxable to the bondholder, interest on Treasuries is exempt from state (but not federal) income tax. Interest on municipal bonds is exempt from federal income tax. If the municipal bond is issued by the jurisdiction in which the bondholder resides, the interest is tax-exempt by both the federal government *and* the state government. If there is a local income tax, the interest is tax-exempt at this level, too. Thus in some instances the bondholder has a triple exemption. Because of the tax-exempt nature of municipal bonds, their rates are usually one- to two-percentage points lower than that of comparable taxable corporate bond, for which there is no tax exemption.

INVESTING IN BONDS

There is no centralized market for corporate bonds excepted for those listed on exchanges. An investor who wishes to buy or sell bonds must contact a broker or dealer who might carry that particular bond in inventory. A dealer who does not have that bond would contact another dealer who did. Because of the transaction costs involved in buying and selling corporate bonds in the secondary market, they may not be an attractive investment for investors. Treasuries may be purchased directly from the government. They are also much more easily obtained in the secondary market from brokers because they are generally available.

Bonds typically earn a return greater than that offered by a bank on its savings account or certificates of deposit (CDs), which are among the safest of investments since they are currently guaranteed up to a value of $100,000 in insured banks.

Bonds are considered relatively safe for several reasons. When buying a bond, the bondholder knows how much interest will be paid periodically from the issuing corporation (or government). Thus, there is little uncertainty regarding the return.

Bonds are also considered relatively safe because the issuers of bonds most likely will be evaluated by one of the credit-rating agencies—Moody's, Standard & Poor's (S & P), or Fitch. These agencies evaluate the creditworthiness of corporations and of state and local governments.

Although bonds are among the safer investments, there are several risks associated with them. Probably the biggest risk to the investor is *market risk*. This is the risk an investor faces should interest rates *rise* after the bonds have been purchased. As mentioned above, when interest rates rise, the price of bonds falls (and vice versa). If an investor bought bonds that were yielding 6 percent, the return is 6 percent as long as the bonds are held, possibly until maturity. If interest rates rise above 6 percent, however, the bonds are no longer paying the market rate of interest. Furthermore, if the investors were to sell the bonds, they would sell for less than what was paid for them. *All* bonds—corporate, Treasuries, and munis—are subject to market risk.

Another risk associated with investing in corporate and municipal bonds (but not Treasuries) is the *credit risk* (or *credit-rating risk*) of the issuer. Since a bond is a loan, a bondholder has to assess the likelihood that the issuer will be able to pay the periodic interest payments and the bond's par value at maturity. Credit rating agencies are well respected and widely used to help an investor assess the credit risk of corporate and municipal bonds. Although the ratings the agencies use and how they determine them vary

slightly, they generally rate the bonds from extremely safe investments to wildly speculative ones.

With Treasury bonds, there is virtually no credit risk since most investors see them as having the full faith of the U.S. government behind them. Because of this perceived absence of default, investors typically use the rate offered on Treasuries as the *benchmark* against which other investments are evaluated.

Another risk associated with investing in bonds is *call risk*. As mentioned previously, some bonds are *callable* at the discretion of the issuer. This means that the issuer may retire the bonds, paying the bondholder the par value (and usually a small "call premium" as well) and any accrued interest since the last interest payment date. The issuer returns the money to the investor. A corporation (or municipal government) usually calls bonds only when interest rates have fallen. If bonds are called, the investor now would be back in the market buying bonds yielding a lower return. Furthermore, if the investor had originally purchased the bonds at a premium, it is likely that the original purchase price would not be realized when the bond is called. Corporate and municipal bonds may be callable. U.S. Treasuries are not.

In spite of the risks mentioned, bonds are still considered an attractive investment for many investors. Prices of bonds are much less volatile when compared to prices of stocks. Defaults on bonds are also quite rare. Furthermore, even if a corporation faces liquidation because of financial distress, bondholders would be among the first to receive corporate assets, since they are creditors of the corporation. According to conventional wisdom, bonds strike an acceptable compromise between risk and return.

(SEE ALSO: *Capital markets*; *Finance*; *Financial institutions*)

BIBLIOGRAPHY

Bodie, Zvi, Kane, Alex, and Marcus Alan J., (1999). *Investments*. Boston: Irwin/McGraw-Hill.

Emery, Douglas R., Finnerty, John D., and Stowe, John D. (1998). *Principles of Financial Management.* Upper Saddle River, NJ: Prentice-Hall.

Levy, Haim, and Alderson, Michael J. (1998). *Principles of Corporate Finance.* Cincinnati, OH: South-Western College Publishing.

Mahony, Stephen. (1996). *Mastering Government Securities.* London: Pitman.

Ross, Stephen A., Westerfield, Randolph W., and Jaffe, Jeffrey. (1999). *Corporate Finance.* Boston: Irwin/McGraw-Hill.

ALLIE F. MILLER

BRANDING

(SEE: *Product Labeling*)

BREAK-EVEN ANALYSIS

(SEE: *Cost-Volume-Profit Analysis*)

BROKERS AND DEALERS

(SEE: *Financial Institutions*)

BUDGETS AND BUDGETING

A *budget* is a financial plan for the upcoming period. A *capital budget*, on the other hand, involves an organization's proposed long-range major projects. The focus of this section is on budget. Public and private entities both engage in the budgetary process. A government budget starts with the projection of sources and amounts of revenue and allocates the potential receipts among projects and legislatively mandated programs based on projected needs and public pressure. Government entities actually record budgets in the accounting records against which expenditures can be made.

A budget is a quantitative plan of operations that identifies the resources needed to fulfill the organization's goals and objectives. It includes both financial and nonfinancial aspects. *Budgeting* is the process of preparing a plan, commonly called a budget. A *master budget* comprises *operating budgets* and *financial budgets.* Operating budgets identify the use of resources in operating activities. They include production budgets, purchase budgets, human resources budgets, and sales budgets. Financial budgets identify sources and outflows of funds for the budgeted operations and the expected operating results for the period. Some variations of budgets are *continuous budgets* and *continuously updated budgets.* Rather than preparing one budget for the upcoming year, in a continuous budget one updates the budget for the following twelve months at the end of each month or each quarter. Such a budget remains more current and relevant. A good budget uses historical data as a base and for reference but at the same time incorporates anticipated costs and volumes based on a comprehensive knowledge and understanding of both internal and external factors that affect the business.

COMPONENTS OF THE MASTER BUDGET

The master budget includes a sales budget, which shows expected sales in units and in dollars. A merchandising firm needs to budget for the goods it needs to purchase for resale; these purchases become its cost of sales. A manufacturing organization's master budget includes a production budget, which uses the sales budget and inventory levels anticipated at the beginning and end of the period to determine how much to produce.

The production budget needs to be exploded into budgets for direct material, direct labor, and manufacturing overhead. Direct material and direct labor are items clearly identifiable in the finished product. Manufacturing overhead includes all costs of manufacturing *except for* direct material and direct labor, such as machine depreciation, utilities, and supervision. The direct material budget explodes the production into basic ingredients; quantities to be purchased are anticipated based on expected inventory levels at the beginning and end of the period. With the help of the purchasing department, the prices for the needed materials are computed to arrive at the material purchases budget. The direct labor budget uses industrial engineering guidelines and production needs to estimate labor requirements. The human resources department provides the labor rates for the skill levels required. Overhead costs are estimated based on production level and appropriate cost drivers (i.e., the factors that cause costs to vary). Some overhead costs are considered variable because they vary with the level of output. Others are considered fixed because the level of output does not affect the amount of those costs. For example, the production supervision cost is assumed to be the same regardless of how much is produced within a shift in a plant. One can, then, estimate production costs and cost per unit for goods to be produced. Cost of goods sold can now be determined based on the inventory levels of finished goods. Selling and general administration costs are then estimated, taking into consideration those costs that vary with sales, such as sales commission, as well as fixed costs that remain the same regardless of the level of sales, such as office rent. The information put together so far gives one all one needs to prepare a forecasted income statement.

At this point, one develops the cash budget. This item starts with cash at the beginning of the period plus cash that will be generated through collection of receivables, cash sales, and other sources minus anticipated minus cash disbursements, which include payroll disbursements, payment for taxes, and accounts payable depending on the terms for payment. The resulting cash balance may be negative—more disbursements than receipts; in this case, one determines borrowing needs. A positive cash balance may be more than needed for operating expense; such excess cash may be deposited in a temporary investment account. The final part of master budget preparation is the forecasted balance sheet, where the anticipated cash balance, investments, accounts receivable, inventory, fixed assets, accounts payable, wages payable, taxes payable, long-term liabilities, and equity accounts are recorded to assure that the two sides of the

equation balance; that is assets = liabilities + equity.

THE BUDGETING PROCESS

Budgeting is—or should be—the result of teamwork. A *top-down budget* is a budget that is essentially imposed on the organization by top management. This may be an efficient way to prepare a budget but because of lack of participation by the employees, such budgets often bring with them a level of employee resentment and resistance that leads to problems in implementation of what is proposed. Employees do not feel a sense of ownership in a budget in which they have not been participants. A *participatory* or *bottom-up budget*, on the other hand, starts with the employees in each department determining their needs and requirements in order to achieve the company goals. Because employees feel a sense of ownership in such budgets, they attempt to meet or exceed those expectations. A balance between the two extremes can often be achieved. Top management should be involved in setting the tone and providing the guidelines and parameters within which the budget will be set. Incentives should be put into place so that those who achieve or exceed the budgetary expectations will receive suitable rewards for their efforts.

There must also be guidelines to discourage budgetary *slacks* and abuses whereby the requested budget amounts are in excess of anticipated needs in order for the department to look better and reap some rewards. A very tight budget, on the other hand, may prove discouraging and unattainable. No matter what approach is taken, it is important to realize that the budget should serve as a map and guideline in anticipating the future. Top management must take it seriously in order for the employees to take it seriously as well. At the same time, the budget should not be seen as a strict and unchangeable document. If opportunities arise, circumstances change, and unforeseen situations develop, there is no reason why the budget should be an impediment to exploring and taking advantage of such opportunities. Many companies form a budget committee to oversee the preparation and execution of the budget. The budget can also be seen as a tool that helps in bridging the communications gap between various parts of the organization. Sales, production, purchasing, receiving, industrial relations, sales promotion, warehousing, computing, treasury, quality control, and all other departments see their roles and understand the roles of the other players in achieving the goals of the organization. Such participation also necessitates budget negotiation among the various parties to the budgetary process until the budget is finalized. *Goal congruence* occurs when the goals of the employees and the goals of the company become intertwined and meshed together. A budget that does not consider the goals of the employees often fails. The finalization of the budget requires acceptance by the affected departments and approval and sign-off by top management. If circumstances change due to factors such as change in product mix, costs, selling prices, negotiated labor rates, or engineering specifications, there may be a need for budget revision.

OTHER BUDGETING TECHNIQUES

An *incremental budget* is a budget that is prepared based on prior-year figures, allowing for factors such as inflation. Although such an approach is used by some government entities, most people frown upon such a practice because it is contrary to the whole notion of a budget, which is supposed to be a calculated and wise anticipation of the future course of events with due consideration of all potential factors. A *zero-based budget*, on the other hand, is a budget that does not take anything for granted. It starts from point zero for each budgetary element and department each year and attempts to justify every dollar of expenditure. Although some industries had implemented such a method earlier, it was first used in preparing the state of Georgia's budget in the early 1970s and was later used to prepare the federal budget in late 1970s during President Carter's administration. However, it was soon abandoned because the paperwork generated and timeframe necessary to do this task proved to be too cumbersome for the federal government. *Kaisen budgeting*, a term borrowed from Japanese, is a budgeting approach that explicitly demands continuous improvement and incorporates all the expected improvements in the budget that results from such a process. *Activity-based budgeting* is a technique that focuses on costs of activities or cost drivers necessary for production and sales. Such an approach facilitates continuous improvement. An easily attainable budget often fails to bring out the employees' best efforts. A budget target that is very difficult to achieve can discourage managers from even trying to attain it. So budget targets should be challenging and at the same time attainable.

MONITORING THE BUDGET

A *flexible budget* modifies the budget to the actual level of performance. Obviously, if the original budget is prepared for say, one thousand units of a product, but two thousand units are produced, comparing the original budget to the actual volume of output does not provide meaningful information. Accordingly, the budgeted costs per unit for all variable costs can be used and multiplied by the actual volume of output to arrive at the flexible change proportionately to the level of output for the former and to the level of sales for the latter cost. Fixed costs, such as rent, however, do not normally change with the level of production or sales. These budgeted costs, therefore, are not adjusted and left intact even though the volume of sales and output may be different from the originally budgeted levels.

Ultimately, a good budget is one which not only uses good budgeting techniques but is also based on a sound knowledge of the business as well as the external factors that affect it. The budget serves as a planning tool for the organization as a whole as well as its subunits. It provides a frame of reference against which actual performance can be compared. It provides a means to determine and investigate variances. It also assists the company in planning again based on the feedback received considering the changing conditions. An attainable, fair, and participatory budget is also a good tool for communication, employee involvement, and motivation.

BIBLIOGRAPHY

Blocher, Edward J., Chen, and Lin. (1998). *Cost Management: A Strategic Emphasis.* Boston, MA: McGraw-Hill.

Horngren, Charles T., Foster, and Datar. (1999). *Cost Accounting: A Managerial Emphasis*, 10th ed. Upper Saddle River, NJ: Prentice Hall.

Raiborn, Cecily A., Barfield, and Kinney. (1966). *Insights: Readings in Managerial Accounting*, 2nd ed. St. Paul, MN: West.

Schick, Allen, ed. (1980). *Perspectives on Budgeting.* Washington, DC: American Society for Public Administration.

Willson, James D. (1995). *Budgeting and Profit Planning Manual.* Boston, MA: Warren, Gorham, Lamont.

Young, Mark S. (1997). *Readings in Management Accounting*, 2nd ed. Englewood Cliff, NJ: Prentice Hall.

ROGER K. DOOST

BUREAU OF LABOR STATISTICS

"Is employment below or above the level of last month?" "What has happened to prices during the past month?" Such questions—and thousands of others about a wide range of labor-related topics—are answered by personnel of the Bureau of Labor Statistics (BLS). When the BLS was established by Congress on June 27, 1884, its mission was stated in these words: "The general design and duties of the Bureau of Labor shall be to acquire and diffuse among the people of the United States useful information on subjects connected with labor, in the more general and comprehensive sense of that word, and especially upon its relation to capital, the hours of labor, social, intellectual, and moral prosperity." The BLS is an independent national statistical agency that collects, processes, analyzes, and disseminates essential statistical data to the citizens of the United States, the U.S. Congress, other federal agencies, state and local governments, businesses, and labor. The president appoints the head of the BLS, the commissioner, with approval by the Senate for a specific term that does not coincide with that of his administration.

The BLS is distinct from the policy-making and enforcement activities of the Department of Labor. The BLS is impartial, with a strong commitment to integrity and objectivity; its data have credibility because of the standards maintained throughout the agency. The major areas of BLS activity are as follows:

- Employment and unemployment
- Prices and living conditions
- Compensation and working conditions
- Productivity and technology
- Employment projections
- Safety and health statistics

Employment and unemployment: In addition to monthly figures on employment and unemployment, the BLS does a comprehensive breakdown of the age, sex, and racial and ethnic composition of the work force as well as of industries and occupations in which the workers are employed. Other characteristics are also tracked, including patterns of regional employment and the extent of participation in work by teenagers, blacks, Hispanics, women, and older Americans.

Price and living conditions: Each month the Consumer Price Index (CPI) and the Producers Price Index (PPI) are prepared. The BLS also reports how households spend their incomes.

Compensation and working conditions: Comprehensive studies of employee compensation—wages and benefits—are undertaken that relate to occupations, industries, and areas of the country. An initiative begun in 2000 will produce national employment cost indexes, employment cost levels, and employee benefit incidence.

Productivity and technology: This office produces productivity measures for industries and for major sectors of the U.S. economy. Additionally, it provides comparisons for key BLS labor statistics series as well as training and technical assistance in labor statistics to people from other countries.

Employment projections: There is much interest in the projections provided by this unit of the BLS. Information about future employment growth—and the nature of that growth—is of critical importance to public officials, businesses, young people preparing for careers, and those who design educational programs at all levels.

Safety and health statistics: The extent of workplace injuries and illnesses is the concern of the office that compiles safety and health statistics. Information analyzed and summarized includes job-related injuries and illnesses by industry, nature of the injury or illness, and the workers involved. There is also a compilation of work-related deaths. The statistics provided are useful in developing safety and health standards, in controlling work hazards, and in the allocation of resources for workplace inspection, training, and consultation services.

THE MANNER OF WORK AND SOURCES OF INFORMATION

The BLS, as is the case for all federal agencies, functions in an open environment. As changes are contemplated, they are discussed with users and advisory committees and described in published materials. Fair information practices are used; maintaining confidentiality of individual responses is assured. The BLS promises the public that users will be provided assistance in understanding the uses and limitations of data provided.

The BLS gathers its information from business and labor groups throughout the country through voluntary advisory councils. The councils were established in 1947; current members meet with BLS staff for discussions related to such matters as planned programs and day-to-day problems the BLS faces in collecting, recording, and analyzing statistics as well as in the publishing of reports.

KEY PUBLICATIONS

The most widely distributed publications, which are available in public as well as other libraries,

include: *Monthly Labor Review, Employment and Earnings,* and *Occupational Outlook Quarterly.* Additionally, a variety of surveys, including those related to the Consumer Price Index and the Producer Price Index, are published.

RESPONSE TO CHANGE IN THE WORKPLACE

Rapid technological changes, globalization of world markets, and demographic shifts are all forces that are reshaping the U.S. workplace in relation to the nature and types of jobs, the composition of the work force, and workers' education, skills, and experiences. The BLS in its Revised Strategic Plan 1997-2002 stated that it "has been and will continue to be responsive to users' need to understand changes."

The BLS has undertaken efforts to improve its programs so that they capture workplace and work-force changes. The *Current Population Survey,* which provides monthly data on the demographic and educational characteristics of the work force, includes supplemental surveys on workplace issues such as contingent employment, worker displacement, and work schedules. A new monthly survey of job openings and labor turnover for the country and major industry sectors will provide information that had not been available earlier.

EMPLOYMENT OPPORTUNITIES

As of the end of 1999, there were approximately twenty-six hundred BLS employees working in Washington, D.C., and in the regional offices in eight cities: Boston, New York, Philadelphia, Atlanta, Chicago, Dallas, Kansas City, and San Francisco. The BLS reports that there is a continuing need for economists, mathematical statisticians, and computer specialists. There is a more limited need for administrative and financial specialists as well as for many types of technicians and assistants. Employment is restricted by law to U.S. citizens. Most professional jobs require a bachelor's degree or its equivalent in experience. Specific qualifications and educational requirements are described in BLS pamphlets available from the agency and also on the Internet (http://www.usajobs.opm.gov/).

BIBLIOGRAPHY

Goldberg, Joseph P., and Moye, William J. (1985). *The First Hundred Years of the Bureau of Labor Statistics.* Washington, DC: U.S. Government Printing Office.

BERNARD H. NEWMAN

BUSINESS CYCLE

The business cycle is the ups and downs of the general level of economic activity. All modern, industrialized countries have fluctuations in their rates of economic activity, leading to the observation that one nation's economy is "booming" while another economy is in a "recession." When an economy goes from a positive to a negative rate of growth, it is said to have reached a "peak" and entered a recession. When an economy goes from a negative to a positive rate of growth, it is said to have reached a "trough" and entered a "recovery."

WHAT IS *THE* BUSINESS CYCLE?

Although something worthy of being called "the business cycle" does exist, attempts at finer classifications or subcategories of business cycles have not been particularly fruitful. Some economists have simply used a broad dichotomy between "major" and "minor" cycles. Descriptively this can be meaningful. A particularly severe recession is referred to as a "depression." The Depression of the 1930s was quantitatively different from the 1990-1991 recession. The output of the economy fell by almost 50 percent in the former and by less than 1 percent in the latter.

It is sometimes useful to speak of the cycles of specific time series; that is, the interest rate cycle, the inventory cycle, the construction cycle, and so forth. Given the diversity of general economic cycles, one can find turns in the general level of economic activity in which individual sectors of the economy do, at least for a time, appear to be independent of the rest of the economy. The most frequently mentioned individual cycles are the inventory cycle, the building or construction cycle, and the agricultural cycle. The standard business cycle is sometimes referred to as the inventory cycle, and some business cycle theorists popularly explain the severity of turns in the economy by the coincidence of timing in the individual cycles.

The idea of the timing of individual time series relative to the general level of business implies specific dates for the business cycle. How does one establish the peaks and troughs for the business cycle? To say whether something leads or lags the business cycle, one must have some frame of reference; hence, the business cycle is referred to as the *reference cycle* and its peaks and troughs as *reference turning points.* (See Table 1.)

For the United States, the reference turning points are established by the National Bureau of Economic Research (NBER), a nonprofit research organization. This organization, originally under the guidance of Wesley Claire Mitchell (1874–1948), pioneered business cycle research in the late 1920s. Today the NBER's decisions regarding the reference cycle are taken as gospel, although they are, in fact, quite subjective. No single time series or group of time series is decreed to be *the* reference cycle. A committee of professional business cycle analysts convened by the NBER establishes the official peaks and troughs in accordance with the following definition:

> *Business cycles are a type of fluctuation found in the aggregate economic activity of nations that organize their work mainly in business enterprises: a cycle consists of expansions occurring at about the same time in many economic activities, followed by similarly general recessions, contractions and revivals which merge in the expansion phase of the next cycle; this sequence of changes is recurrent but not periodic; in duration business cycles vary from more than one year to ten or twelve years; they are not divisible into shorter cycles of similar character with amplitudes approximately their own.* (Burns and Mitchell, 1946, p. 3)

With slight modification, this definition has been used since 1927. Although most of the definition is self-explanatory, it is not all that rigorous. It does not say something like, for example, if the total output of the economy (real GDP) falls at an annual rate of 1 percent for two consecutive quarters, we have entered a recession. The definition does say unambiguously that business cycles are "recurrent but not periodic." The only real constraint in the definition is that if you define a business cycle, say, from peak to peak, you should not be able to find another cycle of equal amplitude between those two peaks. If so, you did it wrong.

As of mid-2000, Table 1 is still relevant. The most recent turning point identified by the NBER was March 1991. As of April 2000, the U.S. economy continued to expand. Notice from the table that all that is established with regard to *the* business cycle is the peak and trough of each cycle. This determination tells us absolutely nothing about the rate of rise or fall in the general level of economic activity, nothing about the magnitude of the boom or the severity of the recession. The most commonly used series as a proxy for the business cycle when more than just turning points is required is real GDP if one can get by with quarterly data, or the industrial production index if monthly data are required. The industrial production index is a measure of economic activity published monthly by the Federal Reserve Board in Washington, D.C. As might be guessed from the attention given them by the media, the consumer price index and the unemployment rate are commonly used measures of the severity of the business cycle. Neither corresponds very closely to the reference cycle.

THEORIES OF THE BUSINESS CYCLE

The first lecture in an introductory economics course usually makes the point that the expenditures of one economic unit are the incomes of other economic units. This provides a fairly firm basis for expecting sympathetic movements in many sectors of the economy. A good theoretical basis and substantial empirical support exist for cumulative upward and downward movement in the economy. One sector's expansion is the basis for another sector's expansion, general prosperity

lowers risk and makes credit more readily available, and so on; but the weakest part of business cycle theory and the toughest problem in forecasting is turning points. Why does the general upward or downward movement end? Sometimes it is obvious. When, for example, a war begins or ends with a commensurate and dramatic change in military expenditures, the cause of the beginning or end of an economic boom is fairly unambiguous. Historically, however, only a small minority of the turning points are the result of specific, identifiable occurrences. There are many theories as to other causes of the business cycle.

In 1917 an eminent American economist by the name of J. M. Clark published an article entitled "Business Acceleration and the Law of Demand: A Technical Factor in Economic Cycles." His technical factor was the observation that with a fixed capital-output ratio, a small percentage change in final sales would give rise to a large percentage change in investment. Each innovation generates a temporary demand for the required investment goods. Once the initial investment has been made, the replacement market requires a lower rate of investment. This is referred to as the *principle of acceleration.* If it takes $10 worth of steel mills to produce $1 worth of steel per year, growth in demand for steel by $1 will *temporarily* generate $10 worth of demand for steel mills.

Another early business cycle theorist, Joseph Schumpeter (1883–1950), noted that nothing is constant over the business cycle and nothing ever really returns to its starting place. That is what makes each business cycle unique. The economy grows and changes with each cycle—new products, new firms, new consumers. As Schumpeter observed in 1939, "As a matter of history, it is to physiology and zoology, not to mechanics, that our science is indebted for an analogous distinction which is at the threshold of all clear thinking about economic matters" (p. 37). The economy *grows* and changes. He referred to this as the process of "creative destruction."

Schumpeter concluded that what most of us consider "progress" is at the source of the prob-

Survey Of Current Business

BUSINESS CYCLE EXPANSIONS AND CONTRACTIONS

Business cycle reference dates		Duration in months			
				Cycle	
Trough	Peak	Contraction (trough from previous peak)	Expansion (trough to peak)	Trough from previous trough	Peak from previous peak
December 1854	June 1857	—	30	—	—
December 1858	October 1860	18	22	48	40
June 1861	April 1865	8	*46*	30	*54*
December 1867	June 1869	*32*	18	*78*	50
December 1870	October 1873	18	34	36	52
March 1879	March 1882	65	36	99	101
May 1885	March 1887	38	22	74	60
April 1888	July 1890	13	27	35	40
May 1891	January 1893	10	20	37	30
June 1894	December 1895	17	18	37	35
June 1897	June 1899	18	24	36	42
December 1900	September 1902	18	21	42	39
August 1904	May 1907	23	33	44	56
June 1908	January 1910	13	19	46	32
January 1912	January 1913	24	12	43	36
December 1914	August 1918	23	*44*	35	*67*
March 1919	January 1920	*7*	10	*51*	17
July 1921	May 1923	18	22	28	40
July 1924	October 1926	14	27	36	41
November 1927	August 1929	13	21	40	34
March 1933	May 1937	43	50	64	93
June 1938	February 1945	13	*80*	63	*93*
October 1945	November 1948	*8*	37	*88*	45
October 1949	July 1953	11	*45*	48	*56*
May 1954	August 1957	*10*	39	*55*	49
April 1958	April 1960	8	24	47	32
February 1961	December 1969	10	*106*	34	*116*
November 1970	November 1973	*11*	36	*117*	47
March 1975	January 1980	16	58	52	74
July 1980	July 1981	6	12	64	18
November 1982	July 1990	16	92	28	108
March 1991		8	—	100	—
Average, all cycles:					
1854–1991 (31 cycles)		18	35	53	[1]53
1854–1919 (16 cycles)		22	27	48	[2]49
1919–1945 (6 cycles)		18	35	53	53
1945–1991 (9 cycles)		11	50	61	61
Average, peacetime cycles:					
1854–1991 (26 cycles)		19	29	48	[3]48
1954–1919 (14 cycles)		22	24	46	[4]47
1919–1945 (5 cycles)		20	26	46	45
1945–1991 (7 cycles)		11	43	53	53

1. 30 cycles.
2. 15 cycles.
3. 25 cycles.
4. 13 cycles.

Table 1

NOTE: Figures printed in bold italic are the wartime expansions (Civil War, World Wars I and II, Korean war and Vietnam war), the postwar contractors, and the full cycles that induce the wartime expansions.

SOURCE: National Bureau of Economic Research, Inc. 1050 Massachusetts Avenue. Cambridge MA 02133.

lem. He felt that as *entrepreneurs* come up with new ways of doing things, this disturbs the equilibrium and creates fluctuations. Schumpeter distinguishes between *inventions* (which may gather dust for years) and *innovations*, which are commercial applications of previous inventions. Inventions occur randomly through time. Innovations tend to be bunched, thereby creating cycles of economic activity.

Many business cycle theorists give a prominent role to the monetary system and interest rates. Early in the twentieth century, a Swedish economist, Knut Wicksell (1851–1926), argued that if the "natural" rate of interest rose above the "bank" rate of interest, the level of economic activity would begin to increase. In contemporary terms, the natural rate of interest is what businesses expect to earn on real investment. The bank rate is the return on financial assets in general and commercial bank loans in particular. The boom begins when, for whatever reason, the cost of borrowing falls significantly below expected returns on investment. This difference between the rate of return on real and financial assets generates a demand for bank loans by investors seeking to exploit the opportunity for profit. The economy booms.

At some point the bank rate will start to rise and/or the real rate will start to fall. When the expected rate of return on investment falls below the rate at which funds can be borrowed, the process will begin to reverse itself—and the recession is on. As bank loans are paid off (or defaulted on), bank credit is reduced, and the economy slows accordingly.

In recent years, business cycles theory has centered on the argument about the source of cyclical instability. The question of the root causes of ups and downs in the level of economic activity received a lot of attention in the 1980s and 1990s.

Figure 1 shows how the parties to the debate are divided up. First, there is the question of whether the private sector of the economy is inherently stable or unstable—which is to say, do the observed fluctuations originate in the government or private sector? On one side are what

might be called *classical* economists, who are convinced that the economy is inherently stable. They contend that, historically, government policy has destabilized it in a perverse fashion. On the other side are what might be called *Keynesians*, named after the famous British economist John Maynard Keynes (1883–1946). Keynesians think that psychological shifts in consumers' purchasing and savings preferences and in businesses' confidence are a substantial source of instability.

There is a whole body of literature on *political business cycles*. As a contemporary economist, William D. Nordhaus, noted in 1989, "The theory of the political business cycle, which analyzes the interaction of political and economic systems, arose from the obvious facts of life that voters care about the economy while politicians care about power" (p. 1). The idea is that politicians in power will tend to follow policies to promote short-term prosperity around election time and allow recessions to occur at other times. The evidence that the state of the economy influences voting patterns is strong, as is the apparent desire of incumbent politicians to influence the economy; but it is difficult to make a case that the overwhelming determinant of the level and timing of business fluctuations is politically determined. At some points in recent history, politically determined policies were apparently a determining factor and at other times not.

With respect to the impact of governmental policies, there is a dispute as to the relative importance of monetary policy (controlling the money supply) and fiscal policy (government expenditures and taxes). Those who believe that monetary policies have had a generally destabilizing effect on the economy are known as *monetarists*. Most economists accept the fact that fiscal policy, especially in wartime, has been a source of cyclical instability.

As noted above, it is the so-called Keynesian economists who think that the private sector is inherently unstable. While noting the historical instability of investment in tangible assets, they have also emphasized shifts in liquidity preference (demand for money) as an independent

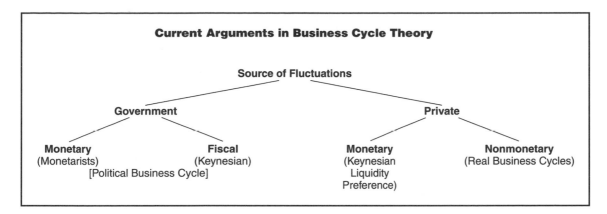

Current Arguments in Business Cycle Theory

Source of Fluctuations

Government — Private

Monetary (Monetarists) — Fiscal (Keynesian) — [Political Business Cycle]

Monetary (Keynesian Liquidity Preference) — Nonmonetary (Real Business Cycles)

Figure 1

source of instability. As a counter to the standard Keynesian position, there has in recent years arisen a school of thought emphasizing *real business cycles*. This school contends that nonmonetary variables in the private sector are a major source of cyclical instability. They contend that the observed sympathetic movements between monetary variables and the level of economic activity result from a flow of causation from the latter to the former. The changes in real factors *cause* the monetary factors to change, not vice versa. In this way they are somewhat like Wicksell, discussed earlier.

(SEE ALSO: *Economic Cycles*)

BIBLIOGRAPHY

Blanchard, Oliver. (2000). "What Do We Know about Macroeconomics That Fisher and Wicksell Did Not?" National Bureau of Economic Research Working Paper No. W7550, February. New York: National Bureau of Economic Research.

Burns, Arthur F., and Mitchell, Wesley C. (1946). *Measuring Business Cycles.* New York: National Bureau of Economic Research.

Clark, J. M. (1917). "Business Acceleration and the Law of Demand: A Technical Factor in Economic Cycles." *Journal of Political Economy* March: 217-235.

Hicks, J. R. (1958). *The Trade Cycle.* London: Oxford University Press.

King, Robert, and Plosser, Charles. (1984). "Money, Credit and Prices in a Real Business Cycle." *American Economic Review* June: 363-380.

King, Robert, and Rebelo, Sergio. (2000). "Resuscitating Real Business Cycles." National Bureau of Economic Research Working Paper No. W7534, February. New York: National Bureau of Economic Research.

Long, John, and Plosser, Charles. (1983). "Real Business Cycles." *Journal of Political Economy* February: 777-793.

Lucas, Robert E. (1981). *Studies in Business Cycle Theory.* Cambridge, MA: MIT Press.

Lucas, Robert E., and Sargent, Thomas J., ed. (1981). *Rational Expectations and Econometric Practice.* Minneapolis: University of Minnesota Press.

Mankiw, N. Gregory. (1989). "Real Business Cycles: A New Keynesian Perspective." *The Journal of Economic Perspectives* Summer: 79-90.

Mitchell, Wesley Claire. (1952). *The Economic Scientist.* New York: National Bureau of Economic Research.

Nordhaus, William D. (1989). "Alternative Approaches to the Political Business Cycle." *Brookings Papers on Economic Activity* 2:1-50.

Rotemberg, Julio J., and Woodford, Michael. (1996). "Real-Business-Cycle Models and the Forecastable Movements in Output, Hours, and Consumption." *The American Economic Review* March: 71-89.

Schumpeter, Joseph. (1939). *Business Cycles.* New York: McGraw-Hill.

Schumpeter, Joseph. (1961). *The Theory of Economic Development.* New York: Oxford University Press.

Su, Vincent. (1996). *Economic Fluctuations and Forecasting.* New York: HarperCollins.

Wicksell, Knut. (1901). *Lectures on Political Economy.* New York: Augustus M. Kelly.

Willet, Thomas D., ed. (1988). *Political Business Cycles: The Political Economy of Money, Inflation, and Unemployment.* Durham, NC: Duke University Press.

Zarnowitz, Victor. (1992). *Business Cycles, Theory, History, Indicators, and Forecasting.* Chicago: University of Chicago Press.

DAVID A. BOWERS

BUSINESS PROFESSIONALS OF AMERICA

Business Professionals of America (BPA) is a national vocational student organization for individuals preparing for careers in business and/or office occupations. With nineteen state associations and 45,000 members in middle, secondary, and post-secondary schools throughout North America, BPA strives to contribute to the preparation of a world-class work force by advancing leadership, citizenship, and academic and technological skills. Using a co-curricular focus, BPA integrates local programs and services into a business classroom curriculum and focuses on real-world teaching and learning strategies. Additionally, BPA develops professionalism in students and teachers through unique programs and services (Business Professionals of America, 1993).

Historically, the need for a student organization serving individuals in vocational office programs was recognized shortly after the passage of the Vocational Education Act of 1963. The articles of incorporation for the Office Education Association, the original name of BPA, were officially filed in 1966. The name was changed to Business Professionals of America on July 1, 1988 (Business Professionals of America, 1996).

Business Professionals of America offers its student, teacher, and alumni members a variety of programs and services. The National Leadership Conference annually hosts national officer elections and competitive events that allow students to demonstrate workplace skills obtained through the business classroom curriculum and Industry Certification and Behavioral Skills Assessment ("Workplace Skills Assessment Program," 1998). Awards programs also recognize successes of members and chapters.

Various written materials and the official quarterly journal, *Communique*, provide members with services, updates, and promotional opportunities. Additionally, scholarship programs are sought at universities to encourage participation in business education at the post-secondary level. More information is available from Business Professionals of America, 5454 Cleveland Ave., Columbus, Ohio 43231-4021, or http://www.bpa.org/.

REFERENCES

Business Professionals of America. (1993). "Today's students. Tomorrow's business professionals" [Brochure]. Columbus, OH: Author.

Business Professionals of America. (1996). "Business Professionals of America (formerly OEA)." Available: http://www.bpa.org/partners/bpa/history.html. 1996.

"Workplace Skills Assessment Program." (1998). *Business Professionals of America*, October:1-3.

JEWEL EVANS HAIRSTON

BUSINESS TO BUSINESS MARKETING

(SEE: *Industrial Marketing*)

C

CABBAGE PATCH DOLLS

(SEE: *Fads*)

CAPITAL

(SEE: *Factors of Production*)

CAPITAL BUDGETING

(SEE: *Budgets and Budgeting*)

CAPITAL INVESTMENTS

Companies make capital investments to earn a return. This is like individuals wanting to "make" money when they invest in stocks and bonds. The amount of money "made" or "lost" is measured as the investment's rate of return. When making an investment, the expected rate of return is determined by the amount, timing, and riskiness of the funds expected from the investment.

RATE OF RETURN

Amount. An investment's rate of return is expressed as a percentage. For example, if a company invests $1,000 and expects to get back $1,100 one year from today, it expects to earn 10 percent (= (1,100 − 1,000)/1,000). If the company expects $1,200 (instead of $1,100), it expects to earn 20 percent. So a rate of return depends first on the *amount* of money expected back from the investment.

Timing. Just as getting more money produces a higher rate of return, getting the money sooner also produces a higher rate of return. If a company earns 10% in six months that's a higher rate of return than 10% earned in one year. So an investment's rate of return also depends on *when* the company expects to get the money back.

Risk. For most capital investments, the amount of money and/or the time at which the company expects to get it back are uncertain. What are the chances it will get exactly what it expects? What are the chances it will get more or less? What are the chances it will get a lot more or a lot less—or even lose all the money invested and get nothing back? The risk of the investment depends on these chances, and, in turn, how the investment's rate of return is calculated depends on this risk. So the third important dimension of an investment's rate of return is the *risk* connected with the amount of money a company expects to get back from the investment.

Time value of money. When a company evaluates a capital investment, the amount of money expected back from the investment is adjusted for its timing and risk. For example, suppose a company expects to get $100 one year from today. If it had that $100 now, it could invest the money—for example, earn interest from a bank—and have more than $100 next year. If the money earned 5 percent, the company would have $105 next year. If we "reverse" this process, the $100 the company expects to get next year is worth less than $100 today. At 5 percent interest, next year's $100 is worth only $95.24 (= $100/ 1.05) today. (This is because if the company had $95.24 now and earned 5 percent on the money, it would have $100 next year.) Similarly, if there is risk connected with the expected money—the company expects $100, but could get more or less—its value today is less than $95.24. And the riskier it is, the lower its value today.

Typically, in order to make "fair" comparisons, the value of all the amounts of money expected back from capital investments are converted into what are called *present values*. The rate of return used to calculate the present value for a capital investment is called the cost of capital. The cost of capital is the minimum rate of return the company must earn to be willing to make the investment. It is the rate of return the company could earn if, rather than making the capital investment, it invested the money in an alternative, but comparable, investment. The cost of capital exactly reflects the riskiness of the money expected back from the capital investment. The mathematical methods used to calculate present values are called the *time value of money* and are explained in more detail in the books in the bibliography.

Net present value (NPV). A capital investment's *net present value* (NPV) is the amount of value the company expects the investment to create. The NPV equals the sum of the present values of all of the money expected back from the investment minus the investment's cost.

MAKING CAPITAL INVESTMENTS

The capital investment process includes the following:

1. Generating ideas for capital investments

2. Classifying capital investments

3. Evaluating and choosing proposed capital investments

Generating Ideas The first—and most important—part of the capital investment process is generating new ideas. Ideas for capital investments can originate anywhere in a company. Often plant managers are responsible for identifying potential projects that will enable their plants to operate on a different scale or on a more efficient basis. For instance, a plant manager might suggest adding 10,000 square feet of production space to a plant or replacing a piece of equipment with a newer, more efficient machine. Ideas for better types of equipment that can help the company operate more efficiently may come from individuals on the plant floor. After screening out undesirable ideas, managers send the ones that appear to be attractive to the divisional level, with supporting documentation.

Division management not only reviews such proposals but also adds ideas of its own. For example, division management may propose the introduction of a new product line. Alternatively, management may want to combine two plants and eliminate the less efficient one. Such ideas are less likely to come from the plant managers!

This bottom-up process results in ideas percolating upward through the organization. At each level, ideas submitted by lower-level managers are screened, and attractive ones are forwarded to the next level. In addition, managers at successively higher levels, who are in a position to take a broader view of the company's business, add ideas that may not be visible—or desirable—to lower-level managers.

At the same time, there is also a top-down process at work in most companies. Strategic planners will generate ideas regarding new businesses the company should enter, other companies it might acquire, and ways to modify its existing businesses to achieve greater profitability. Strategic planning is a critical element in the capital investment process. The processes complement one another; the top-down process generates ideas of a broader, more strategic nature, whereas the bottom-up process generates ideas of a more project-specific nature.

In addition, many companies have a research and development (R&D) group, either within a production division or as a separate department. An R&D group often provides new ideas for products that can be sent on to a marketing research department.

Classifying Capital Investments Analysis costs money. Therefore, certain types of investments receive only cursory checks before approval, whereas others are subjected to extensive analysis. Generally, less costly and more routine investments are subjected to less extensive evaluation. As a result, companies typically categorize investments and analyze them at the level judged appropriate to their category. Potential investments in each category may have a lot in common and are able to be analyzed similarly. A useful set of investment classifications is:

Maintenance projects

Cost-saving/revenue-enhancement projects

Capacity expansions in current businesses

New products and new businesses

Projects required by government regulation or company policy

Maintenance expenditures: At the most basic level, a company must make certain investments to continue to be a healthy, profitable business. Replacing worn-out or damaged equipment is necessary to continue in business. Therefore, the major questions concerning such investments are "Should we continue in this business?" and if so, "Should we continue to use the same production process?" Since the answers to these questions are so frequently "yes," an elaborate decision-making process is not needed, and typically such decisions are approved with only routine review.

Cost savings/revenue enhancement: Projects in this class include improvements in production technology to realize cost savings and marketing campaigns to achieve revenue enhancement. The central issue is increasing the difference between revenue and cost; the result must be sufficient to justify the investment.

Capacity expansion in current businesses: Deciding to expand the current business is inherently more difficult than approving maintenance or cost-saving proposals. Firms have to consider the economics of expanding or adding new facilities. They must also prepare demand forecasts, keeping in mind competitors' likely strategies. Marketing consultants may help, but this class of projects naturally has more uncertain return projections than do maintenance or replacement projects.

New products and new businesses: Projects in this category, which include R&D activities, are among the most difficult to evaluate. Their newness and long lead times make it very difficult to forecast product demand accurately. In many cases, the project may be of special interest because it would give the company an option to break into a new market. For example, a company that has a proprietary technology might spend additional R&D funds trying to develop new products based on this technology. If successful, these new products could pave the way for future profitable investment opportunities. Access to such opportunities represents valuable options for the company.

Meeting regulatory and policy requirements: Government regulations and/or company policies concerning such things as pollution control and health or safety factors are viewed as costs. Often, the critical issue in such projects is meeting the standards in the most efficient manner— at the minimum cost.

Evaluating Proposals The typical stages for the development and approval of a capital investment proposal are the following:

1. Approve funds for research that may result in a product *idea*.

2. Approve funds for market research that may result in a product *proposal*.

3. Approve funds for product development that may result in a usable *product*.

4. Approve funds for plant and/or equipment for the *production* and sale of the new product.

Each stage involves an investment decision at one or more levels of the company. At each stage, the company reestimates the value expected to be created—the NPV—of going ahead. With this kind of sequential appropriation of funds, an automatic progress review is enforced, enabling early cancellation of unsuccessful projects. At each stage there are options to abandon, postpone, change, or continue.

Proposed expenditures that are larger than certain company-set limits generally require a written proposal from the initiator. Typically, such limits are higher in smaller privately owned companies, which tend to have relatively informal organizational structures. Most companies use standard forms, and these are often supplemented by written memoranda for larger, more complex projects. Also, there may be consulting or other studies prepared by outside experts; for example, economic forecasts from economic consultants.

For a successful company, a maintenance project might require only limited supporting information. In contrast, a new product would require extensive information gathering and analysis. At the same time, within a category, managers at each level usually have upper limits on their authority regarding both expenditures on individual assets and the total expenditure for a budgeting period. In this way, larger projects require the approval of higher authority.

For example, at the lowest level, a department head may have the authority to approve $50,000 in total equipment purchases for the year. However, that same person might have to obtain specific approval from higher authority to spend more than $10,000 for any single piece of equipment. A plant manager might have authorization limits of $500,000 per year and $100,000 per piece of equipment, for example.

A system of authorization, such as illustrated in the preceding paragraph, requires more extensive review and a greater number of inputs to approve larger expenditures. The hierarchical review structure reflects the obvious fact that misjudging a larger project is potentially more costly than misjudging a smaller one.

CAPITAL INVESTMENT IN OTHER COMPANIES

Sometimes companies make capital investments in other companies. In concept, these are just like any other capital investment. They range from the simple—such as buying stock in another company in a "passive" investment—to acquiring (purchasing) another company outright or merging with another company. With an acquisition or merger, the details connected with such things as taxes, "corporate cultures," distribution of responsibilities, and logistics, among others, can be exceedingly complex.

Companies give many different reasons for acquisition or merger. In most cases, they want to achieve operating efficiencies and/or economies of scale. For example, in a merger the companies may be able to save money marketing, producing, and delivering their products by combining their operations and eliminating duplication. Combining may also allow greater efficiency in coordinating activities across the companies' units.

A company may be able to expand more cheaply and more quickly through an acquisition or merger. There are also other possible reasons, such as realizing tax benefits and capturing surplus cash. The essence of all the possible reasons is a belief that the merger or acquisition is a good capital investment. Therefore, the analytical tools and basic decision rules are the same for mergers and acquisitions as they are for other capital investments. However, particular care must be taken in applying these tools because of the enormous size and complexity of the investment.

Beyond the basic investment considerations, there can also be important legal considerations connected with a merger or acquisition. These include aspects such as compliance with federal antitrust law, state anti-takeover statutes, financial securities laws, and the charters of the corporations involved.

(SEE ALSO: *Finance*; *Financial Institutions*)

BIBLIOGRAPHY

Brealey, Richard A., Meyers, Stewart C., and Marcus, Alan J. (1999). *Fundamentals of Corporate Finance*. Boston: Irwin/McGraw-Hill.

Emery, Douglas R., Finnerty, John D., and Stowe, John D. (1998). *Principles of Financial Management*. Upper Saddle River, NJ: Prentice-Hall.

Ross, Stephen A., Westerfield, Randolph W., and Jordan, Bradford D. (1998). *Fundamentals of Corporate Finance*. Boston: Irwin/McGraw-Hill.

DOUGLAS R. EMERY
JOHN D. FINNERTY

CAPITALISM

(SEE: *Economic Systems*)

CAPITAL MARKETS

ROLE OF CAPITAL MARKETS

The capital market provides financing to meet the denomination, liquidity, maturity, risk (with respect to credit, interest rate, and market), and other characteristics desired by those who have a surplus of funds and those who have a deficit of funds. The capital market as a whole consists of overnight to long-term funding. The short to medium end of the maturity spectrum is called the money market proper, and the long end is identified as the capital market. The financial instruments range from money market instruments to thirty-year or longer bonds in credit markets, equity instruments, insurance instruments, foreign-exchange instruments, hybrid instruments, and derivative instruments. There has been an explosion of innovation in the creation and development of instruments in the money and capital markets since about 1960 in both debt and equity instruments.

Some of the important (by volume) money market instruments are Treasury bills, federal agency securities, federal funds, negotiable certificates of deposits, commercial paper, bankers' acceptances, repurchase agreements, eurocurrency deposits, eurocurrency loans, futures instruments and options instruments. Similarly, some of the key capital market instruments are U.S. securities; U.S. agency securities; corporate bonds; state and local government bonds; mortgage instruments; financial guarantees; securitized instruments; broker-dealer loans; foreign, international, and global bonds; and eurobonds.

THE CAPITAL MARKET IN THE UNITED STATES

The capital market in the United States is highly developed, marked by sophisticated technology, specialized financing institutions and functions, wide-ranging geographic locations, and continuous innovation in financial products and services to meet the needs of financial investors and those seeking to acquire finances. There are both direct and indirect markets. Corporations, for example, engage in direct finance when they invest in one another's paper directly without the services of brokers and other specialized intermediaries, similar to the proverbial entrepreneur getting finance from an uncle. Most of the financing in the United States, however, is done indirectly through financial intermediaries who substitute their credit for the credit of the borrower (user) of funds. The total amount of credit raised annually in the United States is around $2,200 billion, of which debt instruments account for $2,000 billion and equity instruments (net) for $200 billion.

Money and capital market instruments are traded directly among participants, in the over-the-counter (OTC) markets and in organized exchanges. Many of the exchanges specialize in the type of securities traded, thus giving focus and depth to that instrument or market. The major U.S. exchanges are the New York Stock Exchange (NYSE), Philadelphia Stock Exchange, Pacific Stock Exchange, Boston Stock Exchange, Cincinnati Stock Exchange, Midwest Stock Exchange, Chicago Board of Trade (CBT), Chicago Mercantile Exchange (CME), international money market (IMM), National Association of Securities Dealers Automated Quotations System (American Exchange) (NASDAQ-AMEX), and Globex. The regional exchanges—such as Boston, Cincinnati, Midwest, Pacific, and Philadelphia—

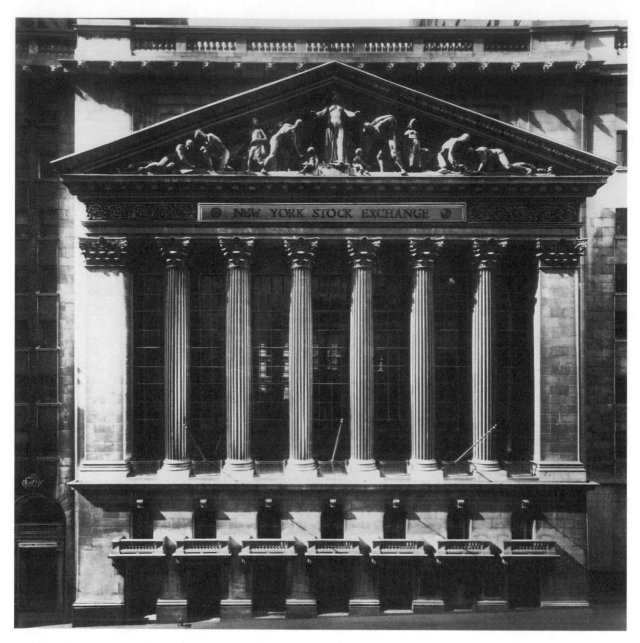

Façade of the New York Stock Exchange in 1928.

each list a small number of regional companies to facilitate their raising of capital in the market. The national/international markets are NYSE, NASDAQ-AMEX, CBT, and CME.

The NYSE, organized by twenty-four brokers in 1792, is the oldest and the largest exchange in the U.S. capital market. It states its mission as follows: "To add value to the capital-raising and asset management process by providing the highest-quality and most cost-effective self-regulated marketplace for the trading of financial instruments, promote confidence in and understanding of that process, and serve as a forum for discussion of relevant national and international policy issues." According to the NYSE, it is "the largest equities marketplace in the world and is home to 3,025 companies worth more than $16 trillion in global market capitalization. As of year-end 1999, the NYSE had 280.9 billion shares listed and available for trading worth approximately $12.3 trillion. Over two-thirds of the roster of NYSE companies have listed here within the last 12 years. These companies include a cross-section of leading U.S. companies, midsize and small capitalization companies. Non-U.S. issuers play an increasingly important role on the NYSE. As of July 1999, 382 non-U.S. companies were listed here—more than triple the number 5 years ago" (www.NYSE.com).

Organized in 1971, NASDAQ was the world's first electronic stock market. According to its mission statement, NASDAQ-AMEX'S purpose is "to facilitate capital formation in the public and private sector by developing, operating and regulating the most liquid, efficient and fair securities market for the ultimate benefit and protection of the investor." Its vision is "to build the world's first truly global securities market . . . a worldwide market of markets built on a worldwide network of networks . . . linking pools of liquidity and connecting investors from all over the world . . . assuring the best possible price for securities at the lowest possible cost." Stocks of over 5000 companies are traded on the NASDAQ-AMEX (www.Nasdaq.com).

INITIAL PUBLIC OFFERINGS AND ROLE OF VENTURE CAPITAL IN THE CAPITAL MARKETS

Stock markets provide high-growth, innovative companies with a means of raising large amounts of long-term capital by selling company shares to outside investors. It is said that the company is "floated" on the stock market through an initial public offering (IPO). An IPO offers many companies the best way of financing their continued growth and for most venture capitalists is the preferred exit route (best way of profiting from venture capital investment) for their investments. However, an IPO involves for the entrepreneur some loss of control over the company, proportional to the amount of equity that is sold to outside investors. The entry standards imposed

for a full listing on traditional stock markets may be too rigorous for young, technology-based companies. Recently, however, a number of initiatives have been taken by traditional stock markets as well as by new market operators to create new stock markets for high-growth, innovative companies. These offer all the benefits of a public equity market, such as an increased public profile and access to new capital and investors, with simplified entry requirements.

Efficient and liquid risk capital stock markets play a large role as a source of financing for high-growth companies and are necessary for the development of venture capital by offering an exit route for investors. In the United States, the NASDAQ market has been developing for more than twenty-five years and has become the market of choice for raising capital to finance fast-growing enterprises. At the turn of the twenty-first century, the 5,500 companies quoted on it employed approximately 9 million people.

Venture capital, which consists of funds raised on the capital market by specialized operators, is one of the most relevant sources of financing for innovative companies. Venture capitalists buy shares or convertible bonds in a company. They do not invest in order to receive an immediate dividend, but rather to allow the company to expand and ultimately increase the value of their investment. Hence, they are interested in innovative small companies with very rapid growth rates. Some venture capitalists specialize in certain business sectors (e.g., biotechnology, information technology). Others may only invest at certain stages in the development of a project or company.

In the United States, the amount offered in the IPO market has been growing exponentially, from $20.7 billion in 1998 to $47 billion in 1999. The fourth quarter of 1999 alone accounted for $22.3 billion.

FINANCIAL INNOVATION AND THE MARKETS IN DERIVATIVE INSTRUMENTS

Financial innovation was one of the most influential trends in international financial markets in the 1980s and 1990s. A large number of new financial products and instruments were created as the traditional barriers between financial institutions were increasingly eroded. Banks, for example, are increasingly competing with markets for what was once considered to be traditional intermediated credits. Markets are becoming more global, and competition between financial institutions has intensified. This increase in financial innovation has taken place in an environment of steady deregulation coupled with significant advances in information and communication technologies. Securitization, perhaps the most important trend in international financial markets in the 1980s and early 1990s, continues to redefine the operations of banks and has important regulatory implications. Both bank and nonbank financial institutions are relying more on income from off-balance-sheet activities. A greater share of credit now flows through capital-market channels, which are characterized by less supervision in comparison to banks. Deregulation, improved technology, growing competition, and volatile exchange and interest rates are the main stimulus for financial innovation. Innovation can improve the efficiency of international financial markets by offering a broader and more flexible range of instruments for borrowing. It also provides hedging instruments that can help banks, borrowers, and investors to manage the risks associated with volatile exchange and interest rate.

The derivatives market took a major step forward with the formation of the Chicago Board of Trade (CBOT) in 1848. It developed standardized agreements as to the quality, quantity, delivery time, and location, and called futures contracts for trading of grains in 1865. The development of financial futures resulted from a changing world economy following World War II. Futures contracts provide for efficient forward pricing and risk-management.

In the early 1970s, approximately 13 million futures contracts were traded in the United States—most of which were agricultural. By the mid 1980s, the number of contracts being traded exploded to over 230 million, with only a quarter related to agricultural products. Today, there are futures contracts for interest rates, stock indexes, manufactured and processed products, non-storable commodities, precious metals, as well as foreign currencies. Furthermore, proposals for new contracts continue to grow.

The Chicago Mercantile Exchange (CME) is another major futures exchange in the U.S. The Merc's diverse product line consists of futures and options on futures in agricultural commodities, foreign currencies, interest rates and stock indexes. In the mid-1960s, it introduced a futures contract on a non-storable commodity—live cattle. In 1972 it launched a contract in foreign currency futures.

The U.S. futures industry operates under an extensive regulatory umbrella. Federal legislation governing the industry has existed since 1924. The Commodity Futures Trading Commission (CFTC), established under the 1974 amendments to the Commodity Exchange Act (CEA), has far-reaching authority over a wide variety of commodity industry activities.

The technology of creating, disseminating, and trading instruments (securities) has increased the efficiency of allocating financing in larger quantities at lower cost of transactions, as well as lower cost of funds because of increased supplies from increased market participation by surplus and deficit units.

ROLE OF THE SECURITIES AND EXCHANGE COMMISSION

The Securities and Exchange Commission (SEC) was organized under the Securities Act of 1934 to create fair market conditions in the securities markets by setting standards for and requirements of information from the issuer of the security to the general public. This process creates competitive and fair pricing and trading of securities, and it prevents abuse and fraud by issuers, brokers, and dealers. Issuers are required to file detailed information with the SEC on all publicly traded securities, which becomes available to the public on an equal basis. Privately traded securities and investments by wealthy individuals are exempt from registration, based on the assumptions that these investors understand the risks involved in a given security and that they are able to tolerate the consequences of those risks if they materialize.

ROLE OF THE FEDERAL RESERVE SYSTEM IN THE CAPITAL MARKET

The Federal Reserve plays a key role in the functioning of the capital market in the U.S. economy and, by extension, in the world economy. It manages the overall liquidity and credit conditions in the U.S. financial system. The Fed maintains a noninflationary level of liquidity in the economy, on an ongoing basis, in order to foster conditions for maximum sustainable growth of the economy. It does so by regulating the money supply through the banking system and its interaction with the public. The Fed pays similar attention to availability of credit; in that regard it is authorized to set the margin rate on stock purchases, thus exercising a direct role in the use of credit in equity market transactions. The Fed is also the commercial and investment banker to the federal government; in this capacity, it conducts the Treasury's operations in the U.S. Treasury securities bond market through the securities dealers recognized by it and so authorized to be dealers in U.S. Treasury bills, notes, and bonds.

ROLE OF THE U.S. TREASURY IN THE CAPITAL MARKET

The U.S. Treasury is the biggest player in the U.S. credit markets. Because the market in U.S. government securities is the largest, most active, and most liquid market, it creates a base for conditions in the U.S. credit markets. The Treasury operations bridge the timing of the cash inflows and outflows of the government. They are also used to finance the budget deficit, which became routine for three decades up to 1999, and beginning in 2000 to begin to retire the accumulated debt out of the government budget surplus.

REGULATORY REQUIREMENTS ON THE CAPITAL MARKET

Regulation plays an important role in a fair and orderly functioning of the capital market. Parts of the market are more heavily regulated than other parts. Commercial banking, for example, is one of the most regulated parts of the financial services industries. This heavy regulation is based on the fact that large bank failures, due to either fraud or mismanagement, can destabilize banking markets and lead to loss of faith in the banking system—and therefore in the currency and money (as the liability of commercial banks). The Gramm-Leach-Bliler (Financial Modernization) Act of 1999 has reduced or eliminated the need for many of the regulations on commercial banks and their activities and affiliations with investment banks and insurance companies by allowing competition for the same or similar products offered by the three.

THE KEY CAPITAL MARKETS OUTSIDE THE UNITED STATES

The increasing integration of the world economy and the growth of other economies have led to the emergence of several key financial centers, the prime examples of which are London, Tokyo, Frankfurt, Zurich, Paris, Hong Kong, and Singapore. As of 2000, the bourses in Paris, Brussels, and Amsterdam had announced their planned merger, as had the London Stock Exchange and Frankfurt Stock Exchange.

The Euromarket has grown steadily since about 1960 with the emergence and growth of the Eurocurrency (initially Eurodollar) market and followed by the Euronote, Eurobond, and Euroequity markets. The euro, introduced as the currency of the European Monetary Union on January 1, 1999, consists of the currencies of eleven countries—Austria, Belgium, Finland, France, Germany, Ireland, Italy, Luxembourg, the Netherlands, Portugal, and Spain. It will begin to circulate in 2002 and will eliminate the need for a significant part of the Euromarket market, as the eleven currencies will be replaced by one European currency. The Euromarket will continue to shrink as further European countries join the European Union and adopt its currency. The Eurocurrency market will, however, continue to provide a mechanism for international and global financing in the euro, the dollar, the yen, and other currencies in international trade and finance. The euro area capital market, the U.S. capital market, and the Asian capital market will be the three key capital markets in the twenty-first century.

(SEE ALSO: *Finance*; *Financial Institutions*)

BIBLIOGRAPHY

Board of Governors of the Federal Reserve System. (1999). *The Federal Reserve System: Purposes and Functions*, Washington, DC.

Gramm-Leach-Bliler (Financial Modernization) Act, 1999.

Hakansson, Nils H. (1989). "Financial Markets." In *The New Palgrave: Finance*, John Eatwell, Murray Milgate, and Peter Newman, eds. (pp. 135-144) New York: The Macmillan Press Limited.

Investment Company Act, 1940.

Kidwell, David S., Peterson, Richard L., and Blackwell, David W. (2000). *Financial Institutions, Markets, and Money*, 7th ed. New York: Dryden Press.

Mishkin, Frederic S. (1997). *The Economics of Money, Banking and Financial Markets*, 5th ed. New York: Addison-Wesley.

Molyneux, Philip, and Shamroukh, Nidal. (1999). *Financial Innovation*. New York: Wiley.

Rose, Peter S. (2000). *Money and Capital Markets*, 7th ed. New York: Irwin McGraw-Hill.

Tobin, James. (1989). "Financial Intermediaries." In *The New Palgrave: Finance*, John Eatwell, Murray Milgate, and Peter Newman, eds. (pp. 35-52). New York: The Macmillan Press Limited.

SURENDRA K. KAUSHIK
MASSIMO SANTICCHIA

CAREERS IN ACCOUNTING

Accounting positions range from bookkeeping clerks who maintain financial data in computer and paper files to chief financial officers who are responsible for providing leadership in the design and operations of a total accounting information system and its output of financial statements.

OVERVIEW OF ACCOUNTING AS AN OCCUPATION FIELD

The U.S. Department of Labor identifies accounting essentially at two levels. At the "executive, administrative, and managerial" occupational level, accountants and auditors are included. Under "bookkeeping, accounting, and auditing clerks," positions are available to those with some training and interest in working with financial records.

Persons employed in accounting are generally expected to have strong computer, analytical, interpersonal, and communications skills in addition to sound knowledge in accounting related to the level of the position. Career opportunities are available for individuals with varying levels of formal education.

In general, the rate of growth of employment in accounting is expected to be the average of that for all occupations through 2008, as projected by the U.S. Department of Labor. The impact of computer technology will continue to change the nature of demand for employees in accounting, but growth in business activity and the turnover of personnel assure appealing opportunities for those individuals who are technically prepared and gain relevant on-the-job experience.

Accounting is a field that is appealing to individuals who enjoy working with figures and who appreciate the need for impeccable accuracy and careful adherence to policies and schedules. Increasingly, those who work in accounting must be computer-savvy. Thus, individuals who are challenged by the continuing need to learn new software, and new ways of work find the field of interest. Those individuals who choose to become certified must continue to be learners, because all certifications have a continuing professional education requirement to maintain certification. Even accountants who are not certified enroll in a range of in-company and other types of programs to upgrade their skills and knowledges.

Accountants must be individuals of high integrity so that those who read financial information prepared or audited by accountants have confidence in the credibility of such information.

Accountants who are certified are expected to adhere to professional codes of ethics that impose rules and regulations to encourage behavior in relation to their work that maintains the credibility of financial reporting, both within the organization and outside the organization.

CAREERS FOR CERTIFIED ACCOUNTANTS

Professional accounting positions that require at least an undergraduate college degree and certification are certified public accountant (CPA), certified management accountant (CMA), certified internal auditor (CIA), and the certified government financial manager(CGFM).

Certified Public Accountant. The most common path for the aspiring CPA is to begin employment in a public accounting firm as a staff accountant. Most states in the United States require experience in auditing for certification. While public accounting firms hire recent graduates of college programs for beginning positions, such firms expect new employees to have taken the examination or be planning to sit for it. While many CPAs leave public accounting to enter other positions in all types of organizations, some remain in public accounting. The promotional opportunities in public accounting for CPAs are related to level of responsibility. Successful staff accountants become seniors; seniors become managers; a limited number of managers become partners. In many public accounting firms, there are more levels of professional staff than indicated in the preceding sentence. In addition to accounting and auditing, public accounting firms provide other services, such as tax advisement and management consulting. Some CPAs choose to move to other services after they gain experience in accounting and auditing. Others decide to establish their own firms; in 1998, for example, 10 percent of accountants were self-employed. Many choose to work in other types of positions after gaining certification and experience. Many accept positions in corporations, not-for-profit entities, and government agencies, where promotional opportunities include both accounting and nonaccounting re-

sponsibilities. Some become chief executive officers in major corporations.

Accountants in Organizations. The range of positions for accountants in organizations is extensive. Accountants are employed in corporate reporting, in controller's offices, and in budget and strategic planning departments. Certification is provided for management accountants through the Institute of Management Accountants. To be certified as a certified management accountant, a candidate must successfully complete a comprehensive examination that includes accounting and related topics relevant to the broad responsibilities assumed by management accountants. There is a requirement for work experience in some aspect of management accounting before a candidate is certified. CMAs have many promotional opportunities in organizations. They are identified for leadership positions, in much the same way as CPAs, at executive levels of their own and other organizations.

Internal Auditors. Many accountants choose to work as internal auditors. The Institute of Internal Auditors provides a certification program for candidates who seek to be certified internal auditors. Certification requires experience as an internal auditor. In many organizations, especially large ones, there is a separate department of internal audit that provides valuable oversight of the total organization. Internal auditors who are certified are expected to adhere to the professional standards as they perform their responsibilities. CIAs have promotional opportunities in internal auditing through moving into managerial positions within the department or moving to operational units where they assume supervisory and executive responsibilities.

Government Accountants. The most common certification for government accountants is that provided by the Association of Government Accountants. An examination and relevant experience are required. The designation achieved by a successful candidate is certified government financial manager. Government accountants are employed throughout the public sector, at federal, state, and local levels.

CAREERS FOR ACCOUNTANTS WITHOUT CERTIFICATION

There are more accountants in the United States who are uncertified than there are those who are certified. Of the slightly more than 1 million workers classified as accountants and auditors in the United States in 1998, fewer than half were certified. Individuals who have studied accounting at the community college, business college, or university level are employed for beginning accounting positions. Through on-the-job training and experience, many of these individuals move into higher-level positions.

Many individuals who study in accounting programs in universities choose not to be certified. Others study some accounting as an elective program and then enter a beginning accounting position as a staff accountant, for example.

Many promotional opportunities are available to accountants. Technical skills and managerial skills are both important if an individual aspires to higher-level positions. Employees who are knowledgeable about accounting and continue to learn as new accounting rules and interpretations are introduced by professional bodies are invaluable to employers. However, such knowledge must be accompanied by strong organizational and interpersonal skills if promotional opportunities are to be realized.

CHANGING REQUIREMENTS FOR ACCOUNTANTS AND AUDITORS

Knowledge of accounting and auditing continues to be critical to handling job responsibilities. However, such knowledge alone is not sufficient. Accountants are expected to have advanced competencies in handling a variety of accounting and auditing software and in designing accounting information systems. Furthermore, accountants and auditors are expected to strategically analyze, interpret, and assess the information from the systems they develop and implement. For example, the need for a broader, yet deeper, education has resulted in many states requiring a 150-hour college program for those who aspire to be CPAs.

It is expected that all states will have such a requirement by 2008.

CAREERS IN ACCOUNTING THAT DO NOT REQUIRE A COLLEGE DEGREE

As noted before, there are positions in accounting that are identified by the U.S. Labor Department as requiring less than a college degree. A variety of bookkeeping, accounting, and auditing clerks are needed in all types of organizations; in 1998, there were 2.1 million such clerks. As reported by the U.S. Department of Labor Statistics, approximately a fourth of these workers were in wholesale and retail trade. The outlook for employment (to 2008) is that virtually all job openings will be related to replacement of individuals who have left positions. There is high turnover in this category of workers as workers move to other types of positions, including ones that represent promotions, or leave the labor force.

Most positions require a high school diploma and exist in virtually every industry in the United States. Such workers are expected to know basic computer software programs. Most U.S. comprehensive and vocational high schools offer courses in accounting and in computer software applications. Also, proprietary business colleges as well as junior and community colleges have programs that prepare students with the basic knowledge and skills needed in many beginning accounting positions. Many employers provide training on the job for the specific applications that new employees need to understand and use. Many employers provide training when there are software or system changes in the accounting information system.

The key task of accounting-related clerks is to maintain financial records. Such workers compute, classify, process, and verify numerical data. In large as well as mid-size businesses, for example, there are departments that handle accounts payable, accounts receivable, or cash. For such departments, companies seek employees who have a basic understanding of accounting principles, possess an organized style of work, and can handle communications with vendors (in accounts payable), customers (in accounts receivable), or personnel in human resources (benefits, pensions). Ability to work under pressure and meet deadlines is also important in some positions. Entry-level workers are generally responsible for handling the details of transactions and for preparing schedules that show the results of processing transactions.

Promotional opportunities are available in many organizations. Individuals who continue their education on a part-time basis and who display maturity and wisdom in their associations with co-workers are considered good candidates for supervisory positions. Responsible, dependable managers often began as clerks but were willing to continue to learn not only all aspects of their jobs but also the total work of the organization in relation to the accounting function.

CAREERS IN ACCOUNTING RELATED TO DOCTORAL DEGREES

University programs that lead to doctoral degrees in accounting provide graduates who find employment in college teaching and in technical positions in public accounting firms, professional standard-setting organizations, and other organizations in which high-level expertise in such specializations as accounting theory, accounting systems design, or accounting policy are in demand.

Opportunities for accountants with doctorates reflect the need for accountants to have leading-edge vision in a rapidly changing global business environment. Advanced studies leading to a doctorate will provide individuals with theoretical understanding who can devise new principles to assure the relevance of financial information that is reported to shareholders and others. Advanced studies will also provide individuals who can design the effective and efficient accounting information systems needed in business and government.

SPECIALIZATIONS WITHIN THE FIELD OF ACCOUNTING

Bodies such as the American Institute of Certified Public Accountants (AICPA) provide specialized credentials in such fields as personal financial planning and information technology for individuals who are CPAs. As of mid-2000, the AICPA began discussion of some type of international business professional designation that would complement the CPA credential. It is the belief of the leadership of the AICPA that holders of a global credential would have national and international recognition and credibility as business professionals who can function in the global marketplace. This effort is relevant because a new international accounting standard-setting structure is scheduled for implementation as of January 1, 2001.

Other initiatives in the United States relate to environmental accounting, forensic accounting, international accounting, and fraud accounting. Organizations with missions related to a specialization are active in establishing standards to guide practitioners who choose to participate in the field.

RELATED FIELDS

Accounting is often referred to as "the language of business." That language has wide application. Many occupations are open to those who have both a background in accounting and analytical skills. Among occupations in which accounting training is perceived to be valuable are budget officers, lending officials in banks, securities advisers, financial analysts, and FBI investigative agents.

(SEE ALSO: *Accounting*; *Assurance Services*; *Auditing*)

BIBLIOGRAPHY

American Institute of Certified Public Accountants. www.aicpa.org.

Institute of Internal Auditors. www.theiia.org.

Institute of Management Accountants. www.imanet.org.

U.S. Department of Labor, Bureau of Labor Statistics. (2000). *Occupational Outlook Handbook.* 2000-2001 Edition. Bulletin 2520. U.S. Department of Labor, Washington, DC.

BERNARD H. NEWMAN
MARY ELLEN OLIVERIO

CAREERS IN ECONOMICS

Economists study how society uses, regulates, and distributes its natural and human-made resources such as land, labor, raw materials, and machinery to produce goods and services (*Horizons*, 2000). In simpler terms, they study how effectively society meets its human and material needs. Economists also study how economic systems address three basic questions: What shall we produce?; How shall we produce it?; For whom shall we produce it? They then compile, process, and interpret the answers to these questions ("Economists," 1997). Economists may analyze the relationship between supply and demand and develop theories and models to help predict these future relationships. They help provide a logical, ordered way of looking at various problems. They attempt to explain social concerns such as unemployment, inflation, economic growth, business cycles, tax policy, or farm prices. Most economists apply their skills to solve problems in specific areas, such as transportation, labor, heath, finance, marketing, corporate planning, energy, or agriculture. Business firms, banks, insurance companies, labor unions, governmental agencies, and others seek advice from economists to use in their decision making (*Horizons*, 2000).

THREE GENERAL TYPES OF ECONOMISTS

Theoretical economists, employing mathematical models, develop theories to examine major economic phenomena, such as the causes of business cycles or inflation or the effects of unemployment, energy prices, or tax laws. Most economists, however, concern themselves with the practical application of economic policy to such areas as finance, labor, agriculture, health, and transportation (Harkavy, 1990). Although there are widely ranging careers open to economists, there are three main career paths: business, government, and academia. Each type of economist applies the economic approach to decision-making in a different setting.

Business economists work in such areas as manufacturing, mining, transportation, commu-

Alan Greenspan, chairman of the Federal Reserve Board.

nications, banking, insurance, retailing, private industry, securities and investment firms, management consulting firms, and economic and market research firms, as well as trade associations and consulting organizations (*Careers*, 2000). Many private firms, both large and small, recruit undergraduate economics majors for jobs. These jobs are general-purpose ones for which employers seek bright, highly-motivated students who can learn a specific business through on-the-job training. To become a professional business economist requires graduate training. Business economists perform such tasks as forecasting the business environment, interpreting the impact of public/governmental policy on the firm, and collecting and processing data. They also supply information to management that affects decisions on the marketing and pricing of company products, as well as providing long- and short-term economic forecasts ("Economics," 1997). For example, a business firm's managers might ask its marketing analysts to

Career Opportunities
For Which An Economics Background is Well Suited

• Economist	• Commodities Trader/Broker
• Business Manager	• Financial Analyst
• Property Manager	• Financial Investment Analyst
• Labor Relations Specialist	• Population Studies Analyst
• Market Research Analyst	• Bank Administrator
• Securities Broker	• Business Administrator
• Urban/Regional Planner	• Investor Relations Manager
• Public Administrator	• Chamber of Commerce Analyst
• Government Economist	• Transportation Planner
• Industrial Traffic Manager	• Commodity Analyst
• Technical Writer	• Data Analyst
• International Trade Specialist	• Cost Analyst
• Farm and Land Appraiser	• Credit Analyst
• Food Store Manager	• Rate Analyst
• Marketing Advisor	• Bank Research Analyst
• Professional Farm Manager	• Compensation/Benefits Coordinator
• Sales Representative	• Financial Researcher
• Statistician	• Investment Banking Analyst
• Journalist (especially business reporting)	• Compensation Analyst
• Actuary	• Cost Estimator
• Researcher	• Demographer
• Agricultural Economist	• Public Administrator
• Tax Economist	• Regional Planner
• Tax Examiner/Collector/Revenue Agent	• Underwriter
• Political Scientist	• Management Consultant
• Stockbroker	

Table 1

provide specific information on which to base marketing and pricing policies. Using econometric modeling techniques, the analysts develop projections of market reactions to various price levels throughout the industry; and on the basis of these projections, the mangers can make informed pricing decisions. Informed, rational decision making on economic matters is what economics is all about.

Government Economists work for federal, state, and local governments in a wide variety of positions involving analysis and policy making. The federal government is a major source of employment for economists with an undergraduate degree; information about job openings in various agencies is available from the Federal Employment Information Center. A bachelor's degree in economics is a good qualification for an entry-level position; a person can advance to higher positions by obtaining a graduate degree or by promotion from within. There are jobs for labor, international, development, and popula-

tion economists, as well as micro- and macroeconomists (*Careers*, 1995). Economists who work for government or private research agencies assess economic trends in order to formulate policy in such areas as agriculture, forestry, business, finance, labor, transportation, urban economics, or international trade and development (*Horizons*, 2000). Working for Congress is a relatively new area for economists. Legislation and the issues facing Congress are becoming more complex and economic in nature, and as a result, members of Congress are turning to economists for advice on these issues.

Academics is another major area in which economists are found. Economics professors teach basic macro- and microeconomics courses (the "big picture" versus individual companies/persons) as well as courses on advanced topics, such as economic history and labor economics. They also do research, write papers and books, and give lectures, contributing their knowledge to the advancement of the discipline ("Econo-

Additional Career Opportunities Available with Certain Skills, Interests, or Further Education

- Business Credit Manager
- Loan Administrator
- Consumer Credit Manager
- Inventory Control Specialist
- Farm Manager
- Purchasing Agent/Buyer
- Lawyer
- Accountant, Public Practice
- Market Interviewer
- System Analyst
- Hospital Administrator
- Consumer Credit Manager
- Underwriter
- Foreign Service Officer
- Cooperative Extension Agent
- Job Analyst
- Personnel Manager
- Marketing/Sales Manager
- Editor
- Demographer
- Consultant
- Real Estate Investor
- Entrepreneur/Businessperson
- Foreign Correspondent
- Soil Conservation Specialist
- Financial Planner Investment Analyst
- Time Management Specialist
- Survey Designer
- Market Research Statistician
- Media Buyer
- Bank Examiner
- Energy Researcher
- Environmental Researcher
- Lobbying Researcher
- Real Estate Development Researcher
- Political Campaign Organizer
- Historical Researcher
- Institutional Researcher
- FBI/CIA Agent
- General Accountant
- Economics Professor

Table 2

Related Occupations

- Insurance Agent/Broker
- Financial Aid Director
- Retail Store Manager
- Legal Assistant
- Real Estate Agent
- Legal Assistant
- Collection Agent
- Public Relations Specialist
- Claim Adjuster/Examiner
- Computer Programmer
- Systems Analyst
- Construction Estimator
- Investment Counselor
- Health Policy Planner
- Affirmative Action Representative

Table 3

mists," 1997). In order to teach at a four-year college, it is essential to have a Ph.D. in economics. Faculty members usually divide their time among teaching, research, and administrative responsibilities. Many academic economists also have the opportunity to consult either for business or government.

RELATED USES FOR AN ECONOMICS DEGREE

Economics is widely recognized as a solid background for many jobs and professions in business, government, and the law. Economics majors have a wide range of choices and a great deal of flexibility when deciding on a profession (Tables 1, 2, 3).

An undergraduate major in economics can be an ideal preparation for work on a Master of Business Administration degree, and many graduate business schools encourage students to take at least some economics courses. Studying economics is also excellent preparation for becoming a lawyer; many believe that economics is one of the best backgrounds for success in law school because of its emphasis on a logical approach to problems, logical reasoning, and analytical skills. Publishing companies and trade associations also employ economists. Newspapers provide economics majors with opportunities to write about economic and business events. The demand for economics teachers in secondary schools is growing as economics becomes an increasingly important and popular course (*Careers*, 1995).

WORK CONDITIONS

Economists generally work in offices or classrooms. The average work week for government economists is forty hours, but the schedules of academic and business economists are less predictable. Regular travel may be necessary to collect data or attend conferences or meetings. International economists may spend as much as 30 percent of their time traveling and 40 percent of their time on the telephone or the Internet researching current trends in foreign economic systems (for this subgroup, language skills are important) (*Economist*, 2000).

Economists in nonteaching positions often work alone writing reports, preparing statistical charts, and using computers, but they may also be part of a research team. Faculty economists have flexible work schedules, dividing their time among teaching, research, consulting, and administrative duties (*Horizons*, 2000). High levels of satisfaction are found throughout this field, which encourages discussion, detailed examination, and lively disagreement.

DESIRABLE PERSONAL QUALITIES

The field of economics rewards creative, curious, analytical, and logical thinkers. Helpful qualities for an economist include the following:

- The ability to work accurately with details
- The ability to work well independently as well as with others
- The ability to be objective and systematic in one's work
- Patience and persistence (since economists and marketing research analysts must spend long hours on independent study and problem solving)
- Effective communication skills
- Intellectual curiosity
- The ability to collect, organize, interpret, and analyze data
- Leadership ability
- The ability to present findings clearly, both orally and in writing
- The ability to make decisions based on experience and using data
- Enjoyment of the research process

Especially for advancement purposes, it is helpful to continue pursuing education and to take graduate-level courses. It is also important to be able to work successfully under the pressure of deadlines and tight schedules and to be able to bear the responsibility of knowing that the infor-

mation provided will affect the future policies of current employers (*Horizons*, 2000).

EDUCATION AND TRAINING

People who are interested in this field should be able to work accurately and precisely, because economics entails careful analysis of data. Good communications skills are also necessary. One should also take as many mathematics and computer science courses as possible in high school ("Economics," 1997).

A college major in economics is the basic preparation for a career in economics. Students should also study political science, psychology, sociology, finance, business law, international relations, statistics, regression analysis, and econometrics. Those who are comfortable with the written and spoken word have a significantly higher rate of advancement and overall job satisfaction than those who are not (*Economist*, 2000).

Although most professional economists hold a master's degree or a doctorate, a bachelor's degree often suffices for an entry-level position in business or government, perhaps in an economics-related area such as sales or marketing, beginning research, or administrative and management training ("Economics," 1997). The primary responsibilities in entry-level positions are the collection, adaptation, and preparation of data. In the federal government, applicants for entry-level economist positions must have a bachelor's degree with a minimum of twenty-one semester hours of economics and three hours of statistics, accounting, or calculus (*Horizons*, 2000). However, additional courses and/or superior academic performance are likely to be required. The importance of quantitative analysis makes it highly desirable for those planning a career in economics to take courses in mathematics, statistics, sampling theory and survey design, and computer science (Harkavy, 1990).

Postgraduate degrees in economics, with concentration in areas such as economic theory, econometrics, comparative economic systems, economic planning, labor economics, and international economics, are generally required for advancement in government or private industry

(Harkavy, 1990). Business economists with a graduate degree and experience may advance to management or executive positions in banks, industry, or other organizations, where they determine business and administrative policy (*Horizons*, 2000). A master's degree is usually the minimum requirement for a job as an instructor in junior and community colleges. For a faculty position in most colleges and universities, however, a Ph.D. is normally required. A Ph.D. plus extensive publications in academic journals are required for a professorship, tenure, and promotion. Economists in education may advance to be department heads or to administrative or research positions ("Economists and Marketing," 2000).

Overall, good mathematical and analytical skills are essential; persistence, objectivity, and creativity in problem solving are important; and computer skills and excellent communication skills are invaluable. No special licensing or certification is required for economists (Harkavy, 1990).

LOCATION OF JOBS

Generally economists who are not in academia work in large cities, where there is the highest concentration of major financial and government power; New York City and Washington, DC, are main centers of employment, along with Chicago and Los Angeles. Academic positions are spread throughout the country. American economists are also employed in foreign countries by international companies and organizations and by U.S. government agencies ("Economists," 1997).

EARNINGS AND PROSPECTIVE JOB OUTLOOK

Economists are the highest-paid social scientists. The highest-paid economists in business are in securities and investment, insurance, and retail and wholesale trade. The lowest-paid economists work in education, nonprofit research institutions, and real estate (Harkavy, 1990).

Job opportunities for economists should be best in manufacturing, financial services, advertising, and consulting firms. The complexity of modern national and international markets will continue to spur a demand for those skilled in quantitative analysis. In addition, lawyers, accountants, engineers, and urban and regional planners, among others, will continue to need economic analysis. The majority of openings will come about as the result of replacement needs for those retiring or leaving the profession for some other reason (Harkavy, 1990).

Demand for qualified marketing research analysts should be strong because of the increasingly competitive economy. Marketing research provides organizations with valuable feedback from purchasers that enables companies to evaluate consumer satisfaction and plan more effectively for the future. As companies seek to expand their market and consumers become better informed, the need for marketing professionals will increase ("Economists and Marketing," 2000).

Economists with a bachelor's degree will face strong competition in securing jobs in business or industry; some may find positions as management or sales trainees or as research or administrative assistants. Those with master's degrees and a strong background in marketing and finance will have the best prospects in business, banking, advertising, and management consulting (Harkavy, 1990). Those holding doctoral degrees in economics and marketing are likely to face strong competition for teaching positions in colleges and universities. However, opportunities should be good in other areas, such as industry and consulting firms.

CONCLUSION

Economics is the only social science for which a Nobel Prize is awarded—an indication of its importance. Economic concepts have been applied in the natural sciences; both the theory of natural selection and the study of ecology, for example, have drawn extensively on economic concepts. Economics is both a theoretical and an applied discipline. It analyzes the way an economy can be changed and improved through learning how the various parts of society affect each other and studying the relationships between government, business, and the individual (Basta, 1991). Economic concepts are so powerful and versatile that they have been applied to attempts to understand nearly every aspect of human activity. Economics provides important insights in areas from government fiscal and monetary policy, to business, to law and property rights, to poverty and health issues, to environmental and natural resource issues, to the choice of marriage partners.

BIBLIOGRAPHY

Basta, Nicolas. (1991). "Economics." *Major Options: The Student's Guide to Linking College Majors and Career Opportunities During and After College.* New York: Stonesong Press.

Careers in Economics. (1995). http://www.sju.edu/~nfox/careers.htm.

Careers in Economics/Student Resources/McGraw-Hill. (2000). McGraw-Hill Higher Education: The McGraw-Hill Companies. http://www.mhhe.com/economics/sharp/student/careers.mhtml.

"Economics," (1997). *VGM's Careers Encyclopedia,* 4th ed. Chicago: NTC Publishing Group.

"Economists." (1997). *Encyclopedia of Careers and Vocational Guidance,* vol. 2. Chicago: J.G. Ferguson Publishing.

"Economists and Marketing Research Analysts." (2000). *Occupational Outlook Handbook.* Washington, DC: U.S. Department of Labor—Bureau of Labor Statistics.

Economist. (2000). [On-line]. Princeton Review Online/Career: Princeton Review Publishing, L.L.C. http://www.review.com.

Harkavy, Michael (1990). "Economists." *101 Careers: A Guide to the Fastest-Growing Opportunities.* New York: Wiley.

Horizons. (2000). [Computer program]. Springfield: Illinois Career Information System, Illinois Occupational Information Coordinating Committee. http://ioicc.state.il.us/etc.htm.

Questions and Answers. (2000). http://www.wiu.edu/users/miecon/wiu/whymajor/questions_answers.html.

WENDY RINHOLEN

CAREERS IN FINANCE

In exploring careers in finance, one quickly begins to realize that there are a variety of jobs, with several types of organizations, requiring varying levels of education and training. Unfortunately, the word *finance* reveals few details about what one actually does as work in a finance career. The *Career Guide to Industries* (edition 2000-2001), produced by the Bureau of Labor Statistics, organizes finance careers according to three broad categories: banking, insurance, and securities and commodities. Careers in the banking industry focus on providing loans, credit, and payment services to individual and large institutional customers. Insurance industry jobs focus on providing clients with protection against financial losses and hardships due to such things as fire. Finally, securities and commodities careers are typically what most people think of when considering a career in finance. These jobs focus on advising and assisting individual and institutional investors with purchasing and selling stocks, bonds, and commodities.

BANKING CAREERS

The majority of jobs in the banking industry are clerical and administrative support positions. Bank tellers make up the bulk of the clerical positions in banking institutions. Tellers work directly with customers, assisting them with basic banking services such as depositing funds and cashing checks. New accounts clerks, also called customer service representatives, assist customers with opening and closing bank accounts and with applying for loans or credit cards. As a result, bank tellers and new accounts clerks need to be knowledgeable about a wide range of banking services and be able educate customers about these services.

There are several other entry-level administrative positions in the banking industry. Bookkeeping, auditing, and accounting clerks are needed to help maintain and update financial records, process deposit slips and checks, and enter data. Credit or loan clerks are responsible for organizing the paperwork needed to complete the required records for approved loans or lines of credit. Banks also need secretaries, receptionists, and computer operators to assist with the many administrative support duties.

According to the *Career Guide to Industries,* 25 percent of the positions in the banking industry are comprised of executive, administrative, and managerial occupations. Examples of these occupations include loan officers, trust officers, and financial managers. Loan officers are responsible for determining whether or not a customer can pay back a loan and then approving or declining the customer's loan application. They also help to bring in new business by developing relationships with customers who will need bank loans in the future. Loan officers and counselors also tend to specialize in either commercial, consumer, or mortgage lending. Trust officers are responsible for managing the finances of customers or organizations that have been placed in trust with the bank. Very often they are called upon to be the executor of an individual's estate upon that person's death. Last, financial managers supervise operations at branch offices or departments to make sure customers receive quality service.

Education and training requirements for finance careers in banking vary according to the special skills required for success and the level of responsibility. Bank tellers and clerks typically need, at minimum, a high school education. Some basic skills and interests needed for success as a teller or clerk are math skills, interpersonal communication skills, and comfort in handling large amounts of money. Typically banks provide tellers and clerks with additional training on the organization's procedures and regulations. The American Institute of Banking, American Bankers Association, and the Institute of Financial Education all offer accredited courses for advanced training. Bank tellers and clerks take these educational courses to prepare for more responsibilities and to assist with career advancement. However, most banks have their own training programs.

Financial managers, loan officers, and trust officers usually have a college degree if not a more advanced professional or graduate degree. Most study business administration or earn a degree with a major in business administration. Any college degree plus a master of business administration or a law degree are excellent preparation for one of these financial management

positions. Managers who also sell securities need to be licensed by the National Association of Securities Dealers.

Earnings in the bank industry reflect the amount of responsibility and education required of the position. As a result, the more responsibility and education a job requires, the higher the salary. As the amount of responsibility increases, so does salary, as can be seen in the salary ranges of commercial loan officers, trust officers, and top executives. Other factors that influence salary are experience, length of time with the bank, and location and size of the bank.

Employment in the banking industry is expected to grow at 3 percent, which is much lower than the growth rate of the overall economy, which is expected to increase 15 percent between 1998 and 2008. The downsizing and cost cutting that occurred in this industry in the early to mid-1990s is expected to decline. Most of the growth in the banking industry is expected to occur in small regional credit unions and banks. As banks become more automated and ATMs are able to provide more services, fewer bank tellers and clerks will be needed. Areas of growth can be found in customer service representatives for staffing call centers and trust officers to administer the estates of an aging population.

INSURANCE INDUSTRY CAREERS

The *Career Guide to Industries* states that more than 40 percent of the positions in the insurance industry are administrative support positions such as secretaries, bookkeepers, word processors, and clerks. These support positions often require skills and knowledge that are specific to the insurance industry. For example, because insurance policy clerks focus on processing insurance policy applications, changes to policies, and cancellations, they need to have a strong understanding of insurance policies. They often verify both the completeness of an application and the accuracy of the insurance company's records. Insurance claims examiners and investigators often investigate questionable claims or claims that exceed the amount the insurance company is willing to pay. Investigators and examiners spend most of their time checking claim applications for accuracy, obtaining information needed for decisions from experts, and consulting current policy about claims.

Executive, managerial, and administrative jobs make up about 30 percent of the positions in the insurance field. Three examples of job titles found at this level of employment in the insurance industry are risk manager, sales manager, and underwriter. Risk managers develop the policies the insurance company follows when making decisions regarding claims. These policies are developed by analyzing historical data about natural disasters, car accidents, and other situations that may result in physical or financial loss. Sales managers sell insurance products, assist clients with questions about policies, and supervise staff. They make up the majority of managers in local sales offices. Finally, underwriters review applications for insurance and the level of risk involved in agreeing to issue an insurance policy. Essentially, the underwriter determines whether to accept or reject the application and how much a client should pay in premiums.

A smaller percentage, about 15 percent, of salaried employees in the insurance industry is made up of salespeople, often called insurance brokers or insurance agents, who focus on selling insurance policies to businesses and individual customers. Insurance agents can sell insurance exclusively for one insurance company or insurance policies issued by several different insurance companies. Some of the typical types of insurance polices an agent or broker may sell include health, life, annuities, property, casualty, and disability. In addition to these services, some agents are now licensed to sell mutual funds, annuities, and securities.

An even smaller career field in the insurance industry is the area of actuary science. Although there may not be as many actuaries as there are salespeople in insurance, they are very important to the industry. Actuaries set rates paid by customers at a level where the premiums that are collected will generate enough money to cover the claims that are paid out. Yet the premiums can't be too expensive or customers will switch to other insurance companies. Actuaries accomplish this by studying the probability of an insured loss and the premium rates of other insurance companies.

Education requirements for jobs in the insurance industry vary, depending on the position and its responsibilities. Many of the entry-level clerical positions in the insurance industry require only a high school diploma. Higher-level executive, managerial, and sales positions require more education, with employers usually preferring to hire college graduates. Most managerial positions are filled by promoting people from within the organization. Such employees usually have a college education, some special training in the insurance industry, and experience with the company. Actuaries typically have a college degree in actuary science, math, or statistics. After completing college, actuaries must pass a series of exams over a period of five to ten years to become fully qualified. Overall, advancement opportunities are good in the insurance industry.

Earnings for insurance clerks and clerical staff are below those of insurance examiners, adjusters, and investigators. Higher yearly salaries are typical for higher-level general managers and top executives. Salaries for sales agents are difficult to pinpoint because many salespeople are paid a salary, plus commissions, plus bonuses for reaching sales goals. In addition, an agent's earnings will rapidly increase as he or she gains experience and develops a client base.

The employment rate for the insurance industry is projected to increase more slowly than the average for all industries combined. Job growth in the insurance field is expected to be limited by the downsizing of large insurance companies, computerization, and a trend that points toward direct-mail and telephone sales campaigns. One area of growth in this industry is that of financial services and products sales. Another growth area stems from the need to cover large liability awards resulting from lawsuits. Finally, the number of claims professionals will grow faster than any other position in the industry because of the need for better customer service and actual inspection of damaged property or consultation with doctors.

SECURITIES AND COMMODITIES CAREERS

There are large numbers of workers in this area of the finance industry. The national brokerage companies have extensive systems of branch offices throughout the country; as a result, these brokerage firms employ the majority of the workers in this industry. Headquarters for these firms are located in New York City, where most of the executives and support personnel work. Mutual fund management companies and regional brokerages also employ many people. Although it is very well known, the New York Stock Exchange actually employs a small number of people compared to the rest of the industry.

A great deal of attention is focused on tracking performance, transactions, and the value of investments. Brokerage clerks are responsible for the majority of the daily operations and for processing much of the paperwork that is generated. These positions are often considered entry-level jobs with the potential for promotion into securities sales and even into higher positions. For example, a sales assistant takes calls from clients, writes up the order, processes the paperwork, and keeps clients updated on their portfolio's performance. With experience and a license to buy and sell securities, brokerage clerks can be promoted into higher-level sales positions.

The largest number of people employed in the securities and commodities industry can be found in three occupations: securities, commodities, and financial services sales. These careers involve buying and selling shares of stocks, mutual funds, and other financial services. The majority of these workers are sales representatives who work directly with individual investors. They are known as brokers, account executives, or financial consultants. Securities and commodities brokers differ in the investments they buy and sell. Securities brokers typically buy and sell stocks, bonds, and mutual funds. Commodities brokers buy and sell futures contracts for metals, energy supplies such as oil, and agricultural products. In addition to buying and selling securities, brokers can advise and educate their clients on investments, saving for retirement, and tolerance for risk. Overall, brokers spend a great deal of time marketing their services and products in order to establish a strong customer following.

Financial planners go a step further in advising and educating their clients. They often provide advice on investments, investing for retirement, tax planning, and employee benefits. Their strategy tends to be more of a comprehensive approach to advising clients on financial matters when compared to brokers. These planners can also buy and sell stock, mutual funds, bonds, and annuities.

Investment bankers and financial analysts make recommendations about potential profits from investments in specific companies by reviewing the companies' financial records and evaluating market trends. They also play a very important role in determining the market value for stocks that are traded publicly or stocks being purchased when a company is merging with or acquiring another company. Financial analysts often specialize in a specific industry sector, such as technology stocks.

Another career in the securities and commodities area of the finance industry is that of portfolio manager. These finance professionals are responsible for investing large amounts of money. The portfolios they manage are often mutual funds, pension funds, trust funds, and funds for individuals who are investing very large amounts of money. Most importantly, portfolio managers must have a clear understanding of a mutual fund's or a client's investment goals in order to ensure that the investment decisions they make meet the financial goals and guidelines set by the mutual fund or client.

As a whole, the workers in this area of the finance industry are well educated and highly trained. Even entry-level brokerage clerk positions often require a college degree. Also, to sell securities professionals are required to pass an examination testing their knowledge of investments. The National Association of Securities Dealers (NASD) conducts this testing and licenses professionals to sell a variety of investment products. Most brokers and sales assistants obtain the Series 7 license from the NASD by passing the General Securities Registered Representative Exam. In addition to passing the exam, these professionals are required to take classes on regulatory issues and new investment products in order to keep their licenses. Currently, there is no special licensing requirement to become a financial planner. However, many financial planners earn a certified financial planning (CFP) or chartered financial consultant (ChFC) designation. The CFP is issued through the CFP Board of Standards and the ChFC is offered by the American College. A series of exams on investments, taxes, insurance, retirement, and estate planning must be passed in order to receive one of these designates. In addition, the CFP must follow the rules and regulations set forth by the CFP Board of Standards.

Most of the workers in the entry-level analyst and managerial positions have a college degree and studied finance, general business administration, economics, accounting, or marketing. In order to advance, many take part in management trainee programs where they briefly work and learn about different departments. To advance further and gain access to higher salaries and more prestigious positions, many people obtain a master's degree in business administration.

For many brokers and commodities dealers, income is based on a salary and on commissions from the sale or purchase of stocks, bonds, or futures contracts. When the economy is strong these commissions and bonuses are much higher than they are when the economy is in a slump. Another factor in determining earnings in this area of finance is the amount of assets the manager is responsible for managing.

Yearly earnings for entry-level brokerage clerks are at the start of the scale. Further up the scale are financial analysts and sales agents. At the next level are the financial managers. The highest-paid professionals in the securities and commodities industry are general managers and top executives. Many firms also offer their employees profit sharing and stock options. Plus, most sala-

ried employees receive health benefits, paid vacation, and sick leave.

Job growth in this industry is being fueled by several factors. First, more than ever, people are investing in securities as a way to save money and plan for retirement, resulting in a large influx of money into the stock market. Second, although on-line trading is reducing the need for direct contact with brokers, there is still a need for investment advice. Finally, the increased demands of investing in a complex global market have created a need for skilled investment managers. According to the *Occupational Outlook Handbook,* these factors have contributed to an employment growth projection of 40 percent for this segment of finance careers, which is much greater than the 15 percent projected for all other industries combined.

(SEE ALSO: *Finance*)

BIBLIOGRAPHY

Career Guide to Industries, 2000-2001 Edition. (1999). Bureau of Labor Statistics. Baltimore: United Press.

Careers in Focus: Financial Services. (1998). Chicago: Ferguson Publishing Company

Occupational Outlook Handbook, 2000-20001 Edition. (1999). Bureau of Labor Statistics. (1999). Baltimore: United Press.

Pandy, Anil, and Okusanya, Omotayo T. (1999). *The Harvard Business School Guide to Careers In Finance 2000 Edition.* Boston: Harvard Business School Publishing.

MARK D. WILSON

CAREERS IN INFORMATION PROCESSING

The demand for computer and information systems professionals exists and continues to grow. The U.S. Commerce Department's Office of Technology Policy (1982) reported that between 1996 and 2006, U.S. businesses and schools will require more than 1.3 million *new* information technology workers to fill jobs. In the twenty-first century, 70 percent of all jobs will require skills in computer and network use.

The U.S. Bureau of Labor Statistics (1998) reported that the fastest-growing computer career positions through the year 2006 will be computer engineer, systems analyst, computer repair technician, and programmer. There is also high demand for systems analysts, computer scientists, network administrators, and database managers.

Careers in computers and information processing, also called information technology (IT), require a unique combination of conceptual skills in creative problem solving and critical thinking, technical hands-on skills, and communications and interpersonal skills, as well as an understanding of business and industry needs.

Career opportunities in computer industries can be grouped into four areas:

- Companies that manufacture computer-related equipment (hardware)

- Companies that develop software

- Companies that hire information systems professionals to work with software and hardware products

- Companies and organizations that provide computer-related training and education

Many service companies exist to support each of these four areas—firms that sell computer supplies or provide consultation on analysis, design, programming, and networking projects.

CAREERS IN THE COMPUTER HARDWARE INDUSTRY

The computer equipment, or hardware, industry consists of manufacturers and distributors of computer systems and computer-related equipment such as monitors, printers, and communications equipment.

Computer equipment manufacturers are organizations with thousands of employees in many locations worldwide. IBM, for example, is one of the largest computer companies, with more than 200,000 employees and sales of more than $80 billion in 1998. Numerous start-up companies have taken advantage of rapid changes in equipment technology to create new products and new job opportunities in areas such as networking, multimedia, and fiber-optics.

In addition to the companies that make end-user equipment, thousands of companies build components such as motherboards, input and output devices, and power supplies. Job titles that involve the design and manufacture of computer equipment include computer engineer, software engineer, and technical writer. A computer engineer designs, builds, tests, and evaluates computer chips, circuit boards, computer systems, and peripheral devices. Computer engineers need a B.S. in electrical or computer engineering. They must be very detailed-oriented and good at problem solving.

Software engineers develop system software such as operating systems, utilities, and software drivers. The minimum education required is a B.S. in computer science. Important capabilities include good analytical skills, an ability to work with abstract concepts, and attention to detail.

Technical writers produce technical publications, such as reference manuals, procedure manuals, and product documentation. The minimum education requirement is a B.S. in engineering, science, or a related discipline. Technical writers need good writing skills as well as knowledge of the products, processes, and procedures.

CAREERS IN THE COMPUTER SOFTWARE INDUSTRY

Companies in the computer software industry develop, manufacture, and support a wide range of software products, such as operating systems and other systems software, productivity software, network software, software development tools, and Internet software and technologies. Some companies specialize in a particular type of software product, such as business productivity software, utility programs, or multimedia and graphic design tools. Other firms produce and sell multiple software products.

The software industry had sales in 1998 exceeding $200 billion. The largest software company, Microsoft, has more than 300 products and technologies, more than 20,000 employees, and sales of more than $11 billion in 1998.

Careers in the software industry involve designing and programming all kinds of software products, such as application software for businesses, productivity software, educational programs, entertainment software, and systems software. Careers in the computer software industry include programmer, software engineer, software analyst, and technical writer. A programmer designs, writes, and tests computer programs. Educational requirements are a B.S. in computer science or computer information systems. Programming requires logical thinking and close attention to detail; it calls for patience, persistence, exacting analysis skills, and the ability to meet deadlines. Ingenuity and imagination are important skills because programmers design solutions and test their work for potential failures. Increasingly, interpersonal skills are important for programmers working in teams and interacting directly with users. Systems programmers who work with the software that controls the computer's operation must have capabilities in technical analysis and abstract concepts.

Systems analysts and software analysts conduct requirements analysis, design software solutions, and oversee the software development process. The minimum education requirement is a B.S. in computer science. Software analysts must have good communication and interpersonal skills, a mastery of the design and development process, and good project management skills.

CAREERS AS INFORMATION SYSTEMS PROFESSIONALS

In many organizations, the information systems (IS) department includes information systems professionals, who set up and manage the computer equipment and software to ensure that it produces information for decision-making. Four basic groups of information systems careers are in operations, systems development, technical services, and end-user computing.

Operations Jobs in operations include computer operator, communications specialist, and local area network (LAN) engineer. A computer operator monitors computer system performance, runs jobs, performs backups, and restores files and systems. A high school diploma is required.

A communications specialist installs, monitors, and evaluates data and/or voice communications equipment and software and is responsible for connections to the Internet and other wide area networks (WANs). The minimum educational requirement is a B.S. in information systems or electrical engineering technology.

A LAN engineer installs and maintains local area networks. An example of a LAN engineer is a Windows NT systems engineer. Network engineers are expected to have the capabilities and experience to take responsibility for entire projects and address issues such as network design, network management, security, scalability, and performance. For network engineers, experience as a senior network engineer plus solid skills in NT troubleshooting, problem solving, teamwork, and communications are essential.

Systems Development Systems development careers include systems analyst, application programmer, Webmaster, Web designer/site builder, Internet specialist, and technical writer. Systems analysts assess user requirements and design information systems solutions. They must think logically, have good communication skills, and like working with ideas and people. They often deal with a number of tasks and projects simultaneously. Although computer scientists and systems analysts may work independently, they often work in teams on large projects. They must communicate effectively with computer personnel, such as programmers and managers, as well as with other staff who have a limited technical computer background but are subject-matter experts in a business functional area. A B.S. in management information systems is required.

Application programmers convert the system design into the appropriate computer language, such as C, Java, or Cobol. The minimum educational requirement is an A.A.S. in information systems. The application programmer's skills are similar to those of the systems programmer. A Webmaster maintains an organization's Web site and creates or helps users create Web pages. The minimum educational requirement is an A.A.S. in information systems. A Web designer/site builder's minimum educational requirement is a B.S. in computer science of information systems. The skill set for both jobs includes abilities in Web-site development languages such as C++, Java, and HTML. This job involves the automation of customer service and help desk functions, as well as ongoing maintenance and development. A strong understanding of the business is essential. Strong prioritizing and customer service skills are necessary. This career involves project work and consulting.

The Internet specialist's minimum education is a B.S. in information systems or electrical engineering technology. This position requires skills in senior-level networking, LANs and WANs, the Internet, security, e-commerce, Unix, Windows NT, and Novell applications. Effective communication skills are essential. This career requires an outgoing personality and the ability to work well with users.

Technical writers work with analysts, programmers, and users to create system documentation and user manuals. The minimum educational requirement is a B.S. in information systems.

Technical Services Three primary careers in technical services are database analyst, system programmer, and quality assurance specialist. Database analysts assist systems analysts and programmers in developing or modifying applications that use an organization's database. The minimum education is a B.S. in computer science or information systems.

A system programmer installs and maintains operating system software and provides technical support to the programmer's staff. The minimum educational requirement is a B.S. in computer science or information systems.

A quality assurance specialist reviews programs and documentation to ensure that they meet the organization's standards. The minimum educational requirement is a B.S. in computer science or information systems.

End-User Computing End-user computing positions include PC support specialists and help desk analysts. The PC support specialist installs and supports personal computer equipment and software. The minimum educational requirement is an A.A.S. in information systems. The help desk analyst provides user/customer telephone support for hardware, software, or telecommunications systems. The minimum educational requirement is an A.A.S. in information systems.

Executive Positions Executive positions in information services are senior-level positions in an organization, such as chief technology officer. The chief technology officer develops a strategic technology organizational plan and oversees the implementation of the plan and high-level IT policy issues. A chief technology officer must be able to provide creative solutions, have solid technology skills, and understand the business being supported. Excellent analytical skills and the ability to balance priorities while paying attention to the bottom line are crucial. A prerequisite for the position is a background as a technical strategist; both in-depth and broad-based knowledge and experience are important, as are excellent communications, interpersonal, and management skills.

CAREERS IN EDUCATION AND TRAINING

Extensive opportunities in computer-related education and training exist because of the increased sophistication and complexity of today's computer products and the rapid development and deployment of new products. Schools, colleges, universities, and private companies all need qualified instructors. The high demand for instructors, in fact, has led to a shortage of qualified instructors and trainers in universities and corporate environments.

CONTINUING EDUCATION

Rapid technological changes and the global marketplace continue to increase the need for ongoing continuing education to keep knowledge and skills current. Employers, hardware and software vendors, colleges and universities, and private training institutions offer continuing education opportunities. Additional training is provided by professional development seminars offered through professional organizations.

INDUSTRY CERTIFICATIONS

Industry certifications provide employers assurance of a standard level of competency, skill, or quality in a particular area. Many organizations offer technical certification programs for their products. Standard curricula, training programs, and examinations are used to determine if a person is qualified for certification. A certificate is proof of professional achievement, a level of competence accepted and valued by the industry. Certificates enhance employment portfolios and career opportunities. Many employers give preference in hiring to applicants with certification. In addition, certification can lead to promotions and help advance careers.

BIBLIOGRAPHY

Cannings, Terence R., and Finkel, Leroy. (1993). *The Technology Age Classroom*. Wilsonville, OR: Franklin, Beedle, & Associates.

Edwards, John. (1999). "Employment in 1999: Opportunities amid Challenges." *Computer* 32 (January):19.

Enhanced Occupational Outlook Handbook, The. (1997). Indianapolis, IN: JIST Works.

Fafard, Lina. (1999). "New Career Chart Toppers." *Computerworld*, May 24:57.

Kleinman, Carol. (1992). *100 Best Job$ for the 1990s and Beyond.* Chicago, IL: Dearborn Financial Publishing.

New Book of Knowledge, The. (1994). Danbury, CT: Grolier.

Saettler, Paul. (1990). *The Evolution of American Educational Technology*. Englewood, CO: Libraries Unlimited.

Shelly, Gary, Cashman, Thomas, Vermaat, Misty, and Walker, Tim. (1999). *Discovering Computers 2000: Concepts for a Connected World*. Cambridge, MA: Course Technologies.

Terry, George, and Stallard, John. (1984). *Office Management and Control*. 9th ed. Richard D. Irwin.

U.S. Bureau of Labor Statistics and Source EDP, 1998 Salary Survey.

U.S. Bureau of Labor Statistics. "Occupational Employment, Training, and Earnings." [stats.bls.gov]. March 30, 1998

U.S. Commerce Department. Office of Technology Policy (1998).

York, Thomas. (1999). "Shift in IT Roles Ahead: Changes in Business and Technology will alter IT careers." *InfoWorld* 21(3)(January 18): 75.

LINDA J. AUSTIN
DEBBIE HUGHES

CAREERS IN LAW FOR BUSINESS

A wide variety of choices are available for a career in law. However, work and determination are required to complete law school and pass a state bar examination.

To be admitted to law school, students must have completed a bachelor's degree, although generally without restriction concerning the choice of undergraduate major. Law students have bachelor's degrees in business, engineering, science, history, politics, and many other disciplines.

ENGAGING IN LAW PRACTICE

The individual states administer the licensing of lawyers. Requirements for attorneys to enter the law field vary from state to state. Generally, a prospective lawyer must pass a state bar examination following graduation from law school. In a very few states, a person is automatically admitted to practice upon graduation from law school. It is possible for a person to sit for bar examinations and become licensed to practice in more than one state.

The states also control discipline once lawyers are admitted to practice. Complaints from clients or others may be made to the state bar, which reviews them and imposes discipline, if necessary. Discipline may range from fines or suspensions up to disbarment. In many states, the state supreme court reviews disciplinary actions imposed upon lawyers.

AREAS OF LEGAL PRACTICE

Lawyers deal with business organizations, individuals, international business, labor relations, educational law, poverty law, legal research and writing, and other areas.

Legal practice with domestic business organizations In the United States, attorneys engage directly with business organizations in many fields in which they practice.

Publicly held corporations: Many areas of law involve publicly held corporations (stock available for purchase by any investor). For example, control and management have legal ramifications, as do capital procurement and maintenance. Attorneys are called upon to settle a wide range of disputes, such as those developing between stockholder and corporation.

Antitrust legislation: Antitrust laws prohibit price fixing, which could result when businesses gain monopoly power in their field. Major legislation in this realm includes the Sherman Act of the 1890s, the Clayton Act of 1914, and the Cellar-Kefauver Act of 1950. The Robinson-Patman Act prohibits manufacturers from discriminating against small retailers in favor of large chains. These acts are enforced by the Federal Trade Commission and the Antitrust Division of the Department of Justice.

Unfair trade practices: These laws involve various types of business competition, especially with reference to trademarks, price maintenance, and price discrimination.

Patents: Patents are issued by the Patent and Trademark Office of the U.S. government. They grant inventors exclusive rights to make, sell, and use inventions in the United States for a given period of time. Patents often require an attorney's counsel.

Copyrights: Copyrights provide protection for original works of literary, dramatic, musical, or artistic expression. The Copyright Office of the Library of Congress administers these laws.

Trademarks: Trademarks are used to distinguish one business firm's products from another. Their symbols may be a word or

words, name, design, picture, or sound. Trademark rights have an indefinite life. A company may register its trademark with the U.S. Patent and Trademark Office in Arlington, Virginia, or with the trademark office in its state.

Accounting: Accounting statements provide financial details concerning the operation of a business or other form of organization. Balance sheets list assets (things that are owned), liabilities (debts), and net worth (assets minus liabilities). Income statements show net income for a period of time (income minus expenses). Business firms, particularly those with stockholders, must prepare honest and conservative financial statements. Very stringent laws have been passed dealing with accounting practices.

Negotiations: Attorneys orchestrate a variety of negotiations. including those involving injury claims, criminal charges, family disputes, and commercial disputes.

Business organizations: Business organizations become involved with the law of employment, agency, partnership, limited partnership, and other types of unincorporated associations.

Regulated industries: Price, supply, and services are a part of Regulation C control in various industries, such as transportation agencies and public utilities. Regulatory policy can involve interaction among legislatures, administrative agencies, and the courts. Advanced legal work may be required for business planning and counseling concerning corporate and tax issues. Clients often need representation before regulatory bodies and at administrative hearings.

Contracts: Attorneys become involved in the creation of promissory liability, the interpretation of words and conduct as well as the nature of obligations assumed by entering into contracts. They also solve problems relating to breach of contract, unfairness as a reason for avoiding contractual liability, and the rights of those not a party to the contract.

The Uniform Commercial Code: Articles 3, 4, and 5 concern negotiable instruments, bank collection systems, and letters of credit. Article 9 deals with secured transactions; Article 7, with documents of title.

Creditors' and debtors' rights: Attorneys deal with consumer credit regulation, including attachments, garnishments, assignments for the benefit of creditors, judgments, and bankruptcy.

Insurance law: This branch as law deals with property, life, and liability insurance; fire and automobile insurance forms; and the regulation of insurance companies' policies and practices.

Remedies: Remedies of quasi-contract, constructive trust, equitable lien, and reformation must be applied to redress enrichment secured by tort, part performance of contract, duress, or mistake.

Government contracts: Laws and regulations apply to contracts with governmental bodies and agencies.

Legal practice for individuals Individuals need a wide range of legal services in the area of business. Some services are provided for investors or owners in business situations; others, for persons finding themselves in difficulty.

Trust and estates: Legal consideration must be given to community property systems, federal gift and estate taxes on property transfers, estate planning not involving property, living wills, delegation of health care decision-making, and gifts to as well as guardianship of minor children. Related legal forms involve living trusts and gift strategies.

Family law: Family law can involve relationships of married couples, unmarried couples, or couples undergoing divorce. Additional family relationships that may involve lawyers include parent and child.

unmarried parents, neglected children, foster care, and adoption.

Taxes: Attorneys can assist in tax planning for individuals. especially where issues arise between the taxpayer and the Internal Revenue Service or state taxing authorities. They also deal with taxation implications for corporate organization, reorganization, and liquidation. Some attorneys deal with international tax problems, such as jurisdictional rules, tax situations between industrialized countries and developing countries, and host country taxation of foreign persons.

Real estate transactions: In this field, lawyers deal with options, binder contracts, and rights and duties between vendor and vendee among other things. Lawyers also practice in basic land contract and mortgage law as well as real estate recording systems. They work with both land-use controls and water-rights laws. They may also deal with environmental law and institutions.

Legal practice for international business International trade in the world is becoming more prevalent and increasingly legally complex. This increases openings for interested attorneys.

International legal practice may involve issues of recognition and nonrecognition of governments and nations, interpretation of treaties and other international agreements, the effect of peace and war, and international claims.

Lawyers may advise on the risks, assumptions, and benefits of doing business in a foreign country. Questions may arise concerning international commercial transactions and investments, the impact of U.S. securities and antitrust laws, and trade laws of the United States and other countries.

Labor relations law State and federal laws deal with employee representation, collective bargaining, and employer-union practices. These laws, the National Labor Relations Act, and related federal and state labor laws often make legal counsel necessary.

Attorneys provide counsel in collective bargaining and with the negotiation and arbitration processes.

Statutes such as these involving fair employment practices, workers' compensation, fair labor standards, unemployment compensation, and Social Security protect workers against insecurity, discrimination, economic exploitation, and physical damage. Their purpose is to guard against unequal opportunity linked to race, sex, religion, age, physical disability, and other factors.

Legal questions linked to public policy arise from representation questions, limitations on the right to strike, grievance arbitration, impasse procedures, and the scope of bargaining.

Educational law practice Legal issues arise from educational financing, integration and segregation, punishment methods applied to children, and alternatives to public school education.

Poverty law Although often unable to pay, the poor frequently require legal services. Some indigents make contact with public-interest law firms or offices that provide legal services for the poor. In this area, lawyers deal with issues such as welfare rights, health, education, public assistance, or housing.

Legal research and writing Some lawyers engage in legal research and writing. This work involves library and computerized research, brief and memorandum writing, organization of legal material, and prediction of rules of law. Much of this activity takes place in law schools or at the appellate court level.

Other areas of law practice There are a number of additional areas of law practice. These include legal problems related to technology and society, bioethics, science, psychiatry, and attempts to achieve progress in developing countries.

U.S. COURT SYSTEM

The court system also offers career opportunities. An understanding of our court system is relevant to a career discussion. The courts in the United States fall within two classifications: the federal court system and the state court systems.

Federal court system The federal court system comprises the Supreme Court, circuit courts of appeal, and district courts. There are also specialized federal courts.

The U.S. Supreme Court is the final court of appeal for both civil and criminal law. It was created by Section 1, Article III of the U.S. Constitution. Title 28 of the U.S. Code establishes its jurisdiction. The Court's organization is specified by legislation, although the rules governing case presentations are formulated by the Court itself.

Judicial review is an important power given to the U.S. Supreme Court. This refers to (1) declaring invalid laws that violate the U.S. Constitution, (2) asserting the supremacy of federal laws or treaties if they differ from state and local laws, and (3) serving as the final authority on the interpretation of the U.S. Constitution.

The U.S. Supreme Court includes a chief justice and eight associate justices. Appointed by the president with the approval of the Senate, they serve for life or until they retire, resign, or are impeached.

The U.S. Supreme Court has original jurisdiction in some cases, particularly where a state is a party or diplomatic personnel are involved. The remaining cases come from lower courts. Requests for review number approximately 4,500 annually; less than 200 cases are selected for decision by the U.S. Supreme Court.

Some appeals to the U.S. Supreme Court come from any of the twelve federal courts of appeal or the ninety-four federal district courts. These cases involve the U.S. Constitution, federal laws or cases in which the U.S. government is a party, disputes between residents of different states ("diversity" jurisdiction), or matters assigned by federal legislation.

Appeals also come from specialized federal courts. The Court of Military Appeals reviews courts-martial cases appealed from military courts. These cases concern offenses committed by members of the armed forces and are sometimes brought before the U.S. Supreme Court.

The U.S. Court of Claims hears cases dealing with claims against the federal government. Its decisions may also be appealed to the U.S. Supreme Court. In addition, the U.S. Supreme Court may rule on cases involving decisions of U.S. Custom offices, such as import duties.

State court systems Each state has its own court system. These courts are created by state statute or constitution to enforce state civil and criminal laws. Most of the states have trial courts, intermediate courts of appeal, and a supreme court.

Most states have local trial courts—municipal, county, district, and small-claims courts. Millions of civil and criminal cases are tried at this level. Other state courts may include police courts, magistrate's courts, justices of the peace, and probate or surrogate courts that handle wills and inheritances. There are also traffic courts, juvenile courts, and domestic relations courts.

State appeals courts (sometimes called "error-correcting" courts) review trial court cases to determine if errors caused an incorrect decision. Their decisions may be appealed to the federal courts, including the U.S. Supreme Court in certain instances.

Supreme courts in each state, like the U.S. Supreme Court at the federal level, interpret their state constitutions, statutes enacted by their state legislatures, and the body of state common law.

BIBLIOGRAPHY

Martindale Hubbell Law Directory, Areas of Practice Index. (1998). Reed Elsevier. (www.martindale.com)

The Official Guide to U.S. Law Schools, the annual joint publication of the Association of American Law Schools and the Law School Admission Services, published each fall. Available at most college book stores or can be ordered directly from Law School Admission Services, Box 2000, Newtown PA 18940

University of Wisconsin Law School. "Preparation for Law Study." www.law.wisc.edu/admissions/lawatwis/pret.htm. December 1998.

U.S. Court System. www.syr.edu/jajcarro/compulegal/court.html.

CRAIG A. BESTWICK
G. W. MAXWELL

CAREERS IN MANAGEMENT

Management is a very exciting and rewarding career. A career in management offers status, interesting work, and the satisfaction of working closely with other people. People are considered the most important resource in organizations. If they perform effectively, the organizations will succeed. Managers work closely with people, ranging from top managers to clerical workers, to ensure that organizations achieve their objectives.

A management career also offers the opportunity to make the world a better place. Managers help organizations succeed. When organizations are successful, there is better utilization of resources, less stress among employees, less chaos in society, and a better quality of life for all. Effective managers play an important role in shaping the world in which we live. Certo (1997) emphasized this point when he stated that our society would not be as developed as it is today without effective managers to guide its organizations.

WHAT DO MANAGERS DO?

Management is a people job. The manager coordinates the work of other people to ensure that the unit is run efficiently and profitably. A manager may have direct responsibility for a group of people in one department or a team of people from several different departments. For some managers, it could mean supervising one person.

Managers provide overall direction and leadership for the organization. The manager sets clear objectives for the team and makes sure they know what the focus is, assigns duties to team members, and encourages them to perform those duties. The manager also evaluates the team's actual performance against organizational objectives and decides on promotions and salary increases where appropriate. When team members are not performing satisfactorily, the manger makes the changes necessary to ensure that they reach the company's objectives. Managers use their people skills and business skills, such as marketing and cost controls, to achieve the company's objectives while at the same time making sure to stay within budget.

The manager's job is varied. Managers are involved with planned and unplanned activities. These activities include scheduled and unscheduled meetings, inspection tours, report writing, new product launches, disagreements among employees, customer grievances, and changes in business trends. According to Miller and associates (1996), a manager should be able to shift continually from person to person and from one subject or problem to another. A manager who is also the business owner makes all the daily decisions involved in the business.

Managers make things happen in organizations. They decide what will be done, who will do it, when will it be done, and what resources will be used. They hire and train new employees, and they coordinate their departments' activities with other departments. Managers are the heart of organizations, the force that unites everything in the organization to ensure optimum efficiency and profitability.

TYPES OF MANAGEMENT CAREERS

In large organizations, managers work in a variety of areas, including operations, human resources, finance, and marketing:

- Operations managers see that the company's products and/or services meet quality standards and satisfy the needs of customers and clients. They plan production schedules to ensure the most efficient use of plant, manpower, and materials. The operations manager is responsible for production control, inventory control, quality control, plant layout, and site selection. New graduates will start as management trainees. After successfully completing the program they will be promoted to production supervisor, then to plant manager. The top management position is vice president for operations.

- Human resources managers provide the organization with competent and productive employees. The duties of the human resources manager include human resource planning, recruiting and selecting employees, training and development, designing compensation and

benefits systems, and formulating performance appraisal systems. In small firms one person may be responsible for all the human resource activities, while in large firms separate departments deal with each function.

- Financial managers deal with the financial resources of the organizations. They are responsible for such activities as accounting, cash management, and investments. They also keep up-to-date records for the use of funds, prepare financial reports, and gather information to assess the financial status of the organization.

- Marketing managers are responsible for getting customers and clients to buy the organization's products or services. They develop the business marketing strategy, set prices, and work closely with advertising and publicity personnel to see that products are promoted adequately.

Apart from the career opportunities in the specialized areas of management discussed above, management careers are also available in government agencies, hospitals, not-for-profit agencies, museums, educational institutions, and even political organizations. Good managers are also needed in foreign and multinational companies. All organizations exist for certain purposes and need good managers to guide their operations to achieve the best possible results. Regardless of the type of organization, managers are obviously one of its most important resources.

There are many specific management positions. Their titles and duties are described below.

Management trainees work under the supervision of an experienced manager while learning. They receive formal training in a variety of management areas. The management trainee position is designed to prepare trainees for work as administrators or managers. Their duties include providing customer service, preparing work schedules, and assisting with coordination of support services.

Labor relations managers have an interest in labor law and are good communicators. They negotiate collective bargaining agreements and develop grievance procedures to handle complaints. When problems arise between management and labor, they interpret and administer the labor contract and resolve the disputes according to the terms of the contract. They also work closely with the human resources director on issues such as wages, benefits, pensions, and work practices.

Administrative services managers coordinate and direct supportive services of larger businesses and government agencies. They are responsible for services such as clerical support, records management, payroll, conference planning, information processing, and materials distribution and scheduling. However, recent corporate restructuring has resulted in many organizations outsourcing their administrative services. This means that the demand for administrative services managers will greatly increase in companies providing management consulting, management services, and facilities support services.

Food service managers have very similar duties to restaurant managers, catering managers, and fast-food restaurant managers. In fact, the food service manager works in a variety of facilities, including fast-food restaurants, hospitals, and school cafeterias. Food service managers coordinate all aspects of the food and beverage activities for the organization. They set the standard for quality food service, hire and assign employees, and plan menus. They also perform some clerical duties, such as payroll and inventory.

Building managers, also called real estate managers, administer rental properties—such as apartment buildings and office buildings—for the owners. As the agents of the owners, they market vacant space, negotiate leases, set and collect rents, and arrange for security and maintenance of the properties. They also handle all the bookkeeping and accounting records and provide periodic reports to the owners.

Fitness center managers are physically fit and interested in exercise science. Companies, government agencies, and cruise ships with fitness facilities are looking for managers who can develop programs that satisfy customers' health and fitness needs. The fitness center manger conducts research to identify customer needs, develops and manages programs for the center and its

clients, and monitors health and safety requirements. In small centers, the manager is also responsible for delivering fitness training and maintaining center equipment.

City managers, also called town managers, are responsible for the day-to-day operations of various departments of city government. A main responsibility of city managers is to prepare budgets for the city council's approval. The city manager must also provide reports to the council members on ongoing and completed projects.

Health services managers work in clinics, hospitals, and health maintenance organizations (HMOs). They make most of the business or operational decisions in the health care facility. The health services manager establishes billing procedures, handles budgets, supervises staff, and interacts with the public. Health services managers start as management trainees or assistant administrators.

Hotel and motel managers are responsible for the full range of activities in a lodging establishment. These include guest registration and checkout, housekeeping, accounting, maintenance and security, and food service. The manager is also responsible for coordinating activities, such as meetings and other special events. In large hotels, assistant managers are responsible for the operations of various departments. Hotel managers begin as department heads and, after gaining experience, are promoted to manager.

Retail managers supervise employees and deal with customer complaints. In addition, they are responsible for managing the store inventory. They keep up-to-date records of merchandise, make pricing decisions, and decide on advertising and promotions. The retail manager works long hours and may be employed in a wide variety of stores, including department stores, discount stores, or specialty stores. Retail managers often begin as assistant managers responsible for a department in a large store. They are then promoted to merchandising manager or to store manager.

Sales managers exist in almost every firm and perform one of the most important functions in the organization. They find customers for the company's products and/or services and therefore provide revenues for the company. They recruit, hire, train, and supervise the company's sales force. Sales managers begin as sales representatives. Being a successful sales representative leads to promotion to senior sales representative or sales supervisor, then to a sales manager.

Procurement managers, sometimes called purchasing agents or industrial buyers, buy the supplies and materials needed by a company. They must be knowledgeable about the various vendors and their offerings. They must acquire the best possible deals for their company in terms of price, quality, delivery, and payment schedules. Managers in large companies sometimes specialize in specific types of purchases.

EDUCATIONAL REQUIREMENTS

Educational requirements for a career in management vary. However, most employers require a college degree in either the liberal arts, social sciences, or business administration. A master's degree in business administration (MBA) is also a common requirement. For students interested in getting into management trainee programs in major corporations, an MBA gives the best opportunity for these top programs. An MBA or the master's degree in health services administration is generally required for a career in health service management.

Apart from major corporations, many other organizations have management trainee programs that college graduates can enter. Such programs are advertised at college fairs or through college job placement services. These programs include classroom instruction and might last one week or as long as one year. Training for a department store manager, for example, might include working as a salesperson in several departments, in order to learn about the store's business, before being promoted to assistant manager.

In small organizations, depending on the type of industry, experience may be the only requirement needed to obtain a position as manager. When an opening in management occurs, the assistant manager is often promoted to the

position, based on past performance. In large organizations a more formal process exists. The management position to be filled is advertised with very specific requirements concerning education and experience.

Persons interested in a career in management should have good communication skills and be able to work well with a variety of people, ranging from other managers, supervisors, and professionals, to clerks and blue-collar workers. They should be analytical, flexible, and decisive. They should also be able to coordinate several activities simultaneously and be able to solve problems quickly. Ability to work under pressure and cope with deadlines is also important.

Recruiters look for self-starters who can use their initiative, recognize what needs to be done, like responsibility, and have high ethical standards. Self-starters and team players are the types of people corporations are looking for.

CAREER OPPORTUNITIES IN MANAGEMENT

According to the U.S. Bureau of Labor Statistics (1996), the number of managerial jobs is expected to increase by 17 percent by 2005. The greatest increase in management positions is projected to be in health services, management consulting, marketing, advertising, and public relations fields. Opportunities for management careers in financial services, restaurant and food service, and real estate industries will also grow at a faster than average rate through 2005. Educational institutions, industrial production, and administrative services are expected to grow about as fast as the average for all occupations through 2005.

The outlook for management careers is good, despite the headlines about downsizing and corporate restructuring. As the economy continues to grow, many businesses are expanding, and this creates additional opportunities for management jobs. Also, as the economy becomes more global, an increasing number of American firms are expanding overseas, and an equally large number of foreign companies are doing business in the United States. This means that despite the layoffs of some middle-level managers, there continues to be a worldwide need for good managers.

Women and minority managers. The future is bright for women and minorities interested in management. Title VII of the Civil Rights Act 1964 bans discrimination in employment on the basis of race, color, religion, sex, or national origin. Many companies, because of affirmative action rules, are actively seeking out women and minorities to fill management positions.

As a result, women are well represented at the lower levels of management; however, the number of top executive positions remains low. Only about 10 percent of the top jobs in the 500 largest U.S. companies are held by women. However, companies are taking steps to attract and promote women executives.

Minority groups remain underrepresented at all levels of management. A Rutgers University study (cited in Certo, 1997) found that in 400 *Fortune* 1000 companies, less than 9 percent of all managers were members of a minority group (p. 16). Since more and more new entrants into the labor market are members of various minority groups, it is becoming essential for business to recruit talented minority managers.

There are numerous opportunities for management careers available in all types of organizations, especially small and medium-sized companies. Every organization is looking for competent managers who can increase employee performance and help the company to be successful. Mosley and associates (1996) put it best when they said: "Managers in organizations of all sizes, in all industries, and at all levels have an impact on performance ... they make the difference between success and failure for their companies" (p. 7).

SOURCES OF ADDITIONAL INFORMATION

American Hotel and Motel Association
1201 New York Avenue, NW
Washington, DC 20005-3931

American Management Association
135 West 50th Street
New York, NY 10020

Administrative Management Society
4622 Silver Road
Trevose, PA 19047

National Management Association
2210 Arbor Boulevard
Dayton, OH 45439

Women in Management
30 North Michigan Avenue
Chicago, IL 60602

BIBLIOGRAPHY

Boone, Louis E., and Kurtz, David L. (1998). *Contemporary Business.* Forth Worth, TX: Dryden Press, Harcourt Brace and Company.

Certo, Samuel C. (1997). *Modern Management.* Upper Saddle River, NJ: Prentice-Hall.

Griffin, Ricky W. (1999) *Management.* Boston: Houghton Mifflin.

Miller, Donald S., Catt, Steven E., and Carbon, James R. (1996). *Fundamentals of Management.* St. Paul, MN: West Publishing Company.

Mosley, Donald C., Pietri, Paul H., and Megginson, Leon C. (1996). *Management: Leadership in Action.* New York: HarperCollins.

Robbins, Steven P., and Coulter, Mary. (1999). *Management.* Upper Saddle River, NJ: Prentice-Hall.

U.S. Bureau of Labor Statistics. (1996). *Occupational Projections and Training Data.* (Bulletin No. 2471). Washington, DC: Author.

THADDEUS MCEWEN

CAREERS IN MARKETING

Is a career in marketing for you? To be successful in a marketing career, an individual must have good communication, critical thinking, and people skills. In addition to these skills, a majority of individuals employed in marketing-related occupations possess excellent time-management skills, the ability to work with a wide variety of people, and a capacity for self-motivation. These individuals must be able to establish timelines, goals, and objectives—and adhere to them.

According to the U.S. Bureau of Labor Statistics, the number of individuals who earn a living in marketing-related careers—advertising, sales, or public relations—is projected to increase rapidly between the turn of the century and the year 2005 (Levine and Salmon, 1999). Currently, almost a third of all Americans are employed in marketing-related positions, and marketing principles are being applied to more and more business and nonbusiness organizations—service firms, nonprofit institutions, political candidates, and so forth (http://www.bls.gov/opub/rtaw/rtawhome.htm). Therefore, a high demand for individuals with marketing training is emerging as a critical criterion for employment in the early years of the twenty-first century. Two major explanations have been offered for the continuously increasing demand for marketing skills—(1) deregulation of major industries (banking, telecommunications, and transportation) and (2) increased foreign competition.

Considering the increased role of marketing in the U.S. economy, members of the twenty-first-century work force need to be familiar with the major marketing-related occupations. According to Kotler (1994) and Khlupin and Shibiko (1998), the major marketing occupations are: (1) advertising, (2) brand and product management, (3) industrial marketing, (4) international marketing, (5) marketing research, (6) new-product planning, (7) physical distribution/distribution management, (8) public relations, (9) retail marketing, and (10) sales and sales promotion marketing. A discussion of each of these major marketing occupations follows.

Advertising. Advertising is a vital business activity that requires planning skills, fact-gathering ability, creativity, artistic talent, and written and verbal communication skills. Individuals who are employed in advertising typically perform the following tasks: (1) search for factual information, (2) read avidly, (3) borrow ideas, (4) talk to customers, (5) develop print layouts, package designs, storyboards, corporate logotypes, trademarks, and symbols, (6) specify style and size of typography, and (7) arrange advertisement details for reproduction. Thus, advertising involves all components of marketing—product, price, promotion, and place. Because all the above tasks require working with people who are clients or potential clients, an individual must be personable, diplomatic, and sincere. Further, he or she needs to be self-motivated and able to present

information about a product to varying audiences.

Brand and product management (BPM). Individuals involved in BPM are planners, directors, and controllers of the positioning of consumer packaged goods for sale in a dramatically and quickly changing marketplace. BPM marketers use research as well as packaging, manufacturing, and forecasting to position products for sale to the most appropriate audience. Individuals employed in this aspect of marketing must have the leadership capability to move a product from obscurity to a national awareness in a relatively short period of time. Usually BPM marketers' job-related responsibilities increase with the growth and development of a particular product. Thus, successful BPM marketers operate in a high-pressure, fast-paced, and constantly changing environment, since a major component of BPM marketing focuses on the financial position of the product under development. In addition, BPM marketers must be results-oriented and creative; possess strong interpersonal, communication, and analytical skills; have entrepreneurial leanings; and exhibit high levels of diplomacy, perseverance, and drive.

Industrial marketing. Industrial marketing involves the planning, sale, and service of products used for commercial or business purposes. In addition to having excellent oral and written communication skills, industrial marketers must be self-reliant individuals with the ability to understand customer requirements as well as the knowledge to propose the purchase of a particular product that will satisfy customers' needs and wants. In essence, industrial marketers are consultants who assist clients in ascertaining the appropriate product for their particular needs. Whether employed in sales, service, product design, or marketing research positions, industrial marketers must develop and maintain ongoing business relationships with suppliers of goods and services as well as with clients. Therefore, the selling relationship is a process of maintaining and building a continuous business relationship. As in any marketing-related career, industrial marketers must have excellent people skills as well as good oral and written communication skills. In addition, a successful industrial marketer should have a broad educational background with an emphasis in technology in order to be able to link that technology to human needs and wants.

International marketing. With the increasing role of foreign industry in the United States as well as increasing U.S. interests abroad, individuals with relevant foreign language skills, as well as an understanding of selected foreign cultures, are needed to assist with the day-to-day operations of business. In order to be able to conduct business effectively and efficiently and to implement marketing strategies abroad, international marketers need to understand the social, economic, and political climates of foreign countries. Marketing personnel interested in this area may be required to travel and/or relocate to a foreign country to oversee company operations and to create a presence in that country's economy. In addition to the language requirement, potential international marketers need appropriate communication skills as well as diplomatic skills in order to work with foreign leaders and function in foreign economic systems.

Marketing research. Marketing researchers are asked to ascertain the reason(s) that a particular product is or is not being purchased by consumers. Based on the interpretation of data collected in marketing research, market researchers make recommendations for enhancing or eliminating existing products as well as developing new products. In addition, promotional activities are based on data collected by marketing researchers. Individuals employed in marketing research occupations must understand statistics, data/information-processing analysis, psychology, consumer behavior, and communication. Marketing researchers interact with other marketing occupations to define problems within a particular product line as well as to identify the appropriate processes to be used to analyze and resolve those problems. A critical component of this position is the ability to present solutions to business problems in a manner that is easily understood by colleagues and constituents. Spe-

cifically, marketing researchers provide information concerning consumers, marketing environment, and competition to relevant internal and external publics. Therefore, strong analytical, methodological, and communication skills are a must for success in this arena.

New-product planning. New-product planning involves the creation and development of new products for an organization. Because individuals who enter this arena typically have been successful in other areas of marketing, they tend to have an excellent knowledge of and background in marketing, to be familiar with the processes for conducting marketing research, to be capable of generating sales forecasts, and to have a background in technology. A new-product-planning marketer conceptualizes, researches, and evaluates new ideas. During the evaluation process, the new-product-planning marketer considers both the feasibility of the production of the product and the product's potential profitability. These individuals must also possess the ability to motivate, coordinate, and direct others. New-product planning is applicable to the marketing of consumer products, consumer services, hospital and medical services, and public service programs, to name only a few areas. Because new-product development is constantly changing, a person who enters this field should have a high degree of tolerance for uncertainty and the unknown, yet nonetheless be able to develop a definite "agenda" and a "report card" to inform superiors about success with new products.

Physical distribution/distribution management. Physical distribution is one of the largest arenas of marketing and has been defined as the analysis, planning, and control of activities concerned with the procurement and distribution of goods. Activities involved with the physical distribution process include transporting, warehousing, forecasting, processing orders, inventorying, production planning, selecting sites, and servicing customers. Individuals employed in this marketing area are concerned with the processes or methods needed to deliver the product from the manufacturer to the wholesalers to the retailers to, ultimately, the consumer. The physical distribution process is an extensive and diverse area that involves the physical transportation of products and the various activities associated with purchasing, selling, and channel-management functions. Individuals who enter physical distribution marketing need interpersonal leadership ability in order to deal with diverse and challenging internal and external publics as well as excellent analytical and communication skills.

Public relations. Public relations marketers either assist in the management of the images of products or individuals or anticipate and handle public problems or complaints. Thus individuals employed in the public relations aspect of marketing create an image or message for or about an individual or an organization as well as maintaining that image with the media. This image or message needs to be communicated effectively, efficiently, and persuasively to the intended audience. To be successful in public relations, an individual needs to be people-oriented and to have excellent oral and written communication skills as well as a background in journalism.

Retail marketing. Individuals in retailing occupations deal directly with consumers or customers. Retail marketing also involves the management of sales personnel, selection and ordering of merchandise, and promotion of selected merchandise, as well as inventory control, store security, and product accounting. Typical jobs are as buyers, sales managers, department managers, and store managers. To be successful in retail marketing, individuals must be self-motivated and possess excellent people skills. A rapidly growing component in retail marketing is direct-response marketing (DRM). DRM attempts to deliver the product from the manufacturer to the consumer by the use of direct mail, print and broadcast media, telephone marketing, catalogues, in-home presentations, door-to-door marketing, electronic ordering and funds transfer, and video text. Attributes needed for success in the area of DRM include creativity, initiative, perseverance, and quantitative competence. In essence, retail marketers use their professional knowledge and competence to improve company

profits by informing various publics of appropriate assortments of goods and service in locations that are easily accessible.

Sales and sales promotion marketing. Sales and sales promotion marketers (SSPMs) need a thorough understanding of their company's products. SSPMs must not only sell a product but also develop and maintain effective relationships with customers. The main goal of SSPMs is to inform customers about and provide them with appropriate products in an expeditious manner. Such individuals focus on providing information to potential clients/customers by interacting with them directly and personally. Beyond this, they close sales and maintain existing accounts to ensure client/customer satisfaction and loyalty. To be successful, an individual must know the product, the customer(s), and the market(s). Further, a good understanding of people and appropriate people skills are a must in order to deal with diverse and challenging internal and external publics. Because the process of selling involves persuasive two-way communication between a seller and a client, individuals in this area of marketing must be people-oriented as well as knowledgeable about the product and the manner in which the product can be used to satisfy buyers' needs and wants.

CONCLUSION

In the twenty-first century, the role of marketing in the U.S. economy will change as consumers react to ever-changing technology and as businesses respond to an ever-changing marketplace. Because of changing technology and the changing marketplace, the roles and functions of conventional marketing as it is known today will be constantly rethought and redefined. In addition, the four Ps of marketing—product, price, place, and promotion—will also be redefined and restructured. With the dynamic changes facing the marketing environment, the demand for marketing-oriented personnel will continue to increase, making marketing-related careers an exciting occupational choice for the twenty-first century.

BIBLIOGRAPHY

http://www.careers-in-marketing.com/ad.htm. (March 2000).

http://www.cob.niu.edu/mktg/career.html. (March 2000).

http://www.cob.ohio-state.edu/dept/mkt/career.html. (March 2000).

http://www.hayek.cob.niu.edu/mktg/career.html. (March 2000).

Khlupin, M. M., and Shibiko, D. (1998). http://www.cob.ohio-state-eud/~mkt/careers/.

Kotler, P. (1994). *Principles of Marketing*, 6th ed. Upper Saddle River, NJ: Prentice-Hall.

Levine, C., and Salmon, L. (1999). "The 1998 SOC: Bridge to Occupational Classification in the 21st Century." *Occupational Outlook Quarterly* 43:27-33.

http://www.marshall.use.edu./marketing/course_career/career-models.html. (March 2000).

National Retail Federation http://www.nrf.com/services/info/careers. (March 2000).

Report on the American Workforce. http://www.bls.gov/opub/rtaw/rtawhome.htm. (1999).

RANDY L. JOYNER

CAREERS OVERVIEW

The concept of careers ranges from descriptions of jobs, occupations, or vocations to the pattern of work and work-related activities that develop through a lifetime. *Career* is defined in the *Merriam-Webster Collegiate Dictionary* (1999) as "a field for or pursuit of consecutive progressive achievement especially in public, professional, or business life."

The perception of a career has various connotations. A "career" could be a "job." A job, again as defined in the *Merriam-Webster Collegiate Dictionary* (1999), is "a regular remunerative position; something that has to be done: task." A job might be washing dishes or typing reports. In other works, a job is a task.

An occupation, yet again as defined in the *Merriam-Webster Collegiate Dictionary* (1999), is "an activity in which one engages; the principal business of one's life: vocation." An occupation may mean practicing law, teaching school, and so forth. In other words, an occupation is a vocation.

Careers are the patterns of work and work-related activities that develop through a lifetime. Having several careers during a lifetime is not uncommon. One may train to become a business teacher—a satisfying occupation (vocation) for years. After that, one may leave teaching and train to become a financial planner (a second vocation).

Also, having more than one job within a career is common. A business teacher might begin teaching middle school general business subjects (a first job), then progress to teaching secondary-level business subjects (another job). While teaching secondary business subjects, the same person might supervise the publication of the school's yearbook (still within the career field of education).

CHOOSING A CAREER

To be successful in a vocation, it is first necessary to obtain knowledge about choosing a career and then to acquire the education needed to grow in that career and in the job(s) pursued within that career.

The Myers-Briggs Personality Test, available at employment offices, at school career/college centers, or on the Internet, could be a first step in choosing a career. Based on the work of Karl Jung, the test was developed by Katherine Briggs and her daughter Isabel Briggs Myers, to determine whether someone was primarily extroverted or introverted, sensing or intuitive, thinking or feeling, judging or perceiving. Combining these traits, they formed sixteen distinct personality types, known as the Myers-Briggs Personality Types. Understanding your own and other people's personality types can help in finding the "perfect" job and make it easier to manage personal and professional relationships.

Along with the Myers-Briggs Personality Test, a person should consider the following when choosing a career:

1. Skills you currently possess and need to acquire
2. Education you have and will need
3. Salary you will accept

4. Working conditions in which you would be comfortable

5. Working schedule you prefer (day or night shift, part-time, or full-time work, etc.)

Anyone searching for a position—whether this is a first job or the next step up the career ladder—needs to go through the following steps.

Know which jobs are for you. The information from the Myers-Briggs Personality Test will give an idea of your abilities and interests. However, this is not the sole source of information for determining the "perfect" job(s). School or public libraries, job counselors, and employment agencies all have information and testing facilities to assist in finding the "perfect" job.

Prepare a flawless resume. Sales representatives know that when calling on a potential customer, displaying their product in the most favorable way enhances the prospect of a sale. The same principles apply when searching for a job. You are selling yourself based largely on your resume—your education, experience, abilities, and talents that apply to their company or organization.

There are two primary resume formats. One is the traditional hard-copy format. The second is the "scanner ready format" meaning that the resume is ready to be posted on the Internet, distributed via e-mail, or submitted to employers with scannable databases. Because a computer software program will probably read your resume initially, you must be sure to include a keyword paragraph in the resume. Keywords are critical words matching you up with the required job qualifications. For instance, if you were applying for a job as a programmer, the keyword paragraph might look like this:

Keywords: Programmer, Unix, C, C++, Cobol, Java, Systems Engineer, and Solaris

The keywords are critical if an employer has resume-tracking software. Make sure they fit the positions for which you are applying. It is also important that your experience and background match the job you want.

Your resume and cover letter are the first documents that the potential employer or resume-tracking system sees or scans. Even if the company has resume-tracking software, when your resume pops up from a search, a human resources professional will read it. You must create that all-important excellent first impression.

Search for jobs. Acquire knowledge about various career choices. The following is a list of the most popular careers for the twenty-first century (*Occupational Outlook Handbook, 2000*). (*The 21st Century*, 1999): (1) air transportation-related occupations, (2) engineering and engineering technicians, (3) architects and surveyors, (4) computer, mathematical, and operations research, (5) scientists and science technicians, (6) legal, (7) social scientists, (8) social and recreation workers, (9) teachers and instructors, counselors, and library occupations, (10) health diagnosticians, (11) health assessment and treating, (12) health technologists and technicians, (13) communications-related, (14) visual arts and design, (15) performing arts.

Determine what education is needed. Research the qualifications necessary. Use the Internet to begin gathering facts on a particular career. Firm-specific data can be found in books such as *Hoover's Handbook of American Business, Dunn's Regional Business Directory*, and other business directories available on-line or in library reference sections. Judy Kaplan Baron, a nationally certified career counselor in San Diego, recommends reading about your target occupation in resources such as the *Occupational Outlook Handbook* published by the U.S. Department of Labor.

Baron believes that it does not occur to most people to use friends, co-workers, and neighbors as referral sources: "You may have what you need as a referral living right next door."

Research the company and/or industry. The task of business research has gotten easier, since the Internet contains information on almost every business. Use search engines to gather information on public and private companies or use information gleaned from your local library.

Prepare for an interview Knowledge is power, especially in an interview. The more you know about the company and what is going to occur in an interview, the more likely you are to be an intelligent candidate. If you familiarize yourself with the interview procedure, you can talk confidently to a potential employer. Rather than worrying about the upcoming interview, spend your time rehearsing and preparing for the interview.

Be aware of implicit rules during the interview. Never ask for a job and respect the interview's time limits. When time is up, offer to end the meeting. Maintain the conversation only if urged by the interviewer to do so.

Close the interview by asking the interviewer to suggest other people with whom you might talk. Then ask if you may mention the interviewer's name when you contact those recommended.

Within twenty-four hours of the interview, send a thank-you note. John Klube, site manager for the Army Career and Alumni Program at Fort Carson, Colorado (1998), also recommends additional follow-up, stating that never hearing from a candidate again makes interviewers feel used. He recommends contacting interviewers again four or five weeks after the initial interview to thank them again and to let them know how any referrals worked out.

Figure the Level of Your Salary. Check with employment agencies, read the want ads in local papers, and talk with others to find out what your salary should be. There are Internet sites, such as salary.com or homefair.com, that will calculate and compare the cost of living in cities worldwide. You choose the origin and destination sites. For example, if you currently live in Denver, Colorado, and want to move to Boston, Massachusetts, input that information. The on-line calculator would tell you that if you make $100,000 in Denver, you would need to make $154,621 in Boston.

SEARCH STRATEGIES

The Myers-Briggs Personality Test, discussed earlier, is useful in helping determine your interests and capabilities. The figures published by Bernard Haldane Associates (Vincent, 1998), a nationwide career search firm, show that nearly 70 percent of all jobs are acquired by those who mix personal initiative with a compelling search strategy: building professional contacts and making themselves known to employers. A job seeker does this through brief, data-gathering dialogues with corporate managers and referrals by those managers to other knowledgeable sources; candidates can gather real-world tips for career success and gain valuable professional contacts.

Roles of colleges and universities. Most of the careers listed earlier require education beyond high school. The length and type of education varies from technical training to a doctoral degree.

Advances in technology have changed the traditional role of the college and university. The Internet, computer-assisted training (enhanced by video technology and courseware authoring tools), interactive CD-ROMs, and distance learning can provide education beyond high school. Training for a career involves competencies consistent with the demands of business and industry. Computer skills, subject-matter skills, and the soft skills of human relations and workplace ethics are central to the curriculum.

BIBLIOGRAPHY

Graham, Donna M. (1998). "Your Resume Gets You the Interview; Your Portfolio Gets You the Job." *Career Magazine.* http://www.careermag.com/db/cmag_articles_resume_graham.

Klube, John. (1998). "The Interview." http://www.acap.army.mil/acap/conusall.htm.

Merriam-Webster Collegiate Dictionary. (1999). http://www.m-w.com/.

"Myers Briggs Personality Test. Career Finder—Personality." America Online. (1999).

The 21st Century—Meeting the Challenges to Business Education—NBEA Yearbook. (1999). http://www.nbea.org.

Vincent, Lynn. (1998). "Company Research Pays Off in a 'Special Needs' Job Search." http://www.intranet .csupomona.edu/~sciman/html/library/internet/ eresumes/crm21.com.html.

JUDITH CHIRI

CELLER-KEFAUVER ANTI-MERGER ACT OF 1980

(SEE: *Antitrust Legislation*)

CENTRALIZATION AND DECENTRALIZATION

(SEE: *Organizational Structure*)

CERTIFIED INTERNAL AUDITOR

A certified internal auditor (CIA) is an individual who has met the requirements for certification as established by the Institute of Internal Auditors (IIA). Requirements relate to education, experience, and successful completion of an examination. Achieving the credential as a certified internal auditor is tangible evidence of meeting professional qualifications established by the IIA.

The IIA, established in 1941 at a meeting in New York City, now has a worldwide membership of more than 70,000 in more than 100 counties. The CIA examination was first administered in 1974.

THE EXAMINATION

The CIA examination is offered twice a year, once in May and once in November. The exam has four parts:

Part I: Internal audit process

- Auditing
- Professionalism
- Fraud

Part II: Internal audit skills

- Problem solving and evaluating audit evidence

- Data gathering, documentation, and reporting
- Sampling and mathematics

Part III: Management control and technology

- Management control
- Operations management
- Information technology

Part IV: Audit environment

- Financial accounting
- Finance
- Managerial accounting
- Regulatory environment

Each part of the exam consists of 80 multiple-choice questions. To complete the examination successfully, a candidate must be familiar with the Institute of Internal Auditors' *Standards for the Professional Practice of Internal Auditing* and the institute's *Code of Ethics*. It is not necessary to be a member of the IIA in order to take the examination. However, a one-year free membership is offered to any nonmember who passes the CIA examination.

The Board of Regents, which administers the CIA exam, recognizes the accomplishments of other professional certifications. Therefore, individuals who already have a certification are eligible to receive credit for part of the exam. Part IV of the exam was designed to offer a Professional Recognition Credit. Candidates who wish to apply for the Professional Recognition Credit need to submit a registration form with a copy of the certificate or letter from the sponsoring organization noting that the person has completed the exam requirements. The sponsoring organization may be contacted to verify the information supplied by the candidate.

For example, in the United States an individual who is a certified public accountant, certified management accountant, certified information systems auditor, or certified bank auditor is eligible to receive Professional Recognition Credit for Part IV of the CIA examination. In Australia, Canada, and the United Kingdom, the chartered accountant designation would receive Professional Recognition Credit by the Board of Regents.

The exam is nondisclosed. Individuals taking the exam sign a statement indicating that they will not disclose questions and answers subsequent to taking the exam. The IIA considers disclosure of the exam questions by a person who took the examination to be a violation of the code of ethics.

The passing score for the exam is 75 percent. In 1996 there were 4646 candidates; the average pass rate by exam part is 45 percent. (*Careers in Accounting* 1997).

EXPERIENCE REQUIREMENT

In order to become a CIA, there is an experience requirement of twenty-four months of internal auditing or its equivalent. Representative equivalent experience can include quality assurance, internal control assessment, or external auditing. A master's degree can be substituted for one year of experience. The Board of Regents determines the acceptability of equivalent work experience.

More information is available from the Institute of Internal Auditors at 249 Maitland Ave., Altamonte Springs, Florida 32701-4201; (407)830-7600; or http://www.theiia.org.

(SEE ALSO: *Institute for Internal Auditors*)

BIBLIOGRAPHY

Careers in Accounting. (1997). Gainsville, FL: Gleim Publications.

CHARLES H. CALHOUN

CERTIFIED MANAGEMENT ACCOUNTANT (CMA) CERTIFIED IN FINANCIAL MANAGEMENT (CFM)

The certified management accountant (CMA) and the certified in financial management (CFM) programs are designed to recognize the unique qualifications and expertise of those professionals engaged in management accounting and financial management. These certifications provide distinction in today's economic climate and afford the opportunity to certify expertise in the business areas that are critical to the decision-making process. The CMA and CFM certifications, introduced by the Institute of Management Accountants (IMA) in 1972 and 1996, respectively, have global recognition and have received the endorsement of approximately 200 corporate and academic organizations.

The CMA and CFM Programs have four objectives:

- To establish management accounting and financial management as recognized professions by identifying the role of the professional, the underlying body of knowledge, and a course of study by which such knowledge is acquired

- To encourage higher educational standards in the management accounting and financial management fields

- To establish an objective measure of an individual's knowledge and competence in the fields of management accounting and financial management

- To encourage continued professional development

The content of the certification examinations represents the knowledge, skills, and abilities required by business professionals in the fields of management accounting and financial management. The content is validated periodically by a practice analysis conducted by the IMA. The content, covered in four examination parts for each program, encompasses:

- Economics, finance, and management

- Financial accounting and reporting (CMA) or corporate financial management (CFM)

- Management reporting, analysis, and behavioral issues

- Decision analysis and information systems

The Financial Accounting and Reporting Exam is waived, upon request, for individuals who have passed the U.S. CPA Exam; this is not the case, however, for the Corporate Financial Management Exam.

Candidates for certification must meet the following criteria to become a CMA or CFM:

- Education: Candidates must hold a baccalaureate degree, in any area, from an accredited college or university. Students attending accredited U.S. universities may take the examinations but must satisfy the education requirement prior to certification. Degrees from institutions outside the United States must be evaluated by an independent agency. The education requirement may also be satisfied by holding a CPA license to practice or other comparable professional qualification.

- Employment: Candidates must complete two continuous years of professional experience in management accounting and/or financial management. Qualifying experience consists of positions requiring judgments regularly made employing the principles of management accounting and financial management. This experience may be completed prior to or within seven years of passing the examination.

- Character references: The names of two character references must be submitted at the time of application.

- Ethics: Candidates for certification must agree to comply with the Standards of Ethical Conduct for Practitioners of Management Accounting and Financial Management.

- Membership: Candidates for certification must be a member of the IMA because the certification programs are a privilege of membership.

The CMA and CFM programs have been designed to meet the evolving needs of business and are focused on the dynamic roles that management accountants and financial managers play in business, public, and government accounting. Certified professionals are more frequently identified for promotion and have greater earning potential than those professionals who are not certified. To gather more information or to join the CMA/CFM programs, visit the IMA Web site at www.imanet.org or call (800)638-4427 for a certification information booklet.

PRISCILLA PAYNE

CERTIFIED PUBLIC ACCOUNTANT (CPA)

The designation certified public accountant (CPA) is conferred by a state or jurisdiction to individuals to practice as a licensed certified public accountant. The licensing of CPAs protects the public from incompetent individuals performing substandard accounting work. In the United States, there are fifty-four states or jurisdictions with laws and regulations on the requirements and obligations of licensed CPAs. In 1896, New York State passed the first accountancy law to test the qualifications of public accountants. This led to the issuance of a state license to practice as a certified public accountant and the emergence of accounting as a profession with licensing requirements, professional standards, and a code of professional ethics. Other states followed this lead, and eventually all of the fifty-four states and jurisdictions enacted public accounting legislation. The Boards of Accountancy of each jurisdiction are responsible for licensing candidates and for compliance with the state accountancy laws.

The Boards of Accountancy make licensure decisions based on three factors: (1) the fulfillment of an educational requirement, (2) passing a Uniform CPA Examination and, (3) having a number of years of work experience. The educational and experience requirements vary among the fifty-four jurisdictions. All require at least a bachelor's degree; however, a majority of the jurisdictions require one hundred and fifty semester hours of coursework before a candidate can take the CPA exam, which is typically a bachelor's degree, plus thirty hours of advanced study. The years of experience required vary among the jurisdictions from no experience to two or three years, depending on educational background. As an example, in Texas candidates planning to take the examination need to have one hundred and fifty semester hours of coursework and at least one year of public accountancy experience. In Florida candidates, since 1983, must complete at least one hundred and fifty hours of coursework, but need no experience.

All the jurisdictions in the United States require CPA candidates to pass a Uniform CPA

Examination that is prepared by the American Institute of Certified Public Accountants (AICPA) and graded by its Advisory Grading Service. The objective of the examination is to provide reasonable assurance to Boards of Accountancy that candidates passing the examination possess the level of technical knowledge, skills, and abilities necessary to protect the public interest. The current Uniform CPA Examination is a two-day paper and pencil linear examination with questions in a predetermined sequence to be answered manually on paper answer sheets. The examination is offered semi-annually in May and November on a Wednesday and Thursday. The current examination covers four sections: (1) Auditing; (2) Financial Accounting and Reporting; (3) Accounting and Reporting—Taxation, Managerial, and Governmental and Not-for-Profit Organizations; and (4) Business Law and Professional Responsibilities. Since May 1996, the examination has been nondisclosed, meaning that candidates are no longer allowed to retain or receive their question booklets after the examination or to reveal questions on the examination in any manner. The Board of Examiners of the AICPA maintains overall responsibility of exam preparation and issuance of grades to the state boards. The examination is continually reviewed to maintain its currency and to reflect current practice. Future examinations will be computer-based examinations, which would permit the examination to be given more frequently and to test an expanded range of knowledge and skills that closely reflect current practice.

Additional information on the Uniform CPA Examination is available from the AICPA Examinations Team, Harborside Financial Center, 201 Plaza Three, Jersey City, New Jersey 07311-3881; http://www.aicpa.org. Information on state requirements may be obtained by contacting the state board or the National Association of State Boards of Accountancy, the organization that coordinates the activities of the fifty-four boards of accountancy, located at 150 Fourth Avenue North, Suite 700, Nashville, Tennessee 37219-2417; http://www.nasba.org.

(SEE ALSO: *American Institute of Certified Public Accountants*; *National Association of Boards of Accountancy*; *State Societies of Certified Public Accountants*; *Uniform Certified Public Accounting Examination*)

BIBLIOGRAPHY

American Institute of Certified Public Accountants. (1998). *Information for Uniform CPA Examination Candidates*, 15th ed. New York: Author.

Booker, Quinton, Brenner, Vincent C., and Blum, James D. (1998). "Brave New World for the CPA Exam." *Journal of Accountancy* January:61-64.

Flesher, Dale L., Miranti, Paul J., and Previts, Gary John. (1996). "The First Century of the CPA." *Journal of Accountancy* October:51-57.

ANTHONY T. KRZYSTOFIK

CHAIN DISCOUNTS
(SEE: *Pricing*)

CHAIN OF COMMAND
(SEE: *Organizational Structure*)

CHANGE PROCESS

Companies that are able to compete successfully in today's rapidly changing business environment—characterized by globalization of the economy, exploding information technology, downsizing, restructuring, and new employer-employee relationships—must be ready to make significant changes in the way they operate. Changes can be realized in a number of areas; they can, for example, be observed in attitude or behavior. Many major organizational changes, however, are technological ones. Sometimes these changes are not intended to change behavior, but they almost always do in some respect. Another type of change is replacement of personnel; when top management is impatient with the pace of productivity, they often replace key individuals. Changes also occur in organizational structure, formal roles and jobs, control systems, work processes, and other elements of the organization's internal environment.

The motivation for change typically stems from the fact that something isn't working—for example, continued negative feedback from customers, reduced profitability, threats of acquisition, or other market pressures. For most organizations, a crisis is the catalyst for change. While a crisis may be sufficient to initiate a change, it takes much more to successfully integrate the change into the work processes. Managers must have more than an extensive knowledge of the marketplace, how to compete in it, and what internal structures must be in place to make the company successful.

Every change effort should be accompanied by an action plan. Once a compelling reason to change has been identified, it is necessary to create a picture of what the change will require, how the organization will effect it, and what the organization will look like when the change has been implemented. Although each action plan for change will be unique, all plans should follow a basic structure: (1) identification of a course of action and allocation of resources to achieve the organization's change goals; (2) designation of the authority, responsibility, and relationships that will drive the change efforts; (3) determination of who will lead the change effort and the specific roles and responsibilities of these individuals; (4) a description of the procedures and processes that will expedite implementation of the change; (5) identification of the training that will be required to enable people to incorporate the change into their work processes; and (6) identification of the equipment, tools, or machinery that will affect the way work is accomplished.

Many organizational changes are initiated and implemented through the authority of top levels of management. The problems are defined and solutions are developed by top-level managers based on information that is gathered by others with help from a limited number of people. Once a decision is made, the changes are often communicated to people in the organization through memo, speech, policy statement, or verbal command. Since only a few people, usually

at the top, are involved in making the decisions, the change is usually introduced very rapidly. However, this strategy has proved to be largely ineffective in dealing with organizational change processes, particularly for successful integration. A common misconception about carrying out a change is that it must be directed from the top. The foundation of successful change management lies in involving the people who will be affected by the change.

Sharing responsibility for change is a process whereby those at the top and those at lower levels are jointly involved in identifying problems and/or developing solutions. Virtually continual interaction takes place between top and bottom levels. The shared responsibility or participative approach can be addressed in several ways: (1) Top management defines the problem and uses staff groups or consultants to gather information and develop solutions. These identified solutions are then communicated to lower-level groups in order to obtain reactions. The feedback from the lower levels is then used to modify the solution, and the communication process starts again. The assumption underlying this approach is that although involving others in the definition of the problem or its solution may be impractical, the solution can be improved and commitment obtained by involving lower levels. (2) Top management defines the problem but seeks involvement from lower levels by appointing task forces to develop solutions. The task forces provide recommendations to top management, where the final decision is made. These task forces are composed of people who will be affected by the change and have some level of expertise in the areas that will be affected by the proposed change. The assumption here is that those who have the expertise to solve the problems are those groups that are closer to the situation. Also, the group's commitment to the change may be made deeper by this involvement. (3) Task forces composed of people from all levels are formed to collect information about problems in the organization and to develop solutions. The underlying assumptions in this approach are that people at the top, middle, and lower levels are needed to develop quality solutions and that commitment must build at about the same rate at all levels. These approaches emphasizing shared responsibility usually take longer to implement but result in more commitment from all levels of the organization and more successful integration of the change into the work processes.

Understanding the factors that drive change, and how people react to change, is critical to the successful implementation of change. It is part of human nature to resist change; people prefer the security of familiar surroundings and often don't react well to changes in their work or social environment. Resistance to change often takes some typical forms. One typical reaction is denial, which individuals use to protect themselves. If the change never really occurs, it won't need to be dealt with. Another common reaction is passive resistance—individuals agree on the surface with the need for change but are quietly unsupportive of it. Still others may respond with active resistance by openly disagreeing with the proposed change, lobbying against it, and encouraging others to do the same.

Many managers assume that if people think the change is a good idea, they will not resist it. Why would the work force resist changes if the changes will fix what they wanted fixed? People may want change—but not necessarily the changes that have been identified in the plan. Workers may have their own ideas about what should change; and frequently the changes they think "fix" the problem involve someone else's changing, not them. In addition workers may think the ways to make things better is simply to adjust and manipulate their work processes, not to implement the drastic changes identified in the proposed plan. Alternatively, workers may not think that is wrong with the current way of working. Often the process of changing looks too hard, looks like it will take too much energy, and seems confusing. A strictly structured change process often ignores the ingrained human resistance to change. When that happens, people who are affected by the change end up expending most of their time and energy figuring out how to stop the change or altering the change until it

looks like something they can live with. If the desired change is not very desirable to the work force, managers need to find out why. Insufficient information about the driving force behind the change and the benefits expected from it is likely to cause distress among those affected by the change. People tend to act in their own perceived self-interest. Managers often think of change initiatives in broader terms; the work force tends to think of it differently, in more narrow terms of how the change will affect their work. Sometimes managers forget or overlook this reaction to change. Effective strategies for organizational change involve an understanding of the human beings in the work force.

Cultivating a sense of involvement and ownership in all individuals affected by the proposed change is critical. The more involved people feel in shaping their future, the less likely they are to criticize the outcome. An essential factor in managing effective change is communication—no amount is too much. Managers should identify the groups/individuals affected by the proposed change in order to determine the best communication methods to use. Newsletters, focus groups, bulletin boards, intranet pages, and lunchtime seminars are all effective ways of communicating to the work force. Managers need to be aware of how information flows through the organization and which communication methods will be most effective.

Also crucial to successful integration of change in an organization is the level of support from its leaders. Top levels of management must believe that the proposed course of action is the right one for the future of the organization. At all phases of the change process, top-management representatives must strongly support the change processes and communicate that support to the work force. During the planning phase, top-management representatives should explain the business reasons for the changes and the costs of not changing, tell employees what they can expect to happen and when, and enlist the support of other senior managers and stakeholders in the process. During the design phase, top-management representatives should listen and respond to feedback from the organization and provide updates on the progress of the change. During the implementation phase, top-management representatives should continue to listen to resistance and respond to feedback, stay involved in the process, ensure that adequate resources and training are available, measure performance toward expected results, and reward role models.

Effective and efficient methods of communication, education/training, and rewards/reinforcements should be built into the implementation plan. Appropriate training should be incorporated into the change plan to ensure that the work force can be productive with the new work processes and systems. However, communication and training may not be the only required elements to help ensure effective change implementation. As the work force envisions the change, managers may need to ensure that rewards are in place for changing—in other words, identification of "what's in it for me?" Recognition is needed to reinforce changes in an organization. Tangible and intangible rewards for changed behavior, new attitudes, and enhanced skills can be effective both in building support and advancing the changes.

Companies and people have no choice: They must change to survive. They do have a choice, however, in how they change. Understanding the forces that effect change, the process for change, and how to manage that process is critical to an organization's survival in today's turbulent world.

BIBLIOGRAPHY

BPR OnLine Learning Center http://www.prosci.com. 1999.

Brill, Peter L., and Worth, Richard (1997). *The Four Levels of Corporate Change.* New York: AMACOM, American Management Association.

Harvard Business Review on Change. (1998). Boston: Harvard Business School Press.

Hesselbein, Frances, Goldsmith, Marshall, and Beckhard, Richard, eds. (1997). *The Organization of the Future.* San Francisco: Jossey-Bass.

Nixon, Bruce. (1998). *Making a Difference: Strategies and Tools for Transforming Your Organization.* New York: AMACOM, American Management Association.

Cheryl L. Noll

CHANNELS OF DISTRIBUTION

The word *channel* might bring to mind a waterway such as the English Channel, where ships move people and cargo. Or it might bring to mind a passageway such as the Chunnel, the railroad tunnel under the English Channel. Either image implies the presence of paths or tracks through which goods, services, or ideas flow. This imagery offers a good starting point for understanding channels of distribution.

The term *marketing channel* was first used to describe trade channels that connected producers of goods with users of goods. Any movement of products or services requires an exchange. Whenever something tangible (such as a computer) or intangible (such as data) is transferred between individuals or organizations, an exchange has occurred. Therefore, marketing channels make exchanges possible. How do they facilitate exchanges? Perhaps the key part of any distribution channel is the intermediary. Channel *intermediaries* are individuals or organizations who create value or utility in exchange relationships. Intermediaries generate form, place, time, and/or ownership values between producers and users of goods or services.

Marketing channels were traditionally viewed as a bridge between producers and users. However, this traditional view fails to fully explain the intricate network of relationships that underlie marketing flows—the exchanges of goods, services, and information. To illustrate, consider a prescription drug purchase. To get authorization to purchase the drug, one must visit a physician to obtain a prescription. Then, one might acquire the drug from one of several retail sources, including grocery store chains (such as Kroger's), mass discounters (such as Wal-Mart), neighborhood pharmacies, and even virtual pharmacies (such as Drugstore.com).

Each of these prescription drug outlets is a marketing channel. Pharmaceutical manufacturers, distributors, and their suppliers are all equally important links in these channels of distribution for pharmaceuticals. Sophisticated computer systems track each pill, capsule, and tablet from its point-of-production at a pharmaceutical manufacturer all the way to its point-of-sale in retail outlets worldwide.

To appreciate the complexity of marketing channels, exchange should be recognized as a dynamic process. Exchange relationships themselves continually evolve as new markets and technologies redefine the global marketplace. Consider, for example, that the World Wide Web's arrival created a new distribution channel now accounting for over $1.3 trillion in electronic exchanges. It may come as a surprise that the fastest-growing segment of electronic commerce involves not business-to-consumer, (called *B2C* in today's Web language) but business-to-business (*B2B*) channels.

Whether these exchange processes occur between manufacturers and their suppliers, retailers and consumers, or in some other buyer-seller relationship, marketing channels offer an important way to build competitive advantages in today's global marketplace. This is so for two major reasons:

- *Distribution strategy lies at the core of all successful market entry and expansion strategies.* The globalization of manufacturing and marketing requires the development of exchange relationships to govern the movement of goods and services. As you sip your preferred coffee blend at your neighborhood Starbucks, consider that consumers in China, Lebanon, and Singapore may be sipping that same blend. Then consider how the finest coffee beans from Costa Rica or Colombia get to thousands of neighborhood coffee shops, airports, and grocery stores around the world.

- *New technologies are creating real-time (parallel) information exchange and reducing cycle times and inventories.* Take as an example Dell Computer, which produces on-command, customized computers to satisfy individual customer preferences. At the same time, Dell is able to align its need for material inputs (such as chips) with customer demand for its computers. Dell uses *just-in-time* production capabilities. Internet-based organizations now compete vigorously with traditional suppliers, manufacturers, wholesalers, and retailers. Bricks-and-mortars (organizations having a physical location) and clicks-and-mortars (organizations having a virtual presence) are in a virtual face-off.

DEFINING MARKETING CHANNELS

The Greek philosopher Heraclitus wrote, "Nothing endures but change." Marketing channels are enduring but flexible systems. They have been compared to ecological systems. Thinking about distribution channels in this manner points out the unique, ecological-like connections that exist among the participants within any marketing channel. All marketing channels are connected systems of individuals and organizations that are sufficiently agile to adapt to changing marketplaces.

This concept of a *connected system* suggests that channel exchange relationships are developed to build lasting bridges between buyers and sellers. Each party then can create value for itself through the exchange process it shares with its fellow channel member. So, a channel of distribution involves an arrangement of exchange relationships that create value for buyers and sellers through the acquisition (procurement), consumption (usage), or elimination (disposal) of goods and services.

EVOLUTION OF CHANNELS

Marketing channels always emerge from the demands of a marketplace. However, markets and their needs are always changing. It's true, then, that marketing channels operate in a state of continuous evolution and transformation. Channels of distribution must constantly adapt in response to changes in the global marketplace. Remember: *Nothing endures but change.*

At the beginning of the nineteenth century, most goods were still produced on farms. The point-of-production had to be close to the point-of-consumption. But soon afterward, the Industrial Revolution prompted a major shift in the American populace from rural communities to emerging cities. These urban centers produced markets that needed larger and more diverse bundles of goods and services. At the same time, burgeoning industrialization required a larger assortment of production resources, ranging from raw materials to machinery parts. The transportation, assembly, and reshipment of these goods emerged as a critical part of production.

During the 1940s, the U.S. gross national product (GNP) grew at an extraordinary rate. After World War II ended, inventories of goods began to stockpile as market demand leveled off. The costs of dormant inventories—goods not immediately convertible into cash—rose exponentially. Advancements in production and distribution methods now focused on cost-containment, inventory control and asset management. Marketers soon shifted from a *production* to a *sales* orientation. Attitudes like "a good product will sell itself" or "we can sell whatever we make" receded. Marketers confronted the need to expand sales and advertising expenditures to convince individual customers to buy their *specific brands*. The classic *four Ps* classification of marketing mix variables—product, price, promotion and place—emerged as a marketing principle. Distribution issues were relegated to the *place* domain.

This new *selling* orientation inspired the development of new intermediaries as manufacturers sought new ways to expand market coverage to an increasingly mobile population. The selling orientation required that more intimate access be established to a now more diversified marketplace. In response, wholesale and retail intermediaries evolved to reach consumers living in rural areas, newly emerging suburbs and densely populated urban centers.

Pioneering retailers such as John Wanamaker in Philadelphia and Marshall Field in Chicago quickly sprouted as goliaths in this brave new retail world. Small retailers came of age, as well, offering specialized operations tailored to meet the needs of a changing marketplace. Retailers and their channels evolved in lockstep with the movements and needs of the consumer marketplace. As always, marketing channels were evolving in response to changing marketplace needs.

The impact of two remarkable innovations taken for granted today—the car and the interstate highway system—cannot be ignored. These transforming innovations simultaneously stimulated and satisfied Americans' desire for mobility. Manufacturers suddenly began selling their wares in previously inaccessible locations. Millions of Americans fled from the cities to the suburbs in the 1950s and 1960s. Retailers quickly followed. Yet another channel phenonenom emerged, this one involving groups of stores situated together at one site. The suburban shopping center was born. Its child, the mall, soon followed.

In 1951, the earth moved. That was the year marketers first embraced the marketing concept. The *marketing concept* decrees that customers should be the focal point of all decisions about marketing mix variables. It was accepted that organizations should only make what they could market instead of trying to market whatever they could make. This new perspective had a phenomenal impact on channels of distribution. Suppliers, manufacturers, wholesalers, and retailers were all *forced* to adopt a business orientation initiated by the needs and expectations of each channel member's *customer*.

The marketing concept quickly reinforced the importance of obtaining and then applying customer information when planning production, distribution, and selling strategies. A sensitivity to customer needs became firmly embedded as a guiding principle by which emerging market requirements would be satisfied. The marketing concept remained the cornerstone of marketing channel strategy for some thirty years. It even engendered the popular 1990s business philosophy known as total quality management. Small wonder, then, that in today's Japan the English word *customer* has become synonymous with the Japanese phrase *honored guest*.

The customer focus espoused within the marketing concept has a broad, intuitive appeal. Yet the marketing concept implicitly suggests that information should flow unidirectionally from customers to intermediaries, and from intermediaries to manufacturers. This unnecessarily restrictive and reactive approach to satisfying customers' needs has been supplanted by the relationship marketing concept. As modern communication and information management technologies emerged, channel members found they could now establish and maintain interactive dialogues with customers. Ideas and information now were exchanged—bidirectionally—in real time between buyers and sellers. Channel members learned that success comes from anticipating one's customer's needs before they do. The earth had moved, again, as the relationship marketing philosophy was widely adopted.

How important is a customer dialogue? Sophisticated database and interactive technologies enable channel members to quickly identify changes in customers' preferences. This, in turn, allows manufacturers to modify product designs nimbly. Relationship marketing allows manufacturers to mass-customize offerings and to reduce fixed costs associated with production and distribution. Retailers and wholesalers make better-informed merchandising decisions. This is yet another lesson in the costs of carrying unwanted products. Relationship marketing yields greater customer satisfaction with the products and services they acquire and consume. And why not? The customer's voice was heard when the offering was being produced and distributed.

Relationship marketing is driven by two principles having particular relevance to marketing channel strategy:

- Long-term, ongoing relationships between channel members are cost-effective. (Attracting new customers costs more than ten times more than retaining existing customers.)
- The interactive dialogue between providers and users of goods and services is based on mutual trust. (The absence of trust imperils all relationships. Its presence preserves them.)

THE ROLE OF INTERMEDIARIES

This progression from a production to a relationship orientation allowed many new channel intermediaries to emerge because they created new customer values. Intermediaries provide many utilities to customers. The provision of contactual efficiency, routinization, assortment or customer confidence all create value in channels of distribution.

One of the most basic values provided by intermediaries is the optimization of the number of exchange relationships needed to complete transactions. Contactual efficiency describes an aspiration shared among channel members to move toward the point where the quantity and quality of exchange relationships is optimized. Without channel intermediaries, each buyer would have to interact directly with each seller. This would be extremely inefficient. Imagine its impact on the total costs of each exchange.

When only two parties participate in an exchange, the relationship is a simple dyad. Exchange processes become far more complicated as the number of channel members increases. The number of exchange relationships that can potentially develop within any channel equals:

$$\frac{3^n - 2^{n+1} + 1}{2}$$

where n is the number of organizations in a channel. When n is 2, only one relationship is possible. When n doubles to 4, up to 25 relationships can unfold. Increase n to 6, and the number of potential relationships leaps to 301. The number of relationships unfolding within a channel quickly becomes too large to efficiently manage when each channel member deals with all other members. Channel intermediaries are thus necessary to facilitate *contactual efficiency*. But as the number of intermediaries approaches the number of organizations in the channel, the law of diminishing returns kicks in. At that point, additional intermediaries add little new value within the channel.

McKesson Drug Company, the nation's largest drug wholesaler, acts as an intermediary between drug manufacturers and retail pharmacies. About 600 million transactions would be necessary to satisfy the needs of the nation's 50,000 pharmacies if these pharmacies had to order on a monthly basis from each of the 1000 U.S. pharmaceutical drug manufacturers. When our example is extended to the unreasonable possibility of daily orders from these pharmacies, the number of transactions required rises to more than 13 billion. The number of transactions is nearly impossible to consummate. However, introducing 250 wholesale distributors into the pharmaceutical channel reduces the number of annual transactions to about 26 million. This is contactual efficiency.

The costs associated with generating purchase orders, handling invoices, and maintaining inventory are considerable. Imagine the amount of order processing that would be necessary to complete millions upon millions of pharmaceutical transactions. McKesson offers a computer-networked ordering system for pharmacies that provides fast, reliable, and cost-effective order processing. The system processes each order within one hour and routes the order to the closest distribution system. Retailers are relieved of many of the administrative costs associated with routine orders. Not coincidentally, the system makes it more likely that McKesson will get their business as a result of the savings.

Routinization refers to the means by which transaction processes are standardized to improve the flow of goods and services through marketing channels. Routinization has several advantages for all channel participants. To begin with, as transaction processes become routine, the expectations of exchange partners become institutionalized. The need to negotiate on a transaction-by-transaction basis disappears. Routinization permits channel partners to concentrate more attention on their *own* core businesses. Routinization clearly allows channel participants to strengthen their relationships.

Organizations strive to ensure that all market offerings they produce are eventually converted into goods and services consumed by members of their target market. The process by which this market conversion occurs is called sorting. In marketing channels, *assortment* is often described as the *smoothing function*. The smoothing function relates to how raw materials are converted to

increasingly more refined forms until the goods are acceptable for use by final consumers. The next time you purchase a soda, consider the role intermediaries played in converting the original syrup to a conveniently consumed form. Coca-Cola ships syrup and other materials to bottlers throughout the world. Independent bottlers carbonate and add purified water to the syrup. The product is then packaged and distributed to retailers. And we buy it. That's assortment. That's what channels of distribution do. Two principal tasks are associated with the sorting function:

- *Categorizing.* At some point in every channel, large amounts of heterogeneous supplies have to be converted into smaller homogeneous categories. Returning to pharmaceutical channels, the number of drugs available through retail outlets is huge. More than 10,000 legal drugs exist. In performing the categorization task, intermediaries first arrange this vast product portfolio into manageable therapeutic categories. The items within these categories are then categorized further to satisfy the specific needs of individual consumers.

- *Breaking bulk.* Producers want to produce in bulk quantities. Thus, it is necessary for intermediaries to break homogeneous lots into smaller units. Over 60 percent of the typical retail pharmacy's capital is tied to the purchase and resale of inventory. The opportunity to acquire smaller lots means smaller capital outflows are necessary at a single time. Consequently, pharmaceutical distributors continuously break bulk to satisfy retailers' lot-size requirements.

The role intermediaries play in building customer confidence is their most overlooked function. Several types of risks are associated with exchanges in channels of distribution, including need uncertainty, market uncertainty, and transaction uncertainty. Intermediaries create value by reducing these risks.

Need uncertainty refers to the doubts that sellers have regarding whether they actually understand their customers' needs. Usually neither sellers nor buyers understand exactly what is required to reach optimal levels of productivity. Since intermediaries act like bridges linking sellers to buyers, they are much closer to both producers and users than producers and users are to each other. Since they understand buyers' and sellers' needs, intermediaries are well positioned to reduce the uncertainty of each. They do this by adjusting *what is available* with *what is needed*.

Few organizations within any channel of distribution are able to accurately state and rank their needs. Instead, most channel members have needs they perceive only dimly, while still other firms and persons have needs of which they are not yet aware. In channels where there is a lot of need uncertainty, intermediaries generally evolve into specialists. The number of intermediaries then increases, while the roles they play become more complex and focused. The number of intermediaries declines as need uncertainty decreases.

Market uncertainty depends on the number of sources available for a product or service. Market uncertainty is difficult to manage because it often results from uncontrollable environment factors. One means by which organizations can reduce their market uncertainty is by broadening their view of what marketing channels can and perhaps should do for them. Channels must be part of the strategic decision framework.

Transaction uncertainty relates to imperfect channel flows between buyers and sellers. When considering product flows, one typically thinks of the delivery or distribution function. Intermediaries play a key role in ensuring that goods flow smoothly through the channel. The delivery of materials frequently must be timed to coincide precisely with the use of those goods in the production processes of other products or services. Problems arising at any point during these channel flows can lead to higher transaction uncertainty. Such difficulties could arise from legal, cultural, or technological sources. When transaction uncertainty is high, buyers attempt to secure multiple suppliers, although this option is not always available.

Uncertainty within marketing channels can often be minimized only through careful actions taken over a prolonged period of exchange. The frequency, timing, and quantities of deliveries typify the processes involved in matching channel functions to the need for efficient resource management within marketing channels. Channel members are often unaware of their precise delivery and handling requirement needs. By minimizing transaction uncertainty, channel intermediaries help clarify these processes. Naturally, as exchange processes become standardized, need, market, and transaction uncertainty is lessened. As exchange *relationships* develop, uncertainty decreases because exchange partners know one another better.

WHERE MISSIONS MEET THE MARKET

The functions performed by marketing intermediaries concurrently satisfy the needs of all channel members in several ways. The most basic way that market needs can be assessed and then satisfied centers on the role channel intermediaries can perform in helping channel members reach the goals mapped out in their strategic plans. Because they link manufacturers to their final customers, channel intermediaries are instrumental in aligning all organizations' missions with the market(s) they serve. Channel intermediaries foster relationship-building activities and are indispensable proponents of the relationship marketing concept in the marketing channel.

Channels of distribution are not all there is to marketing, but without them all the behaviors and activities known as marketing become impossible. Channels of distribution represent the final frontier within which most sustainable strategic marketing advantages can be achieved. Channels of distribution are the instruments through which organizational missions meet— come face to face with—the marketplace. Strategic success or failure will take place there.

LOU E. PELTON
DAVID STRUTTON

CHECKING ACCOUNTS

(SEE: *Financial Institutions*)

CHIEF FINANCIAL OFFICERS ACT AND FEDERAL FINANCIAL MANAGEMENT ACT

The Chief Financial Officer Act of 1990 (CFO Act) provided for tight financial control over agency operations and the central coordination of financial management functions to support an efficient administration of the executive branch. It centralizes organization of federal financial management, required long-term strategic planning to sustain modernization, and began the development of projects to produce audited financial statements for the federal government. As Title IV of the Government Management Reform Act of 1994, the Federal Financial Management Act of 1994 extended the scope of the CFO Act by requiring agency-wide financial statements and a consolidated government-wide financial statement.

RATIONALE FOR CFO ACT

By the late 1980s, it was apparent that the financial systems of the federal government were in a deplorable state. The savings and loan crisis had developed undetected, financial scandals had occurred in the Department of Housing and Urban Development, numerous high-risk programs had been identified, and seriously deficient systems of internal control were common.

Financial management systems were obsolete and inefficient. Management, program funding, and revenue-generating activities were impaired. Hundreds of separate accounting systems made monitoring, comparison, and auditing difficult. Enormous investments to upgrade financial systems were failing to achieve the benefits of integration because planning and coordination were lacking.

No one federal official or agency had statutory responsibility for coordination of federal financial management practices. Congress was concerned that management functions and innovations were being neglected as a result of the preoccupation of the Office of Management and Budget (OMB) with the budget.

In 1990 the CFO Act was adopted to improve the general and financial management practices of the federal government by establishing a structure for the central coordination of financial management. The act provided for the implementation of accounting systems and internal controls to produce reliable financial information and to deter waste, fraud, and abuse. Additionally, the act required extensive changes in reporting to improve the information available to administrators and to the Congress.

REQUIREMENTS OF THE CFO ACT AND ITS 1994 EXPANSION

The CFO Act changed federal financial management in three ways: It created a new organizational structure for financial management, it encouraged the development of new and compatible accounting systems, and it required new forms of reporting.

Three basic changes to organizational structure were introduced in the CFO Act to provide for central coordination of financial management. In addition, a coordinating council was created. First, to heighten management priorities and centralize primary accountability, the act provided for the statutory appointment by the president of a deputy director for management to report directly to the director of OMB. This individual, one of two deputy directors at OMB, is the chief financial officer of the United States with responsibility for general management and financial management policies. His or her responsibilities include guiding improvements in government-wide financial systems, monitoring the quality of financial management personnel, and working to ensure that the executive branch has a financial structure capable of producing quality financial information.

The second component of organizational reform was the creation within OMB of the Office of Federal Financial Management under the control of the deputy director for management. A controller, who functions primarily in the area of financial management, heads this office and serves as principal adviser to the deputy director for management.

The final component of organizational reform was the designation of CFOs and deputy CFOs for fourteen cabinet departments and eight major agencies of the executive branch. Accounting, budgeting, and financial activities were consolidated under agency CFOs who report directly to agency heads. These positions were created to foster organizational uniformity in management operations and to facilitate coordination of federal financial management. Additionally, the chief financial officers council was created to coordinate improvements in federal financial management among agencies.

Under the CFO Act, the deputy director of management has overall responsibility for the development of management systems, including systems to measure performance. Each agency CFO has specific responsibility to develop and maintain integrated financial management systems. These responsibilities include directing the design of agency financial management systems and enhancement projects as well as overseeing assets management systems that encompass cash management, debt collection, and inventory management and control.

In creating new financial management systems, the primary objective was to develop comprehensive financial management systems that would integrate agency accounting, financial information, and financial management systems. Priorities include the elimination of duplicate systems and establishment of strong internal controls. With respect to accounting systems, conformity with applicable accounting principles and standards were required. Integrated systems were needed to support the production of financial statements and to generate quality financial information for a variety of decision-making purposes.

To encourage the availability of sufficient resources to adequately support financial systems, the deputy director of management was required to review and monitor agency budgets for financial systems and to assess the adequacy of agency personnel. The Office of Federal Financial Management was funded under a separate and distinct line item. And agency CFOs were empowered with budget responsibility for financial management functions.

The Federal Financial Management Act provided for specific improvements in financial management. To reduce the cost of disbursements, it required the use of electronic transfers in making wage, salary, and retirement payments. To encourage debt collections, it provided that agencies could retain a percentage of delinquent debts collected. To promote internal markets and competition, it established four franchise funds on a pilot basis. To reduce duplication, it empowered the OMB director to consolidate and streamline management reporting processes.

The CFO Act altered reporting by instituting five-year strategic planning reports, the production of financial statements, and issuance of annual management reports. The director of OMB was required to develop and annually to revise government-wide plans with a five-year horizon for improving the government's financial management systems. The director's report is supported by agency reports that identify changes needed to achieve modern, integrated financial systems. Deliberate long-range planning is intended to curb the proliferation of unique systems and to provide for the common elements necessary for central reporting. The five-year plans to improve financial management include details about the type and form of information that is to be produced: kinds of projects proposed to integrate systems, equipment, and personnel needs, and the costs of implementation.

Under the CFO Act, all covered departments and agencies are required to prepare annual financial statements for trust funds, revolving funds, and commercial activities. A pilot project provided for the preparation of agency-wide statements in six agencies. A gradual pilot approach was adopted with respect to the production of agency-wide financial statements because federal accounting standards were inadequate. The Federal Accounting Standards Advisory Board (FASAB) was established one month before the CFO Act was passed.

The production of agency-wide financial statements and a consolidated government-wide financial statement for the executive branch was intended to strengthen accountability and to provide the information needed for effective management, including performance evaluation. For example, financial statements include information about the ways budgeted funds were spent, the proportion of taxes and other receivables collected, the condition of physical assets, and the extent of financial obligations associated with various commitments.

Under the CFO Act, the director of the OMB is required to submit an annual financial management report to Congress. This report analyzes the status of financial management in the executive branch; summarizes agency financial statements, audits, and audits reports; and reviews reports on internal accounting and administrative controls. Also, government corporations are required to file an annual management report in addition to financial statements, which have to include a statement about internal accounting and administrative controls. Management reports must include plans for correcting internal control weaknesses.

RESPONSIBILITIES OF AUDITORS

The Federal Financial Management Act required the production and audit of agency-wide financial statements covering all accounts and activities of the twenty-three CFO-covered agencies and a consolidated government-wide financial statement for the executive branch as a whole. Additionally, the Act provided that the director of OMB may require audited financial statements of components of agencies such as the Departments of the Army, Air Force, and Navy. All financial statements produced under the CFO and Federal Financial Management Acts must be audited in accordance with generally accepted government auditing standards.

The inspector general of an agency determines who performs the audit. In the absence of an inspector general, the agency head makes this determination. The inspector general, certified public accountant (CPA) firms, or other qualified parties may perform audits. Additionally, the comptroller general may conduct the audit at his or her discretion or at the request of Congress. The Federal Financial Management Act specifies that the comptroller general has responsibility for auditing the consolidated government-wide financial statements of the executive branch.

Special previsions apply to the auditing of government corporations. The CFO Act replaced a requirement that these corporations be audited at least once every three years by the comptroller general with a requirement of annual audits. The corporation was assigned responsibility for arranging the audit, and the comptroller general retained authority to review financial statement audits performed by others. Additional information about the acts is available at http://www.financenet.gov.

(SEE ALSO: *Government Accounting*)

BIBLIOGRAPHY

Chief Financial Officers Act of 1990. (1990). *U.S. Congressional and Administrative News*, 101st Congress 2nd Session, Vol. 3, Laws (Public Law 101-576). St. Paul, MN: West.

Chief Financial Officers Act of 1990. (1990). *U.S. Congressional and Administrative News*, 101st Congress 2nd Session, Vol. 6, Legislative History (Public Law 101-576). St. Paul, MN: West.

Ewer, Sid R. (1997). "Federal Government Accountability." *CPA Journal* 67(3):22-27.

Government Management Reform Act of 1994. (1994). *U.S. Congressional and Administrative News*, 103rd Congress 2nd Session, Vol. 3, Laws (Public Law 103-356). St. Paul, MN: West.

Government Management Reform Act of 1994. (1994). *U.S. Congressional and Administrative News*, 103rd Congress 2nd Session, Vol. 3, Legislative History (Public Law 103-356). St. Paul, MN: West.

Hodsoll, Frank. (1992). "Facing the Facts of the CFO Act." *Public Budgeting & Finance* Vol. 12 (4):72-74.

Jones, L. R. (1993). "Counterpoint Essay: Nice Reasons Why the CFO Act May Not Achieve Its Objective." *Public Budgeting & Finance* Vol. 13 (1):87-94.

Jones, L. R. (1997). "Implementing the Chief Financial Officers Act and the Government Performance and Results Act in the Federal Government." *Public Budgeting & Finance* Vol. 17 (1):35-55.

Jones, L. R., and McCaffery, Jerry L. (1992). "Federal Financial Management Reform and the Chief Financial Officers Act." *Public Budgeting & Finance* Vol. 12 (4):75-86.

Jones, L. R., and McCaffery, Jerry L. (1993). "Implementation of the Federal Chief Financial Officers Act." *Public Budgeting & Finance* Vol. 13 (1):68-76.

Kendig, William L. (1993). "The Evolution of Private Sector Accounting and its Relationship to The Federal Chief Financial Officers Act." *Government Accountants Journal* Vol. 42 (3)9-18.

Steinberg, Harold I. (1996). "The CFO Act: A Look at Federal Accountability." *Journal of Accountancy* 181 (3):55-57.

JEAN E. HARRIS

CIRCULAR FLOW

Circular flow describes how a market economy works. A market economy is one in which individuals influence directly what is produced, marketed, and consumed. Individuals do this by spending money on what they want. This then directs producers to produce goods and services that individuals will consume. The amount of goods and services that are made available is related to the laws of supply and demand.

A model that best depicts how goods and services flow in exchange for money is called the circular flow model, shown in Figure 1.

PARTICIPATION

The primary participants in the circular flow of goods and services are businesses and households. Households are made up of individuals who both spend money and are the recipients of money. Businesses do the same—they spend money and also receive money from households. It is important to note that the flow of goods and services is in one direction in Figure 1, while the flow of money expenditures is in the opposite direction. Both flows make a complete circle—hence, it is called the circular flow of goods and service.

MARKETS

There are two types of markets in the circular flow of goods and services. The *resource market* is where businesses purchase what they use to produce goods and services. Resources are in the form of labor, natural resources, capital, and entrepreneurship, all of which are supplied by households.

If, for example, a business wants to build a small plant to produce electronic equipment, it must have land on which to build the plant. In the process of building the plant, it uses human laborers who in turn use natural resources to construct the building. Capital to complete the building comes ultimately from households, usually by means of some type of financial institution that lends money to the entrepreneurs (who also come from households) to construct the electronics plant.

Product markets are where goods and services are sold. In the case of the plant that produces electronic equipment, the outlets for its products might be retail stores. Members of households purchase the equipment for their own use in the household. Pieces of electronic equipment are purchased by the households that also provided the resources that made it possible to build the product. The outside circle of the process shown in Figure 1 has been completed.

In the reverse direction is the flow of spending. Beginning with households, the individuals therein spend money for the purchase of goods and services that are provided by businesses. In our example, the purchase is of a finished piece of electronic equipment. The money that is spent on the equipment flows from households to the business, making it possible for the business to sustain operations.

To sustain operations, the business must pay workers and purchase resources. Money continues to flow through the business into the resource markets. Bear in mind that one of the vital resources for the operation of a business is human resources, which are supplied by households. Some of the money that passes through the business goes back into the households as pay for the use of the human resources. Once again, the circular flow is complete: Money that came from households through the purchase of electronic

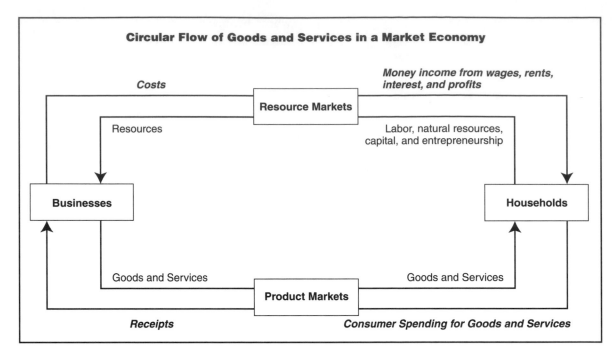

Circular Flow of Goods and Services in a Market Economy

Costs

Money income from wages, rents, interest, and profits

Resource Markets

Resources

Labor, natural resources, capital, and entrepreneurship

Businesses

Households

Goods and Services

Goods and Services

Product Markets

Receipts

Consumer Spending for Goods and Services

Figure 1

equipment passes back to households in the form of wages.

The money flow is more extensive than just wages, as shown in Figure 1. Households do not spend all their wages on goods and services. Some of the money goes into banks, financial investments, real estate, and numerous other places. From those resources, households expect to receive interest or rent as the resource is used. Banks and other financial institutions do not simply hold the money that is deposited by the households—instead, they use it to provide capital for building electronic plants and for numerous other reasons. The money flows back and forth through the circle.

The two flows of income and expenditures are equal. Expenditures on products are ultimately someone's household income. Income that flows into households is expended in some way, either for goods and services or to purchase stock in companies, CDs, land, or another type of investment.

LIMITATIONS

The circular flow model presented here is an accepted way to show the flow of goods and services in a market economy. In a mixed economy, the government plays an important role as well, but this is not shown in the circular flow model. Local, state, and federal governments also produce, or cause the production of, goods and services. Schools, highways, water-treatment plants, parks, and other facilities are examples of government spending. Governments take part of household incomes in the form of taxes, but they also inject money back into households in the form of wages. Some of that money goes back to the government in the form of taxes and still more goes into other places.

The government has considerable control over the economy, which in turn affects production, employment, and economic growth. If interest rates go up, households will purchase fewer goods and services. If interest rates go down, households will spend more. This spending adds to or takes away from businesses' operations and the amount of goods and services being produced.

Governments can influence the mix of goods and services offered to households. Good examples, although they might seem rather extreme, are when the government ordered the breakup of the Bell Telephone System and later of Microsoft Corporation because it was determined that they violated antitrust legislation and had become monopolies. This kind of breakup affects business operations and households.

The model that is shown in Figure 1 could also be influenced by pricing factors—that is, the laws of supply and demand. The model does not take into consideration changes in prices or how prices are determined. Nor does it take into consideration how businesses choose the products or services they produce and market.

Another limitation of the model as presented here is that not all the products and services offered by businesses go to the households that provide the resources. For example, some of the electronic equipment produced in the plant described earlier might be exported to another country. In that case, the goods and services leave the circular flow and the resources to pay for the goods and services come from outside the circle. It might be easier to simplify the explanation and include all households and all businesses in the world, but most economists would not agree with that simplification.

While readers should be aware of the influence that government, exporting and importing, and pricing and production has on businesses and households, it is not necessary to alter the circular flow model. It remains a viable illustration of what happens in a macroeconomic sense without microeconomic influences.

It is also considered by some to be a limitation when money leaves the circular flow to be invested in savings, stocks, bonds, and other financial investments. However, the discussion here assumes that the money that is invested does not really leave the circle, but rather is passed on as a resource to others. It is true that some money does leave the circle because banks and other financial institutions are required by law to maintain a certain amount of money on deposit. And because some individuals in households don't trust banks or other financial institutions, they use the "coffee can" approach to saving their money—they simply keep their savings at home.

SUMMARY

The circular flow of goods and services is a simplified illustration of basically two flows: the flow of incomes to households from businesses, and the flow of resources to businesses from households. This model excludes the more complex influences of microeconomic factors. In the macroeconomic perspective, resources flow from households to businesses, which change the resources into goods and services for consumption in the product markets. Households are rewarded for the resources they provide in the form of money. It is a circular process that flows in both directions.

BIBLIOGRAPHY

Amacher, Ryan C., and Ulbrich, Holley, H. (1989). *Principles of Economics.* Cincinnati, OH: South-Western College Publishing.

Gitman, Lawrence J., and McDaniel, Carl. (2000). *The Future of Business.* Cincinnati, OH: South-Western College Publishing.

McConnell, Campbell R., and Brue, Stanley L. (1999). *Economics.* New York: Irwin/McGraw-Hill.

ROGER L. LUFT

CIVIL RIGHTS ACT

In 1964, the United States passed one of its strongest civil rights laws in history, the Civil Rights Act. The act bans discrimination because of a person's color, race, national origin, religion, or sex; it primarily protects the rights of African Americans and other minorities. Major features of the Civil Rights Act include the freedom to vote and use hotels, restaurants, theaters, parks, and all other public places. The law also encouraged the desegregation of public schools and authorized the withdrawal of federal funds from programs practicing discrimination. Other major

President Lyndon B. Johnson (center, seated) at the signing of the Civil Rights Act.

features included the prohibition of job discrimination and the creation of the Equal Employment Opportunities Commission.

The Civil Rights Act was an attempt to improve the quality of life for African Americans and other minority groups. Historical momentum for civil rights legislation grew in the mid-1940s due to the extensive black migration to northern cities. During this time, Congress became active in the pursuit of civil rights, with the judicial branch of the government at its heels. Shortly afterwards, the Supreme Court joined the civil rights forces and in doing so added to the historical pressure for the Civil Rights Act of 1964. One of the most important and influential Supreme Court decisions involving civil rights legislation was the 1954 ruling in *Brown* v. *Board of Education of Topeka, Kansas*, which desegregated American public schools and paved the way for the civil rights movement.

The specific source of the Civil Rights Act of 1964 was President John F. Kennedy. He began gaining support for it in a televised national address by urging Americans to take action to guarantee equal treatment for all. Kennedy then proposed an act dealing with voting rights, public accommodations, desegregation of public schools, and many more items on the civil rights agendas. On July 2, 1964, President Johnson signed the bill that Kennedy had fought for, which created a major piece of civil rights legislation. Although the Civil Rights Act did not resolve all problems of discrimination, it did open the door to further progress by lessening racial restrictions on the use of public facilities, providing more job opportunities, strengthening voting laws, and limiting federal funding of discriminatory programs.

BIBLIOGRAPHY

Congress Link Web Site. http://www.congresslink.org.

Western Area Power Administration Web Site. http://www .wapa.gov/CSO/eeo.eeomgr27.htm.

World Book Web Site. http://www.worldbook.com.

NIKOLE M. POGEMAN

CLASSICAL MANAGEMENT

(SEE: *Management*)

CLASSIC BRANDS

Classic brands are a part of modern society that have become so deeply ingrained into our everyday experiences that they have become unobtrusive. A classic brand can be defined as one that, through careful and thorough advertising, marketing, and product positioning, has become synonymous with the product category of which it is a part. Additionally, a classic brand may also be one for which there is no other recognizable competition within its product class. In this sense, a classic brand is one that has been raised above the commodity level, creating its own product classification in the consumer's mind. This is not to say that it is the only item of its type, but rather that the other competing products hold such a small market share that they are considered obscure, making the classic brand a "category killer" within its market segment.

EXAMPLES OF CLASSIC BRANDS

Based on the aforementioned definition of what constitutes a classic brand, there are many products and services that may be considered classic. Coca-Cola, (or Coke, as it is commonly referred to) is the undisputed leader in the soft-drink industry, so much so that a consumer in a restaurant who wants a cola drink is programmed to ask for a Coke, whether the establishment serves Coke, Pepsi, or any other brand. In the same sense, an adhesive bandage is better known as a Band-Aid, facial tissue is referred to as Kleenex, and Xerox has become a verb for the act of photocopying, as well as a noun used for what the photocopy machine produces.

Household products such as Arm & Hammer Baking Soda, Clorox Bleach, and Barbie dolls provide strong examples of classic brands that have no major market competition. Of course there are other baking sodas, bleaches, and dolls on the market, but even a savvy consumer would be hard-pressed to name them. This is true not only of tangible products but of services as well. Service providers such as H & R Block and AAA (The American Automobile Association) are classic brands whose names are synonymous with the markets that they represent.

VISUAL IMPACT OF CLASSIC BRANDS

Much of the initial recognition of a classic brand stems not from its performance but from its visual impact on the consumer's memory. Granted, the product must perform superbly to maintain its status; however, the initial impression is often the result of a memorable logo. Classic brands generally have logos or brandmarks that have changed little since the inception of their product. The Coke bottle shape, the Golden Arches of McDonald's, the yellow and red Arm and Hammer box—these are all brand identifiers that need no written words to explain what they represent. Consumers instantly recognize these symbols and associate them with the brands that they depict. In the twenty-first century, with Internet advertising becoming more and more prevalent, such simple images as these are a low-cost means of further perpetuating the brands' success.

HISTORY OF A CLASSIC BRAND

Taking a brand from common to classic is no small task and does not happen overnight. It involves strong commitment from many levels of the organization, along with a well-executed plan for remaining the leading player. A fine example of a classic brand through history is Coca-Cola, probably one of the best-known classics in the world.

Coca-Cola was created by Dr. John Smyth Pemberton, an Atlanta pharmacist, in 1886 as a beverage served at his soda fountain. He described it to his patrons as "delicious and refreshing," a line still used in Coke's advertising in the twenty-first century. In 1892, Dr. Pemberton joined forces with Asa G. Candler, an Atlanta businessman who understood the power of advertising, and registered the Coca-Cola trademark one year later. In order to create brand recognition, Candler created a wide range of promotional memorabilia for soda fountains—clocks, fans, and other novelties, all depicting the Coca-Cola trademark.

In 1915, Candler introduced the contour bottle, which itself was granted trademark protection in 1977—something not usually done for product packaging. The emergence of the contour bottle, along with bottling plants, allowed consumers to enjoy Coca-Cola in their own homes. World War II had a major impact in the building of the brand, since sixty-four of these bottling plants supplied the armed forces with more than five million bottles of Coke. It was also at this time that Coke became associated with the American spirit of a can-do attitude and became a global depiction of camaraderie and refreshment.

After the war, Coca-Cola capitalized on the technology of radio and television to continue to spread its brand imagery. Its longstanding slogans and ad campaigns, such as "It's the Real Thing," have permeated American life to the point that they are no longer just advertising; rather, they have become cultural icons. Coca-Cola's commitment to quality advertising continues in the modern day through its use of not one but five well-known creative agencies whose primary focus is to maintain Coke's classic status.

This rich history, however, is not perfect. In the early 1980s, Coca-Cola tampered with perfection and launched New Coke, a reformulated version of its product with a new taste and new packaging design. Within weeks, consumers were dissatisfied with the change, and Coke moved swiftly to repair the damage that had been done. It quickly produced "Classic Coke," which was the original formula that consumers had come to know and love. This proved very costly to Coke not only from the production and bottling side but also from the marketing side, where a corrective marketing plan had to be rapidly implemented. Of course, Coca-Cola rebounded with a resounding success, and it continues to be the market leader.

FORCES BEHIND CLASSIC BRANDS

The success stories of the countless other classic brands read much the same as Coca-Cola's. These classic brands all have one common thread throughout their history—successful utilization of the four Ps of marketing, which are product, placement, pricing, and promotion. It is the balance of these four significant factors that takes a brand from a name to a classic.

First and foremost is *product*. Brands must outperform their competition in order to become a classic. The best placement, pricing, and promotion will not raise a mediocre product to classic status, regardless of how many marketing dollars are pumped into it. Before becoming a classic brand, the product must taste better, go faster, work harder, or last longer than other products it competes against.

Second, a product must be properly *placed* in the market in order to overshadow the competition. Its target market must be carefully decided on and, in the case of most classic brands, be rather broad. Most classic brands appeal to a wide demographic range, rather than a small slice of consumers. People from all walks of life use most of the brands that have come to be considered classics. Band-Aids, Coke, Levi's, and Timex can be found in just about any home in America, regardless of income, geographic region, education, or age.

Next, *pricing* must be addressed. When looking at the cost of classic brands in comparison to their competition, the classic brands generally fall in the median price range of the product category. While higher in price than the store house brands and "generics," they are not usually at the costly end of the spectrum either. In part, this is because in order to be well received by the masses, the product must be neither overpriced nor undervalued. There are many quality wristwatches on the market, but Timex, one of the least expensive, has made a name for itself as a classic brand.

Lastly, a product must be adequately and appropriately *promoted* to become a classic brand. Timex, for example, has created memorable television commercials over the years by using the same premise over and over—"Timex takes a licking and keeps on ticking." The public has grown accustomed to seeing what the wristwatch can endure and remain functional. Such a promotional idea stems from a creative department committed to the success of the brand through consistent promotional processes. Promotion must also be constant. There must always be some kind of promotional vehicle in motion to keep the brand name in the forefront of the consumer's mind. Point-of-purchase displays, radio, television, print, and Internet advertising, corporate sponsorships, and contests are all used, often simultaneously, to maintain the public's awareness of the brand.

These four traditional guidelines of product marketing are crucially important for classic brands, for the competition is generally aimed directly at them. Pepsi, for example, spends millions of dollars a year targeting itself directly against Coke. Coca-Cola cannot afford to rest on its classic brand status—they must be constantly engaged in maintaining the perfect balance of product, placement, pricing, and promotion, or risk having its market share overtaken by the hungry competition.

Classic brands are not likely to change over the next several generations. They will not disappear overnight or be swept away by increasing technology. Companies fortunate enough to have classic brands in their product lineup protect their esteemed place vigilantly through careful marketing, innovative ideas, and respect for their place in history.

BIBLIOGRAPHY

Battle, John D. (1999). "Brand Names, Durable and Adorable." *Aftermarket Business* June: 49.

Carmichael, Matt. (2000). "Coca-Cola's No Brainer Still Reinforces Brand." *Advertising Age*. February 14: 56.

"From Soda Fountain to American Icon." (1999) *Playthings*. February 3.

KAREN J. PUGLISI

CLASSIC COKE

(SEE: *Classic Brands*)

CLAYTON ANTITRUST ACT OF 1914

(SEE: *Antitrust Legislation*)

CLIMATE IN ORGANIZATIONS

(SEE: *Organizational Behavior and Development*)

CLOSED MANAGEMENT SYSTEMS

(SEE: *Management*)

COGNITIVE DISSONANCE

(SEE: *Consumer Behavior*)

COLLECTIVE BARGAINING

Collective bargaining is "a process of negotiation between management and union representatives for the purpose of arriving at mutually acceptable wages and working conditions for employees" (Boone and Kurtz, 1999, pp. 424-425). Various methods may be used in the bargaining process, but the desired outcome is always mutual acceptance by labor and management of a collective bargaining agreement or contract.

THE BARGAINING PROCESS

The collective bargaining process begins when the majority of workers of an organization vote to be represented by a specific union. The National Labor Relations Board (see Labor Unions) then certifies the union. At this point, the management of the organization must recognize the union as the collective bargaining agent for all the employees of that organization. Once this part of the process is completed, collective bargaining can begin.

Bargaining always takes place between labor and management, but negotiations can include more than one group of workers and more than one employer. Single-plant, single-employer agreements are the most common. However, if an employer has more than one plant or work site, multiplant, single-employer agreements can be bargained. Several different union groups representing the workers of the same employer can use coalition bargaining. Industrywide bargaining involves one national union bargaining with several employers of a specific industry.

Many different negotiation styles can be used when union and labor representatives sit down at the bargaining table. The two basic modes of bargaining are traditional bargaining and partnership bargaining, though there are many variations of each style.

The traditional style of bargaining has been used since collective bargaining began between management and the early labor unions (see Labor Unions). It is an adversarial style of negotiating, pitting one side against the other with little or no understanding of, or education about, the other on the part of either party. Each side places its demands and proposals on the table, and the other side responds to them with counterproposals. The process is negative and involves a struggle of give-and-take on most issues. Even with its negative connotations, however, the traditional style of negotiating is still used effectively in bargaining many union contracts.

The partnership style of bargaining is the more modern approach to negotiations. It strives for mutual understanding and common education on the part of both labor and management, and it focuses on goals and concerns common to both parties. Because of its emphasis on each side's being aware of the issues concerning the other side, partnership-style bargaining is also known as interest-based bargaining. In this process, labor and management each list and explain their needs, and the ensuing discussion revolves around ways to meet those needs that will be not only acceptable but also beneficial to both parties. This style of bargaining is very positive and imparts a much more congenial atmosphere to the negotiating process. Many modern union-management contracts are bargained very successfully using the partnership style.

A blending of the traditional and partnership styles is widely used in labor-management negotiations. The combination approach is used for many reasons, including the fact that many union and management leaders are more familiar with the traditional style. However, with today's more participatory relationship between labor and management in the workplace, the partnership style is becoming more accepted and is being used more frequently. The negotiating process may also include both styles of bargaining because of the variety of issues being negotiated.

The partnership style may be used to negotiate certain issues, while the traditional style may be invoked when bargaining other terms.

COLLECTIVE BARGAINING ISSUES

Labor unions were formed to help workers achieve common goals in the areas of wages, hours, working conditions, and job security. These issues still are the focus of the collective bargaining process, though some new concepts have become the subjects of negotiations. Table 1 lists the issues most often negotiated in union contracts.

THE SETTLEMENT PROCESS

Union contracts are usually bargained to remain in effect for two to three years but may cover longer or shorter periods of time. The process of negotiating a union contract, however, may take an extended period of time. Once the management and union members of the negotiating team come to agreement on the terms of the contract, the union members must accept or reject the agreement by a majority vote. If the agreement is accepted, the contract is ratified and becomes a legally binding agreement remaining in effect for the specified period of time.

If the union membership rejects the terms of the agreement, the negotiating teams from labor and management return to the bargaining table and continue to negotiate. This cycle can be repeated several times. If no agreement can be reached between the two teams, negotiations are said to have "broken down," and several options become available.

Mediation is usually the first alternative when negotiations are at a stalemate. The two parties agree voluntarily to have an impartial third party listen to the proposals of both sides. It is the mediator's job to get the two sides to agree to a settlement. Once the mediator understands where each side stands, he or she makes recommendations for settling their differences. The mediator merely makes suggestions, gives advice, and tries to get labor and management to compromise on a solution. Agreement is still voluntary at this point. The mediator has no power to

force either of the parties to settle the contract, though often labor and management do come to agreement by using mediation.

If mediation fails to bring about a settlement, the next step can be arbitration, which can be either compulsory or voluntary. Compulsory arbitration is not often used in labor-management negotiations in the United States. Occasionally, however, the federal government requires union and management to submit to compulsory arbitration. In voluntary arbitration, both sides agree to use the arbitration process and agree that it will be binding. As in mediation, an impartial third party serves in the arbitration process. The arbitrator acts as a judge, listening to both sides and then making a decision on the terms of the settlement, which becomes legally binding on labor and management. Ninety percent of all union contracts use arbitration if the union and management can't come to agreement (Boone and Kurtz, 1999).

SOURCES OF POWER

If the collective bargaining process is not working as a way to settle the differences between labor and management, both sides have weapons they can use to bolster their positions. One of the most effective union tactics is the strike or walkout. While on strike, employees do not report to work and, of course, are not paid. Strikes usually shut down operations, thus pressuring management to give in to the union's demands. Some employees, even though allowed to belong to unions, are not allowed to strike. Federal employees fall into this category. The law also prohibits some state and municipal employees from striking.

During a strike, workers often picket at the entrance to their place of employment. This involves marching, carrying signs, and talking to the media about their demands. The right to picket is protected by the U.S. Constitution as long as it does not involve violence or intimidation. Problems sometimes arise during strikes and picketing when management hires replacement workers, called scabs or strikebreakers, who

Collective Bargaining Issues

Wages	Hours	Working Conditions	Job Security
Regular Compensation Overtime Compensation Incentives Insurance Pensions	Regular Work Hours Overtime Work Hours Vacations Holidays	Rest Periods Grievance Procedures Union Membership Dues Collection	Seniority Evaluation Promotion Layoffs Recalls

Table 1

need to cross the picket line in order to do the jobs of the striking workers.

The boycott is another union strategy to put pressure on management to give in to the union's demands. During a primary boycott, not only union members but also members of the general public are encouraged to refuse to conduct business with the firm in dispute with the union.

Though it is rarely done, management may use the lockout as a tactic to obtain its bargaining objectives. In this situation, management closes down the business, thus keeping union members from working. This puts pressure on the union to settle the contract so employees can get back to their jobs and receive their wages.

Management sometimes uses the injunction as a strategy to put pressure on the union to give in to its demands. An injunction is a court order prohibiting something from being done, such as picketing, or requiring something to be done, such as workers being ordered to return to work.

GRIEVANCE PROCEDURES

Once a collective bargaining agreement is settled and a union contract is signed, it is binding on both the union and management. However, disagreements with contract implementation can arise and violations of the contract terms can occur. In these cases, a grievance, or complaint, can be filed. The differences that must be resolved are usually handled through a step-by-step process that is outlined in the collective bargaining agreement. The grievance procedure begins with a complaint to the worker's immediate supervisor and, if unresolved at that level, moves upward, step by step, to higher levels of management. If no resolution is found at any of these levels, the two parties can agree to have the grievance submitted to an impartial outside arbitrator for a decision binding to the union and management.

Collective bargaining is a successful way for workers to reach their goals concerning acceptable wages, hours, and working conditions. It allows workers to bargain as a team to satisfy their needs. Collective bargaining also allows management to negotiate efficiently with workers by bargaining with them as a group instead of with each one individually. Though traditional bargaining can be negative and adversarial, it does produce collective bargaining agreements between labor and management. Partnership bargaining can lead to increased understanding and trust between labor and management. It is a positive, cooperative approach to collective bargaining that also culminates in contracts between labor and management.

BIBLIOGRAPHY

Boone, Louis E., and Kurtz, David L. (1999). *Contemporary Business.* Fort Worth, TX: Dryden Press.

Davey, Harold W. (1972). *Contemporary Collective Bargaining.* Englewood Cliffs, NJ: Prentice-Hall.

Miernyk, William H. (1965). *The Economics of Labor and Collective Bargaining.* Boston: Heath.

Voos, Paula B., ed. (1994). *Contemporary Collective Bargaining in the Private Sector.* Madison, WI: Industrial Relations Research Association.

Wray, Ralph D., Luft, Roger L., and Highland, Patrick J. (1996). *Fundamentals of Human Relations.* Cincinnati, OH: South-Western Educational Publishing.

PAULA DEA LEE

COMMAND ECONOMIES

(SEE: *Economic Systems*)

COMMON MARKET

(SEE: *Trading Blocs*)

COMMUNICATION CHANNELS

In the basic communication process, a sender puts a message in words and transmits it to a receiver who interprets the message. The medium the sender chooses to transmit the message is called the communication channel.

Traditionally, it was thought that the words chosen and way they were interpreted were solely responsible for a successful message. However, beginning in the 1960s with Marshall McLuhan, many came to believe that the medium was the message. Today, with the help of media richness theory (Lengel and Daft 1998), most people realize that the appropriate choice of communication channel (medium) contributes significantly, along with the words, to the success of a message. Appropriate choice helps senders communicate clearly, saving them and their businesses time and money. Therefore, examining various communication channels to understand their appropriate use is important.

Media richness theory ranks communication channels along a continuum of richness, defining highly rich channels as those handling multiple inherent cues simultaneously, such as using feedback, nonverbal cues, and several senses. A face-to-face meeting, which employs feedback as well as audio and visual senses, is considered extremely rich. However, a newsletter or brochure is lean, involving only the visual sense and slow or no feedback. Several of these channels—brochures, letters, e-mail messages, video e-mail messages, telephone conversations, videoconferencing, and face-to-face meetings—will be reviewed, along with some guides for appropriate use.

BROCHURES

Writers usually create brochures to provide information on a product or service. While often used for persuasive purposes, they are usually presented as routine informational documents. Writers lay out the information carefully, often designing the visual layout as carefully as they compose the text of the content. This lean channel works effectively when one-way communication in a visual medium is needed. In choosing this channel, the sender is eliminating any extraneous information a richer source might include in order to keep the content of the message clear and focused.

LETTERS

Letters are primarily printed, formal business documents. They are best used today when one wants to convey important, nonroutine information, such as job offers or refusals, promotions, awards and honors, and other kinds of special announcements. Also, they are an appropriate channel for certain attempts at persuasion, such as soliciting contributions to a special cause, asking someone to speak to a group, or proposing the acceptance of an idea. Today print letters are still used as advertising tools; however, the most effective ones are those that are individually customized, making them a special message.

E-MAIL MESSAGES

E-mail messages are widely used in business as well as in personal life. While e-mail is a fast and efficient channel, it is considered lean because it allows for no eye contact and few nonverbal cues. Therefore, e-mail messages are primarily used in routine contexts. The notes writers send to family and friends are usually accounts of day-to-day activities, with more important, special messages communicated through richer channels. Business users, too, choose e-mail for conducting the rou-

Videoconferencing allows people in different locations to interact.

tine affairs of the business, leaving special or nonroutine messages for other channels.

VIDEO E-MAIL MESSAGES

A relatively new variant of e-mail is video e-mail. While much richer than text-based e-mail, video e-mail is still a one-way communication channel. The lack of interactivity makes it appropriate for messages that need richness but not real-time feedback. Even with today's improved compression technologies, video e-mail messages can be very large files. For example, a thirty-second video message might typically require around one megabyte—the upper limit of many e-mail systems. Personal use of this channel might be appropriate for such situations as showing a new haircut, introducing new friends, and even showing a new baby. On the other hand, business use of video e-mail is still evolving. Obviously, when one needs to show something—say a new package design—it would be a good choice. A short sales message might be appropriate in some

contexts. At this time, the best use of this channel appears to be special messages.

TELEPHONE CONVERSATIONS

A somewhat richer channel is the telephone. It transmits sound rather than printed words and sound can enrich the message's words with emphasis and emotion. It also allows for immediate feedback, qualifying it as a richer channel one would use to get important, immediate responses. The choice of this channel to transmit a message is highly contextual. Some receivers view the telephone as invasive, relying on voice-mail systems to get messages. Others view the telephone as an important way of doing business. These receivers often carry cell phones or pagers so they can get important messages wherever they go. Knowing the importance of your message as well as the receiver's preferred way of doing business is critical to choosing—or not choosing—this channel.

VIDEOCONFERENCING

As a communication channel, videoconferencing is extremely rich. Its technology allows people in different locations to see and talk with one another interactively. Its users choose it for its convenience as well as its cost-effectiveness. It is available in most large companies as well as in business centers for use by smaller companies and individuals. For example, a company might want to have the vice president for sales in on its planning meeting for a new product launch without asking that person to travel to its site for a thirty-minute meeting. Or a company might want to screen job candidates and then bring in only the top candidates for on-site interviews. As a rule, this channel is best used when the communication needs are special, immediate, or otherwise expensive.

FACE-TO-FACE MEETINGS

Face-to-face meetings are ranked at the top of the richness scale because they allow complete use of all senses and continuous feedback. Companies find such meetings to be a good choice for nonroutine business, such as planning new products, analyzing markets and business strategy, negotiating issues, and solving or resolving problems. Additionally, the face-to-face meetings of teams often provide a synergistic effect that improves the outcome of their actions. The collaboration efforts face-to-face meetings evoke are often worth the time and expense of using this channel.

SUMMARY

While these channels are not the only ones available, they clearly show that the sender of a message has range of choices from lean to rich. To help ensure successful communication, the sender needs to select the channel appropriate for the context. Additionally, in choosing an appropriate channel, one needs to consider not only richness but also other factors such as training and accessibility. For example, while a fax is relatively easy to send, some people may not have easy access to receiving it, while others could easily have it forwarded to a pager or a wireless phone wherever they are.

Appropriate choice of communication channel leads to productivity increases and positive social effects. Understanding how the appropriate choice affects the success of a message helps senders decide which communication channel to use.

BIBLIOGRAPHY

Donabedian, Baorji, McKinnon, Sharon M., and Burns, William J., Jr. (1998). "Task Characteristics, Managerial Socialization, and Media Selection." *Management Communication Quarterly* 11(3):372-400.

Lengel, Robert H., and Daft, Richard L. (1988). "The Selection of Communication Media as an Executive Skill." *The Academy of Management EXECUTIVE* 2(3):236.

McLuhan, Marshall, and Fiore, Quentin. (1967). *The Medium is the Message.* New York: Random House.

MARIE E. FLATLEY

COMMUNICATIONS IN BUSINESS

Communication, stated simply, is conveying a message, through a channel, from one person to another; that is, connecting or sharing thoughts, opinions, and intelligence. Communication is a mechanism for all types of interaction and connectivity. It can instantaneously bring people together. It can link ideas and things. It can deliver news and facts. It can impart knowledge. Because communication can be expressed as words, letters, pictures, gestures, signals, colors, and so forth, it is credited with being the single element that has brought all corners of the world closer together. In business, communication is the critical backbone of an organization's ability to operate internally and externally as well as nationally and internationally.

COMMUNICATION BASICS

Communication, in its most basic definition, involves a sender (encoder) and a receiver (decoder). The sender encodes a message, deciding what content and relationship codes to use, and sends it via a communication channel (face to face, e-mail, telephone, etc.). The receiver (decoder) takes the message and, in the decoding process, attempts to understand its content and relationship meaning. After decoding, the receiver then may respond, via a communication channel, to the sender with a new message based on the receiver's perception of what the message imparted in terms of information and the relationship with the sender. To be most effective, the feedback loop (the receiver's decoded interpretation of the original message) should go forward; that is, the receiver should respond to the sender. This provides the sender with two vital pieces of information: (1) whether the original message was correctly understood as sent and (2) the new message. This allows for early correction of incorrectly decoded messages. The decoding, encoding, and feedback loop continue as the parties communicate.

In the decoding of a message, miscommunication and/or missed communication can occur. In the feedback loop, it is critical both that the sender provide the intended message, and that the receiver clarify how that message was perceived. The greater the number of people involved in the message exchange process and the greater their differences in values, beliefs, attitudes, and knowledge of the subject matter, the greater are the chances that the message will be decoded improperly and a communication breakdown will occur.

Communication is most successful when it is understood by all persons involved in the process. That is, good communication is free from social colloquialisms, intercultural mores, and gender-based styles. Because communication may be conveyed in many forms, it is frequently described in two general categories: verbal and nonverbal. Nonverbal communication includes body language, gestures, and signals. In general, successful communication depends on how well a sender conveys a message to a receiver relying on the six senses (seeing, hearing, speaking, smelling, touching, and tasting) and feedback.

COMMUNICATION RULES

There are several rules for successful communication. The following checklist provides a guide to creating successful communication:

- Make messages clear, correct, comprehensive, and concise.
- Include an action step with deadlines in messages that requires a response.
- Select correct channels of communication based on message content and relationship components.
- Structure the message so as not to overload the receiver with information.
- Develop sensitivity to the receiver's communication style and create the message accordingly.
- Be aware of how cultural patterns affect communication style and take this into consideration in sending and receiving messages.
- Be aware that people operating in a second language may still code/decode messages based on their first culture's communication patterns.
- Enhance listening skills as an aspect of effective use of the feedback loop.
- Recognize that all messages should be received with a positive attitude.

COMMUNICATION TRANSMISSION MODES

Technology-mediated communication has become the norm in today's worldwide business environment. Messages are communicated regularly via e-mail, fax, and phones. People still meet face to face, but they also use express mail and courier services, messaging and paging systems, caller identification and transfer/forwarding telephony (phone, telex, etc.) systems, and many other combinations of message transfer and delivery methods. Signaling, biometrics, scanning, imagery, and holography also have a place in business communication. Additionally, many professionals work in virtual groups using satellite uplink/downlinks, videoconferencing, and computer groupware. In using these technologies, it is important to recognize the limits of the channel of communication selected. For example, e-mail is efficient but does not convey the nuances of a message that can be gained from facial expressions or gestures. The use of multiple channels of communication may be critical if the content is quite complex; thus, a verbal message may not be sufficient. The importance of using the feedback loop becomes more critical as the content and/or relational aspects of the messages expand. Also, as more workgroups operate globally in a virtual medium, cultural patterns must be considered in the quest for clear and effective communication. The expansion of global business combined with advances in technology has created more cross-cultural opportunities. When working in a cross-cultural, multinational/multicultural environment, it is necessary to understand that culture influences people's behavior as well as their attitudes and beliefs. We encode/decode messages with perceptions learned from our cultural filters. In intercultural situations, the professional is careful to use the feedback loop to clarify understanding of the received message. Just because a message has been received rapidly or with use of high-level technology does not mean that the receiver has decoded it properly.

TYPES OF COMMUNICATION

Written communication usually takes the form of letters, memos, reports, manuscripts, personal correspondence, notes, forms, applications, resumes, legal and medical documents, and so on.

Spoken communication includes, among other things, presentations, verbal exchange (e.g., one-on-one, to a group), and voice messaging. Speaking distinctly, with appropriate speed, as well as paying attention to voice inflection, tone, resonation, pitch clarity, and volume are important to the way a spoken message is received. Frequently, the way a spoken message is delivered is as or more important than the content of the message (a good example is a joke that has perfect timing). More than 90 percent of what a message conveys may actually be based on a positive attitude and nonverbal elements.

Nonverbal communication includes body language (e.g., facial expression, eye contact, body stance or sitting position, distance between sender and receiver, gesturing), which can send signals to the receiver that are much stronger than the message itself. If a picture truly speaks louder than a thousand words, communication by means other than the spoken and written word—such as colors worn, signals or mannerisms reflecting personality or preferences, gesturing—can make a big difference in the message that is conveyed.

COMMUNICATION CHANNELS

Communication in a society, whether personal or business, is critical. Individuals or organizations depend on it to function. Most businesses need both internal and external communication to be productive. Internal communication is communication that is exchanged within an organization. Usually it is less formal than communication that goes to those outside the business. Informal communication may range from chats in the hallway and lunchroom, team and group meetings, casual conversations over the phone or e-mail, and memos and preliminary reports to teleconferencing, brainstorming idea sessions, department or division meetings, and draft documents. Informal communication also includes the grapevine, gossip, and the rumor mill; these communication channels rely on people passing on messages to co-workers, friends, and others. If accurate, they can be very effective.

External communication usually refers to messages that extend beyond the business organization. Because it reflects the organization's image, external communication is usually more formal. External communication is an extension of the organization and can be an important channel for marketing the company's image, mission, products, and/or services.

COMMUNICATION PARAMETERS

The selection or type of business communication takes many factors into consideration, including (1) the nature of the business (e.g., government, commerce, industry, private or public organization, manufacturing or marketing firm); (2) the mission and the philosophy of the organization (open verses limited or closed communication patterns); (3) the way the business is organized (e.g., small or large company, branch offices, subsidiaries); (4) the leadership styles of the organization's managers and supervisors the (democratic, authoritarian, dictatorial, pragmatic, etc.); (5) the number and types of personnel as well as the levels of employees (hierarchy or status of positions, managerial or laborers, supervisors or team leaders, etc.); (6) the proximity of work units (closeness of departments, divisions, or groups that depend on information from each other); and (7) the need for communication (who needs to know what, when, why, and how for informed decision making to take place).

COMMUNICATION SYSTEM

Every group (from an organization, to a family) has a communication system or network. Some are very effective and efficient while others are just the opposite. Even if communication appears to be (or is) nonexistent within an organization or group, the group has a communication system. That is, poor or nonexistent communication still conveys a message: no communication is taking place or there is a lack of exchange of information or messages within the group.

COMMUNICATION STYLES

Without realizing it, most people communicate with others (verbally as well as nonverbally) according to a dominant style. Essentially, people communicate in one of four basic styles: (1) directly or authoritatively (an in-charge person or one who is a driving force to get things done); (2) analytically or as a fact finder (a person who plans, researches, and analyzes the facts and weighs the alternatives carefully); (3) amiably or as a coach (a supportive team builder who gets people to work together toward a common goal); and (4) expressively or flamboyantly (a cheerleader with a positive attitude who has lots of ideas and motivates others toward taking action). Communication styles are developed over time and with practice. They may also reflect cultural

norms. It is important to understand one's own communication style as well as those of others in order to maximize one's communication interactions.

BARRIERS TO COMMUNICATION

Effective communication relies in part on eliminating as many communication barriers as possible. Some of the ways to avoid common barriers to communication include the following:

- Stay focused on the topic.
- If timing is important, adhere to the deadline.
- Be willing to use communication strategy appropriate to the situation; listen, negotiate, compromise, modify, and learn from feedback.
- Avoid relying on the grapevine as a source of facts even though it may have been an accurate communication channel in the past.
- Be sincere, empathetic, and sensitive to others' feelings; one's voice, actions, and other nonverbal cues speak loudly.
- Seek out information about unknowns, especially when cultural and gender differences are involved.
- Be tactful, polite, clear, prepared, and, above all, let a positive attitude guide all communication.

SHARON LUND O'NEIL
D. GAYE PERRY

COMMUNISM

(SEE: *Economic Systems*)

COMPARISON SHOPPING

(SEE: *Shopping*)

COMPETITION

Competition is the battle between businesses to win consumer acceptance and loyalty. The *free-enterprise system* ensures that businesses make decisions about what to produce, how to produce it, and what price to charge for the product or service. Competition is a basic premise of the free-enterprise system because it is believed that having more than one business competing for the same consumers will cause the products and/or services to be provided at a better quality and a lower cost than if there were no competitors. In other words, competition should provide the consumers with the best value for their hard-earned dollar.

ASPECTS OF COMPETITION

To be successful in today's very competitive business world, it is important for businesses to be aware of what their competitors are doing and to find a way to compete by matching or improving on the competitors' product or service. For example, if Pepsi-Cola offers a new caffeine-free soda, Coca-Cola may offer a new caffeine-free soda with only one calorie. By offering an improvement on the competitor's product, Coca-Cola is trying to convince soft-drink consumers to buy the new Coke product because it is an improvement on Pepsi's product.

While being aware of the competition and making a countermove is important, it is also very important to pay attention to changing consumer wants, needs, and values and to make the needed changes before the competition does. Doing research and development and being the first to provide a new product or service can give a company a *competitive advantage* in the marketplace. Once consumers purchase a product or service and are satisfied with it, they will typically purchase the same product again. Having a *competitive advantage* means that a company does something better than the competition. Having a competitive advantage might mean inventing a new product; providing the best quality, the lowest prices, or the best customer service; or having cutting-edge technology. To determine an area where a company might have a competitive advantage, a *SWOT analysis* is often done to identify the company's internal Strengths and Weaknesses and the external Opportunities and Threats. A SWOT analysis lets the company know in which area(s) it has a competitive ad-

vantage so it can concentrate on those areas in the production and marketing of its product(s) or service(s).

In addition to staying on top of changing consumer preferences, companies must constantly be looking for ways to cut costs and increase productivity. Companies must provide consumers with the best-quality product at the lowest cost while still making a profit if they are to be successful competitors in the long run. One way to remain competitive is through the use of technology. Technology can help speed up production processes through the use of robots or production lines, move information more accurately and more quickly through the use of computer systems, and assist in research and development proceedings.

Global competition has made gaining consumer acceptance an even tougher challenge for most businesses. Firms in other countries may be able to produce products and provide services at a lower cost than American businesses. In order to compete, American businesses must find other ways to win consumers. One way for businesses to accomplish this is through competitive differentiation. *Competitive differentiation* occurs when a firm somehow differentiates its product or service from that of competitors. Competitive differentiation may be an actual difference, such as a longer warranty or a lower price, but often the difference is only perceived. Difference in perception is usually accomplished through advertising, the purpose of which is to convince consumers that one company's product is different from another company's product. Common ways to differentiate a product or service include advertising a better-quality product, better service, better taste, or just a better image. Competitive differentiation is used extensively in the monopolistic form of competition, discussed below.

FORMS OF COMPETITION

Although each form has many aspects, not all of which can be considered here, competition can generally be classified into four main categories: perfect competition, monopolistic competition, oligopoly, and monopoly. (Table 1 summarizes the basic differences among these four types of competition.)

Perfect Competition *Perfect competition* (also known as *pure competition*) exists when a large number of sellers produce products or services that seem to be identical. These types of businesses are typically run on a small scale, and participants have no control over the selling price of their product because no one seller is large enough to dictate the price of the product. Instead, the price of the product is set by the market. There are many competitors in a perfect competition industry, and it is fairly easy to enter or leave the industry. While there are no ideal examples of perfect competition, agricultural products are considered to be the closest example in today's economy. The corn grown by one farmer is virtually identical to the corn grown by another farmer, and the current market controls the price the farmers receive for their crops. Perfect competition follows the law of supply and demand. If the price of a product is high, consumers will demand less of the product while the suppliers will want to supply more. If the price of a product is low, the consumers will demand more of the product, but the suppliers will be unwilling to sell much at such a low price. The *equilibrium point* is where the supply and the demand meet and determine the market price. For example, if the going market price for wheat is $5 a bushel and a farmer tries to sell wheat for $6 a bushel, no one will buy because they can get it for $5 a bushel from someone else. On the other hand, if a farmer offers to sell wheat for $4 a bushel, the crop will sell, but the farmer has lost money because the crop is worth $5 a bushel on the open market.

Monopolistic Competition *Monopolistic competition* exists when a large number of sellers produce a product or service that is perceived by consumers as being different from that of a competitor but is actually quite similar. This perception of difference is the result of product differentiation, which is the key to success in a monopolistic industry. Products can be differen-

tiated based on price, quality, image, or some other feature, depending on the product. For example, there are many different brands of bath soap on the market today. Each brand of soap is similar because it is designed to get the user clean; however, each soap product tries to differentiate itself from the competition to attract consumers. One soap might claim that it leaves you with soft skin, while another soap might claim that it has a clean, fresh scent. Each participant in this market structure has some control over pricing, which means it can alter the selling price as long as consumers are still willing to buy its product at the new price. If one product costs twice as much as similar products on the market, chances are most consumers will avoid buying the more expensive product and buy the competitors' products instead. There can be few or many competitors (typically many) in a monopolistic industry, and it is somewhat difficult to enter or leave such an industry. Monopolistic products are typically found in retailing businesses. Some examples of monopolistic products and/or services are shampoo products, extermination services, oil changes, toothpaste, and fast-food restaurants.

Oligopoly An oligopoly (which is described more completely in another article) exists when there are few sellers in a certain industry. This occurs because a large investment is required to enter the industry, which makes it difficult to enter or leave. The businesses involved in an oligopoly type of industry are typically very large because they have the financial ability to make the needed investment. The type of products sold in an oligopoly can be similar or different, and each seller has some control over price. Examples of oligopolies include the automobile, airplane, and steel industries.

Monopoly A monopoly (which is described more completely in another article) exists when a single seller controls the supply of a good or service and prevents other businesses from entering the field. Being the only provider of a certain good or service gives the seller considerable control over price. Monopolies are prohibited by law in the United States; however, government-regu-

Types of Competition

Characteristics	Perfect Competition	Monopolistic Competition	Oligopoly	Monopoly
Number of competitors	Many	Few to many	Very few	No direct competition
Ease of entry or exit from industry	Easy	Somewhat difficult	Difficult	Regulated by U.S. government
Similarity of goods/services offered by competing firms	Same	Seemingly different but may be quite similar	Similar or different	No directly competing products
Individual firm's control over price	None (set by the market)	Some	Some	Considerable (in true monopoly) Little (in regulated one)
Examples	Farmer	Fast-food restaurant	Automotive manufacturer	Power company

Table 1

lated monopolies do exist in some business areas because of the huge up-front investment that must be made in order to provide some types of services. Examples of monopolies in the United States are public utility companies that provide services and/or products such as gas, water, and/or electricity.

BIBLIOGRAPHY

Boone, Louis E., and Kurtz, David L. (1999). *Contemporary Business*, 9th ed. Orlando, FL: Harcourt Brace.

Bounds, Gregory M., and Lamb, Charles W., Jr. (1998). *Business*. Cincinnati, OH: South-Western College Publishing.

Burnett, John, and Moriarty, Sandra. (1998). *Introduction to Marketing Communication: An Integrated Approach*. Upper Saddle River, NJ: Prentice-Hall.

Clancy, Kevin J., and Shulman, Robert S. (1994). *Marketing Myths That Are Killing Business: The Cure for Death Wish Marketing*. New York: McGraw-Hill.

French, Wendell L. (1998). *Human Resources Management*. New York or Boston: Houghton Mifflin.

Goldzimer, Linda Silverman, and Beckmann, Gregory, L. (1989). *"I'm First": Your Customer's Message to You*. New York: Rawson Associates.

Madura, Jeff. (1998). *Introduction to Business*. Cincinnati, OH: South-Western College Publishing.

Moore, James F. (1996). *The Death of Competition: Leadership and Strategy in the Age of Business Ecosystems*. New York: HarperBusiness.

Nickels, William G., McHugh, James M., and McHugh, Susan M. (1999). *Understanding Business*, 5th ed. Boston: Irwin-McGraw-Hill.

Pfeffer, Jeffery. (1994). *Competitive Advantage Through People*. Boston, MA: Harvard Business School Press.

Pride, William M., Hughes, Robert J., and Kapoor, Jack R. (1999). *Business*, 6th ed. New York: Houghton Mifflin.

Zikmund, William G., Middlemist, Dennis R., and Middlemist, Melanie R. (1995). *Business: The American Challenge for Global Competitiveness*. Homewood, IL: Irwin.

MARCY SATTERWHITE

COMPILATION AND REVIEW SERVICES

Public accountants are qualified to provide a range of services related to financial statements. Among the services are reviews and compilations, which are less comprehensive than audits, which are required for publicly owned companies. Statements on Standards for Accounting and Review Services are issued by the Accounting and Review Services Committee, which is the senior technical committee of the American Institute of Certified Public Accountants (AICPA) designated to issue pronouncements in connection with the unaudited financial statements or other unaudited financial information of a nonpublic entity.

NATURE OF ENGAGEMENTS CONTRASTED WITH AN AUDIT

A review is less than an audit inasmuch as a review does not involve obtaining an understanding of internal control, assessing control risk, testing accounting records, and obtaining corroborating evidence to support the financial information shown in the financial statements. The public accountant provides limited assurance with a review. This type of assurance is limited in that the CPA firm states that it is not aware of any modifications that should be made to the financial statements in order for them to be in accordance with generally accepted accounting principles (GAAP). While the CPA firm is not stating that the statements are in accordance with GAAP, it is noting that nothing came to its attention to indicate that the statements are *not* in accordance with GAAP. In order to express this type of limited assurance, the CPA firm should perform more work than in a compilation, but less than in an audit.

A review requires that public accountants make inquiry and perform analytical procedures, which is a type of analysis that examines the relationships among data. For example, if CPAs notice that a company's reported sales are much larger than in the prior year, they should ask management why this is the case. However, the extent of investigation of this change would be much less than if the CPAs were performing an audit. When CPAs issue a review report, the report states explicitly that the procedures performed were much less stringent than what would be required to express an opinion on an audit and that they do not express such an opinion.

A compilation offers *no assurance* that the financial statements are in accordance with GAAP. The word "compilation" is a good de-

scription of the type of service performed—the CPAs actually "compile," or put together, the information supplied by the company's management. While CPAs should be familiar with the practices specific to the client's industry, they do not have to perform the verification types of procedures associated with an audit. All the CPAs must do is to make sure the financial statements are free from obvious errors (e.g., the balance sheet should balance!) and make sure necessary footnote disclosures are included. In their compilation reports, CPAs state explicitly that they have not performed a review or an audit and that they do not express an opinion or offer any type of assurance on the financial statements.

Accountants performing a compilation should possess a level of knowledge of the accounting principles and practices of the industry in which the entity operates so that the financial statements compiled will be appropriate in form for a company operating in that industry. This does not mean accountants cannot accept an engagement to prepare a compilation for a company in an industry with which they are unfamiliar. However, accountants in this situation have the responsibility to obtain the required level of knowledge. There are many resources—including AICPA guides, industry publications, financial statements of other companies in the industry, periodicals, and Web sites—that provide the required background information.

To compile financial statements, accountants should have a general understanding of the nature of the company's business transactions, the nature and extent of accounting records maintained, the qualifications of the accounting personnel responsible for the accounting process, and the accounting basis on which the financial statements are to be presented, as well as the form and content of the financial statements. Accountants are not required to make inquiries or perform other procedures to verify, corroborate, or review information supplied by the entity. However, inquiries are likely to be needed in order to become acquainted with the entity's accounting system.

REQUIREMENT FOR INDEPENDENCE

Another important difference among these services provided by the CPA is the level of independence required of the CPA who performs the service. Independence is a state of separation between the CPA and the client. There are two types of independence mentioned in the standards—*independence in fact*, which is an impartial state of mind, and *independence in appearance*, which relates more to how others would perceive the relationship. For example, if the CPA were related to the client or served on the firm's board of directors, readers of the report might perceive it as biased. In order to provide any type of assurance, CPAs must be independent in fact and appearance. Therefore, both audits and reviews require independent CPAs. However, CPAs do not have to be independent to perform a compilation; but if they are not independent, they must disclose this to readers of their compilation report.

APPROPRIATE USE OF COMPILATIONS AND REVIEWS

So, what type of a client hires a CPA to perform a compilation or a review instead of a full-blown audit? To understand this issue, it is first necessary to understand why some companies need audits. If the management of the company is separate from the suppliers of funding (i.e., stockholders or banks), there is a "monitoring" problem. Basically, banks or stockholders cannot be sure the information provided is reliable, so they charge the company a higher interest rate (or offer them a lower return on their investment) because of the increased risk they face due to this uncertainty. The management of the company, therefore, hires an auditor to attest to the fact that the information is reliable in order to lower the company's "cost of capital."

Now, picture the case of a small sole practitioner who is both the owner and manager of her company. It might be the case that she wants financial statements prepared so that she can assess her own performance, but does not require a great deal of assurance regarding the reliability of the numbers because she is the one who provided them to the CPA. In essence, the person providing the information is also the user of the report, so it would not be necessary to have an independent auditor provide assurance on the reliability of the financial statements. In this case, the owner/manager would probably hire the CPA to perform a compilation because it would cost less money and would be sufficient for her purposes.

Many banks want some form of assurance from small-business owners before lending them money but realize that an audit might be too expensive. They therefore require an independent CPA to provide a review report to give them limited assurance that the financial statements are fairly presented. This type of review is most often performed for nonpublic companies whose securities are not traded on an exchange.

Reviews are also performed for public companies. These companies are audited annually, but the Securities and Exchange Commission (SEC) also requires them to file quarterly financial statements, which are unaudited. Public companies often hire CPAs to perform a review of these interim financial statements. While a review is not required for quarterly reports, the Big Five international CPA firms in 1999 announced that they would not audit any public company that would not allow them to review their quarterly financial statements. They feel that this will provide them with ongoing access to firms' information and thus prevent any big audit surprises at the end of the year. While this Big 5 agreement is not an official accounting standard, it is an important development. Smaller accounting firms have not disclosed whether they will also follow this practice of requiring reviews of quarterly data, but it seems likely that a lot more review reports will be issued in the near future.

SUMMARY

Audits require an independent CPA to perform a substantial amount of work in order to provide positive assurance that the client's financial statements are fairly presented in accordance with GAAP. A review requires an independent CPA to perform more limited procedures to see if the financial statements seem reasonable enough to allow the CPA to provide negative assurance that no problems were noted. To perform a compilation, the CPA does not have to be independent and does not provide any assurance as to whether or not the financial statements are presented in accordance with GAAP.

(SEE ALSO: *Accounting*)

BIBLIOGRAPHY

AICPA Professional Standards. New York: Author.

VICKY B. HOFFMAN

COMPLIANCE AUDITS

(SEE: *Auditing*)

COMPUTER GRAPHICS

The basic building block of images on a computer screen is a dot of light called a *pixel*—the word created by combining the words "picture" and "element."

The computer, because it can present thousands of pixels on a computer screen in millions of different colors, can create shapes that the human eye recognizes as an image—a computer graphic.

It is hard now to imagine a world without computer graphics. Today's children have grown up with video games, and graphic designers work almost exclusively with computer programs to create images once laboriously drawn with pen, compass, ruler, and T-square on paper. Pilots learn the latest techniques of flying in flight simulators; engineers and architects design everything from aircraft to skyscrapers, making three-dimensional models with their computers; TV weather maps display precipitation as it occurs; and doctors can look inside a patient's body without breaking the skin.

It was in the early 1960s that computer pioneers at leading universities began developing computers and the graphics programs that have revolutionized the way we create visual images. The invention of the video display terminal, or computer monitor or screen, and its widespread use beginning in the 1970s, led to the revolution in the way computers were put to use. This revolution was accelerated by the introduction of the photocopier and the electronic spreadsheet to the computer field.

The photocopier was invented by Chester Carlson in 1940 and first produced commercially by Xerox Corporation in 1959. The photocopier's cousin, the desktop laser printer, along with software for desktop publishing (a term coined in the early 1980s), made it possible for amateurs to create polished newsletters, flyers, party invitations, and other documents for modest-sized audiences. Now, with the use of scanners, individuals can produce documents containing color photos, original drawings, or any graphic image from a publication or the Internet with permission from the owners of those images.

Electronic *spreadsheets*, which appeared in 1978, incorporated mathematical formulas behind each element in a table of data. These formulas could refer to other elements of the table. Any change in one value would immediately affect the other cells, so business projections such as sales, growth, or changes in interest rates could be manipulated to explore "what if" scenarios; the impact of every change would be instantly apparent. Such tables can then be imported via computers into a text document to clarify and enhance the information in the document.

Computer memory and speed seem to expand by the day, along with the sophistication of graphics programs, allowing individuals in their own homes and offices to produce graphic materials that match or exceed the capabilities of even the most advanced printing firms only a few years ago.

To create a graphic image, a computer program will supply a series of instructions. Those instructions will tell a computer how to connect two points to form a straight line, draw a circle, or form a letter in printed text. To accomplish

Computer airplane simulators used to help train pilots feature extensive graphics.

this, computer scientists have devised methods to break down complex drawing tasks to simple components. The computer program then repeats those drawing tasks over and over to form a complete image.

Drawing an image of a brick wall by hand, for example, would require an artist or draftsperson to draw hundreds or thousands of rectangles individually. The computer, on the other hand, would draw one brick, then using the same mathematical formula it used to create the first brick, would duplicate it thousands of times almost instantaneously.

Computers are excellent number crunchers. The thousands of calculations—even simple addition or subtraction calculations—needed to create a computer image would be an immensely time-consuming process without computers. But with these calculations written into a computer graphics program, the computer will quickly and precisely light up the pixels needed to create the desired graphic image on the video monitor.

Pixels are arranged in rows and columns on a screen. The number of pixels in rows times the number of pixels in columns determines their density, or *resolution*. Resolution is one component of the computer's ability to form a distinguishable image. A typical computer screen contains 640 pixels in a line and 480 pixels vertically. Multiplied, the number of pixels on a typical screen equals 307,200.

To draw the simplest graphics—those in black and white—the computer program will assign the number 1 to those pixels that are to be lighted and 0 to those that will remain unlit. The contrast created between lighted and unlighted dots forms the graphic image. Numbers written into computer programs likewise determine the color of each pixel in a color system.

Although the ability of computer hardware and software to produce a dense or high-resolution image is important to creating a quality image, their ability to duplicate colors is even more important.

Primary colors—reds, greens, and blues—can be combined to produce full or true color. Their lightness or darkness—or values—as well as their color create shapes, just as they would in a painting or drawing.

The number of pieces of information (*bits*) set aside for each pixel in a region of computer memory known as the *video buffer* determines how many colors the screen can display at once. A true color system is capable of displaying more than 16.7 million colors. However, because of the limits of computer memory, ordinary computers employ a 256-color system.

A program will command the use of one of the 256 colors from a *color palette*, which in turn will transfer that color to a pixel. Determining the numbers to achieve the desired color and value is the core of the science of computer graphics.

By limiting the possible colors to 256, each pixel cannot be illuminated with the perfect color. However, the computer, through a process called *dithering*, can fool the eye by blending colors among adjacent pixels. If a particular red color is not available from the color palette, the computer will spread its available red values around adjacent pixels—giving more red values and fewer green and blue values to some while giving fewer red values and more green and blue values to others to achieve the desired overall color. The process of dithering starts at the image's upper-left corner. In turn the computer will dither each pixel's red, blue, and green color values to make the image appear to the eye as color-accurate, ending at the lower-right corner of the image.

In addition to dithering, a computer can reproduce a true color image, such as a photograph containing thousands of colors, with accuracy by optimizing the use of the 256 colors available through the computer's palette.

One such technique counts the number of colors in an image and gives priority to the ones used the most. But this leaves some colors unrepresented and thus unavailable where needed. To solve this problem, a computer program will carve up an image containing several thousand colors into 256 equal "blocks" grouped accord-

ing to their intensity of color. It discards the blocks with no or few dots. The remaining pixels are then divided up into 256 blocks with an equal number of pixels.

With color space divided up this way, the average of all the pixel values in each block represents an optimal choice for a palette color.

When a computer graphics program draws a line or circle, it chooses which of the pixels to illuminate on a line from point A to point B, for example, by a simple method of addition and subtraction. First the computer illuminates the pixel at point A. Then the computer moves toward B one pixel closer. Should it illuminate the pixel on the same row or one on the row above or below? A simple calculation shows the computer which of the two pixels lies closer to the ideal line, and it illuminates that pixel.

In milliseconds, the program continues to move along the line, calculating which pixel to illuminate until it reaches point B, creating a line that is not strictly straight, but straight enough to appear so to the eye.

Just as with lines, the program will create any shape—triangle, square, or polygon—using a mathematical formula pertaining to that shape. Circles are created in much the same way. The program will choose which pixel to illuminate by measuring its distance from the center of the circle and calculating whether the one at that point along the circumference will help create the circle's ideal shape. Again, the circle is not perfectly circular, but the eye is somewhat deceived because each pixel that is illuminated differs only slightly from its neighbor.

Because computer graphic images can require large amounts of computer memory to be reproducible, techniques have been developed to reduce, or compress, the number of bits of memory needed to store the image.

One such image compression technique is named *run-length encoding (RLE)*. It uses markers that stand for runs of repeating numbers in a graphics file, reducing to two—one specifying the number and another the number of that number in a run—in a file. For example, a file that contains 50 identically colored red pixels with a value of 200 can be substituted with the numbers 50 and 200. With this process, the computer knows the image requires 50 characters with a 200 red value, but it stores only those two commands, a one-twenty-fifth reduction.

Another compression method, *JPEG*, takes its name from, the *Joint Photographic Experts Group*, the organization that invented it. It uses mathematical formulas to segregate information about an image by its importance, and then discards the less important information. The image that results after such compression will not exactly match the original, since some information has been lost in the process.

Another important file format is the *Tagged-Image File Format (TIFF)* which can be read in either IBM-PC-compatible or Macintosh computers.

To create three-dimensional images, a computer uses a mathematical transformation called a *projection*. Although the images are presented on a two-dimensional screen, the computer, through using the principle of perspective—foreshortening, shading, and hidden surface removal—and through its ability to make quick calculations, can portray the object so as to make it appear to the human eye as a three-dimensional object. These techniques are the basis for computer-aided drafting and computer animation.

Rapidly changing 3-D images on the computer screen creates the illusion of motion, or animation. An animated movie will use slightly differing images on a filmstrip to create the illusion of motion. A computer acts much the same way, although it cannot produce the twenty-four full-screen images per second typical in an animated film.

The computer, however, will accomplish the same effect by displaying one image on the screen while creating a new image in the background and swapping the screen. This eliminates the time between display of the images, creating the illusion of motion.

BIBLIOGRAPHY

Gates, Bill. (1995). *The Road Ahead.* New York: Viking Penguin.

Prosise, Jeff. (1994). *How Computer Graphics Work.* Emeryville, CA: Ziff-Davis Press.

WALTER A. HAMILTON

COMPUTERS

(SEE: *Information Technology*)

CONFLICT MANAGEMENT

(SEE: *Management Theories*)

CONSUMER ADVOCACY AND PROTECTION

Consumer advocacy refers to actions taken by individuals or groups to promote and protect the interests of the buying public. Historically, consumer advocates have assumed a somewhat adversarial role in exposing unfair business practices or unsafe products that threaten the welfare of the general public. Consumer advocates use tactics such as publicity, boycotts, letter-writing campaigns, Internet "gripe sites," and lawsuits to raise awareness of issues affecting consumers and to counteract the financial and political power of the organizations they target. Since even large, multinational businesses can be visibly wounded when their mistreatment of consumers or other constituencies arouses the ire of consumer advocacy organizations, it should be obvious to business owners that they can ill afford to engage in business practices that could draw the attention of consumer advocates.

Periods of vocal consumer advocacy around the turn of the twentieth century and in the late 1960s have left a legacy of federal legislation and agencies intended to protect consumers in the United States. The rights of consumers have expanded to include product safety, the legitimacy of advertising claims, the satisfactory resolution of grievances, and a say in government decisions.

President Lyndon B. Johnson, surrounded by advisors and staff, signing a consumer bill.

In the early days of industry, companies could afford to ignore consumers' wishes because there was so much demand for their goods and services. As a result, they were often able to command high prices for products of poor quality. The earliest consumer advocates to point out such abuses were called "muckrakers," and their revelations of underhanded business practices spurred the creation of several federal agencies and a flurry of legislation designed to curb some of the most serious abuses. At the same time, increased competition began to provide consumers with more choices among a variety of products of higher quality. Still, some notable cases of corporations neglecting the public welfare for their own gain continued, and corporate influence in American politics enabled many businesses to resist calls for reform in advertising, worker or consumer safety, and pollution control.

This situation led to the consumer movement of the 1960s. One of the country's most outspoken and controversial consumer advocates, lawyer Ralph Nader, came to the forefront during this time. Nader's effective and well-publicized denunciations of the American automobile industry included class-action lawsuits and calls for recalls of allegedly defective products, and many of his actions served as a tactical model for future advocacy organizations.

The efforts of Nader and other activists led to the formation of several federal agencies designed to protect consumer interests. The U.S. Office of Consumer Affairs, created in 1971, investigates and resolves consumer complaints, conducts consumer surveys, and disseminates product information to the public. The Consumer Product Safety Commission, formed in 1973, sets national standards for product safety and testing procedures, coordinates product recalls, and ensures that companies respond to valid consumer complaints. Other government agencies that benefit consumers include the Better Business Bureau and state consumer agencies. The Consumer Federation of America is the largest consumer advocacy group in the United States, consisting of about two hundred twenty member organiza-

tions. The International Organization of Consumers Unions, based in the Netherlands, actively promotes consumer interests on a global scale.

CONSUMER ADVOCACY IN CYBERSPACE

In the early 1990s, the widespread use of home computers advanced consumer advocacy by making it easier for citizens to gather information and make their views known. And by the late 1990s, the Internet had become one of the primary weapons of consumer advocates. As of 1998, according to Simon Reeve in the *European*, there were more than 8000 "so-called global 'gripe sites' established by campaigners or disgruntled customers with the aim of harassing and haranguing large companies."

Before the advent of the World Wide Web, it was difficult for individuals or small groups, which lacked the resources of major corporations, to make their voices heard over their targets' advertising messages. "But the Internet has created a level playing field for advocacy," Reeve wrote. "With little more than a personal computer and a subscription to an Internet service provider, anyone can open a site on the World Wide Web and say more or less whatever they like." Current and potential customers of major corporations typically use common Internet search engines to access the companies' carefully prepared home pages. Yet these search engines also lead the customers to sites created by protesters that are filled with complaints and allegations against the companies, ranging from the use of child labor to the exploitation of resources in less-developed countries. Thus, for consumer advocates, "the Internet means a new freedom to take on the mightiest corporations, in an environment where massive advertising budgets count for little," Reeve stated.

For businesses, on the other hand, Internet "gripe sites" pose a difficult problem. Although the material posted on such sites might be distorted, false, or even outright libelous, it can still prove damaging to a company's image. Moreover, few legal remedies exist as the law struggles to keep up with technology. It is often difficult for companies to trace the operators of gripe sites, for example, and suing the Internet service providers that provide access to protesters has not proved successful. In addition, turning to the law for help can turn into a public relations disaster for companies, making a small problem into a much bigger one. "The Internet is an uncontrollable beast," attorney Simon Halberstam told Reeve. "While legally the firm may have recourse to law, the reality is that they may just have to accept the problem and carry on with their business."

(SEE ALSO: *Antitrust Legislation; Consumer Bill of Rights; Consumer Product Safety Act of 1972; Consumer Protest; Environmental Protection Agency; Fair Packaging and Labeling Act of 1966; Food and Drug Administration; Food, Drug, and Cosmetic Act; Price Fixing; Product Labeling*)

BIBLIOGRAPHY

"A Consumer Warning on New Ripoffs." *Money*, March 1992: 34.

Cook, Gareth G. (1995). "The Case for (Some) Regulation." *Washington Monthly*, March: 34.

"Is Lawsuit Reform Good for Consumers?" *Consumer Reports*, May 1995, 312.

Kemper, Vicki. (1995). "A Citizen for All Seasons." *Common Cause Magazine*, Spring: 12.

Mayer, Robert N. (1989). *The Consumer Movement: Guardians of the Marketplace*. Boston: Twayne.

Reeve, Simon. (1998). "Web Attack." *European*, January 26: 20.

Saucer, Caroline. (1998). "Small Group, Big Impact." *Best's Review*, March: 50.

"Unsafe at Any Megahertz: Ralph Nader Is Taking on Bill Gates. Is Consumerism Still a Force in America?" *Economist*, October 11, 1997: 80.

LAURIE COLLIER HILLSTROM

CONSUMER AND INDUSTRIAL GOODS

The classification of goods—physical products—is essential to business because it provides a basis for determining the strategies needed to move them through the marketing system. The two main forms of classifications are consumer goods and industrial goods.

CONSUMER GOODS

Consumer goods are goods that are bought from retail stores for personal, family, or household use. They are grouped into three subcategories on the basis of consumer buying habits: convenience goods, shopping goods, and specialty goods.

Consumer goods can also be differentiated on the basis of durability. Durable goods are products that have a long life, such as furniture and garden tools. Nondurable goods are those that are quickly used up, or worn out, or that become outdated, such as food, school supplies, and disposable cameras.

Convenience Goods Convenience goods are items that buyers want to buy with the least amount of effort, that is, as conveniently as possible. Most are nondurable goods of low value that are frequently purchased in small quantities. These goods can be further divided into two subcategories: staple and impulse items.

Staple convenience goods are basic items that buyers plan to buy before they enter a store, and include milk, bread, and toilet paper. Impulse items are other convenience goods that are purchased without prior planning, such as candy bars, soft drinks, and tabloid newspapers.

Since convenience goods are not actually sought out by consumers, producers attempt to get as wide a distribution as possible through wholesalers. To extend the distribution, these items are also frequently made available through vending machines in offices, factories, schools, and other settings. Within stores, they are placed at checkout stands and other high-traffic areas.

Shopping Goods Shopping goods are purchased only after the buyer compares the products of more than one store or looks at more than one assortment of goods before making a deliberate buying decision. These goods are usually of higher value than convenience goods, bought infrequently, and are durable. Price, quality, style, and color are typically factors in the buying decision. Televisions, computers, lawnmowers, bedding, and camping equipment are all examples of shopping goods.

Because customers are going to shop for these goods, a fundamental strategy in establishing stores that specialize in them is to locate near similar stores in active shopping areas. Ongoing strategies for marketing shopping goods include the heavy use of advertising in local media, including newspapers, radio, and television. Advertising for shopping goods is often done cooperatively with the manufacturers of the goods.

Specialty Goods Specialty goods are items that are unique or unusual—at least in the mind of the buyer. Buyers know exactly what they want and are willing to exert considerable effort to obtain it. These goods are usually, but not necessarily, of high value, and they may or may not be durable goods. They differ from shopping goods primarily because price is not the chief consideration. Often the attributes that make them unique are brand preference (e.g., a certain make of automobile) or personal preference (e.g., a food dish prepared in a specific way). Other items that fall into this category are wedding dresses, antiques, fine jewelry, and golf clubs.

Producers and distributors of specialty goods prefer to place their goods only in selected retail outlets. These outlets are chosen on the basis of their willingness and ability to provide a high level of advertising and personal selling for the product. Consistency of image between the product and the store is also a factor in selecting outlets.

The distinction among convenience, shopping, and specialty goods is not always clear. As noted earlier, these classifications are based on consumers' buying habits. Consequently, a given item may be a convenience good for one person, a shopping good for another, and a specialty good for a third. For example, for a person who does not want to spend time shopping, buying a pair of shoes might be a convenience purchase. In contrast, another person might buy shoes only after considerable thought and comparison: in this instance, the shoes are a shopping good. Still another individual who perhaps prefers a certain brand or has an unusual size will buy individual shoes only from a specific retail location; for this buyer, the shoes are a specialty good.

INDUSTRIAL GOODS

Industrial goods are products that companies purchase to make other products, which they then sell. Some are used directly in the production of the products for resale, and some are used indirectly. Unlike consumer goods, industrial goods are classified on the basis of their use rather than customer buying habits. These goods are divided into five subcategories: installations, accessory equipment, raw materials, fabricated parts and materials, and industrial supplies.

Industrial goods also carry designations related to their durability. Durable industrial goods that cost large sums of money are referred to as capital items. Nondurable industrial goods that are used up within a year are called expense items.

Installations Installations are major capital items that are typically used directly in the production of goods. Some installations, such as conveyor systems, robotics equipment, and machine tools, are designed and built for specialized situations. Other installations, such as stamping machines, large commercial ovens, and computerized axial tomography (CAT) scan machines, are built to a standard design but can be modified to meet individual requirements.

The purchase of installations requires extensive research and careful decision making on the part of the buyer. Manufacturers of installations can make their availability known through advertising. However, actual sale of installations requires the technical knowledge and assistance that can best be provided by personal selling.

Accessory Equipment Goods that fall into the subcategory of accessory equipment are capital items that are less expensive and have shorter lives than installations. Examples include hand tools, computers, desk calculators, and forklifts. While some types of accessory equipment, such as hand tools, are involved directly in the production process, most are only indirectly involved.

The relatively low unit value of accessory equipment, combined with a market made up of buyers from several different types of businesses, dictates a broad marketing strategy. Sellers rely heavily on advertisements in trade publications and mailings to purchasing agents and other business buyers. When personal selling is needed, it is usually done by intermediaries, such as wholesalers.

Raw Materials Raw materials are products that are purchased in their raw state for the purpose of processing them into consumer or industrial goods. Examples are iron ore, crude oil, diamonds, copper, timber, wheat, and leather. Some (e.g., wheat) may be converted directly into another consumer product (cereal). Others (e.g., timber) may be converted into an intermediate product (lumber) to be resold for use in another industry (construction).

Most raw materials are graded according to quality so that there is some assurance of consistency within each grade. There is, however, little difference between offerings within a grade. Consequently, sales negotiations focus on price, delivery, and credit terms. This negotiation plus the fact that raw materials are ordinarily sold in large quantities make personal selling the principal marketing approach for these goods.

Fabricated Parts and Materials Fabricated parts are items that are purchased to be placed in the final product without further processing. Fabricated materials, on the other hand, require additional processing before being placed in the end product. Many industries, including the auto industry, rely heavily on fabricated parts. Automakers use such fabricated parts as batteries, sun roofs, windshields, and spark plugs. They also use several fabricated materials, including steel and upholstery fabric. As a matter of fact, many industries actually buy more fabricated items than raw materials.

Buyers of fabricated parts and materials have well-defined specifications for their needs. They may work closely with a company in designing the components or materials they require, or they may invite bids from several companies. In either case, in order to be in a position to get the business, personal contact must be maintained with the buyers over time. Here again, personal selling is a key component in the marketing strategy.

Industrial Supplies Industrial supplies are frequently purchased expense items. They contribute indirectly to the production of final products or to the administration of the production process. Supplies include computer paper, light bulbs, lubrication oil, cleaning supplies, and office supplies.

Buyers of industrial supplies do not spend a great deal of time on their purchasing decisions unless they are ordering large quantities. As a result, companies marketing supplies place their emphasis on advertising—particularly in the form of catalogues—to business buyers. When large orders are at stake, sales representatives may be used.

It is not always clear whether a product is a consumer good or an industrial good. The key to differentiating them is to identify the use the buyer intends to make of the good. Goods that are in their final form, are ready to be consumed, and are bought to be resold to the final consumer are classified as consumer goods. On the other hand, if they are bought by a business for its own use, they are considered industrial goods. Some items, such as flour and pick-up trucks, can fall into either classification, depending on how they are used. Flour purchased by a supermarket for resale would be classified as a consumer good, but flour purchased by a bakery to make pastries would be classified as an industrial good. A pick-up truck bought for personal use is a consumer good; if purchased to transport lawnmowers for a lawn service, it is an industrial good.

BIBLIOGRAPHY

Boone, Louis E., and Kurtz, David L. (1992). *Contemporary Marketing*. IL: Dryden.

Diamond, William T. (1963). *Distribution Channels for Industrial Goods*. OH: Bureau of Business Research.

Eckles, Robert W. (1990). *Business Marketing Management: Marketing of Business Products and Services*. Englewood Cliffs, NJ: Prentice-Hall.

Levy, Michael, and Weitz, Barton. (1992). *Retail Management*. IL: Irwin.

Reid, T. J. (1991). *What Mother Never Told Ya About Retail*. LA: Retail Resources Publications.

EARL C. MEYER
SHARON K. SLICK

CONSUMER BEHAVIOR

In September 1999, Polaroid Corparation introduced to the U.S. market a small, instant camera with a cheap lens that produced fuzzy, postage-stamp-sized photographs that could double as stickers. Scientists and engineers at Polaroid, holding true to the company's long-standing reputation for building high-quality, technologically innovative products, were skeptical. They worried that this new instant camera, called the I-Zone Instant Pocket Camera, would taint their reputation. Before becoming one of I-Zone's ardent supporters, Ed Coughlan thought the camera was crazy, "I'm an old engineer. I couldn't for the life of me figure out who'd buy it" (quoted in Klein, 2000, p. A1).

Figuring out not only *who* would buy it, but *why* they would buy it, *where* they would buy it, *how often* they would buy it, and *how* they would use it is the cornerstone of understanding consumer behavior. Consumer behavior is the study of people: how we buy, consume and dispose of products. There were 275 million people in the U.S. alone in 2000. Each of us is a consumer of hundreds of products every day. As consumers, we can benefit from a better understanding of how we make our decisions so that we can make wiser ones. Marketers can benefit from an understanding of consumer behavior so that they can better predict what consumers want and how best to offer it to them. Trusting their understanding of the changing consumer market, the marketing specialists at Polaroid convinced the company to launch the I-Zone. Less than three months after its launch, the I-Zone Instant Pocket Camera became America's number-one-selling camera (Klein, 2000).

There are two major forces that shape who we are and what we buy. Our personal motives, attitudes, and decision-making abilities guide our consumption behavior. At the same time, our families, cultural background, the ads we see on TV, and the sites we visit on the Internet influence our thoughts and actions (see Figure 1).

UNDERSTANDING CONSUMERS: INTERNAL FACTORS

Our consumption behavior is a function of who we are as individuals. Our thoughts, feelings, attitudes, and patterns of behavior determine what we buy, when we buy it, and how we use it. Internal factors have a major impact on consumer behavior.

Consumer motivation. A marketer's job is to figure out what needs and wants the consumer has, and what motivates the consumer to purchase. Motivation is the drive that initiates all our consumption behaviors, and consumers have multiple motives, or goals. Some of these are overt, like a physiological thirst that motivates a consumer to purchase a soft drink or the need to purchase a new suit for an interview. Other motives are more obscure, like a student's need to tote a Kate Spade bookbag or wear Doc Martens to gain social approval. Most consumption activities are the result of several motives operating at the same time. Researchers specially trained in uncovering motives often use qualitative research techniques in which consumers are encouraged to reveal their thoughts (cognitions) and feelings (affect) through probing dialogue. Focus groups and in-depth interviews give consumers an opportunity to discuss products and express opinions about consumption activities. Trained moderators or interviewers are often able to tap into preconscious motives that might otherwise go undetected. Sentence completion tasks (e.g., Men who wear Old Spice are . . .) or variants of the Thematic Apperception Tests (TAT), in which respondents are shown a picture and asked to tell a story surrounding it, are additional techniques that provide insight into underlying motives.

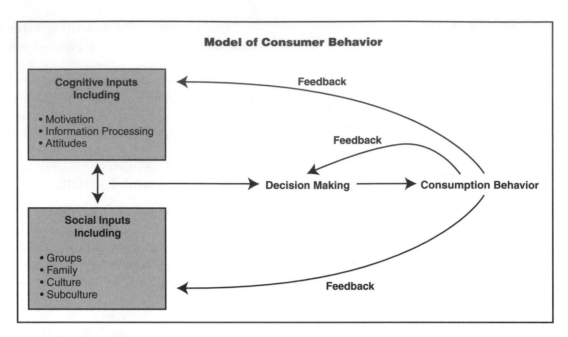

Figure 1

Consumer motives or goals can be represented by the values they hold. Values are people's broad life goals that symbolize a preferred mode of behaving (e.g., independent, compassionate, honest) or a preferred end-state of being (e.g., sense of accomplishment, love and affection, social recognition). Consumers buy products that will help them achieve desired values; they see product attributes as a means to an end. Understanding the means-end perspective can help marketers better position the product and create more effective advertising and promotion campaigns.

Consumer information processing. The consumer information-processing approach aids in understanding consumptive behavior by focusing on the sequence of mental activities that people use in interpreting and integrating their environment.

The sequence begins with human *perception* of external stimuli. Perception is the process of sensing, selecting, and interpreting stimuli in one's environment. We begin to perceive an external stimulus as it comes into contact with one of our sensory receptors—eyes, ears, nose,

mouth, or skin. Perception of external stimuli influences our behavior even without our conscious knowledge that it is doing so. Marketers and retailers understand this, and they create products and stores specifically designed to influence our behavior. Fast-food chains paint their walls in "hot" colors, like red, to speed up customer turnover. Supermarkets steer entering customers directly into the produce section, where they can smell and touch the food, stimulating hunger. A hungry shopper spends more money.

Close your eyes and think for a moment about the hundreds of objects, noises, and smells surrounding you at this very moment. In order to function in this crowded environment, we choose to perceive certain stimuli while ignoring others. This process is called *selectivity*. Selectivity lets us focus our *attention* on the things that provide meaning for interpreting our environment or on the things that are relevant to us, while not wasting our limited information-processing resources on irrelevant items. Did you even notice that after you decide on, say, Florida, for your vacation destination, there seems to be an abundance of ads for Florida resorts, airline promotions for Florida, and articles about Florida restaurants and attractions everywhere? Coincidence? Not really. There are just as many now as there were before, only now you are selectively attending to them, whereas you previously filtered them out. Marketers continuously struggle to break through the clutter and grab consumers' attention. Advertising and packaging is designed to grab our attention through a host of techniques, like the use of contrast in colors and sound, repetition, and contextual placement.

Did you watch TV last night? You may have paid attention to many of the ads you saw during the commercial breaks; you may even have laughed out loud at a few of them. But how many can you recall today? Consumers' ability to store, retain, and retrieve product information is critical to a brand's success. When information is processed, it is held for a very brief time (less than one minute) in *working*, or *short-term*, memory. If this information is *rehearsed* (mentally repeated), it is transferred to *long-term memory*; if not, the information is lost and forgotten. Once transferred to long-term memory, information is *encoded* or arranged in a way that provides meaning to the individual. Information in long-term memory is constantly reorganized, updated, and rearranged as new information comes in, or learning takes place. Information-processing theorists represent the storage of information in long-term memory as a *network* consisting of nodes (word, idea, or concept) and links (relationships among them). Nodes are connected to each other depending on whether there is an association between concepts, with the length of the linkages representing the degree of the association. Figure 2 illustrates a network model of long-term memory. When Edwin Land invented the first Polaroid instant camera, knowledge structures for cameras changed to reflect the association between photography and instant output. Now, knowledge structures are changing to reflect the new I-Zone camera.

The complete network brought to mind when a product is activated is called the product *schema*. Knowing the set of associations that consumers retrieve from long-term memory about a particular product or category is critical to a

successful marketing strategy. For new products or services, marketers must first select the set of associations they want consumers to have. This is called *positioning* the product, or selecting the brand *image*. Peak Freans' unique positioning as an adult cookie was accomplished by establishing a link between the concept "serious" and "cookie." The brand position is then translated into clever ads, reinforced on product packaging, and integrated into all promotion and communication strategies. Over time, a brand's image can fade or become diluted. Sometimes consumers associate concepts that are not favorable to a brand. When this occurs, marketers *reposition* the brand, using advertising and other marketing tools to help consumers create new links to positive association and discard links to the unfavorable ones. In the mid-1990s, Hush Puppies shoes made a comeback after decades of low sales. Introducing exciting, vibrant colors, Hush Puppies repositioned their basic comfort shoe as fashionable, youth-oriented, and "cool." Strategies for successful *brand extensions* also depend on the brand schema. Generally speaking, a brand extension is more likely to be successful if the set of associations for the extension matches the set of associations of the core product. Would Lifesavers brand toothpaste sell? Probably not, because the associations for Lifesavers (sweet, candy, sugar, fruity) are not the same as those for toothpaste (mint, clean, noncandy). On the other hand, a Lifesavers brand sugared children's cereal with colorful, fruity rings has a much better match of associations.

Attitude formation and change. The set of beliefs consumers have stored in long-term memory provides another critical function to marketers: It provides the basis for a consumer's *attitude* toward a brand or an ad. An attitude is an overall evaluation of an object, idea, or action. Attitudes can be positive or negative, and weakly or strongly held. The statement "I love Ben & Jerry's Vanilla Toffee Crunch" is a strong, positively valenced attitude toward a product. The statement "I dislike the new Toyota ad" is a weak, negatively valenced attitude toward an advertisement. Marketers work hard to continuously

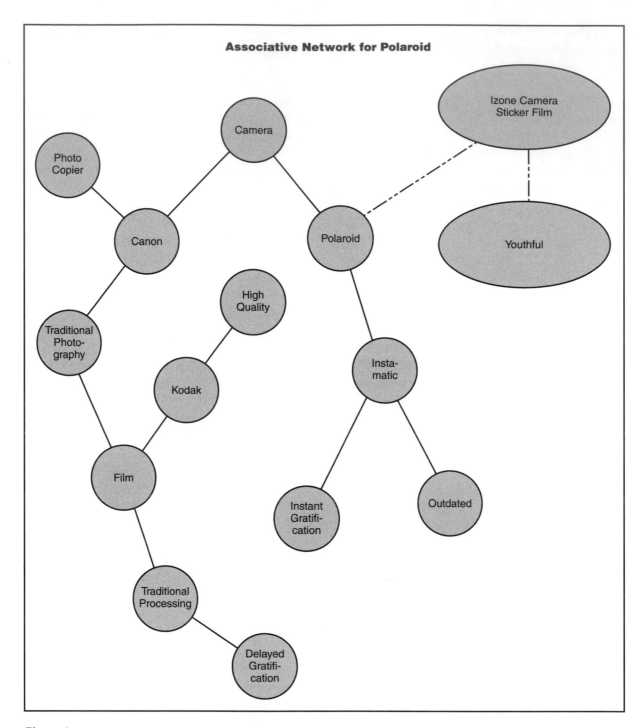

Associative Network for Polaroid

Figure 2

monitor consumer attitudes toward their products. Among other things, attitudes can indicate problems with a product or campaign, success with a product or campaign, likelihood of future sales, and overall strength of the brand or brand equity.

A popular perspective is that attitude has three components: cognitive, affective, and conative. The cognitive component reflects the knowledge and beliefs one has about the object (e.g., "Digital Club Network is an on-line live music Internet site."), the affective component reflects feelings (e.g., "I like the Digital Club Network site") and the conative component reflects a behavioral tendency toward the object (e.g., "I will become a registered user of digitalclubnetwork.com"). Thus, attitudes are predispositions to behave in a certain way. If you have a favorable attitude toward a politician, you will likely vote for him or her in the next election. Because of this, many marketers use attitude measures for forecasting future sales. It is important to note, however, that the link between attitudes and behavior is far from perfect. Consumers can hold positive attitudes toward multiple brands but intend to purchase only one. External economic, social, or personal factors often alter behavioral plans.

Attitudes are dynamic, which means they are constantly changing. As an individual learns new information, as fads change, as time goes on, the attitudes you once held with confidence may no longer exist. Did you ever look at old photos of yourself and wonder "What was I thinking wearing clothes like that? And look at my hairstyle!"

UNDERSTANDING CONSUMERS: EXTERNAL FACTORS

In addition to the internal factors, consumer behavior is also shaped to a large extent by social factors, such as culture, family relationships, and other aspects of the external environment. Awareness of these influences can help marketers to identify groups of consumers who tend to think, feel, or act similarly and separate them into unique market segments. Aspects of the marketing program—such as product design, advertising, and pricing—can then be tailored to meet the unique needs, values, and goals of these distinct groups.

Group influences on individual consumer behavior. Group influences on consumer behavior can impact motivation, values, and individual information processing; they can come from groups to which consumers already belong or from groups to which they aspire to belong (aspirational groups). Groups can exert a variety of influences on individuals, including: (1) *informational influences* where the group acts as a source for expert opinions; (2) *comparative influences* such that the group provides opportunities to manage the individual's self-concept with respect to the group's identity; and, (3) *normative influences*, whereby the group specifies guidelines and sanctions for appropriate or inappropriate individual behaviors.

The influence of groups on consumer behavior tends to vary with a variety of group- and product-related factors. For example, the more the group is perceived to be a credible, valued source of approval or disapproval to the consumer, the more likely that consumer is to conform to group values. In addition, the more frequently group members interact, and the more outwardly visible use of the product is to group and non-group members, the greater the group's influence on individual consumption behavior.

Family influences on consumer behavior. Families have a particularly significant influence on consumer behavior. For example, consumption behavior often changes substantially as family status changes over time. Thus, young unmarried adults, who are often focused on individual self-definition, tend to purchase products that enhance or define their self-concepts. In contrast, couples with children may be more interested in purchasing items or experiences that can be shared by all family members and, as a result, may spend less on individually oriented products.

Family membership also leads to a greater need for joint rather than individual decision making, further complicating consumer behavior at the household level. For example, the person who buys a product may not be the ultimate consumer of the product. Or perhaps the husband and wife have differing levels of involvement with certain product decisions, leading to different types of separate decision processes that must be integrated before a choice is ultimately made. Understanding the dynamics involved in joint decision making and which family members influence which types of decisions has important implications for marketers interested in directing marketing efforts to the right person. Importantly, these family dynamics and lifestyle transitions are complicated by the decline in traditional households and the accompanying rise in nontraditional family structures, such as cohabitating couples or couples integrating families from previous marriages.

Cultural and sub-cultural influences on consumer behavior. *Culture* comprises the common meanings and socially constructed values accepted by the majority of members of a society or social group. It includes such things as shared values, beliefs, norms, and attitudes, as well as affective reactions, cognitive beliefs, and patterns of behavior. Typically, when we think of culture, we tend to think of differences among individuals from different countries or regions of the world. With the increasing globalization of the world economy, understanding differences and similarities in consumer behavior across cultures becomes increasingly meaningful, with important implications about the degree to which marketing strategies can be standardized across countries and cultures, or localized to reflect country- or region-specific cultural distinctions.

One important cultural difference is the degree to which the self is defined as *independent* from others versus *interdependent* with important others. *Individualistic cultures,* such as the United States, tend to foster an independent sense of self, with the self believed to be a set of internal attributes unique to each person. *Collectivist cultures,* however, such as China, foster an interdependent sense of self, with the self believed to be inseparable from others and the social context; person-specific attributes are less important in self-definition than are interpersonal relations. These differences in self-definition affect a variety of consumer behaviors, including emotional reactions to advertisements, the degree to which information from others is valued when making consumption decisions, and gift-giving behavior.

In addition to cultural differences that exist across countries, marketers are also increasingly recognizing the importance of cultural differences within a society. *Subcultures* are distinctive groups within a society that share common meanings. Subcultures can often be identified based on demographic characteristics, such as geographic location (e.g., the southern United States), ethnicity (e.g., Hispanic Americans), or age (e.g., baby-boomers). Polaroid's I-Zone camera is targeted in the United States to appeal to the teenage subculture.

Subcultures can also be identified based on common lifestyles. For example, a strong subculture exists around Harley-Davidson motorcycles and the Harley Owner's Group (HOG). Members of this group share a core cultural value of personal freedom, which is exemplified in both the experience of using the product (taking to the open road) and in the company's marketing strategy (e.g., the open-winged insignia [Schouten and Alexander, 1995]). Importantly, identification of lifestyle subcultures, and the corresponding development of an inventory of shared meanings, is typically more difficult than the development of such understanding of subcultures based on observable demographic characteristics.

Increasingly, Internet marketers have come to realize the value of subculture segments and have tailored product offerings and/or Web site content to appeal to particular subcultures, most often demographically based, and to foster a greater sense of community and connection among subculture members. For example, iVillage.com features content of particular interest to women and offers forums for discussion of issues relevant to its users. Similarly, Hispanic.com aims to provide services and information to Hispanic Americans as well as to provide a virtual meeting space for Hispanic Americans to meet and help one another. These represent early attempts to use the Internet to target and serve subculture populations. Future sites are likely both to target more narrowly defined subcultures (e.g., Hispanic Americans with an interest in gourmet cooking) and to focus on reaching more lifestyle-based subcultures.

THE CONSUMER DECISION-MAKING PROCESS

What consumers think and the social environment they live in determine what they buy and how that purchase decision is made. Typically, the decision process is described as a series of five stages. The first stage, *need recognition*, occurs when consumers perceive a difference between their ideal and actual states. Need recognition is often prompted by persuasive advertising. Consumers then begin the *information search* process by conducting an *internal search* of their own knowledge structures, followed by an *external search* for information from friends, family members, salespeople, and advertisements. This step can clarify the problem, providing criteria to use for assessing product alternatives and resulting in a subset, or "consideration set," of potential choices. These options are then assessed more completely in the third stage, *alternative evaluation*. In this stage, products in the consideration set are compared with one another. Sometimes a simple heuristic rule of thumb, such as "I'm going to buy the cheapest product" is used. At other times a more complex strategy, such as a weighted-average model that compensates for product strengths and weaknesses, is used. After examining each alternative, consumers are ready to *purchase*, the fourth step in the decision process. Finally, after buying, the consumers enter the *post-purchase phase* of the process, during which the performance of the chosen alternative is evaluated in light of prior expectations. Consumers will be satisfied with the product if it meets or exceeds expectations; dissatisfaction occurs if the product does not meet expectations.

This model of consumer behavior, while very useful, is highly simplified and does not always accurately reflect the decision process consumers follow. Consumers may not always proceed linearly through the five steps as described, and sometimes they may skip certain steps entirely. However, the model is a close approximation of the process for most consumers for most purchase occasions.

We are all consumers. Understanding why we behave as we do is integral to an efficient transfer of goods and services in a market-driven economy.

BIBLIOGRAPHY

Klein, Alec. (2000). "On a Roll: The Techies Grumbled, but Polaroid's Pocket Turned into a Huge Hit." *The Wall Street Journal* May 2: A1.

Schouten, John W., and Alexander, James H. (1995). "Subcultures of Consumption: An Ethnography of the New Bikers." *Journal of Consumer Research* 22 (June): 43-61.

Wilkie, William L. (1994). *Consumer Behavior*, 3rd ed. New York: Wiley.

LAUREN G. BLOCK
PATTI WILLIAMS

CONSUMER BILL OF RIGHTS

Webster's dictionary defines consumerism as "a movement for the protection of the consumer against defective products, misleading advertising, etc." Limited consumer protection was present until the 1950s and early 1960s. In the 1950s, a significant breakthrough occurred with the establishment of the product-liability concept, whereby a plaintiff did not have to prove negligence but only had to prove that a defective product caused an injury. In his 1962 speech to Congress, President John F. Kennedy outlined four basic consumer rights, which later became known as the Consumer Bill of Rights. Later, in 1985, the United Nations endorsed Kennedy's Consumer Bill of Rights and expanded it to cover eight consumer rights. Consumer protection can only survive in highly industrialized countries because of the resources needed to finance consumer interests.

Kennedy's Consumer Bill of Rights included the right to be informed, the right to safety, the right to choose, and the right to be heard. The right to be informed involves protection against misleading information in the areas of financing, advertising, labeling, and packaging. Several laws of the 1960s and 1970s were aimed at this right. The Cigarette Labeling Act (1965), Fair Packaging and Labeling Act (1966), and the Wholesome Meat Act (1967) all addressed packaging. This legislation dealt with the accurate identification of the content of the product and any dangers associated with the product. The Truth-in-Lending Act required full disclosure of all costs and the annual percentage rate on installment loans. Prior to Truth-in-Lending, the actual cost was hidden and confusing to calculate. Another significant piece of legislation, the Magnuson-Moss Warranty Act, requires a warranty which states that a product will meet performance standards and affirms that a warranty can be stated or implied. Other regulation took place at the state level. Forty states have a cooling-off law, which allows a consumer to change his or her mind when purchasing products from direct salespeople.

The second consumer right, the right to safety, is aimed at injuries caused by using products other than automobiles. To address this problem, the government established the Consumer Product Safety Commission (CPSC) in 1972. The CPSC has jurisdiction over thirteen thousand diverse products. The powers of the CPSC include the right to require warning labels, to establish standards of performance, to require immediate notification of a defective product, and to mandate product testing. However, its greatest power is product recall.

The right of consumer choice means the consumer should have a range of products from various companies to choose from when making a purchasing decision. To ensure these rights, the government has taken a number of actions, such as imposing time limits on patents, looking at mergers from the standpoint of limiting consumer choice, and prohibiting unfair price cutting and other unfair business practices.

The final consumer right is the right to be heard. Presently, no government agency is responsible for handling consumer complaints. However, a number of government agencies do attempt to protect certain consumer rights. The Office of Consumer Affairs publishes a Consumer's Resource Handbook listing agencies that work in the area of consumer rights. In addition, a number of consumer groups issue complaints to the government and industry groups.

The growth of consumerism in this country has not been without opposition. Although corporations have taken positive steps in many areas, they have also opposed advancement of some consumer rights. Because corporations can have deep pockets, they are able to appeal court cases and slow down litigation. Today, however, because of past successes, the need for consumer protection is not nearly as great as it was in previous years.

BIBLIOGRAPHY

Alexander, Richard. "The Development of Consumer Rights in the United States Slowed by the Power of Corporate Political Contributions and Lobbying." 1999. Archived at: http://consumerlawpage.com/article. 1999.

"Consumer Rights." Archived at: http://www.nolo.com.

"Consumer Rights." Archived at: http://www.consumer.gld.gov.

"Consumer Rights." Archived at: http://www.consumer.gld.gov.av/teacher.

"Protection for the Consumer." Archived at: http://www.hes.eku.edu.

MARY JEAN LUSH
VAL HINTON

CONSUMERISM

(SEE: *Consumer Behavior*)

CONSUMER PRICE INDEX

The Consumer Price Index (CPI) provides a standardized method for comparing the average level of prices faced by the consumers and households of a nation over time. Price-level information is vital to a wide range of personal, government, and business decision makers. The CPI focuses solely on the prices faced by consumers and does not attempt to reflect prices faced by all buying entities in a country. Nevertheless, it is the most commonly used price-level indicator in a nation. It is the basis for the calculation of a country's inflation rate.

COMPUTATION

The Bureau of Labor Statistics (BLS) publishes CPI data monthly. BLS workers collect price data on a set market basket of goods and services in selected cities across the country each month. The market basket includes hundreds of goods and services typically purchased by consumers. The price data is then weighted to represent the mix of goods and services typically purchased by consumers. The mix of goods and services and the weights are based on the Consumer Expenditure Survey, a national survey of the spending habits of 29,000 families (BLS, "How BLS Measures"). The decennial census of the population is used for selection of the urban areas included in the monthly surveys.

The CPI is computed by dividing the weighted price of the market basket in a time period by the weighted price of the market basket in a designated base time period. The resulting ratio times 100 yields an index with a value of 100 for the base time period. CPI values above or below 100 indicate that the price level is higher or lower than it was during the base period. For example, an index value of 140 indicates that the average price level is 40 percent higher than it was in the base year.

The prices of hundreds of goods and services are surveyed each month. The goods and services are organized into eight main groups: food and beverage, housing, apparel, transportation, medical care, recreation, education and communication, and other goods and services.

Each month the BLS publishes numerous CPIs based on the data collected. The two main CPI series are the CPI-U (Consumer Price Index for All Urban Consumers) and the CPI-W (Consumer Price Index for Urban Wage Earners and Clerical Workers) Separate indices are published for twenty-six selected urban areas and four geographic regions of the country. There are also indices for three classes of cities (population of over 1.5 million, mid-sized to small metropolitan areas, and nonmetropolitan areas) and for categories of goods and services.

MEASUREMENT ISSUES

The CPI provides a general approximation of the price level faced by consumers in a given time period. It is not designed to measure the exact price level faced by any one consumer. The BLS collects data only in urban areas. Thus the CPI does not attempt to provide a measure of rural price levels. However, the CPI-U should be serviceable for approximately 87 percent of the U.S. population (BLS, "Guide to Available.") A two-week lag time exists between the completion of data collection and the publication of CPI data. The measure has limitations. The computational methodology has been gradually adjusted over time to allow for more accurate measurement of changing price levels. Measurement issues include index bias due to product innovation and quality changes that affect prices and consumption patterns, as well as uneven price changes across retail outlets and geographic areas.

Historically, the CPI has been calculated as a Laspeyres index, or an index based on a fixed market basket of goods and services. This has been criticized as an inaccurate approach because it does not allow for changing consumption patterns. Consumption patterns may change due to the availability of new products, changing features of current products, changing consumer preferences, or changes in the relative prices of goods and services. The impact of the availability of new products on purchasing patterns is exemplified by products such as videocassette recorders and microwave ovens, which were not available for consumer purchase until the late 1970s but became common household purchases in less than a decade. The emergence of audio CDs and CD players reduced purchases of audio-cassette tapes.

Price changes due to changes in product quality or features can be seen in the development of the manual typewriter, electric typewriter, and word processor. Adjustments are made in the computation of the CPI for the impact of quality changes on price. Also, periodic adjustments in the market basket have been made every eight to twelve years to allow for changing consumption patterns due to new products. This creates a situation in which price-level comparisons may be more accurate when made over relatively short periods of time rather than over many years or decades during which the nature and mix of goods and services in the market basket changed considerably. The base year is also changed periodically. For example, in January 1988 the CPI base year was changed from 1967 = 100 to 1982-1984 = 100.

Beginning with January 1999 data, the BLS changed to a geometric-mean-estimator method of indexing. This method does not employ the Laspeyres fixed market basket; rather, it allows consumers to adjust purchases within broad categories of goods and services due to changes in the relative prices of the goods or services within each category. The consensus of experts was that the Laspeyres method led to a CPI which systematically overestimated the price level actually paid by consumers, because consumers would substitute away from goods that increased in price in favor of similar goods with lower increases in price. The geometric-mean-estimator method was adopted to reduce this overestimation. As part of this change, the BLS reports that CPI expenditure weights are to be updated on a regular two-year schedule (BLS, "Future Schedule").

During a year the prices of many goods and services fluctuate because of seasonal factors, such as increases in supply affecting vegetable prices during harvest season. The BLS also publishes monthly seasonally adjusted CPI measures, which factor out the monthly variation due to the season of the year.

The CPI does not provide any explanation for price-level changes, nor does it forecast future price levels. However, historical CPI data are used extensively by analysts in research on these issues.

HISTORICAL TREND

The CPI tracks an ongoing trend of increasing prices in the United States. When making com-

parisons of the CPI over time, it is important to make sure that all data use the same base year.

RELATED MEASURES

The CPI is not the only measure of price level published by the government. Other common price indexes include a producer price index, which tracks the average prices producers pay for inputs, and the GDP deflator, which includes not only consumer prices but also the prices paid by other purchasers such as investors and the government.

Several other measures are based directly on the CPI. A country's inflation rate is the annual rate of change in its CPI. Also, purchasing power indices are based on CPI data. Typically a purchasing power index is the reciprocal of a price index. In essence, the price index relates how much it would cost to purchase the same group of goods and services compared to a base-time period. A purchasing power index reflects the percentage of the base-period group of goods and services that could be purchased at current prices if income were constant.

USES

Households, businesses, and governments use price-level data in a variety of ways. One of the most common uses is to adjust other statistics for the changes in price level. The resulting price-adjusted measures go by several terms including: real, in constant dollars, in (list base year) dollars, or deflated. For example, if an individual received a 10 percent raise while the CPI rose 3 percent, the individual would have a 7 percent increase in real income. Data which are not adjusted for price-level changes go by the descriptive term *nominal*. Real measures are commonly used in media reports and by decision makers. Other examples of real measures are real gross domestic product, real interest rates, real exchange rates, and real government purchases.

Individuals and households rarely make direct use of the CPI, although they use CPI-based information frequently. Examples of this include comparisons of the cost of living in different cities, planning how much income will be needed to provide a comparable standard of living in retirement, negotiating with employers for raises, and determining the real return received on savings.

Businesses use the CPI extensively in forecasting future average price levels and consumer expenditures. The expected price level also becomes an important issue in negotiating escalator clauses in long-term contracts. Labor contracts and pension plans may include cost-of-living-adjustment (COLA) clauses that tie wage or pension increases to CPI increases. International business decision makers closely monitor differences in the inflation rates of relevant countries.

Many branches of government use the CPI. A stable price level is one of the three main goals of economic stability, and the CPI is the main measuring tool to assess a nation's progress toward this goal. Thus both fiscal and monetary policy makers use this statistic. Levels of many government expenditures, such as transfer payment levels and government employee salaries, are tied to changes in the CPI. The legal system may integrate CPI adjustments into alimony or child-support agreements. In the 1980s the U.S. began to index progressive income tax brackets to the inflation rate. Under an indexed income tax system, an individual will end up in a higher marginal income tax bracket only if his or her income rises more rapidly than the CPI.

BIBLIOGRAPHY

Bureau of Labor Statistics. "BLS to Maintain Current Reference Base of 1982-84 = 100 for Most CPI Index series." *Public Briefings on the 1998 CPI Revision.* http://stats.bls .gov/cpibase1.htm. 1999.

Bureau of Labor Statistics. "Consumer Price Indexes." http://stats.bls.gov/epi0698c.htm. 1999.

Bureau of Labor Statistics. "Future Schedule for Expenditure Weight Updates in the Consumer Price Index." http://stats.bls.gov/cpiupdt.htm. 1999.

Bureau of Labor Statistics. "Guide to Available CPI Data." http://stats.bls.gov/cpifact8.htm. 1999.

Bureau of Labor Statistics. "How BLS Measures Changes in Consumer Prices." http://stats.bls.gov/cpifact2.htm. 1999.

Bureau of Labor Statistics. "Measurement Issues in the Consumer Price Index." *JEC Report: Quality and New Products Bias.* http://stats.bls.gov/cpigm697.htm. 1999.

Bureau of Labor Statistics. "Planned Change in the Consumer Price Index Formula April 16, 1998." http://stats .bls.gov/epigm02.htm. 1999.

"ESBR: Prices." *Economic Statistics Briefing Room.* http://www.whitehouse.gov/fsbr/prices.html. 1999.

C. BETH HAYNES

CONSUMER PRODUCT SAFETY ACT OF 1972

Congress passed the Consumer Product Safety Act in 1972 to "assist consumers in evaluating the comparative safety of consumer products; to develop uniform safety standards for consumer products and to minimize conflicting state and local regulations; and to promote research and investigation into the causes and prevention of product related death, illnesses, and injuries." The act also established the Consumer Product Safety Commission (CPSC) to "protect the public against unreasonable risks associated with consumer products." The CPSC has authority to set mandatory standards, ban products, order recalls of unsafe products, and institute labeling requirements.

The CPSC is an independent regulatory agency charged with protecting consumers from unreasonable risk of injury associated with consumer products. The most serious risks include amputation, electrocution, burns, asphyxiation, and cancer. Examples of recent product liability lawsuits in which defendant companies lost include breast implants that leaked silicone gel and football helmets that did not have enough padding. The commission has jurisdiction over about 15,000 types of consumer products, such as automatic coffee makers, toys, furniture, clothing, and lawn mowers. The CPSC works to reduce the risk of injury and death from consumer products by:

- Developing voluntary standards with industry

- Issuing and enforcing mandatory standards and banning consumer products if no feasible standard would adequately protect the public

Important Safety Recalls

DON'T LET THESE RECALLED PRODUCTS KILL OR INJURE A CHILD IN YOUR HOME!

Pokemon Balls

Lane Cedar Chests

Swimming Pool Dive Sticks

Cosco Arriva Car Seats/Carriers

Cosco Turnabout Car Seats/Carriers

Playskool Travel-Lite Portable Cribs

For More Information Contact:

U.S. CONSUMER PRODUCT SAFETY COMMISSION (CPSC)
Recall Roundup List
Washington, D.C. 20207

TOLL-FREE HOTLINE
(800) 638-2772

WEBSITE:
WWW.CPSC.GOV

U.S. CONSUMER PRODUCT SAFETY COMMISSION IN COOPERATION WITH THE U.S. POSTAL SERVICE

A safety recall poster highlighting possible dangers to children.

- Obtaining the recall of products or arranging for their repair

- Conducting research on potential product hazards

- Informing and educating consumers through the media, state and local governments, and private organizations, and by responding to consumer inquiries. (CPSC, 1999).

The CPSC has three key program areas:

1. The Office of Hazard Identification and Reduction, which collects and analyzes consumer injury and death data to determine trends in consumer product hazards.

2. The Office of Compliance and Enforcement, which supervises compliance and administrative activities related to the act. This office also reviews proposed standards and rules with respect to their enforceability.

3. The Office of Information and Public Affairs, which is responsible for the development, implementation, and evaluation of a comprehensive national information and public affairs program designed to promote product safety. (Fise, 1998).

In recent years, the CPSC has been involved in actions to protect children. In 1987, for example, the commission began to examine toys that pose choking hazards. This led Congress to pass the Child Safety Protection Act of 1994. A sample of child safety issues investigated by the commission includes bicycle helmets, public playgrounds, upholstered furniture, walkers, drawstrings on children's clothing, baseball protective equipment, and toys. More than 160 deaths from toys were reported between 1990 and 1997, and at least seventy-two different toys that posed a small-parts hazard were recalled between October 1996 and September 1997 by the CPSC. (Public Interest Research Group [PIRG], 2000). PIRG reports that in 1998 fewer toys posing choking hazards appeared on shelves.

In addition, the commission has also written rules to establish performance, design, composition, packaging, and construction standards for many products. Examples of products with mandatory safety standards include matchbooks, walk-behind power lawn mowers, residential garage door openers, swimming pool slides, chainsaws, home-use pesticides, and cellulose insulation (Garman, 1997).

Consumers have benefited in the areas where the CPSC has taken action. The commission is constantly challenged to keep abreast of new products and potential hazards that may be associated with them. The commission is usually able to react, however, only after a consumer has been injured or died. The CPSC has changed the way many products are designed and manufactured. Continuing education by consumer groups, the media, and the CPSE has helped increase public awareness of possible consumer safety hazards. The CPSC is an important consumer protection agency, protecting consumers by assuring that products they use every day are safe.

BIBLIOGRAPHY

Consumer Product and Safety Act (1972). Section 2051.

Consumer Product Safety Commission (CPSC). "Who Are We—What We Do for You." www.cpsc.gov/about/who.html. March 1999.

Fise, M. E. R. (1998). "Consumer Product Safety Regulation." In *Regulation and Consumer Protection: Politics, Bureaucracy and Economics*, ed. K. J. Meier, E. T. Garman, and L. R. Keiser. Houston, TX: DAME Publications.

Garman, E. T. (1997). *Consumer Economic Issues in America*, 5th ed. Houston, TX: DAME Publications.

Public Interest Research Group (PIRG). "Trouble in Toyland; Positive Signs in 1998." www.pirg.org/consumer/products/toy/98/page6.htm. March 2000

PHYLLIS BUNN

CONSUMER PROTEST

The United States was built on the philosophy of ensuring citizens' rights. Specifically, individuals have rights set forth in the Constitution and Bill

Consumer advocate Ralph Nader.

of Rights. Throughout history, American citizens and consumers have expended considerable energy toward ensuring that organizations, retailers, and governments recognize and adhere to these rights. Further, when citizens believe one of those rights has been overlooked or denied, they join in protest to rectify the perceived injustice.

For example, even before the American Revolution, when they were still English subjects, colonists were disgruntled by the British Parliament's imposition of a tax on tea imports. On December 16, 1773, to protest the tea tax (which had been implemented to help the poorly managed and corrupt East India Tea Company avoid bankruptcy), citizens donned Mohawk Indian disguises, boarded three East India Tea Company ships docked in Boston harbor, and threw 342 chests of Ceylon and Darjeiling tea overboard.

Since the Boston Tea Party, consumers' quests to attain and maintain their rights have continued as an undercurrent of resistance to unfair business and industry practices that di-

rectly affected consumers' health, welfare, and safety. However, during certain volatile times (the Progressive era of the late 1890s, the Depression years of the 1930s, and the 1960s through the 1970s), consumer concerns have been more strongly emphasized.

Further, women's magazines (*McClure's* and *Ladies' Home Journal*, for example) awakened women to the activist movement as a way of ensuring safe products, achieving justice, and attaining a level of equality (Nader, 1999). Women have been concerned about such issues as price rigging, monopolies, dishonest labeling of medicines, and contaminated food. Outcomes of these efforts have included both self-policing and external policing by some business, industry, and government agencies to protect the environment and consumers.

Upton Sinclair's 1906 novel *The Jungle* exposed unsanitary food-processing and meat-packing conditions. The graphic nature of the book sparked a public outcry that led to the passage of legislation by Congress, including the Pure Food and Drug Act of 1906, which created the Food and Drug Administration (FDA).

When use of a liquid sulfur drug, Elixir Sulfanilamide, resulted in the deaths of more than 100 people in 1937, the Pure Food and Drug Act was proven to be inadequate. In 1938 the federal Food, Drug, and Cosmetic Act, became law; before marketing new drugs, manufacturers were required by this law to prove their safety to the FDA.

Consumer concerns were minimized by World War II and did not retake the stage until the early 1960s. President John F. Kennedy, considering consumer protection an important issue, suggested improvements in existing programs and also proposed two new consumer-protection programs: creation of the position of special assistant for consumer affairs (created by President Lyndon B. Johnson in 1964) and creation of a national oversight board made up of labor, cooperative, and consumer groups, the Consumer Federation of America (established in 1967).

Individuals have played, and continue to play, integral roles in ensuring consumer protection. Ralph Nader, for instance, has led a crusade to ensure consideration and enforcement of consumer rights for more than three decades. Nader and his advocacy groups, known as Nader's Raiders, have investigated complaints, documented harm, determined responsibility, disseminated information about consumer abuse, proposed alternatives, instigated reform, and campaigned to provide the consumers' viewpoint to a wide range of audiences, including government and large corporations. Often these activities not only resulted in important consumer victories; they also resulted in positive changes in the political climate and in the institution of self-regulation to ensure that regulations are met.

From the appearance of the automobile on the American landscape through 1966, when a federal auto safety law was enacted, corporate decision makers had determined the level of safety for their automobiles. From the first death in 1899 until 1966, about 2 million automobile-related deaths occurred as well as about 100 million injuries, a figure three times greater than U.S. combat losses in all military actions. Consumer advocates postulated that many of those deaths and injuries might have been avoided had automobile producers included certain safety features as part of the standard package. Consumers began to demand automobile safety features such as turn signals, seat belts, and air bags.

Nader began his first consumer campaign in 1965 with his book *Unsafe at Any Speed*, which detailed Detroit automakers' negligence and calling the Corvair "one of the nastiest handling cars ever built (quoted in Watson, 1997). In 1969, after considerable consumer activism, Chevrolet ceased Corvair production. Later, in 1972, the Department of Transportation (DOT) tested the Corvair and found the handling "at least as good as the performance of some contemporary vehicles, both foreign and domestic" (quoted in Watson, 1997); however, Nader contested the DOT findings.

Another federal agency, the National Highway and Traffic Safety Administration (NHTSA), was established to ensure highway and automobile safety. It was responsible for setting minimal

safety standards for automobiles, as well as ensuring consumer notification of automobile safety defects. NHTSA developed and issued thirty standards in 1967 aimed at reducing crash potential and resulting damage. However, consumers were generally not aware of these safety requirements, which included, among others, installation of simple components that would reduce head trauma (laminated windshields), prevent injury to the upper body (collapsible steering columns), and prevent occupants from being ejected from the car on impact (stronger door locks). Consumer rights are also protected by local and state governments. For instance, establishing minimum safety standards to ensure highway safety is the responsibility of the individual states; and consumer complaints against specific businesses are often resolved with assistance from local consumer affairs offices.

Over the years, Nader and his associates formed several consumer watchdog groups and instigated activist movements. Included among these were the Critical Mass research project, which was directed at nuclear power's negative impact on citizens' health, and the Public Interest Research Group (PIRG), which addressed banking and corporate accountability as well as tax exemptions and government subsidies for big business.

Based on the initial successes of the PIRG, Nader formed the Public Citizen Tax Reform Research Group in 1972. The tax group's *People and Taxes* was the first publication to explain the manipulation of the tax system to subsidize big corporations, thereby burdening the average taxpayer. In 1976, after many successful tax-reform actions, Tom Stanton, and his colleagues Bob Brandon and Jonathan Rowe, published a succinct, understandable tax analysis: *Tax Politics: How They Make You Pay and What You Can Do About It.*

Nader and his Raiders have played major roles in addressing and resolving consumer matters involving, among others, consumers', workers', and airline passengers' rights; telecommunications; education; banking; automobile safety; environmental protection; and legal issues. Their campaigns, publications, and books have also resulted in the emergence of public opinion in support of environmental protection. Additionally, John C. Esposito's 1970 book, *The Vanishing Air*, presented the Clean Air Act of 1967 as having failed to initiate effective air pollution controls. At about the same time, the Environmental Protection Agency increased its focus on environmental issues, and the Clean Water Act (1972) was passed, both resulting from public reaction to the publication of David Zwick's *Water Wasteland*, which critiqued the failures of pollution-control laws. Further, in response to statistical findings in 1970 that worker deaths and disabilities totaled over 14,000 annually, Nader sponsored Joseph Page's report *Bitter Wages*, which helped turn the public and political tide toward enacting the Occupational Health and Safety Act legislation.

While OSHA has often been perceived by consumer activists as being slow to act or react, it has established standards that ensure business compliance with workplace safety mandates. Additionally, OSHA standards aid in reducing and, hopefully, minimizing cancer risks resulting from use of ordinary carcinogens, including industrial chemicals, such as benzene; pesticides, such as DBCP; ethylene oxide, a carcinogenic gas that is used for medical equipment sterilization; and formaldehyde, which is used in countless educational and industrial environments. All these standards stemmed from the work (from 1974 through 1983) of the Public Citizen Health Research Group headed by Dr. Sidney M. Wolfe.

Nader and his Raiders managed to pinpoint and report dozens of consumer inequities, including ones involving such corporations as Du Pont and Citicorp, but they have not been alone in the quest to establish and enforce consumer rights. Individuals and other traditional and newly established groups (such as the Rainforest Action Network, People for Ethical Treatment of Animals, Earth First) have used various means, including boycotts, to make their displeasure known to business, industry, and government entities. Manufacturers suffered from more than 200 boycotts in 1990 (Rice, 1990), and the numbers have continued to increase as technology has facilitated ease of information access.

Friedman (1995) defines a consumer boycott as an action that deprives the organization of sales, thus threatening its survival. Such action is "an attempt by one or more parties to achieve certain objectives by urging individual consumers to refrain from making selected purchases in the marketplace." (p. 199) Local, state, and international boycotts appear to be less common than national boycotts, and the duration of boycotts varies. Short-term boycotts usually last three months or less, whereas long-term boycotts sometimes last more than a year. Friedman (1995) also noted that boycott characteristics evolve over time. From the beginning announcement that a boycott is being considered, the level of militancy builds, and many media-oriented boycotts combine the power of the media with their own actions to achieve the desired outcome.

In 1994, protesters boycotted dairy products in an effort to prevent products from cows injected with BGH, a hormone to increase bovine milk production, from being marketed. The hormone has potential to create other medical complications, which could result in potential health risks to consumers. The FDA affirmed that the concerns expressed by boycott participants might be valid. Additionally, in response to the boycott, several national food distributors and grocery chains announced that they would not sell goods from BGH-treated cows.

In 1996, Consumers Union of the U.S., Inc., published its 60th anniversary article, which detailed consumer action victories over the preceding sixty years and affirmed the value of their publication *Consumer Reports*. This publication's mission is to detail the most urgent consumer issues. That article provided a listing of consumer issues perceived at that time to be most pressing: commercial clutter, health care, the information age, economic insecurity, the environment, and consumer rights.

As mentioned earlier, self-regulation through codes of ethical conduct and establishing, reviewing, and maintaining product standards has become essential for maintaining fruitful customer/organizational interaction. Self-regulation, has engendered creation of such consumer-focused organizations, as Better Business Bureaus, the International Business Ethics Institute, and the Internet Law and Policy Forum, to name a few. Additionally, self-regulation programs have been created, such as the Chemical Manufacturer Associations Responsible Care program and the standards of ethical conduct drafted by numerous professional organizations (e.g., American Bar Association, American Medical Association, Institute of Electrical and Electronic Engineers, and American Dental Association). While these self-regulation initiatives generally were responses to consumer concerns in the early days of consumer protest, industries subsequently began to self-regulate voluntarily and now view it a matter of course and as a complement to government regulation.

Today, the consumer movement continues pressuring for consumer protection against such problems as misleading advertising and defective products and for such benefits as safer food and drugs, and affordable utilities. As the level of activism grows greater, challenges are generated for businesses and industries, for some complaints are costly to resolve. In the past, the sides (activist versus business) became polarized, resulting in delayed resolution. Wise business and industry representatives, therefore, are not only proactively assuming responsibility for meeting activist-generated challenges, but also taking an active role in setting the public agenda for consumer concerns.

BIBLIOGRAPHY

"America: History and Life." (1980). http://serials.abc-clio.com/cgibin/nph-appframework/ABC-Clio.Serials.

American Civil Liberties Union. (1991)."The Bill of Rights: A Brief History." *ACLU Briefing Paper*. http://www.aclu.org/library/pbp9.html.

"Anthem Mergers Spark Protest." (1997). *Indianapolis Business Journal* 18(42):7.

"Bank-Bashing Goes Digital at Internet Gripe Sites." (1999). *American Banker* 164(58):1-2.

Better Business Bureau. (1999). "Dow Brands and Lever Brothers Prove Industry Self-Regulation Works." http://www.bbb.org/advertising/nad/nadlever.html.

Bollier, D. "Corporate Abuses, Consumer Power." (UK) In *Citizen Action* (Chapter 5). http://www.nader.org/history/bollier_chapter_5.html.

"Boycotting BGH." (1994). *Environmental Action* 26(1):9. http://gw4.epnet.com/fulltext.asp?...mer%20protests&fuzzyTerm=#FullText.

Brobeck, S. (1990). *The Modern Consumer Movement: References and Resources*. G. K. Hall.

Consumer Bankers Association. (1999). http://www.cbanet.org/.

"Consumer Rights." http://www.nolo.com.

"Consumer Rights." http://www.consumer.gld.gov.

Fair Credit Reporting Act. http://www.moody.af.mil/wg/ja/fcra.htm.

Fair Debt Collection Practices Act (FDCPA). http://www.consumeraid.org/debt.htm.

Friedman, M. (1995). "On Promoting a Sustainable Future Through Consumer Activism." *Journal of Social Sciences* 51(4):197-215.

Furger, R. (1999). "Washington Tackles Internet Law." *PC World Online*. http://www.pcworld.com/shared/printable_articles/0,1440,11862.00.html.

Garner, S. (1997). "Long March to Self-Regulation." *Network World Today*. http://www2.idg.com.au/nwwdb.NSF/8...666e54a2564de000eb51a?OpenDocument.

Historic Tours of America. (1999). "Boston Tea Party Ship and Museum." http://historictours.com/boston/teaparty.htm.

Internet Law and Policy Forum. (1999). "ILPF Announces Self-Regulation Initiative." http://www.ilpf.org/selfreg/announce.htm.

Jacob, J. A. (1997). "Consumer Protests Stall Blues Merger; Opposition Focuses on Loss of Charitable Assets." *American Medical News* 40(39):3-4.

King, A. and Lenox, M. (1999). "Industry Self-Regulation Without Sanctions: The Chemical Industry's Responsible Care Program" (working paper abstract). http://www.stern.nyu.edu/om/aking/workingpaper3.htm.

Miller, J. C., III. (1985). "The FTC and Voluntary Standards: Maximizing the Net Benefits of Self-Regulation." *Cato Journal* 4(3):897-903.

Massachusetts Nurses Association. (1996). More Than 1,000 People Turn Out for Patients Not Profits Forum ... Ralph Nader Encourages Nurses and Consumers to Become Allies for Quality Care. *Nursing*

Murphy, G. (1996). "The Bill of Rights Amendments 1-10 of the Constitution." http://leweb2.loc.gov/const/bor.html.

Nader, Ralph. (1999). "Overcoming the Oligarchy." (1999). *The Progressive* 63(1):58-61.

Noe, T. H., and Rebello, M. J. (1995). "Consumer Activism, Producer Groups, and Production Standards." *Journal of Economic Behavior & Organization*, 69-85.

Nowlan, J. "Self-Regulation Only Way out of Budget Hole and Social Malaise." http://jim.nowlan.nidus.net/selfgov.htm.

Office of Consumer Affairs. (1999). http://cher.eda.doc.gov/agencies/oca/index.html.

Pagan, R. D. (1989). "A New Era of Activism." *Futurist* May/June: 5.

"Right to Protest, The." (1999). http://www.geocities.com/SoHo/Workshop/1813/articles/daishowa.html.

"Role of Litagation and Alternatives Thereto in Consumer Activism, The." (1991). *Canada-United States Law Journal* 17:381-387.

Rotfeld, H. (1998). "Commentary: Misplaced Marketing—When Consumers or Society Are Not Satisfied." *Journal of Consumer Marketing* 15(6):523-524.

Stoffer, H. (1997). "Mitsubishi Hit with Whale of a Problem." (1997). *Automotive News* 71(5725):1-6.

"Six Key Issues: Then and Now." (1996). *Consumers Reports* 61(5)(May):6.

Stewart, T. A. (1989). "The Resurrection of Ralph Nader." *Fortune* (May): 106-111.

Watson, B. (1997). "Biggest Corvair Parts Supplier." *Daily Hampshire Gazette.* http://www.ziplink.net/users/mak/bac/articles/newspaper2.html.

Weidman, K. (1998). "Journalist-Turned-Educator Urges Media Self-Policing." *The Freedom Forum.* http.//www.freedomforum.org/newseumnews/1998/8/4thornton.asp.

"What's in a name?" (1992). *U.S. News & World Report* 112(10):17.

Worcester Polytechnic Institute. (1999). "Military Science: Boston Tea Party." http://www.wpi.edu/Academics/Depts/MilSci/BISI/abs_bostea.html.

MARY JEAN LUSH

CONTEMPORARY MANAGEMENT THOUGHTS

(SEE: *Management*)

CONTINGENCY MODEL

(SEE: *Management Styles*)

CONTINUING PROFESSIONAL EDUCATION

(SEE: *Professional Education*)

CONTRACTS

"A contract is a promise or a set of promises for the breach of which the law gives a remedy, or the performance of which the law in some way recognizes as a duty."

The freedom to contract has not existed throughout history. In medieval England, the courts did not engage in the enforcement of agreements between individuals. Rather, the feudal society that ruled personal interaction was relied upon for all forms of trade. As society evolved to emphasize individual freedoms over social caste, the ability to contract was viewed as a fundamental tenet of individual liberty. Writers and economic theorists such as Adam Smith, David Ricardo, Jeremy Bentham, and John Stuart Mill "successively insisted on freedom of bargaining as the fundamental and indispensable requisite of progress; and imposed their theories on the educated thought of their times."

Article I, Section 10 of the U.S. Constitution protects the individual right to contract by stating that, "No State shall . . . pass any . . . law impairing the obligations of Contracts." Many state constitutions contain similar provisions.

Generally, the law of contracts does not come from statutes passed by Congress or by state legislatures, but rather is a product of the common law, the continuing line of court decisions dating back to pre-colonial English courts. The common law is living and constantly evolving, as modern courts continue to analyze, revise and even disagree on its application. The American Law Institute, a collection of legal scholars and practitioners, attempted to catalogue the common law of contracts in its Restatements of the Law of Contracts in 1932. The Restatement, Second, of the Law of Contracts was published in 1979. The Restatement, although it does not have the force of law itself, is generally regarded as an excellent source. The law of contracts is also significantly influenced by the Uniform Commercial Code (UCC), which has been adopted in forty-nine states. The UCC is an attempt to standardize laws dealing with contracts and commerce. The UCC is beyond the scope of this article.

FORMATION OF A CONTRACT

A contract consists of one individual making an *offer*, another *accepting* the offer, and the existence of *consideration* between the contracting parties.

OFFER

An *offer* is the expression of a willingness to enter into a bargain. An offer must be directed to a particular offeree and be sufficiently clear so as to justify another individual in the belief that acceptance of the offer would constitute an agreement. Although an offer need not set forth all terms of the potential bargain (even the price may be left to be later determined), a valid offer must identify the fundamental elements of the proposed agreement. An offer may be revoked at any time before it is accepted or before it is reasonably relied upon by another individual.

ACCEPTANCE

Acceptance of an offer is the communication by the offeree of *mutual assent*, that is, the agreement to be bound by the terms of an offer. An offer may be accepted only by a person to whom the offer was directed and only before the offer terminates or is revoked. A valid acceptance must be communicated to the offeror by the same or similar means under which the offer was communicated, and must be unequivocal to make the agreement binding. At common law, it is generally held that any deviation from the terms of the offer is not an acceptance, but rather a rejection and a counteroffer. If the offer identifies a specific mode of acceptance, such as form, date, time, or place, that mode must be followed for an acceptance to be valid. Generally, an acceptance is not effective until it comes into the possession of the offeror, although some states employ the *mailbox rule*, which makes acceptance sent by U.S. mail effective upon its deposit in the mail. If an offer specifically invites acceptance by performance of a specified act, performance of that act by the offeree constitutes acceptance without notification of the offeror. Except in very limited circumstances, such as where the parties have a pattern of previous dealings or where it would be inequitable to find otherwise, silence does not constitute acceptance.

CONSIDERATION

An offer and acceptance alone do not create a valid and binding contract. A third element, *consideration*, must exist. Consideration is a *bargained-for exchange*, that is, the existence of *mutuality of obligation*. Both parties must derive some benefit—or, alternatively, both parties must experience some detriment or forbearance—for a contract to exist. Without consideration, an offer and acceptance represent merely a naked, unenforceable promise.

While the existence of consideration is critical to the enforceability of a contract, the quantity or quality of consideration is immaterial. Generally, courts are not concerned with the value or adequacy of consideration and will not interfere with a bargain entered into between the parties because of insufficient consideration. Certain acts or forbearance cannot constitute consideration. A preexisting duty to perform or refrain from performing may not be consideration for a contract. Therefore, fulfilling an existing contractual obligation or refraining from an unlawful act cannot constitute consideration. An exception to this rule is that the agreement to pay a preexisting debt may be consideration. A promise to make a gift is not consideration, nor is a moral obligation. A promise not to sue, so long as the right to sue actually exists, may be consideration.

DEFENSES

In its most basic form, a contract exists where there is an offer, an acceptance of the offer, and consideration to support the contract. Despite the existence of these three elements, enforcement of a contract may be denied if a sufficient *defense* to the formation of a contracts is present.

In order for an individual to enter into a contract, that person must have the legal *capacity* to do so. At common law, minors, individuals who are mentally ill, persons under the influence of alcohol or drugs and those under a legal guardianship lack legal capacity to contract. The rule as to minors is that a contract of a minor is *voidable*, not *void*. That is, a minor has the option to make a contract valid or not. However, if a minor enjoys the benefit of a contract, the minor is obligated either to repay the other party or to fulfill the minor's obligations under the contract. In addition to capacity, an individual must have the legal *competency* to enter a contract. Competency is generally defined as the mental ability of a party to contract. In other words, a legally competent person is one who possesses the ability to recognize and understand the contractual obligations that will result. Courts will assume that capacity and competency exist until it is proved otherwise.

If the parties to a contract make a *mutual mistake* with regard to that contract, such as a mutual misunderstanding, there is no mutual assent and therefore no contract. Clerical errors, known as *scrivener's errors*, will generally be corrected by a court. That is, rather than finding the contract invalid, the court will merely correct the error.

A contract that is based on a *fraudulent misrepresentation* of a material term is unenforceable. A fraudulent misrepresentation is material if the maker intended for the misrepresentation to induce the other party to enter the contract and if the misrepresentation would likely induce a reasonable person to so enter the contract.

Duress may make a contract unenforceable. Physical duress, or forcing a person to accept an offer, invalidates the contract, while the threat of physical harm makes the contract voidable at the election of the victim. Courts are divided on whether economic duress is sufficient to deny the enforceability of a contract.

A contract that is entered into under *undue influence* is also voidable at the election of the victim. Undue influence exists where one improperly takes advantage of one's relationship with another to coerce the other person to enter a contract. Examples are the influence that an adult child may have over an elderly parent who is dependent on the child for care, or the reliance of an unsophisticated individual on a sophisticated adviser, where the adviser is aware of the reliance.

As a general rule, an *illegal* bargain is void as a matter of law and may not be enforced. Therefore, a contract to commit murder, to rob a bank, or to steal a car is void as a matter of law.

A contract may be void because enforcement of the contract would be *unconscionable*. It is important to understand that mere disproportionality of the benefits of a contract, no matter how great, does not make the contract void as unconscionable. Unconscionability may be found only where there is grossly disproportionate bargaining power to the extent that one of the parties had virtually no choice in accepting the terms of the contract. Contracts are rarely found to be unconscionable unless a significant public policy issue is involved.

CONTRACT INTERPRETATION

An offer, acceptance, and consideration must be present to form a contract. The defenses to contract formation, as discussed above, may be used to show that no contract exists. However, even if it is shown that a contract does exist, questions may arise as to the content and meaning of that contract.

RULES OF CONSTRUCTION

In interpreting contracts, courts generally follow certain fundamental *rules of construction*. Under the *four corners rule*, courts will restrict their analyses to the written terms of the agreement itself, wherever possible. Ambiguities will be construed against the drafter. Courts will generally seek to harmonize the terms of a contract in a manner that makes those terms consistent. Courts will generally find that specifics in a contract will control over generalities. Words and phrases used in a contract are given their *plain meaning* absent evidence to the contrary.

PAROL EVIDENCE RULE

The *parol evidence rule* provides that if the parties to a contract intended for their contract to be a complete *integration*, that is, if the parties intended that the written agreement be the full extent of the understanding between them, then evidence other than the contract itself may not be admitted to contradict the written terms. Therefore, in interpreting a contract, the court should generally not look beyond the contract itself for interpretation. The parol evidence rule permits evidence intended to prove or disprove the legitimacy of contract formation, such as evidence showing a party's capacity or showing fraud or mutual mistake, but prohibits evidence intended to vary, contradict, or change the terms of the written agreement. Of course, if a contract refers to another document, that other document may be admitted to explain the terms of the contract at issue.

STATUTE OF FRAUDS

A common mistake is the belief that oral contracts are not enforceable. In fact, most oral contracts, if they fulfill all of the requirements of a contract, are indeed enforceable. However, the *statute of frauds* requires that in certain specific circumstances, contracts must be in writing. While the requirements vary from state to state, generally the statute of frauds requires the following contracts to be in writing: contracts by executors, administrators, or other personal representatives; contracts in consideration of marriage; contracts for the sale of real estate; contracts for the sale of goods exceeding $500; and contracts that will not be performed within one year of the making of the contract. The statute of frauds generally does not require any particular written form, and generally a contract will suffice so long as it identifies the parties, describes the subject matter, states the essential and material terms, states that consideration exists, and is signed by the party against whom enforcement is sought.

REMEDIES AND DAMAGES

Throughout this article, reference has been made to the court's enforcement of a contract. This, of course, begs the question of what course of action may be taken to enforce a contract, to repay the victim of a breach of contract, or to punish those who breach.

Generally, the victim of a breached contract is entitled to be made whole, or put in the same position as that party would have been in had the contract been fulfilled. Commonly, this is done by forcing the breaching party to pay the aggrieved party *compensatory damages*. Compensatory damages are intended to compensate the nonbreaching party for the actual damages suffered. Normally, compensatory damages are measured by the party's *expectancy*, or what the parties should have reasonably foreseen as flowing from the breach. Expectancy damages are often described as conferring the *benefit of the bargain* upon the nonbreaching party. Where expectancy damages are difficult to determine or otherwise impractical, a party may receive reliance damages, which are intended to compensate for the losses incurred in relying on the breaching party's fulfillment of the contract. A third alternative for compensation is *restitution*, where the breaching party must compensate the victim for the benefit conferred upon the breaching party.

Liquidated damages are a method used by contracting parties to estimate the damages that will result in the event of a breach. Liquidated damages may not serve as a penalty against the breaching party, but so long as they are a reasonable estimate of the damages that would be suffered by the nonbreaching party, they will be enforced. A clause in an apartment rental contract that requires a breaching party to pay two months rent is a common form of liquidated damages.

Punitive damages are those intended to punish the breaching party. Punitive damages are available only in very rare cases; they generally are not awarded in contract disputes.

Finally, *equitable relief* is available to nonbreaching parties where none of the above remedies would be sufficient. Under the concept of equity, a court may take corrective action other than by awarding money. In rare circumstances where none of the above described compensatory damages would be sufficient, a court may order *specific performance*. That is, the court will order the parties to fulfill their obligations under the contract. This method is not favored because of the practical difficulty of enforcement, but in some cases, such as the purchase of real estate, art, and the like, it is the only remedy that is sufficient. Also available is an *injunction*, which is a court order preventing a party from taking further action, such as a continued breach of a contract.

KEITH A. BICE

COOPERATIVE

A *cooperative* (also referred to as a *co-op*) is a form of business ownership that consists of a group of people who have joined together to perform a business function more efficiently than each individual could do alone. The purpose of a cooperative is not to make a profit for itself, but to improve each member's situation. However, members of certain types of cooperatives do make a profit by selling their product and/or service to customers who are not co-op members.

Cooperatives can take many forms. For example, a group of single parents may decide to band together to provide a child-care facility so they will have reliable day care for their children. Each parent contributes a certain amount of money and/or time, and in exchange they all have a safe place to leave their children. A credit union is also a type of cooperative. The purpose of a credit union is not to make a profit for itself, but to help each member be more financially secure. By creating their own financial institution, members can receive a higher interest rate on the money they have placed in savings and receive a lower interest rate on loans. Retailers have also started establishing co-ops. Ace Hardware, for example, is a co-op of independent hardware store owners. By banding together, the hardware owners can share advertising costs and receive discounts for bulk ordering of materials and supplies. Sharing costs and discounts allows small hardware stores to compete with large chain hardware stores.

While cooperatives can be found in many different areas of the economy, they are most commonly found in the agricultural area. A group of farmers may band together to allow themselves to be more competitive and to achieve more economic power. Agricultural cooperatives allow members to save money on materials needed to produce and market their product, which means a larger profit margin for all members. Ocean Spray Cranberries, Inc., for example, is a cooperative of several hundred cranberry and citrus growers from all over the country. Other well known cooperatives include Blue Diamond, Sunkist, IGA (Independent Grocers Association), and Land-O-Lakes.

BIBLIOGRAPHY

Boone, Louis E., and Kurtz, David L. (1999). *Contemporary Business*, 9th ed. Orlando, FL: Harcourt Brace College Publishers.

Bounds, Gregory M., and Lamb, Charles W., Jr. (1998). *Business*. Cincinnati, OH: South-Western College Publishing.

Madura, Jeff. (1998). *Introduction to Business*. Cincinnati, OH: South-Western College Publishing.

National Cooperative Business Association. http://www .ncba.org/index.cfm. 1999.

Nickels, William G., McHugh, James M., and McHugh, Susan M. (1999). *Understanding Business*, 5th ed. Boston Irwin-McGraw-Hill.

Pride, William M., Hughes, Robert J., and Kapoor Jack R. (1999). *Business*, 6th ed. New York: Houghton Mifflin.

MARCY SATTERWHITE

COOPERATIVE ADVERTISING

(SEE: *Advertising*)

IGA employees. The Independent Grocers Association is one example of a cooperative business group.

COPYRIGHTS

A copyright gives the owner the exclusive right to reproduce, distribute, perform, display, or license original material. Further, the owner also receives the exclusive right to produce or license the production of derivatives of that material. In essence, a copyright provides protection to the owner guaranteeing that material cannot be copied without the owner's permission. Under the current law, materials are covered whether or not a copyright notice is attached and whether or not the material is registered.

Yet an exception exists for the *fair use* of the material. The fair use of copyrighted material includes such use as reproduction for purposes of criticism, comment, news reporting, teaching

The ACE Hardware name and logo are examples of copyrighted material.

(including multiple copies for classroom use), scholarship, or research and is not considered an infringement of a copyright. Thus, fair use allows an individual to reproduce the material for non-profit activities.

Originally, copyrights referred only to written materials. However, copyrights have been extended to include: (1) literary materials; (2) musical materials, including any accompanying words; (3) dramatic materials, including any accompanying music; (4) pantomimes and choreographic materials; (5) pictorial, graphic, and sculptural materials; (6) motion pictures and other audiovisual materials; (7) sound recordings; and (8) architectural materials. Thus, material must be original and published in a concrete medium of expression to be covered by a copyright. In other words, for material to be eligible for copyright protection, a tangible product must exist. Consequently, copyright protection does not extend to any original material for ideas, procedures, processes, systems, methods of oper-

ation, concepts, principles, or discovery, regardless of the form in which the material is described, explained, illustrated, or embodied.

The owner of a copyright has the right to do and authorize any of the following: (1) to reproduce the copyrighted material in copies; (2) to prepare derivative materials based on the original copyrighted material; (3) to distribute copies of the copyrighted material to the public by sale or other transfer of ownership, or by rental, lease, or lending; (4) in the case of literary, musical, dramatic, and choreographic materials, pantomimes, and motion pictures and other audiovisual materials, to perform the copyrighted material publicly; and (5) in the case of literary, musical, dramatic, and choreographic materials, pantomimes, and pictorial, graphic, or sculptural materials, including the individual images of a motion picture or other audiovisual materials, to display the copyrighted material publicly.

The *Berne Convention* was a convention for the protection of literacy and artistic materials and the *Universal Copyright Convention* is a convention to provide for the adequate and effective protection of the rights of authors and other copyright proprietors in literary, scientific, and artistic materials, which includes writings; musical, dramatic, and cinematographic materials; and paintings, engravings, and sculpture. As a result, international guidelines for identifying materials that were subject to copyright protection were established, and those guidelines included an administrative process for redress if an author believed material to be reproduced without permission. Not only were the materials subject to copyright protection expanded from written materials to audiovisual materials; pictorial, graphic, or sculptural materials; architectural materials; collective materials; and compilation materials; but reproduction of materials was refined to include performing or displaying material as well as transmitting the work without the author's permission. The United States joined the Berne Convention for the Protection of Literary and Artistic Materials in 1989.

The federal agency charged with administering the act is the Copyright Office of the Library of Congress. As previously mentioned, materials are subject to copyright protection with or without copyright notice attached to the material. To obtain a copyright for an original work, an application for copyright registration should be filed with the Register of Copyrights in the Copyright Office of the Library of Congress. The application requests the following information: (1) the name and address of the author of the material; (2) in the case of materials other than anonymous of pseudonymous work, the name and nationality or domicile of the author or authors and, if one of more of the authors is deceased, the dates of their deaths; (3) if the work is anonymous or pseudonymous, the nationality or domicile of the author or authors; (4) in the case of material made for hire, a statement to that effect; (5) if the copyright claimant is not the author, a brief statement of how the claimant obtained ownership of the copyright; (6) the title of the work, together with any previous or alternative titles under which the material may be identified; (7) the year in which creation of the work was completed; (8) if the work has been published, the date and nation of its first publication; (9) in the case of a compilation or derivative material, an identification of any preexisting material(s) that it is based upon, and a brief, general statement of the additional materials covered by the copyright claim being registered; and (10) in the case of published documents containing materials manufactured in the United States, the names of the individuals or organizations who performed the manufacturing process and the location where the manufacturing process was performed. Simply, an author of an original work must file the required information and form to register the copyright with the Register of Copyrights in the Copyright Office of the Library of Congress. The appropriate fee must accompany the form to register the copyright. In addition, the Copyright Office of the Library of Congress has been charged with overseeing the copyright process and reviewing any reported violations. While this office has the major responsibility for adjudicating any alleged copyright violations, the U.S. Supreme Court and the U.S. Circuit Courts of Appeals have both rendered decisions affecting copyrights.

RANDY L. JOYNER

CORPORATE EDUCATION

Civilization has entered the Information Age, where business is knowledge-driven. Industries whose product lines either provide knowledge (e.g., software, information technology, and biotechnology) or process knowledge (e.g., telecommunications, banking, and advertising) place an increasing emphasis on speed, flexibility, technical expertise, and innovation. Consequently, it is imperative to the survival of any business organization to continually upgrade the knowledge base and skill levels of its work force in order to keep up with the ever-changing demands of the global marketplace and advances in technology.

A corporation's future is determined largely by its involvement in the development of its intellectual resources. Enterprises are growing and

A corporate outdoor training session in progress.

expanding the education segment of their business activity, realizing that without this input, they will quickly lose their competitive edge in a highly competitive global economy. Not only is continuing education vital to the future success of any organization; it is of equal importance that employees remain adaptable and agile learners in order to profit personally and professionally from available opportunities generated by this new economy. Investing in the right program, for the right people, at the right time will continue to be a challenge for businesses as they strategically attempt to capitalize on the vast opportunities available to them in the twenty-first century.

Another important reason for the continuing growth of corporate education is that many highly competitive businesses are abandoning the multilayered hierarchical organization in pursuit of a structure that empowers front-line workers with the authority to solve problems and make decisions in areas that affect their realms of expertise. Corporate restructuring, as well as high-

speed technological advances, gives employees broader responsibilities that require more skills and training for self-managed, cross-functional teams (Atkinson and Court, 1999).

TYPES OF CORPORATE EDUCATION

Independent Study Independent study is a growing trend in corporate education geared toward providing employees with interactive Web-based training, also known as virtual classrooms, from the comfort of their own desks. The Web reduces time and company costs by 50 percent over classroom training (Roberts, 1998). Employees are provided with the flexibility to learn at their convenience, at their own pace, and from most locations. This method is beneficial for those who lack the time to attend a regularly scheduled class and for those who are uncomfortable in traditional classroom situations where they would be expected to grasp concepts at the same rate as fellow classmates.

The value of an independent-study program is enhanced when used in conjunction with electronic mail, live chatroom discussions, and desktop videoconferencing. These additional tools and resources allow employees to participate in electronic discussion groups that serve to reinforce learning objectives. On-line learning via the virtual classroom relies more on students' learning from collaborative discussions and team projects than from lectures. As high-speed forms of communication media become available, CEOs of many large corporations are encouraging the training of their work force in on-line skills (Roberts, 1998). In terms of public image, these industries project awareness and competency in leading-edge technology, winning the confidence of customers and associates as well as commanding respect from rivals.

Apprenticeships and On-the-Job Training Apprenticeships are a form of on-the-job training whereby individuals with little or no knowledge of certain trades are prepared for occupations in skilled crafts and earn hourly wages as they learn. Experienced workers train employees to become, for example, accomplished electricians, machinists, operating engineers, and tool-and-die makers. Such programs incorporate a certain prescribed number of hours of related classroom instruction. Examples of coursework include safety, mathematics, schematic reading, and technical courses related to particular job requirements. "Statistics show that program graduates earn higher wages, have more stable work records, and are promoted more often than workers who have not been trained through apprenticeship programs" (Texas Workforce Commission, 1999).

Other on-the-job training programs are customized for participants who have some job-related skills but need to become more knowledgeable and proficient in a particular trade. As with apprenticeships, employees benefit because they are paid to learn. In addition, employers benefit from hosting on-the-job training programs because they have the full-time services of motivated individuals who are training to fulfill specific company needs. Participants also include

long-time employees who need to adapt to new technologies and procedures, "skills essential to the full and adequate performance of the job" (Texas Workforce Commission, 1999).

Traditional Classroom Instruction "Most organizations equate employee development with classroom training. Billions are spent providing classes—mostly classroom-based lectures—to employees at all levels. The material taught is mostly concepts, theories, approaches used by other organizations, and analysis of past events" (Wheeler, 1999). Traditional classroom instruction, however, is becoming obsolete. Whether classes are held in an on-site conference room or at an off-site facility, participants must attend regularly scheduled sessions that frequently interfere with work and personal obligations. In addition, the time spent in the classroom is often unproductive. Individuals who arrive at the specified time may spend several minutes waiting for the others in the class before the session commences. If the instructor is the only active participant, the training objective of the course eludes those required to attend. The lack of interactive learning causes students to lose their focus on the course content, become passive, daydream, and watch the clock.

Corporations with frequent employee turnover, such as the hotel and resort industry, find traditional classroom education to be inefficient, expensive, and pointless. This type of industry must train its staff in order to properly and uniformly satisfy customer service requirements; however, employees are usually seasonal workers, making repeat training an exhausting necessity. Also, tight budgets limit the number of corporate trainers available, creating additional problems for international chains. Lack of proper training prevents workers from doing their jobs well, which negatively impacts the business.

For the reasons explained above and many more, organizations are shifting from traditional classroom instruction to Web-based interactive training that actively involves students in the learning process. These programs are always accessible from designated worldwide locations and are easily modified to reflect cultural and language differences. Students may participate frequently and at their own convenience.

Unconventional Training Programs
Regardless of the method used, the training and education department of an organization should be designed to "maintain tighter ownership of learning outcomes in order to better meet corporate priorities" (Meister, 1999). Educational priorities are not always focused on implementing physical applications. Sometimes the purpose of training is to modify employee attitudes and work ethics, thereby transforming the internal corporate culture into one that is compatible with the corporation's external image and direction. Among the multitude of programs that may be appropriate for this type of application are leadership development, team building, and conflict resolution.

Corporate outdoor training, less conventional than the traditional classroom approach, is gaining in popularity with many international businesses as an informal yet meaningful method of conveying corporate values across a diverse range of cultures. "The outdoors provides a unique learning environment for individual challenge, personal development, and promoting beneficial team behaviors" (Brooks, 2000). Activities include ones such as canoeing, rafting, and climbing that incorporate initiative and problem-solving skills. "Teams provide a vehicle for people to become involved, learn from each other, and work toward constant improvement. Learning is most effective when it involves active participation" (Corporate Outdoor Training, 2000).

Another unconventional type of corporate education program emphasizes the usefulness of humor in the workplace. This program encourages employees, starting with upper management, to laugh and have fun, making work more enjoyable for everyone. The motivation behind this type of training is to create an atmosphere in which employees want to work, are proud of their contributions, and enjoy the company of co-workers. Participating organizations benefit from a reduction in stress-related absenteeism and an increase in work-force creativity and innovation. Many corporations have become suc-

cessful because they realized in the early stages of their development that a happy team is a winning team and that "work can be play, and play can be extremely productive" (LeBrun, 2000).

ONGOING VALUE OF EDUCATING WORKERS

Corporations cannot afford to become complacent in the belief that they possess an abundance of educated employees who are sufficiently familiar with existing technologies. As demonstrated throughout the last century, continuous technological developments altered the course of business from a process standpoint, outdating tools and business practices that were once considered useful, even state-of-the-art. As the world begins its journey through the increasingly competitive global economy of the twenty-first century, continuous employee education remains a critical component in determining an industry's ability to survive. Evolving information systems and peripheral equipment will further facilitate worldwide business communications and transactions, allowing instant access to many types of data from a variety of locations. Speed and proficiency in the use of these systems, which are attained mainly through continuous work-force education, will determine an industry's status within the business community.

It is unlikely that this trend will reverse. The human race is becoming accustomed to information-on-demand and, in the long run, technology is cost-efficient. According to Ken Bryant, Senior Business Specialist for Genicom Corporation, a Virginia-based printer manufacturer and network integration company, "With the growth of technology based businesses, especially within the burgeoning Internet marketplace, it is corporate suicide not to actively encourage and promote ongoing corporate training among staff. Technology companies have revolutionized marketing, customer service and many other facets of business, changing corporate culture and mandating an increasing level of competence. Lack of training, whether through traditional classes, continuing education venues, or informal work (help) groups, puts companies at a distinct disadvantage in global commerce" (personal communication, January 27, 2000). The most important goal of any corporation is to increase profits. Without an ongoing commitment to work-force education, businesses set themselves up for failure. Complacency insures that organizational goals will never be attained.

BIBLIOGRAPHY

Atkinson, R. D., and Court, R. H. (1999, April). *Corporate Expenditures on Training have Slightly Declined.* The New Economy Index: Foundations for Future Growth. http://www.dlcppi.org/ppi/tech/neweconomy_site/section3_page18.html.

Brooks, C. *Team Management Systems.* Corporate Outdoor Training: Teambuilding and Leadership Development. http://www.cot.com.au/cam.htm. January 28, 2000.

Corporate Outdoor Training. *Company Profile.* http://www.cot.com.au/profile.htm. January 28, 2000.

LeBrun, L. *Humour: The Missing Link in the Chain of Command.* http://www.partnersinrenewal.com/humour.htm. January 28, 2000.

Meister, J. C. *Innovators in Educating the Work Force.* Corporate Universities. http://www.fortune-sections.com/corporateuniversities/cu2.html. January 28, 2000.

Roberts, B. (1998, August). "://training via the desktop://." *HR Magazine.* http://www.shrm.org/hrmagazine/articles/0898tra.htm.

Texas Workforce Commission. (1999, November 1). *Apprenticeship in Texas: A Career Opportunity that Lets You Earn While You Learn.* http://www.twc.state.tx.us/svcs/apprentice.html.

Texas Workforce Commission. (1999, July 1). *On-the-Job and Customized Training.* http://www.twc.state.tx.us/svcs/ojtcust.html.

Wheeler, K. (1999, September 1). *If Developing People Is a Recruiting Strategy, What's Wrong with Corporate Education?* Corporate Universities and Human Capital. http://www.glresources.com/columns/if_developing_people_is_a.htm.

DIANE M. CLEVESY

CORPORATIONS

A business corporation is a legal entity permitted by law in every state to exist for the purpose of engaging in lawful activities of a business nature. It is an artificial person created by law, with many of the same rights and responsibilities possessed by humans. Corporations are widely prevalent in the United States; today, virtually every large enterprise is a corporation.

RIGHTS AND PRIVILEGES OF A CORPORATION

Within legal guidelines, corporations may issue stock, declare dividends, and provide owners with limited liability.

Stocks A corporation can issue and attempt to sell stock. Every share of stock owned represents a share of the corporation's ownership.

From the standpoint of stock sale, there are two kinds of corporations: public and private. With a public corporation, anyone can buy shares of stock, which may very well be traded on a stock exchange. With a private corporation, however, sale of stock may be limited to stipulated persons, such as members of the principal stockholder's family.

A corporation can own "treasury stock"; that is, it may repurchase its own stock that it had previously issued and sold.

A corporation may even give its stock away for any reason; for example, as a donation to a charity, or as a reward to employees for industrious service.

Dividends A corporate board of directors has the authority to declare and pay dividends in the form of cash or stock. Cash dividends are ordinarily payable from current net income, although net income "kept" from previous years may also be used. A common name for net income kept is "retained earnings." Recipients of stock dividends receive shares of stock in the corporation, thereby increasing the total number of shares they own. Stock dividends are declared from capital stock that has been authorized but not issued.

Rules exist regarding eligibility for receipt of a dividend. For example, assume that a cash dividend is declared on August 15, payable on September 15. If Stockholder A owns the stock on August 15, he or she receives the dividend on September 15. If Stockholder A sells the stock on August 27, Purchaser B buys it "ex-rights," meaning that on September 15 the dividend still goes to Stockholder A. Purchaser B would not receive a dividend until the next one is declared, perhaps on November 15.

Recipients of cash dividends pay income tax as of the year the dividends are received. Income tax on stock dividends, however, is postponed until the recipients sell the stock.

Occasionally, corporations split their stock. However, this does not change the value of the shareholder's shares on the corporation records or the corporation's net worth.

A stock split is often a good sign as it is often done to reduce the price of a stock that has risen to a point at which its marketability is impaired.

Limited Liability If a corporation suffers large financial losses or even terminates its existence, the shareholders might lose part or all of their total investment. However, that is ordinarily the extent of their loss. Creditors cannot satisfy their claims by looking to the personal assets of corporate shareholders as they can with a sole proprietorship or an ordinary partnership.

Limited liability can be advantageous because it encourages investment in the corporation. With personal assets of $1.1 million, a potential investor might willingly invest $50,000 in a corporation knowing that no risks exist beyond the $50,000.

The limited liability advantage, however, can be lost if the owners directly engage in the company's management and play an influential role in causing corporate losses.

Additional Rights of a Corporation Corporations have the basic right to conduct a business in which they sell products or services and to engage in either a profit-seeking or a non-profit-seeking enterprise.

Corporations have the right to own, sell, rent, or lease real or personal property.

Corporations may sue other business entities, such as another corporation, a partnership, or a sole proprietorship.

Corporations may merge with other corporations.

Example of Stock Split

2 for 1 Stock Split	Smith, A Shareholder Owns	Value of Smith's Shares on Corporation Records	
		Per Share	Total Value
Before	100 shares	$80	$8,000
After	200 shares	$40	$8,000

Corporations may make contracts with either another business or a person.

Corporations may hire or discharge employees of any rank, from entry-level employees to the chief executive officer (CEO).

Corporations may borrow money, and they often do so by issuing corporate bonds. Owning a corporate bond does not grant the bondholder any form of ownership in the company. Instead, corporate bondholders have actually loaned money to the corporation, virtually always with a stated interest rate and with terms regarding dates and methods of repayment. Bondholders may ordinarily sell their bonds to other persons, most often through stockbrokers.

In addition to issuing bonds, corporations may borrow directly from any loan source, such as banks. On occasion, corporations raise needed cash by authorizing and selling additional stock.

Corporations may make any lawful investment. They often invest in the stock and/or bonds of other corporations, personal or real property, mutual funds, money market accounts, certificates of deposit, and government securities.

REQUIREMENTS OR LIMITATIONS OF A CORPORATION

Corporations are subject to risk, to suits, and to income tax liabilities.

Risk By engaging in business activities, corporations are at risk, great or small. Profit-seeking corporations may very well find the large profits they seek. But they risk huge economic losses and even bankruptcy.

Suits Corporations may be sued by any business, including other corporations. And they may be sued by individuals or groups of persons.

Income Tax Corporations must pay federal and state income taxes on the net profit they make during a calendar or fiscal year. People who receive cash dividends must also pay income tax for the year they are received. Thus it is often said that corporation profits are subject to double taxation. Corporations receive no deduction for any cash dividends that they pay. Recipients of stock dividends, however, postpone payment of income tax on stock dividends until they sell the stock.

REGULATION OF CORPORATIONS

Corporations are subject to two kinds of regulation: (1) regulation by the state in which they are incorporated and (2) regulation by the individual corporation's articles of incorporation and bylaws.

State Regulation Corporations are regulated by business corporation laws that exist in all fifty states. Although the statutes prescribe what corporations may and may not do, they are written in broad and general language. In essence, then, the states permit articles of incorporation to be written in a manner that permits corporations to engage in business for almost any legal purpose.

Articles of incorporation are filed publicly and are available to the public. They are subject to amendment. Bylaws are not filed publicly. Consequently, they tend be more detailed than articles of incorporation.

Board of Directors Members of the board of directors make the major decisions of the corporation. When corporations are formed, they draw up Articles of Incorporation, usually for approval by shareholders. The board of directors also draws up the initial and ensuing bylaws.

Board members are most often shareholders and officers of the corporation. They are elected by the shareholders. They may be "internal" directors or, for reasons of good public relations or of obtaining of expertise, may work on the "out-side" and be selected on the basis of their prominent role in the community.

Policies made by the board of directors are carried out by the corporation's executives, who direct the work of employees under their jurisdiction.

CLASSES OF STOCK

Corporations ordinarily have two classes of stock: (1) common and (2) preferred. The two classes differ in many respects but both also share a number of common characteristics. There is no limit to how many classes of stock a corporation may have.

Common Stock Common stockholders participate more in the governance of a corporation than do preferred stockholders. This is accomplished by giving common stockholders the right to vote for members of the board of directors as well as on major decisions (e.g., a merger with another corporation). Common stock, however, can be issued without voting rights.

Cumulative voting, which permits shareholders to cast one vote for each share of common stock owned in any combination, is prevalent. In an election for members of the board of directors, for example, a shareholder owning 2000 shares of common stock could cast all 2000 votes for one candidate or divide them in any way among candidates (e.g., 400 votes each for five candidates). Cumulative voting offers some protection for smaller stockholders.

The market value of common stock tends to fluctuate more than that of preferred stock.

Preferred Stock Preferred stockholders are not ordinarily granted the voting rights given to common stockholders. They cannot participate in elections for members of the board of directors or in major decisions of the corporation.

However, preferred stockholders are almost always given prior rights over common stockholders in the matter of dividends.

Dividends for preferred stockholders are often stated in advance and do not tend to fluctuate as much as those for common stock. Preferred dividends may be stated as a percentage of par value or as a dollar amount per share.

However, preferred dividends are not guaranteed in the same sense as is bond interest. Neither preferred nor common stock dividends can be paid without approval of the board of directors. And boards may "skip" declaring dividends if the directors feel the financial situation so warrants.

Preferred stock is often "cumulative." With this provision, a preferred stock dividend that is not declared or paid is considered to be "owed." As long as the preferred dividend is "owed," no common stock dividend may ordinarily be declared or paid. But even if the preferred stock is not cumulative, a frequently applied policy is that common stock dividends cannot be declared as long as the preferred dividends are "in arrears."

Sometimes preferred stock is "convertible." Shareholders who own convertible preferred stock may, at a price announced when the stock is purchased, turn in their preferred stock and receive common stock in its place. Assume, for example, that an investor purchases preferred stock at $36.50 per share. The stock is convertible four years from its issuance at a ratio of 3:1; that is, three shares of preferred stock can be traded at the shareholder's option for one share of common stock. At the 3:1 ratio, after discounting any related transfer costs, the preferred stockholder would find it profitable to convert if the common stock value rises above $109.50 per share ($36.50 × 3).

Preferred stock may be "callable." At the option of the corporation, callable preferred stock may be surrendered to the corporation, usually at a price a little above par value (or a stated value). If the stated value is $50, the callable price on or after a specified date might be $51.25. If the stock's market value rises to, say, $55, it might be profitable for the corporation to call for its surrender.

Occasionally preferred stock is given the right to "participate" with common stock in being granted dividends above a stated value. For example, assume the board of directors declares a regular preferred stock dividend at $3 per share

and a common stock dividend at $13 per share. With participating rights, it would have been stipulated that preferred stockholders would receive $1 per share more for every additional $5 given to common stockholders.

If a corporation closes down its operation, preferred stockholders have prior claim over common stockholders upon dissolution of the assets. A sufficient amount of the corporation's assets would need to be turned over to the preferred stockholders before common stockholders could claim any part of the assets. In practice, however, assets of a closed-down corporation are rarely sufficient to pay off the preferred shareholders in full.

RELATED FORMS OF BUSINESS OWNERSHIP

Five types of business entities have regulations similar to those of corporations.

Professional Corporations Professional corporations, organized under corporation laws of their respective states, involve incorporation by persons engaged in professional practice, such as medical doctors, lawyers, and architects. They are granted limited liability against claims from their clients, except for malpractice.

Not-for-Profit Corporations Not-for-profit corporations, formed under the nonprofit laws of their respective states, have members instead of stockholders. Any income made cannot be distributed to the members.

Some apply to the Internal Revenue Service for tax-exempt status, becoming "501(c)(3)" organizations, which permits donor gifts to be declared tax-deductible.

Closed Corporations Closed corporations, not permitted by statute in all states, limit shareholders to fifty. They permit the firm to operate informally either by eliminating the board of directors or curtailing its authority. Closed corporations also restrict transferability of the owners' shares of stock.

Limited-Liability Companies Limited-liability companies enjoy the benefits of limited liability while being taxed like a general partnership.

Owners' net income is taxed at an individual personal rate rather than at the rate of a corporation (taxation of both corporate net income and dividends).

Not all states permit formation of limited-liability companies. They are neither a partnership nor a corporation. They generally have a limited life span. Management must be by a small group. States do not restrict the number or the type of members. Unlimited transferability of ownership is not permitted.

S Corporations S corporations' major benefit is that they are taxed like partnerships. The owners' income tax is based on their share of the firm's total net income, whether or not it is distributed to them. The second huge benefit is limited liability.

However, an S corporation is limited to thirty-five shareholders, none of whom can be nonresident aliens. Only one class of stock may be issued or outstanding. The S corporation may own only 80 percent of a subsidiary business firm.

BIBLIOGRAPHY

Dicks, J. W. (1995). "Corporation." In J. W. Dicks, *The Small Business Legal Kit and Disk.* Holbrook, MA: Adams Medica Corporation.

Snifen, Carl R. J. (1995). *The Essential Corporation Handbook.* Grants Pass, OR: Oasis Press/Psi Research.

G. W. MAXWELL

COST ACCOUNTING

(SEE: *Accounting*)

COST ALLOCATION

A cost is generally understood to be that sacrifice incurred in an economic activity to achieve a specific objective, such as to consume, exchange, or produce. All types of organizations—businesses, not-for-profits, governmental—incur costs. To achieve missions and objectives, an organization acquires resources, transforms them in some manner, and delivers units of product or service to its customers or clients. Costs are incurred to perform these activities. For planning and control, decisions are made about areas such as pricing, program evaluation, product costing, outsourcing, and investment. Different costs are needed for different purposes. In each instance, costs are determined to help management make better decisions.

When incurred, costs are initially reviewed and accumulated by some classification system. Costs with one or more characteristics in common may be accumulated into cost pools. Costs are then reassigned, differently for specified purposes, from these cost pools to one or more cost objects. A cost object is an activity, a unit of product or service, a customer, another cost pool, or a segment of an organization for which management needs a separate measurement and accumulation of costs. Costs assigned to a cost object are either direct or indirect. A direct cost can be traced and assigned to the cost object in an unbiased, cost-effective manner. The incurrence of an indirect cost cannot be so easily traced. Without such a direct relationship to the cost object, an indirect cost requires an in-between activity to help establish a formula relationship. When the indirect cost is assigned through the use of this formula, the cost is considered allocated. The activity used to establish the in-between linkage is called the basis of allocation.

TYPES OF ALLOCATIONS

Cost allocations can be made both within and across time periods. If two or more cost objects share a common facility or program, the cost pool of the shared unit is a common cost to the users and must be divided or allocated to them. Bases of allocation typically are based on one of the following criteria: cause-and-effect, benefits derived, fairness, or ability to bear. The selection of a criterion can affect the selection of a basis. For example, the allocation of the costs of a common service activity across product lines or programs based on relative amounts of revenue is an ability to bear basis, whereas the same allocation based on the relative number of service units consumed by each product line or program would reflect either the benefits derived or the cause-and-effect criteria. Cost allocation then is the assignment of an indirect cost to one or more cost objects according to some formula. Because this process is not a direct assignment and results in different amounts allocated depending on either the basis of allocation or the method (formula) selected, some consider cost allocation to be of an arbitrary nature, to some extent.

Costs of long-lived assets are allocated and reclassified as an expense across two or more time periods. For anything other than land, which is not allocated, the reclassification of tangible assets is called depreciation (for anything other than natural resources) or depletion (for natural resources) expense. The bases for these allocations are normally either time or volume of activity. Different methods of depreciation and depletion are available. The costs of long-lived intangible assets, such as patents, are allocated across time periods and reclassified as amortization expense. The basis for these allocations is normally time.

Cost allocations within a time period are typically across either organizational segments known as responsibility centers or across units of product or service or programs for which a full cost is needed. Allocations may differ depending on whether a product or program is being costed for financial reporting, government contract reimbursement, reporting to governmental agencies, target pricing or costing, or life-cycle profitability analysis. Allocations to responsibility centers are made to motivate the centers' managers to be more goal-congruent in their decisions and to assign to each center an amount of cost reflective of all the sacrifices made by the overall organization on behalf of the center. These allocations can be part of a price or transfers of cost pools from one department to another.

ETHICAL CONSIDERATIONS

Allocations can involve ethical issues. Often the federal government issues contracts to the private sector on a cost-plus basis; that is, all the actual costs incurred to complete a contract plus a per-centage of profit is reimbursed to the contractor performing the contract. A contractor completing both governmental and private-sector contracts may select a formula that tends to allocate more indirect costs to governmental contracts than to nongovernmental ones. A contractor may also try to include in reimbursement requests costs that are not allowable by the governmental agency. A contractor may even try to double-count a cost item by including it as a direct cost of the contract and as a part of an indirect cost pool allocated to the contract. Lastly, a contractor may attempt to have a reimbursement cover some of the costs of unused capacity. Audits are made of costs of government contracts to identify inappropriate costs.

SERVICE FIRMS, NOT-FOR-PROFIT ORGANIZATIONS, AND MERCHANDISERS

Service and not-for-profit organizations allocate costs, too. The cost object can be a unit of service, an individual client, or a cluster (category) of clients. The costs of a service firm are typically professional labor and indirect costs in support of the labor. The basis for allocating these indirect costs is often professional labor hours (either billable or total) or the cost of such, reflective of either cause-and-effect or benefits-received criteria. For not-for-profit organizations, the proportions to be allocated are best figured in terms of units of the resource on hand, such as the number of full-time equivalents, amount of square footage, or number of telephone lines. An important point to remember is that the principles of allocation are the same for for-profit and not-for-profit organizations. The only difference is that the cost objects will be dissimilar.

Merchandisers, unlike most service and not-for-profit organizations, have inventory that must be costed for external and internal reporting purposes. In these cases, the cost object is a unit of inventory. Incidental costs associated with the acquisition and carrying of the inventory are mostly direct costs easily traceable clearly assignable to the entire inventory, if not to individual units.

MANUFACTURERS

Manufacturers need to cost the resources required to complete their products. In costing a unit of product for inventory valuation, costs of production are assigned. With the unit of product as the cost object, production costs are either direct costs (traceable usage of materials and labor) or indirect costs (all of the other production costs, referred to as overhead). The indirect production costs are allocated. Traditionally, manufacturers using labor-intensive technologies used a single basis of allocation based on labor, either in hours or in cost, associated with a single indirect cost pool. A manufacturer using a more capital intensive technology might use a nonlabor basis such as machine hours. Today many firms produce a varied set of products, using varied technologies with many levels of complexity. Such firms need a more refined cost assignment system that uses multiple bases of allocation with multiple indirect cost pools, such as activity based costing.

While for product costing a unit of output remains the final cost object, the technology a producer uses can require a cost assignment to an intermediate cost pool (object) prior to an assignment to a unit of output. For instance, a batch technology has a cost assignment first to an individual job order (batch); the total cost assigned to the job order is then unitized over the units in the batch to determine cost of one unit of output. Alternatively, for a given period in a process technology, costs are accumulated by (assigned to) each production process; the total cost assigned is then unitized across the total number of (equivalent) units produced by that process to cost-out a unit of output.

Manufacturers also incur service department costs (such as computer center costs) in support of production departments. These service department costs are indirect to a unit of production and for full costing must be allocated, first to respective production areas and then to the units of output. Such allocations are called service department allocations, and the basis of allocation is normally an activity reflective of the nature of demands made on the service department by other departments, both service and production.

JOINT PRODUCTION ALLOCATIONS

Allocations are also required in a joint production process. When two or more separately identifiable final products initially share a common joint production process, the products are called joint products. The point at which they become separately identifiable is referred to as the split-off point. Manufacturing costs incurred prior to this split-off point are referred to as joint costs and need to be allocated across the different joint products for product costing purposes. The bases for allocating the joint costs typically include (1) relative sales value at split-off, (2) net realizable value at split-off (as an approximation of the sales value at split-off), (3) final sales value at the completion of the production process, and (4) the number of physical units of the joint products at split-off.

Many would consider this list of bases to be in an order of descending preference of use. Normally there are additional production costs beyond the split-off point. These additional costs are incurred in order to complete each joint product. For a given joint product, the net realizable value at split-off is calculated by subtracting the additional costs to complete from the final sales value of the finished joint product.

SERVICE DEPARTMENT (RE)ALLOCATIONS

There are three basic methods to allocate service department costs to production departments or programs in a not-for-profit: (1) the direct method; (2) the step method; and (3) the reciprocal method. The basis for allocation of service area costs should ideally be causally related to the demands made on that area by other areas. Both cause-and-effect and benefits-received criteria are taken into account. If the service areas provide service to each other (referred to as reciprocal services), the reciprocal method is the most accurate, the step method next, and the direct method the least accurate. With different service and production departments as cost objects, costs are initially accumulated on a department-by-department basis. Departments working directly on programs or units of product or service are production departments. The other departments are service departments. The allocation problem then is to reassign service department costs to production departments or programs for both performance evaluation and product or program costing. Within a production department, these allocated service costs are then reallocated to units of service or product according to the bases of allocation that each respective production department uses for its indirect costs.

The direct method ignores reciprocal services. A service department's costs are allocated to the production departments according to the extent to which each production department uses (or, for budgeting purposes, intends to use) the services of the service department. This "extent" is determined on a percentage basis by either the amount of services actually provided by the service department to all the production departments or by the amount of services the service department is capable of providing at normal or full capacity. Variable and fixed costs may be allocated separately, resulting in a dual allocation process (for example, variable costs based on actual usage and fixed costs based on budgeted usage).

The step method partially takes reciprocal services into account by allocating service department costs to production departments on a sequential basis. The service department that provides the greatest amount of service to the other service departments is allocated first; the one providing the second greatest amount of service to the other service departments is allocated second; and so forth. The absolute dollar amounts of costs incurred within service departments can be used to break a tie in usage, the larger amount allocated first. Once a service department has been allocated, it is ignored for all subsequent allocations.

The reciprocal method takes into account all the reciprocal services by setting up a set of simultaneous equations, one equation per service department. For any given service department, its equation is: Total allocable cost = direct costs of the service department + costs allocated from each of the other service departments based on this department's use of the other service departments. Once these equations are solved, the resultant allocable cost (sometimes referred to as the reciprocal or artificial cost) is reallocated across all the other departments, service and production, according to the original percentage usages.

Two additional issues, fairness and acquiring the service from the inside or from the outside, concern the allocation of a common cost. The amount of common service cost allocated to a using department may be greater that what it would cost that department to obtain the same service from the outside. A variation of the reciprocal method provides an analysis to help the manager of a using department decide whether to obtain the service from another department within the organization or to contract outside for the service from another organization. The amount of a particular service department's cost allocated to a using department may be dependent on the extent to which other departments also use this service department. This does not seem to be fair.

(SEE ALSO: *Accounting*; *Costs*)

BIBLIOGRAPHY

Blocher, Edward J., Chen, Kung H., and Lin, Thomas W. (1999). *Cost Management: A Strategic Emphasis.* New York: Irwin/McGraw-Hill.

Brown, Clifford D. (1999). *Accounting and Reporting Practices of Nonprofit Organizations—Choices and Applications.* New York: American Institute of Certified Public Accountants.

Horngren, Charles T., Foster, George, and Datar, Srikant M. (2000). *Cost Accounting: A Managerial Emphasis.* Upper Saddle River, NJ: PrenticeHall.

Ijiri, Yuji. (1975). *Theory of Accounting Measurement.* Sarasota, FL: American Accounting Association.

Kaplan, Robert S., and Atkinson, Anthony A. (1989). *Advanced Management Accounting.* Englewood Cliffs, NJ: Prentice-Hall.

Statements on Management Accounting (4B): Allocation of Service and Administrative Costs. (1985). Montvale, NJ: National Association of Accountants.

Willson, James D., and Colford, James P. (1990). *Controllership: The Work of the Managerial Accountant.* New York: Wiley.

LAWRENCE A. KLEIN
CLIFFORD BROWN

COST-BENEFIT ANALYSIS

Cost-benefit analysis is used for determining which alternative is likely to provide the greatest return for a proposed investment. Sometimes referred to as cost-effectiveness analysis, it is relevant to businesses as well as to not-for-profit entities and governmental units.

A business might find it helpful to use cost-benefit analysis to determine if additional funds should be invested in a facility in the home country or in another country. A community not-for-profit organization that provides a variety of programs for children might use cost-benefit analysis to assist management in determining which activities will provide the most services for the costs specified. A federal governmental agency might use cost-benefit analysis to determine which of several projects planned for the national parks is likely to be most used, given the costs, by interested citizens.

Because resources such as money and time are limited, an organization usually cannot undertake every project proposed. To decide whether to undertake a project, decision makers weigh the benefits from the project against the cost of the resources it requires, normally approving a project when its benefits exceed its costs. Cost-benefit analysis provides the structure and support for making such decisions.

Benefits increase the welfare of the organization. Some benefits are monetary benefits, such as the dollar amount of cash inflows from additional sales of a product or the saving in cash outflows that a project enables. Other benefits are important but harder to quantify. For example, a project may increase customer satisfaction; increased customer satisfaction may increase future sales, but the exact relationship between sales and satisfaction is often hard to specify.

Costs are the outlays or expenditures made in order to obtain a benefit. Many costs are measured monetarily, such as the cost of buying a new machine or of hiring an additional employee.

COST-BENEFIT ANALYSIS IN BUSINESS

A cost-benefit analysis is straightforward when all costs and benefits are measurable in monetary terms. Assume that Company A must decide whether to rent an ice cream machine for the summer for $900. The ice cream machine will produce additional cash inflows of $1,000 during the summer. The benefit of additional cash inflows ($1,000) exceeds the additional cost ($900), so the project should be undertaken. Not all cost-benefit analyses are this simple, however. If the benefits and costs occur in different time periods, it may be necessary to discount the future cash flows to their equivalent worth today.

In another example, cost savings is a benefit. Assume that Company B makes about 100,000 photocopies a year. Company B does not have its own copy machine and currently pays 4 cents per copy, or $4,000 a year, to Copycat Copiers. Company B can lease a copy machine for $2,500 a year. It must also pay 2 cents per page for paper for the leased machine, or $2,000. In this example, the cost of leasing the machine and buying paper ($2,500 + $2,000 = $4,500) exceeds the benefit of saving the $4,000 normally paid to Copycat Copiers. Company B should continue to use Copycat Copiers for its photocopies. However, Company B must have a pretty good estimate of the number of copies it needs to be comfortable with its decision. If Company B needs 150,000 copies this year instead of 100,000, the cost of the leasing the machine and buying paper ($2,500 + $3,000 = $5,500) is cheaper than the $6,000 (150,000 × $0.04) savings in fees to Copycat Copiers.

A third example involves a project with benefits that are difficult to quantify. Assume that Company C is deciding whether to give a picnic costing $50,000 for its employees. Company C would receive the benefit of increased employee morale from the picnic. Better employee morale might cause employees to work harder, increasing profits. However, the link between increased morale and increased monetary profits is tenuous. The decision maker must use his or her judgment to compare the nonmonetary benefit to the monetary cost, possibly deciding that increased employee morale is worth the $50,000 cost but would not be worth a $100,000 cost.

In the preceding examples, cost-benefit analysis provided a framework for decision making. The range of objectivity related to measurement of the factors is typical. Techniques used in business as a basis for determining costs and benefits, such as return on investment, are generally quantifiable and thus appear to be objective. However, it is not uncommon for qualitative factors to enter into the decision-making process. For example, providing a product that individuals with limited incomes will be able to purchase may not provide the highest monetary return on investment in the short run, but might prove to be a successful long-term investment. Careful decision makers attempt to deal with a difficult-to-quantify factor in as objective a manner as possible. However, cost-benefit analysis in most situations continues to introduce measurement problems.

COST-BENEFIT ANALYSIS IN NONBUSINESS ENTITIES

Cost-benefit analyses are also common in non-business entities. Boards of not-for-profit organizations establish priorities for their programs, and such priorities often specify desired program outputs. For example, assume a not-for-profit organization is interested in reducing the level of illiteracy among the citizens of a rural community in a state that has one of the lowest per-capita incomes in the United States. As alternative programs for those who need to learn to read are considered, there will be cost-benefit analyses that focus on a number of factors, including the extent to which a particular program can attract those who are illiterate. A program in the downtown area of a small town might be considered because a facility is available there at low cost—and that low cost is appealing. Focus on cost is

not sufficient, however. When benefits are considered, it might become clear that those who are eager for such a program do not have cars and that there is no public transportation from where they reside to the center of the small town. Further consideration of relevant factors and of alternatives, undertaken in good faith, should result in cost-benefit analyses that provide valuable information as the agency makes decisions.

At all levels of government in the United States, cost-benefit analyses are used as a basis for allocating resources for the public good to those programs, projects, and services that will meet the expectations of citizens. For example, decision makers at the federal level who have policy responsibility for environmental standards, air-quality rules, or services to the elderly often find information from cost-benefit analyses to be critical to the decision-making task.

CONTINUING EFFORTS TO QUANTIFY COST-BENEFIT FACTORS

As possibilities for the use of funds increase, there is motivation for better measurement of both costs and benefits as well as for speedier ways of accomplishing analyses for alternatives that are appealing. All types of entities—businesses, not-for-profit organizations, and governmental units—strive to improve the measurments used in cost-benefit analyses. The capabilities of electronic equipment provide promising assistance in accumulating data relevant for analyses. Wise use of resources is an important goal in every organization; cost-benefit analyses make a key contribution to this goal. Therefore, attention is given to improving both the effectiveness and efficiency of such analyses.

BIBLIOGRAPHY

Boardman, Anthony, E. (1996). *Cost-Benefit Analysis: Concepts and Practice.* Upper Saddle River, NJ: Prentice-Hall.

Nas, Tevik F. (1996). *Cost-Benefit Analysis: Theory and Application.* Thousand Oaks, CA: Sage Publications.

MARY MICHEL
MARY ELLEN OLIVERIO

COST OF LIVING INDEX

(SEE ALSO: *Consumer Price Index*)

COSTS

The word *cost* appears in many terms, some with subtle distinctions in meaning, used in accounting, economics, and business. The single word *cost* rarely has a clear meaning. (Neither does the word *value* have a clear meaning. Avoid using *value* without a modifying adjective, such as *market* or *present* or *book*.) The word *cost*, without modifying adjectives, typically means the sacrifice, measured by the price paid or required to be paid, to acquire goods or services. Hence, the single word *cost* often carries the meaning more precisely represented by the following.

> *acquisition cost. historical cost.* Net price plus all expenditures to ready an item for its intended use at the time the firm acquired the item. The other expenditures might include legal fees, transportation charges, and installation costs.

Accountants can easily measure acquisition cost, but economists and managers often find it less useful in making decisions. Economists and managers more often care about some measure of current costs, which accountants find harder to measure.

> *current cost.* Replacement cost or net realizable value.
>
> *replacement cost.* Acquisition cost at the date of measurement, typically the present, in contrast to the earlier date of acquisition.
>
> *net realizable value.* The amount a firm can collect in cash by selling an item, less the costs (such as commissions and delivery costs) of disposition.

When accountants use a notion of current cost, they most often refer to *fair value.*

> *fair value.* Price negotiated at arm's length between willing buyers and willing sellers,

each acting rationally in their own self-interest. Sometimes measured as the present value of expected cash flows. [See the entry **Time value of money.**]

Accountants often contrast (actual) historical cost with *standard cost.*

> *standard cost.* An estimate of how much cost a firm should incur to produce a good or service. This measurement plays a role in cost accounting, in situations where management needs an estimate of costs incurred before sufficient time has elapsed for computation of actual costs incurred.

The following terms desegregate historical cost into components.

> *variable cost.* Costs that change as activity levels change. (The term *cost driver* refers to the activity that causes cost to change.) Strictly speaking, variable costs are zero when the activity level is zero. Careful writers use the term *semivariable costs* to mean costs that increase strictly linearly with activity but have a positive value at zero activity level. Royalty fees of 2 percent of sales are variable; royalty fees of $1,000 per year plus 2 percent of sales are semivariable.
>
> *fixed cost.* A cost that does not change as activity levels change, at least for some time period. In the long run, all costs can vary.

In accounting for the costs of product or services or segments of a business, accountants sometimes desegregate total costs into those that benefit a specific product and those that benefit all products jointly produced.

> *traceable cost. direct cost.* A cost the firm can identify with a specific product, such as the cost of a computer chip installed in a given personal computer, or with some activity.
>
> *common cost. joint cost. indirect cost.* A cost incurred to benefit more than one product or activity, such as the cost of rent of a

factory building in which the firm makes several different kinds of personal computers or the cost of a steer from which the firm manufactures leather and hamburger. Some restrict the term *common cost* to situations such as the first, where the firm chooses to produce products together, while restricting *joint costs* to situations, such as the second, where the firm must incur the cost simultaneously. The major problem in cost accounting is allocation of common and joint costs to individual products. Managers and regulators (e.g., the Securities and Exchange Commission and the IRS) often insist on such allocations, while economists and some accountants recognize that such allocations do not aid decision making.

Virtually all costs recorded by accountants require a cash outlay at some time. Analysts sometimes need to distinguish between costs associated with current or future cash expenditures and those where the expenditure already occurred.

out-of-pocket cost. outlay cost. cash cost. An item requiring a current or future cash expenditure.

book cost. sunk cost. A cost incurrence where the cash expenditure has already occurred, such as the cost of depreciation for a machine purchased several years ago. (In accounting, depreciation is an allocation of a previous expenditure, while in economics depreciation represents a decline in current value.)

In decision making, the cost concepts above often get further refined, as follows.

incremental cost. marginal cost. differential cost. avoidable cost. The firm will incur (save) incremental costs if it carries out (or stops) a project. These four terms tend to have the same meaning, except that the economist restricts the term *marginal cost* to the cost of producing one more unit. Thus the next unit has a marginal cost; the

next week's output has an incremental cost. If a firm produces and sells a new product, the related new costs would properly be called *incremental*, not *marginal*. If a factory is closed, the costs saved are incremental, not marginal.

unavoidable cost. inescapable cost. sunk cost. Unavoidable costs will occur whether the decision is made to go ahead or not, because the firm has already spent, or committed to spend, the cash. Not all unavoidable costs are book costs; consider a salary promised, but not yet earned, that the firm will pay if it makes a no-go decision. *Sunk costs* are past costs that current and future decisions cannot affect and, hence, are irrelevant for decision making (aside from income tax effects). For example, the acquisition cost of machinery is irrelevant to a decision of whether to scrap the machinery. In making such a decision, one should consider only the sacrifice of continuing to own it and the cost of, say, the electricity to run the machine, both incremental costs. Sunk costs become relevant for decision making when the analysis requires taking income taxes (gain or loss on disposal of asset) into account, since the cash payment for income taxes depends on the tax basis of the asset. Avoid using the ambiguous term *sunk costs*. Consider, for example, a machine costing $100,000 with current salvage value of $20,000. Some would say that $100,000 is "sunk"; others would say that only $80,000 is "sunk." Those who say $100,000 have in mind a gross cost, while those who say $80,000 have in mind a net cost—original amount reduced by current opportunity cost.

In deciding which employees to reward, management often cares about desegregating actual costs into those that are *controllable* and those not controllable by a given employee or division. All costs can be affected by someone in the firm; those who design incentive schemes attempt to hold a person responsible for a cost only if that person can influence the amount of the cost.

A firm incurs costs because it perceives that it will realize benefits. Careful usage of cost terms distinguishes between incurrences where the firm will enjoy the benefits in the future from those where the firm has already enjoyed the benefits. Accounting distinguishes costs that have future benefits by calling them *assets* and contrasting them with costs whose benefits the firm has already consumed, by calling them *expenses*. Other pairs of terms involving this distinction are *unexpired cost* versus *expired cost* and *product cost* versus *period cost*.

Economists, managers, and regulators make further distinctions between cost concepts, as follows.

fully absorbed cost versus *variable cost*. Fully absorbed costs refer to costs where the firm has allocated fixed manufacturing costs to products produced or divisions within the firm as required by generally accepted accounting principles. Variable costs, in contrast, may be more relevant for making decisions, such as in setting prices or deciding whether a firm has priced below cost for antitrust purposes.

fully absorbed cost versus *full cost*. In full costing, the analysis allocates all costs, manufacturing costs as well as central corporate expenses (including financing expenses), to products or to divisions. In full absorption costing, the firm allocates only manufacturing costs to product. Only in full costing will revenues, expenses, and income summed over all products or divisions equal corporate revenues, expenses, and income.

opportunity cost versus *outlay cost*. Opportunity cost refers to the economic benefit forgone by using a resource for one purpose rather than another. If the firm can sell a machine for $200,000, then the opportunity cost of using that machine in operations is $200,000 independent of its

outlay cost or its book cost or its historical cost.

future cost versus *past cost*. Effective decision making analyzes only present and future outlay costs, or out-of-pocket costs. Optimal decisions result from using future costs, whereas financial reporting uses past costs.

short-run cost versus *long-run cost*. For a given configuration of plant and equipment, short-run costs vary as output varies. The firm can incur long-run costs to change that configuration. This pair of terms is the economist's analogy of the accounting pair, above, variable and fixed costs. The analogy is inexact because some short-run costs are fixed, such as property taxes on the factory.

imputed cost versus *book cost*. Imputed costs do not appear in the historical cost accounting records for financial reporting. The actual cost incurred is recorder and is called a *book cost*. Some regulators calculate the cost of owners' equity capital, for various purposes; these are imputed costs. Opportunity costs are imputed costs and are relevant for decision making.

average cost versus *marginal cost*. This is the economic distinction equivalent to fully absorbed cost of product and variable cost of product. Average cost is total cost divided by number of units. Marginal cost is the cost to produce the next unit (or the last unit).

differential cost versus *variable cost*. Whether a cost changes or remains fixed depends on the activity basis being considered. Typically, but not invariably, analysts term costs as *variable*, or *fixed*, with respect to an activity basis such as changes in production levels. Typically, but not invariably, analysts term costs as *incremental*, or not, with respect to an activity basis, such as the undertaking of some new venture. Consider the decision to undertake the production of food processors, rather than food blenders, which the manufacturer has been making. To produce processors requires the acquisition of a new machine tool. The cost of the new machine tool is incremental with respect to a decision to produce food processors instead of food blenders, but, once acquired, becomes a fixed cost of producing food processors. Consider a firm that will incur costs of direct labor for the production of food processors or food blenders, whichever the firm produces. Assume the firm cannot produce both. Such labor is variable with respect to production measured in units, but not incremental with respect to the decision to produce processors rather than blenders. This distinction often blurs in practice, so a careful understanding of the activity basis being considered is necessary for understanding of the concepts being used in a particular application.

Analysis of operating and manufacturing activities uses the following subdivisions of fixed (historical) costs. Fixed costs have the following components:

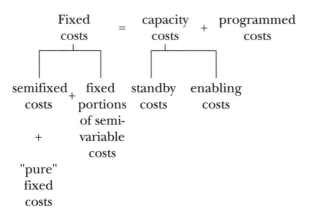

Capacity costs (committed costs) give a firm the capability to produce or to sell, while *programmed costs (managed costs, discretionary costs)*, such as for advertising or research, may be nonessential, but once the firm has decided to incur them, they become fixed costs. The firm will incur *standby costs* even if it does not use existing capacity; examples include property taxes and depreciation on a building. The firm

can avoid *enabling costs*, such as for a security force, if it does not use capacity. A cost fixed over a wide range but that can change is a *semifixed cost* or "step cost." An example is the cost of rail lines from the factory to the main rail line, where fixed cost depends on whether there are one or two parallel lines but are independent of the number of trains run per day. *Semivariable costs* combine a strictly fixed component cost plus a variable component. Telephone charges usually have a fixed monthly component plus a charge related to usage.

(SEE ALSO: *Cost Allocation*; *Cost-Benefit Analysis*)

BIBLIOGRAPHY

Buchanan, James. M., and Thirlby, G. F. (1973). *L.S.E. Essays on Cost*. London: Weidenfeld and Nicholson.

Horngren, Charles T., Foster, George, and Datar, Srikant M. (2000). *Cost Accounting: A Managerial Emphasi*, 10th ed. Upper Saddle River, NJ: Prentice-Hall.

Maher, Michael W., Stickney, Clyde P., and Weil, Roman L. (1997). *Managerial Accounting: An Introduction to Concepts, Methods, and Uses*, 6th ed. Ft. Worth, TX: Dryden Press.

Stickney, Clyde P., and Weil, Roman L. (2000). *Financial Accounting: An Introduction to Concepts, Methods and Uses*, 9th ed. Ft. Worth, TX: Dryden Press.

ROMAN L. WEIL

COST-VOLUME-PROFIT ANALYSIS

Cost-volume-profit analysis (CVP), or break-even analysis, is used to compute the volume level at which total revenues are equal to total costs. When total costs and total revenues are equal, the business organization is said to be "breaking even." The analysis is based on a set of linear equations for a straight line and the separation of variable and fixed costs.

Total variable costs are considered to be those costs that vary as the production volume changes. In a factory, production volume is considered to be the number of units produced, but in a governmental organization with no assembly process, the units produced might refer, for example, to the number of welfare cases processed. There are a number of costs that vary or change, but if the variation is not due to volume changes, it is not considered to be a variable cost. Examples of variable costs are direct materials and direct labor. Total fixed costs do not vary as volume levels change within the relevant range. Examples of fixed costs are straight-line depreciation and annual insurance charges. Total variable costs can be viewed as a 45° line and total fixed costs as a straight line. In the break-even chart shown in Figure 1, the upward slope of line DFC represents the change in variable costs. Variable costs sit on top of fixed costs, line DE. Point F represents the breakeven point. This is where the total cost (costs below the line DFC) crosses and is equal to total revenues (line AFB).

All the lines in the chart are straight lines: Linearity is an underlying assumption of CVP analysis. Although no one can be certain that costs are linear over the entire range of output or production, this is an assumption of CVP. To help alleviate the limitations of this assumption, it is also assumed that the linear relationships hold only within the relevant range of production. The relevant range is represented by the high and low output points that have been previously reached with past production. CVP analysis is best viewed within the relevant range, that is, within our previous actual experience. Outside of that range, costs may vary in a nonlinear manner. The straight-line equation for total cost is:

Total cost = total fixed cost + total variable cost

Total variable cost is calculated by multiplying the cost of a unit, which remains constant on a per-unit basis, by the number of units produced. Therefore the total cost equation could be expanded as:

Total cost = total fixed cost + (variable cost per unit × number of units)

Total fixed costs do not change.

A final version of the equation is:

$$Y = a + bx$$

where a is the fixed cost, b is the variable cost per unit, x is the level of activity, and Y is the total cost. Assume that the fixed costs are $5,000, the volume of units produced is 1,000, and the per-unit variable cost is $2. In that case the total cost would be computed as follows:

$$Y = \$5,000 + (\$2 \times 1,000) \quad Y = \$7,000$$

It can be seen that it is important to separate variable and fixed costs. Another reason it is important to separate these costs is because variable costs are used to determine the contribution margin, and the contribution margin is used to determine the break-even point. The contribution margin is the difference between the per-unit variable cost and the selling price per unit. For example, if the per-unit variable cost is $15 and selling price per unit is $20, then the contribution margin is equal to $5. The contribution margin may provide a $5 *contribution* toward the reduction of fixed costs or a $5 contribution to profits. If the business is operating at a volume above the break-even point volume (above point F), then the $5 is a contribution (on a per-unit basis) to additional profits. If the business is operating at a volume below the break-even point (below point F), then the $5 provides for a reduction in fixed costs and continues to do so until the break-even point is passed.

Once the contribution margin is determined, it can be used to calculate the break-even point in volume of units or in total sales dollars. When a per-unit contribution margin occurs below a firm's break-even point, it is a contribution to the reduction of fixed costs. Therefore, it is logical to divide fixed costs by the contribution margin to determine how many units must be produced to reach the break-even point:

$$\frac{\text{Break-even}}{\text{in units}} = \frac{\text{total fixed costs}}{\text{contribution margin per unit}}$$

Assume that the contribution margin is the same as in the previous example, $5. In this example, assume that the total fixed costs are increased to $8,000. Using the equation, we determine that the break-even point in units:

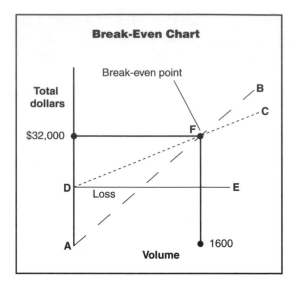

Break-Even Chart

Break-even point

Total dollars

$32,000

B

C

F

D

Loss

E

A

1600

Volume

Figure 1

$$\text{Break-even point in units} = \frac{\$8,000}{\$5}$$

$$= 1,600 \text{ units}$$

In Figure 1, the break-even point is shown as a vertical line from the x-axis to point F. Now, if we want to determine the break-even point in total sales dollars (total revenue), we could multiply 1600 units by the assumed selling price of $20 and arrive at $32,000. Or we could use another equation to compute the break-even point in total sales directly. In that case, we would first have to compute the contribution margin ratio. This ratio is determined by dividing the contribution margin by selling price. Referring to our example, the calculation of the ratio involves two steps:

$20   (selling price)
−15   (variable cost)
$ 5   (contribution margin)

$$\text{Contribution margin ratio} = \frac{\text{contribution margin}}{\text{selling price}}$$

$$= \frac{5}{20}$$

$$= 25\%$$

Going back to the break-even equation and replacing the per-unit contribution margin with the contribution margin ratio results in the following formula and calculation:

$$\text{Break-even in total sales} = \frac{\text{total fixed costs}}{\text{contribution margin ratio}}$$

$$= \frac{\$8,000}{.25}$$

$$= \$32,000$$

Figure 1 shows this break-even point, at $32,000 in sales, as a horizontal line from point F to the y-axis. Total sales at the break-even point are illustrated on the y-axis and total units on the x-axis. Also notice that the losses are represented by the DFA triangle and profits in the FBC triangle.

The financial information required for CVP analysis is for internal use and is usually available only to managers inside the firm; information about variable and fixed costs is not available to the general public. CVP analysis is good as a general guide for one product within the relevant range. If the company has more than one product, then the contribution margins from all products must be averaged together. But, any cost-averaging process reduces the level of accuracy as compared to working with cost data from a single product. Furthermore, some organizations, such as nonprofit organizations, do not incur a significant level of variable costs. In these cases, standard CVP assumptions can lead to misleading results and decisions.

(SEE ALSO: *Accounting; Costs*)

G. STEVENSON SMITH

COTTAGE INDUSTRIES

"Cottage industries" is a term that was used prevalently during the eighteenth and nineteenth and centuries to describe the home-based system of manufacturing. This term is also used today to refer to goods or services that are produced at home. Sewing, craft production, sales and mar-

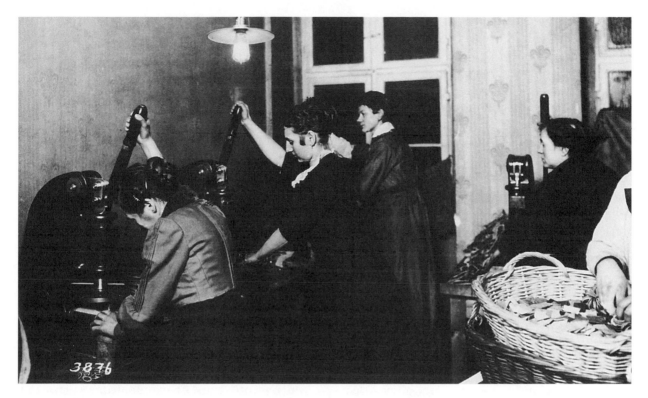

Women working in a cottage industry at the beginning of the twentieth century.

keting, typing, bookkeeping, and auto repair are just a few examples of home-based employment.

HISTORY

Rural families were some of the first to become involved in the cottage industry. They added to their agricultural income by making products at home. Merchants provided the raw materials to the families, collected and marketed the finished product, and then paid the family a percentage of the price charged to the end consumer. Some of the items made by these at-home workers were cloth and clothing, shoes, cigars, and hand-decorated items.

Cottage industries developed in cities around 1870, resulting in the harsh tenement housing system. Immigrant families lived and worked in these crowded, unsafe apartment buildings. They worked for extremely low wages, usually making garments. This system lasted until around 1920, when better management of factories made home-produced goods less competitive.

Hand-decorating of items, sewing, and other highly specialized activities still operate as cottage industries today. Economists point to the rise of a new type of cottage industry whereby people can stay at home to perform work on their computers that formerly had to be done at the office. "Tele-commuters" is another term used more frequently today to refer to home-based employment. Many jobs that used to require workers' physical presence in the office can now be performed from home. Running a business from home today requires only a couple of phone lines with call forwarding and call waiting, a computer with e-mail and a modem, a fax machine, a copier, and office supplies. For executives on the go, a cell phone and laptop computer can keep them up and running from just about any location.

HOME EMPLOYMENT BENEFITS

There are many reasons that people choose to work from their homes. They can be experienced or inexperienced, young or elderly, healthy or physically challenged, single or married, with or without children.

Many mothers and/or fathers of young children find it more productive, more cost-effective, and safer to keep their children with them while they work at home. They can have the flexibility of arranging their job around their family's needs. Many parents enjoy being able to spend time with their children during the day. Parents maintain responsibility for the safety of their own children and can keep abreast of how much they are learning, know who they are playing with, and save money on day-care expenses at the same time.

Another reason people choose to work from home is that they don't have to commute to and from their workplace. By not commuting to work, they can save on wear and tear of their vehicle, get lower insurance rates, and spend less money on gas.

Working from home also saves money that would normally be spent on a workplace wardrobe. Much more informal clothing can be worn when working at home. Not spending money on uniforms, suits, and/or dresses provides more money for other expenses.

Home employment gives control of one's life to oneself. There is freedom and flexibility in setting work schedules. Parents can be home for their children, there are no commuting hassles, and no one looks over shoulders or determines break time. The individual, not the employer, determines the work schedule. A parent has the flexibility of scheduling work flow around school activities such as field trips and sports activities.

DECISIONS TO MAKE

Despite all the benefits listed above, home employment is not for everyone. For example, those who start their own business must be able to generate work. There are advertising costs involved in getting the company name out to the general public. Careful consideration should be given to the possible advertising avenues to use. Advertising can be very expensive and may not generate enough business if it does not reach po-

tential customers. People who do good work but cannot get others to recognize this or cannot do well in promoting themselves may be spending more than they are earning.

Detailed record keeping is a must for the self-employed as well as the work-at-home person. Some deductions are available only if the business is making a profit, while others are used yearly to determine expenses. Depending on the type of business a person wishes to become involved in, start-up costs need to be considered and information gathered on the best equipment/tools necessary. Some businesses may require a starting inventory, while others do not. When considering start-up costs, one should shop wisely and consider purchasing used equipment and supplies. This will save money for other expenses, and the depreciation on these items will be more reasonable. Advertising, mileage expenses, cost of supplies, phone, electricity, and entertainment are just some of the expenses for which records must be maintained. Tax laws can and do change frequently. The person who is unsure about what records need to be kept should contact a tax adviser for detailed and up-to-date information.

Another factor to consider before deciding to work from home is motivation. One must be able to set one's own schedule and follow through on it. If a person is used to working for someone else and having supervision and direction provided, it can be very easy to let work slide. Setting goals and following through on them is a necessity when working for oneself.

Finally, one should check local authorities before starting a home-based business as towns vary greatly in their local ordinances. They will explain any rules the town has established regarding home-based businesses and give guidance in the necessary paperwork or approval process.

HOME EMPLOYMENT RESOURCES

For those people who wish to become self-employed and work out of their home, there are several organizations available to help get started.

One major resource for the self-employed is an association called SCORE (Service Corps of

Retired Executives). SCORE is a nonprofit group sponsored by the U.S. Small Business Administration that has provided successful, free business counseling since 1964. SCORE matches volunteer counselors with clients needing their expert advice. It also maintains a national skills roster to help identify the best counselor for a particular client. SCORE is made up of more than 13,000 retired or active executives and has more than 400 chapters nationwide. These executives volunteer their time, skills, and experience to help the self-employed get started in their own business or help those who are already in business when they have problems or need advice. SCORE also offers many seminars and workshops and posts this information at its local chapters. Since its inception, SCORE has advised, counseled, and mentored more than 300,000 small businesses, helping nearly 4 million Americans with face-to-face counseling, e-mail counseling, and training. For more information on SCORE, contact a local chapter personally or visit its Web site at http://www.score.org/.

Home Employment Resource is an organization dedicated to helping people who want to work at home. It provides information on companies nationwide that hire people to work from home. A partial listing of jobs that have been available to the home-employed include typists, graphic artists, auto appraisers, editors, reporters, financial analysts, cartoonists, claims processors, photographers, proofreaders, recruiters, and writers. There are many jobs available for home-based workers if one knows where to look. This organization assists in contacting the companies that hire work-at-home people. The Web site for Home Employment Resource is http://www.home-employment.com/.

The Independent Homeworkers Alliance (IHA) is an organization dedicated to helping people who want to work from home. The IHA offers its members valuable benefits that are designed specifically for the work-at-home person. Included in its database are more than 43,000 job listings. Membership and maintenance fees that are charged to members are applied directly to the organization itself to improve, enhance, and add to the existing services provided to its members, who number more than 27,000. More information about Independent Homeworkers Alliance is available through their Web site at http://www.homeworkers.org/.

There are also home study schools that offer training in fields such as medical billing and claims processing, medical transcription, bookkeeping, and paralegal work. For more information on home-study schooling, contact At-Home Profession ... America's First Home Study School for Work-at-Home Careers, 2001 Lowe Street, Fort Collins, CO 80525.

BIBLIOGRAPHY

Home Employment Resource. http://www.home-employment.com/.

Independent Homeworkers Alliance. http://www.homeworkers.org/.

SCORE, Johnson City, Tennessee. http://farad.xtn.net/virtual/mainmenu/newjc/chamber/scoreindex.html.

"The SCORE Association Marks Milestones. Carolina-Upstate Business Journal. http://www.carolina-upstate.com/journal/page20.htm.

The World Book Encyclopedia. (1997) Chicago: World Book.

JULIE A. WATKINS

COUPONS

(SEE: *Promotion*)

CREDIT/DEBIT/TRAVEL CARDS

Until the 1920's, consumer purchases in the United States were made primarily in one of two ways: cash or personal check. But in that decade, a new means of payment was introduced—the credit account. While credit transactions had been common for a long time in business to business dealings, they were new to the consumer market. The credit account allowed a consumer to defer payment on a purchase made today to some time in the future: thus, the expression "buy now, pay later" was born. Evidence of the credit account typically took the form of a card—the credit card.

Since the 1920's, different types of credit cards have emerged. In addition, related types of cards have also appeared on the consumer scene: the debit card, as well as the ATM card and the smart card, and the travel card and charge card. Each type of card will be defined and explained in this entry.

CREDIT CARDS

A **credit card** is a pocket size, plastic card that allows the holder to make a purchase on a credit account that will be repaid at some time in the future. Repayment may be in a single amount or in a series of amounts. At a minimum, the credit card will include identification of the user by name, account number, and signature.

The earliest issuance of credit cards in the United States was by gasoline companies and retail stores. Thus, it was quite common in the first half of the twentieth century to carry a credit card from Esso, Sears, and/or a local department store. These early cards were issued by the private company itself based on the credit policy of that company. Many of the accounts were expected to be paid in the month following purchase. Others were revolving charge accounts in which partial payment was expected every month, with a charge for interest on amounts not paid promptly.

If the balances of the credit accounts were not paid, the issuing firm took the loss. Thus, deciding to issue a credit card was a thoughtful process on the part of the firm. Often, the three C's of credit were applied to a credit applicant: character, capacity, and capital. Character referred to the record of the applicant in paying previous accounts—his or her credit history. Capacity meant the earnings potential (salary) of the applicant. Capital referred to the net assets (assets minus liabilities) of the person. Obtaining a credit card was far from an automatic process.

Major changes in the nature and types of credit cards occurred in the 1950's. Two types of credit cards emerged in that decade: the charge card and the bank credit card. The charge card is discussed as a travel card later in this entry.

The bank credit card expanded the idea of a credit card company to a much broader usage—virtually every merchant and service provider worldwide. The 1959 BankAmericard from the Bank of America in California is today the VISA card. The 1970's saw the birth of Master Charge, today's MasterCard. These cards are issued by banks, so one applies to a bank for the credit card. A preset credit limit is assigned to the card user. After an item is charged at a firm, the firm receives payment from the bank. The bank charges a fee to the firm, pays the firm the net amount, and then collects from the consumer. The consumer usually pays an annual fee to the bank and is charged interest on the unpaid balance at the end of each month. Credit cards may also be used to make a cash advance from the bank. However, it should be remembered that interest rates on cash advances using a credit card can be much higher than the rates for credit card purchases. Thus, the cash advance feature should be used wisely.

While at one time it was difficult to earn credit, the process is far easier at the present time. Banks compete for customers for their credit cards and often solicit college students with limited capital and offer them credit cards. Telemarketing of credit cards is frequent. Low credit limits are relatively easy to obtain at present. Demonstrating a solid payment record and growth in earnings then leads to higher limits.

Managing one's credit becomes important to the consumer. It is critical never to get into a position in which one has so many credit cards and so many high balances that the credit bills never get paid off. For example, if you have a bank credit card with a balance of $1,000 and an interest rate of 18% a year or 1 ½% a month (18% divided by 12 months), the interest for the current month will be $15 ($1,000 × .015). If the payment made on the account this month is only $25, then the first $15 is for interest; the remaining $10 ($25-$15) reduces the principal of $1,000 to $990 for the next month. In other words, more has been paid for interest than for what was purchased; the situation in the following month will change very little. At this rate of payment, it could be several years before the balance is reduced to zero. In the meantime, if the card has been used for more purchases, the cycle of remaining in debt continues. Credit card management is critical to a consumer. In fact, one who has difficulty in dealing with credit cards might be better off with debit cards.

DEBIT CARDS

A **debit card** is also issued by a bank and looks like a credit card, but it works very differently. When one uses a debit card, the amount spent is deducted immediately from the user's bank account. It is as if one is paying by check without having to write a check. There will be no unpaid future bills, for the payment is made at the time of the expenditure. For example, many people today purchase groceries with the debit card by running it through the card reader at the grocery store check out counter. In addition, people often get extra cash while paying for the groceries with that debit card.

It is helpful to know how a bank account works from the bank's point of view to fully understand the debit card. When an amount is added to a bank account, such as by a deposit, the individual's account is "credited;" when an amount is subtracted from that bank account, such as by writing a check, the account is "debited." Thus, the term debit card states what happens to the bank account when the card is used—an immediate subtraction.

A common function of the debit card is as an ATM card. ATM stands for the Automated Teller Machine that so many use today. ATMs allow for 24-hour banking. The card holder is able to make deposits, find out bank balances, transfer money from account to account, and make a loan payment. The ATM/debit card can also be used to obtain cash; the amount withdrawn is subtracted immediately from the bank account; thus it is another use of a debit card.

The user of the debit card must take particular care in keeping records of expenditures with the debit card. Unlike the check that usually is recorded at the time of payment, the debit card expense has its record in the form of a sales slip, a register receipt, or a record of an ATM withdrawal or deposit. Debit card expenditures must be deducted from the bank account balance by the user in a regular accurate manner to avoid losing track of the account balance.

A variation on the debit card is the **smart card**. While the debit card uses a magnetic strip, the smart card typically uses an embedded semiconductor to store and maintain information. Smart cards have many uses, but in general are used for prepayment of an expense, such as when a phone card is purchased. The phone card has so many dollars in it that have been paid for in advance of use. As the card is used, money value is deducted. Other applications of the smart card are for the payment of tolls and for the purchase of gasoline. In both cases, the card can be waved at a reader that will record the toll or the purchase of gasoline. Food plans at colleges and transit cards on subway systems are other uses of the smart card. Using a smart card saves that sudden search for change to pay a toll or to make a phone call.

TRAVEL CARDS

Travel cards, also called travel and entertainment cards, fall into two categories. The first is the charge card mentioned earlier. A **charge card** is issued by a firm whose main product is credit granting in order to purchase a service. The first two companies in this field were Diners' Club, Inc. and American Express Company. In both cases, one is issued a card based on a credit check and then uses the card at designated establishments and with designated types of firms to pay for services or products. Payment is made not to a store nor to a bank, but rather to Diners' Club or to American Express. Diners' Club cards are used primarily at eating establishments. American Express cards are used for airlines, hotels, and other travel-related activities. No credit limits are established for charge cards, but payment is expected in full within the next billing period to maintain one's credit record. However, a current change in the approach to the charge card has been made by American Express to allow monthly payments, just as if it were a bank credit card account.

A second type of travel card is issued by airlines or hotel chains. This card does not have direct money use, but serves instead as an upgraded service provider. Thus, included in this category are such cards as frequent flyer cards, with which airline mileage is accumulated, to be later used for upgraded or free flights. In addition, services are provided to the cardholder such as early boarding of flights and/or other amenities. Also included in this category are hotel chain cards that accumulate services at hotels in that chain. Room upgrades, speedy check in and check out, and help with reservations are among the benefits of this type of card. Furthermore, many hotels are partners with airlines, so money spent at a hotel can result in additional miles on the airline mileage account.

A growing trend among the airlines is the issuance of airline MasterCards or VISA cards. The airlines work with a bank to issue standard bank credit cards with one modification: every dollar spent using that credit card is turned into airline mileage. Thus, the benefit of the bank credit card is joined with the value of the airline travel card.

SUMMARY

From a time when what was bought was paid for on the spot, "plastic" has changed the way that consumers do business and handle personal financial functions. Credit cards allow a purchase now with payment in the future. Debit cards result in an immediate deduction from a bank account without writing a check. Smart cards allow for prepayment of expenses to aid in convenience when the expense needs to be paid. Travel cards permit charging of travel related expenses and the accumulation of travel services and benefits. All of these items are part of what seems to be arriving in the fairly near future—a paperless financial society accessed by cards of various types. In fact, it is possible that the day of cards will at some point end and another means will be found to connect the individual with those purchases

needed for functioning. Until then, given the many ways to purchase, wise consumerism is needed to result in the correct choice of cards for an individual.

BURTON S. KALISKI

CREDIT UNIONS

(SEE: *Financial Institutions*)

CRIME AND FRAUD

Both individuals and businesses commit many criminal activities that cost businesses, consumers, government agencies, and stockholders considerable sums of money each year. Business crime is not new; in fact, fraudulent activities have been a common part of business operations for thousands of years. For instance, in 360 B.C. in Syracuse, Sicily (then a Greek colony), Xenothemis and a shipowner, Hegestratos, persuaded a customer to advance cash by claiming that a vessel was fully laden with corn. Maritime trade was at that time very risky, and many vessels were subsequently lost at sea. Hegestratos intended to exploit this risk of loss at sea three days after the ship sailed from port by sinking it. When the other passengers discovered Hegestratos' plot, he panicked, jumped overboard, and drowned. This early example illustrates that criminal, and especially fraudulent, activities have existed within the world of business for some time and, unfortunately, will probably continue to do so.

Under modern law, for a crime to have occurred, an illegal act must have been committed *and* intent to commit the act must be shown. A crime is a violation of local, state, or federal law and is punishable by the appropriate government authority. Criminal activities are usually defined as applying to a specific type of behavior or action. Embezzlement and fraud are two common business-related crimes. Embezzlement occurs when a person has the right to possess business property or money but then converts that property or money to personal possession or use. Fraud is often thought of as intentional deception of another person in order to deprive that person of property or to injure that person in some other way. Criminal activities can be committed by individuals against a business as well as by businesses through the actions of their employees against consumers, the general public, and/or stockholders.

INDIVIDUAL CRIMES AGAINST BUSINESS

Business-related individual criminal activities are normally broken down into two categories: internal and external.

Internal Crimes Internal crime occurs when an employee steals from or commits some other offense against the business. For example, depending on their jobs, employees may have access to business files, records, or sensitive financial information. The dishonest employee could then use this information to commit a crime against the business. Generally, the higher in the business the employee, the greater the potential for serious criminal activities against the firm.

A number of internal crimes are frequently committed against a business. Among the most common are abuse of power, accounting embezzlement, misuse of business time, computer and electronic information manipulation, intellectual property theft, supply and equipment pilferage, travel expense abuse, and vandalism and sabotage.

Abuse of Power. One form of employee criminal activity is making inappropriate financial decisions on behalf of the business that are really intended to benefit the employee. An example of this activity may be seen when an employee is empowered to sign purchase contracts on behalf of the employer with the objective of getting the lowest price available from outside vendors. Instead of doing this, an employee could sign contracts with more expensive outside vendors and receive a kickback in return. Acceptance of kickbacks is an abuse of power and, depending on the size of the contracts, may cost a business a considerable amount of money.

Accounting Embezzlement. One of the most common internal criminal activities is the manipulating of accounting records to steal business funds. An employee who is well trained in accounting techniques may be able to devise sophisticated schemes to cover his or her connection to the stolen business funds. Such criminal accounting violations have and can go on for years and end up costing a business many thousands of dollars. These criminal accounting practices can be detected through a variety of methods, such as changes in accounting procedures, co-worker concerns, and regular internal and/or external audits.

Accounting crimes are very serious matters that have adverse consequences for a business. The stealing of funds hurts the business's profit margin and, in turn, stockholders. Stock value is hurt because of the reduced profits showing on the books, which, in turn, can cost a business the lost value of its securities. Such internal accounting crimes must be reported to the appropriate law enforcement agencies, making the embezzlement part of the business's public record. Thus the business faces the embarrassment associated with having been a victim of accounting crimes, possibly weakening its image and public confidence in it. An employee who gets caught committing such crimes faces severe penalties if convicted. Depending on the amount of funds stolen, an employee could be charged with and convicted of a felony and face a long prison sentence. In addition, once convicted of such a crime, it will be next to impossible for a person to get another job in the business world.

Misuse of Business Time. Employees who perform non-work-related functions while at work are involved in fraudulent activities because they are getting paid to do work for the business but in reality are not performing those functions. An example of this practice is an employee who surfs the Internet for several hours a day for personal reasons, depriving the business of employee production during that time. A few hours of lost time here and there may not seem like much to an employee, but the aggregate loss of work time in the business as a whole can add up to a sizable loss.

Computer and Electronic Information Manipulation. The advent of modern technology has provided more opportunities for employees to commit computer or electronic fraud. One of the most common forms of embezzlement involves the electronic manipulation of business funds so as to deposit them into personal or other third-party accounts. Once the rerouted business funds are deposited into such an account, the employee is free to withdraw and spend them at will. Initially, such electronic fraud might seem easy to carry out, but computers leave behind clues that will lead auditors to the final destination of the funds and to the dishonest employee.

Intellectual Property Theft. One of the fastest-growing areas of business-related criminal activity is the theft of cutting-edge technology by a worker from the employing business. Typically, the dishonest employee will sell the stolen technological knowledge to a competing firm. Criminal activity in this area can be extremely damaging to any business. One reason is that most businesses invest considerable sums of money in research and development to improve or create new technology. The theft and resale of this information to competitors could easily cost a business many thousands of dollars in lost profits. Another is that the business's competitors can stay competitive for only a fraction of the price and thus reap even larger profits. In response to this serious issue, businesses have tightened security and have asked law enforcement to vigorously prosecute anyone involved with this type of criminal behavior.

Supply and Equipment Pilferage. Another example of internal employee criminal activity is the theft of business supplies and office equipment. Businesses are concerned with employees who steal supplies and office equipment, such as laptop computers, paper, paper clips, pens, printers, and so forth. The theft of such business property reduces business profits and, if its stock is publicly traded, earnings for its stockholders. The consequences for dishonest employees who

are caught engaging in these activities include job termination and criminal prosecution.

Travel Expense Abuse. Employees who travel for a business as part of their jobs often commit fraud by putting personal items on the firm's expense account. For example, employees may include higher amounts on their expense voucher than were actually paid. This practice is common when reporting the amount paid in the form of a tip, as usually no receipt is involved. Individually, the funds embezzled by one employee in this way might not add up to much, but collectively this type of crime could cost a business many thousands of dollars each year.

Vandalism and Sabotage. Another type of internal crime is an employee's intentional destruction of business property or equipment. The employee does not receive any monetary benefit from destroying business property; rather, it is done to get back at a business or a supervisor for a myriad of reasons, such as being passed over for promotion, a pending layoff, or a poor performance evaluation. Traditional employee vandalism involves destruction of physical property, including computer equipment, office furniture, business vehicles, or other business property. Physical destruction of business property can be deterred by the use of surveillance equipment and the visible presence of adequate security staff.

The real threat to modern businesses is the effort to sabotage computer systems. An employee with extensive knowledge of a business's computer system could create a computer virus or some other highly technical method to incapacitate some or all of the business's computer system. The destruction or failure of a business's computer system would cause enormous trouble for the business. In addition, if business files were to be damaged or erased, it could cost the business a considerable amount of time and resources to fix them, not to mention the lost sales or poor customer service that might occur as a result. Since the computer security issue is so important, businesses normally discontinue computer access for employees who are going to be separated from the firm. In addition, business security typically monitors employees who have exhibited strong negative feelings toward the business or a supervisor.

External Crimes Among the more common external crimes committed against a business are burglary, robbery, shoplifting, and walk-in office/factory thefts.

Burglary. While burglary has been described in many ways, it is usually thought of as breaking into a place of business with the intent of committing a felony or simply stealing something. Although any business may be burglarized, individuals who commit burglary tend to target those firms where they are likely to receive a high monetary return for their efforts. Financial institutions, such as banks, are often targeted because they normally have large amounts of cash or valuable securities on hand. Almost every major financial business uses a variety of elaborate antiburglary devices to deter potential burglaries. Financial institutions also use extensive networks of electronic equipment to notify law enforcement when burglaries do occur. Most major businesses now employ a wide variety of antiburglary strategies in order to provide maximum security to their offices and employees.

Robbery. Robbery is committed when a criminal attempts to steal from a business by use of force or threat of force—usually with a weapon, such as a gun or knife—during its normal operating hours. Robberies are very serious because of their potential to inflict bodily injury on employees and/or customers who are on the premises at the time of the robbery. Moreover, any property or money that is stolen also hurts the business from a profit-and-loss point of view. The most common example of a robbery would be a criminal attempting to steal money from a store during business hours.

Shoplifting. One of the most prominent threats to any retail business is shoplifting, which costs businesses millions of dollars in lost sales and stolen merchandise each year. Unfortunately, the cost associated with this type of criminal activity is passed on to honest consumers in the form of higher prices. Because of the high costs associated with shoplifting, many retail businesses use sophisticated electronic surveillance systems in order to deter shoplifting and to catch those who commit the crime. In fact, most retailers have adopted a zero-tolerance policy relative to shoplifting and prosecute anyone caught stealing regardless of the amount. The combination of strong antitheft measures and vigorous prosecution of those caught has resulted in fewer numbers of shoplifting cases.

Walk-In Office/Factory Thefts. Some individuals commit thefts by simply walking into an office and attempting to steal something of value. The criminal then walks out of the office or factory with the item and tries to resell the product. Individuals who commit such crimes normally use a disguise (i.e., a delivery person) in order to get past business security.

CRIMES COMMITTED BY BUSINESS

Occasionally, businesses are sources of crime against consumers, the general public, government, and/or stockholders. Examples of crimes committed by businesses include fraudulent reporting, price fixing, and product misrepresentation.

Fraudulent Reporting A business might partake in fraudulent activities by manipulating or misrepresenting business accounting records, profit information, sales data, or other pertinent financial information. This type of behavior is usually on attempt to hide serious financial problems in order to prevent the general public, regulatory agencies, or stockholders from getting poor status reports. Unfavorable financial information can be devastating to a business's stock value, which, in turn, will likely cause the business to lose a considerable amount of money in business equity. For example, business X might intentionally misreport higher profits than were actually accrued to maintain the stock price and value of the business. If the actual lower profits had been reported, then the stock would almost surely go down, causing a decrease in the value of the business. Another reason a business might report inaccurate financial data is because most corporate officers have some form of stock options, and a serious drop in the stock price might be very costly on a personal basis. This type of fraud is usually carried out at the top levels of the business.

When this type of crime is committed by a business through its officers, serious consequences accrue to both. Once the crime is uncovered, regulatory and law enforcement agencies at both the federal and state levels may begin an investigation of the alleged fraudulent activities. If the criminal activities are substantiated and convictions occur, the business, at a minimum, faces large fines, while the officers face long prison terms. In addition, the business faces a humiliating defeat in the arena of public opinion that will, in turn, hurt future sales.

Price Fixing Businesses may engage in another type of crime known as "price fixing," or conspiring with competitors to charge a minimum price for their products. This practice forces consumers to pay more for a particular product than would be charged in a "non-price fixing" competitive environment. Businesses are rewarded with higher profit margins because this practice does not force them to conform to market forces. Price fixing is a violation of the Sherman Anti-Trust Act of 1890, which was passed to ensure that a competitive free market exists, which results in competitive pricing. The Federal Trade Commission (FTC) and the United States Department of Justice have primary jurisdiction over businesses that engage in violations of the Sherman Anti-Trust Act. When a business and its officers are prosecuted for price fixing, the business often faces large fines while individual officers usually go to prison.

Product Misrepresentation When a business knowingly produces a defective or substandard product and sells it to the public anyway, the firm has committed product fraud. Product fraud is extremely serious because consumers depend on safe products in every aspect of daily life. Defective or unsafe products can cause serious harm to both the individual consumer and the general public. An example of product fraud would be when an automobile manufacturer produces and markets a vehicle that has shown, in presale trials, to be unsafe. For instance, a vehicle may be unsafe when hit from behind or from the side, causing the gas tank to explode because of design flaws. The obvious results of such flaws in vehicle design are the severe injury and/or death of people. Naturally, responses to product fraud include numerous lawsuits and lack of public trust in businesses that knowingly release defective or poorly designed products.

SUMMARY

Business-related criminal activity is not new. In fact, crimes in business, such as fraud, can be traced by thousands of years. Crimes can be committed both by and against a business. Common crimes that influence the health of businesses and their customers include burglary, embezzlement, fraud, robbery, and shoplifting. Since crimes, both by and against businesses, are so costly, elaborate measures have been put in place to decrease the likelihood of their occurrence.

BIBLIOGRAPHY

Anderson, R. A., Fox, I., and Twomey, D. P. (1980). *Business Law*, 11th ed. Cincinnati, OH: Southwestern Publishing Company.

Clarke, M. (1990). *Business Crime—Its Nature and Control.* New York: St. Martin's Press.

Coleman, J. W. (1985). *The Criminal Elite.* New York: St. Martin's Press.

Comer, Michael J. (1998). *Corporate Fraud*, 3d ed. Brookfield, VT: Gower.

Loewy, A. H. (2000). *Criminal Law in a Nutshell*, 3d ed. St. Paul, MN: West.

Mann, R. A., and Roberts, B. S. (1998). *Essentials of Business Law and the Legal Environment*, 6th ed. St. Paul, MN: West.

ALLEN D. TRUELL
MICHAEL MILBIER

Money traders at work.

CURRENCY EXCHANGE

Money is any medium that is universally accepted in an economy by sellers of goods and services as payment and by creditors as payment for debts. Money serves as a medium of exchange; indeed, without money, we would have to resort to barter in doing business. *Barter* is simply a direct exchange of goods and services for other goods and services. For instance, a wheat farmer who wants a pair of eyeglasses must find an optician who, at exactly the same time, wants a dozen bushels of wheat; that is, there must be a double coincidence of wants, and the elements of the desired trade must be of equal value. If there isn't a double coincidence of wants, the wheat farmer must go through several trades in order to obtain the desired eyeglasses; for example, this might involve trading wheat for a computer, then the computer for several lamps, then the lamps for the desired eyeglasses.

The existence of money means that individuals do not need to hold a diverse collection of goods as an exchange inventory. Money allows them to specialize in any area in which they have a comparative advantage and to receive money payments for their labor. Money can then be exchanged for the fruits of other people's labor. The use of money as a medium of exchange permits individuals to specialize and promotes the economic efficiencies that result from specialization.

In the same way that money facilitates exchange in a single economy, exchange of currencies facilitates the exchange of goods and services across the boundaries of countries. For instance, when you buy a foreign product, such as a Japanese car, you have dollars with which to pay the Japanese carmaker. The Japanese carmaker, however, cannot pay workers in dollars. The workers are Japanese, they live in Japan, and they need Japanese yen to buy goods and services in that country. There must be some way of exchanging dollars for the yen that the carmaker will accept in order to facilitate trade. That exchange occurs in a *foreign-exchange market*, which in this case specializes in exchanging yen for dollars.

The particular exchange rate between yen and dollars that would prevail depends on the current demand for and supply of yen and dollars (see Figure 1). If one cent per yen is the equilibrium price of yen, then that is the foreign-exchange rate determined by the current demand for and supply of yen in the foreign-exchange market. A person going to the foreign-exchange market would need one hundred yen (1/.01) to buy one dollar or one dollar to buy one hundred yen.

SUPPLY AND DEMAND FOR FOREIGN CURRENCY

Suppose you want to buy a Japanese car. To do so, you must have Japanese yen. You go to the foreign-exchange market (or your American bank). Your desire to purchase the Japanese car causes you to offer (*supply*) dollars to the foreign-exchange market. Your *demand* for Japanese yen is equivalent to your supply of U.S. dollars to the foreign-exchange market. Indeed, every U.S. import leads to a supply of dollars and a demand for some foreign currency. Likewise, every U.S. export leads to a demand for dollars and a supply of some foreign currency by the purchaser.

For the moment assume that only two goods are being traded—Japanese cars and U.S. steel. Thus, the U.S. demand for Japanese cars creates a supply of dollars and a demand for Japanese yen in the foreign-exchange market. Similarly, the Japanese demand for U.S. steel creates a supply of yen and a demand for dollars in the foreign-exchange market. The equilibrium exchange rate will tell us how many yen a dollar can be exchanged for (the dollar price of yen) or how many dollars a yen can be exchanged for (the yen price of dollars).

The demand for and supply of foreign-exchange determine the *equilibrium* foreign exchange rate. For the moment, ignore any speculative aspects of foreign exchange; that is, assume

that there are no individuals who wish to buy yen simply because they think that the price of yen will go up in the future.

The idea of an exchange rate is similar to the idea of paying a market-determined price for something you want to buy. If you like soda, you know you have to pay about fifty cents a can. If the price went up to one dollar, you would probably buy fewer sodas. If the price went down to twenty-five cents, you might buy more. In other words, the demand curve for soda, expressed in terms of dollars, slopes downward, following the law of demand.

The demand curve for Japanese yen also slopes downward. Suppose it costs you one cent to buy one yen—this would be the exchange rate between dollars and yen. If tomorrow you had to pay two cents for a yen, then the exchange rate would have changed. Looking at such an increase with respect to the yen, we would say that there has been an *appreciation* in the value of the yen in the foreign-exchange market. But this increase in the value of the yen means that there has been a *depreciation* in the value of the dollar in the foreign-exchange market. When one currency appreciates, the other currency depreciates.

DETERMINANTS OF THE VALUE OF FOREIGN EXCHANGE

Supply and demand in the foreign-exchange market are determined by changes in many market variables, including relative price levels, real interest rates, productivity, product preferences, and perceptions of economic stability.

Different countries have different rates of inflation, which are an important factor in determining exchange rates. *Purchasing power parity* (PPP) is one widely used theory of the determination of exchange rates. PPP exists between any two currencies whenever changes in the exchange rate exactly reflect relative changes in price levels in two countries. In the long run, the average value of exchange rates depends on their purchasing power parity because in that way the relative prices in the two countries will stay the same (when measured in a common currency). That is, changes in the relative values of the two

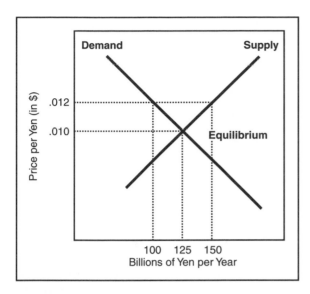

Figure 1

currencies compensate exactly for differences in national exchange rates. The PPP theory seems to work well in the long run when the differences in inflation rates between two countries are relatively large. When differences in inflation rates are relatively small, other market-oriented forces may dominate and often distort the picture.

A factor that may affect equilibrium currency prices is the interest rate of a country. If the U.S. interest rate, corrected for people's expectations of inflation, abruptly increased relative to interest rates in the rest of the world, international investors elsewhere would increase their demand for dollar-denominated assets, thereby increasing the demand for dollars in foreign-exchange markets. An increased demand in foreign-exchange markets, other things held constant, would cause the dollar to appreciate and other currencies to depreciate.

Another factor affecting equilibrium is a change in relative productivity. If one country's productivity increased relative to another's, the former country would become more competitive in world markets. The demand for its exports would increase, and so would the demand for its currency.

Changes in consumers' tastes also affect the equilibrium prices of currencies. If Japan's citizens suddenly developed a taste for a U.S. prod-

uct, such as video games, this would increase the demand for U.S. dollars in foreign-exchange markets.

Finally, economic and political stability affect the supply of and demand for a currency, and therefore the equilibrium price of that currency. If the United States looked economically and politically more stable than other countries, more foreigners would want to put their savings into U.S. assets than in assets of another country. This would increase the demand for dollars.

FIXED- VERSUS FLEXIBLE-EXCHANGE-RATE SYSTEMS

Under the *flexible-exchange-rate system* described above, the equilibrium exchange rate reflects the supply and demand for the currency. Under a *fixed-exchange-rate system* a country's central bank intervenes by buying or selling its currency to keep its foreign-exchange rates from changing. As with most systems in which the price of a good or service is fixed, the only way that it can remain so is for the government to intervene. Consider the two-country example above. Suppose that there were an increase in the prices of all goods and services made in the United States, including steel. The Japanese yen would now buy less steel than before. The Japanese would supply fewer yen to the foreign-exchange market and demand fewer dollars at the fixed exchange rate. But suppose Americans continued to demand Japanese cars. In fact, they would demand more Japanese cars because, at the fixed exchange rate, the relative price of Japanese cars would fall. Americans would now supply more dollars to the foreign-exchange market and demand more yen. In the absence of intervention by a central bank, the exchange rate would change. In order to maintain the foreign-exchange price of the yen, the Japanese central bank would buy (demand) dollars and sell (supply) yen.

If the central bank didn't act to support the stated foreign-exchange rate, then too much or too little of one currency would be supplied or demanded. This lack of balance (i.e., disequilibrium) in the foreign-exchange market would impede trade between the two countries and could potentially result in a black market (i.e., underground market or illegal trade) in the two currencies.

CURRENCY CRISES

The only way for the United States to support the price of the dollar is to buy up excess dollars with foreign reserves—in our case, with Japanese yen. But the United States might eventually run out of Japanese yen. If this happened, it would no longer be able to stabilize the price of the dollar, and a currency crisis would result. A currency crisis occurs when a country can no longer support the price of its currency in foreign-exchange markets under a fixed-exchange-rate system. Many such crises have occurred in the past several decades when countries have attempted to maintain a fixed exchange rate that was in disequilibrium.

One alternative to a currency crisis or to continuing to try to support a fixed exchange rate is to devalue unilaterally. Currency devaluation is equivalent to currency depreciation, except that it occurs under a fixed-exchange-rate regime. The country officially lowers the price of its currency in foreign-exchange markets; this is a deliberate public action by a government following a fixed-exchange-rate policy. Revaluation is the opposite of devaluation. This occurs when, under a fixed-exchange-rate regime, there is pressure on a country's currency to rise in value in foreign-exchange markets. Unilaterally, that country can declare that the value of its currency in foreign-exchange markets is higher than it has been in the past. Currency revaluation is the equivalent of currency appreciation, except that it occurs under a fixed exchange rate regime and is mandated by the government. Managed exchange rates, sometimes referred to as dirty float, occur when a central bank or several central banks intervene in a system of flexible exchange to keep the exchange rate from undergoing extreme changes.

SUMMARY

Thus, a well-functioning foreign-exchange market is vital for worldwide trade. In a flexible-exchange-rate system, supply of and demand for a currency determine the exchange rate. In a fixed-exchange rate system, a government imposes the exchange rate; given the mandated exchange rate, consumers determine how much of the currency they wish to supply or demand. In a managed-exchange-rate system, the exchange rate is determined through the markets, but the central bank will intervene by buying and selling the currency in order to influence the price.

DENISE WOODBURY

CUSTOMER SERVICE

A growing number of organizations are giving increased attention to customer service. Financial institutions, hospitals, public utilities, airlines, retail stores, restaurants, manufacturers, and wholesalers face the problem of gaining and retaining the patronage of customers. Building long-term relationships with customers has been given a high priority by the majority of America's most successful enterprises. These companies realize that customer satisfaction is an important key to success. *Customer service* can be defined as those activities that enhance or facilitate the purchase and use of the product. Today's emphasis on customer satisfaction can be traced to a managerial philosophy that has been described as the marketing concept.

EVOLUTION OF THE MARKETING CONCEPT

What is the "marketing concept"? When a business firm moves from a product orientation to a customer orientation, we say it has adopted the *marketing concept*. This concept springs from the belief that the firm should dedicate all its policies, planning, and operation to the satisfaction of the customer.

The marketing era in the United States began in the 1950s. J. B. McKitterick, a General Electric executive, is credited with making one of the earliest formal statements indicating corporate interest in the marketing concept. In a paper written in 1957 he observed that the principal marketing function of a company is to determine what the customer wants and then develop the appropriate product or service. This view contrasted with the prevailing practice of that period, which was to develop products and then build customer interest in those products.

The foundation for the marketing concept is a business philosophy that leaves no doubt in the mind of every employee that customer satisfaction is of primary importance. All energies are directed toward satisfying the consumer. L. L. Bean, the Freeport, Maine, mail-order firm, provides a good example of a company that has embraced the marketing concept. This well-known supplier of outdoor products offers the customer an unconditional guarantee of satisfaction that has been in place since the company was founded in 1912. If you are unhappy with an L. L. Bean product, simply request replacement or a refund (Comarow, 1999).

We have entered the age of boundless competition, triggered in large part by an expanding global economy. Multinational competition has increased dramatically in recent years, and this means a one-world market exists for products ranging from cars to computers. To compete successfully in markets where products are the same or very similar, and prices are basically the same, service is often the only competitive advantage available.

WINNING CUSTOMER SERVICE STRATEGIES

According to the marketing concept, an organization must determine what customers want and use this information to create satisfying products and services (Pride and Ferrell, 1997). Federal Express redefined mail service by providing overnight, door-to-door delivery of packages and letters. The company discovered a need for speed, reliability, and courteous service by well-trained employees. The marketing concept is a management philosophy guiding all the organizational activities, including production, personnel, finance, distribution, and marketing.

Excellent customer service is achieved by a three-dimensional process (see Figure 1) that includes a well-conceived service strategy, customer-driven systems, and customer-friendly

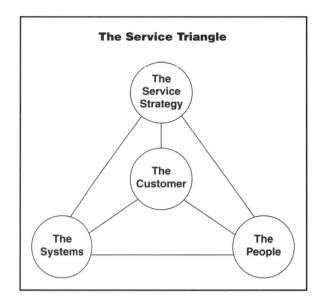

Figure 1

people (Albrecht and Zemke, 1985). Each dimension must reflect the important needs and wants of the customer. The "service triangle" can be developed for any type of business. Each piece of the triangle is explained in the following sections.

SERVICE STRATEGY

A well-conceived service strategy includes three important elements: market research to discover the customers' needs and wants; a clear vision of the firm's "reason for being"; and clearly stated beliefs and values that guide the enterprise (Albrecht and Zemke, 1985).

Many organizations are creating a written vision or mission statement that directs the energies of the company and inspires employees to achieve greater heights. Ortho Biotech, based in Raritan, New Jersey, begins its vision statement with a bold prediction: "We will be the best in our business by providing customers with innovative solutions to significant medical problems through biotechnology and related science" (quoted in Lee, 1993, p. 27). Senior managers must serve as "cheerleaders" to unify employees behind the vision.

The creation of a sound set of beliefs and values can give stability to an organization. Customer service priorities also become clearer. Ben

Edwards, chairman of A.G. Edwards and Sons, Inc., the seventh-largest securities firm in the nation, says following the Golden Rule is still the best way to achieve success in business (Kegley, 1990). This attitude has had a positive influence on the company's 7400 employees.

CUSTOMER-FRIENDLY SYSTEMS

Service systems are made up of all the various practices and procedures that personnel can use to meet customer needs. When you check into the Hyatt Regency Crown Center in Kansas City, Missouri, you are given a card that says, "Call 50 for a response to any concern within five minutes" (Manning and Reece, 1998). MBNA, a Wilmington, Delaware, financial services company wants every phone call answered within two rings. Employees achieve this goal nearly 100 percent of the time (Reece and Brandt, 1999). If you have a problem with your Dell computer, you can check the detailed troubleshooting guide provided by the company or get help from a member of the technical support staff. These examples are typical of the steps being taken by companies that want to meet, and in some cases exceed, the expectations of their customers.

Customer-friendly systems are designed to make things easy for customers. Complaints should be handled in a timely fashion. Returning or exchanging products should not be difficult. Requests for assistance should be handled in a courteous and efficient manner. Customer-friendly systems add value and build customer loyalty.

CUSTOMER-FRIENDLY FRONTLINE PEOPLE

In many cases, the customer's first impression of an organization comes during contact with frontline people. The cashier at the supermarket, the receptionist at the doctor's office, and the front-desk clerk at the hotel often have the first opportunity to serve the customer. Unfortunately, too often these employees earn low pay, receive little formal training, and are given little

recognition for the important duties they perform. The best frontline employees are both competent and caring. They have a certain level of maturity and possess the social skills needed to build customer loyalty.

SUMMARY

The ultimate purpose of every business should be to satisfy the customer. Increased levels of competition require a greater commitment to customer service. Firms that invest the time, energy, and money needed to achieve excellent customer service will be the ones that thrive and grow.

BIBLIOGRAPHY

Albrecht, K., and Zemke, R. (1985). *Service America!* Homewood, IL: Dow Jones-Irwin.

Carlzon, Jan. (1987). *Moments of Truth.* Cambridge, MA: Ballinger.

Comarow, A. (1999). "Broken? No Problem." *U.S. News and World Report* January 11:68-70.

Fromm, Bill, and Schlesinger, Len. (1994). *The Real Heroes of Business . . . and Not a CEO among Them.* New York: Currency Doubleday.

Kawasaki, Guy. (1999). *Rules for Revolutionaries.* New York: Harper Business.

Kegley, G. (1990). "Broker with a Difference: A. G. Edwards, Chairman." *Roanoke Times World News* April 13:B-6.

Lavington, Camille. (1997). *You've Only Got Three Seconds.* New York: Doubleday.

Lee, C. (1993). "The Vision Thing." *Training* February 27:27.

Manning, G. L., and Reece, B. L. (1998). *Selling Today: Building Quality Partnerships.* Upper Saddle River, NJ: Prentice-Hall.

Peppers, Don, and Rogers, Martha. (1999). *The One to One Fieldbook.* New York: Currency Doubleday.

Pride, W. M., and Ferrell, O. C. (1997). *Marketing.* Boston Houghton Mifflin.

Reece, B. L., and Brandt, R. (1999). *Effective Human Relations in Organizations.* Boston: Houghton Mifflin.

Sewell, Carl. (1998). *Customers for Life.* New York: Pocket Books.

BARRY L. REECE

D

DATABASES

With the rise of business data-processing systems on a very large scale during the 1960s and 1970s came the development of databases and database management systems. *Databases* are large collections of interrelated data stored on computer disk systems from which they can be immediately accessed and revised. *Database management systems* are large computer programs that "manage" or control the databases.

Data is normally defined as "facts" from which *information* can be derived. For example, "Janene Clouse lives at 1411 Sycamore Avenue" is a fact. A database may contain millions of such facts. From these facts the database management system can derive information in the form of answers to questions such as "How many people live on Sycamore Avenue?" The popularity of databases in business is a direct result of the power of database management systems in deriving valuable business information from large collections of data.

RELATIONAL DATABASES

Most modern databases are *relational*, meaning that data are stored in tables, consisting of rows and columns, and that data in different tables are related by the meanings of certain common columns. (The tables in a database are sometimes called "files," the rows are called "records," and the columns are called "fields." However, this is an older terminology, left over from the early days of business computer systems.) The following is an example of a simple relational database consisting of three tables—one for customers, one for products, and one for sales:

Customers

Customer_no	name	address	phone
1001	Jones	320 Main	555-8811
1002	Smith	401 Oak	555-8822
1003	Brown	211 Elm	555-8833
1004	Green	899 Maple	555-8844

Products

product_no	description	price
25	Ring	3.25
33	Gasket	1.23
45	Shaft	4.55

Sales

sale_no	date	customer_no	product_no
841	3/11	1002	45
842	3/12	1001	25
843	3/12	1002	45
844	3/13	1004	33
845	3/14	1003	25
846	3/15	1002	33

Suppose we want to know the customer's name for sale number 845. We look in the customer number column of the Sales table, and we see that it was customer 1003. Next, we refer to the Customers table and find customer 1003. Here we see the customer's name is Brown. So, Brown was the customer for sale number 845.

STRUCTURED QUERY LANGUAGE

The foregoing is a simple example of a database query. In a modern database, queries are expressed in a query language, which requires a particular format that can be recognized and interpreted by the database management system (DBMS). The standard query language for relational databases, as adopted by the American National Standards Institute (ANSI), is SQL, which is generally understood to be an abbreviation for "Structured Query Language." Let us look at a few examples of queries expressed in SQL.

Query: Which products have a price over $2?

SQL Solution: Select product_no, description

From Products
Where price > 2.00

Result: **product_no**   **description**

Ring
Shaft

This query's SQL solution illustrates the SQL format. In general, SQL "statements" have a Select "clause," a From "clause," and a Where "clause." The Select clause lists the columns that are to be shown in the result, the From clause lists the database tables from which data is to be taken, and the Where clause gives the condition to be applied to each row in the table. If a row satisfies the condition, then it is selected, and the values in that row for the columns listed in the Select clause are included in the result.

Query: When have we sold product number 45 to customer 1002?

SQL Solution: Select date
From Sales
Where product_no = 45
and customer_no = 1002

Result: **date**
3/11
3/12

In this example you can see that the condition in the Where clause includes the connector "and," which indicates that both conditions (product_no = 45 and customer_no = 1002) must be fulfilled. In our sample database there are two rows that satisfy this condition, and the query's result yields the dates from those two rows.

Our next query gives the SQL solution to the original query we discussed above.

Query: What is the customer's name for sale number 845?

SQL Solution: Select name
From Customers, Sales
Where sale_no = 845 and
Sales.customer_no =
Customers.customer.no

This query illustrates how we can query more than one table at once in SQL. First, we list all tables needed to answer the query. In this case then, we list the Customers and the Sales tables. Then in the Where clause we give two conditions:

sale_no = 845 and

Sales.customer_no = Customers.customer_no

The first condition indicates that the sale_no column must have a value of 845. Since there is only one row in the Sales table having that value, we have limited our query to that single row. The second condition indicates that we want only that row in the Customers table which has the same value for its customer_no column as the Sales row has for its customer_no column. This condition then limits our result to the joining together of one row from the Sales table and one row from the Customers table. Finally, the Select clause,

Select name

tells us that we should give the value from the name column as our result. As we showed before, the resulting customer name is "Brown."

Queries can also be used to perform calculations:

```
Query: What is the average price of our products?

SQL Solution:    Select Avg (price)
                 From Products

Result:          3.01
```

SQL also provides statements that can be used to make changes to data in the database. For example, let's suppose we want to increase the price of our products by 3 percent. Then we can use the following statement:

Update Products

Set price = 1.03 * price

This statement will cause the price of every product in our Products table to be increased by 3 percent. Note that it doesn't matter whether we have 3 products, as shown in our sample database, or 300,000 products. A single statement will update the prices of all products. Of course, if we only want to change the prices of selected products we can do that, too:

Update Products

Set price = 1.03 * price

Where product_no = 33

This statement will only change the price of product number 33. SQL also provides statements to Insert new rows into tables and to Delete rows from tables.

These queries show only a very small number of the capabilities of SQL. The Where clause can be used to select rows based on where names are in the alphabet, whether dates are before or after certain other dates, based on averages, and based on many other conditions.

SMALL AND LARGE DATABASES

Databases can be *single-user* or *multi-user*. A single-user database exists on a single computer and is accessible only from that computer. Many single-user databases exist, and there are a number of commercial DBMSs that address this market. A multi-user database may exist on a single machine, such as a mainframe or other powerful computer, or it may be *distributed* and exist on multiple computers. Multi-user databases are accessible from multiple computers simultaneously. With the rise of the Internet, many databases are publicly accessible. For example, the holdings of university libraries are maintained on databases that can be browsed from remote locations. A person interested in locating a book in a library can enter the book's title, author, or subject, and a database query will be automatically performed. Information on the desired book or list of books will be returned to the person's computer.

SELECTING A DATABASE SYSTEM

A person or business seeking to purchase a database management system for use in managing a database should consider the following factors:

Relational: Virtually all major commercial database management systems are relational, since the desirability of relational databases is well-accepted in the database community.

SQL: In addition, since the American National Standards Institute has adopted SQL as it standard for relational databases, the desired DBMS should support SQL.

Capacity: As noted above, database management systems are designed for a variety of environments. Some are designed to be single-user systems, others are designed for medium-sized businesses, while still others are designed for large businesses. The system chosen should naturally be one that has been shown to be successful in and appropriate for the environment it is chosen for.

Disaster recovery capability: More sophisticated systems are more capable of recovering from power outages, computer hardware failure, and the like than are the single-user systems. They use sophisticated *logging* and database *locking* facilities that make such recovery possible. Often, these facilities are unnecessary for single-user systems.

SUMMARY

Databases and database management systems are central to modern business information systems. Relational databases using the SQL language provide substantial logical power to help businesses make informed decisions based on their own data. Database systems can be small and handled by a single user, or they can be large and available to multiple users. They are even publicly available through the Internet. Database management systems can be sophisticated and expensive, and consequently their purchase requires careful, informed consideration.

BIBLIOGRAPHY

Dunham, Jeff. (1998). *Database Performance Tuning Handbook.* New York: McGraw-Hill.

Groff, James R. and Weinberg, Paul N. (1999). *SQL: The Complete Reference.* Berkeley: Osborne/McGraw-Hill.

Hansen, Gary W. and Hansen, James V. (1996). *Database Management and Design*, 2d ed. Upper Saddle River, NJ: Prentice Hall.

Kroenke, David M. (2000). *Database Processing*, 7th ed. Upper Saddle River, NJ: Prentice Hall.

Rob, Peter and Coronel, Carlos. (2000). *Database Systems: Design Implementation, and Management*, 4th ed. Cambridge, MA: Course Technology.

GARY HANSEN

DECA

DECA is a national student organization for individuals preparing for marketing, management, and entrepreneurship careers. With 180,000 members, DECA serves as the companion to marketing education programs within secondary and post-secondary schools across all fifty states of the United States, its territories, and Canada. As a co-curricular organization, DECA is an integral part of classroom instruction—a vehicle through which students learn marketing and management, and are motivated to succeed.

In partnership with businesses throughout the country, DECA offers learning experiences that contribute to the integration of academic and career-focused instruction, resulting in heightened student achievement and student recognition. For example, each year more than 60,000 student members participate in a competitive events program, culminating in state and national secondary and post-secondary Career Development Conferences that allow members to demonstrate academic and marketing excellence.

Organized in 1946, DECA meets the needs of marketing (then, distributive) education students seeking professional and personal growth. The association is governed by a board of directors. Until July 1991, DECA was referred to as the Distributive Education Clubs of America. Although that continues to be the legal name, the organization uses the commonly recognized acronym, DECA, along with the tag line, An Association of Marketing Students." The official logo of DECA is a diamond, whose four points emphasize civic consciousness, leadership development, vocational understanding, and social intelligence. DECA is advised by a national advisory board, consisting of business representatives, and a congressional advisory board, comprised of federal legislators.

The official publications of DECA are the *DECA Advisor, Dimensions, Chi Connection, Highwired.Net*, and the *DECA Guide.* Such scholarships as the Harry A. Applegate, J. C. Penney, and Sears Scholarships are available to support the academic endeavors of members. More information is available from DECA at 1908 Association Dr., Reston, Virginia 20191; (703)860-5000: or http://www.deca.org.

BIBLIOGRAPHY

Berns, Robert G. (1996). *DECA: A Continuing Tradition of Excellence.* Reston, VA: DECA.

Cahill, Julie, and Brady, Kathleen. (1999). "Sweetening the Deal." *Techniques*, March:26-28.

Distributive Education Clubs of America DECA: An Association of Marketing Students. http://www.deca.org/. 1999.

JEWEL E. HAIRSTON
ROBERT G. BERNS

DECISION MAKING

Decision making, also referred to as problem solving, is the process of recognizing a problem or opportunity and finding a solution to it. Decisions are made by everyone involved in the business world, but managers typically face the most decisions on a daily basis. Many of these decisions are relatively simple and routine, such as ordering production supplies, choosing the discount rate for an order, or deciding the annual raise of an employee. These routine types of decisions are known as *programmed decisions*, because the decision maker already knows what the solution and outcome will be. However, managers are also faced with decisions that can drastically affect the future outcomes of the business. These types of decisions are known as *nonprogrammed decisions*, because neither the appropriate solution nor the potential outcome is known. Examples of nonprogrammed decisions include merging with another company, creating a new product, or expanding production facilities.

Decision making typically follows a six-step process:

1. Identify the problem or opportunity

2. Gather relevant information

3. Develop as many alternatives as possible

4. Evaluate alternatives to decide which is best

5. Decide on and implement the best alternative

6. Follow-up on the decision

In *step 1*, the decision maker must be sure he or she has an accurate grasp of the situation. The need to make a decision has occurred because there is a difference between the desired outcome and what is actually occurring. Before proceeding to step 2, it is important to pinpoint the actual cause of the situation, which may not always be obviously apparent.

In *step 2*, the decision maker gathers as much information as possible because having all the facts gives the decision maker a much better chance of making the appropriate decision. When an uninformed decision is made, the outcome is usually not very positive, so it is important to have all the facts before proceeding.

In *step 3*, the decision maker attempts to come up with as many alternatives as possible. A technique known as "brainstorming," whereby group members offer any and all ideas even if they sound totally ridiculous, is often used in this step.

In *step 4*, the alternatives are evaluated and the best one is selected. The process of evaluating the alternatives usually starts by narrowing the choices down to two or three and then choosing the best one. This step is usually the most difficult, because there are often many variables to consider. The decision maker must attempt to select the alternative that will be the most effective given the available amount of information, the legal obstacles, the public relations issues, the financial implications, and the time constraints on making the decision. Often the decision maker is faced with a problem for which there is no apparent good solution at the moment. When this happens, the decision maker must make the best choice available at the time but continue to look for a better option in the future.

Once the decision has been made, *step 5* is performed. Implementation often requires some additional planning time as well as the understanding and cooperation of the people involved. Communication is very important in the implementation step, because most people are resistant to change simply because they do not understand why it is necessary. In order to ensure smooth implementation of the decision, the decision maker should communicate the reasons behind the decision to the people involved.

In *step 6*, after the decision has been implemented, the decision maker must follow-up on the decision to see if it is working successfully. If the decision that was implemented has corrected the difference between the actual and desired outcome, the decision is considered successful. However, if the implemented decision has not produced the desired result, once again a decision must be made. The decision maker can decide to give the decision more time to work, choose another of the generated alternatives, or start the whole process over from the beginning.

STRATEGIC, TACTICAL, AND OPERATIONAL DECISIONS

People at different levels in a company have different types of decision-making responsibilities. *Strategic decisions*, which affect the long-term direction of the entire company, are typically made by top managers. Examples of strategic decisions might be to focus efforts on a new product or to increase production output. These types of decisions are often complex and the outcomes uncertain, because available information is often limited. Managers at this level must often depend on past experiences and their instincts when making strategic decisions.

Tactical decisions, which focus on more intermediate-term issues, are typically made by middle managers. The purpose of decisions made at this level is to help move the company closer to reaching the strategic goal. Examples of tactical decisions might be to pick an advertising agency to promote a new product or to provide an incentive plan to employees to encourage increased production.

Operational decisions focus on day-to-day activities within the company and are typically made by lower-level managers. Decisions made at this level help to ensure that daily activities proceed smoothly and therefore help to move the company toward reaching the strategic goal. Examples of operational decisions include scheduling employees, handling employee conflicts, and purchasing raw materials needed for production.

It should be noted that in many "flatter" organizations, where the middle management level has been eliminated, both tactical and operational decisions are made by lower-level management and/or teams of employees.

GROUP DECISIONS

Group decision making has many benefits as well as some disadvantages. The obvious benefit is that there is more input and therefore more possible solutions to the situation can be generated. Another advantage is that there is shared responsibility for the decision and its outcome, so one person does not have total responsibility for making a decision. The disadvantages are that it often takes a long time to reach a group consensus and that group members may have to compromise in order to reach a consensus. Many businesses have created problem-solving teams whose purpose is to find ways to improve specific work activities.

BIBLIOGRAPHY

Boone, Louis E., and Kurtz, David L. (1999). *Contemporary Business*, 9th ed. Orlando, FL: Harcourt Brace College Publishers.

Bounds, Gregory M., and Lamb, Charles W., Jr. (1998). *Business*. Cincinnati, OH: South-Western College Publishing.

Clancy, Kevin J., and Shulman, Robert S. (1994). *Marketing Myths That are Killing Business: The Cure for Death Wish Marketing*. New York: McGraw-Hill.

French, Wendell L. (1998). *Human Resources Management*. New York: Houghton Mifflin.

Madura, Jeff. (1998). *Introduction to Business*. Cincinnati, OH: South-Western College Publishing.

Nickels, William G., McHugh, James M., and McHugh, Susan M. (1999). *Understanding Business*, 5th ed. Boston: Irwin McGraw-Hill.

Pride, William M., Hughes, Robert J., and Kapoor, Jack R. (1999). *Business*, 6th ed. New York: Houghton Mifflin.

MARCY SATTERWHITE

DEFLATION

(SEE: *Economic Cycles*)

DELEGATION

(SEE: *Mangement: Authority and Responsibility*)

DEMAND

(SEE: *Supply and Demand*)

DEMAND CURVES

(SEE: *Supply and Demand*)

DEPARTMENTALIZATION

(SEE: *Organizational Structure*)

DEPRESSION

(SEE: *Economic Cycles*)

DEREGULATION

Most societies rely on competitive markets to handle the allocation of scarce resources to their highest and best uses. Yet markets are not without their shortcomings. For this reason, governments sometime institute regulatory control. In 1887, the first regulatory agency, the Interstate Commerce Commission, was created to regulate monopolistic pricing policies of railroads.

When private firms gain monopoly power, usually because of economies of scale, they are in a position to restrict production and raise price with little worry of competition; these are known as natural monopolies. The government may permit a single producer (e.g., of natural gas or electricity) to exist in order to gain lower production costs but simultaneously empower a regulatory agency to set the firm's prices.

A second reason for regulation stems from the fact that society declares certain activities illegal. Prostitution, gambling, and certain drugs are either not permitted or allowed only under certain conditions. Through a licensing system, government agencies control who enters such industries, their prices, and their methods of operation.

Another reason for government regulation arises because society establishes standards for particular professions, such as medicine, law, accounting, and real estate. The government guarantees compliance with these standards by imposing tests and other requirements. Those failing to meet these standards are not permitted to engage in that business. Hundreds of agencies administer tests and police the professions, all done ostensibly in the interest of protecting the consumer. Interestingly, license holders often push for even higher licensing requirements, often grandfathering in all current license holders, because higher salaries are possible when the number of competitors is restricted.

Many government regulations are designed to protect people from the negative consequences (i.e., externalities) of buyers and sellers who have little incentive to look out for the welfare of third parties. For example, slaughterhouses may have the freedom to kill animals for sale to their customers in grocery stores without taking into account obnoxious odors or sounds emanating from the slaughterhouse. Neighborhood residents, however, incur externality costs. Through agencies such as the Environmental Protection Agency (EPA), the government controls what slaughterhouses can and cannot do in order to lessen the negative effects on the population.

Although government regulation is pervasive for the reasons presented above, it is apparent that regulation may not achieve the lofty goals set out in the initial effort to regulate. Governments can also fail, and government failure often aggravates the problems it sets out to solve. Public choice economists have identified several specific causes of government failure. Voters are often rationally ignorant about many things, and they vote for political candidates who are uninformed or misinformed. Also, politicians are often indebted to their financial supporters, some of whom are regulated industries, and will often enact laws favorable to their supporters regardless of the negative impact on the public. Politicians may even be willing to sacrifice the future for the sake of short-term benefits for their financial supporters. Recognition of such limitations to government regulation has caused Congress to rethink regulation, especially as it relates to certain industries.

Beginning in the mid-1970s, increased dissatisfaction with the burdens of regulation, especially the costs imposed on consumers, led to the *deregulation* of a number of industries, including

Protesters at a deregulation rally.

the airlines (Airline Deregulation Act of 1978), natural gas (Natural Gas Policy Act of 1978), trucking (Motor Carrier Act of 1980), and banking (Depository Institutions Deregulation and Monetary Control Act of 1980).

In 1997 some states began deregulating the production and sale of electricity. New technologies now permit small companies to produce electricity at reduced costs. Under the new system (much like the system in the telephone industry), local utilities must permit competitors to use their electric lines for a fee.

Benefits from deregulation include reduced prices and increased choices for consumers. Competition among long-distance telephone suppliers is keen, no longer requiring government regulation, and is demonstrated by the fact that from 1985 to 1998 prices declined by 72 percent. Expanded service and reduced prices have occurred in both airlines and trucking. Eleven thousand new trucking lines started up

within three years of deregulation, and savings may be as high as $50 billion per year.

Some concerns have arisen about deregulation, however. The airline industry has become more concentrated since deregulation. In 1978 eleven carriers handled 87 percent of the traffic, while in 1995 seven carriers handled 93 percent of the traffic. Although some feared reduced safety, that has not materialized. Some of the bank failures in the 1980s were attributed to deregulation; yet depositors receive higher interest. On balance, deregulation effects have been positive.

A significant change in direction has also taken place with regard to government regulation of industries producing externalities. Many externalities arise because of the lack of property rights; consequently there is greater emphasis on establishing clearly defined property rights, which allows the market to automatically internalize the cost to buyers and sellers, making government regulation costly and unnecessary.

The EPA now depends less heavily on its command-and-control approach and more heavily on tradable permits, reducing the overall level of pollution and allowing firms to avoid pollution in a more cost-effective way.

Although Congress has deregulated specific industries, *social* regulation designed to "protect" consumers has expanded. Through such agencies as the Occupational Safety and Health Administration, the Consumer Product Safety Commission, the Food and Drug Administration, the Equal Employment Opportunity Commission, and the EPA, the government is attempting to provide safer products, better health care, fairer employment practices, and a cleaner environment. Government at federal, state, and local levels has also continued to increase license requirements for numerous occupations and professions.

Many economists wonder if the benefits are high enough to warrant the cost of regulation. In addition to regulatory-imposed limits on consumer freedom, product prices rise, administrative costs are high, and some firms are driven out of business, thereby reducing competition. To further complicate things, many special-interest groups use such laws to increase their wealth at the expense of others. It has been estimated that federal regulation costs each household $6000 per year. Clearly the issues surrounding regulation/deregulation will continue to be discussed into the twenty-first century.

BIBLIOGRAPHY

Kahn, Alfred E. (1988). *The Economics of Regulation: Principles and Institutions.* Cambridge, MA: MIT Press.

Teske, P., Best, S, and Mintrom, M., (1995). *Deregulating Freight Transportation.* Lavergne, TN: AEI Press.

Winston, C. (1993). "Economic Deregulation" *Journal of Economic Literature* September: 1263-1289.

JAMES R. RINEHART
JEFFREY J. POMPE

DERIVATIVES

Derivative instruments are used as financial management tools to enhance investment returns and to manage such risks relative to interest rates, exchange rates, and financial instrument and commodity prices. Several local and international banks, businesses, municipalities, and others have experienced significant losses with the use of derivatives. However, their use has increased as efforts to control risk in complex situations are perceived to be wise strategic decisions.

SFAS 133'S DEFINITION OF A DERIVATIVE INSTRUMENT

In 1998, the Financial Accounting Standards Board (FASB) issued Statement on Financial Accounting Standards No. 133 (SFAS 133), *Accounting for Derivative Instruments and Hedging Activities*, which is effective for companies with fiscal years beginning after June 15, 2000. SFAS 133 establishes new accounting and reporting rules for derivative instruments, including derivatives embedded in other contracts, and for hedging activities. Derivatives must now be reported at their fair values in financial statements. Gains and losses from derivative transactions must be reported currently in income, except from those transactions that qualify as effective hedges.

According to Statement on Financial Accounting Standards (SFAS) 133, a derivative instrument is defined as a financial instrument or other contract that represents rights or obligations of assets or liabilities with all three of the following characteristics:

- It has (1) one or more underlyings and (2) one or more notional amounts or payment provisions or both. Those terms determine the settlement amount of the derivative. An *underlying* is a variable (i.e., stock price) or index (i.e., bond index) whose market movements cause the fair value market or cash flows of a derivative to change. The *notional amount* is the fixed amount or quantity that determines the size of the change caused by the change in the underlying; possibly a number of currency units, shares, bushels, pounds, or other units specified in the contract. A *payment provision* specifies a fixed or determinable settlement to be made if the underlying behaves in a specified manner.

- It requires no initial net investment or an initial net investment that is smaller than would be required for other types of similar instruments.

- Its terms require or permit net settlement. [SFAS 133, paragraph 6]

USERS OF DERIVATIVES

The derivatives market serves the needs of several groups of users, including those parties who wish to hedge, those who wish to speculate, and arbitrageurs.

- A *hedger* enters the market to reduce risk. Hedging usually involves taking a position in a derivative financial instrument, which has opposite return characteristics of the item being hedged, to offset losses or gains.

- A *speculator* enters the derivatives market in search of profits, and is willing to accept risk. A speculator takes an open position in a derivative product (i.e. there is no offsetting cash flow exposure to offset losses on the position taken in the derivative product).

- An *arbitrageur* is a speculator who attempts to lock in near riskless profit from price differences by simultaneously entering into the purchase and sale of substantially identical financial instruments.

Other participants include clearinghouses or clearing corporations, brokers, commodity futures trading commission, commodity pool operators, commodity trading advisors, financial institutions and banks, futures exchange, and futures commission merchants.

TYPES OF DERIVATIVE INSTRUMENTS

Derivative instruments are classified as:

- Forward Contracts
- Futures Contracts
- Options
- Swaps

Derivatives can also be classified as either forward-based (e.g., futures, forward contracts, and swap contracts), option-based (e.g., call or put option), or combinations of the two. A forward-based contract obligates one party to buy and a counterparty to sell an underlying asset, such as foreign currency or a commodity, with equal risk at a future date at an agreed-on price. Option-based contracts (e.g., call options, put options, caps and floors) provide the holder with a right, but not an obligation to buy or sell an underlying financial instrument, foreign currency, or commodity at an agreed-on price during a specified time period or at a specified date.

Forward Contracts Forward contracts are negotiated between two parties, with no formal regulation or exchange, to purchase (long position) and sell (short position) a specific quantity of a specific quantity of a commodity (i.e., corn and gold), foreign currency, or financial instrument (i.e., bonds and stock) at a specified price (delivery price), with delivery or settlement at a specified future date (maturity date). The price of the underlying asset for immediate delivery is known as the spot price.

Forward contracts may be entered into through an agreement without a cash payment, provided the forward rate is equal to the current market rate. Forward contracts are often used to hedge the entire price changed of a commodity, a foreign currency, or a financial instrument. irrespective of a price increase or decrease.

Futures Contracts Futures are standardized contracts traded on a regulated exchange to make or take delivery of a specified quantity of a commodity, a foreign currency, or a financial instrument at a specified price, with delivery or settlement at a specified future date. Futures contracts involve U.S. Treasury bonds, agricultural commodities, stock indices, interest-earning assets, and foreign currency.

A futures contract is entered into through an organized exchange, using banks and brokers. These organized exchanges have clearinghouses, which may be financial institutions or part of the futures exchange. They interpose themselves between the buyer and the seller, guarantee obligations, and make futures liquid with low credit risk. Although no payment is made upon entering into a futures contract, since the underlying (i.e. interest rate, share price, or commodity price) is at-the-market, subsequent value changes require daily mark-to-marking by cash settlement (i.e. disbursed gains and daily collected losses). Similarly, margin requirements involve deposits from both parties to ensure any financial liabilities.

Futures contracts are used to hedge the entire price change of a commodity, a foreign currency, or a financial instrument since the contract value and underlying price change symmetrically.

Options Options are rights to buy or sell. For example, the purchaser of an option has the right, but not the obligation, to buy or sell a specified quantity of a particular commodity, a foreign currency, or a financial instrument, at a specified price, during a specified period of time (American option) or on a specified date (European option). An option may be settled by taking delivery of the underlying or by cash settlement, with risk limited to the premium.

The two main types of option contracts are call options and put options, while some others include stock (or equity) options, foreign currency options, options on futures, caps, floors, collars, and swaptions.

- *American call options* provide the holder with the right to acquire an underlying product (e.g., stock) at an exercise or strike price, throughout the option term. The holder pays a premium for the right to benefit from the appreciation in the underlying.

- *American put options* provide the holder with the right to sell the underlying product (e.g., stock) at a certain exercise or strike price, throughout the option term. The holder gains as the market price of the underlying (stock price) falls below the exercise price.

- An *interest rate cap* is an option that allows a cap purchaser to limit exposure to increasing interest rates on its variable-rate debt instruments.

- An *interest rate floor* is an option that allows a floor purchaser to limit exposure to decreasing interest rates on its variable-rate investments.

Generally, option contracts are used to hedge a one-directional movement in the underlying commodity, foreign currency, or financial instrument.

Swaps A swap is a flexible, private, forward-based contract or agreement, generally between two counterparties to exchange streams of cash flows based on an agreed-on (or notional) principal amount over a specified period of time in the future.

Swaps are usually entered into at-the-money (i.e. with minimal initial cash payments because fair value is zero), through brokers or dealers who take an up-front cash payment or who adjust the rate to bear default risk. The two most prevalent swaps are interest rate swaps and foreign currency swaps, while others include equity swaps, commodity swaps, and swaptions.

- *Swaptions* are options on swaps that provide the holder with the right to enter into a swap at a specified future date at specified terms (stand-alone option in a swap) or to extend or terminate the life of an existing swap (embedded option on a swap).

Swap contracts are used to hedge entire price changes (symmetrically) related to an identified hedged risk, such as interest rate or foreign currency risk, since both counterparties gain or lose equally.

RISK CHARACTERISTICS OF DERIVATIVES

The main types of risk characteristics associated with derivatives are:

- Basis Risk This is the spot (cash) price of the underlying asset being hedged, less the price of the derivative contract used to hedge the asset.

- Credit Risk Credit risk or default risk evolves from the possibility that one of the parties to a derivative contract will not satisfy its financial obligations under the derivative contract.

- Market Risk This is the potential financial loss due to adverse changes in the fair value of a derivative. Market risk encompasses legal risk, control risk, and accounting risk.

BIBLIOGRAPHY

Hull, John. (1998). *Introduction to Futures and Options Markets*, 3rd ed. Upper Saddle River, NJ: Prentice Hall.

Kolb, Robert. (1995). *Futures, Options and Swaps*, 2nd ed. London: Blackwell.

Statement of Financial Accounting Standards (SFAS) No. 133, Accounting for Derivatives Instruments and Hedging Activities. (1998). Norwalk, CT: Financial Accounting Standards Board (FASB).

PATRICK CASABONA

DESKTOP PUBLISHING

Desktop publishing, or *DTP*, is the term applied to the process of creating and publishing professional-looking documents using microcomputers. DTP systems can produce many types of documents, from simple to sophisticated, including business cards, letterhead stationery, brochures, newsletters, flyers, maps, coupons, posters, invitations, business graphics, annual reports, proposals, and magazines. For such projects, a company would need photography equipment, photo-editing software, illustration software, and page-layout software.

For example, creating a brochure would require photographs of people or products. Photo-editing software would be used to edit, combine, and give special treatment to the photographs. Illustration software would be needed to create line drawings or other special effects. And page-layout software would be needed to arrange all the text and graphic elements. The following sections review the history, system components, design process and guidelines, features, and management guidelines pertaining to DTP.

HISTORY

Historically, the creation and publication of professionally designed documents involved a variety of separate processes and people. To create a brochure, for example, a designer would develop the overall idea and create a drawing of the finished document. A writer would create the text, a typesetter would type the text in the desired fonts, an illustrator would draw needed line art, a photographer would shoot photos, and a service bureau would develop the film and create color separations from the photos for color work. The designer would then create the final comprehensive, pasting text, illustrations, and other elements on a board for filming. The comprehensive would be photographed, after which photo negatives would be cut out and placed on a sheet from which printing plates would be made. The plates would then be mounted on a printer, and the final document would be printed, cropped, folded, and bound as necessary.

Today's DTP technology automates many of these steps and enables just one person with a computer and DTP software to become a stand-alone publishing business. Photos can be taken with digital cameras, bypassing the film-development stage required of traditional film-type photography. Photo-editing software enables photos to be cropped, scaled, and edited. Word-processing software is used to capture and process text, and illustration software is used to create drawings. Finally, page-layout software is used to assemble all the components and print output from which printing plates are made. The final document is then printed on a computer printer or on a large commercial press. Alternately, electronic documents can be published on the Internet, making them available to a worldwide audience.

SYSTEM COMPONENTS

DTP system hardware requires a fast computer with a high-capacity hard disk, scanner, high-resolution printer, modem or other connection to the Internet, large amount of random-access memory (RAM), and digital camera. In addition, the system must have word-processing software, illustration software, photo-editing software, page-layout software, Internet-publishing software, clip art, and multiple type fonts. DTP periodicals can be helpful in selecting appropriate hardware and software.

DESIGN PROCESS AND GUIDELINES

Being successful at desktop publishing requires more than just learning how to operate all the DTP hardware and software. One must first develop a design, which requires creativity and knowledge of design principles, and then use the hardware and software to make the design a reality. The first phase of document creation involves planning. This phase focuses on identifying the goals of the publication. For example, to design a business card, the designer will want to give the customer the information needed to contact the business and to make a good impression on the customer.

The second step is to analyze the audience, the people who will be using and reading the document. If a newsletter focuses on mountain biking, for example, the audience might be primarily younger outdoor enthusiasts. Additional audience research would provide additional information about mountain biker characteristics.

The third step is to develop a strategy, or theme. A total communication line for a mountain biking retail business might include an Internet Web site, brochures, business cards, letterhead and envelopes, forms, and information sheets. To achieve unity, a carefully selected concept or theme should be carried throughout all these items. For example, all the documents might carry a common theme of a knobby bicycle wheel as the company logo, the same typeface for text and headings, and the same color scheme. Repetition of document characteristics and elements is a key characteristic of effective documents.

The final step in the planning phase is to develop a prototype of documents to be developed. Designers usually create numerous sketches and then gradually refine the more preferred sketches until a final selection is made. The final design must include appropriate empty space, called *white space*, so the document does not look too crowded. Obviously, the greatest requirement of the final design is that it will appeal to and persuade the intended audience.

After the planning phase, the document is created. Creation requires writing appropriate text, called *copy*, and choosing the appropriate fonts (typefaces, type styles, and type sizes) for the various parts of the text. To achieve a harmonious appearance, the fonts must complement the graphic styles. The text must be skillfully organized for easy reading, and the wording must be understandable and meaningful to the intended audience.

Graphics also have to be obtained, either illustrations or photographs. Professional artists can be hired to create needed illustrations, and photographers can be hired to shoot the desired photographs. Alternately, a person can take a photograph with a digital camera or with a regular camera, and afterward use a scanner to insert the image into the DTP software. Illustrations of many types can be created using illustration software, or commercially prepared clip art and clip photos can be purchased for use in business documents. As allowed by software-licensing agreements, graphic software can be used to manipulate or combine these graphics to produce the final desired graphic.

The graphics and text must then be assembled on the page, using page-layout software, so that all elements contribute to a pleasing and effective product. Principles of color, size, position, shape, pattern, and other contrast techniques must be applied so that documents will attract readers' attention. Documents should also be attractively balanced on the left and right sides of a page. *Symmetrical balance* means that the left and right sides of the page are visually similar. *Asymmetrical balance* means that the left and right sides are visually different. Asymmetrical balance is less formal and usually attracts readers' attention better; symmetrically balanced documents convey a message of formality and stability.

Elements of the document should be appropriately aligned with other parts of the document, rather than being randomly positioned. For example, a block of text and its related graphic could be aligned by the top, bottom, left, or right sides. Using a page *grid* (guidelines dividing a page into rectangular rows and columns) will help to achieve a good layout.

In addition to alignment, related items should be grouped and placed more closely together, while unrelated items should be separated. Extra white space or borders can be used to divide or frame elements.

After the document is designed and created, it can then be published. Publishing can include desktop printers, photocopy machines, or large commercial presses. If commercial printers are used, document designers should confer with the press personnel regarding special procedures and file formats required in creating the document. In addition to being published as paper documents, documents can also be electronically published on the Internet for viewing by a worldwide audience.

FEATURES

The features typically found in page-layout software include the following:

Alignment guidelines: places nonprinting alignment lines on the computer screen for easy alignment of graphics and text

Automatic threading: links various parts of related text segments throughout multipage publications, such as magazines, and connects them with appropriate text, such as "continued on page x" and "continued from page x"

Color separation printing: enables the printing of different printing plates required in color offset printing

Frames: creates rectangular or circular boxes to contain graphics or text

Graphic cropping: provides the ability to cut, or *crop*, unwanted portions of photographs

Grid lines: displays multiple borders on the screen for consistent positioning of text and graphics

Imposition: arranges long publications, like booklets, books, and magazines, for printing and subsequent folding into the proper page sequence

Independent text and graphic placement: enables the placement of text and graphic objects anywhere on the page without having nearby text and graphics affect them

Indexing: provides automatic generation of indexes and tables of contents

Layers: provides the ability to stack text or graphics on top of one another

Master pages: provides automatic layout, pagination, headers and footers, and graphic elements for multiple pages

Object grouping: enables various graphic and text objects to be combined so they can be moved as a single object

Page-size flexibility: gives the ability to create documents in a wide variety of page sizes

Printer's marks: prints crop marks and registration marks needed by commercial printers when running color jobs

Spacing: manipulates the amount of white space on a page, including leading, kerning, tracking, margins, indentations, and column and paragraph borders

Spell checking: provides automatic spell checking for text

Styles: automatically adds appropriate typographical and layout attributes to text and graphics

Text curving and rotation: enables text to be angled or curved

Typography: manipulates all aspects of type, such as typeface, height, width, color, and dropped capitals

MANAGEMENT GUIDELINES

Not every organization needs to have a fully equipped DTP system. The decision regarding what elements to purchase should be based on a realistic needs analysis. Several questions should be answered in making this decision, such as (1) what documents are being planned for the organization? (2) can existing word-processing software be used to create most of the documents the company needs? (3) does the organization have trained personnel to design and create professional documents? and (4) how much will an outside agency charge to produce the documents the firm is wants to publish?

After a careful needs and resource analysis, a firm might decide to develop in-house DTP design and software expertise. If such a decision is made, the firm can hire someone who is already trained in DTP, or the organization can send current employees to DTP seminars or enroll them in formal classes at a local college. Also, high-quality periodicals provide useful design guidelines as well as information on cutting-edge technology and product comparisons. In addition, helpful Web sites give useful learning tips, and numerous DTP books offer additional assistance in document design.

BIBLIOGRAPHY

Conover, Theodore E. (1995). *Graphic Communications Today*, 3d ed. St. Paul, MN: West Publishing Company.

Devall, Sandra Lentz. (1998). *Desktop Publishing Style Guide*. Albany, NY: Delmar Publishers.

Parker, Roger C. (1997). *Looking Good in Print*. Research Triangle Park, NC: Ventana Communications Group.

Shushan, Ronnie, Wright, Don, and Lewis, Laura. (1996). *Desktop Publishing by Design*. Redmond, WA: Microsoft Press.

WILLIAM H. BAKER

DIRECT MAIL ADVERTISING

(SEE: *Advertising*)

DISCOUNT STORES

A discount store is a departmentalized retail operation that sells at prices substantially lower than conventional retailers. To offset the lower prices, expenses are kept down by minimizing free customer services, maximizing the use of self-service, and using inexpensive fixtures, decorations, and displays. In addition, improvement of operational efficiency is continually sought to control costs. Modern discount stores typically sell a mix of hard goods (e.g., refrigerators, televisions) and soft goods (e.g., apparel) and other general merchandise.

Discount stores evolved from a series of retailing changes that began in the United States in the late nineteenth century. Following the Civil War, the development of mass-production processes and a mass-distribution system, along with population increases, paved the way for a new approach to retailing—mass merchandising. The first type of mass-merchandising operation was the department store. The second was the chain store, which included variety stores and "junior department stores." The third was the mail-order house. These patterns for mass merchandising remained relatively constant through the 1920s.

The Great Depression of the 1930s and the accompanying economic hardships set the stage for another retailing change and the beginning of discount operations. Grocery supermarkets, the fourth type of mass-merchandising operation, appeared in 1930. Supermarkets were comprehensive grocery stores that were designed for self-service and consumer accessibility. Their size and low-cost facilities enabled them to operate on low margins and sell below the competition. Their inventories were quickly expanded to include nonprescription drugs. Drugstores, in turn, added variety merchandise, and variety stores expanded their mix while keeping prices relatively low. The starting point for the fifth type of mass merchandising, discount stores, is often traced to the opening of a radio and appliance store by the Masters brothers in Manhattan in 1937.

Price competition among supermarket, drug, and variety chains in the 1930s also brought about legislative constraints in several states to protect small retailers. These resale-price-maintenance, or "fair-trade," laws provided that manufacturers could establish retail prices for products that carried their brand name, thus legally fixing prices. In 1937, these laws were strengthened by the Miller-Tydings federal legislation. Even though the laws were difficult to enforce, they would present a major challenge to discount merchandisers over the years to come.

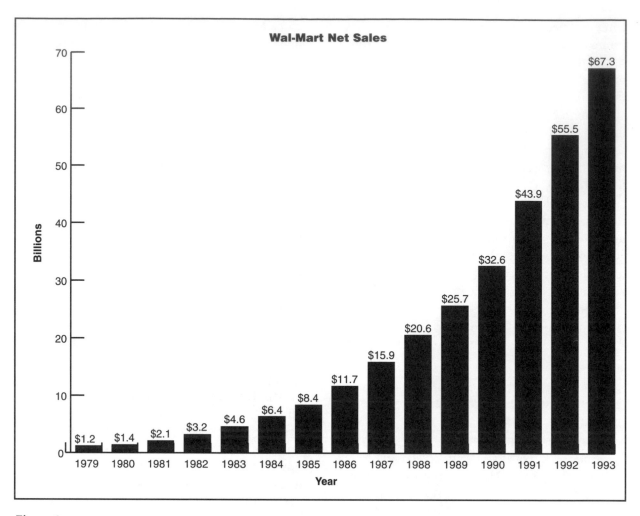

Wal-Mart Net Sales

Figure 1

SOURCE: Stone, Kenneth E. (1995). *Competing with the Retail Giants: How to Survive in the New Retail Landscape.* New York: Wiley.

By the early 1940s, a significant number of retail operations called *discount houses* had been established in several major cities. These discounters carried nationally advertised hard goods such as cameras and appliances. They targeted specific groups, such as teachers and labor unions, and sold from catalogues or samples. They were able to offer goods at exceptionally low prices because they bought directly from manufacturers and kept expenses down through low inventories, low-cost facilities (often in office buildings), and no credit/no delivery policies.

After World War II, discount merchandising grew rapidly. This explosion in growth was fueled by consumer bargain-hunting in the face of rising prices, the pent-up demand for goods created by wartime shortages, and the establishment of homes and families by returning GIs. Discount stores sprang up across the country to satisfy the demand for consumer goods, including television sets and other new products. Many of these new discounters sold their merchandise out of other existing businesses or set up in low-cost facilities such as abandoned factories and lofts. Despite these often makeshift origins, the modern discount industry was beginning to take shape.

Sparked by increased consumer confidence in discount stores and increased availability of goods from manufacturers, discounting contin-

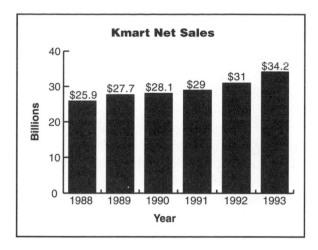

Figure 2

SOURCE: Stone, Kenneth E. (1995). *Competing with the Retail Giants: How to Survive in the New Retail Landscape.* New York: Wiley.

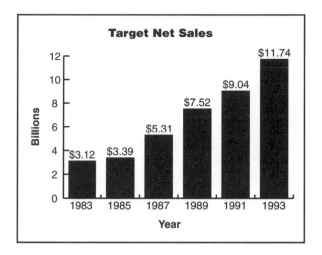

Figure 3

SOURCE: Stone, Kenneth E. (1995). *Competing with the Retail Giants: How to Survive in the New Retail Landscape.* New York: Wiley.

ued to grow rapidly during the 1950s and became an important part of the retail landscape. New chains were drawn to the field, and established chains opened new outlets. Variety stores, specialty retailers, traditional department stores, and supermarkets were looking into discounting and, in some cases, launching ventures.

The look of discount stores also began to change in the 1950s as leading discounters (e.g., Masters, Two Guys, Korvettes) took on a department store-like appearance by adding household goods, apparel, and other soft goods. "Mill store" discount operations further contributed to this change as they began to surface with their base of soft goods.

In addition to the national and regional chains that entered the industry in the 1950s, several others opened their doors in the early 1960s. Many of the new additions were inexperienced and underfinanced, but among the new entries were four that would become the giants of the industry—K-Mart, Woolco, Target, and Wal-Mart. All four began their operation in 1962.

K-Mart was formed by Kresge, one of the nation's leading chain stores, in response to competition from drugstores, supermarkets, and the new discount stores. Kresge's new venture was

unique in two respects. First, the marketing plan was based on the idea of offering quality merchandise—predominantly national brands—at discounted prices. Second, the location strategy was to "surround" cities with their stores.

Woolco was organized by Woolworth, another longtime leader among variety stores. Faced with the same problem as Kresge, they also responded by shifting their efforts to discounting. Their strategy was built around carrying department store merchandise, auto parts and accessories, and soft goods, all at discount prices.

Target was a spin-off of the Dayton Corporation, a Minneapolis-based regional department store chain. It was conceived as a chain of regional upscale discount stores designed to attract affluent suburbanites. The product lines were higher quality and higher priced, with an emphasis on furniture and household appliances.

Wal-Mart was started from scratch by Sam Walton, the owner of a group of Ben Franklin variety stores in the south-central states. Walton's strategy was to establish stores only in small and medium-size towns so that he could capture a substantial part of the total local market. His key policy was to sell at "everyday low prices," rather than hold periodic sales.

In addition to their marketing innovations, these four industry leaders played a major role in setting the pattern for other aspects of the industry. In particular, they established large facilities with standardized layouts in or near shopping centers. Their merchandise lines included both hard and soft goods. And, once they were established, they reduced the number of leased departments to a minimum.

Many discount businesses failed in 1962 and 1963 because of the fierce competition brought on by the proliferation of new discounters and the experimentation of other retailers in discounting in the early 1960s. Many were marginal operators that had expanded too quickly; others were well-established chains.

In spite of the failures, the industry continued to expand in the mid-1960s, both in terms of number of stores and amount of sales. The larger chains, especially, were expanding through acquisition of closing operations as well as opening new units. By 1966, discount stores were attracting approximately 60 percent of the nation's shoppers (1969).

By the late 1960s, Woolco had opened ninety-two stores (1968), Target had eleven (1968), and Wal-Mart had reached thirteen (1969). At this time, K-Mart had grown to more than 300 stores.

The 1970s were a decade of expansion for the successful chains. Woolco and K-Mart focused on national expansion, and by 1974 K-Mart had become the first truly national chain with stores in the forty-eight contiguous states. Wal-Mart expanded into the Southeast and Midwest. And Target established a strong presence in the Midwest. Some chains were forced into bankruptcy by the recessions of the 1970s, but their stores were bought up by the major chains and others. The decade also witnessed the end of federal "fair-trade" laws and the adoption of retailing technologies such as computerized cash registers, point-of-sale (POS) checkout scanning, and satellite communications.

Acquisitions and failures were still common at the beginning of the 1980s, reaching a high point in 1982. Most notably, Woolco closed during that year, while several others filed Chapter 11 bankruptcy and closed shortly thereafter. Other well-known chains folded in the years that followed. As in the previous decades, these failures provided the opportunity for quick expansion by survivors.

Two distinct trends were underway as the discount industry entered the 1990s. One was the bankruptcy of several remaining discounters. The other was the spectacular growth of the (now) three major players: Target, K-Mart, and Wal-Mart. Target sales more than doubled between 1987 and 1993. K-Mart sales grew by more than $8.3 billion during the period 1988-1993. Meanwhile, in 1991, Wal-Mart passed Sears to become the nation's largest retailer. Their combined sales had increased by more than $46.7 billion during the period 1988-1993. As a result of these trends, the industry fragmented into four segments: the three major chains and a group of regional operators.

Along with the departure of large numbers of discounters and the acquisition of others by stronger chains, new kinds of discounters have emerged. They include membership warehouses, specialty discounters, factory mall outlets, and specialty mail-order houses.

Based on the trends of the 1990s, continued growth and consolidation as well as new applications are safe predictions for discounting at the beginning of the twenty-first century. In addition, deep discounting promises to provide strong competition for others in the industry. And all indications are that e-commerce discount retailing will grow, rapidly changing the shape of discounting and impacting the current industry members.

BIBLIOGRAPHY

"Discounting: Chronicles of its Evolution (30 Years of Discounting)." (1992). *Discount Store News* September: 49-50.

Liebeck, Laura. (1994). "Deja Vu: K-Mart to Remake Itself." *Discount Store News* September: 54-55.

Lisanti, Tony. (1999). "It's Time to Look Ahead." *Discount Store News* December: 8.

Stone, Kenneth E. (1995). *Competing with the Retail Giants: How to Survive in the New Retail Landscape*. New York: Wiley.

Vance, Sandra S., and Scott, Roy V. (1994). *Wal-Mart: A History of Sam Walton's Retail Phenomenon*. New York: Twayne.

EARL C. MEYER
WINIFRED L. GREEN

DISPLAYS

(SEE: *Promotion*)

DISPOSABLE INCOME

(SEE: *Income*)

DISTRIBUTION

(SEE: *Channels of Distribution*)

DIVERSITY IN THE WORKPLACE

Diversity in the workplace is a reality for all employers. Managing that diversity is an idea whose time has come. Employers of all kinds are awakening to the fact that a diverse work force is not a burden, but a potential strength.

OUR CHANGING FACE

One of the reasons for this awakening is the increasing diverse marketplace. Today, when you call many airlines to make flight reservations, the automated attendant asks if you would feel more comfortable talking to a Spanish-speaking customer service representative. Who can best understand and serve this changing market? It takes a diverse work force at all levels.

Changing demographics is an urgent reason for the increased interest in managing diversity in the workplace. The growing numbers in the U.S. labor force and its customer base will be composed largely of women, minorities, and immigrants. This group will constitute about 85 per-

cent of the new entrants into the work force, according to the landmark Hudson Institute Study. With more diversity come varied expectations of service as well as language barriers. Customer service training consultants are adding diversity to their curriculum because customers have varied backgrounds and expect customized service. Employers realize they must attract, retain, and promote a full spectrum of people to be successful. So great is their need that advice on management of diversity has become a growth industry.

Progressive employers have developed specialized programs to deal with the work-force diversity issue. Some of these programs, known as "valuing differences programs," are geared to the individual and interpersonal level. Their objective is to enhance interpersonal relationships among employees and to minimize blatant expressions of racism and sexism. Often these programs focus on the ways that men and women or people of different races or cultures have unique values, attitudes, behavior styles, and ways of thinking. These educational sessions can vary in length from one day to several days or they can occur on an ongoing basis. They usually concentrate on one or several of the following general objectives:

- Fostering awareness and acceptance of human differences
- Fostering a greater understanding of the nature and dynamics of individual differences
- Helping participants understand their own feelings and attitudes about people who are different from themselves
- Exploring how differences might be tapped as assets in the workplace

HARASSMENT

The Equal Employment Opportunity Commission (EEOC) is the federal agency responsible for enforcing antidiscrimination efforts. The EEOC has identified what constitutes unlawful harassment: It is verbal or physical conduct that denigrates or shows hostility or aversion toward an individual because of his or her race, color, reli-

President Bill Clinton speaks to corporate leaders about diversity.

gion, gender, national origin, age, or disability or that of his or her friends, relatives, or associates. It must also create a hostile work environment, interfere with work performance, and affect one's employment opportunities. Some states, cities, and employers have also included sexual orientation in their antidiscrimination policies.

Examples of harassment include epithets, slurs, negative stereotyping, or threatening acts toward an identified person or group. Other examples include written or graphic material placed on walls, bulletin boards, or elsewhere on the employer's premises that denigrates or shows hostility or aversion toward an individual or group. Included in this definition are acts that purport to be pranks but in reality are hostile or demeaning.

To be illegal, harassment must be sufficiently severe or pervasive to alter the conditions of employment and create an intimidating or abusive work environment. Although courts do not usu-

ally hold employers liable for violations based on isolated derogatory remarks in the workplace, many recognize that in the right context one slur can effectively destroy a working relationship and can create a hostile environment, particularly if the comment is made by a supervisor.

At the organizational level, employers must be sensitive to a wide array of both state and federal regulations that address all types of discrimination in employment. With today's diverse workplace, the goal is to increase the chances of equal opportunity for all workers and mutual respect in the workplace.

EMPLOYER RESPONSIBILITIES

Providing a workplace free from harassment is one of the basic responsibilities of an employer. Although sexual harassment has received most of the public attention, harassment can take many forms. As employers add staff from a variety of ethnic, religious, age, and cultural groups, maintaining a harmonious workplace is critical. Given our increasing litigious society, it is inevitable that court decisions related to other forms of harassment will increase.

Senior citizens, immigrants, and employees with disabilities are being employed in all levels of positions. They might suffer from a hostile environment because of their differences. To avoid future litigation, prudent managers need to create a hospitable environment.

A major challenge for all employers is to assimilate a variety of employees into the mainstream of corporate life. Women and minorities are sometimes excluded from social activities or left out of informal communications networks. The result appears to be a sense of isolation, lower organizational commitment, and ultimately a decision to seek employment in a more welcoming environment. For example, a woman feeling left out may think that two much emphasis is placed on getting along with others in senior management: "As a woman, I do not fit into the group of males who go to lunch together and play golf together. These are the guys who get the promotions."

As work-force diversity increases, exclusion and isolation may disappear. In the meantime, a few organizations are encouraging women's support groups, black caucuses, and other ways to help subgroups tie into social and communications networks. More importantly, organizations are becoming more sensitive to sponsoring social activities that will allow full participation by all employees.

DISCRIMINATION

Making prejudgments is part of human nature because we cannot anticipate every event freshly in its own right. Although prejudgments help give order to our daily living, our minds have a habit of assimilating as much as they can into categories, which can cause irrational judgments. A person acts with prejudice because of his or her personality, which has been formed by family, school, and community environments.

Prejudice has been defined as an attitude, not an act—an opinion based partly on observation

and partly on ignorance, fear, and cultural patterns, none of which have a rational basis. A prejudiced person tends to think of all members of a group as being the same, giving little consideration to individual differences. This kind of thinking gives rise to stereotypes. Stereotypes, like prejudices, are based partly on observation and partly on ignorance and tradition. For example, a person who assumes that all women are overly emotional is subscribing to a widely held but false stereotype of women.

Stereotypes are difficult to overcome because they usually develop over long periods of time. Some stereotypes are shared by many people, giving them an illusion of rationality. However, many people today are trying to rid themselves of stereotyped thinking about others. This effort reflects a growing consciousness that people are individuals and can and should be treated as such.

The basis of prejudice toward a subgroup of society is often found in economic or psychological factors. Most free-market countries have a diversity of social groups. The social mobility concept postulates that as one subgroup moves up in economic terms, it is replaced by a less fortunate subgroup that is seeking a better way of life.

Since the mid-1800s, various ethnic groups have immigrated to the United States in waves. Tension between subgroups is often a result of economic competition for jobs, shelter, and social status. When physical differences, religious beliefs, ethical values, and traditions differ, subgroups can feel threatened and can sometimes take inappropriate actions.

Unfortunately, there is macroeconomic gain for employers in aiding and abetting discrimination in the workplace. Competition for jobs among workers can help employers lower wages and neglect working conditions. Employers often threaten striking workers with the prospect of being replaced, since there are usually members of minority groups who are willing to take jobs that pay lower wages because they previously had little or no chance of being hired at all.

As the United States becomes more involved in international markets, business managers are becoming aware that discrimination can make a disastrous impression on potential buyers and sellers. When we preach democracy but practice discrimination, our credibility is lost. Establishing oil trade with African countries, for example, becomes more complex when Africans see the U.S. establishment discriminating against African Americans.

RACIAL PREJUDICE

From its beginnings, the United States was divided by racial tensions. White settlers drove out Native Americans and, in the South, set up a system of labor based on slavery. Racism toward blacks and Native Americans is still with us today.

Minority groups come from subcultures that often have their own norms and values, which are not always understood by the majority group. For example, African Americans' social relations are sometimes characterized by an outlook they describe as ecosystem distrust. Ecosystem distrust subsumes such phenomena as lower interpersonal trust and suspicion of authority figures. When this type of outlook is brought into a traditional white, middle-class work environment, there can be misunderstandings and mistrust. Lack of awareness of these phenomena can easily lead to false assumptions by management about the worker. Due to cultural differences, many employers are conducting cross-cultural training for employees from both majority and minority groups.

GENDER ISSUES

Many women have felt discriminated against in the workplace. Advancement into management positions for women has been difficult. In the past decade, more and more woman have not only entered the work force but also have been promoted into management positions. Some would argue that men and women influence the workplace differently. Women exercise leadership through strong interpersonal skills, producing positive results. Male leadership can be more direct, impersonal, and focused on results. Because of the individual strengths of both men and women, a diverse leadership team incorporating different styles of leadership will do more to help employers succeed in today's marketplace.

Traditionally, women have been discriminated against in terms of pay. The wage gap continues to narrow, however. For various reasons, women's pay is gaining parity with men's. For example, many high-paying manufacturing jobs have disappeared, forcing many men into jobs in lower-paying service industries.

Organizations that continue to exclude some segments of the population from their work force risk sending the subtle message that some employees and perhaps some customers are less valued, less important, and less welcome. This will have a negative effect on the bottom line.

BIBLIOGRAPHY

Champagne, Paul, McAfee, Bruce, and Moberg, Phillip. (1992). "A Workplace of Mutual Respect." *HR Magazine* October: 78-81.

Rosen, Benson, and Lovelace, Kay. (1994). "Fitting Square Pegs into Round Holes." *HR Magazine* January: 86-88.

Smith, Vernita. (1993). "Glass Ceiling: Take Two." *Human Resources Executive* October: 30-33.

PATRICK J. HIGHLAND

DIVISION OF LABOR

In the early 1900s, Max Weber, one of the pioneers of modern sociology, designed a perfectly rational organizational form, called a bureaucracy. Among the characteristics of this "ideal" organization were specialization, division of labor, and a hierarchical organizational design.

Division of labor is a form of specialization in which the production of a product or service is divided into several separate tasks, each performed by one person. According to Weber's design, inherent within the specialization and division of labor is knowledge of the precise limit of each worker's "sphere of competence," and the authority to perform individual tasks without overlapping others.'

Sociology pioneer Max Weber.

Adam Smith, an early economist, suggested that productivity would rise significantly when the division of labor principle was used. Output per worker would be raised while costs per unit produced would be reduced. Division of labor was applied, for example, in manufacturing plants that incorporated mass production techniques. In organizations that used mass production, each worker specialized in completing one specialized task; the combined work of several specialized workers produced the final product. For example, in manufacturing an automobile, one worker would assemble the dashboard, another would assemble the wheels, and yet another would paint the exterior.

Since the time of Adam Smith, division of labor has been perceived as a central feature of economic progress. Two aspects of labor exist. First is the division of labor within firms; this concerns the range of tasks performed by workers within a particular firm. Second is the division of labor between firms; this concerns the range of products or services the firm produces.

CURRENT APPLICATION OF DIVISION OF LABOR

Fred Luthans (1998) describes the bureaucratic model proposed by Max Weber as an "historical starting point" for organizational analysis. Citing "complex, highly conflicting relationships, advanced information technology, and empowered employees," Luthans (p. 519) discusses the functional and dysfunctional consequences of specialization uncovered in several research studies. For example, although specialization has enhanced productivity and efficiency, it has also led to conflict between specialized units, hindering achievement of the overall goals of the organization. Further, specialization can impede communication among units, as highly specialized units tend to "withdraw into themselves and not fully communicate with other units above, below, or horizontal to it: (Luthans, p. 519). In addition, highly specialized jobs can lead to employee boredom and burnout.

Given these concerns, a significant change is under way in management of work in organizations. According to Richard Walton (1991), the work force can be managed in two ways, one based on control and the other based on commitment. Key factors that differ between the control and commitment approaches are job design principles, performance expectations, management organization (structure, systems, and style), compensation policies, employment assurances, employee input in policies, and labor-management relations (Walton, 1991).

The control-oriented approach is based on the classic bureaucratic principles of specialization and division of labor. In the control-oriented environment, worker commitment does not flourish. Division of labor can ultimately reduce productivity and increase costs to produce units. Several reasons are identified as causes for reduction in productivity. For example, productivity can suffer when workers become bored with the monstrous repetition of a task. Additionally, productivity can be affected when workers lose pride in their work because they are not producing an entire product they can identify as their own work. A breakdown in the mass production line can bring an entire production line to a standstill. And, with highly specialized jobs, worker training can be so narrowly focused that workers cannot move among alternate jobs easily. Consequently, productivity can suffer when one key worker is absent. Finally, discontent with control is increasing in today's work force, further hindering the long-term success of the classic bureaucratic application of specialization and division of labor.

In contrast to the control-oriented approach, the commitment-oriented approach proposes that employee commitment will lead to enhanced performance. Jobs are more broadly designed and job operations are upgraded to include more responsibility. Control and coordination depend on shared goals and expertise rather than on formal position. The control and commitment-oriented approaches are only one way to view the concepts of division of labor and specialization. These concepts influenced organizations in the late 1990s by a complex array of organizational dynamics.

In response to such complex organizational dynamics as intense competitive pressures, organizations were being restructured. Hierarchies were becoming flatter, meaning that fewer levels of management existed between the lowest level of worker and top management. In some organizations, web-like and network organizational structures were replacing traditional hierarchical organizations (Kerka, 1994). In these redesigned organizations, the shift was away from departments that focused on traditional organizational functions such as production, administration, finance, design, and marketing (Lindbeck and Snower, 1997).

In these redesigned organizations, the shift was away from highly-specialized jobs toward workers performing a multitude of tasks within relatively small autonomous customer-oriented teams. In these working groups, workers were given a broad task specification by management and within those loose constraints, the teams were allowed to organize, to allocate roles, to schedule tasks, and so forth (Bessant, 1991). With this design, traditional occupational barriers and clear-cut specialized job descriptions began evaporating as workers were empowered to define their own job tasks; this movement resulted in a decrease of the division of labor and specialization within firms.

As a consequence of these changes, during the 1990s, increased division of labor between firms was often accompanied by a reduction in the division of labor within firms. In other words, while firms were becoming more specialized in the products and services they offered, individual workers within firms were handling an increasing range and depth of job responsibilities. As mentioned earlier, this work was often completed in autonomous teams.

EFFECTS OF SIZE, COST, AND PERFORMANCE ON DIVISION OF LABOR

In some organizations, division of labor and the degree of specialization are being reduced, while in other organizations, division of labor and specialization are increasing. A number of factors can influence this discrepancy among organizations.

For example, the degree of specialization and division of labor can be related to the size of the organization; typically, small and mid-sized employers are not able to cost justify specialized division of labor. Lindbeck and Snower (1997) report that, as the costs of communication among workers declines, the degree of specialization, and consequently, division of labor within organizations, may rise. Some literature reports that, as the size of the market increases, it supports more division of labor. The degree of division of labor within firms can also depend on the degree to which performance on particular tasks is measurable, and the degree to which wages affect task performance. Implementation of technology can also have a profound influence on the division of labor in organizations.

EFFECTS OF TECHNOLOGY ON DIVISION OF LABOR

Computerization has enabled organizations to increase the variety of tasks performed by workers, consequently reducing specialization and division of labor. For example, information technology—flexible machine tools and programmable multipurpose equipment—can reduce the division of labor within firms as workers transfer their knowledge from task to task more easily. Information and manufacturing technology can also enable individual workers or work teams to combine different tasks more readily to meet a customer's needs while enhancing productivity. For example, customer information gained from production activities can be used to improve financial accounting practices, and employee information gained from training activities can be used to improve work practices.

Eric Alsene (1994) reported that increased integration of computer databases has the potential to profoundly alter task and functional assignments in organizations, consequently affecting division of labor and specialization. Originally, the purpose of integrating computers into organizations was to merge the various functions of labor. Computer integration was designed to restructure businesses around their core business processes, outsourcing some activities to specialized external organizations and strengthening partnerships with suppliers and subcontractors. In the new culture shaped by computer integration, every worker was to have a broader view of the organization. Workers were expected to work in teams with enhanced communication, participation, teamwork, and an enhanced sense of belonging and continuous learning. In this new organizational model enabled by technology, the classic bureaucratic mass production model in which workers performed functions separately and sequentially was eliminated.

The computer integration model was designed to ultimately lead to the dismantling of vertical and horizontal barriers while supervisory control concentrated increasingly on work methods rather than on final products (Child, 1987). In other words, the new design enabled organizations to focus on how products and services were delivered rather than on what products or services were delivered. This design facilitated continuous improvement in the organization. The new technologies assisted in blurring the boundaries among departments while information flowed freely throughout the organization, thereby disregarding the traditional bureaucratic hierarchy. As work groups and task forces were formed, units no longer worked in isolation.

The new model enabled by technology calls into question the traditional division of labor in organizations. For example, flexible manufacturing systems eliminate the barrier between maintenance and production. This increased automation supports the movement described earlier of work becoming more diversified, independent, intellectual, and collective.

SUMMARY

The classic principles of division of labor and specialization still exist; however, their application produces both functional and dysfunctional consequences in the increasingly complex organizations of the twenty-first century. A number of factors affect the modern application of division of labor. Along with other complex organizational and market dynamics, these factors include information technology, worker empowerment, human factors, communication systems, organizational size, competitive pressures, and organization structure.

BIBLIOGRAPHY

Alsene, Eric. (1994). "Computerization Integration and Organization of Work in Enterprises." *International Labor Review*. 133(5-6) 657-676.

Bessant, J. (1991). *Managing Advanced Manufacturing Technology: The Challenge of the Fifth Wave*. Oxford, Blackwell.

Child, J. (1987). "Organizational Design for Advanced Manufacturing Technology," in T.D. Wall, C.W. Clegg, and N.J. Kemp eds. *The Human Side of Advanced Manufacturing Technology*. Chichester: Wiley.

Kerka, Sandra. (1994). "New Technologies and Emerging Careers. Trends and Issues Alerts." Columbus, OH:

ERIC Clearinghouse on Adult, Career, and Vocational Education.

Lindbeck, Assar, and Snower, Dennis J. (1997). "The Division of Labor Within Firms." Stockholm, Sweden: Institute for International Economic Studies, University of Stockholm.

Luthans, Fred. (1998). *Organizational Behavior*. Boston, MA: Irwin McGraw-Hill.

Walton, Richard E. (1991). "From Control to Commitment in the Workplace: In Factory After Factory, There Is a Revolution Under Management of Work." *Readings on Labor-Management Relations*. Washington, DC: Bureau of Labor-Management Relations and Cooperative Programs.

DONNA L. MCALISTER-KIZZIER

DOCUMENT PROCESSING

Document processing involves the equipment, software, and procedures for creating, formatting, editing, researching, retrieving, storing, and mailing documents. A document is any written, printed, or electronically prepared business communication that conveys information. The most common types of documents are those that comprise correspondence: letters, memos, reports, forms, statistical tables, and e-mail.

Document processing can be viewed as an integral part of information resource management (IRM), which includes the management of (1) a broad range of information resources, such as printed materials, electronic information, and microforms; (2) the various technologies and equipment that manipulate these resources; and (3) the people who generate, organize, and disseminate those resources. The overall purpose of IRM is to increase the usefulness of information to both internal users and external customers.

Information resource management is a philosophical and practical approach to managing information. Because information is a valuable resource to be managed like other resources, IRM contributes directly to accomplishing organizational goals and objectives. It provides an integrated approach to managing the entire life cycle of information—from creation, to dissemina-

tion, to archiving or destruction—so as to maximize the overall usefulness of information.

DOCUMENT ORIGINATION AND PREPARATION

The procedures for creating a document include formatting the layout of a document, inputting and editing it, and proofreading it.

SETTING FORMATS

In correspondence, formats are selected that are appropriate for the type of document (e.g., letter, memorandum, or report). Format settings include margins (left, right, top, and bottom of page), tab settings, page length, line spacing, header and footers, page numbering, type style (font typeface and size)

INPUTTING DOCUMENTS

Documents are most often keyed into a computer so that they can be stored, revised as needed, and updated and reused when appropriate. Sometimes voice-recognition software—which keys in words that appear on a computer monitor as one dictates material—is used.

EDITING DOCUMENTS

A document may be edited, or changed, several times before it is finished. Sometimes certain kinds of formatting are done after a document has been initially keyed in, including alignment (e.g., centering or justifying); and such formatting enhancements as bold face or italic type, underscoring, bulleted lists, and tables. Editing functions include copy and move, cut and paste, search and replace, insert and delete, merge, and save, among others.

PROOFREADING

After a document is keyed, checks are made for errors, such as keying errors, spelling errors, and grammatical errors. Many software packages have tools that check for spelling and grammar errors. These tools enhance, but do not replace, careful proofreading.

COMPOSITION OF BUSINESS CORRESPONDENCE

The essentials of effective communication are courtesy, clarity, completeness, and conciseness. Business correspondence includes memos, minutes of meanings, agendas, e-mail messages, and letters. Electronic technology has increased the use of written communications in the office, which often take the form of an interoffice memos or e-mail; employees of a large corporation may send hundreds of thousands of pieces of e-mail every month. Interoffice memos and e-mail can be in a more casual form than traditional letters.

Because many businesses have offices around the world, it is important to understand international business communications and to accommodate cultural differences. Customs, values, religion, decision-making processes, and manners, vary from country to country; international correspondence should reflect an understanding of these differences. International correspondence is often more formal than domestic correspondence.

Tone is an important part of a message because it reflects the attitude of the writer; a positive tone—which includes tact and courtesy—encourages a positive reaction from the reader. Letters should have a natural style, with short sentences and active verbs. Typical business communications include cover letters, reference letters, "good news" and "bad news" letters, reminders, acknowledgments, and letters of introduction. A variety of business reports, ranging from briefing reports to comprehensive research reports, are also typical business communications.

Business correspondence can also include forms, such as invoices, purchase requisitions, and purchase orders. Document processing also includes the creation, distribution, and use of such forms.

DESKTOP PUBLISHING

Desktop publishing is a method for using a computer, a laser printer, and various software programs to prepare and print documents ranging from a single page of text to flyers, advertisements, pamphlets, books, and magazines. Desktop publishing became possible for small businesses on a broad scale around 1985, with the introduction of the first relatively inexpensive laser printer able to produce "letter-quality" type and visuals when used with a personal computer.

A basic desktop publishing system, besides providing a variety of type fonts and sizes, can also create graphics as well as use art and photographs stored in sources inside the computer.

HISTORY OF DOCUMENT PROCESSING

Documents have been processed in business since the beginning of formal systems of writing. Prior to the invention of the typewriter, documents were handwritten, and the particular style of penmanship preferred by businesses was studied. The manual typewriter was introduced into businesses after its invention in the 1870s, followed by the electric typewriter. In the early 1960s, IBM introduced the Selectric typewriter, with a golf-ball type element that tilted and rotated to transfer characters onto paper. This innovation, by eliminating the movable carriage, allowed for faster document production. In 1964, IBM introduced the Magnetic Tape Selectric Typewriter (MT/ST). The magnetic tape stored keystrokes electronically, so that text could then be edited. The MT/ST is considered to be a "first-generation" automated document processor. Office equipment manufacturers then began to develop and market word-processing or document-processing hardware and software, which included the addition of a cathode-ray tube (CRT), to view text and provide additional flexibility in manipulation of the text copy and format prior to printing. The storage media was expanded to include not only magnetic tape and cards but also floppy disks, hard disks, and mainframe computers.

REPROGRAPHICS

Reprographics, which is the multiple reproduction of images, today involves the use of two primary types of equipment: copiers and duplicators. Copiers use an image-forming process similar to a camera to create copies directly from existing originals. Duplicators make copies from masters on specially prepared paper.

Copying, printing, and distributing information has been with us for thousands of years. For much of that time, it was a largely manual task performed by scribes. The first major success in automation was by Gutenberg's invention of movable type in the fifteenth century, a milestone in the history of printing, duplicating, and copying, methods. Reprographics can be traced through four basic historical periods: printing (letterpress; 1500 to present), duplicating (offset, spirit, and stencil; 1900 to present), copying (photochemical, thermofax, dye transfer, electrofax, xerography, and liquid toner transfer; 1940 to present), and electronic printing (intelligent copier/printers, ink jet, magnetography, thermography, and laser xerography; 1976 to present).

COMPUTERIZED RECORDS MANAGEMENT

The processing capabilities and storage capacity of computers have made electronic storage and retrieval of information a common practice in business. Computer-generated document management, records-management software, and imaging systems assist businesses with large volumes of records. Imaging systems convert all types of documents to digitized electronic data that can be easily stored and retrieved. These systems include scanners that convert paper documents to a digitized form, processors that compress the image, storage media that retain the image, retrieval mechanisms to convert the image for viewing on a monitor, and output devices that process the image into hard-copy format. Laser optical disks are well suited for high-volume record management because of their high capacity and durability.

Micrographics is the process of creating, using, and storing images and data in microform. The most common type of microform is microfilm. Images, reduced in size, are stored on reels, in cartridges, on cassettes, on aperture cards, on microfiche, and in jackets. Information stored in

a computer can be converted to microfilm. Computer-output microfilm (COM) is imaged directly from magnetic media. The electrical impulses on the media are converted to visual images and stored on microfilm. Computer-input microfilm (CIM) can be converted to electrical impulses, stored on magnetic media, and used as input. CIM can be used to introduce information from a large microfilm file, such as census data, into a computer for processing. Computer-assisted retrieval (CAR) systems are used for high-speed microform indexing and retrieval.

For many businesses, however, manual records-management systems are still the norm. Businesses use one or more of the five basic filing methods—alphabetic, subject, numeric, geographic, and chronological—to store records in vertical and lateral files, open-shelf files, and rotary files. Good records-management practices include establishing complete archives, developing retention schedules, and using timelines for transferring records to permanent storage.

SEARCHING FOR INFORMATION ON THE INTERNET

The ease and availability of using the Internet to find information has added another dimension to document processing. A search engine is a software program that is used to find Web sites, Web pages, and Internet files. Examples include AltaVista, Excite, Yahoo!, HotBot, Lycos, and Infoseek. Single or multiple keywords can be entered into a search engine, which will search indices to return a list of hits, which can number from zero to more than a million. The hits are Web pages that contain information relevant to the search criteria. Users must beware that the quality of the sites may differ; some sites may be those of Fortune 500 companies, while others may be those of a 10-year-old child.

The Internet contains Web sites, composed of multiple related Web pages, connected by hyperlinks. A hyperlink, also called a link, is a built-in connection to another related Web page. These links allow information to be obtained in the order desired by the user, not necessarily in the linear fashion provided in books. Information found on the Web can be easily copied and pasted into other documents or used alone, with only minor editing.

BIBLIOGRAPHY

Academic American Encyclopedia (Grolier Multimedia Encyclopedia Version). (1995). Danbury, CT: Grolier.

Blass, Gary D., et al. (1991). "Finding Government Information: The Federal Information Locator System (FILS)" *Government Information Quarterly* 8 (1):11-32.

Boldt, Dennis, and Groneman, Nancy. (1998). "Internet Use in Document Processing and Computer Application." In Dennis LaBonty (ed.), *Integrating the Internet into the Busines Curriculum* (1998 NBEA Yearbook, No. 36) (pp. 117-127). Reston, VA: National Business Education Association.

Shelly, Gary, Cashman, Thomas, Vermaat, Misty, and Walker, Tim. (1999). *Discovering Computers; 2000 Concepts for a Connected World.* Cambridge, MA: Course Technology.

Stallard, John J., and Terry, George R. (1984). *Office Systems Management.* Homewood, IL: Irwin.

Swanson, Marie L. Reding, Elizabeth Eisner, Beskeen, David W., and Johnson, Steven M. (1997). *Microsoft Office 97, Professional Edition—Illustrated, A First Course.* Cambridge, MA: Course Technology.

Tilton, Rita Sloan, Jackson, J. Howard, and Rigvy, Sue Chappell. (1996). *The Electronic Office: Procedures & Administration.* Cincinnati, OH: South-Western Educational Publishing.

LINDA J. AUSTIN
DEBBIE HUGHES

DOUBLE-ENTRY ACCOUNTING

(SEE: *Accounting*)

DOW-JONES INDEX

(SEE: *Stock and Bond Issues*)

DURABLE GOODS

(SEE: *Goods and Services; Shopping*)

E

ECONOMIC ANALYSIS

Economic forces affect decisions made in personal business activities, as well as within business organizations, government entities, and nonprofit organizations. Changes in economic conditions affect and are affected by supply and demand, strength of buying power and the willingness to spend, and the intensity of competitive efforts. These changes propel fluctuations in the overall state of the economy and influence courses of action and the timeliness of actions. Nonprofit organizations, for example, may find that fund-raising efforts fueled by personal contributions are more successful during periods of economic prosperity. A first-time home buyer may be more inclined to purchase a house when interest rates are low and prices are likely to increase in future months. Since decision makers cannot control economic forces, a concerted effort should be made to monitor such forces. All business executives know that it is important to gain some idea of what general business conditions will be in the months or years ahead. Fortunately, certain economic indicators or indices enable decision makers to forecast oncoming changes in economic forces. Since both individuals and organizations operate in a dynamic economic environment, losing sight of what is going on can be disastrous for either.

THE BUSINESS CYCLE

Fluctuations in the economy tend to follow a general pattern that is commonly referred to as the business cycle. The business cycle, in the traditional view, consists of four stages—each of which may vary in terms of duration and intensity. The four stages are prosperity, recession, depression, and recovery.

Up-to-date charts, tabulations, and measures of relevant economic indicators are published by the Bureau of the Census in the monthly report, *Business Cycle Developments*. Economic indicators are predictors or gauges that signal cyclical movement of the economy within each stage of the business cycle or from one stage to another. A few examples of economic indicators include average workweek in manufacturing, new building permits for private housing, new orders for durable goods, and changes in consumer installment debt. While various government agencies collect and report monthly, quarterly, semi-annual, and annual measures of numerous economic indicators, economists representing various industries and other decision makers analyze and interpret the data.

Timing is everything when it comes to making good business cycle-sensitive decisions. Just as a truck driver starts braking before reaching an intersection with a flashing red light, decision makers need to make appropriate plans before the business cycle passes from one stage to the next. Prosperity, a period characterized by low unemployment and relatively high incomes, is followed by recession, a period during which unemployment rises and total buying power declines, leading to decreased spending by business firms and consumers. A production manager should make appropriate cutbacks prior to the onset of a recession. Failure to do so, in the face of decreasing sales, leads to bloated inventories and idle productive resources. On the other hand, when a period of recession (during which unemployment is extremely high and wages are very low), gives way to a period of recovery (characterized by increases in employment and income), a production manager should begin to plan for increased outputs. Just as the truck driver saw the red light and recognized it as a signal to start braking, decision makers must see changing economic conditions and make appropriate responses.

THE PROCESS OF CONDUCTING AN ECONOMIC ANALYSIS

Conducting an economic analysis requires the application of scientific methods to break down economic events into separate components that are easier to analyze. The remainder of this article discusses the steps included in this process.

Step 1—Identify Appropriate Economic Indicators The first step in the process of conducting an economic analysis is to identify appropriate economic indicators for specific economic forecasts or trends. While various indicators may be selected, they are usually classified as indicators that lead, lag, and/or are coincident with economic conditions. Measures of data derived from economic indicators yield valuable information for the identification of economic trends and the preparation of specific economic forecasts.

Step 2—Collect Economic Data Once the identification of indicators has been completed, the second step, which is the collection of economic data yielded by the indicators, can begin. Data collection is accomplished through observation and/or by reviewing measures of economic performance, such as unemployment rates, personal income and expenditures, interest rates,

business inventories, gross product by industry, and numerous other economic indicators or indices. Such measures of economic performance may be found in secondary sources such as business, trade, government, and general-interest publications. The Bureau of Economic Analysis (BEA), contained in the U.S. Department of Commerce, provides economic information via news releases, publications, diskettes, CD-ROMs, and the Internet. The information may be accessed through the Bureau's Web site (http://www.bea.doc.gov), on recorded telephone messages, and in printed *Bureau of Economic Analysis Reports*. Such economic data are also available online through STAT-USA's Economic Bulletin Board.

Step 3—Prepare or Select an Economic Forecast Of course, simply gathering information about economic indicators is not enough. Decision makers must use the data to identify trends and project forecasts. Decision makers know that it is important to gain some idea of what economic conditions will be in months or years ahead. As a result, they either use the collected data to prepare their own forecasts or they use economic forecasts that have been prepared by experts who monitor economic activity. Regardless of its origin, the forecast itself is essential if the decision maker is to recognize opportunities and threats posed by the economic environment. Thus, using economic data to predict the future is the third step in the process.

Economic forecasting can be and often is a complicated process. While accurate, relevant data are the basis for predictions, forecasters must be careful not to gather so much data that sheer volume makes analyzing impossible. Forecasts may be classified as short term (with spans or distances to the target period of up to one or two years), intermediate (two to five years), and long term (relating to more persistent developments and distant occurrences). Because of the possibility of unforeseen events occurring over a long interval, short-term forecasts are usually more accurate than long-range ones. There are four principal techniques used to forecast:

- Judgmental forecasting is the oldest and still the most important method of forecasting the future. Judgmental forecasters often blend several forecasters' judgments together to produce a forecast. This may be a complicated process, since various "Delphic" methodologies are used to integrate inputs from people experienced in forecasting.

- Indicator forecasts are nearly as old as judgmental forecasts. This technique requires that economic indicators be used to estimate the behavior of related variables. The index of leading indicators published by the Commerce Department is the best-known overall measure, but decision makers can use many other indicators for their own purposes.

- Time-series techniques use trend projections of past economic activity to extend into the future. Projecting is done by plotting data for the past years on a chart and, from the latest data, extending a line into future time periods that follows the pattern of prior years.

- Structural models of the economy try to capture the interrelationships among many variables, using statistical analysis to estimate the historic patterns. Large models of the U.S. economy, used by major forecasting firms and the government, may have up to a thousand interlinked equations. Simple models used by individual organizations, however, can have as few as one equation.

These four methods are not mutually exclusive. Combinations of methodologies are perhaps more commonly used in formulating forecasts today.

Step 4—Interpret the Economic Data The fourth step requires decision makers to examine, assess, and interpret the economic data collected and the subsequent forecast generated from the economic data. Decision makers evaluate the data and forecast for accuracy, try to resolve inconsistencies in the information, and—if it is warranted—assign significance to the findings. By analyzing economic data and forecasts, decision makers should be able to recognize and identify potential opportunities and threats linked to economic changes and developments. As a result, they are better able to understand the influence that the economy is exerting and better prepared to make decisions and plan strategy. The process, however, should not be viewed in an oversimplified manner. Today's global economic links make economic forecasting and analysis especially complex.

Step 5—Monitor Intervening Forces Then, too, intervening forces can and do influence economic activity. Such forces can shift or alter economic performance and trends and must be anticipated by decision makers. Thus, anticipating and monitoring the government's manipulation of two powerful sets of economic instruments, fiscal policy and monetary policy, becomes the fifth step in the process. Fiscal policy is the government's combined spending and taxation program, while monetary policy represents actions by the Federal Reserve System that affect the supply and availability of money and credit. The two arms of policy can work to supplement each other when powerful stimulus or restraint is sought. Or they can work in beneficial or damaging opposition, when one or the other is driven off-course into excessive stimulation or excessive restraint. Observers can often anticipate the government's implementation of fiscal and/or monetary policies based on prevailing economic conditions. The outcomes of such implementations must be considered by analysts.

Step 6—Use the Economic Analysis for Decision Making Finally, decision makers use the results of an economic analysis for decision making. Astute decision makers recognize that economic forces are uncontrollable and that current strategies may need to be adjusted to cope with or overcome obstructing economic changes. They approach with caution opportunities and threats discovered as a result of economic scanning and analysis. They pursue a proactive approach, however, knowing that an economic analysis enables them to choose from alternative approaches how to employ scarce or uncommon resources and achieve objectives in the most efficient and cost effective manner.

BIBLIOGRAPHY

Cross, Wilbur. (1995). *Encyclopedia of Business Terms Dictionary.* Englewood Cliffs, NJ: Prentice Hall.

Economic Information Systems Incorporated. http://econline.com/.

Economic Statistics Briefing Room. http://www.whitehouse.gov/fsbr/esbr.html.

FEDSTATS. http://www.fedstats.gov.

Geahigan, Priscilla Cheng, ed. (1994). *American Business Climate and Economic Profiles.* Detroit, MI: Gale Research.

Maddison, Angus. (1995). *Explaining the Economic Performance of Nations: Essays in Time and Space.* Brookfield, VT: Edward Elgar Publishing.

Office of Economic Analysis Main Page. http://www.oea.das.state.or.us/welcome.html.

Rao Tummola, V. M. (1973). *Decision Analysis with Business Applications.* New York: Intext Educational Publishers.

Schumpeter, Joseph A. (1954). *History of Economic Analysis.* New York: Oxford University Press.

STAT-USA Internet. http://www.stat.usa.gov.

Trueman, Richard E. (1981). *Quantitative Methods for Decision Making in Business.* Dryden Press.

RALPH D. WRAY

ECONOMIC CYCLES

Economic cycles, more commonly called business cycles, are the recurring expansion and contraction of the national economy. This is a phenomenon that is unique to a private or free-enterprise economic system, also called a capitalist economy. Other systems do experience some of the same characteristics of the free-enterprise economy; however, business/economic cycles in the capitalistic economy are the focus of attention in this discussion.

The individual who is most famous for research on the business/economic cycle is Wesley Mitchell. He defined the business cycle as follows:

> Business cycles are a type of fluctuation found in the aggregate economic activity of nations that organize their work mainly in business enterprises; a cycle consists of expansions occurring at about the same time in many economic activities, followed by similarly general recessions, contractions, and revivals which merge into the expansion phase of the next cycle; this sequence of changes is recurrent but not periodic; in duration business cycles vary from more than one year to ten or twelve years; they are not divisible into shorter cycles of similar character with amplitudes approximately their own. (Burns and Mitchell, 1946, p. 3)

This definition illustrates Mitchell's point that business/economic cycles occur in private-enterprise but not other systems. He also pointed out that business cycles are not unique to a single firm or industry; they affect an entire economy. Although all cycles follow the same basic pattern, they differ in many ways, such as longevity and severity. Mitchell also points out that an economic cycle can last from one to twelve years.

UNDERSTANDING THE BUSINESS CYCLE

Business/economic cycles go through increases and decreases while reaching peaks and troughs. To begin thinking about a cycle, think about a trough, or the low flat part of the cycle, which moves to a peak and then to a terminating trough. In order to determine and isolate a specific cycle, it is necessary to determine the dates of the initial trough and the terminal trough. Most cycles are measured from cycle to cycle regardless of length or magnitude.

Cycle Divisions Every business/economic cycle goes through divisions. The period from the initial trough to the peak is called *expansion*. The declining period of the cycle is called *contraction*. Within the expansion period there are two phases, which are called *recovery* and *prosperity*. After the cycle reaches its peak and contraction begins, the cycle goes through *crisis* and *depression*. Another term used for a mild depression is *recession*.

The business cycle is often further divided into nine stages. Stage I is centered at the time of the initial trough; Stage V is at the time of the peak; and Stage IX is centered at the terminal trough. Stages II through IV are equally divided into thirds across the expansion period, and Stages VI through VIII are equally divided into thirds across the contraction period. These divi-

Men waiting for job openings during the Great Depression of the 1930s.

sions are made so economists can more easily analyze date and time periods for the cycles.

Cycle Terminology There is considerable terminology that is related to business/economic cycles, terms such as *expansion, contraction, depression, recession,* and others. To better understand business cycles, it is important to understand the terminology.

Expansion: When the economy is growing and businesses in general are doing well, the period is known as expansion. There are several ways in which economic growth is measured. One way is gross domestic product (GDP), which is the total value of all goods and services that are produced in a country in a specific time period, such as a month, a quarter, or a year. If production is increasing, this is an indicator that the economy is growing.

Another measure of economic expansion is personal income. If workers have increasing income, the indications are that the economy is

growing and workers can be paid more. Likewise, if unemployment rates are declining or remain low, this means that people who want to work are finding jobs and the economy is expanding. One fear is that the economy will expand too rapidly, leading to inflation.

Inflation: In simplest terms, inflation means that there is too much money in the economy and not enough goods and services to purchase. Inflation is a general rise in the prices of goods and services. In economics, this relates to supply and demand. If consumers have high demands for goods and services, but the supply of these goods and services doesn't increase to meet the demands, producers can raise prices and consumers will still be willing to purchase the goods and services at higher prices. There is considerable competition for limited resources. Inflation is measured using the Consumer Price Index (CPI). The CPI is a market basket of goods and services that consumers regularly buy. As the prices of these goods and services rise, so do the

Consumer Price Index and all prices in general. This explains why the shoes that cost $50 last year now cost $55.

Contraction: The economy will reach a point where expansion first slows and then stops. There might be a period of stagnation during which there is no growth or even a decline in economic activity. An economic decline, or contraction, typically follows this period. This is the result of business activity slowing, less money being spent, unemployment rising, and wages and salaries declining or remaining stable.

Recession: If there are two consecutive quarters of decline in economic activity as measured by a decrease in GDP, the economy is said to be in a recession. During a recession, prices fall, consumers don't buy as many products (especially high-priced items), and businesses begin to fail. A recession has severe consequences for the economy, highlighted by high unemployment and an overall drop in living standards. When the fear of a recession begins to surface, the federal government expends considerable effort to change the course of activities. Those activities will be discussed later.

Depression: A depression is a very severe recession. History books talk about the Great Depression of the 1930s in the United States, one of the most severe in the history of the U.S. and world economies. Depressions are characterized by extremely high unemployment, low wages, business failures due to little money to purchase goods and services, and appalling living standards.

Deflation: The opposite of inflation, deflation means that prices are going down. The CPI goes down because the prices of the goods and services that are used to measure it are in general decline. Deflation often follows inflation but normally is shorter in length and of a lesser magnitude.

Stagnation: Stability in growth is a goal of the private-enterprise system. This means that there aren't any drastic changes in prices and the economy is moving forward at an acceptable rate. However, stability can lead to stagnation, a time when there is too much complacency, which in turn leads to a decline in new-product development and marketing. If this occurs, consumers become dissatisfied with what is available and spending slows down, followed by a decline in the economy. For example, if consumers are spending at a steady rate and they are willing to pay reasonable prices for goods and services, manufacturers don't feel the need for innovation and growth in new areas. This causes stagnation, which leads to decline.

Stagflation: The term stagflation is sometimes used to describe a situation in which there is slow to zero growth in real output, high inflation exists, and unemployment is higher than normal. This situation usually begins with rising prices at times when production is declining. Because of declining production, unemployment also increases. All three of these factors combined cause stagflation—stagnation in production and employment together with increasing inflation.

HISTORICAL PERSPECTIVE

The economies of the United States and of the world generally have been through numerous economic cycles. This discussion will not be an extensive one, but rather an overview to show the effects and relationships of the economy and business cycles.

The First Cycle Following the end of The Revolutionary War in 1783, the U.S. economy experienced rapid development and growth. This was a period when the population was growing rapidly and there was expansion to the West. Even though the manufacturing and agricultural processes were primitive by today's standards, the country was full of new activities. There were new outlets for goods and services, and trade opportunities were enhanced. This new growth and expansion lasted until the beginning of the Civil War.

The Second Cycle Rapid growth in economic activity continued in the period between the beginning of the Civil War and the start of World War I. This was caused in part by the steady increase in population growth, with immigrants arriving in the United States virtually daily. During this time, manufacturing became more dominant and replaced agriculture as the primary industry. At the beginning of this period, about 30 percent of production in the United States was from agriculture; and at the end of the period, it had declined to about 20 percent.

This period wasn't without setbacks, however. In 1873 a major depression began that lasted until the middle of 1879. This depression resulted from a financial panic that caused banks to call for repayment of many of their loans. Very few banks failed, but in the wake of the panic many businesses were affected and did fail.

The Third Cycle The third cycle of economic activity began in 1914 and lasted through 1950. This period was one of major economic variations. Following World War I, demand for goods and services was high, so the economy flourished. Manufacturing continued to flourish and grow, and mechanization in agriculture increased the efficiency of production and reduced the demand for labor. People who were farm laborers became laborers in the manufacturing sector, especially after the introduction of the gasoline-powered tractor.

In 1929, signs of a troubled economy began to surface. The stock market was greatly affected because investors were borrowing large amounts of money to purchase stocks. In late October, the stock market crash had a profound effect on all business activity. Business activity continued to decline through 1932. This was the Great Depression—a worldwide depression. In 1933, a recovery began that lasted until 1937. There was again a decline in economic activity and a recession, which lasted until late in 1938.

The United States entered World War II in December 1941. Because of military operations, the demand for goods and services rose dramatically, employment levels increased, and consumers had more money to spend. The economy was on the mend but rising too rapidly, causing fears of inflation. These fears caused the government to set price ceilings on some products and to ration others. Following the war, the country converted from wartime to peacetime produc-

tion, causing many industries to slow down; but the economy continued to grow.

The Fourth Cycle This period, which began with 1950, has been characterized by many economic cycles. The first twenty years of this period saw satisfactory economic growth. The Korean conflict and the Vietnam War greatly influenced the economy. There were some downturns in the economy, but they were minimal. These occurred in 1953, 1957, and 1960. During this period, unemployment was becoming a problem because the demand for unskilled labor was decreasing and the labor force was growing at a rate faster than the demand for employees.

In more recent years, the economy has grown and prospered. There has been a shift to a service economy, which has largely resulted from rapid changes in technology. In this last cycle, there have been recessions that have been relatively short but have caused hardships for some business sectors. There was a period of recession from 1973 to 1975, in 1980, and again in late 1981. Inflation was a severe problem in 1981, and recovery didn't start again until late in 1982. Then, in late 1987, the stock market crash caused problems for many businesses and investors. In addition to those events, there have been several smaller cycles.

CONCLUSION

This overview of business/economic cycles has provided some insight to the cause of changes in the U.S. economy, highlighting terminology that it is important to understand. The role of the U.S. government in controlling changes in economic activity could not be discussed for reasons of length.

(SEE: *Fiscal policy, Monetary policy*)

BIBLIOGRAPHY

Burns, Arthur, and Mitchell, Wesley. (1946). *Measuring Business Cycles.* New York: National Bureau of Economic Research.

Dolan, Edwin G., and Lindsey, David E. (1991). *Economics.* Chicago: Dryden Press.

Griffin, Ricky W., and Ebert, Ronald. (1999). *Business*. Upper Saddle River, NJ: Prentice-Hall.

Nickels, William G., McHugh, James M., and McHugh, Susan M. (1998). *Understanding Business*. Chicago: Richard D. Irwin.

Sherman, Howard J., and Kolk, David X. (1996). *Business Cycles and Forecasting*. New York: HarperCollins.

Valentine, Lloyd M. (1987). *Business Cycles and Forecasting*. Cincinnati: South-Western Publishing.

PAULA LUFT

ECONOMIC DEVELOPMENT

Economic development, generally speaking, is a process of change that is focused on the betterment of the community, state, and/or nation. Defining economic development can be difficult. The first term in this phrase—"economic"—refers to an accepted paradigm for organizing the business and financial and even to some extent the governmental sectors of a nation. Economics is viewed as the foundation for building a prosperous society. However, it is the second term—"development"—over which there is considerable debate. People's perceptions of development vary. For some, development has the appearance of successful commercial enterprise; for others, the face of development is one of economic equality. Nevertheless, the concept of "economic development" has the attention of government, the business sector, and the citizenry. We pursue economic development as one of the goals of a successful country, state, or city. It captures the attention of the news media and impacts, as well as is impacted by, political objectives.

MEASUREMENT OF ECONOMIC DEVELOPMENT

Economic development in a community can take many forms. However, before we can discuss the process of economic development, we must first understand how economic development has been measured, particularly at the national level. It is within this framework that communities have pursued their goal of improving the local economic environment. In fact, standardized measures of economic development are being used throughout the world, not just in the United States.

Standardized measures of economic development are used to identify the status of one's country, state, or local community. We use these measures for a number of different purposes, including identifying trends and understanding patterns of economic development in communities that face different resource opportunities and constraints.

One of the most common methods of measuring economic growth is by calculating the gross national product of a country. Gross national product (GNP) is the value of goods and services produced *by* an economy's factors in a given period of time (e.g., the value of all goods and services produced by U.S. operations throughout the world in a given year). Gross domestic product (GDP), on the other hand, is the value of goods and services produced *in* an economy in a given period of time (e.g., the value of goods and services produced in the United States in a given year). When these measures are adjusted for inflation, we correct for any changes in the GNP or GDP that are due simply to increases in the price level in the economy. Real GDP, for example, is the value of goods and services produced in an economy adjusted for changes in the price level. This is particularly important when comparing across different economies because changes in price levels will not necessarily be uniform from one country to the next.

The general purpose of using measures such as real GNP or real GDP is to collect and analyze information related to a country's economic transactions. Real GNP or real GDP provides analysts with an indication of how quickly the business sector of the economy is growing in a country. It also serves as a guidepost for local communities as they address economic development issues at a local level.

Trends in national economic development reflect changes occurring at the state and local levels and can impact local economic develop-

Economic development in Portland, Oregon.

ment planning. For instance, if the real GD of a country has increased, then we conclude that the country has experienced economic growth and the economy has improved. This information sends a signal to local economies suggesting that the national economy is in the growth phase of the business cycle. Communities can use this in-

formation to identify their position relative to the current trend and to plan future economic development. If, however, real GNP has declined, then the economy is thought to have experienced an economic downturn and a community can use this information to anticipate the impact of future economic downturns.

TRENDS IN ECONOMIC DEVELOPMENT IN THE UNITED STATES

Positive trends in growth at the national level do not guarantee that individual communities are or will be successful in developing their local economies. The needs of local communities have changed as the patterns of growth at the local level have changed. Thus the rules of local economic development as they relate to attracting new business in order to promote economic growth also have changed. As communities compete with each other to attract new businesses and hence jobs to the local environment, they are discovering that the traditional methods of tax abatement and low-interest loans, coupled with job training, are not sufficient to guarantee a level of development that improves the economic base of the community. In fact, communities are looking for ways to ensure that they will get more from the investment than it will cost them in terms of tax abatements and infrastructure costs.

As firms increasingly engage in multilocation operations, communities are finding that, in addition to attracting new businesses, encouraging local firms to develop is a valuable economic development tool. The community's view of its resources has expanded beyond providing the traditional tax incentives to expand a community's economic resources to include factors such as a well-educated work force and adequate public services. Communities are now more likely to target the type of firm that is "right" for the community. The emphasis on locating manufacturing enterprises has diminished as communities look to "healthy" businesses that fit the changing needs of the work force and infrastructure. Explicit consideration of the impact of the new business on economic equity in the community is also becoming more important, and growth and equity are increasingly recognized as complementary rather than opposing goals.

Many of these changes can be summarized in the phrase "sustainable development." The case of sustainable development is appearing more and more frequently in discussions of community economic development. What is "sustainable development"? Sustainable development is a process of development that "ensures the needs of the present are met, without compromising the ability of future generations to meet their own needs." (World Commission on Environment and Development, 1987, p. 9) The vision of sustainable development is one of developing within the capacity of our resources an ability to replenish themselves; by analogy to the financial sector, it means living off of the interest as opposed to the capital of our investment.

In the sustainable development context, economic development is managed and controlled in a way that recognizes the dynamic nature of social, political, technological, and economic factors in a local community. Ultimately, the process of economic development is changed from one of identifying incentives for business growth to one of comprehensive planning to address social, economic, and environmental concerns. The themes of economic development also change. Traditional local economic development policies pursue increases in economic activity and thus in the income levels of local residents. A larger tax base and lower levels of unemployment are equated with business expansion. Sustainable development means that growth occurs alongside community goals of increased self-sufficiency and improved environmental quality. In fact, different forms of growth are encouraged. The sustainable development initiative is not opposed to growth but rather focuses its efforts on answering the question, "*How* do we grow?"

Successful economic development has been achieved in many communities pursing a sustainable development approach. Among the success stories is Kansas City, Missouri. This city faced one of the most urgent economic development problems of urban areas—urban sprawl. From 1960 to 1990, the population in the metropolitan area grew by less than one-third while the land area developed more than doubled. The city's population was moving to the suburbs while the inner city was slowly being abandoned. As a result, the jobs moved with the population, and the communities in the outer ring of the city used traditional economic development tools, such as tax incentives, to attract new business.

The central city attempted to compete by providing additional incentives. The burden, however, was clearly felt by taxpayers, as this increased over this period.

Recently, however, a Metropolitan Development Forum was formed to address the community development issues associated with urban sprawl. The forum has been successful in many areas: they have identified regional transportation needs, achieved agreement on the role of tax incentives in the region as a whole, created a metropolitan greenway, and created local initiatives for economic development planning.

One community that has achieved long-term success is Portland, Oregon. Portland has channeled the economic growth in the city such that employment in the formerly dying downtown area grew from 50,000 jobs in 1975 to 105,000 jobs in 1998. This strategy has been successful because they focused the development of business in areas that are close to developed transit systems, limited commuter parking, and controlled the expansion of growth into the rural areas.

Kansas City and Portland are only two of many examples of successful sustainable development initiatives across the country. As a community's needs change and as development is more broadly defined to include social as well as economic indicators of progress, sustainable development and planned growth initiatives will continue to take hold. There are many opportunities ahead for local economies to grow and prosper in ways that recognize the importance of improving the quality of life as well as the economy's overall productivity and income levels.

BIBLIOGRAPHY

Parkin, Michael. (1998). *Macroeconomics*, 4th ed. Addison-Wesley.

Shaffer, Ron. (1998). "Playing by New Rules in Local Economic Development." *Community Economics Newsletter*, No. 263. Center for Community Economic Development, University of Wisconsin-Madison.

Shaffer, Ron. (1995). "Sustainable Community Economic Development." *Community Economics Newsletter*, No. 224. Center for Community Economic Development, University of Wisconsin-Madison.

Thomas, Margaret G. (1999). "Strategies for Sustainable Economic Development." *Community Economics Newsletter*, No. 267. Center for Community Economic Development, University of Wisconsin-Madison.

World Commission on Environment and Development. (1987). *Our Common Future*. Oxford: Oxford University Press.

ELLEN JEAN SZARLETA

ECONOMICS

Economics is often described as a body of knowledge or study that discusses how a society tries to solve the human problems of unlimited wants and scarce resources. Because economics is associated with human behavior, the study of economics is classified as a social science. Because economics deals with human problems, it cannot be an exact science and one can easily find differing views and descriptions of economics. In this discussion, the focus is an overview of the elements that constitute the study of economics, that is, wants, needs, scarcity, resources, goods and services, economic choice, and the laws of supply and demand.

Every person is involved with making economic decisions every day of his or her life. This occurs when one decides whether to cook a meal at home or go to a restaurant to eat, or when one decides between purchasing a new luxury car or a low-priced pickup truck. People make economic decisions when they decide whether to rent or purchase housing or where they should attend college.

WANTS, NEEDS, AND SCARCITY

As a society, and in economic terms, people have unlimited wants; however, resources are scarce. Don't confuse wants and needs. Individuals often want what they don't need. In the automobile example used above, someone might want to drive a large luxury car, but a small pickup truck may be more suited to the purchaser's needs if he or she must have a vehicle for hauling furniture. Economic decisions must be made.

Robert Mundell, 1999 Nobel Economics winner.

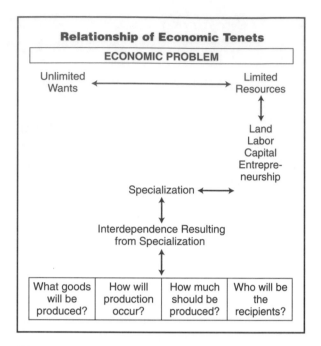

Figure 1

A resource is scarce when there is not enough of it to satisfy human wants. And human wants are endless. Because of unlimited wants and limited resources to satisfy those wants, economic decisions must be made. This problem of scarcity (limited resources) must be addressed, which leads to economics and economic problems.

Figure 1 illustrates the relationships that exist relative to wants and scarcity. Many elements influence economic decisions. To better understand economics, it is critical to understand what is shown in this Figure.

RESOURCES

Economic resources, often called factors of production, are divided into four general categories. They are land, labor (sometimes referred to as human resources), capital, and entrepreneurship.

Land. *Land* describes the ground that might be used to build a structure such as a factory, school, home, or church, but it means much more than that. *Land* is also the term used for the

resources that come from the land. Trees are produced by the land and are used for lumber, firewood, paper, and numerous other products, so they are referred to as land. Minerals that come from the ground, such as oil that is used to make gasoline or to lubricate automobile engines, or gold that is used to make jewelry, or wheat that is grown on the land and is used in the production of bread and other products, or sheep that are raised for the wool they produce that is used to make sweaters are all described as land.

Labor (Human Resources). Labor is the general category of the human effort that is used for the production of goods and services. This includes physical labor, such as harvesting trees for lumber, drilling for oil or mining for gold, growing wheat for bread, or raising the sheep that produce wool for a sweater. In addition to physical labor, there is mental labor, which is necessary for such activities as planning the best ways to harvest trees and making decisions about which trees to harvest. Labor is also involved when a doctor or surgeon analyzes and diagnoses (mental labor) before performing a medical procedure, then performs the procedure (physical labor).

Capital. Capital is input that is often viewed in two ways, much as is labor. Capital might be viewed as human capital—the knowledge, skills, and attitudes that humans possess that allow them to produce. The other type of capital is physical capital, which includes buildings, machinery, tools, and other items that are used to produce goods and service. Traditionally, physical capital has been a prerequisite for human capital; however, because of rapid changes in technology, today human capital is less dependent on physical capital.

Entrepreneurship. One special form of human capital that is important in an economic setting is entrepreneurship (often thought of as the fourth factor of production). Entrepreneurial abilities are needed to improve what we have and to create new goods and services. An entrepreneur is one who brings together all the resources of land, labor, and capital that are needed to produce a better product or service. In the process of doing this, the entrepreneur is willing to assume the risk of success and failure.

Many people associate entrepreneurship with creating or owning a new business. That is one definition of entrepreneurship but not the only one. An entrepreneur might create a new market for something that already exists or push the use of a natural resource to new limits in order to maximize efficiency and minimize consumption. See "entrepreneurship" for a more general discussion as it relates to business ownership.

GOODS AND SERVICES

It takes land, labor, and capital that are used by an entrepreneur to produce goods and services that will ultimately be used to satisfy our wants. *Goods* are tangible, meaning they are something that can be seen or touched. The production of goods requires using limited resources to produce in order to satisfy wants. An example might be a farmer who grows grain. The farmer uses farm equipment manufactured from resources; ground is a natural resource that is used to grow the grain; and because the growth of grain depletes the nutrients in the soil, the farmer must use fertilizers to restore the nutrients. Limited resources are used to produce natural or chemical fertilizers, but they are necessary for crop production. Water might be used to irrigate the crop and enhance production. When the crop is ready for harvest, the farmer uses additional resources to complete the process—equipment, gasoline, labor, and so on—which results in a good that can be used or sold for use by others.

Services are provided in numerous ways and are an intangible activity. There is no doubt that one can often see someone providing a service, but the service is not something that someone can pick up and take home to use. An example of a service is a ride in a taxi through a crowded city. It takes resources for the owner or driver to provide the service, and a passenger is consciously aware of riding in a taxi. When the ride is completed and the provider has been paid, the passenger doesn't have anything tangible to hold except the receipt. However, resources have been used to provide the service. The automobile used as the cab, the fuel used to operate the cab, and the labor of the driver are all examples of resources being used to provide a service that will satisfy a want.

It is important to understand that because goods and services utilize resources that are limited, goods and services are also scarce. Scarcity results when the demand for a good or service is greater than its supply. Remember that society has unlimited wants but scarce resources. It is scarcity, then, that causes consumers to have to make choices. If individuals can't have everything they want, they must decide which of the goods and services are most important and which they can do without.

ECONOMIC CHOICE

Opportunity Cost. When one makes economic decisions, it is because of limited resources. Alternatives must be considered. People make such decisions based on expecting greater benefits from one alternative than another. There is an *opportunity cost* involved in the choice. Opportunity cost is the benefit forgone from the best alternative that is *not* selected: Individuals give up an opportunity to use or enjoy something in order to select something else.

Opportunity costs can't always be measured, because it might be satisfaction that is lost. At other times, however, opportunity cost can be measured. Here are examples of each. Perhaps a student is studying hard for a final examination in a difficult course because a good exam score is critical to achieve the desired grade. Friends call to invite the student out for the evening. The alternatives are to study or to have fun. Being wise, the student selects studying instead of going out. It is difficult to measure the opportunity cost of having fun with friends. In the second example, the same studying student is asked to help someone clean a garage. If the person offers to pay the student $50 to clean the garage and the student chooses to study, the opportunity cost is easily measured at $50. In both these examples, opportunity cost is directly related to what was given up, not any other benefits that might result from the decision.

Circumstances also play a role in opportunity cost. Sometimes people are forced into a decision because of circumstances and the results may not always be optimal. For example, if someone is planning to relocate to a new city to start a new job and wants to sell a house before the move in order to be able to purchase a new house in the new location, the person may sell the house for less than the market price in order to complete the process. The opportunity cost is the value of what was given up in order to be able to purchase a new home. Every time a choice is made, opportunity costs are assumed.

Production. Another economic choice that must be made is related to production. This is illustrated in Figure 1. All four of the decisions must be made: What goods will be produced? How will production occur? How much should be produced? Who will be the recipients? All are decisions that influence production efficiency.

Efficiency is the primary element in deciding what to produce and how to go about the production process. Efficiency is producing with the least amount of expense, effort, and waste, but not without cost. If you take something away from a person to satisfy another person, one will be less happy and the other will be more happy. If a way can be found to make one person more happy without making the other person less happy, this would be efficient.

An example of economic efficiency might be the following. Assume someone owns a car and a friend doesn't own a car but does drive. The friend needs transportation regularly for a week. It happens to be a time when the car owner will be away on a business trip and therefore won't be using the car. It makes no sense for the friend to buy a car to use for such a short period of time, so the owner loans the friend the car for that week. The car owner is no worse off and the friend is better off. Economic efficiency has occurred in this situation. If the car owner had not loaned the car to the friend, there would have been waste because the friend would have had to buy or rent a car. It is wasteful to fail to take advantage of opportunities in which there is no loss of satisfaction to either party.

Production efficiency is a situation in which it is not possible to produce any more units of a good without giving up the opportunity to produce another good unless a change occurs in available productive resources. If a farmer is growing wheat to be sold for the production of bread, there is a point at which adding additional fertilizer to the soil would do no good. If the fertilizer were used on an oat crop in a different field, production could be increased for that crop. The way to increase the wheat production is to find different resources to make the crop better, such as irrigating the land to provide more moisture.

In the above example, it was suggested that different or additional resources might be used to increase production. This is necessary only after efficiency has been achieved. Additional resources would have to come from land, labor, capital, or entrepreneurship. It is most common that capital will be used most often to increase production. Capital is productive input that is increased by people. This is known as investment. Investment involves giving up what might presently be consumed in favor of producing something to consume in the future. If the farmer wants to increase wheat production in the future, something will have to be given up now in order to increase the resources available for future production.

Increasing human capital is critical to increasing production. This does not mean that more people must be produced, but rather that the knowledge and skills of humans must be increased. This can happen because of improvements in technology and new ways of satisfying wants. This involves the entrepreneurial factor that was described previously—the human element that figures out ways to improve and expand the resources that already exist.

Product Distribution. Getting goods into the hands of those who want them involves many choices. The economic system must decide how to divide the products that are produced among the potential recipients. Sometimes products can be divided equally among recipients, but normally this is not the situation. It must then be determined how the division will take place. In a capitalistic economic system, distribution is often determined by wealth. If two people have the same wants, the person who can most afford something will be able to acquire it.

THE LAWS OF SUPPLY AND DEMAND

Production decisions are made based on demand for goods and services. Supply of goods and services is dependent upon demand for the same. Why do movies that are much more popular stay at theaters longer than those that aren't as popular? Demand for the movie causes the theater operators to supply the showings that the consumer wants. Why does the room rate in a convention hotel go down on weekends? There is less demand on weekends because most convention-goers leave on Friday or Saturday and others don't arrive until Monday, so the supply of available rooms goes up. Hotel operators try to create more demand for their vacant weekend rooms by lowering prices and offering attractive amenities.

The *law of demand* states that during a specific time period the quantity of a product that is demanded is inversely related to its price, as long as other things remain constant. The higher the price, the lower the demand; the lower the price, the higher the demand. Don't confuse demand with wants. Consumers have unlimited wants, as was established at the beginning of this discussion. Nor are demands and wants the same as needs. A consumer may need to have a crown put on a tooth but may not want to have it done because of the high cost. At some point, the suffering patient may demand the services be provided regardless of the price.

Often when prices are too high and demand for a product or service lessens, it is because consumers have found a suitable substitute. Substitution happens all the time as a result of economic decisions that are made by consumers. For example, if someone needs a winter coat and likes one with a designer name and a price that reflects that name, the purchase may not be made. Instead, the person finds a similar coat that does not have a designer label and purchases it instead at a much lower cost.

Demand for goods or services determines the amount that will be supplied. The *law of supply* states that the greater the demand, the more that will be supplied; the lower the demand, the less that will be supplied. The amount that will be supplied by a producer of the good or service is based on capacity and willingness to supply the product at a specific price. A producer will not supply goods and services just because there is demand for them—price for the good or service is an important consideration.

If consumers are willing to pay more for a good or service, the producer will likely be willing to shift more resources in order to increase the supply of the demanded product. If a rancher is raising prime beef cattle and there is high demand for this good and consumers are willing to pay more for high-quality beef, then the rancher might be willing to supply more even if it is necessary to shift resources or acquire additional resources to be able to do so.

Demands change, supplies change, and prices change. So how does a producer know how much is enough and what price to charge for the goods and services? Very simply, the demand for and supply of goods and services can be plotted on graphs using different prices. The supply and demand for a good or service intersect on the graph at what is called the equilibrium price, or the price where all of what is supplied will be demanded. If the price is below equilibrium, there will be a shortage of the good or service, and if the price is above equilibrium, there will be a surplus of the good or service. For a more detailed explanation on this aspect of economics, see the discussion of supply and demand.

SUMMARY

Economics is a complex topic that is studied constantly and thoroughly. This article has given an overview of some of the main tenets of economics; however, there is much that was not even introduced. There are other topics throughout this encyclopedia, such as macroeconomics and microeconomics, that will further define and expand the topic of economics.

BIBLIOGRAPHY

Dolan, Edwin G., and Lindsey, David E. (1991). *Economics*. Chicago: Dryden.

Heilbroner, Robert L., and Thurow, Lester C. (1987). *Economics Explained*. New York: Simon & Schuster.

Lipsey, Richard G., Steiner, Peter O., Purvis, Douglas D., and Courant, Paul N. (1990). *Economics*. New York: Harper & Row.

McEachern, William A. (1991). *Economics: A Contemporary Introduction*. Cincinnati, OH: South-Western Publishing.

ROGER L. LUFT

ECONOMICS: A HISTORICAL PERSPECTIVE

Economics has been around since the beginning of time, but the study of economics dates back only a few hundred years. Since the beginning of human history, people have had to confront the problem of scarce resources and unlimited wants. The study of economics will continue until the end of time because each day uncovers new evidence that supports or revolutionizes economic theory.

THE DEVELOPMENT OF ECONOMIC SYSTEMS

The United States has a capitalistic economic system. Sometimes this system is called the free-enterprise system because that term is more acceptable to certain individuals. A capitalistic system includes a market society, or market system—a system of mercantilism in which participants react freely to the opportunities and challenges of the marketplace. This is in contrast to systems in which participants follow tradition or the commands of others. In a market system, anyone can buy land or sell it of his or her own free will or produce products and/or services that are sold at a market price. In earlier societies, participants responded not to the demands of the marketplace but to the demands of tradition or law as well as the threat and fear of punishment.

The factors of production, key to a capitalistic system, are the result of historical changes that made labor a key to creating wealth, made real estate out of land that had been in families for generations, and made capital out of possessions. Capitalism, a free-market system, was the cause of much unrest and insecurity, but it also gave birth to progress and, ultimately, fulfillment. There have been several key individuals whose work and economic writing help to clarify current thought about economic systems. The ideas of four are presented here.

ADAM SMITH (1723–1790)

Perhaps the best known and one of the most revered economists, Adam Smith wrote *The Wealth of Nations* in 1776, the same year the Declaration of Independence was signed. In this famous work, Smith explained how an independent society works. He answered several questions that people had at the time regarding the concepts of a free-market system.

Of primary concern was the question of how those consumed with greed might be controlled so they wouldn't take over society. Smith introduced the concept of competition. Anyone bent on bettering only him- or herself with no regard for others will be confronted by others with the same goals. In this new system, those who are buying or selling are forced to meet the prices offered by competitors.

Smith also illustrated that a market system also has another important function. That function is to produce goods and services that society wants, and in quantities that society wants. A good example of this is when products such as hula-hoops, cabbage patch dolls, or beanie babies became the rage, there weren't enough being produced to satisfy all the potential buyers. As a result, the manufacturers had to increase production and were also able to increase prices because the demand for the products was so great and buyers were willing to pay higher prices. In fact, many buyers bought quantities they didn't need precisely so they could, in turn, sell the high-demand products to others who were willing to pay the higher price. That is the capitalistic market system.

Smith was extremely visionary and foresaw that if a free market is to grow and prosper, there must be little government intervention. He saw that a free market must be self-regulating in order to become wealthy and robust. He made it clear that it was truly individuals' greed and desire for profits that would create a working free-enterprise system that is self-regulating.

KARL MARX (1818–1883)

The mere mention of Karl Marx might be disturbing to some; however, his thoughts and writings on economics have stirred many to more intense economic analysis. His role in economic history is quite different from that of Adam Smith. Smith was the visionary regarding the orderly processes and growth of capitalism while Marx diagnosed its disorderliness and eventual demise. Marx believed that growth is fraught with crises and pitfalls.

Karl Marx stressed the instability of capitalism.

Marx was the first economic theorist to stress the instability of capitalism, maintaining that economic growth is wavering and uncertain. He pointed out that even though accumulation of wealth is primary in a free-market system, it may not always be possible. Marx believed that increasing instability would occur until the system collapsed.

Marx discussed how the size of businesses would continue to grow because of the inherent instability and demise of smaller, noncompetitive businesses. Failing businesses would be bought by successful ones; hence, the growth cycle would continue. He realized that a trend toward larger businesses is typical in a capitalistic system.

Marx also speculated that there would be a class struggle in a capitalistic society. He thought that as small businesses were forced out of the marketplace and acquired by larger businesses, the social structure would also evolve into two classes. He predicted that there would be one class of wealthy property owners and another class of propertyless workers. There are arguments for and against Marx's economic beliefs, but he has more critics than supporters in capitalistic countries.

JOHN MAYNARD KEYNES (1883–1946)

John Maynard Keynes was the father of a "mixed economy" in which the government plays a crucial role. Many believe that government should not have a role in a capitalistic system, viewing such a role with considerable distrust and suspicion. As a result, many find Keynes's theories to be as offensive as those of Marx.

One of the main tenets of Keynes's theory—in conflict with both Smith and Marx—is that economic problems in a capitalistic society are not self-correcting and that economies cannot keep growing indefinitely. He believed that if there is nothing to support capital growth, a depressed economy requires outside intervention or a substitute for business capital spending. Keynes believed that only government intervention could get a country out of a depression and the economy back on track.

ALFRED MARSHALL (1842–1924)

Alfred Marshall was a mathematician who applied his mathematical training to his explanation of economics. Marshall's economic theories, although very elaborate, have been viewed as eclectic and lacking in internal consistency. He was noted for taking a series of formal economic thoughts and analyses and linking them. He thought that his writings would present a detailed picture of economic reality.

His complex thoughts are much too detailed to go into here, but he did develop theories of value and distribution that combine marginal utility with real cost. The forces behind both supply and demand determine value. Behind demand is marginal utility, which is reflected in the prices at which given quantities will be demanded by buyers. Marshall stated that behind supply is marginal effort and sacrifice, reflected in the prices at which given quantities will be produced.

J. Maynard Keynes, father of the "mixed economy."

SUMMARY

There are, of course, many other noted economists who have influenced the study of economics. Many contemporary economic theorists have used the writings of the early economists to further develop economic thought. Economics is a continually evolving study, and its history will be constantly changing.

BIBLIOGRAPHY

Blaug, Mark, ed. (1990). *The History of Economic Thought.* Brookfield, VT: Elgar.

Deane, Phyllis. (1978). *The Evolution of Economic Ideas.* New York: Cambridge University Press.

Galbraith, John Kenneth. (1987). *Economics in Perspective: A Critical History.* Boston: Houghton Mifflin.

Heilbroner, Robert L., and Thurow, Lester C. (1987). *Economics Explained.* New York: Simon and Schuster.

Heimann, Eduard. (1964). *History of Economic Doctrines: An Introduction to Economic Theory.* New York: Oxford University Press.

Rostow, W. W. (1990). *Theorists of Economic Growth from David Hume to the Present With a Perspective on the Next Century.* New York: Oxford University Press.

ROGER L. LUFT

ECONOMIC SYSTEMS

The fundamental economic problem in any society is to provide a set of rules for allocating resources and/or consumption among individuals who can't satisfy their wants, given limited resources. The rules that each economic system provides function within a framework of formal institutions (e.g., laws) and informal institutions (e.g., customs).

In every nation, no matter what the form of government, what the type of economic system, who controls the government, or how rich or poor the country is, three basic economic questions must be answered. They are:

What and how much will be produced? Literally, billions of different outputs could be produced with society's scarce resources. Some mechanism must exist that differentiates between products to be produced and others that remain as either unexploited inventions or as individuals' unfulfilled desires.

How will it be produced? There are many ways to produce a desired item. It may be possible to use more labor and less capital, or vice versa. It may be possible to use more unskilled labor to substitute for fewer units of skilled labor. Choices must be made about the particular input mix, the way the inputs should be organized, how they are brought together, and where the production is to take place.

For whom will it be produced? Once a commodity is produced, some mechanism must exist that distributes finished products to the ultimate consumers of the product. The mechanism of distribution for these commodities differs by economic system.

MARKET VS. COMMAND SYSTEMS

One way to define economic systems is to classify them according to whether they are market systems or command systems. In a *market system*, individuals own the factors of production and individually decide how to use them. The cumulative decisions of these individuals are reflected in constantly changing prices, which result from the supply and demand for different commodities and, in turn, impact that supply and demand. The prices of those commodities are signals to everyone within the system indicating relative scarcity and abundance. Indeed, it is the signaling aspect of the price system that provides the information to buyers and sellers about what should be bought and what should be produced.

In a market system the interaction of supply and demand for each good determines *what and how much to produce.* For example, if the highest price that consumers are willing to pay is less than the lowest cost at which a good can be produced, output will be zero. That doesn't mean that the market system has failed. It merely implies that the demand is not high enough in relation to supply to create a market; however, it might be someday.

In a market economy the efficient use of scarce inputs determines *how output will be produced.* Specifically, in a market system, the least-cost production method will have to be used. If any other method was used, firms would be sacrificing potential profit. Any firm that fails to employ the least-cost technique will find that other firms can undercut its price. That is, other firms can choose the least-cost or any lower-cost production method and be able to offer the product at a lower price, while still making a profit. This lower price will induce consumers to shift purchases from the higher-priced firm to the lower-priced firm, and inefficient firms will be forced out of business.

In a market system, individuals make the choice about what is purchased; however, ability to pay, as well as the consumer's willingness to purchase the good or service, determine that choice. *Who gets what* is determined by the distribution of money income. In a market system, a consumer's ability to pay for consumer products is based on the consumer's money income. Money income in turn depends on the quantities, qualities, and types of the various human and non-human resources that the individual owns and supplies to the marketplace. It also depends on the prices, or payments, for those resources. When you are selling your human resources as labor services, your money income is based on the wages you can earn in the labor market. If you own non-human resources—capital and land, for example—the level of interest and rents that you are paid for your resources will influence the size of your money income, and thus your ability to buy consumer products.

Critics commonly argue that in a market system the rich, who begin with a disproportionately large share of resources, tend to become richer while the poor, who begin with a disproportionately small share of resources, tend to become poorer. They further argue that a government, which is designed to protect private-property rights, will tend to be exploited by those in power, which tends to be the economically wealthy. These critics argue that a market economy leads to selfish behavior rather than socially desirable outcomes.

In contrast, a *command system* is one in which decision making is centralized. In a command system, the government controls the factors of production and makes all decisions about their use and about the consumption of output. The central planning unit takes the inputs of the economy and directs them into outputs in a socially desirable manner. This requires a careful balancing between output goals and available resources.

In a command system the central planners determine *what and how much* will be produced by first forecasting an optimal level of consumption for a future period and then specifically allocating resources projected to be sufficient to support that level of production. The "optimal" level of production in a command economy is determined by the central planners and is consistent with government objectives rather than being a function of consumer desires.

As a part of the resource allocation process, the central planners also determine *how production will take place*. This process could focus on low-cost production or high quality production or full-employment of relatively inefficient resources or any number of other governmental objectives.

Finally, the command system will determine for *whom the product is produced*. Again, the focus is on socially-desirable objectives. The product can be allocated based on class, on a queuing process, on a reward system for outstanding or loyal performance, or on any other socially-desirable basis for the economy.

Critics commonly argue that because planned economies cannot effectively process as much relevant information as a market does, command economic systems cannot coordinate economic activity or satisfy consumer demand as well as market forces do. For example, consider an economic planning board of twenty people, that must decide how many coats, apartment buildings, cars, trains, museums, jets, grocery stores, and so forth should be built in the next five years. Where should these planners begin? How would they forecast the future need for each of these? Critics argue that, at best, planners would make a guess about what goods and services would be needed. If they guess wrong, resources would be misallocated and too much or too little production would take place. These critics argue that private individuals, guided by rising and falling prices and by the desire to earn profits, are better at satisfying consumer demand.

CAPITALISM

Under a capitalist economic system, individuals own all resources, both human and non-human. Governments intervene only minimally in the operation of markets, primarily to protect the private-property rights of individuals. Free markets in which suppliers and demanders can enter and exit the market at their own discretion are fundamental to the capitalist economic system. The concept of laissez-faire, that is, leaving the coordination of individuals' wants to be controlled by the market, is also a tenet of capitalism.

What and how much will be produced? How will it be produced? For whom will it be produced? In a capitalist system, individuals own resources, either through inheritance or through industry. The individual receives compensation for the use of resources by others. This, combined with inherited wealth of the person, determines an individual's spending power. The accumulated spending power and the willingness of individuals to allocate resources to consumption determine demand. The availability and costs of resources, together with the potential for profits of firms, determine supply. In a market system the demand of consumers combined with the supply of producers determine what and how much will be produced.

Because of the economic competitiveness of the market system, the lowest-cost production method will be used. If anything other than the lowest-cost production method was being used, a competing firm would have an incentive to enter production to earn a greater profit and could afford to sell at a lower price, thus driving the original firm out of production. Consumers could then purchase more of the product at a lower price, allowing their limited resources to purchase more.

Production will be allocated to those with available resources and a willingness to purchase the output of production. These purchases then become information for suppliers in determining what and how much to produce in the future.

Thus, pure capitalism is an economic system based upon private property and the market in which—in principle—individuals decide how, what, and for whom to produce. Under capitalism, individuals are encouraged to follow their own self-interests, while the market forces of supply and demand are relied upon to coordinate economic activity. Distribution to each individual is according to his or her ability, effort, and inherited property. Typically the economies of Canada, the United States, and Western Europe are considered to be capitalist.

SOCIALISM

Under a socialist economic system, individuals own their own human capital and the government owns most other, non-human resources— that is, most of the major factors of production are owned by the state. Land, factories, and major machinery are publicly owned.

What and how much will be produced? How will it be produced? For whom will it be produced? A socialist system is a form of command economy in which prices and production are set by the state. Movement of resources, including the movement of labor, is strictly controlled. Resources can only move at the direction of the centralized planning authority. Economic decisions about *what and how much, how,* and *for whom* are all made by the state through its central planning agencies.

In theory, socialism is an economic system based upon the individual's good will toward others, rather than a function of his or her own self-interest. Socialism attempts to influence individuals to take other people's needs into account and to adjust their own needs in accordance with what's available. In socialist economies, individuals are urged to consider the well-being of others; if individuals don't behave in a socially desirable manner, the government will intervene. In practice, socialism has become an economic system based on government ownership of the means of production, with economic activity governed by central planning. The economies of Sweden and France are examples of a socialist economic system.

COMMUNISM

Under a communist economic system, all resources, both human and non-human, are owned by the state. The government takes on a central planning role directing both production and consumption in a socially desirable manner.

What and how much will be produced? How will it be produced? For whom will it be produced? Central planners forecast a socially beneficial future and determine the production needed to obtain that outcome. The central planners make all decisions, guided by what they believe to be good for the country. The central planners also allocate the production to consumers based on their assessment of the individual's need. Basic human needs and wants would be met according to the Marxist principle, "From each according to his ability to produce, to each according to his need."

The economies of China, the former Soviet Union, and the former East Germany are examples of communist economies.

MIXED ECONOMIC SYSTEMS

In practice, most economies blend some elements of both market and command economies in answering the three fundamental economic questions: *What and how much will be produced? How will it be produced? For whom will it be produced?* Furthermore, within any economy, the degree of the mix will vary.

The economy of the United States is generally considered to be a free market or capitalist economic system. However, even in the United States the government has determined a "minimum wage," has set rules and regulations for environmental protection, has provided price supports for agricultural products, restricts the imports of items that might compete with local production, restricts the exports of sensitive output, provides for public goods such as a park system, and provides health and retirement services through Medicaid and Medicare. All of these detract from the essential nature of a capitalist economy. However, most decisions continue to be left to free markets, leaving the United States as a mixed economy that leans heavily toward the capitalist economic system.

In contrast, the economy of the former Soviet Union is generally considered to be communist. However, the strict controls of the central planning unit of the country tended to be more intensely focused on heavy industry, including the defense and aerospace industries, than on agricultural industries. Farmers often had significant freedom to produce and sell (or barter) what they wished.

SUMMARY

Countries have scarce resources. The economic systems of countries are designed to allocate those resources, through a production system, to provide output for their citizens. The fundamental questions that these systems answer are:

- *What and how much will be produced?*
- *How will it be produced?*
- *For whom will it be produced?*

Market economies leave the answers to these questions to the determination of the forces of supply and demand while command economies use a central planning agency to direct the activities of the economy. Pure capitalist economies are market economies in which the role of government is to ensure that the ownership of the resources used in production are privately held. Socialist economies are primarily command economies where most non-human resources are owned by the state but human capital is owned by the individual. Communist economies are also command economies but all resources, both human and non-human, are owned by the state.

In practice, all economies are actually mixed economies, incorporating some facets of both market and command economies. The relative importance of the particular economic system in the country is the determinant of the type of economic system that it is generally considered to be.

DENISE WOODBURY

EDUCATION

(SEE: *Corporate Education; Training and Development*)

ELECTRONIC COMMERCE

"No single force embodies our electronic transformation more than the evolving medium known as the Internet. Internet technology is having a profound effect on the global trade in services," according to a White House paper in

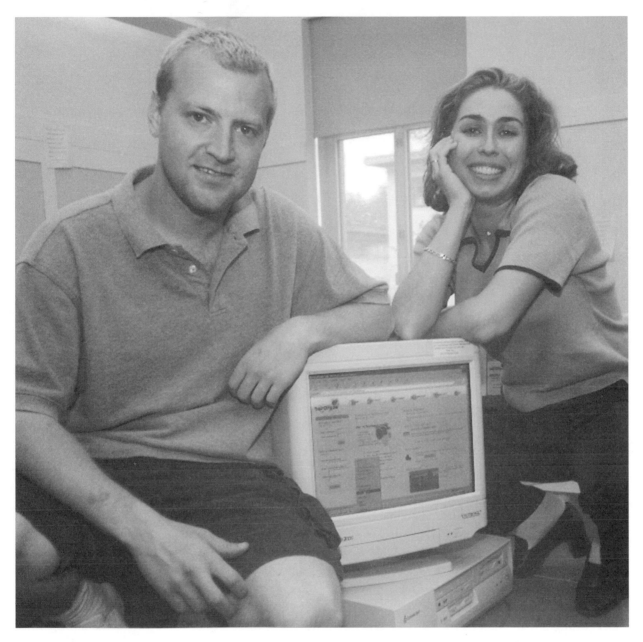

These Carnegie Mellon University students were among the first to graduate with a Master of Science in Electronic Commerce.

1997. Electronic commerce is estimated to have been in the range of $63 billion in 1999 and is expected to soar to $1,444 trillion by 2003 (Forrester Research, 1999). *Electronic commerce* is a broad term describing business activities with associated technical data that are conducted electronically. It is an entire set of different, digitally enabled activities that are progressively replacing the more traditional brick-and-mortar commercial functions. While the wider phenomenon of "electronization of economic activities" encompasses the digitalization of all processes of economic wealth generation—including economic analysis, production, storage, information provi-

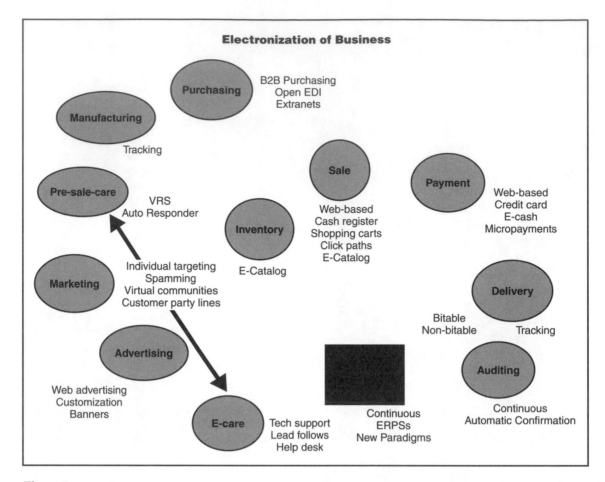

Electronization of Business

Figure 1

sioning, marketing, and so on—it is the area of sales and related processes facilitated by electronic media that have been popularly termed "electronic commerce." Consequently within the more general phenomenon of digitalization of modern life, we find its most important component electronic commerce.

NEW WAYS OF DOING BUSINESS

Corporate, not-for-profit, and governmental systems are incorporating many increasingly digitalized processes that are leading to astounding productivity gains in the world economy because these processes are becoming less expensive, less time consuming, and more useful ("Why the Productivity Revolution," 2000). For example, a directory-assistance call formerly required an op-

erator, look-up in paper-based directories, and a localized search. Now it involves a national (or international) computer database, voice synthesis, and automatic connection. Furthermore, the process has been expanded; one can do reverse searches through the Internet that will point to the owner of a telephone number, link this to one's telephone bill, and not involve any individual as the service provider. Thousands of "system processes" are undergoing this type of mutation, leading to cheaper, less time-consuming, and expanded types of services. Figure 1 shows several components of the business process (e.g., marketing) and electronic commerce tools (e.g., Web banners) that are structurally changing ways of doing business.

The marketing, advertising, and care triad are the core of the phenomenon. One-to-one

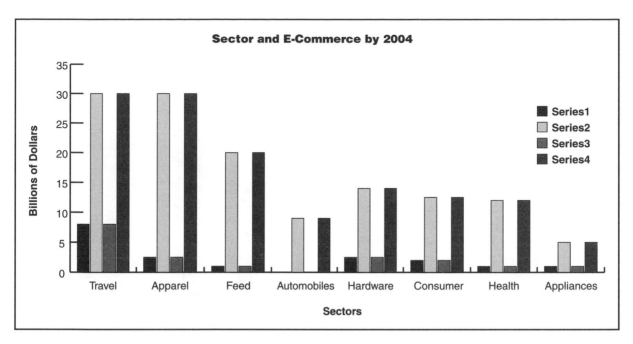

Figure 2

marketing (whereby large customer databases link much information about clients, thus creating very efficient leads) is linked to very tailored advertising: The firm knows the client when he or she is connected to the Internet, and it fires off a series of individually targeted banners catering very closely to the client's needs. These advertising banners can explore the geography of the client at that moment (for example, if in a car, the closest gas station, drug store, or sports bar), linkages among products or recent purchase (bought a computer, needs parts and software), personal factors (getting married, needing a dress, birthday, death in the family), and other factors. The e-care part of the triad is the emerging process of the new organization. Technologically rich products need superior, technologically based support. E-care—a mix of e-mail, Web-based support, and, when essential, phone support—is cheaper and more powerful if properly done than the traditional means. Organizations are finding that the same stringent standards of traditional care must be applied in the e-organization.

The electronic commerce revolution is in its initial phases and will progressively take over all processes either directly or indirectly. The distinction between "snail" commerce and e-commerce will disappear, with all processes becoming either digital or aided by digital supporting processes. The pace of this transformation is what differentiates winning from losing competitors, industries, and investors. The intrinsic nature of the product and processes, as well as the dynamics and resistance to change of corporations and industries, will determine the pace of change and the gains in productivity. Together with the telephone, railroads, and electricity, the Internet is one of the major agents of change of modern life.

Two major factors affect the speed of change in terms of product: (1) bitability and (2) e-commoditization. A product is bitable or not. If it can be transmitted over the Internet, the product (or service) is bitable. Software, information, remote support services, banking, brokerage, and insurance, for example, fall into this category. If a product is bitable it does not ultimately have to be physically delivered, although

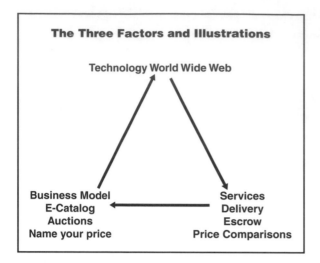

The Three Factors and Illustrations

Technology World Wide Web

Business Model
E-Catalog
Auctions
Name your price

Services
Delivery
Escrow
Price Comparisons

Figure 3

it may take some time to acquire sufficient bandwidth or get consumers used to the idea. The e-commoditization factor is more complex. An e-commodity is an item that one does not need to touch, see, try on, try out, taste, or squeeze before buying. Clearly high-fashion clothes, cars, foods, meats, vegetables, and girlfriends tend not to fall into this category. On the other hand, this is very much a question of attitude and need. Busy executives will forgo the examination of food items for the convenience of having them at home when they arrive there. Once a teenager has tried on an item of brand-name clothing for size, it becomes a commodity, since sizes tend to be quality controlled. A buyer who lives in a very remote location may consider an item to be a commodity because the cost of its examination does not warrant extensive travel—and, in the case of clothes, they can be altered. Ultimately, bitable goods and bitable commodity goods present the highest potentials for e-commerce.

Research predicts that there will be a wide range of business expansion on the Internet. This is reflected on Figure 2, which incorporates a series of predictions from four different organizations.

Travel and apparel are expected to be the largest B2C (business to consumer) areas. At the same time, the volumes of B2B (business to business) trade are expected to be six to ten times larger than B2C, but with much narrower margins.

EMERGING PRINCIPLES OF ELECTRONIC COMMERCE

An entirely new set of principles of commerce is emerging. First is the realization that a Malthusian physical world is giving way to a place where information is abundant and eyeballs limited. Second is the realization that paradoxes exist because of technology, and that giving things away for free, not protecting software against privacy, and paying for visitors, may be the paradigms of the e-world. Third, the meaning of the words *competitor* and *industry* are changing. In the faceless world of the Internet, one's current and future customers and suppliers are both one's competitors and one's allies. Fourth, industries are blending and changing, and affiliation agreements allow for the creation of entire product cycles without the ownership of inventory or production facilities. Finally, pricing models are changing; hybrids of fixed pricing, auctions, variable pricing, contingent pricing, and name-your-price pricing are emerging and creating new business models. While technology gets most of the credit, actually successes are usually based on the triad of: (1) technology, (2) business model innovation, and (3) a family of facilitating (profitable) services. (See Figure 3)

The B2B sector of e-commerce will present both vertical and horizontal models. In the vertical model, the firm will focus on an industry and develop great industry expertise in order to develop its markets. In the horizontal model the firm will focus on one type of product or service and offer it across industries (e.g., Internet payroll services). The B2B sector is intrinsically different from B2C. Buyers are well informed, possess many resources and can negotiate based on volume. Brand name is much less of a consideration than price, quality, delivery time, and reliability. Three different models have emerged for B2B transactions: (1) the e-catalog model for situations in which there are many different items at distributed locations and the price is fixed (e.g., auto parts); (2) the auction model, in which products are not standardized and there are great differences in the perceptions of value (e.g., auctions of used capital plant products); and (3) the commodity auction model, in which there are not too many variations on the type of product and there are large buyers and sellers (e.g., natural gas, pork bellies, coffee, etc.).

Electronic commerce is progressively and irreversibly changing the face of many businesses because of three dominant phenomena: (1) disintermediation, whereby one party to a transaction is eliminated (e.g., brokers in on-line trading); (2) re-intermediation, whereby a new electronic intermediary comes between the seller and the buyer (e.g., electronic booksellers that take orders and farm them out to providers that have the book in stock); and (3) cannibalization, whereby businesses progressively give up their traditional brick-and-mortar ventures for the superior electronic model (e.g., traditional pharmacies opening on-line drug stores).

PROBLEMS IN SEARCH OF SOLUTIONS

The e-commerce juggernaut is not without its dangers and shortcomings. It is drastically affecting traditional firms that cannot continue to do business according to the traditional economic model. For example, a stock brokerage firm that on average charged $90 per trade cannot compete with $10 on-line trades; if any adaptations meet with strong resistance, the organization could be dooming itself to extinction. The security weaknesses of the e-commerce infrastructure have been well publicized: Viruses, security intrusions, and inability to provide services because of volume attacks are not phenomena that will disappear. A continuous struggle is evolving among facilitating technologies, intrinsic technological dangers, and the management of these factors.

Privacy issues present a different set of challenges. The same technology that facilitates business activities and provides wonderful services is also a major threat to individual freedom. Large databases linking information about economic activity from different sources (purchases, banking activity, medical records) provide great economic advantages by making marketing more ef-

ficient, loans more targeted, and medical information ubiquitous. They also create great dangers for privacy potentials for abuse. Doubleclick.com, a marketing analysis technology firm, tracks customer activities in Web sites. Its click-path analysis allows firms to understand customer behavior and improve their offerings. However they have 11,000 clients, and linking together the buyers' profiles from these sites is considered to be far too intrusive by many people. Complaints have been filed with the Federal Trade Commission and boycotts proposed. As a response, Doubleclick lured bigger profile "primary" officers for its board."

Solutions, however, are not as straightforward as they might seem. Making certain actions illegal can actually create arbitrage opportunities and extraordinary advantages for Internet players. Because gambling rules are strict in the United States, electronic casinos are created in cooperative havens in the Bahamas: A legal obstacle in the United States is a business opportunity for another country. When restrictions are placed on the use and content of databases in Germany, offshore database havens appear immediately. When Web-site censorship appears in China, free-Chinese Web sites are constructed. Telephone systems are monitored and taxed by PTTs, supranational satellite telephone networks are being created.

Consequently, easy fixes are not possible and new methods of establishing order, efficiency, and decency will have to be created. Because the Internet is truly a supranational entity, nations need to band together to maintain order and efficiency and reasonableness in cyberspace. The same economic factors that allow for arbitrage can also be used for self-policing and monitoring of the e-commerce environment. To benefit fully from this medium, companies/entities and nations must have payment-clearing solutions, customs solutions, and access to the large markets of the economy. Rogue countries can be excluded from the payment-clearing chains; rogue companies behaving in unacceptable ways can be boycotted and excluded from any affiliation and linking deals. Self-policing seals such as the American Institute of Certified Public Accountants' (AICPA) Web Trust and SysTrust products, inspections, and certificates can be used for monitoring and supervision. International information structures, involving many cooperating organizations, can be on the alert for rogue behavior and spearhead a drive to create reasonable and unbiased rules. Technology can be used to monitor and detect money laundering, illegal product flows, and information trafficking. But such monitoring must be carefully conceived and supervised, because it could turn into a "Big Brother" type of behavior. Most important of all is not to succumb to the easy temptation of creating restrictive and ill-thought-out laws of the sort that legislators tend to create when some local scandal occurs.

BIBLIOGRAPHY

American Institute of Certified Public Accountants and Canadian Institute of Chartered Accountants. (1999). *SysTrust (TM/SM) Principles and Criteria for Systems Reliability.*

American Institute of Certified Public Accountants. (updated annually). *CPA WebTrust: Practitioner's Guide for Business to Consumer Electronic Commerce.*

Forrester Research. (1999, November).

Kilmer, William E. (1999). *Getting Your Business Wired: Using Computer Networking and the Internet to Grow your Business.* New York: AMACOM.

Rosen, Anita. (2000). *The e-Commerce Question and Answer Book: A Survival Guide for Business Managers.* New York: American Management Association.

U.S. Government's Framework for Electronic Commerce, The. (1997, July 1). The White House, http://www.ecommerce.gov/framewrk.htm#BACKGROUND.

"Why the Productivity Revolution Will Spread." (2000). *Business Week.* February 14. http://www.businessweek.com.

MIKLOS A. VASARHELYI

E-MAIL

Electronic mail, or e-mail, is a method of communicating whereby an individual uses a computer or other electronic device to compose and send a message to another individual. Messages may be sent through computer systems linked by a network, through modems using telephone lines, or, in some cases, through wireless transmissions.

While some systems provide links only within a company's particular e-mail system, the prevailing trend is for e-mail users to be able to send e-mail to anyone in the world. In order to send an e-mail message, each party must have an e-mail address. The address is composed of an identifying name, an @ sign, the name of the fileserver where the account is located, and a domain name. Typical domain names are com (commercial), gov (government), edu (schools), and org (organization). An example of an e-mail address would be marysmith@linc.lincoln.com. In order to send a message outside the company e-mail system, the complete address must be used.

Address book: Most electronic mail systems offer an address book feature. The address book provides a place to store e-mail addresses, which can often be complex and difficult to remember. The address book can also be used to develop mailing lists. For example, if six friends frequently communicate, a user might list all their addresses in a folder in the address book. The folder would have a name such as "My Friends." Then the user could quickly send a message to all six friends at one time by addressing the message to "My Friends" rather than to each individual user.

Attachments: While the majority of e-mail messages are composed of text, e-mail users are sending increasingly complex messages with accompanying attachments. Users can send documents by using an attachment feature of the e-mail package. The attachment feature allows the user to specify where an electronic file—such as a text document, a spreadsheet, or a graphics presentation—is located and then to send a copy by e-mail. Attachments can also be sent to a list of people in one e-mail message. This feature has greatly enhanced the ability of people at a distance to work together. For example, if two people are planning a presentation at a conference, they can attach outlines of the presentation as well as slides of the actual presentation and transmit them for revision or review.

Photographs can also be attached to e-mail messages, in the same way as another file can. One caution is that multimedia files including photos can be quite large and take a longer time to send. With the additional use of digital cameras and/or scanners, photographs that are valuable to business are easier to send than ever before.

Deleting a message: After reading an incoming e-mail message, the reader may decide that the message does not need to be saved. All e-mail systems have a feature to allow for quick deletion of messages. However, many systems convey the deleted message to a trash file that will allow the message to be recalled. To delete the message from the individual computer, the message in the trash file must also be deleted. Even after this double deletion, the message may still be accessible. Large computer systems periodically back up all mail, so the message may be floating around in the organization's computer memory backup for a much longer time.

Forwarding a message: At times, the reader of a message may decide to forward a message to a third party. The person sending e-mail has no control over what the receiver will do with the message. The receiver can easily forward the message to one individual or a list of individuals.

Replying to a message: If the reader wishes to respond to an e-mail message, the reply feature provides a quick way to answer the message without keying in the e-mail address of the person who sent it. There is a common e-mail faux pas, however, that should be avoided. If a message has been sent to a list and one reader replies to the person who sent the message by using the reply feature, that reply may be sent to everyone on the list. For example, a conference coordinator sends a reminder message to a list of 500 people who will be attending a conference. One of the respondents has a question about whether his or her registration has arrived and replies to the message using the reply feature. Since the original message was sent to a list, it is quite possible that using the reply feature will result in that individual's message being transmitted to all 500 people on the list instead of only to the original sender. This is a common violation of "netiquette," a term that refers to using courtesy on the Internet.

Netiquette: Using the correct etiquette helps people respond correctly in their environment. For example, eating peas with a knife, interrupting a speaker, and not introducing people are examples of poor etiquette. Poor etiquette can also exist in the electronic environment. A few things that could be considered violations of netiquette are flaming (sending an immediate, angry overreaction to an e-mail message), shouting (typing a message in all capital letters), forwarding personal messages without permission, and sending a personal message to an entire list. Other problems include preparing a list that includes individuals who have no interest in the topic and bombarding them with e-mail, sending e-mail messages that criticize others, and using emoticons (typed symbols to indicate expressions) in business e-mail. Just as an understanding of good manners helps one move effectively in society, so an understanding of netiquette helps one perform effectively in electronic communication.

Privacy of e-mail: One of the controversies surrounding electronic mail has been the issue of privacy. The term "mail" seems to imply the same safeguards that one has when using the U.S. Postal Service. These safeguards include the right to open your own mail and legal protection from those who would tamper with your mail. Electronic mail, however, may not include these safeguards.

Courts have upheld the right of corporations to review the e-mail of employees who use company resources such as hardware, software, and/or company time to compose and send e-mail messages. It is the court's position that a company has the right to read the e-mail of employees is especially strong for those companies who have an e-mail policy in place.

Employees should be judicious in their use of e-mail and should not put in electronic writing anything they would not write on paper for public distribution. Both individuals and companies have seen their e-mail communications come back to haunt them in the media and in court. For example, some plaintiffs in sexual harassment cases have used negative e-mail messages sent by company employees to establish the legal definition of a hostile working environment. Others have seen their e-mail admitted in court as proof of their beliefs and actions that may disagree with their sworn testimony.

Electronic mail policy: Many organizations have implemented e-mail policies in the workplace. A good policy clearly defines an employer's expectations about how e-mail should be used by employees. If personal e-mail is acceptable, conditions for its use are outlined in the policy. In addition, a process should be developed so employees can indicate their understanding of the e-mail policy in place.

Volume of electronic mail messages: A concern for many employees is the large number of e-mail messages that they receive and are expected to respond to on a daily basis. Some e-mail systems allow the sender to assign a priority rating to the message. In this way priority messages are flagged. Other systems rely on the subject line. For that reason, a concise subject line that clearly defines the message is an asset when a reader reviews the message. The subject line will help the reader decide when the message should be read. A message from an unknown sender with no subject line may not be evaluated very quickly.

Organizing electronic mail messages: As e-mail messages arrive, the reader can reply, forward, or delete them. The reader can also save or store messages. E-mail systems allow the reader to set up filters to organize incoming messages and folders to organize messages that should be stored. The reader then merely transfers the message to the appropriate folder. This action will clear the inbox of messages and provide a logical arrangement to locate messages by sender or by topic.

Response speed: Just as it is easier to send an e-mail message than to mail a letter or, in many cases, to attempt to phone someone, the amount of time allowed for a response has also decreased. While a letter may take two to three days to travel to its destination, an e-mail message is transmitted almost instantaneously. Few would expect an answer to a letter within a week of sending it. However, the tolerance for a slow e-mail response has dwindled. Seldom would a person sending an e-mail message expect to wait two to three days for a response. If the first e-mail message elicits no response, the sender may send follow-up messages or attempt some other means of communication if a timely response is not received.

Junk mail or spam: Junk mail, or spam, can arrive in the inbox in the form of chain letters, unsolicited advertisements, warnings (usually not founded in fact) about viruses or files, and other nonbusiness information. The difference between the junk mail received via the U.S. Postal Service and the junk mail received through e-mail is that the former can be quickly discarded. The junk mail received via e-mail, however, is more difficult to get rid of and ties up the company's resources as well. Some corporations use procedures to block junk mail, or spam, from entering their e-mail systems. Some users find that friends or acquaintances can be the worst violators and are too willing to pass along unnecessary information they have found on the Internet.

BIBLIOGRAPHY

Bicknell, David. (1999). "E-Mails That Could Cost Millions." *Computer Weekly* January 28:26.

Flynn, Nancy, and Flynn, Tom. (1998). *Writing Effective E-Mail: Improving Your Electronic Communication.* Menlo Park, CA: Crisp Publications.

Gleeson, Kerry. (1998). *The High-Tech Personal Efficiency Program: Organizing Your Electronic Resources to Maximize Your Time and Efficiency.* New York: Wiley.

Hartman, Diane B., and Nantz, Karen. (1996). *The 3 R's of E-Mail: Risks, Rights, and Responsibilities.* Menlo Park, CA: Crisp Publications.

Levin, John R., and Baroudi, Carol. (1997). *E-Mail for Dummies,* 2d ed. Foster City, CA: IDG Books Worldwide.

Mead, Hayden, and Hill, Brad. (1997). *The On-Line/E-Mail Dictionary.* New York: Berkley Publishing Group.

Overly, Michael R. (1999). *E-Policy: How to Develop Computer, E-Policy, and Internet Guidelines to Protect Your*

Company and Its Assets. AMACOM. Boulder, CO: Net Library, Inc.

Schwartz, Alan, and Ferguson, Paula. (1998). *Managing Mailing Lists.* Cambridge, England: O'Reilly and Associates, Inc.

Tuten, Tracy L., Urban, David J., and Gray, George. (1998). "Electronic Mail as Social Influence in Downsized Organizations." *Human Resource Management* 37(3,4):249-261.

MARSHA L. BAYLESS

EMPLOYEE ASSISTANCE PROGRAMS

The term *employee assistance program (EAP)* refers to a program that provides business and industry with the means of identifying employees whose job performance is negatively affected by personal or job-related problems. The EAP arranges for structured assistance to solve those problems, with the goal of reestablishing the employee's effective job performance. The services of an EAP may be contracted, or the program may be an employer's own creation, designed to fit the unique needs of a company. EAPs typically provide professional, confidential, no- or low-cost assistance for employees with personal problems.

EAPs help employers by identifying troubled workers, by either supervisory referrals or self-referrals. Each referred employee is assessed, and a plan of action is designed to suit his or her needs. The ability to uncover the employee's primary problem is required. The goal is to enable the employees to work again at peak levels. An effective EAP requires a knowledge of resources available in the community.

HISTORY

No one knows when the first employer offered counseling and social work services to its employees. But in 1917 Macy's, the New York City department store, opened an office specifically devoted to helping employees deal with personal problems. Metropolitan Life Insurance Company and Western Electric were also pioneers in the field, but it was not until the years immediately following World War II that a limited form of EAP became relatively common.

In those days, Alcoholics Anonymous was a new organization gaining widespread attention. For the first time, alcohol abuse was perceived by business to be a workplace problem, and many companies started alcoholism programs for their workers. These programs were usually staffed by recovering alcoholics who trained supervisors to spot alcoholics by looking for such symptoms as shaking hands, bloodshot eyes, and alcohol on the breath. These early programs produced gratifying results, but they were severely limited because they identified only late-stage problems. Alcoholics in the early stage whose hands did not shake and who did not drink on the job did not receive help.

Today, most EAPs pay close attention to the specific needs of clients. For example, until recently few EAPs dealt with gambling-related issues; but now counselors are being trained to deal with gambling addiction and related problems. A number of companies also have EAPs that offer financial and legal referrals to employees with consumer credit or bankruptcy problems and legal concerns. These services are in addition to assistance offered for emotional, family, work, and substance-abuse problems.

Another area that EAPs frequently deal with is critical incident intervention—helping workers handle deaths, suicides, hostage situations, major accidents, and natural disasters, including fires, earthquakes, mudslides, floods, and hurricanes. Employees often need assistance in dealing with the emotional and physical trauma of these natural disasters.

MODERN PROGRAMS

Organizational development, managed care, workers' compensation, child care, and catastrophic disasters are just a few of the issues that are expanding the scope of today's EAPs. The changes going on in corporate America are tremendous. As a result, the role and scope of the company's employee assistance program has evolved with the times. Some EAPs offer workers

In 1917, Macy's department store in New York City opened an office to help employees deal with personal problems.

professional organizational counseling. This service runs the gamut from counseling work-group members who are having problems getting along with one another to counseling survivors of downsizing on how to handle stress.

Managers may have to terminate good employees as well as difficult ones. Besides the emotional effects, there is also a practical side to letting workers go: There is documentation and a procedure to follow. Human resources staff members are stretched to the limit in some cases.

Many EAPs provide disability management services. Companies today want to complement the traditional disability arrangement with a whole-person approach. In many cases workers' self-esteem is tied to their jobs. As workers sit at home recuperating from injuries or disabilities, they may become bored and depressed. In some cases their disabilities may put financial strains on their families. Therefore, there is a need to supplement the medical care a person is receiving with counseling on issues he or she is facing. The goal is to keep the worker connected to the workplace.

Today's EAPs have grown in size and sophistication. In some businesses EAPs are operated through employee associations. Sometimes professional groups or similar businesses and small industries unite to form a consortium. Although all EAPs aim to help both management and employees, there are differences in how they do it. Boiled down to the essentials, these differences come under two headings: who is helped and how that help is provided.

SINGLE-ISSUE PROGRAMS

Single-issue programs aim to help only employees impaired by a specific problem. Their focus is clear, and they are generally small enough to cost the employer relatively little. A disadvantage of single-issue programs is that they may become stigmatized because of the negative connotations of terms such as *addiction* and *alcoholism*. Some people may be afraid to use the program for fear of being labeled "drunks" or "addicts." Since the per-person cost of an EAP decreases with the number of people who use it, this stigmatization is an important issue to consider. Furthermore, supervisors tend to look only for symptoms of abuse instead of concentrating on declining job performance.

The greatest weakness of single-issue programs is their lack of preventative power. Late-stage alcoholics and addicts have the highest relapse rate and the least chance for permanent recovery. Single-issue programs tend to find these late-stagers, but recognizing those in the early stages for whom help can be most effective is much more difficult.

BROAD-BRUSH EAPS

Broad-brush EAPs offer help to employees suffering from all kinds of problems, including chemical dependency. For example, a broad-brush program may provide crisis-management services for those whose problems can be dealt with over the short term. Sometimes all that is needed is a chance to talk a problem over with a sympathetic listener. The great advantage of broad-brush programs is their ability to uncover drug and alcohol problems in their early stages. Often early-stagers come to their EAP presenting problems that make no mention of alcohol or drugs. At first clients complain about financial trouble, a stressful marriage, or abuse of problem children. It is only after working with a skilled counselor that the truth is revealed: cocaine bankrupting an executive; a marriage in trouble because the wife drinks and the husband enables her; children acting out because they cannot get the nurturing they need from addicted parents.

One disadvantage of broad-brush programs is that they are usually more expensive than single-issue programs. There are, however, ways to minimize costs by designing a program customized to specialized businesses. Costs can be reduced when multiple businesses form an EAP alliance. In the long run, EAPs can save businesses money by making them more efficient and productive, by reducing accidents, by reducing employee absenteeism/turnover, by raising employee morale and decreasing grievances, and by cutting back on the number of unnecessary insurance claims.

MODES OF SERVICE

Today's EAPs differ from their predecessors in the mode of service they deliver. It would be impossible to describe all variations that exist, but a short description of several of the most common varieties will provide some insight.

Some EAPs are just a hotline. Employees are encouraged to call a particular number and ask for help. The EAP provides the names and numbers of local public service agencies that may be able to address employees' personal problems. Alone, this just barely qualifies as employee assistance. However, a hotline in conjunction with other services may prove helpful in attracting fearful employees for whom anonymity is essential. And hotlines can be extremely beneficial when depression is a serious problem.

Other EAPs amount to no more than a single individual in the personnel department or the medical office who can direct an employee off-site on the basis of his or her problem. This is not much better than the hotline, and employees may not go near the office for fear of being labeled. Employees required to report to this office because of poor performance evaluations and fear of losing their livelihoods may complain about the lack of confidentiality.

A few very large companies have elaborate on-site EAP divisions with full staffs, including doctors and nurses. Or several geographically close companies with similar concerns or products may join together to form an EAP consortium that contracts with a consulting EAP organization to provide services to employees from each site.

Most EAP providers emphasize the confidential nature of their services and will give the employer numerical information only, without divulging names of EAP-assisted employees. Otherwise, many employees would be hesitant, if not totally unwilling, to admit a personal problem for fear that it would jeopardize their job status or chances for promotions.

However, there may be situations in which an employer may need to know certain types of information. For example, when an employee is engaged in dangerous duties, supervisory personnel may need to know general information about the employee's condition for safety reasons. Therefore, the employer's promise of confidentiality and privacy to employees is extremely important. Whatever level of confidentiality the employer establishes must be maintained; notice must be given to employees and consent obtained for variances. Also, it is important that an employer give employees clear warnings that such disclosures are permitted. Specific state privacy laws may affect the availability of such information.

Some EAP programs provide services to groups of employees during a crisis. For example, a team of counselors from an EAP may work with an entire department affected by a violent workplace incident.

EAPS CAN DETER VIOLENCE

Stress at home or on the job, burnout, or relationships that have soured can result in violent acts at work. Experts estimate that more than 100,000 incidents of workplace violence occur annually in the United States. The typical workplace killer is a middle-aged man, most likely a loner frustrated by problems on the job with few personal contacts outside the workplace. One study showed men were responsible for 98 percent of all violence committed at work. The average age was 36, and firearms were used 81 percent of the time. Following workplace homicides, one-fourth of the murderers killed themselves.

Workplace violence, whether it involves harassment, threats, or physical attack, is a serious and growing problem for employers. Lack of attention to the issue can mean lost lives, discontent, and fear among employees, as well as tremendous cost to companies.

Corporations without preventative measures are particularly subject to lawsuits and higher costs. The best way to prevent workplace violence is to have an effective employee assistance program. Other precautions companies can take to prevent violence are establishing clear guidelines on appropriate behavior, screening applicants carefully, training employees to identify warning signs, and setting up procedures for managers to respond to cries for help. Companies also should look closely at the procedures they use when they terminate employees. Perhaps most important is maintaining a healthy work environment. It really boils down to one person's relationship with another and whether or not the environment fosters mutual respect.

EXTERNAL PROVIDERS

A unique feature of employee assistance programs is the dual responsibility that its professionals have toward both the companies they work for and the individual workers in those organizations who require assistance. The special responsibilities toward the organization go beyond those that social workers have toward their agencies because the occupational setting also is a client to which they have service obligations. At times this dual responsibility creates ethical dilemmas for practitioners. The very existence of a well-functioning EAP is a major source of assistance to the organization as a whole, not just the individual clients who receive direct services.

Both managers and employee clients expect staff members of in-house EAPs to be especially adept in matching an employee's needs with resources that provide prompt and effective intervention. The depth and thoroughness of the assessment is a means of increasing the probability that key problems will be identified and prioritized accurately. Failure to meet these expectations can adversely affect the credibility of the EAP. As a result, most EAPs devote a significant part of program resources to locating, evaluating, and updating their network of providers. The referral function is distinct from the procedures governing the internal services. Referring is the process of locating one or more providers external to the employer to supply ongoing services to deal with employee concerns. These external resources may assume responsibility for all of a client's needs or they may be ancillary to the work being done in-house by an EAP counselor.

Most employees are not well informed about treatment programs, community agencies, or even self-help groups. EAPs must educate them about available services, their relative benefits, and how these resources are viewed in the community. In addition, clients often need to be encouraged to assume a consumer orientation regarding referral sources. Having to apply for any kind of help is intimidating, and it is difficult for the uninitiated to recognize appropriate or inappropriate requirements. Clients should be told that if they decide a resource is not acceptable they may return to the EAP for other options.

PERSONAL PROBLEMS

People thrive on things they do well. Often it is their work. A happy, healthy worker is likely to be a productive one. Conversely, personal problems can hamper an employee's performance. Sometimes problems can be alleviated quickly, but often the problems extend over long periods of time. The impact on the employee will vary, but there will usually be noticeable change in behavior and attitude. Personal problems are significant hurdles that every person living in today's complex society will confront in one fashion or another.

Employees' personal problems can have many sources. Most can be categorized into one of the following categories: substance abuse, health related, family related, and financial. Almost every adult will deal with one or more of these problems. It is how individuals deal with these problems, and the level of support they receive in addressing the issue, that will determine the intensity of the problem's impact.

BIBLIOGRAPHY

Browning, Darrell. "Stamping Out Violence." *Human Resources Executive.* 1994: 22-25.

PATRICK J. HIGHLAND

EMPLOYEE BENEFITS

Employee benefits are compensations given to employees in addition to regular salaries or wages. These compensations are given at the entire or partial expense of the employer. Benefit packages usually make up between 30 and 40 percent of an employee's total compensation for employment, which makes them an important aspect of the terms of employment. While some employee benefits are required by law, many employers offer additional benefits in order to attract and retain quality workers and maintain morale. Some types of benefits are also used as incentives to encourage increased worker productivity.

LEGALLY REQUIRED BENEFITS

While some benefits are offered as incentives to attract workers, some are legally required. For example, employers must provide workers' compensation insurance, which pays the medical bills

Target stores offer employees a 10 percent discount on merchandise.

for job-related injuries and provides an income for employees who become disabled because of a job-related injury. Social Security must be paid by the employer (in addition to the amounts deducted from employee's pay) to help meet employees' retirement needs, and employers must pay for unemployment insurance to compensate workers in the event that their job is eliminated. The Family and Medical Leave Act, passed by Congress in 1993, requires large employers to provide workers with unpaid leave for family or medical emergencies (up to 12 weeks of unpaid, job-protected leave per year). Under this law, employees are guaranteed that they can return to the same or a comparable position and that their health care coverage will be continued during the leave.

TRADITIONAL TYPES OF EMPLOYEE BENEFITS

Because of continually rising health care costs, one of the most desirable types of benefits for employees to have is a health insurance plan. These plans can be set up to cover the individual worker and, in many cases, the worker's family as well; they may or may not include such options as dental, eye, chiropractic, hospital, and other types of health care. Health insurance plans may be provided at no cost to employees, or they may be made available at a more desirable rate than employees could get on their own. The health insurance aspect of a benefit package is often the major deciding factor in whether a person accepts a position with a company. The degree of health insurance is often more important to a potential employee than the salary level; especially when children are an issue.

Most benefit plans also include a certain number of paid sick days, personal days, and/or vacation days. Many companies are finding ways of increasing the flexibility of employee benefits. One way to increase flexibility is to group sick, vacation, and personal days into a certain amount of *paid time off* (PTO). PTO allows employees to take days off—for example, to care for a sick child, observe a religious holiday, or go on vacation—without having to explain why. The PTO benefit helps employees because their time is more flexible, and it helps employers by maintaining morale and reducing unanticipated absenteeism.

Life insurance and retirement options are another type of benefit many companies offer their employees. These types of benefits often encourage employees to remain with the same company because they do not want to cash in their life insurance or retirement plans. This tends to make employees more loyal to the company because their future is invested with the company. It also gives the employee a feeling of power by having some control over planning for retirement.

EXPANDED TYPES OF EMPLOYEE BENEFITS

While health care, paid time off, and retirement plans are the most common types of benefits employees receive, some companies offer even more types of benefits to help attract and retain employees as well as increase employee morale and improve job performance. One example of this type of benefit is tuition reimbursement, which allows employees to further their education while working. Motivating employees to better themselves at the employer's expense, helps the company keep knowledgeable employees.

With the growing number of single parents and dual-career couples in the work force, many companies have opened day-care facilities in the workplace where employees can feel safe about leaving their children. On-site child care is obviously a very desirable benefit for parents because it allows them to check up on the children, cut down on travel time, and be available in case of an emergency. However, some childless workers feel that this benefit discriminates against them because they get no use out of the day-care facility. One way many companies are handling this type of concern is through a *cafeteria plan.* While there are several different ways to set up a cafeteria plan, such as setting aside pre-tax dollars for medical expenses, one of the most useful ways is

to give employees many different benefit options to choose from. Each employee is given a set allowance that can be used toward any benefit the employee chooses, allowing the employees to pick the options that will most benefit them. The cafeteria plan is one fair way to handle benefits for everyone concerned.

Another characteristic of the work force is its increasingly older age. As a result, there are an increasing number of workers with aging parents who need care. Many companies recognize the need for elder care and are providing benefits to help, such as referral services for quality nursing homes and flexible work hours and/or days off so employees can care for aging parents.

Other benefits provided by some employers include credit unions to help employees with financial needs, gym facilities to allow employees to fit exercise into their busy schedules, cafeterias that sell reduced price meals to working employees, and on-site laundry services where employees can have laundry done while they are at work. Making the work environment seem more like a family helps boost employee morale and improve working relationships. Many companies provide uniforms for their employees, so that workers do not have to worry about ruining their own clothing. The uniforms also help with the feeling of unity because everyone in the company is dressed similarly. Because transportation can often be a problem for employees, some companies are even providing transportation options as a benefit to employees. Disney World, in Orlando, Florida, has a shuttle that picks employees up from their living quarters and takes them to work. Corn detasslers meet in a central location and a bus takes them to the site. Sales people are often provided with a company car.

While these types of benefits are meant to attract and retain employees as well as create a positive work environment, some types of employee benefits are used to encourage increased performance. The following are the four main types of benefits used as incentives to encourage employees to exhibit superior performance:

1. *Profit sharing* gives the employee a portion of the company profits. Profit

sharing is often done through making shares of company stock part of the employee benefit package. Employees receive a certain number of shares of stock each year, which provides employees an incentive to help the company succeed. This might also be accomplished through a yearly profit-sharing bonus.

2. *Gain sharing* rewards employees for exceeding a predetermined goal by sharing the extra profits. If profits exceed the goal, employees share in the extra profits.

3. *Lump-sum bonuses* are a one-time cash payment based on performance. Lump-sum bonuses may be an annual reward, such as a Christmas bonus, where the purpose is to share profits with the employees, and thus motivate them.

4. *Pay for knowledge* rewards employees for continuing their education and/or learning new job tasks. The more education or experience an employee has, the higher he/she moves up on the pay-for-knowledge pay scale. Pay for knowledge is an incentive for employees to continue their education because it results in immediate rewards on the job.

PERKS

In addition to what we typically think as employee benefits, many employers also offer "*perks*" to their employees. Typically limited to employees in management positions, these perks include such benefits as country club or health club memberships, a company car, special parking privileges at work, tickets for sporting events, first-class travel accommodations, and generous expense accounts. However, certain types of perks are also being extended to employees in many different types of positions. One type of perk that is common in many retail stores is an employee discount on merchandise bought from the place of employment. For example, Dayton Hudson's Target stores offer a 10 percent discount to employees and their immediate families when purchasing merchandise from any Target

store. Employees of local movie theaters often receive free movie tickets as a perk, while many restaurant employees receive free or reduced-price meals. By offering employees such perks, the company is providing a strong incentive for employees to continue working there.

FLEXIBLE WORK PLANS

A flexible work plan is another type of employee benefit that has been proven to have a positive influence on employee productivity, attendance, and morale. A flexible work plan allows employees to adjust their working conditions within constraints set by the company and may include such options as flex-time, a compressed workweek, job sharing, and home-based work. Flex-time involves adjusting an employee's daily time schedule; it can be as simple as allowing a worker to come into work an hour earlier and leave an hour earlier than the normal 8-to-5 workday. Usually there are some time constraints set up by the company, but employees who work within those constraints can basically set their own schedules. A compressed workweek involves working longer hours each day for fewer days than the normal Monday-through-Friday workweek. For example, at many businesses employees work ten-hour days, four days a week.

Job sharing allows two or more people to divide the tasks of one job. It allows the same consistency as a full-time person, because the work is simply divided among the people who share the job responsibility. Job sharing is popular among people who only want to work part time but want a job with full-time responsibilities. These types of people include older workers, retirees, students, and working parents. Home-based work programs allow employees to perform their jobs at home instead of in an office setting. These people are often know as telecommuters, because they "commute" to work through electronic mail, faxes, and other types of telecommunications. Home-based work is popular with disabled workers, elderly workers, parents with small children, and workers who have had to relocate far away from the workplace because of a spouse's job change. Through home-based work, all of these types of employees are able to take care of personal and family responsibilities while maintaining and enjoying their job and/or career.

CONCLUSION

Finally, it should be noted that the various types of benefits offered to employees can depend greatly on the size and type of the business as well as its geographic location. For example, a small business might be unable to afford to provide complete health care coverage for employees because there are not enough employees to divide the risk. This would cause the cost of the insurance to be high. On the other hand, a large company may not want to give all 1,000 employees a turkey for Thanksgiving because of the enormity of the undertaking. A video store would be more likely to give employees free movie rentals, while a restaurant would offer employees free or reduced-price meals. Employee benefits may be the major deciding factor for many people when choosing a company for employment. In order to attract and retain the best-quality employees, companies must be willing to offer flexible and extensive types of benefits to meet various employee needs.

BIBLIOGRAPHY

Boone, Louis E., and Kurtz, David L. (1999). *Contemporary Business*, 9th ed. Orlando, FL: Harcourt Brace College Publishers.

Bounds, Gregory M., and Lamb, Charles W., Jr. (1998). *Business*. Cincinnati, OH: South-Western College Publishing.

French, Wendell L. (1998). *Human Resources Management*. New York: Houghton Mifflin.

Jenks, James M., and Zevnik, Brian L. P. (1993). *Employee Benefits Plain and Simple*. New York: Macmillan.

Madura, Jeff. (1998). *Introduction to Business*. Cincinnati, OH: South-Western College Publishing.

Nickels, William G., McHugh, James M., and McHugh, Susan M. (1999). *Understanding Business*, 5th ed. Boston, MA: Irwin-McGraw-Hill.

Pfeffer, Jeffery. (1994). *Competitive Advantage Through People*. Boston, MA: Harvard Business School Press.

Pride, William M., Hughes, Robert J., and Kapoor Jack R. (1999). *Business*, 6th ed. New York: Houghton Mifflin.

MARCY SATTERWHITE

EMPLOYEE COMPENSATION

In exchange for job performance and commitment, an employer offers rewards to employees. Adequate rewards and compensations potentially attract a quality work force, maintain the satisfaction of existing employees, keep quality employees from leaving, and motivate them in the workplace. A proper design of reward and compensation systems requires careful review of the labor market, thorough analysis of jobs, and a systematic study of pay structures.

There are a number of ways of classifying rewards. A commonly discussed dichotomy is intrinsic versus extrinsic rewards. Intrinsic rewards are satisfactions one gets from the job itself, such as a feeling of achievement, responsibility, or autonomy. Extrinsic rewards include monetary compensation, promotion, and tangible benefits.

Compensation frequently refers to extrinsic, monetary rewards that employees receive in exchange for their work. Usually, compensation is composed of the base wage or salary, any incentives or bonuses, and other benefits. Base wage or salary is the hourly, weekly, or monthly pay that employees receive. Incentives or bonuses are rewards offered in addition to the base wage when employees achieve a high level of performance. Benefits are rewards offered for being a member of the company and can include paid vacation, health and life insurance, and retirement pension.

A company's compensation system must include policies, procedures, and rules that provide clear and unambiguous determination and administration of employee compensation. Otherwise, there can be confusion, diminished employee satisfaction, and potentially costly litigation.

DETERMINANTS OF COMPENSATION

Fair and adequate compensation is critical to motivating employees attracting high-potential employees, and retaining competent employees. Compensation has to be fair and equitable among all workers in the same company (internal equity). Internal equity can be achieved when pay is proportionate to the individual employee's qualifications and contributions to a company. On the other hand, compensation also has to be fair and equitable in comparison to the external market (external equity). If a company pays its employees below the market rate, it may lose competent employees. In determining adequate pay for employees, a manager must consider the three major factors: the labor market, the nature and scope of the job, and characteristics of the individual employee.

Potential employees are recruited from a certain geographic area—the labor market. The actual boundary of a labor market varies depending on the type of job, company, and industry. For example, an opening for a systems analyst at IBM may attract candidates from across the country, whereas a secretarial position at an elementary school may attract candidates only from the immediate local area of the school.

Pay for a job even within the same labor market may vary widely because of many factors, such as the industry, type of job, cost of living, and location of the job. Compensation managers must be aware of these differences. To help compensation managers understand the market rate of labor, a compensation survey is conducted. A compensation survey obtains data regarding what other firms pay for specific jobs or job classes in a given geographic market. Large companies periodically conduct compensation surveys and review their compensation system to assure external equity. There are professional organizations that conduct compensation surveys and provide their analysis to smaller companies for a fee.

Several factors are generally considered in evaluating the market rate of a job. They include the cost of living of the area, union contracts, and broader economic conditions. Urban or metro-politan areas generally have a higher cost of living than rural areas. Usually, in calculating the real pay, a cost-of-living allowance (COLA) is added to the base wage or salary. Cost-of-living indexes are published periodically in major business journals. During an economically depressed period, the labor supply usually exceeds the demand in the labor market, resulting in lower labor rates.

The characteristics of an individual employee are also important in determining compensation. An individual's job qualifications, abilities and skills, prior experiences, and even willingness to work in hardship conditions are determining factors. Within the reasonable range of a market rate, companies offer additional compensation to attract and retain competent employees.

In principle, compensation must be designed around the job, not the person. Person-based pay frequently results in discriminatory practices, which violates Title VII of the Civil Rights Act, and job-based compensation is the employer's most powerful defense in court. For job-based compensation, management must conduct a systematic job analysis, identifying and describing what is happening on the job. Each job must be carefully examined to list the necessary tasks and actions, identify skills and abilities required, and establish desirable behaviors for successful completion of the job.

With complete and comprehensive data about all the jobs, job analysts must conduct systematic comparisons of them and determine their relative worth. Numerous techniques have been developed for the analysis of relative worth, including the simple point method, job classification method, job ranking method, and the factor comparison method.

Information resulting from the comprehensive job analysis will be used for establishing pay or wage grades. Assume that twenty-five jobs range from 10 to 50 points in their job scores based on the job point method. All twenty-five of these jobs are reviewed carefully for their relative worth and plotted on Figure 1. The x-axis represents job points and the ordinate (y-axis) represents relative worth or wage rates. Once a man-

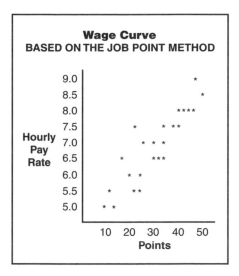

Figure 1

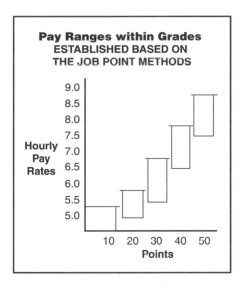

Figure 2

ager can identify fair and realistic wages of two or more jobs, desirably top and bottom ones, then all the rest can be prorated along the wage curve in the diagram.

In order to simplify the administration of a wage structure, similar jobs in the approximate cluster are grouped together into a class or grade for pay purpose. Figure 2 shows how twenty-five jobs are grouped into five pay grades. Employees move up in their pay within each grade, typically by seniority. Once a person hits the top pay in the grade, he or she can only increase the pay by moving to a higher grade. Under certain unusual circumstances, it is possible for an outstanding performer in a lower grade to be paid more than a person at the bottom of the next-highest level.

INNOVATIONS IN COMPENSATION SYSTEMS

As the market becomes more dynamic and competitive, companies are trying harder to improve performance. Since companies cannot afford to continually increase wages by a certain percentage, they are introducing many innovative compensation plans tied to performance. Several of these plans are discussed in this section.

Incentive Compensation Plan. Incentive compensation pays proportionately to employee performance. Incentives are typically given in addi-

tion to the base wage; they can be paid on the basis of individual, group, or plant-wide performance. While individual incentive plans encourage competition among employees, group or plant-wide incentive plans encourage cooperation and direct the efforts of all employees toward achieving overall company performance.

Skill-Based or Knowledge-Based Compensation. Skill-based pay is a system that pays employees based on the skills they possess or master, not for the job they hold. Some managers believe that mastery of certain sets of skills leads to higher productivity and therefore want their employees to master a series of skill sets. As employees gain one skill and then another, their wage rate goes up until they have mastered all the skills. Similar to skill-based pay is knowledge-based pay. While skill-based pay evolved in the manufacturing sector, pay-for-knowledge developed in the service sector (Henderson, 1997). For example, public school teachers with a bachelor's degree receive the lowest rate of pay, those with a master's degree receive a higher rate, and those with a doctorate receive the highest.

Team-Based Compensation. As many companies introduce team-based management practices such as self-managed work teams, they begin to offer team-based pay. Recognizing the importance of close cooperation and mutual development in a work group, companies want to encourage employees to work as a team by offering pay based on the overall effectiveness of the team.

Performance-Based Compensation. In the traditional sense, pay is considered entitlement that employees deserve in exchange for showing up at work and doing well enough to avoid being fired. While base pay is given to employees regardless of performance, incentives and bonuses are extra rewards given in appreciation of their extra efforts. Pay-for-performance is a new movement away from this entitlement concept (Milkovich and Newman, 1996). A pay-for-performance plan increases even the base pay—so-called merit increases—to reflect how highly employees are rated on a performance evaluation. Other incentives and bonuses are calculated based on this new merit pay, resulting in substantially more total dollars for highly ranked employee performance. Frequently, employees also receive an end-of-year lump sum bonus that does not build into base pay.

EXECUTIVE COMPENSATION

Recently, people have been concerned with the excessively high level of executive compensation. According to *Business Week*'s annual executive pay survey, in 1997 Sanford Weill, CEO of Travelers Group, collected $7.5 million in salary and bonuses plus $223.2 million for long-term compensation, totaling $230.7 million. In the same year, Roberto Goizueta, CEO of Coca-Cola, earned a total of $111.8 million, including annual salary, bonuses, and long-term compensation. Compensations of the twenty highest-paid executives ranged from $28.4 million to $230 million.

Frequently, executive compensation becomes controversial. Are these compensations excessive? What justifies such a large compensation for executives? Justification of such a large sum of compensation is linked to the company's performance. In fact, a significant portion of executive compensation results from exercising stock options, which were quite valuable in the recent "bull" market. And yet ordinary working-

class Americans are outraged by the shocking contrast in pay raises: Annual executive pay at large companies rose 54 percent in 1996, whereas the pay raises of most working-class people were in the 3 percent to 5 percent range during the same period.

An executive compensation package is typically composed of (1) base salary, (2) annual incentives or bonuses, (3) long-term incentives (e.g., stock options), (4) executive benefits (e.g., health insurance, life insurance, and pension plans), and (5) executive perquisites. Considering the high turnover rate of competent executives, offering a competitive salary is crucial in attracting the top candidates.

Frequently, annual bonuses play a more important role than base salary in executive compensations. They are primarily designed to motivate better performance. In order to underscore the importance of financial performance, usually measured by the company's stock price, top executives are offered stock options. Sometimes, exercising stock options yields more cash benefits to executives than do annual salaries.

In addition to monetary compensation, executives enjoy many different types of perquisites, commonly called "perks." Such executive perks include the luxurious office with lush carpets, the executive dining room, special parking, use of a company airplane, company-paid membership in high-class country clubs and associations, and executive travel arrangements. Many companies even offer executives tax-free personal perks, including such things as free access to company property, free legal counseling, free home repairs and improvements, and expenses for vacation homes or boats.

Another perk that became popular recently is the so-called golden parachute—a protection plan for executives in the event that they are forced out of the organization. Such severance frequently results from a merger or hostile takeover of the company. The golden parachute provides either a significant one-time sum to the departing executive or a guaranteed executive position in the newly merged company.

BIBLIOGRAPHY

Henderson, Richard I. (1997). *Compensation Management in a Knowledge-Based World*, 7th ed. New York: Prentice-Hall.

Henderson, Richard I. (1994). *Compensation Management: Rewarding Performance*, 6th ed. New York: Prentice Hall.

Klein, Andrew L. (1996). "Validity and Reliability for Competency-Based Systems: Reducing Litigation Risks." *Compensation and Benefits Review* 28(4): 31-37.

Milkovich, George T., and Newman, Jerry M. (1996). *Compensation*, 5th ed. Chicago: Irwin.

Pauline, George B. (1997). "Executive Compensation and Changes in Control: A Search for Fairness." *Compensation and Benefits Review* 29 (March/April): 30-40.

Reingold, Jennifer, and Borrus, Amy. (1997). "Even Executives Are Wincing at Executive Pay." *Business Week*, May 12: 40-41.

Reingold, Jennifer, and Melcher, Richard A. (1998). "Executive Pay." *Business Week*, April 20: 64-68.

LEE W. LEE

EMPLOYEE DISCIPLINE

Discipline refers to the actions imposed by an organization on its employees for failure to follow the organization's rules, standards, or policies. Traditional approaches to discipline, based on punishment, are known to promote adversarial relationships between leaders and followers. A more effective approach now being used by many companies recognizes good performance and encourages employee commitment to the organization and its goals. Once employees see the discrepancy between actual and expected performance, the burden is on the employee to change. Even with more positive approaches to discipline, organizations still need to have some form of disciplinary procedure, whether formal or informal, that carries successively stiffer penalties for repeated or more serious offenses.

ESTABLISHING AND COMMUNICATING WORK RULES

A first step in the disciplinary procedure is to establish work rules that are in line with the organization's goals or objectives. These work rules become the basis for disciplinary actions when the rules are broken. They are generally established jointly by management, the organization's human resources unit, and employees, who should have an opportunity for input to ensure that rules are fair and can reasonably be followed. Work rules are directly related to work behavior and productivity. Employees who continually violate the rules are candidates for a disciplinary procedure.

Employees must know the rules that have been established. Even though employees might have had input in the development of the rules, it is the employer who creates the final version. The organization's work rules should be presented in a printed format, and each employee should be given a copy. This is usually accomplished in the form of an employee handbook. The handbook may have other information, but the work rules are a critical part of it.

In some organizations, these work rules are discussed at meetings, seminars, or training sessions. Employees with long tenure in the organization typically review the rules periodically. Work rules should be reviewed from time to time and, if necessary, revised. If an organization makes major changes in the way it operates because of new equipment, expansion or contraction, or new ownership, it will need to revise its work rules accordingly. Small companies with only a few employees also need to have written work rules. Such companies may not have an employee handbook, but it is still wise for the rules to be written down and presented to each employee. Additionally, these rules may be posted in a spot where all employees can read them easily.

EVALUATING EMPLOYEES

In the employee evaluation process, either formal or informal, behaviors requiring disciplinary actions are often revealed. Informal evaluation might occur at all times as supervisors monitor employees. Formal evaluations of each employee should be completed regularly so that deficiencies can be discovered and discussed with the employee. When employees violate work rules, a change of behavior is sought. Although small companies with only a few employees may not use a formal written evaluation, it is still important that employees be evaluated regularly. Small companies may find it easier to take corrective actions than large companies because of the closeness of the supervisor to each of the work situations. In contrast, a supervisor in a large organization might be responsible for fifty, a hundred, or more workers.

When employees break the rules of the organization, they often need assistance to change their behavior so as to operate within the established parameters. Counseling and coaching could be a part of this process, but they usually take place prior to disciplinary actions. If employees change their behavior as a result of disciplinary actions and conform to the established work rules, there is no need for further discipline. If a change in behavior does not occur, then a harsher disciplinary procedure will need to be implemented.

The need to resort to disciplinary procedures may be lessened by (1) smart hiring, using background checks and extensive interviews; (2) performance evaluations with clear goals and objectives; (3) training and development to improve skills and increase performance; and (4) rewarding performance and goal achievement.

USING THE DISCIPLINARY PROCEDURE

Although most employees do follow the organization's rules and regulations, there are times when the employer must use the discipline procedure. Frequent reasons for using the procedure include the following:

Absence from work

Absenteeism

Abusing customers

Abusive language toward supervisor

Assault and fighting among employees

Causing unsafe working conditions

Damage to or loss of machinery or materials

Dishonesty

Disloyalty to employer (includes competing with employer, conflict of interest)

Falsifying company records (including time records, production records)

Falsifying employment application

Gambling

Horseplay

Incompetence (including low productivity)

Insubordination

Leaving place of work (including quitting early)

Loafing

Misconduct during a strike

Negligence

Obscene or immoral conduct

Participation in a prohibited strike

Possession or use of drugs or intoxicants

Profane or abusive language (not toward supervisor)

Refusal to accept a job assignment

Refusal to work overtime

Sleeping on the job

Slowdown

Tardiness

Theft

Threat to or assault of management representative

A formal disciplinary procedure usually begins with an oral warning and progresses through a written warning, suspension, and, ultimately, discharge. Formal disciplinary procedures also outline the penalty for each successive offense and define time limits for maintaining records of each offense and penalty. For instance, tardiness records might be maintained for only a six-month period. Tardiness prior to the six months preceding the offense would not be considered in the disciplinary action. Less formal procedures generally specify the reasons for disciplinary action as being for just or proper cause.

Preventing the disciplinary procedure from progressing beyond the oral warning stage is obviously advantageous to both the employee and management. Discipline should be aimed at correction rather than punishment. If the behavior can be corrected by a friendly talk between the supervisor and the employee, there is less chance that the problem will become a source of bitterness. Formal oral or written warnings are less likely to cause animosity than would a suspension. Of course, the most costly and least acceptable form of discipline is discharge. Disciplinary procedures should be viewed as a means of encouraging employees to abide willingly by the rules and standards of the organization.

The importance of having a procedurally correct performance evaluation system receives constant emphasis. There is a need to adopt procedural due process for performance evaluation systems in order to rate employee job performance accurately because those ratings might be challenged. Legal problems regarding employee disciplinary measures can be prevented by making sure that these measures follow prescribed guidelines, such as these:

- Employees are given advance notice of disciplinary action.
- Disciplinary rules are reasonable.
- Offenses are properly investigated.
- Investigations are conducted objectively.
- Rules are enforced equally.
- Penalties are related to the severity of offenses.

LABOR UNION INVOLVEMENT

Numerous employees in the United States are represented by labor unions. In a unionized organization, the supervisor is the primary link between the organization and union members. The supervisor's first responsibility is to uphold the interests of management. At the same time, the supervisor must fulfill the contractual obligations of management and see that the union fulfills its obligations. Collective bargaining between management and the union determines terms of worker contracts, legal documents that cover a specified period of time. Union contracts include

provisions for a worker grievance and disciplinary procedures. For example, the union contract may stipulate that an employee can be disciplined for just cause. To fulfill this provision, management must develop a system of discipline that supervisors must follow.

FEATURE OF AN EFFECTIVE DISCIPLINARY PROCESS

A disciplinary procedure is directed against the worker's behavior rather than the person. Key features of an effective process include the following principles of disciplining workers.

1. The length of time between the misconduct and the discipline should be short. For discipline to be most effective, it must be administered as soon as possible, but without making an emotional, irrational decision.

2. Disciplinary action should be preceded by advance warning. Noting rule infractions in an employee's record is not sufficient to support disciplinary action. An employee who is not advised of an infraction is not considered to have been given a warning. Noting that the employee was advised of the infraction and having the employee sign a discipline form are both valid employment practices. Failure to warn an employee of the consequences of repeated violations of a rule is a frequently cited reason for overturning a disciplinary action.

3. Consistency in the discipline procedure is key. Inconsistency lowers morale, diminishes respect for the supervisor, and leads to grievances. Consistency does not mean that an absence of past infractions, long length of service, a good work record, and other mitigating factors should not be considered when applying discipline. However, an employee should feel that under essentially the same circumstances any other employee would have received the same punishment/penalty.

4. Supervisors should take steps to ensure impartiality when applying discipline. The employee should feel that the disciplinary action is a consequence of behavior, not of personality or relationship to the supervisor. The supervisor should avoid arguing with the employee and

should administer discipline in a straightforward, calm manner. Administering discipline without anger or apology and then resuming a pleasant relationship aid in reducing the negative effects of discipline.

5. Ordinarily, the supervisor should administer discipline in private. Only in the case of gross insubordination or flagrant and serious rule violations is a public reprimand desirable. Then a public reprimand helps the supervisor regain control of a situation. Even in such situations, however, the supervisor's objective should be to regain control, not to embarrass the employee.

6. The supervisor should warn the employee of the result of repeated violations. Sometimes suggestions to the employee on ways to correct behavior are beneficial. Supervisors should be very reluctant to impose disciplinary suspensions and to discharge workers. Usually, discipline of this degree is reserved for higher levels of management. However, even though supervisors usually lack the power to administer disciplinary suspensions or to discharge workers, they are nearly always the ones who must recommend such action to higher management.

7. Finally, it is necessary to document the action taken and inform others in the organization. Any time an organization takes disciplinary action, it must consider the possibility of an Equal Employment Opportunity complaint. The documentation should be sufficiently detailed that another manager at a similar level in the organization would come to the same conclusions or least see clearly why the decision was made. Sufficient documentation does not mean that every detail of an individual's work needs to be recorded. Rather, the manager should keep accurate records of those elements that significantly contribute to or hamper the work effort. In addition, this information, both positive and negative, should be communicated to the employee either orally or in writing.

SUMMARY

If a company is to have a successful employee disciplinary procedure, both the organization and the manager have important roles to play. In practice, companies assume the responsibility of establishing rules, communicating them to employees, and developing a penalty system for enforcing them. The manager's role in the disciplinary procedure is distinct from that of the organization, yet the two overlap and support each other. Managers are responsible for implementing the organization's discipline procedure. This requires them to do several things: They must compare their organization's rules with employee behavior to determine whether a rule has been broken; they must determine whether they have sufficient proof that the employee did indeed break the rule; they must decide what corrective action should be taken and then take it; and they must document whatever action is taken. To the extent that all managers perform these steps effectively, the disciplinary procedure will be effective and there is a very good chance that employee behavior on the job can be significantly improved.

BIBLIOGRAPHY

Benton, Douglas A. (1998). *Applied Human Relations*. Upper Saddle River, NJ: Prentice-Hall.

Champagne, Paul J., and McAfee, R. Bruce. (1989). *Motivating Strategies for Performance and Productivity*. New York: Quorum Books.

Greenberg, Jerald. (1999). *Managing Behavior in Organizations: Science in Service to Practice*. Upper Saddle River, NJ: Prentice-Hall.

Hersey, Paul, Blanchard, Kenneth H., and Johnson, Dewey E. (1996). *Management of Organizational Behavior*. Upper Saddle River, NJ: Prentice-Hall.

Rue, Leslie W., and Byars, Lloyd L. (1990). *Supervision: Key Link to Productivity*. Homewood, IL: Irwin.

Whetten, David A., and Cameron, Kim S. (1995). *Developing Management Skills*. New York: HarperCollins.

Wray, Ralph D., Luft, Roger L., and Highland, Patrick J. (1996). *Fundamentals of Human Relations*. Cincinnati, OH: South-Western Educational Publishing.

Yukl, Gary. (1994). *Leadership in Organizations*. Englewood Cliffs, NJ: Prentice-Hall.

MARCIA ANDERSON

EMPLOYEE MOTIVATION

(SEE: *Motivation*)

ENTREPRENEURSHIP

A subject taught in many high schools and colleges, *entrepreneurship* is actually defined as "the state of being an entrepreneur." An entrepreneur is an individual who owns, organizes, and manages a business and, in so doing, assumes the risk of either making a profit or losing the investment. According to the Small Business Administration (1999), the total number of businesses in the United States in 1995 was somewhere between 16 million and 24 million, of which approximately 15,000 were large. In 1997, there were an estimated 8.5 million businesses owned by women.

For any business to be successful, an adequate level of funding must be furnished. The amount needed varies according to the scope and nature of the business. Another key factor in the success of an entrepreneurial organization is planning, including planning for the marketing, management, and financial aspects of the business.

From a personal perspective, becoming an entrepreneur is not a simple task. It certainly has its drawbacks. However, it can also be quite rewarding.

BENEFITS AND DRAWBACKS OF ENTREPRENEURSHIP

Choosing to create a new business, or even to purchase an existing one, is a decision that has a far-reaching impact. Long hours, poor pay, and an unclear future are only three of the challenges a budding entrepreneur must face. And, of course, losing everything one invests in a business is a very real risk. In fact, while 885,416 "new employer firms" were created in 1997, as reported by the U.S. Department of Labor, 857,073 businesses were terminated during the same year, with 53,826 of these being bankruptcies and 83,384 being failures. Failures and bankruptcies

Computer entrepreneur Bill Gates.

are business closures that occur while the business owes debts.

However, the potential rewards are unlimited. Business owners can profit greatly. Many of the wealthiest people on earth are entrepreneurs, including William Henry Gates III, the world's richest person and co-founder, chairman, and CEO of Microsoft Corporation. Another reward entrepreneurs tend to appreciate is independence. However, entrepreneurs' time is not necessarily their own. The work of the business must be completed, and often the entrepreneur is the one who must perform the most complex tasks of the business. Although others may work for the owner and manager of the business, it is ultimately the responsibility of the entrepreneur to make sure that the work gets done. Other rewards cited by entrepreneurs include personal satisfaction gained while performing the duties of the business and the resulting prestige.

BUSINESS PLAN

Planning is a key ingredient in the success of an entrepreneur. A business plan helps to guide the decision making needed to operate a business. The first decision is to choose what sort of business to own. The business may be:

- a retail business that markets a tangible product (such as clothing, houses, food)
- a wholesale business that acquires goods from a producer and distributes requested quantities to retailers
- a service business that offers an intangible product (such as insurance, haircuts, consultant services, construction, financial services)
- a manufacturing business that produces a product

Of course, a business may perform more than one of these functions. The scope of the business will also be dependent on the breadth and depth of the products or services offered as well as the geographic region served.

One option available to someone interested in purchasing a business is a franchise. A franchise is a license to organize a business that markets products manufactured or owned by a parent company, such as a Kwik Copy, Sleep Inn, McDonald's, Play It Again Sports, or other businesses.

Another early decision involves choosing the legal form of ownership. Three options are sole proprietorship, partnership, and corporation. In a sole proprietorship, a single person owns and operates the business. The owner assumes all risks and responsibilities for the business, including debts. Two or more individuals may form a partnership and serve as co-owners of the business. If the partnership is a general partnership, all partners assume unlimited liability. However, if the partnership is a limited partnership, one or more of the partners assumes unlimited liability while the remaining partner(s) do(es) not. Instead, they may lose up to the amount of their investment, while having limited involvement in the business.

The third form of ownership is the corporation. A corporation is a group of individuals who obtain a charter giving the organization formed by the group legal rights and privileges. This organization can perform such functions as buying and selling, as well as owning property, as if the group were an individual person. The corporation is actually owned by individuals who purchase stock. A major advantage of this form of ownership is that the stockholders themselves have limited liability, thus minimizing financial risks.

The Small Business Administration (1999) reports that in 1996, according to the Internal Revenue Service, 16,471,000 sole proprietorships, 1,679,000 partnerships, and 5,005,000 corporations filed nonfarm business tax returns.

A business plan often contains three major sections: the marketing plan, the management plan, and the financial plan.

Marketing Plan Marketing is a process in which the decisions of the business are based upon the goals of the organization. One of these goals is usually that of satisfying the needs and wants of potential customers or a target market. Potential customers can be divided into specific market segments that represent groups based on specified characteristics. For example, a business may strive to serve those in their late teens and early twenties who live primarily in large cities. Narrowing the segment even further, the business may offer goods or services for those interested specifically in sports—both as active players and as spectators or fans. Thus the business may sell athletic shoes and clothing, sports equipment, and "how-to" books. The owner(s) would locate this business in an area with a large number of people in that age group. Other factors to consider when defining a target market include such demographic factors as income level, sex, marital status, and ethnic group, and such geographic factors as climate and region of the country.

Part of the marketing plan is the marketing mix. A marketing mix has four basic components: product, place, price, and promotion.

Product: The product is the goods and/or services offered by the business. A travel agent may offer the service of arranging any type of trip to anywhere in the world or may specialize specifically in cruises. Choosing products is dependent on the market segment the business intends to serve. Other considerations include the amount of physical space available for storing the product, the amount of funds needed to purchase the product from the wholesaler or manufacturer, and the profitability potential of offering the product. Another important consideration is the product's life cycle. A life cycle has four sections: introduction, growth, maturity, and decline. When a new product is introduced to the market, it is in the introduction phase. Over time, it may grow in popularity and sales, reaching a point of maturity. Maturity is then followed by decline. An entrepreneur must be careful to avoid offering products or services that are in decline. That is one of the reasons for continually monitoring the sales of products and adjusting the product mix to reflect such changes in the product life cycle.

Place: Another factor in the marketing mix is place. Marketers often say that the success of a business is dependent upon "location . . . location . . . location." Choosing the location of the business is an important decision that must take into consideration such factors as the chosen target market, traffic patterns, parking availability, population trends, competitive businesses, rental costs, and other expenses. The place function also includes business activities that involve physical distribution, such as transporting goods, handling the goods, storing the goods, and keeping track of the goods (inventory).

An increasing number of businesses are locating on the Internet. Entrepreneurs create World Wide Web pages on which they promote their offerings. Consumers may either telephone the business to order the product or service or use a credit card to purchase the item over the Internet. The actual location of the business is less important since the Web is available throughout the country and, indeed, the world. However, the location still must be considered relative to business expenses (e.g., rent, utility prices) and transportation prices (e.g., cost of

transporting products purchased on the Internet from the business to the customer).

Businesses can also be located in the home; in fact, home-based businesses represent a large portion of businesses in the United States. Many entrepreneurs begin their businesses in the home and eventually outgrow the space available there, at which point the owner usually seeks an outside facility.

Price: Price is the third component of the marketing mix. A pricing structure must be developed that includes specific goals and reflects policies of the business. A goal may reflect an intended image of the business or a particular profit margin that is sought. Factors to consider when identifying goals and policies related to price are: the amount of sales that are sought, pricing policies of competitors, profits that are projected, supply of the product that is available and projected demand for that product, the location of the business, and the expenses of the business.

Promotion: The fourth component of the marketing mix is promotion—the activities of the business that are intended to inform potential customers about the product or service and persuade them to purchase it. Methods include personal selling, advertising, visual merchandising (the coordination of all physical elements in a business such as displays, counters, offices, windows, signs, fixtures, lighting, and such), and publicity. The effectiveness of promotional strategies must be monitored so that promotional dollars are spent on strategies that are contributing to the achievement of business goals.

Management Plan Another major section of a business plan is the management plan. The four basic functions of management are planning, organizing, directing, and controlling.

Planning involves the determination of goals and objectives for the business, including the actual results sought by the firm. A set of policies and procedures are determined that guide the identification of specific activities that will lead to these goals. Planning does not end with the creation of a business plan, however; it continues throughout the life of the business.

To implement the plan, the entrepreneur organizes the personnel and other resources of the business. An organizational chart is created that shows the hierarchy of the people working in the business. After the number of employees and their qualifications are determined, applicants are recruited and, once hired, are trained. Other types of resources that are organized by management are facilities, equipment, materials, and supplies.

The third management function is directing. Managers direct the work of the business by applying leadership and management skills. They model desired behavior while supervising, motivating, and evaluating their employees. Finally, comparing the plan with the actual results is called "controlling." By observing and studying financial statements, managers can understand the status of the business and adjust activities where necessary to contribute toward the achievement of the business goals. The controlling function also includes evaluation of employees.

Financial Plan The financial aspects of the business must also be planned. The financial plan includes several financial statements. One of these statements is the "statement of financial requirements," which identifies the projected expenses and the assets they will create for a specified time period. Among the expenses listed are those for rent, insurance, telephone, and inventory. The entrepreneur also needs money to meet personal expenses as the business grows. These expenses are also included in this statement. The expenses are used to create assets. Assets are items of value that are owned by the business. For example, if a business purchases land upon which to place a facility for the business, the money needed for the purchase is an expense that then creates the asset of land.

The financial plan also includes the source(s) of the funds needed to meet the financial requirements. Sometimes an entrepreneur will already have all the funds needed; more often these must be acquired from family members, private lending agencies, and/or governmental loan programs.

Another statement included in the financial plan is the income statement, which may be referred to as a profit-and-loss statement or operating statement. This statement is a projection of the sales expected in a given period of time, the cost of the merchandise that will be sold, and the operating expenses of the business. From this information, projected profits or losses are determined.

A financial plan also includes a beginning balance sheet. This form provides a list of the assets, liabilities, and net worth of a business on a given day. Assets are tangible items that are owned by the business, liabilities are the debts of a business, and net worth is the amount of investment that the owner(s) has in the business.

The financial plan also includes a cash-flow analysis and a break-even analysis. The cash-flow analysis identifies the cash generated after expenses and loan principal payments are deducted. This projection is calculated for several years into the future. The break-even analysis identifies the break-even point, which is the level of sales and expenses, including loan principal payments, at which a business has no profit and no loss.

RESOURCES

Information that can help the budding entrepreneur is available from people, printed material, and the Internet. All entrepreneurs need people they can go to for advice. Accountants and attorneys are especially important. An accountant not only provides the financial data and statements for the business but also interprets the information for the entrepreneur. This is important because business decisions must be based on a variety of considerations, including financial ones. Attorneys provide legal advice throughout the process of purchasing or creating a business and owning and managing it.

Other sources of information include financial institutions, the Chamber of Commerce, educational institutions, insurance agents, and suppliers of products used in the business. Publications provide up-to-date information: Books from major publishers, magazines such as

Entrepreneur and *Inc.*, and newsletters and journals offered by associations are available. Many types of businesses are served by trade associations such as the American Hotel and Motel Association, which is comprised of owners and operators of lodging businesses throughout the country. Along with providing publications, these organizations hold conferences and workshops and provide networking opportunities. Various government agencies are also available for advice, such as the Small Business Administration and the Internal Revenue Service.

The Internet provides information from a variety of people and organizations. Although the Internet is a valuable resource, the information available on it is not screened for accuracy. Relevant Web sites can be located by use of search engines that pinpoint specification on categories and topics.

Although it is important that the entrepreneur seeks advice throughout the planning and operation of a business, the ultimate decision maker on matters related to the business is the entrepreneur.

SUCCESSFUL ENTREPRENEURS

Successful entrepreneurs can be found in just about every community in the country. From small businesses employing only a few persons to megabusinesses employing thousands, successful entrepreneurs abound. The following successful entrepreneurs represent a few of those at the high end of success as measured by wealth:

> William (Bill) H. Gates is the co-founder, chairman, and CEO of Microsoft Corporation, the world's leading provider of software for personal computers. Gates was a student at Harvard when he developed BASIC, a programming language for the first microcomputer. He founded Microsoft in 1975 with a childhood friend, Paul Allen. According to Microsoft Corporation, Gates's determination to develop Microsoft stemmed from his belief that the personal computer would be a valuable tool for ev-

ery home and office; thus he began developing software for personal computers.

Mary Kay Ash launched Mary Kay Cosmetics on September 13, 1963. Mary Kay, Inc. reports that, with a life savings of $5000, Ash launched what is now the largest direct seller of skin care products and the best-selling brand of skin-care and color cosmetics in the United States. Mary Kay Cosmetics originated from an idea of writing a book to help women survive in the male-dominated business world. From there, Ash inadvertently created the marketing plan for Mary Kay Cosmetics.

Gozi Samuel Oburota founded the Gozi Samuel Oburota Certified Public Accountancy Corporation (GSO) in 1994. According to the GSO Corporation, before founding the company, Oburota had served as a senior accountant at IBM, trusted with worldwide accounting responsibility for the DASD 3390 mainframe computer project from product development through manufacturing and general availability. GSO is a full service certified public accounting firm with offices in San Jose, Los Angeles, and Washington, D.C. By 1999, GSO was one of the fastest-growing professional firms headquartered in Silicon Valley. GSO is 100 percent minority owned.

(SEE ALSO: *Factors of Production*)

BIBLIOGRAPHY

Ely, Vivien K., Berns, Robert G., and Popo, Debbi. (1990). *Entrepreneurship.* New York: Glencoe/McGraw-Hill.

Entrepreneur Magazine 2392 Morse Avenue, Irvine, California 92614.

GSO Corporation. http://www.gsocorp.com. 1999.

Kent, Calvin A., ed. (1990). *Entrepreneurship Education Current Developments, Future Directions.* Westport, CT: Quorum Books.

Inc. 477 Madison Ave., New York, New York 10022.

Longenecker, Justin G., Moore, Carlos W., and Petty, Bill (1997). *Small Business Management: An Entrepreneurial Emphasis.* Cincinnati, OH: South-Western College Publishing.

Mary Kay, Inc. http://www.marykay.com. 1999.

Meyer, Earl C., and Allen, Kathleen R. (1994). *Entrepreneurship and Small Business Management.* New York: Glencoe.

Microsoft Corporation. http://www.microsoft.com. 1999.

Moorman, Jerry W., and Halloran, James W. (1996). *Contemporary Entrepreneurship.* Cincinnati, OH: South-Western Educational Publishing.

U.S. Association for Small Business and Entrepreneurship. *Entrepreneurial Theory and Practice.* Waco, TX: Baylor University.

U.S. Small Business Administration. http://www.sba.gov. 1999.

ROBERT G. BERNS
JEWEL E. HAIRSTON

ENVIRONMENTAL PROTECTION AGENCY

In December 1970, the U.S. Environmental Protection Agency (EPA) was established as an independent agency. Reorganization Plan #3 of 1970 consolidated fifteen components from five agencies for the purpose of grouping all environmental regulatory activities under a single agency. Most of these functions were housed in the Department of the Interior, Department of Agriculture, and the Department of Health, Education and Welfare.

The purpose of the EPA is to ensure that all Americans and the environment in which they live are safe from health hazards. The EPA has a number of goals: clean air, clean and safe water, safe food, preventing and reducing pollution, water management and restoration of waste sites, redirection of international pollution, and credible deterrents to pollution. Also, the EPA engages in education about pollution and its environmental risks.

The first four goals deal with the immediate environment of people: clean air; clean and safe water; safe food; and preventing pollution and reducing risks in our environment. The remaining goals deal with education, the clean-up of existing pollution, and efforts in the global arena. They involve better water management, the reduction of cross-border environmental risks, the expansion of Americans' right to know about their environment, sound service, improved understanding of environmental risks, credible deterrents to pollution, and greater compliance with the law and effective management.

In addition to these goals, the EPA has adopted a number of principles to guide management in establishing priorities. These guidelines are to reduce environmental risks, to prevent pollution, to focus on children's health, to establish partners with local governments, to maximize public participation, to emphasize community-based solutions, to work with Indian tribes, and to choose cost-effective solutions. The EPA also is engaged in ongoing educational programs, which emphasize the community's right to know about its environmental risks.

The EPA has to enforce fifteen or more statutes or laws, including the Clean Air Act; the Clean Water Act; the Federal Food, Drug, and Cosmetic Act; the Endangered Species Act; the Pollution Prevention Act; and the Federal Insecticide, Fungicide, and Rodenticides Act. The EPA also enforces other laws dealing with pollution and toxic substances.

The EPA has had some major successes since its inception. In the area of air quality: (1) More than half of the large cities now meet air-quality standards; (2) emissions of common air pollutants have dropped by an average of 24 percent; and (3) blood lead levels in children have declined by 75 percent. In the area of water quality: (1) 60 percent of the nation's waterways are safe for fishing and swimming; (2) ocean dumping has been banned; and (3) standards for wastewater have been established for fifty industries. In the area of toxic and pesticide management: (1) DDT has been banned; (2) safer pesticides have been introduced; and (3) toxic emissions have been reduced by 39 percent. Finally, the EPA has been able to set many standards covering a wide range of pollutants. More information is available from the EPA at 401 M Street SW, Washington, D.C. 20460-0003; (202)260-2090; or http://www.epa.gov.

American Electric Power, in Beverly, Ohio, was named in a lawsuit by the Environmental Protection Agency.

BIBLIOGRAPHY

Environmental Protection Agency (EPA). "EPA's Mission." Archived at: http://www.epa.gov/epahome. 1999.

EPA. "Frequently Asked Questions." Archived at: http://www.epa.gov.gov/history. 1999.

EPA. "Research Programs." Archived at: http://www.epa.gov/epahome. 1999.

EPA. "Twenty-Five Years of Environmental Progress at a Glance." Archived at: http://www.epa.gov/25years. 1999.

MARY JEAN LUSH
VAL HINTON

EQUAL EMPLOYMENT OPPORTUNITY ACT

The Equal Employment Opportunity Act of 1972 (Public Law 92-261) instituted the federal Equal Employment Opportunity program, which is designed to ensure fair treatment to all segments of society without regard to race, religion, color, national origin, or sex. The goal of this law and program is to make discrimination in employment illegal. Equal Employment Opportunity programs include affirmative action for employment as well as processing of and remedies for discrimination complaints. All employees, including supervisors, managers, former employees, and applicants for employment, regardless of grade level or position, are covered under this legislation. The Equal Employment Opportunity Act of 1972, which amended the Civil Rights Act of 1964 to include public employees, granted enforcement authority to the Civil Service Commission (now the Office of Personnel Management) to ensure nondiscrimination in human resources actions and to establish affirmative employment measures.

Equal Employment Opportunity (EEO) means fair treatment in employment, promotion, training, and other personnel actions without regard to the previously mentioned factors. The main misconception about the EEO is that it applies is only to selected groups, but the EEO

Black Males for Justice campaign for Equal Employment Opportunity.

applies to everyone because it is the law. However, the EEO program is not a guarantee of employment for anyone. Under the EEO law, only job-related factors can be used to determine whether an individual is qualified for a particular job.

The development of the EEO policies and laws can be dated back to the Civil Rights Act of 1883, which prohibited political favoritism in federal employment. In 1940, Executive Order 0948 prohibited discrimination in federal agencies based on race, creed, or color. In 1961, Executive Order 10955 required that positive steps be taken to eliminate workplace discrimination in agencies. The next landmark influencing equal employment opportunity was the Equal Pay Act of 1963, which prohibited the payment of different wage rates to workers for substantially similar work on the basis of sex. Title VII of the Civil Rights Act of 1964, which prohibited discrimination based on race, color, sex, religion, or national origin and established the Equal Employ-

ment Opportunity Commission (EEOC), was another very influential piece of legislation for the EEO movement. Executive Order 11246 in 1965 was also influential because it named the process for achieving equal employment opportunity—affirmative action. Other important milestones were Executive Order 11375 in 1967, which prohibited discrimination based on sex and required affirmative action employment to help women, and the Age Discrimination in Employment Act of 1967, which prohibited discrimination against persons between the ages of 40 and 70. The final piece of legislation that influenced the Equal Employment Opportunity Act of 1972 was Executive Order 11478 of 1969, which mandated that equal employment opportunities be a part of every aspect of human resources policy and practice in the employment, development, advancement, and treatment of civilian employees of the federal government.

In addition to the Equal Employment Opportunity Act of 1972, two other pieces of legislation dealing with equal employment opportunities have been passed. The Equal Employment Opportunity Act of 1995 is one of these more recent laws. This act prohibits discrimination on fourteen grounds: (1) impairment, (2) marital status, (3) political belief or activity, (4) race, (5) religion, (6) sex, (7) societal status as a person, (8) age, (9) role in business dealings, (10) lawful sexual activity, (11) physical features, (12) pregnancy, (13) position or past positions held as employment, and (14) association with a person who is identified by reference to any of the thirteen other listed grounds. The act also prohibits sexual harassment, which applies to both employers and employees. The other piece of legislation dealing with equal employment opportunity is the Further Amendment to Executive Order 11478, Equal Employment Opportunity in the Federal Government. The order provides a uniform policy for the federal government to use in prohibiting discrimination based on sexual orientation in the federal civilian work force, in addition to race, color, religion, sex, national origin, physical disabilities, or age for which discrimination is prohibited in Executive Order 11478.

BIBLIOGRAPHY

African American Internetwork Web Site. http://www.afamnet.com/NationalPage/Politics/052998/_eeo.htm.

Defense Supply Center Web Site. http://www.dscr.dla.mil/eeo/Web-Project-WIP/DCSR-EEO-Terms.htm.

Law Institute of Victoria Web Site. http://liv.asn.au/public/general/employ/employ-Equal.html.

National Archives and Records Administration Web Site. http://www.nara.gov.nara.eeo.html#program.

U.S. Equal Employment Opportunity Commission Web Site. http://www.eeoc.gov

Western Area Power Administration Web Site. http://www.wapa.gov/CSO/eeo.eeomgr27.htm.

NIKOLE M. POGEMAN

EQUAL PAY ACT

The Equal Pay Act of 1963, which is an amendment to the Fair Labor Standards Act of 1938, is a federal law that requires employers to pay all employees equally for equal work, regardless of their gender. In other words, the act prohibits unequal pay for equal or substantially equal work performed by men and women in the same establishment who are performing under similar working conditions. Enforced by the Equal Employment Opportunity Commission, the Equal Pay Act also bars employers from reducing the wages of either sex in order to comply with the law. The act makes no provisions as to wage discrimination based on race or national origin, addressing only the issue of sex-based wage discrimination and covering only situations involving substantially equal work. The Equal Pay Act applies to all employees covered by the Fair Labor Standards Act, which means that virtually all employees are covered. However, in addition to the employees covered by the Fair Labor Standards Act, the Equal Pay Act covers professional employees such as executives and managers and includes administrators and teachers in elementary and secondary schools.

In order to fully understand the Equal Pay Act, it is important to determine the definition of "equal work." Jobs do not have to be identical for them to be considered equal. The courts have ruled that two jobs are equal for the purposes of the Equal Pay Act when both require equal levels of skill, effort, and responsibility and are performed under similar conditions. Although there is a lot of room for interpretation, the focus of equal work should be on only the duties performed. Job titles, classifications, and descriptions may weigh into the determination, but they are not all that is considered.

Significant legal history of employment discrimination began to appear in the early 1960s. The Equal Pay Act of 1963 was established to fix pay contingent upon the job. The act has almost always been applied to situations in which women are being paid less than men for doing similar jobs. Indeed, the law was passed to help rectify the problems faced by women workers because of sex discrimination in employment. The Equal Pay Act was closely followed by Title VII of the Civil Rights Act of 1964, which pro-

President Clinton speaks on Equal Pay.

hibits discrimination in employment. However, the Equal Pay Act provides two advantages over Title VII of the Civil Rights Act. First, a lawsuit can be filed under the Equal Pay Act without first filing a complaint with the Equal Employment Opportunity Commission. In addition, unlike Title VII, the Equal Pay Act does not require proof that the employer acted intentionally when discriminating, which makes an Equal Pay Act case easier to win.

When a worker establishes a pay disparity between a male and a female worker performing substantially equal jobs, the burden of proof shifts to the employer to justify its actions. Employers can defend themselves in one of four ways. The defenses that can be used are to show that the pay disparity was based on (1) a seniority system, (2) a merit system, (3) a system that determines wages based on the quantity or quality of work produced, or (4) some factor other than sex. However, an investigation occurs only if the employee can prove that the male and female are working in the same place, doing equal work, and receiving unequal pay because of their genders. In the event the employer is found guilty of violating the Equal Pay Act, back pay can be doubled if the employer's violation is determined to be willful.

BIBLIOGRAPHY

Law for All. http://www.nolo.com.

National Partnership for Women and Families. http://www.nationalpartnership.org.

U.S. Equal Employment Opportunity Commission Web Site. http://www.eeoc.gov/laws/epa.html.

Western Area Power Administration Web Site. http://www.wapa.gov/CSO.eeo.eeomgr27.htm.

NIKOLE M. POGEMAN

EQUILIBRIUM

(SEE: *Supply and Demand*)

EQUITY THEORY

(SEE: *Motivation*)

ERGONOMICS

Ergonomics is the science of fitting the job to the worker and adapting the work environment to the needs of humans. An overall goal of ergonomics is to promote health and safety and to optimize productivity.

The term *ergonomics* comes from the Greek words *ergon*, meaning "work", and *nomos*, meaning "laws"—thus, laws of work. The study of ergonomics as a way to reduce human error began in the military during the Korean War. In planes used for pilot training, the eject button was poorly placed and pilots sometimes accidentally ejected themselves—often at too low an altitude for their parachutes to open. The button's location was changed and fewer lives were lost.

Principles of ergonomics are now applied to the design of many elements of everyday life, from car seats to garden tools. Many different occupations are involved in implementing these "human factor" principles in the workplace, such as human factors/ergonomics specialists; safety engineers; industrial hygienists, engineers, designers; human resource managers; occupational medicine physicians and therapists; and chiropractors. Research in ergonomics is ongoing.

Knowledge of basic ergonomics principles is important for both workers and employers because both share responsibility for a safe work environment. One can easily imagine the potential hazards in manufacturing settings where equipment is operated and heavy materials are handled, but hazards exist in other environments, too. And technology (especially computer use) has brought about widespread changes in how work is accomplished.

Attention to ergonomics principles helps to reduce workplace injuries and illnesses that result in workers' compensation costs, medical claims, and lost work time. Many disorders and injuries are preventable when work conditions are designed for human safety and comfort. People

need training in how to recognize hazards and safety problems as well as how to control their own behaviors for maximum comfort and health.

One of the key considerations in ergonomics is adjustability of physical elements. People come in all shapes and sizes, and the "average" workstation configuration will not fit everyone. Making changes during a workday in the physical setup of equipment, such as adjusting chair height, can alleviate discomfort and fatigue. Work surfaces should be at comfortable heights in relationship to a chair or to a standing position. Equipment and related items should be arranged conveniently.

Whenever a mismatch occurs between the physical requirements of a job and the physical capacity of a worker, musculoskeletal disorders can result. People working with intense concentration or at high speeds often work with poor posture. Cumulative trauma disorders (also called repetitive strain injuries) are caused by repeating the same motion in awkward positions or with noticeable force, such as in lifting heavy objects. Carpal-tunnel syndrome, a disorder affecting nerves in the wrist that has the potential to permanently disable, is a condition affecting people in a variety of occupations from meatpackers to musicians. Wrist pain can be severe, with treatment involving wrist splints, anti-inflammatory drugs, or even surgery. And people who use a computer extensively are especially prone to developing carpal-tunnel syndrome. Computer use often contributes to vision problems, too.

Posture in standing and in seated positions is important to avoid musculoskeletal disorders. The natural curve of the spine should be maintained, with the head balanced over the spine. When a person is seated:

- Feet should rest on the floor, with legs and body forming 90° to 110° angles.

- The body should be straight, with the neck upright and supporting the head balanced on the spine (not forward or twisted to the sides).

- Upper arms should be perpendicular to the floor; forearms should parallel the floor.

Ergonomic keyboards help ease the strain on computer users' hands and wrists.

Symptoms of musculoskeletal disorders can begin as numbness or stiffness in joints or tingling, aching sensations in muscles. Pain or burning sensations may be evident, too. Often symptoms progress gradually, becoming more severe with prolonged exposure to the condition causing them. Damage to nerves, tendons, joints, or soft tissue can result.

With computer use so prevalent, poor work habits will contribute to musculoskeletal disorders for many people who spend long hours seated at a computer. These include the following:

- Wrists misaligned or excessive force used with a keyboard
- Poor posture used with an incorrect seating height

- A monitor incorrectly positioned, resulting in eye strain and vision problems

- Inappropriate lighting, causing glare on monitors and other work surfaces

- High concentration, causing infrequent breaks

The following paragraphs provide a few guidelines for working conditions when using a computer.

Chair: A well-designed chair with easy-to-implement adjustability is essential. A user can vary angles of back support and the seat pan to control the degree of pressure on the thighs and back. Weight should be evenly distributed, with no extreme pressure points. An upright posture is a little easier to achieve if the seat pan is tilted slightly forward of horizontal. When a person is seated, feet should rest on the floor and the chair seat pan should be even with the back of the knee, ranging from 13 to 19 inches above the floor depending on an individual's height. A foot rest may be used to relieve pressure on the thighs. Both lumbar and mid-level back support are needed. Arm rests, adjustable for height, are helpful to many people. The chair should have a five-point base for stability and casters for easy movement.

Keyboard: The keyboard provides the primary means of interacting with a computer. The keyboard should be in a comfortable position, and wrists should "float" over the keyboard when keying with a light touch so wrists and forearms remain straight. Although wrist pads are helpful for resting when not keying, they can actually create problems when a user keeps wrists on them when keying because the wrists can bend down. Different opinions exist on the appropriate angle of the keyboard; some people prefer a flat position while others find a reverse incline more comfortable. Split and curved keyboards are available, too. However, the most important part of keyboard use is keeping the wrists straight in line with the forearm and not bent to the side. When voice-recognition technology becomes commonly used, dependency on the keyboard will be reduced.

Mouse: A mouse should be positioned next to the keyboard, reachable without extending the arm in an awkward position. Again, a light touch is needed and users should avoid gripping or squeezing the mouse. A wrist support or adjustable mouse platform may be helpful if a user begins to develop wrist problems. A variety of shapes are available for these pointing devices, and a trackball can be used for the same purpose.

Monitor: A monitor should be directly in front of the user, with the top of the screen at or below the line of sight, 18 to 30 inches away from the eyes, and tiltable to avoid glare from overhead lighting and windows. If necessary, antiglare filters can be added. Screen size should be large enough for easy reading of screen character sizes with a screen refresh rate fast enough to avoid a visible flicker. An individual can experience blurred vision or fatigue from a poor monitor viewing angle, reflected glare, or a low-quality monitor. Because glands in the eyelids produce tears that cleanse eyes as the eyelids blink and the eyes move, irritated eyes can develop because one's blink rate tends to decrease when one is concentrating.

To avoid neck and eyestrain, an individual should do the following:

- Use a copyholder positioned near the monitor to support material used with computer work.

- Use lower levels of lighting to reduce glare on monitors. Many older offices have high illumination levels that are necessary for paper-intensive tasks—but are too highly lighted for computer work. Softer overall, or ambient, lighting should be used, with task lighting added to surfaces as needed for more illumination.

- Relax eye muscles by shifting focus from the computer screen to distant objects for a few seconds every 5 to 10 minutes.

- Take microbreaks to stretch the neck, shoulders, hands, wrists, back, and legs as well as to rest the eyes. Stretching exercises can be simple neck rotations, shoulder shrugs, fists clenched and then released, or arms hanging down naturally for a few moments. Get up and move around about every 30 minutes. Take a brisk walk if possible. Exercises with hand weights will help with stretching and will give the body isometric exercise.

While it may be ideal to have individually adjustable temperature controls, this is not feasible in many work situations. For business offices, most people are comfortable with temperature levels at 68° to 72° in the winter and 72° to 76° in the summer. Humidity levels should be maintained between 40 to 60 percent not only for comfort but also for proper functioning of office equipment. Indoor air quality involves more than heating and cooling—air should be cleansed of pollutants (bacteria, dust, fumes, etc.), with fresh air added before circulation. Many factors affect the efficiency of HVAC (heating, ventilation, and air conditioning) systems. These systems must be designed for the number of people and the equipment to be used in each area because computers and other devices can produce almost as much heat as a human body produces.

Another important concept is adjustability of work pace. Jobs may require redesign to allow workers to accomplish tasks at varying speeds or to enable workers to rotate to different tasks or to use a variety of work methods that permit different movements. Rest breaks are important, too, and microbreaks can be taken to interrupt intense situations, to rest arms and wrists, or to rest eyes.

Much ergonomics information is available in print and on the Internet, published by organizations such as the Occupational Safety and Health Administration (OSHA), the National Institute of Occupational Safety and Health (NIOSH), the National Safety Council, the Human Factors and Ergonomic Society, and others. OSHA is developing ergonomics program standards that were to be published in 2000 (OSHA 1999). Consultants can provide technical expertise to help with all phases of ergonomics assessment and the implementation of corrective measures and/or training programs.

BIBLIOGRAPHY

"Occupational Safety and Health Administration." http://www.osha~slc.gov/SLTC/ergonomics/. 1999.

PAT R. GRAVES

ETHICS IN ACCOUNTING

Ethics in accounting is of utmost importance to accounting professionals and those who rely on their services. Certified Public Accountants (CPAs) and other accounting professionals know that people who use their services, especially decision makers using financial statements, expect them to be highly competent, reliable, and objective. Those who work in the field of accounting must not only be well qualified but must also possess a high degree of professional integrity. A professional's good reputation is one of his or her most important possessions.

The general ethical standards of society apply to people in professions such as medicine and accounting just as much as to anyone else. However, society places even higher expectations on professionals. People need to have confidence in the quality of the complex services provided by professionals. Because of these high expectations, professions have adopted codes of ethics, also known as codes of professional conduct. These ethical codes call for their members to maintain a level of self-discipline that goes beyond the requirements of laws and regulations.

CODES OF ETHICS

By joining their professional organizations, people who work in the field of accounting agree to uphold the high ethical standards of their profession. Each of the major professional associations for accountants has a code of ethics. The Code of Professional Conduct of the American Institute of CPAs (AICPA), the national professional association for CPAs, sets forth ethical principles and rules of conduct for its members. The principles are positively stated and provide general guidelines that CPAs (or any professionals, for that matter) should strive to follow. The rules of conduct are much more explicit as to specific actions that should or should not be taken. The Institute of Management Accountants (IMA) Standards of Ethical Conduct applies to practitioners of management accounting and financial management, and the Institute of Internal Auditors (IIA) Code of Ethics applies to its members and to Certified Internal Auditors (CIAs).

ETHICAL RESPONSIBILITIES

A distinguishing mark of professions such as medicine and accounting is acceptance of their responsibilities to the public. The AICPA Code of Professional Conduct describes the accounting profession's public as consisting of "clients, credit grantors, governments, employers, investors, the business and financial community, and others who rely on the objectivity and integrity of CPAs to maintain the orderly functioning of commerce." Many, but not all, CPAs work in firms that provide accounting, auditing, and other services to the general public; these CPAs are said to be *in public practice*. Regardless of where CPAs work, the AICPA Code applies to their professional conduct, although there are some special provisions for those in public practice. Internal auditors, management accountants, and financial managers most commonly are employees of the organizations to which they provide these services; but, as professionals, they, too, must also be mindful of their obligations to the public.

The responsibilities placed on accounting professionals by the three ethics codes and the related professional standards have many similarities. All three require professional competence, confidentiality, integrity, and objectivity. Accounting professionals should only undertake tasks that they can complete with professional competence, and they must carry out their responsibilities with sufficient care and diligence, usually referred to as *due professional care* or *due care*. The codes of ethics of the AICPA, IMA, and IIA all require that confidential information known to accounting professionals not be disclosed to outsiders. The most significant exception to the confidentiality rules is that accounting professionals' workpapers are subject to sub-

poena by a court; nothing analogous to attorney-client privilege exists.

INDEPENDENCE

Maintaining integrity and objectivity calls for avoiding both actual and apparent conflicts of interest. This notion is termed *independence*. Being independent in fact and in appearance means that one not only is unbiased, impartial, and objective but also is *perceived* to be that way by others. While applicable to all accounting professionals, independence is especially important for CPAs in public practice. The AICPA's rules pertaining to independence for CPAs who perform audits are detailed and technical. For instance, a CPA lacks independence and thus may not audit a company if he or she (or the spouse or dependents) owns stock in that company and/or has certain other financial or employment relationships with the client.

ETHICS ENFORCEMENT

To a large extent, the accounting profession is self-regulated through various professional associations rather than being regulated by the government. The AICPA, the IMA, and the IIA have internal means to enforce the codes of ethics. Furthermore, the professional organizations for CPAs in each state, known as *state societies of CPAs*, have mechanisms for enforcing their codes of ethics, which are usually very similar to the AICPA Code. Violations of ethical standards can lead to a person's being publicly expelled from the professional organization. Because of the extreme importance of a professional accountant's reputation, expulsion is a strong disciplinary measure. However, ethical violations can lead to even more adverse consequences for CPAs because of state and federal laws.

The state government issues a CPA's license to practice, usually through an organization known as the *state board of accountancy*. Since state laws governing the practice of accountancy typically include important parts of the AICPA Code, the Code thus gains legal enforceability. Consequently, ethical violations can result in the state's revoking a CPA's license to practice on a temporary or even permanent basis. Because a licensed CPA is also likely to belong to the AICPA and the state society of CPAs, investigations of ethics violations may be carried out jointly by the AICPA, the state society, and the state board of accountancy.

CPAs in public practice who audit the financial statements of public corporations are subject to federal securities laws and regulations, including the Securities Exchange Act of 1934. The Securities and Exchange Commission (SEC), which administers these laws, has broad powers to regulate corporations that sell their stock to the public. One important SEC requirement is that these corporations' financial statements be audited by an independent CPA. The SEC has the authority to establish and enforce auditing standards and procedures, including what constitutes independence for a CPA. The SEC has largely delegated standard setting to the private sector but retains oversight and enforcement responsibilities. In 1998 the SEC and the AICPA jointly announced the creation of the Independence Standards Board (ISB), a private-sector body whose mission is to improve auditor independence standards. In announcing the formation of the ISB, the SEC reaffirmed the crucial importance of the CPA's independence: "[M]aintaining the independence of auditors of financial statements . . . is crucial to the credibility of financial reporting and, in turn, to the capital formation process" (SEC Release FRR-50, 1998).

(SEE ALSO: *American Institute of Certified Public Accountants*; *Institute of Internal Auditors*; *Institute for Management Accountants*; *State Societies of CPAs*)

BIBLIOGRAPHY

AICPA Code of Professional Conduct. (1988). Jersey City, NJ: American Institute of Certified Public Accountants.

IMA. (1997). *Statements on Management Accounting: Objectives of Management Accounting*, Statement No. 1B. New York: Institute of Management Accountants.

IIA Code of Ethics. (1988). Altamonte Springs, FL: Institute of Internal Auditors.

MARY BRADY GREENAWALT

ETHICS IN ECONOMICS

As might be suspected, early writings on ethics were centered not on economics or business, but personal beliefs and actions. It becomes readily apparent from early discussions of ethics that philosophers and writers viewed ethics as a matter of choice. Individuals must make choices in their lives. This is important to note—businesses don't make choices. Choices are made and/or implemented by individuals within the economic enterprise. People in government make choices, people in educational institutions make choices, people in businesses make choices, people with churches make choices; everyone is forced to make choices, and even the choice not to choose is a decision.

ETHICS IN ORGANIZATION

Velasquez (1982) illustrated some important points regarding organizations and their acts relative to individuals in the organization. He stated:

I. A corporate organization "exists" only if (1) there exist certain human individuals placed in certain circumstances and (2) our linguistic rules lay down that when those kinds of individuals exist in those kinds of circumstances, they shall count as a corporate organization.

II. A corporate organization "acts" only if (1) certain human individuals in the organization performed certain actions in certain circumstances and (2) our linguistic rules lay down that when those kinds of individuals perform those kinds of actions in those kinds of circumstances, this shall count as an act of their corporate organization. (p. 16)

Linguistic rules are the rules of either written or spoken language. In the above quote, it is pointed out that individuals make up the corporation or business and that the corporation acts when these individuals carry out their assigned duties within the scope of the corporate authority. However, since it is human individuals on whom the corporation depends, it is these individuals who are seen to be responsible for moral duties and issues.

Businesses are the most significant institution in the economic structure. As such, businesses are expected to produce goods and services that are demanded by members of society, and once produced, these goods and services must be distributed to the numerous societal groups. Decisions are made within the business structure about who will produce, how much will be produced, how production will be implemented, how the work will be organized, and how the finished good or service will be made available to the consuming members of society. All these decisions are necessary in the day-to-day operation of an economic institution, and all these choices are made by people. It could be argued that computer models are used to make decisions, but it can be further counter-argued that computer models are developed by people and people are the ones who implement recommendations made by computer modeling.

In order for people in all institutions to make choices, there must be some guidelines or principles upon which the choices are based. These guidelines are often referred to as values. Everyone develops a set of values, or preferences, beginning in early childhood—or perhaps even immediately from birth. These values stem from how people are raised, where they live, their ancestry, and all the other factors that influence everyone's lives. If everyone has a value system, everyone must have an ethical system upon which to base judgments and choices. Stemming from this personal set of values will come policies and procedures that will guide all organizations within the economic structure.

Boulding (1968) argued that individuals have a "real" personal ethic, which can be deduced from a person's actual behavior, and a "verbal" ethic, which can be deduced from a person's statements. Boulding found that it is basically a universal phenomenon that a person will talk about one set of ethical principles but act according to another. The old statement "Do as I say,

not as I do" seems to reflect an accurate perception of reality.

Ethics, from an economist's perspective, is a matter of choice. Economics is a matter of choice. There are several alternatives from which a choice must be made. A business owner or manager might have to decide between producing weapons for military use or firearms for use by private individuals who pursue the sport of wild game hunting. These decisions are not always easy, especially when guided by the need for the organization to make a profit. The choice that is ultimately made is based on a value system that influences policies and procedures in the organization. In an economic environment, the decision is often made based on values that have been determined to be most important or that are ranked on a scale of best to worst.

A dilemma that faces all decision makers, especially when group decision making is used, is the different value systems that are held by individuals. While organizations have policies and procedures, not every option from which to choose is necessarily easily defined or clearly understood. Many organizations have mechanisms through which those affected by the decision can appeal it for further consideration. In the case of a university student who receives a failing grade but thinks the grade was undeserved because of a conflict with the professor, an appeal by the student might be heard and a decision could be made to overturn the professor's decision. Or the decision might be made in favor of the professor and the student's appeal denied. Such a decision is based on value systems that guide ethical behaviors.

Decisions made by economic institutions do not always match what the general populace thinks is correct. When this happens, the result can be new laws or rules that are passed to try to contain those who are perceived as violating the public trust. For example, many laws have been passed to curb problems with pollution. Antipollution laws are designed to reduce the harmful effects of pollution; when a business does not follow the laws, it can be severely penalized. In some cases, the new laws force the closure of business enterprises because conformity to the laws is cost-prohibitive. This was the case when laws went into effect requiring underground gasoline tanks at service stations to meet Environmental Protection Agency requirements. Many businesses couldn't meet the requirements because of the expenses involved and they closed their doors.

At other times, businesses choose to violate the laws in order to save money. In the long run, this can cost more than the business would have had to pay had the changes been made to comply with the laws. This occurred when a chemical manufacturing company was caught dumping hazardous waste into an Illinois River. The company was told to stop the dumping and was fined a large sum of money. But during the time the environmental inspectors were on the premises, the company chose to dump more waste into the river, saying that if they hadn't done it, there could have been a fatal accident in the plant. They were fined an additional sum. These examples illustrate choices that must be made—not by businesses in economic systems, but by individuals in the businesses.

It was stated earlier that businesses are the most significant institution within the economic structure. It should also be noted, however, that businesses are not the only institutions within an economic structure. There are many other important groups, such as the family, government, churches, and schools. All these institutions play an important role in developing value systems and the moral influences on individuals in businesses.

Because many other institutions influence the thinking of individuals in organizations, different value systems are developed. Some value systems are inconsistent with what is necessary for successful business operations and become a threat to a business and economic system. An example of that is honesty. An individual whose value system does not include complete honesty becomes a threat to successful business operations. Because of threats like these to economic entities, rules are established to deal with those who have different value systems. The rules are called laws, and the government is the largest enforcer of laws.

Governments are important to successful business and economic operations. Governments help to assure fair trade and commerce within a country and internationally. A good example of this is when the U.S. government ordered the breakup of the Bell Telephone System several years ago. It was felt that the system had grown too large and that fair competition wasn't possible. When companies become monopolies, they can set prices and control supplies of goods and services in ways that might not be fair to consumers. A government can intervene to assure fair trade practices. Many laws have been written to influence fair economic trade.

SETTING BUSINESS ETHICAL STANDARDS

Businesses make decisions that influence consumers, employees, and society in general. It is people who make up the businesses, and it is people who must set the standards for ethical conduct. The process for setting standards needs to be a top-down approach—management must develop and support an ethical code. Employees must understand what is expected of them in order to follow the codes. Managers and employees must be trained to interpret and consider alternatives relative to established ethical codes. In larger businesses, compliance offices are often established to assure that ethical codes are followed.

People outside the business must also know what ethical standards are being followed, and they must know that individuals within the company who do not follow the prescribed ethical codes will be dealt with in a manner appropriate to the violation. This illustrates the need to enforce the ethical codes. If a business establishes an ethical code but does not enforce it, the code will not be followed.

SOCIAL RESPONSIBILITY

Closely related to ethical codes are responsibilities that economic enterprises have to society. This is known as social responsibility. This is a difficult element of business operations because it normally means additional costs to the business. Social responsibility could mean making contributions to charitable organizations. An example might be a corporation donating land it is not using to a conservation group for the development of a nature preserve.

Social responsibility also includes internal considerations, such as hiring minorities, establishing on-site child-care facilities, controlling pollution, ensuring safe working conditions, providing substance-abuse programs for employees, and manufacturing safe products. These are all economic decisions that have social effects both within and outside the business.

Businesses that are concerned about social responsibility will conduct social audits. This is a systematic evaluation of the organization's progress toward implementing socially responsible programs. This is not a precise science and depends on interpretations of what is socially responsive behavior. Again, these decisions must be made by individuals within the business. Social audits do illustrate that a business is at least concerned about the social impact it has.

SUMMARY

Ethics is not easy for any business, and there will always be individuals and/or groups who question the behaviors of institutions in our economic system. Our discussion has focused on businesses in the economic system, but other systems such as churches, schools, and governmental agencies are also subjected to critical ethical scrutiny. Ethics and social responsibility are the concern of everyone, and it is up to individuals to establish ethical codes and to follow them.

BIBLIOGRAPHY

Baylis, Charles A. (1958). *Ethics: The Principles of Wise Choice.* New York: Henry Holt.

Boulding, Kenneth E. (1968). *Beyond Economics: Essays on Society, Religion, and Ethics.* Ann Arbor; MI: University of Michigan Press.

Bowne, Borden P. (1895). *The Principles of Ethics.* New York: Harper & Brothers.

Brandt, Richard B. (1979). *A Theory of the Good and the Right.* Oxford: Clarendon Press.

Facione, Peter A., Scherer, Donald, and Attig, Thomas. (1991). *Ethics and Society.* Englewood Cliffs, NJ: Prentice Hall.

Velasquez, Manuel G. (1982). *Business Ethics: Concepts and Cases.* Englewood Cliffs, NJ: Prentice-Hall.

ROGER L. LUFT

ETHICS IN FINANCE

Ethics in general is concerned with human behavior that is acceptable or "right" and that is not acceptable or "wrong" based on conventional morality. General ethical norms encompass truthfulness, honesty, integrity, respect for others, fairness, and justice. They relate to all aspects of life, including business and finance. Financial ethics is, therefore, a subset of general ethics.

Ethical norms are essential for maintaining stability and harmony in social life, where people interact with one another. Recognition of others' needs and aspirations, fairness, and cooperative efforts to deal with common issues are, for example, aspects of social behavior that contribute to social stability. In the process of social evolution, we have developed not only an instinct to care for ourselves but also a conscience to care for others. There may arise situations in which the need to care for ourselves runs into conflict with the need to care for others. In such situations, ethical norms are needed to guide our behavior. As Demsey (1999) puts it: "Ethics represents the attempt to resolve the conflict between selfishness and selflessness; between our material needs and our conscience."

Ethical dilemmas and ethical violations in finance can be attributed to an inconsistency in the conceptual framework of modern financial-economic theory and the widespread use of a principal-agent model of relationship in financial transactions. The financial-economic theory that underlies the modern capitalist system is based on the rational-maximizer paradigm, which holds that individuals are self-seeking (egoistic) and that they behave rationally when they seek to maximize their own interests. The principal-agent model of relationships refers to an arrangement whereby one party, acting as an agent for another, carries out certain functions on behalf of that other. Such arrangements are an integral part of the modern economic and financial system, and it is difficult to imagine it functioning without them.

The behavioral assumption of the modern financial-economic theory runs counter to the ideas of trustworthiness, loyalty, fidelity, stewardship, and concern for others that underlie the traditional principal-agent relationship. The traditional concept of agency is based on moral values. But if human beings are rational maximizers, then agency on behalf of others in the traditional sense is impossible. As Duska (1992) explains it: "To do something for another in a system geared to maximize self-interest is foolish. Such an answer, though, points out an inconsistency at the heart of the system, for a system that has rules requiring agents to look out for others while encouraging individuals to look out only for themselves, destroys the practice of looking out for others" (p. 61).

The ethical dilemma presented by the problem of conflicting interests has been addressed in some areas of finance, such as corporate governance, by converting the agency relationship into a purely contractual relationship that uses a carrot-and-stick approach to ensure ethical behavior by agents. In corporate governance, the problem of conflict between management (agent) and stockholders (principal) is described as an agency problem. Economists have developed an agency theory to deal with this problem. The agency theory assumes that both the agent and the principal are self-interested and aim to maximize their gain in their relationship. A simple example would be the case of a store manager acting as an agent for the owner of the store. The store manager wants as much pay as possible for as little work as possible, and the store owner wants as much work from the manager for as little pay as possible. This theory is value-free because it does not pass judgment on whether the maximization behavior is good or bad and is not concerned with what a just pay for the manager might be. It

drops the ideas of honesty and loyalty from the agency relationship because of their incompatibility with the fundamental assumption of rational maximization. "The job of agency theory is to help devise techniques for describing the conflict inherent in the principal-agent relationship and controlling the situations so that the agent, acting from self-interest, does as little harm as possible to the principal's interest" (DeGeorge, 1992). The agency theory turns the traditional concept of agency relationship into a structured (contractual) relationship in which the principal can influence the actions of agents through incentives, motivations, and punishment schemes. The principal essentially uses monetary rewards, punishments, and the agency laws to command loyalty from the agent.

Most of our needs for financial services—management of retirement savings, stock and bond investing, and protection against unforeseen events, to name a few—are such that they are better entrusted to others because we have neither the ability nor the time to carry them out effectively. The corporate device of contractualization of the agency relationship is, however, too difficult to apply to the multitude of financial dealings between individuals and institutions that take place in the financial market every day. Individuals are not as well organized as stockholders, and they are often unaware of the agency problem. Lack of information also limits their ability to monitor an agent's behavior. Therefore, what we have in our complex modern economic system is a paradoxical situation: the ever-increasing need for getting things done by others on the one hand, and the description of human nature that emphasizes selfish behavior on the other. This paradoxical situation, or the inconsistency in the foundation of the modern capitalist system, can explain most of the ethical problems and declining morality in the modern business and finance arena.

ETHICAL VIOLATIONS

The most frequently occurring ethical violations in finance relate to insider trading, stakeholder interest versus stockholder interest, investment management, and campaign financing. Business in general and financial markets in particular are replete with examples of violations of trust and loyalty in both public and private dealings. Fraudulent financial dealings, influence peddling and corruption in governments, brokers not maintaining proper records of customer trading, cheating customers of their trading profits, unauthorized transactions, insider trading, misuse of customer funds for personal gain, mispricing customer trades, and corruption and larceny in banking have become common occurrences.

Insider trading is perhaps one of the most publicized unethical behaviors by traders. Insider trading refers to trading in the securities of a company to take advantage of material "inside" information about the company that is not available to the public. Such a trade is motivated by the possibility of generating extraordinary gain with the help of nonpublic information (information not yet made public). It gives the trader an unfair advantage over other traders in the same security. Insider trading was legal in some European countries until recently. In the United States, the 1984 Trading Sanctions Act made it illegal to trade in a security while in the possession of material nonpublic information. The law applies to both the insiders, who have access to nonpublic information, and the people with whom they share such information.

Campaign financing in the United States has been a major source of concern to the public because it raises the issue of conflict of interest for elected officials in relation to the people or lobbying groups that have financed their campaigns. The United States has a long history of campaign finance reform. The Federal Election Commission (FEC) administers and enforces the federal campaign finance statutes enacted by the Congress from time to time. Many states have also passed lobbying and campaign finance laws and established ethics commissions to enforce these statutes.

ETHICAL CODES

Approaches to dealing with ethical problems in finance range from establishing ethical codes for financial professionals to efforts to replace the rational-maximizer (egoistic) paradigm that underlies the modern capitalist system by one in which individuals are assumed to be altruistic, honest, and basically virtuous.

It is not uncommon to find established ethical codes and ethical offices in American corporations and in financial markets. Ethical codes for financial markets are established by the official regulatory agencies and self-regulating organizations to ensure ethically responsible behavior on the part of the operatives in the financial markets.

One of the most important and powerful official regulatory agencies for the securities industry in the United States is the Securities and Exchange Commission (SEC). It is in charge of implementing federal securities laws, and, as such, it sets up rules and regulations for the proper conduct of professionals operating within its regulatory jurisdiction. Many professionals play a role within the securities industry, among the most important of which are accountants, broker-dealers, investment advisers, and investment companies. Any improper or unethical conduct on the part of these professionals is of great concern to the SEC, whose primary responsibility is to protect investor interests and maintain the integrity of the securities market. The SEC can censure, suspend, or bar professionals who practice within its regulatory domain for lack of requisite qualifications or unethical and improper conduct. The SEC also oversees self-regulatory organizations (SROs), which include stock exchanges, the National Association of Security Dealers (NASD), the Municipal Securities Rulemaking Board (MSRB), clearing agencies, transfer agents, and securities information processors. An SRO is a membership organization that makes and enforces rules for its members based on the federal securities laws. The SEC has the responsibility of reviewing and approving the rules made by SROs.

Other rule-making agencies include the Federal Reserve System, the Federal Deposit Insurance Corporation (FDIC), and state finance authorities. Congress has entrusted to the Federal Reserve Board the responsibility of implementing laws pertaining to a wide range of banking and financial activities, a task that it carries out through its regulations. One such regulation has to do with unfair or deceptive acts or practices. The FDIC has its own rules and regulations for the banking industry, and it also draws its power to regulate from various banking laws passed by Congress.

In addition to federal and state regulatory agencies, various professional associations set their own rules of good conduct for their members. The American Institute of Certified Public Accountants (AICPA), the American Institute of Certified Planners (AICP), the Investment Company Institute (ICI), the American Society of Chartered Life Underwriters (ASCLU), the Institute of Chartered Financial Analysts (ICFA), the National Association of Bank Loan and Credit Officers (also known as Robert Morris Associates), and the Association for Investment Management and Research (AIMR) are some of the professional associations that have well-publicized codes of ethics.

TOWARD A PARADIGM SHIFT

There has been an effort to address the ethical problems in business and finance by reexamining the conceptual foundation of the modern capitalist system and changing it to one that is consistent with the traditional model of agency relationship. The proponents of a paradigm shift question the rational-maximizer assumption that underlies the modern financial-economic theory and reject the idea that all human actions are motivated by self-interest. They embrace an alternative assumption—that human beings are to some degree ethical and altruistic—and emphasize the role of the traditional principal-agent relationship based on honesty, loyalty, and trust. Duska (1992) argues: "Clearly, there is an extent to which [Adam] Smith and the economists are right. Human beings are self-interested and will not always look out for the interest of others. But there are times they will set aside their interests to act on behalf of others. Agency situations were presumably set up to guarantee those times."

The idea that human beings can be honest and altruistic is an empirically valid assumption; it is not hard to find examples of honesty and altruism in both private and public dealings. There is no reason this idea should not be embraced and nurtured. As Bowie (1991) points out: "Looking out for oneself is a natural, powerful motive that needs little, if any, social reinforcement. . . . Altruistic motives, even if they too are natural, are not as powerful: they need to be socially reinforced and nurtured" (p. 19). If the financial-economic theory accepts the fact that behavioral motivations other than that of wealth maximization are both realistic and desirable, then the agency problem that economists try to deal with will be a nonproblem. For Dobson (1993), the true role of ethics in finance is to be found in the acceptance of "internal good" ("good" in the sense of "right" rather than in the sense of "physical product"), which, he adds, is what classical philosophers describe as "virtue"—that is, the internal good toward which all human endeavor should strive. He contends: "If the attainment of internal goods were to become generally accepted as the ultimate objective of all human endeavor, both personal and professional, then financial markets would become truly ethical" (p. 60).

BIBLIOGRAPHY

Bowie, Norman E. (1991). "Challenging the Egoistic Paradigm." *Business Ethics Quarterly*. 1. 1-4.

Bowie, Norman E., and Freeman, Edward R., eds. (1992). *Ethics and Agency Theory: An Introduction*. New York: Oxford University Press.

DeGeorge, Richard T. (1992) "Agency Theory and the Ethics of Agency." In Norman E. Bowie and Edward R. Freeman, eds. *Ethics and Agency Theory: An Introduction*. New York: Oxford University Press.

Dempsey, Mike. (1999). "An Agenda for Window-Dressing or for Radical Change?" http://panopticon.csustan.edu/cpa99/html/dempsy.html.

Dobson, John. (1993). "The Role of Ethics in Finance." *Financial Analysis Journal*. November-December: 57-61.

Duska, Ronald R. (1992). "Why Be a Loyal Agent? A Systematic Ethical Analysis." In *Ethics and Agency Theory: An Introduction*. Norman E. Bowie and Edward R. Freeman, eds., New York: Oxford University Press.

Frowen, S.F. and McHugh, F.P., eds. (1995). ed. *Financial Decision-Making and Moral Responsibility.* New York: Macmillan.

Goodpaster, Kenneth E. (1991). "Business Ethics and Stakeholder Analysis." *Business Ethics Quarterly.* 1. 53-71.

Nadler, Paul S. (1989). "Ethics and the Financial Community." *Secured Lender.* January-February.

ANAND G. SHETTY

ETHICS IN INFORMATION PROCESSING

New technologies in information processing often raise ethical concerns, resulting from their creating new possibilities for human action. *Computer ethics* can be defined as moral philosophy concerning the ethical dilemmas involved in areas of information processing, including theories, approaches in decision-making situations, and methods of increasing awareness of ethics. These ethical and moral issues are among the most socially important aspects of information processing. There are two major problems in the area: (1) unethical behavior leading to immoral acts such as virus creation and software piracy and (2) lack of awareness about information technology security and information technology-related crimes (Siponen and Kajava, 1999).

Ethics in information processing is considered so important that the Computer Ethics Institute developed the following Ten Commandments of Computer Ethics.

Thou shalt not use a computer to harm other people.

Thou shalt not interfere with other people's computer work.

Thou shalt not snoop around in other people's computer files.

Thou shalt not use a computer to steal.

Thou shalt not use a computer to bear false witness.

Thou shalt not copy or use proprietary software for which you have not paid.

Thou shalt not use other people's computer resources without authorization or proper compensation.

Thou shalt not appropriate other people's intellectual output.

Thou shalt think about the social consequences of the program you are writing or the system you are designing.

Thou shalt always use a computer in ways that ensure consideration and respect for your fellow humans.

INFORMATION-PROCESSING ETHICS AND BUSINESS

Ethical issues raised by information processing in business include confidentiality of data, software piracy, hacking, and stealing the property of others. In order to determine the ethical knowledge and behavior of young people, a survey of 780 high school and university business students was conducted (Vincent and Meche, 1998). The ethical knowledge survey was made up of nineteen questions, six of which were the information-processing questions shown in Table 1.

All of the actions in Table 1 are unethical. The responses shown in the table demonstrate that ethical problems exist among young people. As can be seen, some do not recognize ethical dilemmas, and many would participate in unethical behavior regardless. For instance, revealing confidential information, stealing the ideas of others, copying software, and punching the time clock from home are unethical behaviors. Unauthorized copying of software—software piracy—is stealing. Besides being strictly illegal in many countries, it is morally wrong, because it violates the right of the owners of the software to receive payment for the use of their invention. Illegal software amounts to more than 90 percent of all software used in some Asian countries, at least 75 percent in Eastern Europe, and less than 33 percent in the United States (Siponen and Kajava, 1999). Additionally, according to a *Computerworld* survey of 255 information systems professionals in corporate America, 53 percent have made unauthorized copies of commer-

Use of Information

	% Ethical		% Would You Do It?	
	High School Yes	Univ Yes	High School Yes	Univ Yes
1. You are the payroll clerk and know what everyone's salary is. A raise will be given next month. You feel that it would be OK to tell a few of your closest friends what they will be getting.	0.36	0.27	0.54	0.29
2. Your job is in jeopardy because you have displayed very little initiative. You need this job because you have a family to support. You use a colleague's computer and see a proposal for a new product. You write it up as your own.	0.15	0.12	0.25	0.15
3. Today is the third day you have had trouble getting to work on time. You can punch in by computer from your home. You do it "just for today" so that you do not lose your job.	0.15	0.10	0.48	0.35
4. You work for the phone company and have access to private/unlisted numbers. A friend calls you, saying he must make an emergency call; and he needs to know a number that is unlisted. You give your friend the number.	0.17	0.17	0.39	0.42
5. A really nice word processing program is on the computer in your office. You would like to have it on your home computer, so you copy it.	0.33	0.33	0.59	0.56
6. You work in a bank and have access to all bank account records. Out of curiosity, you check to see what your friends' bank balances are.	0.10	0.13	0.23	0.21

Table 1

cial software ("Results of a Survey," 1995). The typical reason given was to try it out before buying it.

Hacking and virus creations are serious crimes that must be treated just like other criminal offenses. Generally speaking, hacking is breaking into other people's property; it is an immoral action that cannot be justified under any circumstances. One of the most popular hackers' arguments is that "electrons are free—they do not belong to anybody." This premise is invalid; there is no reason why electrically committed crimes should be treated differently from physical crimes (Siponen, 1997).

Information on the Net, including thousands of databases and more than four hundred magazines, is extremely hard to control. Search engines or robots have been designed to search for specific information in this immense collection of data. When a search engine filters or controls all the information that a person accesses, there is the danger that the person's view of the topic will become narrowed (Pedersen, 1996). This offers the designers of search engines an opportunity to manipulate people's minds by controlling the information they receive. Additionally, online shopping creates the possibility of disclosure of financial information, such as credit card information, to unauthorized parties.

Questions have arisen concerning computer graphics. For example, should graphical re-creations of incidents such as automobile accidents be allowed to be used in courtrooms? Is it right for an individual to electronically reproduce and then alter an artistic image originally created by someone else. It is apparent that there should be clear rules and regulations concerning cyberspace (Johnson, 1994).

INFORMATION-PROCESSING ETHICS AND ETIQUETTE

Courtesy in information processing is often referred to as Netiquette—or etiquette on the Internet. E-mail and chat room etiquette is central to courtesy in cyberspace. In both situations people should follow the Golden Rule: "Do unto others as you would have them do unto you."

Regarding e-mail, one should respond promptly to e-mail messages; think twice before sending personal information and private letters on business systems; not send flame mail (mail written in anger); not send duplicate copies of private e-mail without letting the recipient know who else is getting it; and not send unsolicited mail, such as pyramid schemes, chain letters, and junk mail.

Schools and employers should establish e-mail policies, present them in writing, and have training sessions for all involved. Lack of an e-mail policy creates legal risks. Often, the company is responsible for the e-mail of its employees. Additionally, e-mail is not a secure medium. Many company policy statements say that e-mail is owned or co-owned by the company and that the company has a right to inspect it. The federal Electronic Communication Privacy Act of 1986 prohibits the interception of any wire, oral, or electronic communication, but there is a business exception to the law that allows employers to intercept such communications that are deemed work-related.

Chat room etiquette involves communicating with others over the Internet. The same etiquette used in personal conversation should be observed here. Anonymity does not excuse bad behavior.

INFORMATION-PROCESSING ETHICS AND PORNOGRAPHY

Currently computer pornography means depiction of actual sexual contact (hard-core) and depiction of nudity or lewd exhibition (soft-core). The courts and numerous U.S. statutes concur with the distinction between hard-core and soft-core pornography. Not all pornography meets the legal test for obscenity, however, nor are all depictions of sexual activity deemed pornographic (Albee, 1999). Pornography and obscenity certainly raise a few moral questions: Are pornographic materials morally objectionable or not? Is it right for the state to regulate access to

pornographic material by consenting adults? In all the confusion one point should be made: Pornography degrades human beings.

Feminists consider pornography to be demeaning to women, contributing to their being seen as objects of desire and control for men. Some religious leaders maintain that pornography ought to be banned because it is morally wrong. Meanwhile pornography continues to be a huge force in the social and personal context (Albee, 1999).

CODES OF ETHICS IN INFORMATION PROCESSING

The following guidelines should be considered when developing codes of ethics for schools and businesses:

1. Identify prevailing social values before addressing current issues in the school or workplace. Examples of ethical values important to society might include trustworthiness, responsibility, respect, empathy, fairness, and citizenship.

2. In composing the code of ethics, give examples of behaviors that reflect each value.

3. Have key members of the organization review the code and provide input.

4. Review any rules or values incorporated into the code to assure that they adhere to relevant laws and regulations; this ensures that the school or organization is not breaking any of them.

5. Indicate that all employees are expected to conform to the values stated in the code of ethics.

6. Announce and distribute the new code of ethics to all involved.

7. Update the code at least once a year.

Examples of topics typically addressed in codes of ethics include: dressing appropriately; avoiding illegal drugs; following the instructions of superiors; being reliable and prompt; maintaining confidentiality; not accepting personal gifts from stakeholders; avoiding discrimination based on race, gender, age or sexual orientation; avoiding conflicts of interest; complying with laws and regulations; not using the organization's property for personal use; and reporting illegal or questionable activity (McNamara, 1998).

TEACHING INFORMATION PROCESSING ETHICS

In direct and indirect ways people begin to learn ethical values from birth. While the family and religious institutions are assigned the primary responsibility for ethical education, schools have traditionally been charged with teaching and reinforcing moral values, especially those directly related to school behaviors. Since many of the ethical issues that surround technology deal with school behaviors, they are an appropriate and necessary part of the school curriculum. Schools must create technology environments that help students avoid temptations. Computer screens that are easily monitored, use of passwords, and logging in and out of secure network systems, along with videotaping of lab areas, all help remove the opportunities for technology misuse in the media center or classroom.

Teachers and leaders of student groups who want to promote good ethical behavior can use methods such as creating codes of ethics, using stories of good or bad ethical behavior as examples in discussions, inviting speakers, and using case studies, role playing, games, simulations, and mock trials. Of primary importance is the teacher's or student leader's own behavior, which should be exemplary. Technology privileges should not be given to students until they have demonstrated that they know and can apply ethical standards and school policies.

Finally, measures should be taken to improve the solutions to the ethical dilemmas that arise in information processing. There is a need for more specific professional guidelines and codes of ethics; research on ethical problems; education and training; and cooperation among all who are involved with information-processing ethics, including, but not limited to, theologians, philosophers, computer scientists, educators, business people, and attorneys.

BIBLIOGRAPHY

Albee, Reid D. "Ethical Dimensions: Ethical Considerations of Pornography." http://www.umm.maine.edu/BSED/students/ReidAlbee/ra360.html. 1999.

Johnson, Deborah G. (1994). *Computer Ethics*, 2nd. ed. Englewood Cliffs, NJ: Prentice Hall.

McNamara, Carter. "Complete Guide to Ethics Management: An Ethics Toolkit for Managers." http://www.mapnp.org/library/ethics/ethxgde.htm#anchor41892. 1998.

Pedersen, Christian H. (1996). "Agents Searching Information from Networks." *Magazine of Science.*

"Results of a Survey of Information Systems Professionals in the United States." [1995]. *Computerworld* May 2:p. 1.

Siponen, Mikko T. (1997). "The Applicability of Ethical Theories to Computer Ethics—Selected Issues." Unpublished manuscript.

Siponen, Mikko T., and Kajava, Jorma. "Computer Ethics—The Most Vital Social Aspect of Computing: Some Themes and Issues Concerning Moral and Ethical Problems in Information Technology." http://www.ifi.uio.no/isis20/proceedings/12.htm. 1999.

Vincent, Annette, and Meche, Melanie. (1998). "Knowledge of Ethics Among Teens and Young Adults." *Ethics and Critical Thinking* December:Part 1, Section 4, pp. 1-11.

ANNETTE VINCENT
MELANIE A. MECHE

ETHICS IN LAW FOR BUSINESS

This article deals with ethical problems in law in the context of business operations. A lawyer is professionally qualified to give businesspersons advice on what the law is; judges are authorized to decide what the law is; and legislatures, within the limits of the Constitution, may make the law. Religious organizations and other organizations make many statements about what is ethical, but unless the ethical norms are written into law, they are not enforceable and, to some extent, remain a matter of personal opinion.

This article is intended to raise issues of ethics in law for business that may be discussed and debated. It also provides a framework from Aristotle to aid in the discussion of determining the most ethical course. In each case questions may be asked as follows:

1. What are the ethical choices in making this decision?

2. Does the law require the businessperson to make ethical choices?

3. Should the law require the businessperson to make ethical choices?

WHAT IS LAW?

Law for business consists of a set of required norms of behavior. The essence of law is that it commands behavior under threat of punishment or sanction. Tax law requires the payment of money to the government; there is no choice. Contracts are entered into voluntarily, but once entered into they may be enforced through the courts. Many laws have no particular ethical content. Many laws require ethical behavior, and, in rare cases, some laws may require unethical behavior. Frequently the law allows the businessperson the choice to be either ethical or unethical. In those cases the question arises: Should the law require ethical behavior?

WHAT IS ETHICS?

The Greek word *ethos* means "habit." The Greek philosopher Aristotle taught that the ethical person is one who has virtuous habits. Among the virtues are courage, temperance, honor, good temper, truthfulness and justice. Virtues can be learned through education and practice. Aristotle believed virtue and consequent ethical behavior can be learned. He went on to say that we all seek "the good life," which comes when we live in a society of ethical persons—that is, those who behave virtuously. This philosophy can serve as a model for our discussion. We must decide what the elements of "the good life" are (wealth, security, freedom, opportunity). Next, what in a given business situation would be ethical (virtuous behavior), and does the law require or should the law require ethical behavior? In the following paragraphs areas of business law that have ethical issues are considered. The reader is invited to examine the issues in light of the above ethical model.

CONTRACTS AND ETHICS

Business is about making and selling products and exchanging goods and services. When a contractor orders a load of bricks to build a house and then in turn sells the house or hires a worker, it is a constant process of making and fulfilling contracts. A contract is a promise to do something. It may be to deliver goods, to perform a service (say, to paint a house), or possibly to employ or be employed by another. The very process of business is making and fulfilling contracts. Without contracts, no business would be possible. There are many ethical issues involved in making contracts.

For most legal purposes, a person becomes an adult at age eighteen. Before that, a minor may disaffirm an otherwise legal agreement, a provision that exists to protect minors from abuse by overreaching adults. What should the rights and responsibilities of minors be? What about adults who are mentally incompetent or insane?

What about adults of normal intelligence and capacity? Suppose a loan is made on the following terms: "Here is a loan of $20. You will give me $21 back in a week." This is an interest rate of 5 percent a week, which is 5 percent × 52, or 260 percent a year. This contract is illegal in most states. Suppose a fast-talking but honest salesperson sells goods on credit in the buyer's home. Buyers must be told in writing that they have three days to change their minds. Is this ethical?

Under the law of contract, when a transaction is completed, it is final. Suppose a person buys a set of green towels and then decides a couple of days later that red towels would look better. The store could legally say, "you bought them, there's nothing wrong with them; they are yours." If a sign in the store said "All returns must be made within 30 days," that sign becomes part of the contract. Frequently signs warn "No returns on prom and party dresses." This reinforces what the contract already is. A good return policy is simply good business, but the law leaves the ethics of returns up to the store. What return policy is the most ethical for business?

WARRANTIES

A warranty is part of a business contract. It is essentially a binding promise that the product is fit for its intended purposes, is free of defects, and works. Most products of any complexity come with a "limited warranty," which most commonly warrants parts and labor for one year. Also common these days are the sales of extended warranties that extend the one-year warranty up to three or even five years. This allows manufacturers and sellers to write warranties in almost any fashion. The ethical questions are: To what extent should a company stand behind its products? At what point is it ethically correct for the customer to accept the risk of a defective product?

The way warranties are written can raise ethical problems. In an automobile, tires and batteries wear out and are subject to very limited warranties; however, a modern automobile consists of thousands of parts—any one of which may give out or be defective. Warranty descriptions, even when plainly written, can be confusing as to what is included and what is excluded. What, then, is an ethical automobile warranty?

ADVERTISING

Everyone is aware that there is much criticism of the ethics of advertising. False advertising is against the law, and all would agree it is unethical. Famous cases involve a product that was beneficial in many ways but was falsely claimed to prevent colds. In another case, an aspirin company claimed its aspirin was more effective than others.

If a store advertises "apples—5 pounds for $2.50," it must have a "reasonable quantity" on hand; it is considered good business practice to give "rain checks," but doing so is not legally required. It is also against the law to advertise a product at a very low price with the intention of trying to talk customers into higher-priced products. This is known as "bait and switch."

The law allows what is known as sales "puffery." This is an emphasis on subjective qualities, such as that a car is beautiful and will make you "feel good," or that a high-fat food "tastes good" without mentioning the health risks of excess fat. It is easy to look at advertisements and identify sales puffery and half-truths. What is the ethical line?

It is against the law to advertise illegal products, such as controlled substances. But what about legal products that are harmful? Cigarettes may not now be advertised on television or on billboards. Should the ban be extended to advertising in magazines?

Truthful advertising is part of freedom of speech. What other restrictions, if any, should be part of law? What about advertisements for alcohol?

EMPLOYMENT LAW

Few areas of law mix law and ethics as much as employment law. Surely employment is critical to our welfare and thus is of keen interest and subject to much emotional debate.

Employment-at-Will While government employees and unionized workers enjoy more job protection, most employees in the United States are employed at will. The law allows them to be fired for cause or for no cause. A boss, under the law, may fire even a long-term employee simply because the boss does not like the person. In most other industrialized countries employees, after a probationary period, can be fired only for cause (e.g. they are incompetent or steal company property). American law seems to be less ethical. What arguments can be made for American law?

Employment Discrimination Law The United States made a major commitment to putting ethics into law through the Civil Rights Act of 1964, which forbids employment discrimination based on race, religion, creed, national origin, or sex. Other categories, including age and disability status, have been added since then. Most people agree that the United States had great problems of employment discrimination and that today, despite substantial progress, many problems remain. There are many ethical questions. Virtually everyone would agree that it is unethical to discriminate both because it is wrong and because it violates the law. Should the law compel businesses to be ethical and not discriminate?

Jobs Overseas Since almost everyone agrees the American civil rights laws serve an ethical purpose, should American business voluntarily implement these laws as policy in their operations in foreign countries that do not have similar laws?

Wages are substantially lower in many countries, such as Mexico, than in the United States. Many companies have moved all or part of their operations to Mexico. The law allows this. What ethical obligation does a company have to American workers who in many cases will not find comparable employment? What do managers ethically owe to workers and what to the shareholders or owners? What, then, are the ethical obligations to potential Mexican workers who may be eager to take the jobs even though the pay, benefits, and protection are well below U.S. standards? This, in fact, is a whole area of ethical discussion. What standards of employment (pay, benefits, job protection) should American companies and consumers demand when we make or buy goods produced in a foreign country?

ENVIRONMENT

Along with civil rights, the environmental movement has been another great crusade. The purpose of environmentalism is to protect the planet not only for ourselves but also for those who come after us. Compliance with environmental law would seem a basic ethical norm. How far should environmental law go? Chemical companies that make products we all use everyday, by the nature of their business, pollute the environment. What is the ethical position of a chemical company in spending money lobbying the public and Congress on new laws and enforcement of existing ones? Automobiles still pollute the atmosphere, although much less than in the past. Gasohol is a motor fuel made in part from ethanol, which is made from corn, but it is more expensive than gasoline. What are the ethical issues surrounding ethanol?

Global warming is an important environmental issue. According to some, our planet is gradually growing warmer due to pollutants. This could end or radically change life on earth. Others say that the earth naturally warms and cools and that there is no evidence to suggest that there has been any significant change because of pollution. What should be the ethical position of citizens, especially companies that stand to either lose or gain by governmental measures taken?

As with civil rights law, many countries have less stringent laws than the United States regarding environmental issues. American companies with operations in these countries can pollute much more than in the United States. It is also an important point that pollution does not respect national borders. What are the ethical norms that a company should consider in making its policy?

CONCLUSIONS

Aristotle said that deciding what is the best ethical course is not easy. Reasonable people will disagree on what is right. This article is intended to raise questions, not to provide answers. Many more issues of ethics in law for business could be considered. The ultimate, overreaching questions are: What is an ethical company and to what extent should law require ethics?

BIBLIOGRAPHY

Bagley, Constance E. (1999). *Managers and the Legal Environment*, 3d ed. St. Paul, MN: West Publishing Company.

Charley, Robert N. (1996). *The Legal and Regulatory Environment of Business*, 10th ed. New York: McGraw Hill.

Cheeseman, Henry R. (1997). *Contemporary Business Law*, 2d ed. Upper Saddle River, NJ: Prentice-Hall.

Mann, Richard A., and Roberts, Barry S. (1999). *Smith and Roberson's Business Law*, 11th ed. St. Paul, MN: West Publishing Company.

McGuire, Charles. (1998). *The Legal Environment of Business*, 3d ed. Dubuque, IA: Kendall/Hunt Publishing Company.

CARSON VARNER

ETHICS IN MANAGEMENT

Managers in today's business world increasingly need to be concerned with two separate but interrelated concerns—business ethics and social responsibility.

BUSINESS ETHICS

Perhaps the most practical approach to view ethics is as a catalyst that causes managers to take socially responsible actions. The movement toward including ethics as a critical part of management education began in the 1970s, grew significantly in the 1980s, and is expected to continue growing. Hence, business ethics is a critical component of business leadership. Ethics can be defined as our concern for good behavior. We feel an obligation to consider not only our own personal well-being but also that of other human beings. This is similar to the precept of the Golden Rule: Do unto others as you would have them do unto you. In business, ethics can be defined as the ability and willingness to reflect on values in the course of the organization's decision-making process, to determine how values and decisions affect the various stakeholder groups, and to establish how managers can use these precepts in day-to-day company operations. Ethical business leaders strive for fairness and justice within the confines of sound management practices.

Many people ask why ethics is such a vital component of management practice. It has been said that it makes good business sense for managers to be ethical. Without being ethical, companies cannot be competitive at either the national or international levels. While ethical management practices may not necessarily be linked to specific indicators of financial profitability, there is no inevitable conflict between ethical practices and a firm's emphasis on making a profit; our system of competition presumes underlying values of truthfulness and fair dealing.

The employment of ethical business practices can enhance overall corporate health in three important areas. The first area is productivity. The employees of a corporation are stakeholders who are affected by management practices. When management considers ethics in its actions toward stakeholders, employees can be positively affected. For example, a corporation may decide that business ethics requires a special effort to ensure the health and welfare of employees. Many corporations have established employee advisory programs (EAPs) to help employees with family, work, financial, or legal problems, or with mental illness or chemical dependency. These programs can be a source of enhanced productivity for a corporation.

A second area in which ethical management practices can enhance corporate health is by positively affecting "outside" stakeholders, such as suppliers and customers. A positive public image can attract customers. For example, a manufacturer of baby products carefully guards its public image as a company that puts customer health and well-being ahead of corporate profits, as exemplified in its code of ethics.

The third area in which ethical management practices can enhance corporate health is in minimizing regulation from government agencies. Where companies are believed to be acting unethically, the public is more likely to put pressure on legislators and other government officials to regulate those businesses or to enforce existing regulations. For example, in 1990 hearings were held on the rise in gasoline and home heating oil prices following Iraq's invasion of Kuwait, in part due to the public perception that oil companies were not behaving ethically.

A CODE OF ETHICS

A code of ethics is a formal statement that acts as a guide for how people within a particular organization should act and make decisions in an ethical fashion. Ninety percent of the *Fortune* 500 firms, and almost half of all other firms, have ethical codes. Codes of ethics commonly address such issues as conflict of interest, behavior toward competitors, privacy of information, gift giving, and making political contributions. According to a recent survey, the development and distribution of a code of ethics within an organization is perceived as an effective and efficient means of encouraging ethical practices within organizations (Ross, 1988).

Business leaders cannot assume, however, that merely because they have developed and distributed a code of ethics an organization's members have all the guidelines needed to determine what is ethical and will act accordingly. There is no way that all situations that involve ethical decision making an organization can be addressed in a code. Codes of ethics must be monitored continually to determine whether they are comprehensive and usable guidelines for making ethical business decisions. Managers should view codes of ethics as tools that must be evaluated and refined in order to more effectively encourage ethical practices.

CREATING AN ETHICAL WORKPLACE

Business managers in most organizations commonly strive to encourage ethical practices not only to ensure moral conduct but also to gain whatever business advantage there may be in having potential consumers and employees regard the company as ethical. Creating, distributing, and continually improving a company's code of ethics is one usual step managers can take to establish an ethical workplace.

Another step managers can take is to create a special office or department with the responsibility of ensuring ethical practices within the organization. For example, management at a major supplier of missile systems and aircraft components has established a corporate ethics office. This ethics office is a tangible sign to all employees that management is serious about encouraging ethical practices within the company.

Another way to promote ethics in the workplace is to provide the work force with appropriate training. Several companies conduct training programs aimed at encouraging ethical practices within their organizations. Such programs do not attempt to teach what is moral or ethical but, rather, to give business managers criteria they can use to help determine how ethical a certain action might be. Managers then can feel confident that a potential action will be con-

sidered ethical by the general public if it is consistent with one or more of the following standards:

1. *The Golden Rule*: Act in a way you would want others to act toward you.

2. *The utilitarian principle*: Act in a way that results in the greatest good for the greatest number.

3. *Kant's categorical imperative*: Act in such a way that the action taken under the circumstances could be a universal law, or rule, of behavior.

4. *The professional ethic*: Take actions that would be viewed as proper by a disinterested panel of professional peers.

5. *The TV test*: Always ask, "Would I feel comfortable explaining to a national TV audience why I took this action?"

6. *The legal test*: Ask whether the proposed action or decision is legal. Established laws are generally considered minimum standards for ethics.

7. *The four-way test*: Ask whether you can answer "yes" to the following questions as they relate to the decision: Is the decision truthful? Is it fair to all concerned? Will it build goodwill and better friendships? Will it be beneficial to all concerned?

Finally, managers can take responsibility for creating and sustaining conditions in which people are likely to behave ethically and for minimizing conditions in which people might be tempted to behave unethically. Two practices that commonly inspire unethical behavior in organizations are giving unusually high rewards for good performance and unusually severe punishments for poor performance. By eliminating such factors, managers can reduce much of the pressure that people feel to perform unethically. They can also promote the social responsibility of the organization.

SOCIAL RESPONSIBILITY

The term *social responsibility* means different things to different people. Generally, corporate social responsibility is the obligation to take action that protects and improves the welfare of society as a whole as well as organizational interests. According to the concept of corporate social responsibility, a manager must strive to achieve both organizational and societal goals. Current perspectives regarding the fundamentals of social responsibility of businesses are listed and discussed through (1) the Davis model of corporate social responsibility, (2) areas of corporate social responsibility, and (3) varying opinions on social responsibility.

A model of corporate social responsibility developed by Keith Davis (1975) provides five propositions that describe why and how businesses should adhere to the obligation to take action that protects and improves the welfare of society and the organization:

> *Proposition 1*: Social responsibility arises from social power.
>
> *Proposition 2*: Business shall operate as an open system, with open receipt of inputs from society and open disclosure of its operation to the public.
>
> *Proposition 3*: The social costs and benefits of an activity, product, or service shall be thoroughly calculated and considered in deciding whether to proceed with it.
>
> *Proposition 4*: Social costs related to each activity, product, or service shall be passed on to the consumer.
>
> *Proposition 5*: Business institutions, as citizens, have the responsibility to become involved in certain social problems that are outside their normal areas of operation (pp. 20-23).

The areas in which business can become involved to protect and improve the welfare of society are numerous and diverse. Some of the most publicized of these areas are urban affairs, consumer affairs, environmental affairs, and employment practices. Although numerous businesses are involved in socially responsible activities, much controversy persists about whether such involvement is necessary or appropriate.

There are several arguments for and against businesses performing socially responsible activities.

The best-known argument supporting such activities is that because business is a subset of and exerts a significant impact on society, it has the responsibility to help improve society. Since society asks no more and no less of any of its members, why should business be exempt from such responsibility? Additionally, profitability and growth go hand in hand with responsible treatment of employees, customers, and the community. However, studies have not indicated any clear relationship between corporate social responsibility and profitability (Aupperle, Caroll, and Hatfield, 1985; McGuire, Sundgren, and Schneeweis, 1988).

One of the better known arguments against such activities is advanced by the distinguished economist Milton Friedman. Friedman (1989) argues that making business managers simultaneously responsible to business owners for reaching profit objectives and to society for enhancing societal welfare represents a conflict of interest that has the potential to cause the demise of business. According to Friedman, this demise almost certainly will occur if business continually is forced to perform socially responsible behavior that is in direct conflict with private organizational objectives. He also argues that to require business managers to pursue socially responsible objectives may be unethical, since it requires managers to spend money that really belongs to other individuals.

Regardless of which argument or combination of arguments particular managers might support, they generally should make a concerted effort to perform all legally required socially responsible activities, consider voluntarily performing socially responsible activities beyond those legally required, and inform all relevant individuals of the extent to which their organization will become involved in performing socially responsible activities.

Federal law requires that businesses perform certain socially responsible activities. In fact, several government agencies have been established to develop such business-related legislation and to make sure the laws are followed. The Environmental Protection Agency has the authority to require businesses to adhere to certain socially responsible environmental standards. Adherence to legislated social responsibilities represents the minimum standard of socially responsible performance that business leaders must achieve. Managers must ask themselves, however, how far beyond the minimum they should attempt to go—a difficult and complicated question that entails assessing the positive and negative outcomes of performing socially responsible activities. Only those activities that contribute to the business's success while contributing to the welfare of society should be undertaken.

Social Responsiveness Social responsiveness is the degree of effectiveness and efficiency an organization displays in pursuing its social responsibilities. The greater the degree of effectiveness and efficiency, the more socially responsive the organization is said to be. The socially responsive organization that is both effective and efficient meets its social responsibilities without wasting organizational resources in the process. Determining exactly which social responsibilities an organization should pursue and then deciding how to pursue them are perhaps the two most critical decision-making aspects of maintaining a high level of social responsiveness within an organization. That is, managers must decide whether their organization should undertake the activities on its own or acquire the help of outsiders with more expertise in the area.

In addition to decision making, various approaches to meeting social obligations are another determinant of an organization's level of social responsiveness. A desirable and socially responsive approach to meeting social obligations involves the following:

- Incorporating social goals into the annual planning process
- Seeking comparative industry norms for social programs
- Presenting reports to organization members, the board of directors, and stockholders on progress in social responsibility

- Experimenting with different approaches for measuring social performance
- Attempting to measure the cost of social programs as well as the return on social program investments

S. Prakash Sethi (1975) presents three management approaches to meeting social obligations: (1) the social obligation approach, (2) the social responsibility approach, and (3) the social responsiveness approach. Each of Sethi's three approaches contains behavior that reflects a somewhat different attitude with regard to businesses performing social responsible activities. The social obligation approach, for example, considers business as having primarily economic purposes and confines socially responsible activity mainly to conformance to existing laws The social responsibility approach sees business as having both economic and societal goals. The social responsiveness approach considers business as having both societal and economic goals as well as the obligation to anticipate upcoming social problems and to work actively to prevent their appearance.

Organizations characterized by attitudes and behaviors consistent with the social responsiveness approach generally are more socially responsive than organizations characterized by attitudes and behaviors consistent with either the social responsibility approach or the social obligation approach. Also, organizations characterized by the social responsibility approach generally achieve higher levels of social responsiveness than organizations characterized by the social obligation approach. As one moves from the social obligation approach to the social responsiveness approach, management becomes more proactive. Proactive managers will do what is prudent from a business viewpoint to reduce liabilities whether an action is required by law or not.

Areas of Measurement To be consistent, measurements to gauge organizational progress in reaching socially responsible objectives can be performed. The specific areas in which individual companies actually take such measurements vary, of course, depending on the specific objectives of the companies. All companies, however, probably should take such measurements in at least the following four major areas:

1. *Economic function*: This measurement gives some indication of the economic contribution the organization is making to society.

2. *Quality of life*: The measurement of quality of life should focus on whether the organization is improving or degrading the general quality of life in society.

3. *Social investment*: The measurement of social investment deals with the degree to which the organization is investing both money and human resources to solve community social problems.

4. *Problem solving*: The measurement of problem solving should focus on the degree to which the organization deals with social problems.

The Social Audit: A Progress Report A social audit is the process of taking measurements of social responsibility to assess organizational performance in this area. The basic steps in conducting a social audit are monitoring, measuring, and appraising all aspects of an organization's socially responsible performance. Probably no two organizations conduct and present the results of a social audit in exactly the same way. The social audit is the process of measuring the socially responsible activities of an organization. It monitors, measures, and appraises socially responsible performance.

BIBLIOGRAPHY

Aupperle, K. E., Caroll, A. B., and Hatfield, J. D. (1985). "An Empirical Examination of the Relationship Between Corporate Responsibility and Profitability." *Academy of Management Journal* June:446-463.

Davis, L. (1975). "Five Propositions for Social Responsibility." *Busisiness Horizons* June:19-24.

Friedman, M. (1989). "Freedom and Philanthropy: An Interview with Milton Friedman." *Business and Society Review* Fall:11-18.

McGuire, J. B., Sundgren, A., and Schneeweis, T. (1988). "Corporate Social Responsibility and Firm Financial Performance." *Academy of Management Journal* December:854-872.

Ross, T. (1988). *Ethics in American Business*. New York: Touche Ross and Co.

Sethi, S. P. (1975). "Dimensions of Corporate Social Performance: An Analytical Framework." *California Management Review* Spring:58-64.

THOMAS HAYNES

ETHICS IN MARKETING

Ethics are a collection of principles of right conduct that shape the decisions people or organizations make. Practicing ethics in marketing means deliberately applying standards of fairness, or moral rights and wrongs, to marketing decision making, behavior, and practice in the organization.

In a market economy, a business may be expected to act in what it believes to be its own best interest. The purpose of marketing is to create a competitive advantage. An organization achieves an advantage when it does a better job than its competitors at satisfying the product and service requirements of its target markets. Those organizations that develop a competitive advantage are able to satisfy the needs of both customers and the organization.

As our economic system has become more successful at providing for needs and wants, there has been greater focus on organizations' adhering to ethical values rather than simply providing products. This focus has come about for two reasons. First, when an organization behaves ethically, customers develop more positive attitudes about the firm, its products, and its services. When marketing practices depart from standards that society considers acceptable, the market process becomes less efficient—sometimes it is even interrupted. Not employing ethical marketing practices may lead to dissatisfied customers, bad publicity, a lack of trust, lost business, or, sometimes, legal action. Thus, most organizations are very sensitive to the needs and opinions of their

Tobacco marketing has been the target of government regulation.

customers and look for ways to protect their long-term interests.

Second, ethical abuses frequently lead to pressure (social or government) for institutions to assume greater responsibility for their actions. Since abuses do occur, some people believe that questionable business practices abound. As a result, consumer interest groups, professional asso-

ciations, and self-regulatory groups exert considerable influence on marketing. Calls for social responsibility have also subjected marketing practices to a wide range of federal and state regulations designed to either protect consumer rights or to stimulate trade.

The Federal Trade Commission (FTC) and other federal and state government agencies are charged both with enforcing the laws and creating policies to limit unfair marketing practices. Because regulation cannot be developed to cover every possible abuse, organizations and industry groups often develop codes of ethical conduct or rules for behavior to serve as a guide in decision making. The American Marketing Association, for example, has developed a code of ethics (which can be viewed on its Web site at www.ama.org). Self-regulation not only helps a firm avoid extensive government intervention; it also permits it to better respond to changes in market conditions. An organization's long-term success and profitability depends on this ability to respond.

Several areas of concern in marketing ethics are explored in the remainder of the article.

UNFAIR OR DECEPTIVE MARKETING PRACTICES

Marketing practices are deceptive if customers believe they will get more value from a product or service than they actually receive. Deception, which can take the form of a misrepresentation, omission, or misleading practice, can occur when working with any element of the marketing mix. Because consumers are exposed to great quantities of information about products and firms, they often become skeptical of marketing claims and selling messages and act to protect themselves from being deceived. Thus, when a product or service does not provide expected value, customers will often seek a different source.

Deceptive pricing practices cause customers to believe that the price they pay for some unit of value in a product or service is lower than it really is. The deception might take the form of making false price comparisons, providing misleading suggested selling prices, omitting important conditions of the sale, or making very low price offers available only when other items are purchased as well. Promotion practices are deceptive when the seller intentionally misstates how a product is constructed or performs, fails to disclose information regarding pyramid sales (a sales technique in which a person is recruited into a plan and then expects to make money by recruiting other people), or employs bait-and-switch selling techniques (a technique in which a business offers to sell a product or service, often at a lower price, in order to attract customers who are then encouraged to purchase a more expensive item). False or greatly exaggerated product or service claims are also deceptive. When packages are intentionally mislabeled as to contents, size, weight, or use information, that constitutes deceptive packaging. Selling hazardous or defective products without disclosing the dangers, failing to perform promised services, and not honoring warranty obligations are also considered deception.

OFFENSIVE MATERIALS AND OBJECTIONABLE MARKETING PRACTICES

Marketers control what they say to customers as well as and how and where they say it. When events, television or radio programming, or publications sponsored by a marketer, in addition to products or promotional materials, are perceived as offensive, they often create strong negative reactions. For example, some people find advertising for all products promoting sexual potency to be offensive. Others may be offended when a promotion employs stereotypical images or uses sex as an appeal. This is particularly true when a product is being marketed in other countries, where words and images may carry different meanings than they do in the host country.

When people feel that products or appeals are offensive, they may pressure vendors to stop carrying the product. Thus, all promotional messages must be carefully screened and tested, and communication media, programming, and editorial content selected to match the tastes and interests of targeted customers. Beyond the target audience, however, marketers should understand that there are others who are not customers who might receive their appeals and see their images and be offended.

Direct marketing is also undergoing closer examination. Objectionable practices range from minor irritants, such as the timing and frequency of sales letters or commercials, to those that are offensive or even illegal. Among examples of practices that may raise ethical questions are persistent and high-pressure selling, annoying telemarketing calls, and television commercials that are too long or run too frequently. Marketing appeals created to take advantage of young or inexperienced consumers or senior citizens—including advertisements, sales appeals disguised as contests, junk mail (including electronic mail), and the use and exchange of mailing lists—may also pose ethical questions. In addition to being subject to consumer-protection laws and regulations, the Direct Marketing Association provides a list of voluntary ethical guidelines for companies engaged in direct marketing (available at their Web site at www.the-dma.org).

ETHICAL PRODUCT AND DISTRIBUTION PRACTICES

Several product-related issues raise questions about ethics in marketing, most often concerning the quality of products and services provided. Among the most frequently voiced complaints are ones about products that are unsafe, that are of poor quality in construction or content, that do not contain what is promoted, or that go out of style or become obsolete before they actually need replacing. An organization that markets poor-quality or unsafe products is taking the chance that it will develop a reputation for poor products or service. In addition, it may be putting itself in jeopardy for product claims or legal action. Sometimes, however, frequent changes in product features or performance, such as those that often occur in the computer industry, make previous models of products obsolete. Such changes can be misinterpreted as planned obsolescence.

Ethical questions may also arise in the distribution process. Because sales performance is the most common way in which marketing representatives and sales personnel are evaluated, performance pressures exist that may lead to ethical dilemmas. For example, pressuring vendors to buy more than they need and pushing items that will result in higher commissions are temptations. Exerting influence to cause vendors to reduce display space for competitors' products,

promising shipment when knowing delivery is not possible by the promised date, or paying vendors to carry a firm's product rather than one of its competitors are also unethical.

Research is another area in which ethical issues may arise. Information gathered from research can be important to the successful marketing of products or services. Consumers, however, may view organizations' efforts to gather data from them as invading their privacy. They are resistant to give out personal information that might cause them to become a marketing target or to receive product or sales information. When data about products or consumers are exaggerated to make a selling point, or research questions are written to obtain a specific result, consumers are misled. Without self-imposed ethical standards in the research process, management will likely make decisions based on inaccurate information.

DOES MARKETING OVERFOCUS ON MATERIALISM?

Consumers develop an identity in the marketplace that is shaped both by who they are and by what they see themselves as becoming. There is evidence that the way consumers view themselves influences their purchasing behavior. This identity is often reflected in the brands or products they consume or the way in which they lead their lives.

The proliferation of information about products and services complicates decision making. Sometimes consumer desires to achieve or maintain a certain lifestyle or image results in their purchasing more than they need or can afford. Does marketing create these wants? Clearly, appeals exist that are designed to cause people to purchase more than they need or can afford. Unsolicited offers of credit cards with high limits or high interest rates, advertising appeals touting the psychological benefits of conspicuous consumption, and promotions that seek to stimulate unrecognized needs are often cited as examples of these excesses.

SPECIAL ETHICAL ISSUES IN MARKETING TO CHILDREN

Children are an important marketing target for certain products. Because their knowledge about products, the media, and selling strategies is usually not as well developed as that of adults, children are likely to be more vulnerable to psychological appeals and strong images. Thus, ethical questions sometimes arise when they are exposed to questionable marketing tactics and messages. For example, studies linking relationships between tobacco and alcohol marketing with youth consumption resulted in increased public pressure directly leading to the regulation of marketing for those products.

The proliferation of direct marketing and use of the Internet to market to children also raises ethical issues. Sometimes a few unscrupulous marketers design sites so that children are able to bypass adult supervision or control; sometimes they present objectionable materials to underage consumers or pressure them to buy items or provide credit card numbers. When this happens, it is likely that social pressure and subsequent regulation will result. Likewise, programming for children and youth in the mass media has been under scrutiny for many years.

In the United States, marketing to children is closely controlled. Federal regulations place limits on the types of marketing that can be directed to children, and marketing activities are monitored by the Better Business Bureau, the Federal Trade Commission, consumer and parental groups, and the broadcast networks. These guidelines provide clear direction to marketers.

ETHICAL ISSUES IN MARKETING TO MINORITIES

The United States is a society of ever-increasing diversity. Markets are broken into segments in which people share some similar characteristics. Ethical issues arise when marketing tactics are designed specifically to exploit or manipulate a minority market segment. Offensive practices may take the form of negative or stereotypical representations of minorities, associating the consumption of harmful or questionable products with a particular minority segment, and demeaning portrayals of a race or group. Ethical questions may also arise when high-pressure selling is directed at a group, when higher prices are charged for products sold to minorities, or even when stores provide poorer service in neighborhoods with a high population of minority customers. Such practices will likely result in a bad public image and lost sales for the marketer.

Unlike the legal protections in place to protect children from harmful practices, there have been few efforts to protect minority customers. When targeting minorities, firms must evaluate whether the targeted population is susceptible to appeals because of their minority status. The firm must assess marketing efforts to determine whether ethical behavior would cause them to change their marketing practices.

ETHICAL ISSUES SURROUNDING THE PORTRAYAL OF WOMEN IN MARKETING EFFORTS

As society changes, so do the images of and roles assumed by people, regardless of race, sex, or occupation. Women have been portrayed in a variety of ways over the years. When marketers present those images as overly conventional, formulaic, or oversimplified, people may view them as stereotypical and offensive.

Examples of demeaning stereotypes include those in which women are presented as less intelligent, submissive to or obsessed with men, unable to assume leadership roles or make decisions, or skimpily dressed in order to appeal to the sexual interests of males. Harmful stereotypes include those portraying women as obsessed with their appearance or conforming to some ideal of size, weight, or beauty. When images are considered demeaning or harmful, they will work to the detriment of the organization. Advertisements, in particular, should be evaluated to be sure that the images projected are not offensive.

CONCLUSION

Because marketing decisions often require specialized knowledge, ethical issues are often more complicated than those faced in personal life— and effective decision making requires consistency. Because each business situation is different, and not all decisions are simple, many organizations have embraced ethical codes of conduct and rules of professional ethics to guide managers and employees. However, sometimes self-regulation proves insufficient to protect the interest of customers, organizations, or society. At that point, pressures for regulation and enactment of legislation to protect the interests of all parties in the exchange process will likely occur.

BIBLIOGRAPHY

American Marketing Association. (1998). *American Marketing Association Code of Ethics.* New York: Author.

Barnett, Tim, Bass, Ken, Brown, Frederick, and Hebert, J. (1998). "Ethical Ideology and the Ethical Judgments of Marketing Professionals." *Journal of Business Ethics* May: 715-723.

Berman, Barry, and Evans, Joel R. (1998). *Retail Management: A Strategic Approach,* 7th ed. New York: Prentice Hall.

Bone, Paula F., and Corey, Robert J. (1998). "Moral Reflections in Marketing." *Journal of Macromarketing* Fall: 104-114.

"Federal Trade Commission Deception Policy Statement." http://www.webcom.com.lewrose/deceptionpol.html. 1983.

Ferrell, O. C., Hartline, Michael D., and McDaniel, Stephen W. (1998). "Codes of Ethics Among Corporate Research Departments, Marketing Research Firms, and Data Subcontractors: An Examination of a Three-Communities Metaphor." *Journal of Business Ethics* April: 503-516.

"FTC Guides Against Deceptive Pricing." http://www.ftc.gov/bcp/guides/decptprc.htm. 1998.

Gustafson, Robert, Popovich, Mark, and Thomsen, Steven. (1999). "The 'Thin' Ideal." *Marketing News* March 15: 22.

Jones, Thomas M., and Ryan, Lori V. (1998). "The Effect of Organizational Forces on Individual Morality: Judgment, Moral Approbation, and Behavior." *Business Ethics Quarterly* July: 431-445.

Koehn, Daryl. (1999). "Business Ethics Is Not a Contradiction." *San Antonio Business Journal* 12(49) (January): 38.

Kotler, Philip, and Armstrong, Gary. (1999). *Principles of Marketing,* 8th ed. New York: Prentice-Hall.

Mahoney, Ann I. (1999). "Talking About Ethics." *Association Management* March: 45.

Murphy, Patrick E. (1998). "Ethics in Advertising: Review, Analysis, and Suggestions." *Journal of Public Policy and Marketing* Fall: 316-319.

Murphy, Patrick E. (1999). "Character and Virtue Ethics in International Marketing: An Agenda for Managers, Researchers, and Educators." *Journal of Business Ethics* January: 107-124.

Rallapalli, Kuman C. (1999). "A Paradigm for Development and Promulgation of a Global Code of Marketing Ethics." *Journal of Business Ethics* January: 125-137.

Rieck, Dean. (1998). "Balancing Ethics and Profitability." *Direct Marketing* October: 53-56.

Rose, Gregory M., Bush, Victoria D., and Kahle, Lynn. (1998). "The Influence of Family Communication Patterns on Parental Reactions Toward Advertising: A Cross-National Examination." *Journal of Advertising* Winter: 71-85.

Russell, J. Thomas, and Lane, W. Ronald. (1999). *Kleppner's Advertising Procedure,* 14th ed. New York: Prentice Hall.

Self-Regulatory Guidelines for Children's Advertising. (1997). New York: Children's Advertising Review Unit of the Council of Better Business Bureaus.

Sirgy, M. Joseph, Lee, Dong-Jin, Kosenko, Rustan, and Lee, H. (1998). "Does Television Viewership Play a Role in the Perception of Quality of Life?" *Journal of Advertising* Spring: 125-142.

United States Code, Title 15, Section 45. http://www4.law.cornell.edu/uscode/15/45.text.html.

JOHN A. SWOPE

ETHICS OVERVIEW

Ethics is the study of questions of morality, the search to understand what is right, wrong, good, and bad. It is the branch of philosophy that systematically studies moral ideals and goals, motives of choice, and patterns of good and bad conduct. *Ethics* is derived from the Greek *ethikos,* meaning "character." Issues of personal character, and the search for the best patterns for living, were at the core of Greek ethical philosophy. In contrast, *moral* is from the Latin *more* (MOR-ay). The Romans used this term to describe the customary ways that people tended to act. Thus, though the two terms are often used interchangeably today, *morality* has evolved to mean the social norms that people are taught and conditioned to follow, while ethics has come to refer to

Greek philosopher Socrates was a pioneer in virtue-ethical thinking.

the rational investigating and questioning of these norms. This view of ethics is said to be *normative*, since it assumes the existence of at least some universal moral principles and standards.

Ethics tends to be a cross-disciplinary field of study. Theologians study ethics and morality in light of religious teachings and divine commands. Psychologists seek to understand how people's values influence their thinking, behavioral motivations, and personal development. Sociologists attempt to identify and explain varying cultural norms and practices. Business educators try to help companies, employees, and professionals avoid expensive and counterproductive ethical misdeeds. However, the study of normative ethics has historically been dominated by philosophers, who have applied rules of reason and logic to find answers to humanity's perplexing moral questions.

One apparent obstacle to this process is that logical reasoning, at least at first glance, does not seem to lead different people to the same ethical conclusions and answers. If people, ideally, used reason correctly, what would it tell us about ethics? This search for the best, most logical principles to follow is the realm of general ethics. The end results of this search are *ethical systems* or theories—groups of systematically related ethical principles that attempt to describe and prescribe human morality. Scholars in applied ethics then take these ethical systems and principles and apply them to contemporary moral questions, dilemmas, and life-situations. Examples of specific studies in applied ethics include business, government, and professional ethics (medical, legal, etc.).

RELIGIOUS AND PHILOSOPHICAL ETHICS

Perhaps the greatest continual struggle related to ethics throughout history has been between followers of religious ethics and proponents of philosophical ethics. Religious ethics gives preeminence to divine authority. Actions that conform to the will or teachings of this authority are considered good or right; actions that do not conform are seen as bad, wrong, or evil. It is

believed that people can find or discover this divine will through sacred scriptures, the teachings of religious leaders, prayer, and personal revelation. On the other hand, philosophical ethics places its primary emphasis on rational thought and the rules of logic. This view assumes that individuals can use reason to find answers to moral questions, making religious authority unnecessary.

This conflict can reach critical proportions. Many philosophers who have challenged the religious authorities of their times have been branded as dangerous heretics. Foreshadowing the pattern that would repeat itself for centuries, the central charge leading to the conviction and eventual execution of Socrates was that he questioned the gods of Athens and taught others to do the same. However, it is also worth noting that some of history's most influential ethical thinkers have argued that this perceived conflict between reason and faith may only be illusionary; that faith and reason need not be adversaries, but can support and even validate each other.

ETHICAL SYSTEMS

There have been about as many different philosophical viewpoints on ethics as there have been people thinking about them. But these can be roughly grouped into three main families of ethical systems. The first are *virtue-ethics theories*, founded on the teachings of the three great lights of ancient Greek philosophy—*Socrates* (469-399 B.C.), *Plato* (427?-347? B.C.), and *Aristotle* (384-322 B.C.). Most attempts to chronicle Western ethical thinking begin with these three men because of their emphasis on reason and logic as essential tools for finding answers to ethical questions. This assumption has been the cornerstone of philosophical thinking ever since. The central focus in virtue-ethics is personal character. The ancient Greeks believed it was a mandate from nature itself that the purpose of life for humans was to achieve happiness and fulfillment. The goal of ancient Greek ethics, then, was the search for "the good life," the pattern of specific character traits (virtues) that people should integrate into their lives to make happiness and fulfillment most likely. Plato and Aristotle wrote that the virtues of wisdom, courage, temperance, and justice were the most logical choices to help people achieve this goal.

One evidence of the profound influence of these Greek thinkers is that so many other philosophers have adopted and adapted their approach. *Cicero* (106-43 B.C.), the most well known of the Roman intellectuals, leaned heavily on Aristotle's principles and concepts. The Catholic theologian *Thomas Aquinas* (1225?-1274) took Aristotle's writings about the essential roles of reason and nature in ethics and integrated them with medieval Roman Catholic dogma. In doing so, he helped to usher in the Enlightenment, revolutionizing Catholic thinking and doctrine in ways still evident today. Aquinas's ethical system (*natural law*) remained the most influential view throughout much of the Middle Ages, supported in no small part by the power of the Church. This domination continued until the seventeenth and eighteenth centuries, when philosophers began attempting to restore the preeminence of reason over religious authority, perhaps the most significant event in the development of ethical thinking since the time of Plato.

One early leader was the British philosopher *John Locke* (1632–1704). Locke stretched natural law's tenets to include the assumption that all humans are endowed by nature (or God) with certain basic human rights. This fact gives people a clear moral duty to respect the rights of others. Thus, violating the rights of others becomes the only real moral wrong, and all actions that do not violate the rights of other persons must be ethically permissible. Among the most ardent supporters of Locke's *natural rights* system were the founders of the United States, who viewed his principles and assumptions as the moral bedrock of their new republic. These principles, evident throughout the Declaration of Independence and Constitution, remain at the heart of the American legal system.

The second family of ethical sytems is made up of *deontology* theories. These approaches share the view that ethics should be based primarily on moral duty. This approach is probably best ex-

emplified by the writings of the great German philosopher and writer *Immanuel Kant* (1724–1804). Kant maintained that at the heart of ethics lies the moral duty to obey the dictates of reason. People can know what reason commands through intuition and moral reason. Kant's central ethical principle is the *categorical imperative*, which says that the only moral actions are those consistent with the moral standards that we would want everyone else to follow. For example, Kant argued that lying is always wrong, since no rational person would want lying to become the moral standard for everyone. (Kant recognized no exceptions, arguing that even lying to save a life was immoral.) A corollary to this principle is Kant's *respect for persons*, the maxim that it is always wrong to exploit others. People, he argued, must be treated as ends (goals) in themselves, not merely as means to our own ends.

The third major family of ethical systems comprises the *utilitarian* theories. This approach sees the proper goal of ethics as producing good, pleasure, or happiness. Early proponents of utilitarianism were the British philosophers *Jeremy Bentham* (1748–1832) and *John Stuart Mill* (1806–1873). According to utilitarian reasoning, the morally right (or best) action is the one that produces the greatest possible happiness for the greatest possible number. Thus, behaviors are not always moral or always immoral. Instead morality is based on specific variables unique to each situation. In some situations, lying might produce more overall good than telling the truth (e.g., deceiving a kidnapper to save a child). In other situations, truth would clearly produce more good.

BUSINESS AND PROFESSIONAL CODES OF ETHICS

These classical ethical systems are expressed and affirmed in contemporary society in many ways. Codes of ethics are practical examples. A code of ethics is a written document intended to serve as a guideline to those who would follow it. Most larger businesses and corporations have codes of ethics for their employees, as do most professions for their members. Professional codes are usually written by members of the profession through a central national organization. For example, it is generally understood that American doctors are subject to the American Medical Association code of ethics, and American lawyers follow their bar association codes. But many other professions have codes of ethics as well, including such diverse fields as journalism, pharmacy, business management, education, accounting, engineering, nursing, law enforcement, and psychology. Even the best codes of ethics cannot guarantee ethical behavior. Indeed, many codes do not even contain methods of enforcement, but merely express the ideals and values of their respective corporations and professions. The decision to act ethically or unethically is, as it has been through the ages, up to the individual.

BIBLIOGRAPHY

DeGeorge, Richard T. (1990). *Business Ethics*, 3rd ed. New York: Macmillan.

Frost, S. E., Jr. (1989). *Basic Teachings of the Great Philosophers*. New York: Anchor.

Goree, Keith. (1996). *Ethics in American Life*. Cincinnati, OH: South-Western ITP.

Gorlin, Rena A. (1991). *Codes of Professional Responsibility*, 2nd ed. Washington, DC: Bureau of National Affairs.

Holmes, Robert L. (1993). *Basic Moral Philosophy*. Belmont, CA: Wadsworth.

Peterfreund, Denise. (1992). *Great Traditions in Ethics*, 7th ed. Belmont, CA: Wadsworth.

Richardson, Michael, and Baker, Emily. (1999). *Ethics Applied*, ed. 3.0. New York: Pearson.

Ruggiero, Vincent R. (1992). *Thinking Critically About Ethical Issues*, 3rd ed. Mountain View, CA: Mayfield.

Shaw, William H. (1991). *Business Ethics*. Belmont, CA: Wadsworth.

Wagner, Michael E. (1991). *An Historical Introduction to Moral Philosophy*. Englewood Cliffs, NJ: Prentice-Hall.

KEITH GOREE

EUROPEAN UNION

The European Union is an ever-evolving alliance of fifteen European countries designed to foster economic cooperation among its members. With its roots stretching back to just after World War II, this alliance has the ultimate goal of unifying the economic interests of these countries in order to reduce the chance of widespread armed conflict returning to the European continent.

HISTORY

In the early 1950s, Germany and France spearheaded the establishment of the European Coal and Steel Community. At this time, West Germany was in the process of rebuilding its war-ravaged steel industry under the direction of the United States and Great Britain. This was an understandable source of concern for France, as German industrial might had been used against the French in the two world wars earlier in the century. Consequently, a federation that would govern these important economic resources won the approval of both the French and Germans. They were also joined by Italy, Belgium, Luxembourg, and the Netherlands as the original six founding nations of what would eventually become the European Union.

The European Coal and Steel Community was later followed by the establishment of the European Economic Community under the Treaty of Rome, which was signed by the same six countries in 1957. This treaty established the framework for the six member countries to pursue an economic and monetary union by creating a single market to further their economic development. The European Economic Community established a customs union for removing trade barriers, such as tariffs and quotas, between member countries over a period of several years. Also, common external tariffs were phased in for goods entering the union.

The single market established by the European Economic Community also opened the door for the free movement of workers, businesses, and capital throughout the community. Border stops and customs checks were eliminated, companies expanded across national borders, and financial institutions expanded with them.

Romano Prodi (right), president of the European Union Commission.

THE EURO

To further facilitate trade within this single market, European leaders felt a single currency should be created to eliminate foreign-exchange hurdles encountered by companies doing business across European borders. After several intervening rounds of negotiations and agreements, the Treaty on European Union was signed in Maastricht in December 1991. The European Union was formally established as the successor to the European Economic Community, and the treaty laid the groundwork for the completion of the economic and monetary union by calling for a new European currency.

The European Union introduced this new currency on January 1, 1999, christening it the "euro." Like many other changes implemented by the European Union, the euro was not launched without difficulties. By the time the euro was introduced in 1999, nine more countries had joined the original six members. The European Union had added Denmark, Ireland, and the United Kingdom to its ranks in 1973; Greece in 1981; Portugal and Spain in 1986; and Austria, Finland, and Sweden ratified membership in 1995. During the launch of the euro, the United Kingdom, Sweden, and Denmark all chose to "opt out" of participation due to political pressures in each country. One other member, Greece, failed to satisfy the economic criteria for convergence, which required members of the "euro zone" to meet targets for price stability, long-term interest rates, government budget deficits, and government debt. Consequently, the conversion to the euro was initiated in only eleven of the fifteen member states in 1999.

Transactions in member states beginning in 1999 could be denominated in euros. The actual euro currency and coins will begin circulation in 2002. In the "interim period," transactions can be carried out in either euros or the former national currencies of the member states.

GOVERNANCE

The governance of the European Union is quite complex. The European Commission, based in Brussels, introduces legislation and negotiates all trade agreements between the European Union and other countries. The five largest countries in the union appoint two members and other countries one member to the European Commission. The European Parliament, which is the only elected body, also has legislative and veto authority in some specific areas. The Council of Ministers, comprised of civil servants from each country, acts on the legislation proposed by the European Commission. Most decisions are by a majority vote, but some require unanimity.

Monetary policy in the countries adopting the euro is governed by the European Central Bank. The primary mission of this independent institution is to maintain stable prices. It is also responsible for foreign-exchange operations and managing foreign reserves in the euro zone. Although it is a relatively new currency, the euro has joined the U.S. dollar and Japanese yen as a reserve currency held by central banks.

INTERNATIONAL TRADE

The fifteen members of the European Union in 1999 have a combined population 40 percent larger than that of the United States, creating an attractive business marketplace without internal trade barriers. Many American companies—from Ford, which sells 15 million vehicles a year in Europe, to Coca-Cola, Inc., which serves 209 million of its beverages to European customers every day—have a long-established presence in Europe. Other companies, such as software giant Microsoft, have entered the European market in recent years and been successful in the European Union's single market. If the European Union continues to add new members, it may be only a matter of time before the European marketplace begins to challenge the United States as the premier business market in the world.

European companies, with their enhanced size due to expansion across Europe, have also set their sights across the Atlantic. The purchases of Chrysler by Daimler-Benz and Amoco by British Petroleum in the late 1990s were but two of the many examples of large European companies strengthening their positions in the American marketplace. With the majority of foreign investment in the United States coming from members of the European Union, economic interests have continued to become more intertwined as multinational companies now operate on both sides of the Atlantic.

FUTURE EXPANSION

In the future, the size of the European Union will likely expand because numerous other countries, primarily in Central and Eastern Europe, have expressed an interest in joining the union. Many of these countries are in the process of making the structural changes needed to meet the criteria for membership in the European Union. Admitting these countries would add to the European Union's stature in global trade negotiations, further the cause of social stability in the region, and add yet another chapter to the story of this dynamic union.

BIBLIOGRAPHY

Dinan, Desmond, ed. (1998). *Encyclopedia of the European Union.* (1998). Boulder, CO: Lynne Rienner.

How Does the European Union Work?, 2d ed. (1998). Luxembourg: Office for Official Publications of the European Communities.

Leonard, R. L. (1998). The Economist *Guide to the European Union.* London: The Economist in association with Profile.

Redmond, John, and Rosenthal, Glenda G., eds. (1998). *The Expanding European Union: Past, Present, Future.* Boulder, CO: Lynne Rienner.

DAVID MCGRADY

EXECUTIVE COMPENSATION

(SEE: *Employee Compensation*)

EXPECTANCY THEORY

(SEE: *Motivation*)

EXPORT-IMPORT BANK

(SEE: *Financial Institutions; International Trade*)

EXPORTS

(SEE: *International Trade*)

F

FACSIMILE REPRODUCTION

Facsimile reproduction means making an exact copy of anything imprinted on paper by using electronic devices such as copiers, fax machines, and scanners. Material may be reproduced electronically on a computer's monitor (soft copy), or reproduced on paper (hard copy). In reproducing information either electronically or on paper, one wants a quality copy that will be acceptable for the task at hand.

HISTORICAL PERSPECTIVE

The first method used to make a printed copy was carbon paper. Although a Britain named J. W. Swan invented carbon tissue paper coated with gelatin about 1862, it didn't come into general use for office work until the mid-1920s. It provided a somewhat less than perfect copy of typed material. At that time one could choose between very messy carbon paper that made several copies or single-use carbon paper that was much easier to use. The first reverberations of the death knell for carbon paper occurred in 1937 when Chester Carlson invented the xerography process of duplication.

In the late 1890s the mimeograph machine began to be used to produce copies. This process involved typing on a lightly oiled surface called a "master," which involved retyping a preexisting original—a very time-consuming process. As time passed, however, the mimeograph machine was improved enough to permit masters to be reused if stored properly.

In 1906 the Haloid Company was founded to sell photographic paper for its early version of today's copier. This early piece of reprographic equipment was hardly an office tool—it was very expensive, very cumbersome, and very difficult to use. Trained operators were scarce.

In 1913 Edouard Belin invented the Belinograph, a portable facsimile machine capable of using ordinary telephone lines.

In the 1920s, the Gestetner office duplicating machine was considered to be one of the first modern examples of efficient industrial design.

In 1937 an electrostatic copying process known as "xerography" was invented by an American law student named Chester Carlson. This process, which involved the effect of light on photoconductivity, led to the unprecedented success of the "Xerox" commercial copy machine, introduced in 1959. The major problem with this copier was that it was heat-sensitive and resulted in paper scorching.

After World War II, 3M and Eastman Kodak introduced the Thermo-Fax and verifax copiers into the workplace. The copies were of poor quality and continued to darken long after having been pulled from the machine. Although these office machines were relatively inexpensive and easy to use, they required special paper that was extremely expensive.

Chester Carlson invented the xerography process.

As computer use continued to develop, additional copying methods such as fax, Ditto, and Mimeograph appeared.

In 1971 dot-matrix printers were introduced, providing a reasonably efficient way to reproduce computer-generated information on paper.

In 1974 the first international fax standard was set by the United Nations, allowing for fax messages to be transmitted at a rate of one page every six minutes. Special paper was required for these early fax machines. Today's fax equipment will accept either special fax paper of a greatly-improved quality or plain paper. In 1990 facsimile machines (commonly called fax machines) that could transmit in color became available.

In 1975 IBM introduced the first laser printer. Using light lasers in the process of copying greatly improved both the process and the product.

Today's evolving technology provides reprographic-related equipment. Scanners are used in conjunction with digital cameras to reproduce pictures, sounds, and other images electronically and on paper.

COPIERS TODAY

Today's copiers are advancing rapidly, consistent with continuing advances in technology. Although using a copier today is a simple process, choosing one is not. Training is required, along with knowledge of what is best in an individual situation. Cost is a major factor in determining the most appropriate copier to use, as is the type of material that is to be reproduced.

COPIER FEATURES

Copiers are sold by a variety of vendors who offer an array of products to meet individual needs. When selecting a copier for possible lease or purchase, individual features and individual needs should be studied and matched carefully. Doing so can save time and money in the long run.

Copy Speed: The number of copies that can be produced in a minute is an important feature. Most copiers can make from twelve to fifty copies per minute, depending on the model. Most of today's copiers are also capable of creating trans-

parencies, address labels, and letterheads. However, the quality of paper is important because poor-quality paper can cause jamming.

Paper Trays: Only specified amounts of paper can be loaded at one time into today's copiers. Paper can be loaded from the front using either a specified tray or a "bypass" tray. A bypass tray permits two-sided copies or copies on special paper stock or paper sizes to be made by programming the size individually.

Enlargement Options: Copiers today often come with a choice of preset enlargement ratios. For example, one copier's enlargement ratios are preset at 65, 77, 129, and 155 percent. Other models allow one to reduce or enlarge from 65 to 165 percent in 1 percent increments. This feature can save time and money if one has predetermined the common enlargement needs and preset the ratio to assist in copying.

Book Copying: Copiers with a book-copying feature allow copying from books or bound documents without distortion of copy.

Sorting: Copiers are available that can sort with a variety of bin configurations. As paper moves through the copier, it can be sorted into a bin and then stacked, collated, and stapled. This option can save immense time.

Control Panel and Servicing: The easy-to-read control panels on today's copiers permit copying decisions to be made easily. Copiers are often designed with a front opening that allows unobstructed access for easy servicing, including changing toner for the copier. An increasing number of copiers are now designed so that they use toner cartridges, a feature that eliminates messy, time-consuming toner changes.

COPIER COSTS

The cost of a copier is determined by the model selected and the options desired. Prices range from a few hundred dollars to more than $100,000. One modern copier has a suggested list price of $120,000 for the standard configuration and $137,500 for a model equipped with additional options. These options include digital service capabilities such as permitting taking of a photo, putting it on a scanner, bringing it up on the computer and sending out copies.

The Xerox 5800 is suited for use in general office copy rooms, an application encouraged by its user-friendly touch-screen control panel. Additional trays are available that automatically combine a variety of different paper stocks, including full-color offset pages, color covers, specialty stocks, mylar tabs, and heat-sensitive materials in a single document.

It also includes an exclusive computer-based service capability called Xerox Sixth Sense. This remote service system uses leading-edge communications technology and specially developed software to enable rapid diagnosis and resolution of equipment service needs. A copier of this type is truly state of the art.

SCANNERS

A scanner is a small machine that makes a photocopy of virtually any printed matter or illustration and stores it in a computer.

Scanners have a wide variety of applications. For personal use, for example, they can be used for copying photographs and sending them to friends and relatives over the Internet.

Businesses make extensive use of scanners. They are used in doctors' and dentists' offices to photocopy patients' health insurance data for storage in their computer. Manufacturers may use a scanner to store copies of technical matter in a computer for later retrieval. Lecturers may use scanners not only to provide illustrations for brochures advertising their appearance but also to enhance overhead transparencies they may use during their lectures. People who use communications a great deal in their work find scanners invaluable in enriching the e-mails they transmit.

Selection of a scanner should involve consideration of the ease of placing the image into the user's application. One begins the operation of some scanners by merely pressing a button; others require drawing a box around a preliminary scan. Some scanners automatically make the correct setting by recognizing the difference between a photograph and printed material; others require the setting to be done by the operator.

Some scanners automatically select the correct file type for the software program being used; others must have this procedure handled by the operator.

Image quality is another criterion to be studied when selecting a scanner. It is important to have good resolution and bit-depth. But additional factors are large lenses, good optics, and strong light sources. Some scanners have automatic functions that bring these good results; others require considerable adjustments or rescanning of the image.

Image quality can also be observed in color line art. Some scanners leave uneven color line-art halftones; others correct automatically for such a deficiency. In working with black-and-white line art, some scanners bring about perfect edges automatically. Other scanners must resort to rescanning.

Another factor to take into consideration when purchasing a scanner is the manufacturer. What is the manufacturer's reputation? If a question arises about a scanner, it is easy to get a satisfactory answer quickly from technical support? And is prompt service available in the event of a problem?

Finally, thought must be given to resolution. It is not true that the larger the number of dots per inch (dpi), the higher the quality of the image. Rather, the dpi must be appropriate for the scanning project. Most scanning projects require less than 300 dpi. If you could scan an image at 9600 dpi, only a small portion would show on a computer monitor.

Judging a scanner involves studying its ease of operation, the quality of the image, the reputation of the manufacturer, and the resolution of the image.

BIBLIOGRAPHY

"Carbons to Computers." www.educate.si.edu/scitech/carbons/copiers/.html. March 3, 1999.

"HP Scanjet Scanners, Hewlett Packard." www.scanjet.com/products/shoppinglist.html. March 15, 1999.

DOROTHY MAXWELL

FACTORS OF PRODUCTION

Land, labor, capital, and entrepreneurship: These are four generally recognized factors of production. Of course, in a literal sense anything contributing to the productive process is a factor of production. However, economists seek to classify all inputs into a few broad categories, so standard usage refers to the categories themselves as factors. Before the twentieth century, only three factors making up the "classical triad" were recognized: land, labor, and capital. Entrepreneurship is a fairly recent addition.

The factor concept is used to construct models illustrating general features of the economic process without getting caught up in inessential details. These include models purporting to explain growth, value, choice of production method, income distribution, and social classes. A major conceptual application is in the theory of production functions. One intuitive basis for the classification of the factors of production is the manner of payment for their services: rent for land, wages for labor, interest for capital, and profit for entrepreneurship. A discussion of each of the factors follows.

LAND

This category sometimes extends over all natural resources. It is intended to represent the contribution to production of nonhuman resources as found in their original, unimproved form.

For the French physiocrats led by Francois Quesnay in the 1750s and 1760s, land was the only factor yielding a reliable gain to its owner. In their view, laborers and artisans were powerless and in excess supply, and hence they earned on average only a subsistence-level income; and in the same way what they produced outside of agriculture fetched enough to cover only their wages and input costs with no margin for profit. Only in agriculture, due to soil fertility and other "gifts of nature," could a laborer palpably produce more than required to cover subsistence and other costs, so only in agriculture could proprietors collect surplus. Thus the physiocrats explained land rent as coming from surplus pro-

Joseph Schumpeter contrasted the entrepreneur from the capitalist.

duced by the land. They recommended taxes on land as the only sound way to raise revenue and land-grabbing as the best means to increase the government's revenue base.

In 1821 David Ricardo, in *The Principles of Political Economy and Taxation*, stated what came to be known as the classical view: that rent reflects scarcity of good land. The value of a crop depends on the labor required to produce it on the worst land under cultivation. This worst land yields no rent—as long as some of it remains unused—and rent collected on better land is simply its yield in excess of that on the worst land. Ricardo saw rent as coming from differences in land quality (including accessibility) and scarcity. The classical economists assumed only land—understood as natural resources—could be scarce in the long term.

Marginalism, as expounded in 1899 by John Bates Clark in *The Distribution of Wealth*, takes a different approach. It declares that rent reflects the marginal productivity of land—not, as with

Ricardo, the productivity of good versus marginal land. Marginal productivity is the extra output obtained by extending a *constant* amount of labor and capital over an *additional* unit of land of uniform quality. Marginalists held that any factor of production could be scarce. Their theory is based on the possibility of substituting among factors to design alternative production methods, whereby the optimal production method allocates all the factors to equalize their marginal productivity with their marginal costs.

Long thought of as a self-sustaining input, land might depreciate just like produced assets do. In 1989 Herman Daly and Jonathan Cobb, in *For the Common Good*, distinguished between nonrenewable resources that are consumed or depreciate irretrievably, and renewable resources where the rate of natural renewal is important. One consequence of this work in environmental economics is that natural resource accounting increasingly resembles capital accounting.

LABOR

The classical "labor theory of value" was an innovative theory in response to the physiocratic doctrine that only land could yield surplus. In 1776 Adam Smith, in *The Wealth of Nations*, observed that with expansion of production and trade, enterprises were making profits over long periods of time, although they either had nothing to do with agriculture or else as agricultural enterprises. Classical economists tried to answer the question: Where does profit come from? Their answer was that it came from labor. At prevailing prices, labor can yield a surplus over subsistence costs in many industries.

The question arises of why proprietors, but not laborers, earn profit. Ricardo arrived at one answer: Technical innovation increases labor productivity. Owners of innovative equipment, until its general adoption, get the premium from reduced costs. In 1867 Karl Marx in *Capital*, added that wages reflect the cost of subsistence, not what laborers can produce, and that profit is the difference between the two. Even without innovation proprietors would reap surpluses,

Marx held, since laborers lack market power and cannot afford their own equipment.

Why do wages differ for different types of labor? Marx's answer was that higher wages cover costs, beyond personal subsistence, of training and cultivation of skills, acknowledging that one kind of "equipment," now known as human capital, was available at least to some laborers.

Marginalist economists noticed the advance of technology, which according to classical and Marxist views made labor ever more productive, continually throws laborers out of work. This led them to attribute productivity to equipment rather than only to labor. Referring to equipment as capital, they developed production functions featuring labor and capital as substitutes for each other. Choice among production techniques involving different combinations of labor and capital became a major theme in marginalist growth theory.

CAPITAL

This most controversial of factors is variously defined as produced equipment; as finance used to acquire produced equipment; as all finance used to begin and carry on production, including the "wage fund"; and as the assessed value of the whole productive enterprise, including intangibles such as "goodwill." In 1960 Piero Sraffa, in *Production of Commodities by Means of Commodities*, showed that capital in the sense of produced equipment can fail to behave as expected in marginalist production functions when an entire economy is modeled. Specifically, equipment adopted to replace labor after wages rise from a low level, relative to interest on capital, may be abandoned again in favor of labor as wages rise still higher. This counterintuitive "reswitching" can happen because the equipment used is itself a product of labor and equipment, and because the ratio of labor to equipment varies for different products.

Frequently capital is treated as finance, associated with the payment of interest. Yet the connection with equipment, in spite of Sraffa's demonstration, has never been severed entirely. One still studies capital depreciation, distinguishing wear-and-tear from obsolescence, and from the present value of investments in capital. Increasingly, theory has come to treat any investment as a capital investment. Furthermore, acquired skills (as opposed to "know-how," an attribute of society rather than individuals) have come to be viewed as analogous to physical equipment, capable of yielding their owners a return. This analogy suggests their current designation as human capital. Thus capital is a concept still mired in confusion, and care must be taken in its use to be sure what it means.

ENTREPRENEURSHIP

Until the twentieth century, this function was assigned to the capitalist and frequently conflated with capital. In the classical view, profit rather than interest was attributed to ownership of capital. In the marginalist view, capital earned interest, and profit was a mere residual after all the factors of production were compensated. In his *Principles of Economics*, first published in 1890, Alfred Marshall made extensive references to "organization" and "management," referring to the coordination function of entrepreneurship but to neither risk-assuming nor innovation. But in 1912 Joseph Schumpeter, in *The Theory of Economic Development*, featured the revolutionary role of organizer and innovator and contrasted it with that of the conservative financier, thus vividly distinguishing the entrepreneur from the capitalist. The entrepreneur's role in this view is not merely that of manager and risk-taker, but also of visionary—someone who seeks as much to destroy the old order as to create something new. Since innovation usually requires destroying old ways of doing things, Schumpeter gave it the name "creative destruction." Profit is now assigned to entrepreneurship, to innovation. With the rise of "venture capitalists" and other financiers willing to take on more risk and do more for innovation in the hope for supernormal returns, the distinction between capitalist and entrepreneur has again become fuzzier. Now there are entrepreneurial financiers as well as entrepreneurial producers and distributors.

Although in business usage stock dividends are distributed profits, in economic analysis they figure as returns to capital, a kind of interest payment, since they are a return to finance rather than to entrepreneurship. The fact that stocks are legally equity rather than debt shares is thereby ignored. Similarly, salaries of corporate executive officers are treated as profit, a return to entrepreneurship, rather than as wages for labor services.

BIBLIOGRAPHY

Clark, John Bates (1899/1966). *The Distribution of Wealth.* Clifton, NJ: Augustus M. Kelley.

Daly, Herman E., and Cobb, Jonathan. (1989). *For the Common Good: Redirecting the Economy Toward Community, the Environment, and a Sustainable Future.* Boston: Beacon Press.

Marshall, Alfred. (1920). *Principles of Economics.* New York: Macmillan.

Marx, Karl. (1867/1977). *Capital,* vol. I. New York: Vintage Books.

Ricardo, David. (1821/1965). *The Principles of Political Economy and Taxation.* London: Everyman's Library.

Schumpeter, Joseph. (1934/1912). *The Theory of Economic Development.* Cambridge, Mass.: Harvard University Press.

Schumpeter, Joseph. (1954). *History of Economic Analysis.* New York: Oxford University Press.

Smith, Adam. (1776/1965). *An Inquiry into the Nature and Causes of the Wealth of Nations.* New York: Modern Library.

Sraffa, Piero. (1960/1963). *Production of Commodities by Means of Commodities.* London: Cambridge University Press.

MICHAEL BRUN

FADS

The Hula Hoop, Pet Rock, and Cabbage Patch Kid were all crazes known as fads. These products, like most fads, entered the market quickly, created a consumer obsession, sold millions of units in a short amount of time, and declined just as rapidly. Their special product life cycle of quick, dramatic sales and a sharp, drastic decline differs from the five stage product life cycle con-

Hula Hoopers enjoy one of the current fads of their day.

cept of product development, introduction, growth, maturity, and decline. Fads have a limited following and tend to die quickly because they do not satisfy a strong consumer need.

THE PRODUCT LIFE CYCLE

The course that a product's sales and profits take over its lifetime is the product life cycle (PLC).

Marketers know that all products will have some type of life cycle, but the shape and length is not known in advance. In the first stage of the cycle, *product development*, an idea for a product is formulated and development of the product begins. During this stage sales are zero, consumer research begins, and promotion consists of public relations.

The next stage, *introduction*, is characterized by a period of slow sales growth, but no profits are made because of the high initial investment and promotional costs. The company begins to inform consumers about the product through advertising, and distribution of the product is selective.

The third stage of the PLC, *growth*, is a time of rapid market acceptance and increasing profits. Product distribution becomes more widespread, and advertising shifts from being informative to being persuasive. Realizing the opportunity for profit, competitors will enter the market, creating market expansion. Promotional spending remains the same or increases slightly. Prices may be lowered during the growth stage to attract new customers.

The fourth stage of the PLC, *maturity*, is a period of slow sales growth and leveling-off or declining profits. Most potential buyers have been reached, so no new customers are buying the product. This stage presents the greatest challenges to marketers. To prevent entering the decline stage, research and development departments may make product modifications to meet the changing needs of consumers, distribution becomes selective again, and advertising becomes competitive because of the number of competitors who have entered the market.

Sales slow and profits drop in the *decline* stage, usually because of advances in technology, a shift in consumer taste, or increased competition. Distribution becomes exclusive, and sales promotions are developed. Products in the decline stage should have their sales, market share, costs, and profit trends regularly reviewed so that managers can decide whether to maintain the product, harvest the product (reduce various costs associated with the product), or drop the product from the product line. Now let's examine and discuss the product life cycle of fads.

THE PRODUCT LIFE CYCLE OF FADS

The Hula Hoop has been called the "greatest fad of them all." Developed in 1957 by Wham-O creators Richard Knerr and Arthur "Spud" Melin, it was modeled after an Australian toy. A prototype was developed and tested on U.S. playgrounds and was found to have the longest "play value." After only four months on the market, 25 million Hula Hoops had been sold. In less than a year, sales had almost completely stopped and competition was increasing, so Wham-O entered foreign markets and its success continued. Collectively, toy manufacturers made $45 million off the Hula Hoop.

The life cycle of the Hula Hoop was not typical of most products. A prototype was developed and tested during the product development stage, but the Hula Hoop bypassed the introduction stage and, with rapid sales, the toy quickly entered the growth stage. Again, the Hula Hoop skipped the maturity stage and went directly into the decline stage, with sales coming to an almost immediate halt. Other fads' life cycles have followed this model.

Gary Dahl created the Pet Rock in the 1970s, complaining that dogs, cats, and other pets were too messy, misbehaved, and expensive. Instead, Dahl had a pet rock that was easy to care for and cheap; it also had a great personality. Dahl wrote the *Pet Rock Training Manual* and created the Pet Rock out of a Rosarita Beach Stone that cost him a penny. In October 1975, Dahl packaged the Pet Rock in a gift box shaped like a pet carrying case, included the training manual, and sold it for $3.95. Within a few months, Dahl had sold a million rocks and became an instant millionaire. By the next February, sales had stopped.

Unlike the Hula Hoop, the Pet Rock was not tested during the product development stage. Dahl had the idea for the product and quickly produced it with no market testing. Similar to the Hula Hoop, the Pet Rock caught on quickly with consumers, reached its life-cycle peak at the growth stage, and dipped down into the decline stage in a very short period of time.

Artist Xaiver Roberts created Cabbage Patch Kids, originally called "Little People," in 1977. The cloth doll was "delivered" at BabyLand General Hospital, a former medical clinic in Cleveland, Georgia, where Roberts had his employees dress in white nurses' and doctors' uniforms.

Sales of the dolls were termed "adoptions," and each doll came with a birth certificate and adoption papers. Roberts sold 250,000 dolls at prices ranging from $125 to $1000. National Cabbage Patch mania struck when Roberts signed a contract with Coleco in 1982, and $25 models started selling all over the United States. Approximately 2.5 million Cabbage Patch Kids were sold in the first year on the market. But, like the fads before it, the Cabbage Patch Kid had lost its dominating position in the market by 1985.

The Cabbage Patch Kid had a standard product development stage, but its introduction stage was short. Shortly after hitting the toy store shelves, sales skyrocketed and the product entered the growth stage with full force. It entered the maturity stage when sales starting leveling off and the supply was greater than the demand. In an effort to prevent the product from entering the decline stage, marketers at Coleco experimented with product extensions—but to no avail. Eventually, profits began to drop and the Cabbage Patch Kid fell into the decline stage. Figure 1 shows the product life cycle of fads.

Fads are generally mysterious both to their creators and to the public. Although their products were unique, Wham-O, Dahl, and Roberts had no idea they would experience such rapid success. Past fads have included the Rubik Cube, Beanie Babies, and Furbee. Most fads never really completely die, but they never regain their initial popularity. To understand consumer obsessions with fads, marketers must understand consumer buying behavior.

CONSUMER BUYING BEHAVIOR

There are four types of buying behavior: complex buying behavior, dissonance-reducing buying behavior, habitual buying behavior, and variety-seeking buying behavior. Complex buying behavior occurs when the consumer is purchasing something expensive or risky, such as a personal computer. The consumer must learn about the product line, is highly involved in the buying process, and perceives significant differences among brands. Marketers must differentiate their products' features from other brands. Disso-

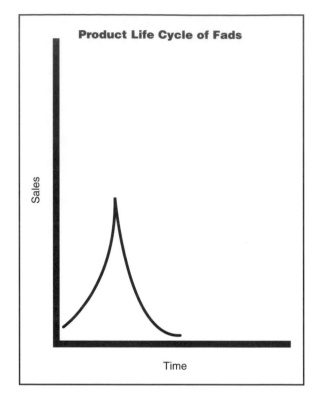

Figure 1

nance-reducing buying behavior occurs when an expensive or risky purchase is being made, but the consumer perceives no difference in brands. They may purchase the brand that offers the best price or that is the most convenient to buy. Habitual buying behavior involves low consumer involvement and little concern for brand differences. Variety-seeking buying behavior is characterized by low consumer involvement but significant differences in brands. Consumers displaying this type of buying behavior often switch brands to experience variety rather than because of dissatisfaction.

Fad purchasers display variety-seeking buying behavior. Buyers of Beanie Babies are loyal to the Ty brand; they will not buy competing brands. Many consumers who buy Beanie Babies switch to the next craze when it hits the shelves. PokeMon became the latest fad in 2000, and the variety-seekers shifted again to this latest trend. Until consumer demands and obsessions cease to exist, fads are here to stay.

BIBLIOGRAPHY

Armstrong, Gary and Kotler, Philip. (1999). *Principles of Marketing*. 8th ed. Upper Saddle River, NJ: Prentice-Hall.

Baig, Edward C. (1983). "The Billion-Dollar Cabbage Patch in Cleveland, Georgia." *Fortune* December 26: 108.

Friedrich, Otto. (1983). "The Strange Cabbage Patch Craze; Troubled Coleco is Cashing in Big On the Year's Hottest Toy." *Time* December 12: 122.

Rakstis, Ted J. (1985). "Cabbage Patch Takes Sudden Sales Plunge." *Playthings* June: 83.

JENNIFER L. JENNESS

FAIR PACKAGING AND LABELING ACT OF 1966

Many consumer problems have been, and in some instances still are, caused by incorrect and even fraudulent information disclosure on products and through advertising. The Fair Packaging and Labeling Act of 1966 was passed during the Johnson administration to ensure that consumers have the information they need to choose wisely among competing products. The act directs businesses to disclose necessary information truthfully. Product labels must include such basic information as ingredients and contents, quantity, and maker of the product. Therefore, any business engaged in producing and distributing consumer products must comply with the Fair Packaging and Labeling Act of 1966. This act comes under the consumer-protection charge of the Federal Trade Commission, which bears the primary responsibility for making sure that labeling is not false and misleading. Textiles and food products are two examples of products regulated under this act, which not only prevents consumer deception but also provides consumers with the opportunity to compare value.

Amendments to the Fair Labeling and Packaging Act of 1966, passed in 1992 and enforced beginning in 1994, require labels to include conversion of quantities into a metric measurement in addition to the customary U.S. system of weights and measures. There was a great deal of opposition to this act from both private and public-sector manufacturers that sold their products only in the United States. For example, some paint manufacturers said that labeling contents in pints and gallons should be sufficient since their paint was sold only in the United States. The minimum federal penalty for not including metric measurements was established at $10,000. State regulators have the authority to remove products from store shelves if they were not compliant with the established guidelines.

Under the Bush administration, the Nutrition Labeling and Education Act of 1990 was passed, which requires detailed information on labels and standardized descriptive phrases such as "low fat" and "light." Manufacturers had to comply with this act by 1994. Since the passage of the Nutrition Labeling and Education Act, people are better satisfied with the information printed on food and drug labels (Kristal et al., 1998). While manufacturers were initially opposed to the new nutrition labeling, mainly because of cost, it was predicted that consumer health benefits would exceed the cost.

In 1993 the Food and Drug Administration issued additional regulations to the Nutrition Labeling and Education Act, stating that restaurant menus must comply with regulations for nutrient and health claims that appear on signs, placecards, and menus. The rule was finalized in 1996, establishing criteria under which restaurants must provide nutrition information for menu items. Thus healthier or "low-fat" menu choices must be highlighted with claims such as "no more than 5 grams of fat per serving." Restaurants are getting excellent customer response—better than expected—to providing healthy food choices. Consumers today are demanding higher quality. Fair labeling and packaging help assure consumers that they are getting the high quality they are demanding.

BIBLIOGRAPHY

Kristal, A. R., Levy, L., et al. (1998). "Trends in Food Use Associated with New Labeling Regulations." *American Journal of Public Health* 88(8):1212-1216.

Kurtzweil, P. (1997). "Today's Special Nutrition Information." *FDA Consumer* 31(4):21-26.

Litvan, L. M. (1994). "Sizing Up Metric Labeling Rules." *Nation's Business* 82(11):62.

PHYLLIS BUNN

FEDERAL RESERVE SYSTEM

To promote the development of a sound economy and a reliable banking system, Congress passed, and President Woodrow Wilson signed, the Federal Reserve Act on December 23, 1913. The act was a response to the recurring bank failures and financial panics that had plagued the nation.

After much disagreement, but eventual compromise, all parties to the discussions—the government, banks, other financial institutions, and a few business and labor leaders—agreed that a central U.S. bank was essential for the economic health of the country. Starting with the goal of stabilizing the nation's monetary and financial system, the Federal Reserves System (Commonly called the Fed) has undertaken a number of responsibilities that are described later in this article.

STRUCTURE OF THE SYSTEM

Designed by Congress and subject to congressional authority, the Fed is a politically independent and financially self-sufficient federal agency. It consists of the following components:

1. A central bank, sometimes called the government's bank, located in Washington, D. C.

2. Twelve regional Reserve Banks, located in the following cities: Atlanta, Boston, Chicago, Cleveland, Dallas, Kansas City, Minneapolis, New York, Philadelphia, Richmond, San Francisco, and St. Louis. Each Reserve Bank relies on advisory groups for information and suggestions. Some of the more important ones concern operations, small business and agriculture, and thrift institutions (savings banks, savings and loan associations, and credit unions). Reserve Bank officials also meet periodically to discuss mutual problems. These groups include the Conference of Presidents, the Conference of First Vice Presidents, the Conference of Chairmen, and the Financial Services Policy Committee.

3. Twenty-five branch banks, located within defined areas of the Reserve Banks. For example, branch banks within the San Francisco Reserve Bank area are located in Los Angeles, Portland (Oregon), Salt Lake City, and Seattle.

4. Member banks, located throughout the country. Some are national banks (all of which are commercial banks) chartered by the federal government and, by law, are members of the Fed. Others are state commercial banks that have chosen to be members. Of the more than 9000 commercial banks in the country, more than 3700 are members of the Fed. Other depository institutions, including nonmember commercial banks and thrift institutions, are subject to many of the Fed's rules and regulations. A member bank is required to purchase stock from its Reserve Bank in an amount equal to 3 percent of its combined capital and surplus. However, this investment does not represent control of or a financial interest in the Reserve Bank. In return for its investment, however, a member bank receives a 6 percent annual dividend and the right to vote in elections of directors of its Reserve Bank.

GOVERNANCE OF THE SYSTEM

These are three basic components in the governance structure of the Fed:

1. The Fed's primary policy-making group is the seven-member Board of Governors. Appointed by the president and confirmed by the Senate, members serve for one fourteen-year term only. A member who is appointed to fill an unexpired term may be appointed for an additional

The Federal Reserve building.

full term. From among the seven members, the Board's chairman and vice chairman are also appointed and confirmed by the president and the Senate for four-year terms.

2. There are three advisory groups that aid the Board of Governors:

   a. Federal Advisory Council, consisting of one member from each Reserve Bank. Its major concerns involve banking and economic issues.

   b. Consumer Advisory Council, consisting of thirty specialists in consumer and financial matters.

   c. Thrift Institutions Advisory Council, consisting of people representing thrift institutions. This Council is concerned with issues affecting those institutions.

3. The Federal Open Market Committee (FOMC) consists of the seven-member Board of Governors, the New York Federal Reserve Bank president, and an additional four Reserve Bank presidents who serve on a one-year rotating basis. By tradition, the Committee elects the Board of Governors chairman as its chairman and the New York Reserve Bank president as its vice chairman. Although all twelve Reserve Bank presidents attend the FOMC's eight-times-a-year formal meetings, only the Board, the New York Reserve Bank president, and the four rotating presidents are voting members.

ACTIVITIES AND RESPONSIBILITIES OF THE FEDERAL RESERVE SYSTEM

In conjunction with the FOMC and the twelve Reserve Banks, the Board of Governors' main concern is the development of monetary policy, which it carries out through three means:

1. The establishment of reserve-level rates; that is, amounts that member banks must

Woodrow Wilson created the Federal Reserve.

set aside to be reserved against deposits. These amounts depend on the nation's economic activity status, with emphasis placed on price levels and the volume of business and consumer expenditures. By the lowering of the required reserve-level rate, banks can increase the proportion of funds they are able to lend to customers. By raising the required reserve-level rate, the opposite effect takes place. Thus, the Fed can influence such factors as economic activities, the money supply, interest rates, credit availability, and prices. However, a change in a reserve-level rate usually causes banks to change their strategic plans. In addition, a reserve-level rate increase is costly to banks. Consequently, changes in reserve-level rates are uncommon.

2. The approval of discount rates (interest rates at which member banks may borrow short-term funds from their Reserve Bank). When inflation threatens, a discount-rate increase tends to dampen economic activity because then banks charge higher interest rates to borrowers. On the other hand, a discount-rate decrease is designed to stimulate business activity. The term "discount window" is often used when describing a Reserve Bank facility that extends credit to a member bank.

Another rate, the federal funds rate, is an important factor affecting day-to-day bank operations. This is the rate charged by one depository institution to another for the overnight loan of funds. This happens when one bank is short of funds while another has a surplus. The rate is not fixed; it may change from day to day and from bank to bank.

3. Open-market operations (the purchase and sale of U.S. government securities in the open market). These activities are conducted by the FOMC, of which the Board of Governors comprises the majority. The Fed buys and sells U.S. government securities such as Treasury bills from banks and others several times a week. As a result, the amounts banks have available to lend to borrowers are affected. For example, when the Fed buys securities, banks have more funds, so interest rates tend to drop. The opposite occurs when the Fed sells its securities. By and large, open-market operations comprise the most powerful tool the Fed has to influence monetary policy.

Other activities and responsibilities of the Federal Reserve System include the following:

1. Supervision of the twelve Reserve Banks and their branches. With regard to the latter, the Board of Governors, through the Reserve Banks, uses both on- and off-site examinations to maintain awareness of each member bank's activities. These activities include the quality of loans, capital levels, and the availability of cash.

2. Cooperative efforts of the U.S. Treasury and the Fed. For example, the Fed acts as the Treasury's fiscal agent by putting paper money and coins into circulation, handling Treasury securities, and maintaining a checking account for the Treasury's receipts and payments.

3. Oversight of banking organizations, such as bank holding companies (companies that own or control one or more banks).

4. Provision of an efficient payments system; for example, check collections and electronic transactions. With billions of checks in circulation each year, the Fed plays a major role in assuring their efficient processing. By arrangements among the Reserve Banks, member banks and nonmember banks, checks are credited or debited (added to or subtracted from) to depositors' accounts speedily and accurately. Electronic methods are being used increasingly to transfer funds (and securities, too). One such method, involving very large sums, is called "Fedwire." Another is the Automated Clearinghouse (ACH), which is used by the government, businesses, and individuals for the receipt or payment of recurring items, such as Social Security.

5. Enforcement of consumer credit protection laws. These laws include the Community Reinvestment Act, which promotes community credit needs; the Equal Credit Opportunity Act, which prohibits discrimination in credit transactions on the basis of marital status, race, sex, and so forth; the Fair Credit Reporting Act, which allows consumers access to their credit records for the purpose of correcting errors; and the Truth in Lending Act, which enables consumers to determine the true amount they are paying for credit.

6. Establishment of banking rules and regulations.

7. Determination of margin requirements (the amount of credit granted investors for the purchase of securities, such as shares of stock). The borrowed funds are usually secured from a bank or a brokerage firm (a company that sells stocks and/or bonds). Margin requirements that are too liberal can damage the stock market and the economy.

8. Approval or disapproval of applications for bank mergers (two or more banks joining together to form one new bank). The Fed also acts if the new bank is to become a state member bank of the Federal Reserve System.

9. Approval and supervision of the Edge Act (named for Senator Walter Edge of New Jersey) and "agreement corporations." Both cases involve corporations that are chartered to engage in international banking. Edge Act corporations are chartered by the Fed, while "agreement corporations" secure their charters from the states. The latter are so named because they must agree to conform to activities permitted to Edge Act corporations. The Fed is also responsible for approving and regulating foreign branches of member banks and for developing policies regarding foreign lending by member banks.

10. Issuance and redemption of U.S. savings bonds. Regardless of how the bonds are purchased—for example, through an employer savings plan or a bank—it is the Fed that processes the applications and sends the bonds.

SUMMARY

Since it holds substantial U.S. government securities, the Federal Reserve System earns sufficient interest to operate without government appropriations. Consequently, it is both a financially self-sufficient and politically independent agency that exerts great influence on the nation's economy. It bolsters domestic consumer confidence and is a major player in global economic activities.

(SEE ALSO: *Financial Institutions*)

BIBLIOGRAPHY

Federal Reserve System. http://www/federalreserve.gov. *Federal Reserve System Structure and Functions.* (1992). Atlanta: Federal Reserve Bank of Atlanta.

Feinman, Joshua N. (June 1993). "Reserve Requirements: History, Current Practice, and Potential Reform." *Federal Reserve Bulletin* 79:569-589.

The Federal Reserve System: Purposes and Functions. (1994) Washington, DC: Board of Governors of the Federal Reserve System.

MELVIN MORGENSTEIN

FEDERAL TRADE COMMISSION ACT OF 1914

The Federal Trade Commission Act of 1914 prohibits unfair methods, acts, and practices of competition in interstate commerce. It also created the Federal Trade Commission, a bipartisan commission of five presidential appointees, confirmed by the Senate, to police violations of the act. The Federal Trade Commission's (FTC) function is to counter deceptive acts and practices and anticompetitive behavior by businesses. The FTC enforces the Clayton and Federal Trade Commission Acts as well as a number of other antitrust and consumer-protection laws. The FTC's rulemaking authority enables it to issue rules interpreting the antitrust laws that govern either all members of industry or apply to specific business practices. When a rule is violated, the FTC can initiate civil proceedings in a federal district court to obtain injunctive relief and civil damages.

The FTC (and the provisions of the antitrust acts that preceded it) promotes free and fair trade competition by investigating and preventing violations of the law. Key areas covered by the Federal Trade Commission Act of 1914, as well as other antitrust laws, include the following:

Price fixing: There are two types of price fixing: vertical and horizontal. Vertical price fixing occurs when manufacturers make express or implied agreements with their customers obligating them to resell at a price dictated by the manufacturer. Manufacturers can suggest retail prices but not fix them by agreement. Few sellers are caught vertically fixing prices; instead, they intimidate retailers by cutting off sales (Garman, 1997). Horizontal price fixing occurs when competitors make direct agreements about the quantity of goods that will be produced, offered for sale, or bought. According to Garman (1997), in one case, an agreement by major oil refiners to purchase and store the excess production of small independent refiners was found to be illegal because the purpose of the agreement was to affect the market price for gasoline by artificially limiting the availability of supply. The government can take action, civil and/or criminal, in cases of price fixing.

Unfair competition: The FTC and antitrust policies that preceded it are in agreement on concepts of unfair competition. Examples of unfair competition are larger businesses using their size or market power to gain lower prices from suppliers or a manufacturer granting discounts for the same products sold to larger firms without granting similar discounts to smaller businesses when selling costs do not vary.

Merger prohibition: A merger is the acquisition of one company by another. The FTC established guidelines and criteria that challenge mergers that lessen competition. The judgment of the courts is that a restraint of trade occurring through a merger must be undue and unreasonable before it is held illegal.

Deceptive practices: False advertising is one example of deceptive practice. The FTC considers an advertisement deceptive if it contains misrepresentation or omission that is likely to mislead consumers acting reasonably under the circumstances to their detriment.

Even though there are differences of opinion as to the effectiveness of antitrust policy, everyone—consumers, competitors, and prospective business owners—benefits from a more competitive economy. Thus, antitrust policy is an important element in public policy regarding business. Unfortunately, there are limits to what is accomplished mainly because the amount of funds provided by Congress for antitrust issues has a significant impact on enforcement. One case, such as the 1999 Microsoft case, can make a major dent in the FTC budget.

(SEE ALSO: *Antitrust Legislation*)

BIBLIOGRAPHY

Garman E. T. (1997). *Consumer Economics Issues in America*, 5th ed. Houston, TX: DAME Publications.

Meier, K. J., Garman, E. T., and Keiser, L. R. (1998). *Regulation and Consumer Protection: Politics, Bureaucracy and Economics*, 3d ed. Houston, TX: DAME Publications.

PHYLLIS BUNN

FEEDBACK

(SEE: *Operations Management*)

FINANCE

Corporate or *Business Finance* is basically the methodology of allocating financial resources, with a financial value, in an optimal manner to maximize the wealth of a business enterprise. There are three major decisions to be made in this allocation process: capital budgeting, financing, and dividend policy. *Capital budgeting* is the decision regarding the choice of which investments are to be made with the resources that have been brought into the business or earned and retained by the business. The choice depends on the returns to be made from the investment exceeding the cost of capital. The method used to

do this is the discounted time-value of money of the cash flow from the investment. This value is the *internal rate of return (IRR)*, a measure of return on investment. When the IRR exceeds the required return, which is equal to the cost of the funds invested—see *weighted average cost of capital*, below—then the investment should be made. If such a required return is used as the *discount rate*, then that is the same as saying the investment will yield a positive *net present value (NPV)*. If there are two or more investments that can be made, but they are mutually exclusive, then they must be ranked; and the one with the highest NPV should be chosen. If there is a limited amount of funds to be invested, then some bankers or advisers who obtain additional funds for a business may require that the business choose among the investments so as not to exceed the limited level of funds available. This selection process, which is called *capital rationing*, should be done in a similar manner to rank the projects by selecting the combination of investments that do not exceed the total funds available and that yield the maximum total net present value.

Financing is the decision of which resources or funds are to be brought into the business from external investors and creditors in order to be invested in profitable projects. The first external source of finance is *debt*, which includes *loans* from banks and *bonds* purchased by bondholders. The debt creditors take less risk of nonrepayment because the business must repay them if there are funds available to do so when the debt becomes due. The second external source of finance is *equity*, which includes *common stock* and *preferred stock*. The equity investors in the business take more business risk and may not receive payment until the creditors are repaid and the management of the business decides to distribute funds back to the investors. The goal of the financing decision is to obtain all the resources necessary, to make all the investments that yield a return in excess of the cost of the funds invested or the required rate of return, and to obtain these funds at the lowest average cost, so as to reduce the required rate of return and increase the net present value of the projects selected.

Dividend policy is the decision regarding funds to be distributed or returned to the equity investors. This can be done with *common stock dividends, preferred stock dividends,* or *stock repurchase* by the business of its own stock. The aim of this decision is to retain the resources in the business that are required to run the business or make additional investments in the business, as long as the returns earned exceed the required return. In theory, management should return or distribute all resources that cannot be invested in the business at levels in excess of the required return. In practice, however, dividends are often maintained at or changed to certain levels in order to convey the proper signals to the investors and the financial markets. For example, dividends can be maintained at moderate levels to demonstrate stability, maintained at or reduced to low levels to demonstrate the growth opportunities for the business, or increased to higher levels to demonstrate the restoration of a strong financial (capital) structure (debt and equity capital) for the business.

Capital is the total of financial resources invested in the business. In terms of the sources, there are two types of capital: *interest-bearing debt* funds, such as loans, bonds, short-term notes, and interest-bearing payables to trade suppliers; and *equity,* such as common and preferred stock and the earnings retained in the business that add to stockholders' share of the entities. In terms of uses, there are also two types of capital: *net working capital,* such as operating cash, inventory, and receivables, less interest-free payables to trade suppliers; and *fixed capital,* such as property, plant and equipment. Capital is managed to maximize wealth by maximizing the rates of return on investments of capital and thus maximizing the total net present value of the business. This can be done by minimizing the amount of capital used for given business investments with given business returns.

Weighted average cost of capital is the weighted average of the returns on investment or future dividends for the stockholders and interest rates on debt for the creditors. This average return should be used as the required return for investments, as mentioned earlier, because it represents the weighted average of the required returns of all the different debt creditors and equity investors. It also represents the weighted average of the costs that can be saved by the business if the resources or financial funds are returned to the creditors and investors instead of being used for investments within the business.

Capital structure is represented by the types of sources of capital funds invested in the business. A common measure of sources is the percentage of debt relative to equity that appears on a company's balance sheet. Usually, the cost or required returns for the debt is much less than the equity, especially on an after-tax basis. Thus, the total cost of capital declines when some debt funds from creditors are substituted for equity funds from investors. Yet as more debt is added, the business becomes riskier because of the higher amount of fixed payments that must be made to creditors, whether or not the business is generating adequate funds from earnings; and then the costs of both the debt and equity funds are increased to the point where the weighted-average cost increases.

Acquisitions, which are purchases of other businesses, are merely another type of capital budgeting investment for a business. Such purchases should be evaluated in the same manner as any other capital investment, as outlined earlier, to obtain the maximum positive net present value, though the issues and data are often more complex to analyze.

Price/earnings ratio is often used in making acquisitions as an abbreviated measure of valuation. This ratio is of the value or price of a business or its stock to its earnings. Yet the actual decision to make an acquisition is a capital budgeting decision; the resultant determination of price or net present value can then be described in relative terms to the earnings in the price/earnings ratio.

Returns for any business or particular debt or investment made in the business are merely the cash flows that will ultimately be earned by the business or particular creditors and stockholders. These can be expressed in dollar terms or as percentages, with the latter being the average annual percentage of the cash flows relative to the overall investment in the business or the particular amounts of debt or stock involved. For debt instruments, these percentage rates are called *interest rates*. For specific investment decisions, the returns used should be those that are incremental of the specific investment.

Return/interest rates are based on three components: *pure return* for the investor or creditor providing funds; coverage of *inflation rates*, so that the purchasing power of the proceeds is maintained apart from the true return; and additional return for additional *risk*, such as an equity investment in a risky business as opposed to a bond from the U.S. government. These components are then compounded with each other, rather than merely added together, to obtain the overall interest rate or required return on equity investment. When calculating return or interest rates, any additional up-front money, such as closing costs, must also be added to the investment; this amount increases or reduces the return, depending on who pays for it.

Residual values are a portion of the returns to be earned in an investment that is returned to the business when the investment is sold or the project is terminated. This can be most important in the liquidation of inventory and receivables when operations of a portion of a business are terminated or when real estate ceases to be required and thus can be sold, for example, when a factory is closed or when a lease term is complete.

Maturities of debt instruments, such as bonds, loans, or notes payable, are the amounts of time outstanding before the debt becomes due. The financial management rule with respect to maturities is to match the duration of the funds being borrowed by the debtor, or invested by the creditor, with the timing of his or her own business needs for funds in the future. Thus, the financing of a new business—with the likely future expansions of property, plant, equipment, inventory, and receivables—can be done with

longer-term debt funds. Yet the financing of a specific shorter-term need, such as the outlays on a construction project before completion payments are made, should be comparably shorter in maturity. Similarly, the investment of temporary excess cash should be in shorter-term instruments, such as short-term CDs or Treasury bills. If maturities are not matched, then the additional time before the debt becomes due from or to you becomes a period of speculation on the rise or fall of future interest rates.

International finance is concerned with the same methodology of allocating financial resources, but with modifications or areas of emphasis required by the restrictions of currency and capital movements among countries and the differences in the currencies used in different countries. The following paragraphs represent some of the major changes to the basic financial decisions:

1. *Foreign capital budgeting* requires the use of foreign cash flows and local tax rates, but U.S. inflation rates and U.S. dollars at the current exchange rates can be used. The required return or cost of capital then need only be adjusted, as with any investment, for the greater or lesser risk of the project in which the investment is made, which includes the greater or lesser risk of the country in which the investment is being made.

2. *Foreign capital markets* are a source for both debt and equity funds, for both foreign subsidiary operations and the general needs of the overall business. *Foreign subsidiary capital structures* often utilize more local debt when legally and practically available in order to reduce the risk of blockages of earned funds from repatriation to the parent company in another country. In addition, local-currency debt reduces the risk for the parent company if the exchange rates for the local currency change adversely.

3. *Foreign-exchange* rates can change dramatically and therefore pose a significant

risk for the value of assets held in or future payments from foreign countries. These exposures may be in dealings with third parties or within a company's own foreign subsidiaries. *Forward currency contracts* or *currency options*, instruments used to purchase one currency for another currency in the future at guaranteed exchange rates, can be used to protect against such risk. While these contracts are often also used to make profits by managers who believe the exchange rates will change in a manner different from the expectations implicit in the overall currency market, such use should be viewed as risky speculation.

4. *Personal finance* is concerned with the same methodology of allocating resources, but with a greater emphasis on allocating some of them to obtain the maximum consumption satisfaction at the lowest cost, as opposed to earning income and cash flow returns on the investments.

5. *Budgeting* and *financial planning* are the processes used by financial managers to forecast future financial results for a business, a person, or a particular investment. Usually, the major components of earnings, cash flow, and capital are projected in the form of *forecasted income statements, cash-flow statements*, and *balance sheets*. The latter show where the capital funds are invested in the components of fixed and working capital, as well as the sources of these capital funds in terms of the debt, stock, and retained earnings.

ISSUES IN APPLIED CORPORATE FINANCE AND VALUATION

Estimation of the Cost of Capital. In recent decades, theoretical breakthroughs in such areas as portfolio diversification, market efficiency, and asset pricing have converged into compelling recommendations about the cost of capital to a corporation. The cost of capital is central to modern finance, touching on investment and di-

vestment decisions, measure of economic profit, performance appraisal, and incentive systems. Each year in the United States, corporations undertake more than $500 billion in expenditures, so how firms estimate the cost is not a trivial matter. A key insight from finance theory is that any use of capital imposes an opportunity cost on investors; namely, funds are diverted from earning a return on the next-best equal risk investment. Since investors have access to a host of financial market opportunities, corporate use of capital must be benchmarked against these capital market alternatives. The cost of capital provides this benchmark. Unless a firm can earn in excess of its cost of capital, it will not create economic profit or value for investors. A recent survey of leading practitioners reported the following best practices:

- Discounted cash flow (DCF) is the dominant investment-evaluation technique.
- Weighted average cost of capital (WACC) is the dominant discount rate used in DCF analyses.
- Weights are based on market, not book, value mixes of debt and equity.
- The after-tax cost of debt is predominantly based on marginal pretax costs, as well as marginal or statutory tax rates.
- The capital asset pricing model (CAPM) is the dominant model for estimating the cost of equity.

Discounted cash flow valuation models. The parameters that make up the DCF model are related to risk (the required rate of return) and the return itself. These models use three alternative cash-flow measures: dividends, accounting earnings, and free cash flows. Just as DCF and asset-based valuation models are equivalent under the assumption of perfect markets, dividends, earnings, and free cash-flow measures can be shown to yield equivalent results. Their implementation, however, is not straightforward. First, there is inherent difficulty in defining the cash flows used in these models. Which cash flows and to whom do they flow? Conceptually, cash flows are defined differently depending on whether the valuation objective is the firm's equity or the value of the firm's debt plus equity. Assuming that we can define cash flows, we are left with another issue. The models need future cash flows as inputs. How is the cash-flow stream estimated from present data? More important, are current and past dividends, earnings, or cash flows the best indicators of that stream? These pragmatic issues determine which model should be used. Although the dividend model is easy to use, it presents a conceptual dilemma. Finance theory says that dividend policy is irrelevant. The model, however, requires forecasting dividends to infinity or making terminal value assumptions. Firms that presently do not pay dividends are a case in point. Such firms are not valueless. In fact, high-growth firms often pay no dividends, since they reinvest all funds available to them. When firm value is estimated using a dividend discount model, it depends on the dividend level of the firm after its growth stabilizes. Future dividends depend on the earnings stream the firm will be able to generate. Thus, the firm's expected future earnings are fundamental to such a valuation. Similarly, for a firm paying dividends, the level of dividends may be a discretionary choice of management that is restricted by available earnings. When dividends are not paid out, value accumulates within the firm in the form of reinvested earnings. Alternatively, firms sometimes pay dividends right up to bankruptcy. Thus, dividends may say more about the allocation of earnings to different claimants than valuation. All three DCF approaches rely on a measure of cash flows to the suppliers of capital (debt and equity) to the firm. They differ only in the choice of measurement, with the dividend approach measuring the cash flows directly and the others arriving at them in an indirect manner. The free cash-flow approach arrives at the cash-flow measure (if the firm is all-equity) by subtracting investment from operating cash flows, whereas the earnings approach expresses dividends indirectly as a fraction of earnings.

The capital asset pricing model. This is a set of predictions concerning equilibrium expected returns on risky assets. Harry Markowitz estab-

lished the foundation of modern portfolio theory in 1952. The CAPM was developed twelve years later in articles by William Sharpe, John Lintner, and Jan Mossin. Almost always referred to as CAPM, it is a centerpiece of modern financial economics. The model gives us a precise prediction of the relationship that we should observe between the risk of an asset and its expected return. This relationship serves two vital functions. First, it provides a benchmark rate of return for evaluating possible investments. For example, if we are analyzing securities, we might be interested in whether the expected return we forecast for a stock is more or less than its "fair" return given its risk. Second, the model helps us to make an educated guess as to the expected return on assets that have not yet been traded in the marketplace. For example, how do we price an initial public offering of stock? How will a new investment project affect the return investors require on a company's stock? Although the CAPM does not fully withstand empirical tests, it is widely used because of the insight it offers and because its accuracy suffices for many important applications. Although the CAPM is a quite complex model, it can be reduced to five simple ideas:

- Investors can eliminate some risk (unsystematic risk) by diversifying across many regions and sectors.

- Some risk (systematic risk), such as that of global recession, cannot be eliminated through diversification. So even a basket with all of the stocks in the stock market will still be risky.

- People must be rewarded for investing in such a risky basket by earning returns above those that they can get on safer assets.

- The rewards on a specific investment depend only on the extent to which it affects the market basket's risk.

- Conveniently, that contribution to the market basket's risk can be captured by a single measure—"beta"—that expresses the relationship between the investment's risk and the market's risk.

Finance theory is evolving in response to innovative products and strategies devised in the financial market-place and in academic research centers.

(SEE ALSO: *Financial Institutions; Financial Markets; Securities and Exchange Commission*)

BIBLIOGRAPHY

Bodie, Zvi, Kane, Alex, and Marcus, Alan J. (1999). *Investments.* New York: Irwin-McGraw-Hill.

Bruner, Robert F. (1998). *Case Studies in Finance: Managing for Corporate Value Creation,* New York: Irwin McGraw-Hill.

Bruner, Robert F. and Eades, Kenneth M., Harris, Robert S., and Higgins, Robert C. (1998). "Best Practices" in Estimating the Cost of Capital: Survey and Synthesis." *Journal of Financial Practice and Education* Spring.

Kaushik, Surendra K., and Krackov, Lawrence M. (1989). *Multinational Financial Management.* New York: New York Institute of Finance.

Krackov, Lawrence M., and Kaushik, Surendra K. (1988). *The Practical Financial Manager.* New York: New York Institute of Finance.

Stein, Jeremy. (1996). "Rational Capital Budgeting in an Irrational World." *The Journal of Business* (October).

White, Gerald I., Sondhi, Ashwinpaul C., and Fried, Dov. (1998). *The Analysis and Use of Financial Statements.* New York: Wiley.

SURENDRA K. KAUSHIK
LAWRENCE M. KRACKOV
MASSIMO SANTICCHIA

FINANCE: HISTORICAL PERSPECTIVES

Corporate finance, which is the acquisition and use of funds by business entities, has evolved as the scope of business enterprises has changed and as American society has become increasingly successful in achieving its economic goals. The history of finance in the United States is a story that began with rudimentary, unregulated means of securing funds in the early years of the newly established nation and reached in the closing decades of the twentieth century, a level of advanced innovation that made the United States the financial leader in the global community. The success of the finance function in corporate America is the result of a combination of business innovation in the design and strategies of securing funds and of governmental regulations that assure integrity in financial markets. Significant aspects in this development are discussed in the sections that follow.

EARLY AMERICAN FINANCE

In the colonial United States, businesses were, for the most part, small and self-financed. However, the first settlers, who had been British subjects, were well acquainted with the corporate form of organization. As Davis (1917) noted, "before the end of the colonial period a considerable number of truly private corporations had been established for ecclesiastical, education, charitable, and even business purposes" (p. 4).

Many of these early efforts were unsuccessful, and those individuals who invested in them often lost their total contributions. The nature of financing problems in these early efforts is illustrated by the story of an organization called *The Society for Establishing Useful Manufacturers.* In November 1791, the legislature of New Jersey passed an act incorporating this enterprise, which likely manufactured various products including paper, textiles, pottery, and wire. Davis (1917) identified this company as "one of the pioneer industrial corporations of the United States and the largest and most pretentious of these" (p. 349). Plans for the new corporation were publicly announced, including the much-criticized strategy of raising capital by issuing public stocks. The emphasis on developing domestic industry and reducing dependence on imports was appealing to potential investors, and private citizens were getting encouragement from the newly formed federal government to undertake business activity on a broader scale than had been common at the time. At the time the prospectus for this new enterprise was being circulated, Alexander Hamilton, the secretary of the Treasury, presented his *Report on Manufacturers,* which was prepared in response to President Washington's direction "to prepare and report to the House, a proper plan for the encouragement and promotion of such manufactories as will tend to render the United States independent of other nations" (quoted in Davis, 1917, p. 362).

The requisite capital was indeed raised, with most of the subscriptions secured in New York. Shortly thereafter, panic ensued because the new enterprise was not progressing as intended. The leading offices and directors were deeply involved in the speculative boom that was widespread at the time and had not given attention to the actual business of the new enterprise. Thereafter, the leaders, who were in possession of most of the paid-in funds, went bankrupt. This story reveals the lure of becoming wealthy quickly and of general incompetence among leadership. There were virtually no rules to restrain the behavior of the leaders, and they appropriated the funds for their own personal use.

The society was saved by a loan of $10,000 from the Bank of New York, and there is evidence that the secretary of Treasury was critical in securing this financing. However, there continued to be serious finance problems, throughout the period when facilities for the envisioned textile mills were being constructed. The newly appointed treasurer was supposed to be bonded, but he refused. He continued in the position nonetheless. When he retired in 1796, the treasurer's books and the funds were supposed to be left with the deputy-governor. The books, though, were never recovered. It is not clear whether all the funds were recovered. The operations were unprofitable and were discontinued in the same year.

FINANCE IN THE 1800s

On the brink of the nineteenth century the United States had a dismal record of successful corporations, as illustrated by the effort in New Jersey discussed above. The country was a world of small mercantile businesses. As of 1790, for example, there were only three banks, three bridge companies, a few insurance associations, and a dozen canal companies (Williamson, 1951). However, some businesspeople began to see the value of the corporation: The risks of manufacturing made the limited liability of the corporation appealing. Several states enacted

useful laws. In 1811 New York enacted a law that allowed for the incorporation of certain kinds of manufacturing concerns with less than $100,000 of capital. Connecticut, in 1817, and Massachusetts, in 1830, granted limited liability, which was the first step in movement for general incorporation acts. The intent of such acts was to encourage the financing of entities through the corporate structure and to protect the public that might be inclined to invest in these new enterprises. In the same period, the government was significantly involved in the financing of businesses. As Cochran (1966) noted:

> The capital needs of banking and transportation brought state participation in business organization. Few such pioneer enterprises seemed possible without substantial state, county, or municipal purchases of stocks and bonds. The credit of the state was generally substituted in part for that of the private company by issuance of state bonds and use of the proceeds to buy the company's securities. (p. 219)

At the same time, Cochran (1966) noted some of the serious drawbacks of the new ownership:

> Free and secret transferability of corporate ownership encouraged grave abuses on the part of unscrupulous financiers. It was possible for managing groups to profit personally by ruining great companies and then selling out before the situation became known. (p. 219)

However, there were conscientious men who were interested in productive efficiency as well as the quest for wealth. Among the individuals Cochran (1966) identified was Nathan Appleton:

> Nathan Appleton ... turning from mercantile pursuits in 1813, joined with some of the Lowells and Jacksons, put his capital into large-scale textile manufacture. ... Appleton came to be looked upon as the business leader of Massachusetts. ... By 1840 he and his Boston associates had created in eastern Massachusetts a miniature of the corporate industrial society of the twentieth century. They controlled banking, railroad, insurance, and power companies as well as great textile mills scattered all over the state. It was the large "modern" corporation controllable by strategically organized blocs of shares, and virtually self-perpetuating boards of directors that made

this concentration of power possible, but it must be remembered that it was also this device for gathering together the savings of thousands of small investors that had produced the great development. (p. 220)

There had been remarkable developments throughout the 1800s. Baskin and Miranti (1997), for example, pointed out that the "last quarter of the eighteenth century saw the start of a great economic expansion that changed corporate finance in fundamental ways" (p. 127). It was during this period that there was extensive development of railroads, which independently became strong bastions of finance capitalism. During this period, preferred stock and debt became popular means of financing corporations. During the final decades of the 1800s, relatively widely distributed financial journals and newspapers began to appear.

THE ROLE OF BANKS FROM THE LATE 1800s THROUGH THE 1920s

Bankers are critical to economic development. Schumpeter, in his theory of economic development, highlighted the role of bankers as the source of funds for enterpreneurs, who themselves often lack financial resource. Schumpeter (1934) noted: "In an economy without development there would be no such money market . . . the kernel of the matter lies in the credit requirements of new enterprises . . . thus, the main function of the money or capital market is trading in credit for the purpose of financing development" (p. 122-127).

Schumpeter undoubtedly was fully aware of the U.S. experience and the influence of American bankers in the impressive growth of the American economy from the mid-1800s through the early decade of the twentieth century. Possibly the most impressive of the bankers were the Morgans. As Chernow (1990), in his history of the Morgans, concluded: "The old pre-1935 House of Morgan was probably the most formidable financial combine in history. It financed many industrial giants, including U.S. Steel, General Electric, General Motors, Du Pont, and American Telephone and Telegraph" (p. xi).

At the end of the 1800s, banks were the critical source of funds for U.S. enterprises. Their role, however, changed during the twentieth century, as businesses became larger and the types of financial institutions increased.

CHANGES IN FINANCIAL STRUCTURE

The financial structure in the United States changed during the twentieth century. Goldsmith's (1969) study provided a comparison of the main types of U.S. financial institutions in 1900 and 1963, shown in Table 1.

As Table 1 shows, in 1900, 62.9 percent of total assets of all the financial institutions were held by commercial banks; by 1963 that percentage was 32.2. While thrift institutions, including mutual savings banks, savings and loan associations, credit unions, and postal savings systems, maintained approximately the same percentage of total assets (18.2 percent in 1900; 16.9 percent in 1963), mutual savings banks held 15.1 percent of total assets in 1900 but only 5.1 percent in 1963. Savings and loan associations, which had 3.1 of total assets in 1900, held 10.9 percent in 1963. In 1900 a group of institutions identified as "miscellaneous" included only mortgage companies and security dealers. By 1963, the "miscellaneous" category included those that had existed in 1900, plus finance companies, investment companies, land banks, and government lending institutions (Goldsmith, 1969).

Goldsmith's analysis revealed that financial superstructure grows more rapidly than the infrastructure of national product and national wealth. He noted that in less than two hundred years within the world community there had developed what he identified as a financial system of the modern type, characterized by:

the existence of several basic forms of financial institutions (banks of issue and deposit, savings banks, mortgage banks, and insurance companies) and of financial instruments (scriptural [nonmetallic] money, bills of exchange, accounts receivable and payable, bank deposits and loans made by financial institutions, life insurance and pension contracts, mortgages, government and corporate bonds, and corporate stock.) (Goldsmith, 1969, 99. 10-11)

Financial Institutions in 1900 and 1963

Type of institution	Distribution of total assets of financial institutions	
	1963 %	1900 %
Federal Reserve Banks	5.9	---
Commercial banks	32.2	62.9
Mutual savings banks	5.1	15.1
Savings and loan associations	10.9	3.1
Credit unions	0.8	---
Postal savings system	0.1	---
Insurance organizations	32.0	13.8
Miscellaneous institutions	13.0	5.1
Total	100.0	100.0

Table 1

SOURCE: Goldsmith, Raymond. (1969). *Financial Structure and Development.* New Haven: Yale University Press.

A parallelism between economic and financial development is observable if periods of several decades are considered. Goldsmith's (1969) data showed that "as real income and wealth increase, in the aggregate and per head of the population, the size and complexity of the financial superstructure grow" (p. 48).

Shares of assets held by banks and thrift institutions continued to decline. While the two types of financial institutions held 55.0 percent of total assets in 1963, the two types held only 22.7 percent by the end of 1999, as reported by the Federal Reserve Board.

IMPETUS FOR REGULATION OF SECURITIES IN THE UNITED STATES

Prior to 1929, there was little support for federal regulation of securities markets in the United States. The optimism of the post-World War I period, with promises of easy credit and instant wealth, was not a time of restraints imposed by regulation. As noted by the Securities and Exchange Commission (SEC), "During the 1920s, approximately 20 million large and small shareholders took advantage of post-war prosperity and set out to make their fortunes in the stock market. It is estimated that of the $50 billion in new securities offering during this period, half became worthless." (SEC, www.sec.gov/)

Public confidence shifted dramatically with the stock market crash of 1929. For the economy to recover, the public's faith in the capital markets needed to be restored. The outcome was the passage of two acts by Congress, the Securities Act of 1933 and the Securities Exchange Act of 1934. These laws were established to provide structure in the functioning of financial markets and to provide government oversight.

THE SECURITIES AND EXCHANGE COMMISSION

The Securities Exchange Act of 1934 included the establishment of the Securities and Exchange Commission, which was charged with enforcing the newly passed securities laws, promoting stability in the markets, and protecting investors.

The Securities and Exchange Commission operates on the premise that all investors should have access to certain basic facts about investments prior to purchase. The key means of achieving this is through requiring that all publicly owned companies disclose relevant financial and other information to all citizens.

The SEC oversees key participants in the financial world, including stock exchanges, broker-dealers, and investment advisers. Through its enforcement authority, the SEC brings civil enforcement actions against individuals and companies that violate securities laws. Typical infractions relate to insider trading, accounting fraud, and providing false or misleading information about securities and the companies that issue them.

THE ROLE OF STOCK EXCHANGES

Stock exchanges have played a significant role in the financing of U.S. business enterprises through providing a means of buying and selling securities. The first stock exchange in the United States was established in 1790 in Philadelphia. Two years later, in 1792, the New York Stock Exchange was formed when twenty-four stockbrokers signed an agreement to trade with one another beneath a buttonwood tree outside what is now 68 Wall Street. The New York Stock

Exchange (NYSE) is the largest stock exchange in the world.

The NYSE's first client, in 1792, was the Bank of New York, and its first office, set up in 1817, was a rented room at 40 Wall Street. It achieved its first million-share day on December 15, 1886, and its first billion-share day on October 28, 1997.

A study of all securities markets by the SEC in 1961 revealed that the over-the-counter securities market was fragmented and obscure, leading the SEC to propose to the National Association of Securities Dealers, that it develop an automated over-the-counter securities system. Such a system was completed and began operations in February 1971; it is known as the National Association of Securities Dealers Automated Quotation—or NASDAQ—system. The world's first electronic stock market, by the end of 1999 it ranked second, below the New York Stock Exchange, among the world's securities markets in terms of dollar volume.

CLOSING DECADES OF THE TWENTIETH CENTURY

With the passage of new laws, the financial industry is being restructured. The scope of services provided by type of institution is not as limited as was the case earlier.

The impact of technology. As the twenty-first century got under way, the ways in which stocks were bought and sold began to receive intensive attention. Stock markets, including the regional ones in the United States, began considering the ways in which current and emerging technologies would affect how they function.

The Federal Government also became involved in assessing the implications of electronic commerce during the final years of the twentieth century. Hearings were held by committees in both the House of Representatives and the Senate. Among those making presentations at hearings of the Senate Banking Committee were leaders of banks and stock exchanges. Traditional firms in these industries assured the members of such committees that they could meet the chal-

lenges of the new technology and continue to be viable players in the financial marketplace.

One example of the appeal of electronic commerce in financial services is the extent of such commerce as of mid-2000. On-line spending in financial services, primarily the buying and selling of securities, was 28.9 percent of all expenditures in this category. A year earlier, the extent of such transactions was 14.6. (as reported in *The Wall Street Journal,* July 17, 2000. "Clicks and Mortar." William M. Bulkeley, p.R4. Source was cited as Boston Consulting Group).

There is considerable interest in developing the rules and regulations to enhance the effectiveness and efficiency of financial transactions electronically. An important new ruling for e-commerce that will allow on-line signatures was passed by Congress in June 2000 and will take effect as of October 1, 2000.

Continuing development of the theory of finance. In the final third of the twentieth century, there were impressive developments in the theory of finance. Although the Nobel Prize was first awarded in 1901, the category "economic science" was not added until 1969. Several leading theorists in the field of finance have been among the recipients of the Nobel Prize in economic science.

The globalization of financial activity. The transformation of capital markets from the national level to the global level increased considerably during the final decade of the twentieth century, fueled by economic progress and supported by rapidly developing technological capabilities. Leadership was provided by an association of the world's securities regulators, the International Organization of Securities Commissions (IOSCO), which was organized in the early 1970s. The IOSCO in 1993 described a core set of standards that would be needed to provide a comprehensive body of accounting principles for companies undertaking cross-border securities offerings. In May 2000, the IOSCO approved the core standards developed by the International Accounting Standards Committee (IASC). In the meantime, the International Accounting Standards Committee designed a new structure for an international accounting standard-setting body, which was accepted by the membership in May 2000 with implementation anticipated in January 2001.

These developments are promising for the development of a functioning global financial marketplace.

(SEE ALSO: *Finance*)

BIBLIOGRAPHY

Baskin, Jonathon Barron, and Miranti, Paul J., Jr. (1997). *A History of Corporate Finance.* New York: Cambridge University Press.

Bulkeley, William M. (2000). "Clicks and Mortar." *The Wall Street Journal.* July 17: p.R4.

Chernow, Ron. (1990). *The House of Morgan: An American Banking Dynasty and the Rise of Modern Finance.* New York: Atlantic Monthly Press.

Cochran, Thomas C. (1966). "Business Organization and the Development of an Industrial Discipline." In Thomas C. Cochran and Thomas B. Brewer, eds. *Views of American Economic Growth: The Agricultural Era.* New York: McGraw-Hill.

Davis, Joseph Stancliffe. (1917). *Essays in the Earlier History of American Corporations.* vol. 1. Cambridge, MA: Harvard University Press.

Goldsmith, Raymond. (1969). *Financial Structure and Development.* New Haven, CT: Yale University Press.

National Association of Securities Dealers Automated Quotation. www.nasdaq.com/.

New York State Exchange. www.nyse.org.

Schumpeter, Joseph A. (1934). *The Theory of Economic Development: An Inquiry into Profits, Capital, Credit, Interest, and the Business Cycle.* cambridge, MA: Harvard University Press.

Securities and Exchange Commission (SEC). www.sec.gov

Williamson, Harold F. (1951). *Growth of the American Economy.* 2nd ed. Englewood Cliffs, NJ: Prentice-Hall.

MARY ELLEN OLIVERIO

FINANCIAL ACCOUNTING STANDARDS BOARD

The United States has a longstanding tradition of accounting standards being set by the private sector (as opposed to the government). Although the federal government's Securities and Exchange Commission (SEC) has the legal authority to establish accounting standards for public companies, the SEC has historically looked to the private sector to set accounting standards.

The first two standard-setting organizations in the United States were the Committee on Accounting Procedure (CAP), which was established in 1938, and the Accounting Principles Board (APB), which replaced the CAP in 1959. Both organizations were committees of the American Institute of Certified Public Accountants (AICPA) and included approximately twenty representatives of the accounting profession who served on a part-time basis. Pronouncements issued by those two bodies are still considered to be generally accepted accounting principles (GAAP) today unless they have been specifically amended or replaced by a subsequent pronouncement.

Largely as a result of criticisms concerning the perceived lack of independence of the APB and the part-time involvement of its members, a major reconsideration of the standard-setting structure in the United States occurred in the early 1970s. This led to the creation in 1973 of a new standard-setting body designed to be independent of all other business and professional organizations. That new group was the Financial Accounting Standards Board (FASB).

The FASB is funded by revenues from the sales of its publications and by voluntary contributions, primarily from public accounting firms and corporations. The board consists of seven full-time members. The usual composition of the board is three members with extensive public accounting experience, two from a corporate background, one academic, and one financial analyst.

The three pillars on which the FASB was built are independence, openness (or "sunshine"), and neutrality. Although independence can never be totally assured, the FASB charter did attempt to protect the board from as much external pressure as possible. The charter gives the FASB exclusive authority to set its own agenda and establish accounting standards. Board members are insulated from external pressures by fixed five-year terms (with a two-term maximum), by the requirements to end all past employment relationships, and by disclosure of (and certain limitations on) investments and outside activities that might create a conflict of interest.

"Sunshine" characterizes the open process that the board follows. It means that all its technical business is conducted in meetings that are announced in advance and are open to the public. Because the board's Rules of Procedure require a supermajority of five votes to approve the issuance of any new standard, no more than four board members can meet privately to discuss technical issues.

Neutrality means that accounting standards should be designed to provide the best possible information for economic decision making without regard to how that information may affect economic, political, or social behavior. Putting it another way, accounting standards should not be intentionally biased for the purpose of promoting either private special interests or government policy goals. Neutrality has been reinforced by adoption and adherence to a broad set of principles called the conceptual framework. That framework was designed to produce standards that result in neutral information that is useful in decision making.

An independent group, the Financial Accounting Foundation, oversees the activities of the FASB. It is responsible for selecting members of the FASB, raising money to fund the FASB's operations, and providing general oversight of the FASB to assure that it is performing its mission. The foundation is composed of a sixteen-member board of trustees that represent the majority of the groups interested in, or affected by, the accounting standard-setting process.

The FASB has the authority to establish GAAPs but has no authority to enforce its standards. The SEC and the AICPA are the organizations that provide the enforcement mechanism. The SEC requires compliance with FASB standards by all public companies, that is, those whose securities are traded in public markets—on stock exchanges or over-the-counter. The

AICPA requires public accounting firms that audit either public or private companies to express an opinion as to whether those companies' financial statements conform with GAAPs.

STANDARD-SETTING PROCESS

Within this overall structure, the FASB has developed an extensive structure of due process to conduct its standard-setting activities. The process usually starts by determining what financial reporting issues are sufficiently pervasive and important that they warrant consideration by the board.

The FASB has a professional staff of approximately forty-five persons; once a project is added to the agenda, staff members are assigned to begin research on the topic. On most larger projects, a task force of outside advisers is appointed; they assist in the staff's research and the board's deliberations by providing expertise, a diversity of viewpoints, and a mechanism for communication with those who may be affected by the proposed standard.

The FASB sometimes asks for written comments from constituents during the research phase through the issuance of a Discussion Memorandum. Such a document analyzes the problem in depth, delineates the issues, identifies alternative solutions, and discusses the merits of those solutions in an objective way. Or the board may issue what is known as a Preliminary Views document, which includes tentative decisions on a few basic issues and again seeks input from constituents.

After completion of initial research by the staff and consideration of comments on a Discussion Memorandum or Preliminary Views, if one of those documents is issued, the board members begin deliberating the issues in earnest. This process can take anywhere from a few months to several years, depending on the number and complexity of the issues involved as well as the strength of the convictions of individual board members. Once at least five board members agree on an overall answer, the board issues an Exposure Draft (ED) of a proposed standard for public comment. The comment period is at least ninety days.

While the ED is out for public comment, the FASB will often conduct a field test, which is designed to test the application of the proposed standard using actual financial information provided by volunteering companies.

The number of comment letters received on an ED can range from a few dozen to more than a thousand, depending on how pervasive and how controversial the proposal is. Comment letters are received primarily from corporations, large public accounting firms, government regulators, academics, and financial analysts, although any interested party is free to express his or her views. After reading the letters, the board redeliberates all the issues in the ED and any additional issues that may have arisen in the comment and field-test processes. At the end of those deliberations, the board again votes; if there is sufficient support among the board members, it issues a final Statement of Financial Accounting Standards.

The steps described above are just an overall outline of the process. Throughout a project's life, discussions are held with the FASB's advisory council, the project task force, and various other interested parties. In addition, the process does not end with the issuance of a Statement. The FASB monitors the application of a Statement to ensure that it is working as planned. Should the standard not work in practice, then the board may consider amending it to provide clarification, issuing additional interpretive guidance, or taking some other action to address problems that arise.

Most FASB projects are controversial. For example, pronouncements on topics such as accounting for employee stock options, postretirement health care benefits, and derivative financial instruments were strongly opposed by many corporations and other affected parties. The board does its best to consider the reasonable arguments expressed by all parties. But in the final analysis, the FASB endeavors to act in the public interest by issuing accounting standards that will result in the most informative and unbiased financial statements possible. Thus investors, creditors, and all others who use financial statements in making economic decisions can take comfort in the fact that the FASB puts the general public interest above any concerns of individual corporations or other self-interested parties.

Despite disagreement over some specific pronouncements, the board's various constituents remain generally supportive. They know that their views are carefully weighed during the FASB's deliberations, but they also recognize that the ultimate determinant of a new standard must be the board's judgment. As the FASB's mission statement states, "The FASB is committed to following an open orderly process for standard setting that precludes placing any particular interest above the interests of the many who rely on financial information."

COMMUNICATING WITH THE FASB

In addition to the Statements, EDs, Discussion Memoranda, and Preliminary Views documents referred to above, the FASB publishes a variety of other documents that provide guidance on financial accounting and reporting. For example, its Emerging Issues Task Force (EITF) develops consensus positions on accounting matters that demand prompt solutions. EITF materials and other FASB publications can be ordered by individual item or through a variety of subscription programs that the organization offers. Special discounts on publications are available to parties who make voluntary contributions to support the overall work of the FASB.

More information on publications or any other related matters is available from the FASB at 401 Merritt 7, Norwalk, CT 06856; (203)847-0700; or at http://www.fasb.org.

BIBLIOGRAPHY

Miller, Paul B. W., Redding, Rodney J., and Bahnson, Paul R. (1998). *The FASB—The People, the Process, and the Politics.* New York: Irwin/McGraw-Hill.

Van Riper, Robert. (1994). *Setting Standards for Financial Reporting—FASB and the Struggle for Control of a Critical Process.* Westport, CT: Quorum Books.

DENNIS R. BERESFORD

FINANCIAL FORECASTS AND PROJECTIONS

Business entities need to plan for the future; they must also consider alternative management strategies and prepare capital and operating budgets; they must also consider alternative funding and cash budget possibilities. An important part of the planning process is the preparation of prospective financial statements that attempt to predict the outcome of the business entity's activities in future periods.

Financial forecasts and *financial projections* are prospective financial statements that present an entity's expected financial position, results of operations, and cash flows in future periods under two different conditions. Financial forecasts assume that the entity will continue to function in the manner in which it is currently functioning. For example, if the entity is a retail store chain, that it will continue to do business in the manner in which it is currently engaged. The financial forecast presents the predicted results for the next year. Financial projections, on the other hand, make one or more hypothetical assumptions about an entity's future course of action. For example, if the retail store chain were considering a Web site at which it would also sell merchandise—in addition to the merchandise sold in the stores—a financial projection would provide expected results. Financial forecasts and projections should be distinguished from *pro forma* financial statements, which show the effect of a hypothetical future event on the historical financial statements results.

PREPARATION OF PROSPECTIVE FINANCIAL STATEMENTS

The preparation of prospective financial statements requires considerable knowledge of the entity's business and the factors that are likely to determine its future results. The following key factors related to future results must be considered in the preparation of such statements:

- Factors related to the specific entity
- Factors related to the industry
- Factors related to the market
- Factors related to the economy

Factors Related to the Specific Entity. The principal cost elements of the entity's doing business must be considered. Depending on the entity, these elements may include such costs as payroll and benefits, needed employees, raw materials, products the entity sells, freight or shipping, and advertising.

Another consideration is the availability of resources. For example, are the expert, specialized, or skilled workers available to meet the needs of the entity under the plan as initially proposed? Are the raw materials and/or products for resale available? Can the delivery system be organized to accomplish the task? Are the company's physical facilities sufficient for the uses and for the capacities contemplated?

Factors Related to the Industry. Factors related to the industry in which the entity is operating must be considered. Is the industry one in which companies are very competitive? Are competitive industries emerging? Is obsolescence emerging within the industry? Are there regulatory considerations and requirements? Is new technology being introduced into the industry? What are the economic conditions within the industry?

Factors Related to the Market. Market factors must be considered. What are the trends in business or consumer demand related to the services or goods being sold by the entity? Are competitive companies emerging, perhaps with new or different products? Is unique marketing required? Are there pricing developments to be factored into the forecast?

Factors Related to the Economy. Numerous factors related to the economy must be considered. What are the economic conditions in the country? What are critical economic trends? Is the economy inflationary, deflationary, or stable? What is the trend with regard to labor availability? What are the financing considerations in relation to the economy? What are interest rates? Are there significant factors related to long-term versus short-term financing? Is a public stock offering a possible financing option?

ATTESTATION SERVICES PROVIDED FOR FINANCIAL FORECASTS AND FINANCIAL PROJECTIONS

Forecasts and projections are important in an organization. They are also of great interest to financial analysts and others in the business environment who make decisions about future business behavior. Because of outsider interest, public accountants are engaged to provide professional services. There are three types of engagements that a certified public accountant may undertake in relation to financial forecasts and projections:

1. Examination: An accountant evaluates the preparation, underlying support, and presentation of the financial statements, and expresses an opinion on them.

2. Applying agreed-upon procedures: Users establish the nature and scope of the engagement, and only the results of the procedures performed are provided.

3. Compilation: An accountant prepares the prospective statements from information and assumptions provided, and no assurance is given.

Examination. The American Institute of Certified Public Accountants (AICPA) has prepared guidelines for prospective financial statements engagements. The person or persons who prepare the financial statements, called the responsible party, are usually the management of the company but may be outsiders, such as the management of an entity considering acquiring the company. The accountants who examine such statements must consider whether the sources of information used by the client are sufficient to

support the assumptions reflected in the prospective statements. For example, external sources that should be considered include industry and government publications; reports on new information; digital, electronic, and mechanical technology; reports on new scientific developments; micro and macroeconomic forecasts; and reports on present and proposed legislation. Examples of internal sources that accountants consider include strategic plans, budgets, contractual agreements, purchase and sale agreements and commitments, intellectual property rights such as copyrights and patents, royalty and commission agreements, employee contracts and labor agreements, and financing and debt agreements.

When the examination is of a financial projection, the accountants must determine whether the hypothetical condition or course of action (which will not necessarily occur) is consistent with the purpose of the projection. The accountants must evaluate the support underlying assumptions in the same manner as is done for a forecast.

Upon completion of a financial forecast examination, assuming the accountants have collected sufficient evidence to provide a reasonable basis for the standard report to be issued, that report will state in part:

In our opinion, the accompanying forecast is presented in conformity with guidelines for presentation of a forecast established by the American Institute of Certified Public Accountants, and the underlying assumptions provide a reasonable basis for management's forecast.

Upon completion of a financial projection examination, the standard report would include a description of the hypothetical assumption and the opinion would state that the underlying assumptions provide a reasonable basis for management's forecast assuming the occurrence of the hypothetical assumption. The report will state in part:

In our opinion, the accompanying projection is presented in conformity with guidelines for presentation of a projection established by the American Institute of Certified Public Accountants, and the underlying assumptions provide a reasonable basis for management's projection [then the hypothetical assumption would be described and assumed to have occurred, for example, "assuming the establishment of a Web site which will . . ."]

Financial forecasts are considered general-purpose financial statements that may be distributed to any interested party, whereas financial projections are considered limited-purpose financial statements only to be used by the responsible party who prepared the statements or by knowledgeable third parties. In both forecasts and prospective financial statement opinions, a warning must be included in the opinion that the prospective results may not be achieved.

If, in the accountants' opinion, the prospective financial statements depart from AICPA guidelines, or one of the significant assumptions does not provide a reasonable basis for the prospective statements, or the accountants could not apply some procedures that were considered necessary, the report would have to be modified.

Applying Agreed-Upon Procedures. Another type of engagement that certified public accountants may undertake is to apply only some procedures, which have been specified by the users, to the financial forecast or projection. An example of such an engagement might be to review the forecast in regard to sales, or payroll costs, or both. Limiting the procedures to only one item, or some of the items, on the prospective financial statements does not enable the accountants to provide an overall opinion. Because of the limitation in regard to the procedures performed, the report is restricted to the users who specified the procedures to be applied.

The standard applying agreed-upon procedures report will state in part:

At your request, we have performed certain agreed-upon procedures, as enumerated below, . . . we make no representation regarding the sufficiency of the procedures described . . . [a list of the procedures performed and related findings would be stated] . . . we do not express an opinion on whether the prospective financial statements . . . provide a reasonable basis for the presentation.

Compilation. A compilation of prospective financial statements by certified public accountants involves only the service of preparing the statements in whole or part from information and significant assumptions provided by the responsible party, usually a member of management. Because such an activity does not envision an examination or even applying agreed-upon procedures, no assurance is provided.

The standard compilation report on a forecast would state in part:

We have not examined the forecast and, accordingly, do not express an opinion or any other form of assurance on the accompanying statements or assumptions.

IMPORTANCE OF FORECASTS AND PROJECTIONS

Forecasts and projections have assumed extraordinary significance in U.S. business. The release of corporate managers' earnings forecasts has become common. Management forecasts have become an important source of information for financial analysts and investors. Stock prices show significant movements after the release of information that shows earnings will be higher or lower than current expectations.

However, some skepticism in regard to these forecasts exists on the part of financial analysts and governmental agencies, such as the Securities and Exchange Commission, because of the fear that forecasts may be biased at times in order to influence capital markets or may simply be inaccurate. In addition, prospective financial information is considered vital in relation to mergers and acquisitions as well as to such business entity management activities as budgeting. In these circumstances, it would appear advisable to obtain certified public accountant examinations and reports before the public release of prospective financial information.

(SEE ALSO: *Assurance Services*; *Auditing*)

BIBLIOGRAPHY

AICPA Professional Standards. Attestation Standards, Financial Forecasts and Projections. (1999). New York:

American Institute of Certified Public Accountants (published annually).

Coller, and Maribeth, and Yohn, Teri Lombardi, (1998). "Management Forecasts: What Do We Know?" *Financial Analysts Journal* (January/February): 58-62.

Guide for Prospective Financial Information. (1999). New York: American Institute of Certified Public Accountants.

Hirst, D. Eric, Koonce, Lisa, and Miller, Jeffrey. (1999). "The Joint Effect of Management's Prior Forecast Accuracy and the Form of Its Financial Forecasts on Investor Judgment." *Journal of Accounting Research* 37 (Supplement): 101-124.

BERNARD H. NEWMAN

FINANCIAL INSTITUTIONS

A financial institution is one that facilitates allocation of financial resources from its source to potential users. There are a large number of different types of financial institutions in the United States, creating a rich mosaic in the financial system. Some institutions acquire funds and make them available to users. Others act as middlemen between deficit and surplus units. Still others invest (manage) funds as agents for their clients. The key categories of financial institutions are the following: deposit taking; finance and insurance; and investment, pension, and risk management. There are also government and government-sponsored institutions that carry out regulatory, supervisory, and financing functions. Historically, each type has performed a specialized function in financing and investment management.

DEPOSIT TAKING

Deposit-taking institutions take the form of commercial banks, which accept deposits and make commercial and other loans; savings and loan associations and mutual savings banks, which accept deposits and make mortgage and other types of loans; and credit unions, which are cooperative organizations that issue share certificates and make member (consumer) and other loans. Altogether there are more than 15,000 deposit taking institutions with more than 100,000 branches spread across the economy.

The U.S. commercial banking system practiced competition through a large number of firms in the industry from 1776 to 1976. It was designed to be a unit-banking system in which state charters of banks allowed only one-office banking. The system also encouraged thrift and use of local savings for investment in the local economy. The unit-banking system not only forced competition among existing and new banks in a given banking market; it deliberately avoided the emergence of monopolies in the industry. The founding fathers in the original thirteen states understood the harm monopolies could inflict on the economic and financial systems. In due course the U.S. Congress passed the Sherman Antitrust Act of 1890, making monopoly and monopolistic practices unacceptable and therefore illegal.

The commercial banking industry dominated the U.S. financial industry from the beginning to the 1970s, when financial product innovation and the resulting business and consumer financial choices exploded to create competition across financial services industries. The commercial banking industry and its limited product offerings on both sides of the balance sheet were the only choices available to the general public. This is because the commercial banks specialized in taking checking account deposits on the liability side and making commercial loans on the asset side. They relied for safety of their operations on maturity-based hedging of mostly short-term liabilities with short-term self-liquidating commercial loans assets. This also meant that households, farmers, students, and other groups did not have access to financial capital.

Savings and loan associations, mutual savings banks and credit unions, and money market mutual funds are other deposit-taking institutions. Savings and loan associations take savings deposits and primarily make mortgage loans throughout the country. They have provided funds to create millions of housing units in the county. Their key function is maturity intermediation when they accept short-term deposit and make long-term mortgage loans. Mutual savings banks exist mainly in the eastern part of the

United States. Like savings and loan associations, they, too, accept short-maturity deposits and make long-term mortgage loans. They also issue consumer and other loans, making then somewhat more diversified and therefore less risky in terms of loan defaults. Credit unions specialize in member savings and loans, although they also make mortgage-type loans and other investments similar to other deposit-taking institutions.

FINANCE AND INSURANCE INSTITUTIONS

Finance (credit) companies are different from deposit-taking banking institutions in that their sources of funds are not deposits. They acquire funds in the market by issuing their own obligations, such as notes and bonds. They, however, make loans on the other side of the balance sheet in full competition with deposit-taking and other types of financial institutions, such as insurance companies. Finance companies specialize in business inventory financing, although they also make consumer loans, mostly indirectly through manufacturers and distributors of goods and services. Some of the finance companies are huge and operate in domestic as well as foreign markets. Several are bigger than most of the commercial banks in the United States.

Insurance companies provide the dual services of insurance protection and investment. There are two types of insurance companies: life insurance companies and casualty and property insurance companies. Insurance companies' sources of funds are primarily policy premiums. Their uses of funds range from loans (thus competing with finance companies, commercial banks, and savings and loan associations) to creation of investment products (thus competing with investment companies). Life insurance companies match their certain mortality-based needs for cash outflows with longer-term riskier investments such as stocks and bonds. Casualty and property insurance companies have more uncertainty of cash outflows and their timing. Therefore they have more conservative investment policies in terms of maturity and credit risk of their investments.

INVESTMENT, PENSION, AND RISK MANAGEMENT

Investment companies pool together funds and invest in the market to achieve goals set for various types of investments, matching liquidity, maturity, return, risk, tax, and other preferences of investors on the one hand and users of funds on the other. Investment companies are organized as open-end or closed-end mutual funds. Open-end funds accept new investments and redeem old ones, while closed-end funds accept funds at one time and then do not take in new funds. Investment companies have become very popular with investors in recent decades, and thus they have mobilized trillions of dollars.

Another investment type of company is investment banks, which provide investment and fund-raising advice to potential users of funds, such as commercial, industrial, and financial companies. They also create venture capital funds or companies. Some of them also have brokerage and dealerships in securities. Many of them underwrite securities and then place them in the market or sell them to investors.

Pension funds in the private and the government sectors collect pension contributions and invest them according to goals of the employees for their funds. Increasingly, employees are able to indicate their personal preferences for risk and reward targets with respect to their own and sometimes their employers' contributions.

Other institutions that are significant parts of the financial system are the stock, bond, commodity, currency, futures, and options exchanges. The various types of exchanges make possible not only creation and ownership of financial claims but also management of liquidity and risk of price changes and other risks in underlying commodities in the market. They greatly expand investment opportunities for savers and access to funds by small, medium, and large business enterprises. They have deepened and broadened markets in financial products and services, helped manage price risk, and improved allocation efficiency in financial markets where every attribute desired in a financial product has a counter party to trade with. The banking and investment intermediaries have extended their services to the global saver-investor with the cross-border flow of funds and trading of financial products facilitated by cross-border investing, listing, and trading of securities in home and foreign markets in home and foreign currencies.

HISTORICAL DEVELOPMENT OF THE U.S. FINANCIAL SYSTEM

Specialization and division of labor, identified as sources of creativity and efficiency by Adam Smith, led to the creation of other specialized deposit-taking and investment-type financial institutions that began to meet the demand not fulfilled by the commercial banking industry. Similar institutions were created to finance agriculture and housing in rural areas, public works, and education. Laws and regulations recognized and strengthened the separation, and thus specialization, of the financial function different intermediaries performed in the financial system.

The system was further strengthened by establishing government and semi-government intermediaries to increase liquidity in the market, manage maturity risk, and broaden the sharing of the market (price) risk through secondary markets for mortgages, agency (government and sponsored) securities, and other asset-based securities. Examples of institutions are: Commodity Credit Corporation, Farm Credit Banks, Farm Credit Financing Assistance Corporation, Farmers Home Administration, Federal Home Loan Mortgage Corporation (FEDMAC), Federal Financing Corporation, Federal National Mortgage Association (FNMA), Federal Housing Administration (FHA), Federal Home Loan Banks, Government National Mortgage Association (GNMA), Resolution Funding Corporation, Small Business Administration, and Student Loan Marketing Association (SLMA).

THE MONETARY SYSTEM

The U.S. monetary system is based on credit. The U.S. currency is issued by its central bank, the Federal Reserve System, as a liability on itself. The value of the currency is based on its purchasing power in the economy and around the world

and has not been linked to or defined in terms of any particular commodity or an index since 1968. The issuance of currency was tied to the U.S. gold holdings prior to 1968. The U.S. money supply consists of currency and coins and checkable public deposits in the banking system. The measures of money are M1, M2, M3, and L.

The Federal Reserve System, created in 1913, was established to furnish elastic currency to the economy and to supervise the banking system. Prior to 1913 there had been financial crises that were due to absence of a systematic way to provide money and credit in the economy. There had also been large bank failures due to fraud and mismanagement, as well as economic fluctuations and boom and bust in commodity prices.

The Federal Reserve System consists of the Board of Governors of the Federal Reserve and the twelve regional or district Federal Reserve banks. The Board of Governors in Washington is the central decision point organization in a decentralized system. The board has seven members who are nominated by the president and confirmed by the Senate. Each board member has a fourteen-year appointment so as to make the board immune from political influence of any administration in office. The board is set up as an independent agency; it does not report to the president, but it does report to Congress. However, it actively coordinates its research and analysis with the White House and the Treasury Secretary in formulating policy. The regional Federal Reserve banks' Board of Directors is also structured to represent banking, industry and commerce, and the general public. There is a formal statutory requirement to have three directors from the three groups in the area on the board.

The monetary policy-making body within the Federal Reserve is the Federal Open Market Committee (FOMC), which meets regularly (generally eight times a year). Its voting members are the seven governors of the Board of Governors and five presidents of the regional banks. The president of the Federal Reserve Bank of New York is a permanent member of FOMC, and the other four serve on annual rotation from among four groups formed from the remaining eleven regional banks. The regional banks are located in Boston, New York, Philadelphia, Richmond, Atlanta, Cleveland, Chicago, Dallas, St. Louis, Kansas City, Minneapolis, and San Francisco. These cities were chosen because they represented the hub of the regional economy of each area of the United States in 1913. It was thought at the time that the regional economies had different characteristics in terms of the type and level of economic activity, so they needed different accommodation with respect to supply of money and finance, rediscounting mechanisms, and interest rates. In other words, it was thought that there were twelve different money markets in the U.S. economy, so each one needed special attention for its needs. This structure of the Federal Reserve System continues to this day, but the money market has become one market due to institutional and technological advancements. Now there are truly national financial institutions, not just in terms of their national charter, with interstate deposit taking and lending of commercial and numerous other types of loans to businesses and households.

The Federal Reserve policy serves the needs of the entire economy and all its parts by taking into account economic and financial information concerning all economic segments and activities in the U.S. economy. There are many advisory committees, such as the Federal Advisory Committee representing the interests of the banking industry, the Consumer Advisory Committee representing consumer interests, and similar other committees representing interests of other segments to the Federal Reserve System. Legislative, regulatory, monetary policy, and day-to-day operations of the central bank consider relevant details in their deliberations and policy decisions, including research from a wide variety of sources, private and public, about the economy.

LEGAL AND REGULATORY STRUCTURE

The key laws governing the U.S. financial institutions are: National Bank Act of 1863; Federal Reserve Act of 1913; McFadden Act of 1927; Banking Act (Glass-Steagall) of 1933 and 1935; Securities Act of 1933; Securities Exchange Act of

1934; Federal Credit Union Act of 1934; Investment Advisors Act of 1940; Investment Company Act of 1940; Bank Holding Company Act of 1956 and Douglas Amendment of 1970; Bank Merger Act of 1966; Employment Retirement Income Security Act of 1974; Depository Institutions Deregulation and Monetary Control Act of 1980; Depository Institutions (Garn-St. Germain) Act of 1982; Competitive Equality in Banking Act of 1987; Financial Institutions Reform, Recovery, and Enforcement Act of 1989; Federal Deposit Insurance Corporation Improvement Act of 1991; Interstate Banking and Branching Efficiency Act of 1994; and Financial Modernization Act of 1999.

The federal agencies that regulate depository institutions are: Office of the Comptroller of the Currency, Federal Reserve System, Federal Deposit Insurance System, National Credit Union Administration, and Office of Thrift Supervision. The Securities and Exchange Commission, Commodity Futures Trading Commission, and the Justice Department monitor and enforce relevant laws and regulations concerning securities and futures markets. State authorities regulate, monitor, and enforce laws concerning depository, insurance, finance companies and other financial institutions. The laws and regulations on financial institutions in the United States have made them competitive, efficient, fair, safe and sound, and transparent with the use of both carrots and sticks.

FINANCIAL SERVICES MODERNIZATION ACT 1999

The U.S. financial system in the twenty-first century has evolved into the largest, most developed, most efficient, and most sophisticated financial system in the world. The financial system has grown enormously since the founding of the first insurance company by Benjamin Franklin, as Philadelphia Contributionship, in 1752. The first banks in the United States were the Bank of New York, founded by Alexander Hamilton in 1784; Bank of Boston, also founded in 1784; and the First Bank of the United States, chartered in 1791. The economic structures and forces that have made this success possible are the concepts (or the foundation stones) of competition, specialization, thrift, entrepreneurial zest, and innovation. These concepts were just as well understood and vigorously practiced in the American colonies as they were expounded on by Adam Smith in Scotland in 1776 in *An Inquiry into the Nature and Causes of the Wealth of Nations*, his synthesis of a competitive market system. The United States has structured its economic and financial systems on Smith's economic model since its founding in 1776.

Some of the key concepts that have been the foundation stones of this financial architecture are: competition, efficiency, entrepreneurial culture, financial capital, innovation, regulation/deregulation/liberalization, reform, risk management, savings, specialization, and thrift.

The Financial Services Modernization Act, signed into law by the president on October 12, 1999, removes many of the restrictions on the banking and securities institutions imposed in the 1920s and 1930s. For example, financial conglomerates will again be able to organize commercial banking, insurance business, investment banking, securities underwriting, and other financial services under the umbrella of a holding/parent company. The McFadden Act and the Glass-Steagall Act are now in the history books. Financial innovation made possible by computer and communications technologies and spawned by competition and deregulation has brought U.S. financial institutions and the entire financial system to the exciting financial structure of the twenty-first century.

(SEE ALSO: *Capital Markets; Finance*)

BIBLIOGRAPHY

Blackwell, David W., Kidwell, D., and Peterson, R. L. (2000). *Financial Institutions, Markets, and Money*, 7th ed. Fort Worth, TX: Dryden Press, Harcourt College Publishers.

Dymski, Gary A., Epstein, G., and Pollin, R. (1993). *Transforming the U.S. Financial System: Equity and Efficiency for the 21st Century*. Armonk, NY: M.E. Sharpe.

Federal Deposit Insurance Corporation, Division of Research and Statistics. (1998). *Statistics on Banking: A Statistical Profile of the United States Banking Industry.*

Washington, DC: Federal Deposit Insurance Corporation.

Federal Reserve System. (1994). *Purposes and Functions*, 8th ed. Washington, DC: Board of Governors of the Federal Reserve System.

Hayes, III, Samuel L., ed. (1993). *Financial Services: Perspectives and Challenges*. Boston: Harvard Business School Press.

Kaufman, George G. (1995). *The U.S. Financial Systems: Money, Markets and Institutions*, 6th ed. Engelwood Cliffs, NJ: Prentice Hall.

Meerschwam, David M. (1991). *Breaking Financial Boundaries: Global Capital, National Deregulation, and Financial Services Firms*. Boston: Harvard Business School Press.

SURENDRA KAUSHIK

FINANCIAL MARKETS

(SEE: *Capital Markets*)

FINANCIAL STATEMENT ANALYSIS

Financial statement analysis is the process of examining relationships among financial statement elements and making comparisons with relevant information. It is a valuable tool used by investors and creditors, financial analysts, and others in their decision-making processes related to stocks, bonds, and other financial instruments. The goal in analyzing financial statements is to assess past performance and current financial position and to make predictions about the future performance of a company. Investors who buy stock are primarily interested in a company's profitability and their prospects for carning a return on their investment by receiving dividends and/or increasing the market value of their stock holdings. Creditors and investors who buy debt securities, such as bonds, are more interested in liquidity and solvency: the company's short- and long-run ability to pay its debts. Financial analysts, who frequently specialize in following certain industries, routinely assess the profitability, liquidity, and solvency of companies in order to make recommendations about the purchase or sale of securities, such as stocks and bonds.

Analysts can obtain useful information by comparing a company's most recent financial statements with its results in previous years and with the results of other companies in the same industry. Three primary types of financial statement analysis are commonly known as horizontal analysis, vertical analysis, and ratio analysis.

HORIZONTAL ANALYSIS

When an analyst compares financial information for two or more years for a single company, the process is referred to as *horizontal analysis*, since the analyst is reading across the page to compare any single line item, such as sales revenues. In addition to comparing dollar amounts, the analyst computes percentage changes from year to year for all financial statement balances, such as cash and inventory. Alternatively, in comparing financial statements for a number of years, the analyst may prefer to use a variation of horizontal analysis called *trend analysis*. Trend analysis involves calculating each year's financial statement balances as percentages of the first year, also known as the base year. When expressed as percentages, the base year figures are always 100 percent, and percentage changes from the base year can be determined.

VERTICAL ANALYSIS

When using vertical analysis, the analyst calculates each item on a single financial statement as a percentage of a total. The term *vertical analysis* applies because each year's figures are listed vertically on a financial statement. The total used by the analyst on the income statement is net sales revenue, while on the balance sheet it is total assets. This approach to financial statement analysis, also known as *component percentages*, produces *common-size financial statements*. Common-size balance sheets and income statements can be more easily compared, whether across the years for a single company or across different companies.

RATIO ANALYSIS

Ratio analysis enables the analyst to compare items on a single financial statement or to examine the relationships between items on two financial statements. After calculating ratios for each year's financial data, the analyst can then examine trends for the company across years. Since ratios adjust for size, using this analytical tool facilitates intercompany as well as intracompany comparisons. Ratios are often classified using the following terms: *profitability ratios* (also known as operating ratios), *liquidity ratios*, and *solvency ratios*. Profitability ratios are gauges of the company's operating success for a given period of time. Liquidity ratios are measures of the short-term ability of the company to pay its debts when they come due and to meet unexpected needs for cash. Solvency ratios indicate the ability of the company to meet its long-term obligations on a continuing basis and thus to survive over a long period of time. In judging how well on a company is doing, analysts typically compare a company's ratios to industry statistics as well as to its own past performance.

CAVEATS

Financial statement analysis, when used carefully, can produce meaningful insights about a company's financial information and its prospects for the future. However, the analyst must be aware of certain important considerations about financial statements and the use of these analytical tools. For example, the dollar amounts for many types of assets and other financial statement items are usually based on historical costs and thus do not reflect replacement costs or inflationary adjustments. Furthermore, financial statements contain estimates of numerous items, such as warranty expenses and uncollectible customer balances. The meaningfulness of ratios and percentages depends on how well the financial statement amounts depict the company's situation. Comparisons to industry statistics or competitors' results can be complicated because companies may select different, although equally acceptable, methods of accounting for inventories and other items. Making meaningful comparisons is also hampered when a company or its competitors have widely diversified operations.

The tools of financial statement analysis, ratio and percentage calculations, are relatively easy to apply. Understanding the content of the financial statements, on the other hand, is not a simple task. Evaluating a company's financial status, performance, and prospects using analytical tools requires skillful application of the analyst's judgment.

(SEE ALSO: *Analytical Procedures*)

MARY BRADY GREENAWALT

FINANCIAL STATEMENTS

Financial statements provide information of value to company officials as well as to various outsiders, such as investors and lenders of funds. Publicly owned companies are required to periodically publish general-purpose financial statements that include a balance sheet, an income statement, and a statement of cash flows. Some companies also issue a statement of stockholders' equity and a statement of comprehensive income, which provide additional detail on changes in the equity section of the balance sheet. Financial statements issued for external distribution are prepared according to generally accepted accounting principles (GAAP), which are the guidelines for the content and format of the statements. In the United States, the Securities and Exchange Commission (SEC) has the legal responsibility for establishing the content of financial statements, but it generally defers to an independent body, the Financial Accounting Standards Board (FASB), to determine and promote accepted principles.

The balance sheet, also known as the statement of financial position or condition, presents the assets, liabilities, and owners' equity of the company at a specific point in time. The assets are the firm's resources, financial or nonfinancial, such as cash, receivables, inventories, properties, and equipment. The total assets equal (balance) the sources of funding for those resources: liabilities (external borrowings) and equity (owners' contributions and earnings from firm operations). The balance sheet is used by investors, creditors, and other decision makers to assess the overall composition of resources, the constriction of external obligations, and the firm's flexibility and ability to change to meet new requirements.

Firms frequently issue a separate statement of stockholders' equity to present certain changes in equity, rather than showing them on the face of the balance sheet. The statement of stockholders' equity itemizes the changes in equity over the period covered, including investments by owners and other capital contributions, earnings for the period, and distributions to owners of earnings (dividends) or other capital. Sometimes companies present a statement of changes in retained earnings rather than a statement of stockholders' equity. The statement of changes in retained earnings, also known as the statement of earned surplus, details only the changes in earned capital: the net income and the dividends for the period. Then the changes in contributed capital (stock issued, stock options, etc.) must be detailed on the balance sheet or in the notes to the financial statements.

The income statement, also known as the statement of profit and loss, the earnings statement, or the operations statement, presents the details of the earnings achieved for the period. The income statement separately itemizes revenues and expenses, which result from the company's ongoing major or central operations, and the gains and losses arising from incidental or peripheral transactions. Certain irregular items (such as discontinued operations, extraordinary items, effects of accounting changes) are presented separately, net of tax effect, at the end of the statement. When revenues and gains exceed expenses and losses, net income is realized. Net income for the period increases equity. The results of the firm's operating activities for the period as presented in the income statement provide information that can be used to predict the amount, timing, and uncertainty of future cash flows. This statement is useful to investors, creditors, and other users in determining the profitability of operations. The income statement must also show earnings per share (EPS), where the net income is divided by the weighted average number of shares of common stock outstanding. Since EPS scales income by the magnitude of the investment, it allows investors to compare diverse companies of different sizes; hence, investors commonly use it as a summary measurement of firm performance.

In 1998, the FASB required that companies present a separate statement that classifies all items of other comprehensive income by their nature. Other comprehensive income includes all equity changes not recorded in the income statement or in the statement of changes in retained earnings and that do not result from contributions by owners. In addition to providing a separate statement, companies must display the total of other comprehensive income separately from retained earnings and additional paid-in capital in the equity section of the balance sheet.

The statement of cash flows replaced the statement of changes in financial position in 1987 as a required financial statement for all business enterprises. The statement of cash flows presents cash receipts and payments classified by whether they stem from operating, investing, or financing activities and provides definitions of each category. Information about key investing and financing activities not resulting in cash receipts or payments in the period must be provided separately. The cash from operating activities reported on the statement of cash flows must be reconciled to net income for the period. Because GAAP requires accrual accounting methods in preparing financial statements, there may be a significant difference between net income and cash generated by operations. The cash-flow statement is used by creditors and investors to determine whether cash will be available to meet debt and dividend payments.

Financial statements include notes, which are considered an integral part of the statements. The notes contain required disclosures of additional data, assumptions and methodologies employed, and other information deemed useful to users.

The financial statements of publicly owned companies also include an auditor's report, indicating that the statements have been audited by independent auditors. The auditor's opinion is related to fair presentation in conformity with GAAP.

The external financial statements required for not-for-profit organizations are similar to those for business enterprises, except that there is no ownership component (equity) and no income. Not-for-profit organizations present a statement of financial position, a statement of activities, and a statement of cash flows. The financial statements must classify the organization's net assets and its revenues, expenses, gains, and losses based on the existence or absence of donor-imposed restrictions. Each of three classes of net assets—permanently restricted, temporarily restricted, and unrestricted—must be displayed in the statement of financial position, and the amounts of change in each of those classes of net assets must be displayed in the statement of activities. Governmental bodies, which are guided by the Governmental Accounting Standards Board (GASB), present general-purpose external financial statements that are similar to those of other not-for-profit organizations, but they classify their financial statements according to fund entities.

(SEE ALSO: *Accounting; Financial Statement Analysis*)

BIBLIOGRAPHY

Engstrom, J., and Hay, L. (1996). *Essentials of Accounting for Governmental and Not-for-Profit Organizations.* Chicago: Irwin.

Financial Accounting Standards Board. (1987). *Statement of Financial Accounting Standards No. 95: Statement of Cash Flows.* Stamford, CT: Author.

Financial Accounting Standards Board. (1993). *Statement of Financial Accounting Standards No. 117: Financial Statements of Not-for-Profit Organizations.* Stamford, CT: Author.

Financial Accounting Standards Board. (1997). *Statement of Financial Accounting Standards No. 130: Reporting Comprehensive Income.* Stamford, CT: Author.

Gross, M., et al. (1995). *Financial and Accounting Guide for Not-for-Profit Organizations.* New York: Wiley.

Revsine, L., Collins, D., and Johnson, B. (1999). *Financial Reporting and Analysis.* Upper Saddle River, NJ: Prentice-Hall.

VICTORIA SHOAF

FISCAL POLICY

Fiscal policy is manifested in a government's policies on taxation and expenditures. To obtain funds for their operation, government units generally collect some form of taxes. The expenditure of these funds not only provides goods and services for constituents, but has a direct impact on the economy. For example, if expenditures are larger than the funds received by the government, the resulting deficit tends to stimulate the economy, as goods and services are produced for government purchase. In contrast, if a government runs a surplus by not spending all the funds it collects, economic growth will generally be curtailed, as the surplus funds are removed from circulation in the economy.

THE FEDERAL BUDGET

In the United States, the fiscal process of the federal government begins each February with the president sending to Congress a proposed federal budget for the coming fiscal year, which begins in October. Congress then develops a budget resolution, which is to be completed by April. The budget resolution contains overall revenue and spending budgets as well as the budgeted amount of discretionary and mandatory spending for each functional area, such as national defense. Mandatory spending is required by prior legislation, while discretionary spending must be approved during the current year's legislative process. The majority of all federal government spending is mandatory spending for established programs.

Using the budget resolution as a guide, bills that provide budget authority for annual discretionary spending must be completed by June each year. Legislative changes can also be made to mandatory spending or tax provisions at this time. However, any legislation that would cut taxes or increase mandatory spending must be accompanied by legislation that would raise revenue or cut spending in other areas to pay for these changes. Consequently, any new legislation in this area must be "budget-neutral."

In fiscal 1998, the federal government had receipts of $1,721 billion and expenditures of $1,651 billion, leaving a surplus of $70 billion. This was the first surplus recorded by the federal government since 1969, ending almost thirty consecutive years of deficits. During this time, the nonstop annual deficits forced the U.S. government to borrow additional money each year to make up the difference between the federal government's receipts and outlays. As a result, the outstanding federal debt reached roughly $5.5 trillion in 1998, representing more than $20,000 per citizen of the country. Paying the annual interest charges on this debt consumes a significant portion of the federal budget.

FEDERAL GOVERNMENT REVENUE

Individual income taxes have been the federal government's largest source of funds for many years. In 1998, $829 billion in individual income taxes were collected, comprising 48 percent of the federal government's receipts. Robust economic growth in the 1990s steadily increased individual income tax payments and was a large factor in turning the mushrooming deficits of the prior thirty years into a surplus in 1998, as tax collections grew faster than government spending.

Social Security taxes, which are paid by most workers in the United States, are the other major source of funds for the federal government. In 1998, payments of $540 billion were made into the Social Security system. These taxes, which are a percentage of a worker's wages, have increased substantially as a result of a growing work force in the 1990s with many workers in their peak earning years.

FEDERAL GOVERNMENT EXPENDITURES

The enormous impact of the Social Security system on the federal government's budget is demonstrated by the fact it is the largest outlay of the federal government each year. In 1998, almost 23 percent of federal government expenditures were payments of monthly benefits to families of retired and disabled workers. In 1940, in the early years of the Social Security program, there were only 222,000 beneficiaries receiving a total of $35 million a year in benefits. By 1998, the federal government was sending $379 billion to almost 45 million Social Security beneficiaries. When these payments are coupled with the burgeoning cost of Medicare, which generally provides health insurance for the same individuals who receive Social Security benefits, it means that the United States spent over 35 percent of the federal budget on this group of retired and disabled individuals in 1998. With the increased life expectancy of senior citizens and the large number of baby-boomers nearing retirement age, Social Security and Medicare will continue to consume a large part of the federal budget dollar in the foreseeable future.

Defense spending is the largest item of discretionary spending in the federal budget. In 1998, $270 billion, 16 percent of the federal budget, was spent on the armed forces of the United States. With an ever-larger portion of the federal budget being consumed by mandatory spending programs, defense spending has been the target of budget cuts since the resumption of normalized relations with the countries that constituted the former Soviet Union.

Interest on the federal government's debt is the other major federal government outlay, in 1998 requiring $243 billion in net interest payments on the federal debt, which exceeded $5 trillion. Declining interest rates and reduced federal government borrowing, however, have slowed the growth of this budget item.

IMPACT ON THE ECONOMY

As discussed previously, the federal government's policies on taxes and spending have a large impact on the economy. The economic theory of the famous English economist John Maynard Keynes advocates the use of the government's fiscal policy to offset imbalances in the economy.

According to Keynes, a government should use fiscal policy to stimulate an economy slowed by a recession by running a deficit, that is, by spending more than it takes from the economy in taxes. On the other hand, to slow down an economy that is threatened by inflationary pressures, Keynes urged increasing taxes or cutting spending to create a budget surplus that would act as a drag on the economy.

Keynes thought fiscal policy could be an automatic stabilizer for the economy because it automatically responds to changes in economic activity. Government spending on items such as unemployment benefits generally increases during a recession, whereas government receipts such as income taxes will fall during a recession, moderating the extremes of the business cycle. Consequently, fiscal policy, along with monetary policy, which is dictated by the Federal Reserve, has an important influence on the health of the economy in the United States.

IMPACT ON FOREIGN COUNTRIES

The impact of fiscal policy in the United States extends far beyond the country's borders. For example, top marginal income tax rates in this country have declined substantially since the late 1970s, when they were as high as 70 percent. This reduction in top rates has made it difficult for Canadian companies to attract and retain key executives because Canadian income taxes on high-income individuals are now substantially greater than in the United States. Even Canadian hockey teams have found that higher income tax rates north of the border encourage many of their players to flee to teams based in the United States, where they can retain a larger portion of their earnings. Consequently, even the balance of power in the National Hockey League is influenced by the fiscal policy of the U.S. government.

BIBLIOGRAPHY

A Citizen's Guide to the Federal Budget: Budget of the United States Government, Fiscal Year 1999. (1999). Washington, DC: Executive Office of the President.

Baker, Dean. (1995). *Robbing the Cradle?: A Critical Assessment of Generational Accounting*. Washington, DC: Economic Policy Institute.

Bruce, Neil. (1998). *Public Finance and the American Economy*. Reading, MA: Addison-Wesley.

DAVID McGRADY

FOOD AND DRUG ADMINISTRATION

The Food and Drug Act of 1906, which prohibited the interstate trade of misbranded or tainted food, drinks, and drugs, was passed by Congress on the same day as the Meat Inspection Act. At this time there was no Federal Drug Administration, but there was a Bureau of Chemistry. In 1927, a separate enforcement agency known as the Food, Drug and Insecticide Administration was created; in 1930, it was renamed the Food and Drug Administration (FDA). In 1938, after five years of battle with Congress, the Federal Food, Drug, and Cosmetic Act was passed. According to the FDA's Web site, it contained the following new provisions:

- Extending control to cosmetics and therapeutic devices.

- Requiring new drugs to be shown safe before marketing—starting a new system of drug regulation.

- Eliminating the Sherley Amendment requirement to prove intent to defraud in drug misbranding cases.

- Providing that safe tolerance is set for unavoidable poisonous substances.

- Authorizing standards of identity, quality, and fill-of-container for foods.

- Authorizing factory inspections.

- Adding the court injunctions to the previous penalties of seizures and prosecutions.

Later the FDA's jurisdiction was expanded to include microwaves and any radiation-emitting consumer products, as well as veterinary drugs and pet food. The agency monitors the manufacture, transportation, and sale of food and drugs. To ensure its efficiency, the FDA operates in 157 cities and employs approximately 9000 people. Among its employees are chemists, microbiologists, and investigators who visit 15,000 locations each year.

FDA inspectors visit businesses that are regulated by the FDA. If a problem exists, the FDA allows the company to voluntarily correct the problem or recall the faulty product. If the company refuses to cooperate, the FDA can go to court to force cooperation. Court action can include criminal prosecution if necessary.

In the area of drug control, the FDA does not conduct its own experiments but closely examines the results of the company's research. FDA inspectors conduct three types of inspections: study-oriented, investigation-oriented, and bioequivalence inspections. Study-oriented inspections are needed in case of new drug or new-product applications for approval. An investigator-oriented inspection may be ordered if other investigators looking at the same study think the findings are inconsistent. If one study is the sole basis for a marketer request, a bioequivalence study is conducted.

Once a drug or device is approved, the agency's responsibility does not end. The FDA monitors any complaints and looks for any adverse reactions associated with the product. As a result, approximately 3000 products are recalled each year.

In addition to ensuring the quality of the product itself, the FDA has had a major influence on businesses and the way goods are packaged; for example, medicines and products dangerous to children are now packaged in childproof bottles, and labels on containers of food products must list the nutritional contents and their amounts.

Any company that produces a product that is under the jurisdiction of the FDA has felt the pressure of its regulations, and complaints have been made about the slowness of the FDA's procedures. However, no country's citizens enjoy more protection regarding the products they use than U.S. citizens.

Demonstrators protest against Food and Drug Administration (FDA) policies.

More information is available from the Food and Drug Administration, Fishers Lane, Rockville, MD 20852 or http://www.fda.gov.

BIBLIOGRAPHY

Food and Drug Administration. *Frequently Asked Questions.* Archived at: http://www.fda.gov/opacom/fgs.

Food and Drug Administration. *FDA Inspections of Clinical Investigators.* Archived at: http://www.verity.fda.gov/search97.

Food and Drug Administration. *Milestones in United States Food and Drug Law History.* Archived at: http://www.fda.gov/opacom/backgrounder.

Food and Drug Administration. *Small Business Guide to FDA.* Archived at: http://www/fda.gov.opacom.

Food and Drug Administration. *Warning Letters.* Archived at: http://www.fda.gov/ora/compliance.

MARY JEAN LUSH
VAL HINTON

FOOD, DRUG, AND COSMETIC ACT OF 1938

The Food, Drug, and Cosmetic Act of 1938 is the most important of the pure food and drug acts passed and administered by the Food and Drug Administration (FDA) of the U.S. Department of Health and Human Services. Food and drug laws were enacted to ensure the safety, proper labeling, and purity of foods, drugs, vaccines, devices, and cosmetics. The 1938 act is a revision of the first food and drug law, enacted in 1906, which brought attention to many abuses in the form of poor health practices and excessive pricing. The 1938 revised law and subsequent amendments, give consumers greater protection from dangerous and impure foods and drugs; they require labeling that discloses the nature of the contents of the package when the buyer cannot see the product or judge its composition and value. They also provide safeguards against the introduction of untested new drugs (Versaware Technologies, 1999).

The Food, Drug, and Cosmetic Act of 1938 addressed the wholesomeness of the food supply by giving the FDA powers to engage in economic regulation, to set legally enforceable food standards, and to establish affirmative labeling requirements (Hardy, 1990). Consequently, the FDA examines food products' adulteration from the perspectives of both wholesomeness and safety. For example, the FDA has investigated several cases involving the alteration of fruit juices by dilution with sugarwater or less expensive juices that represent both reductions in wholesomeness and economic fraud.

Another condition of economic fraud covered by the Food, Drug, and Cosmetic Act is manufacturer misbranding of food: The food is not adulterated, but the consumer is deceived. In 1993, the FDA seized 2400 cases of Procter &

Gamble's Citrus Hill orange juice because the label used the word "fresh" when the product was, in fact, produced from concentrate. (Colford, 1991).

Since the passing of the first food and drug law, food laws and regulations have evolved from (1) concerns centering around food fraud, (2) to concerns about food safety, (3) to protection of the nutritional integrity of food, (4) to truth in labeling, (5) to, most recently, concern about the relationship between health and food. Many amendments to the Food, Drug, and Cosmetics Act of 1938 and other food-related laws and acts have been passed by Congress and will continue to be enacted in response to future technological changes and developments.

Manufacturers of food, drugs, cosmetics, and their related products must comply with the law. Penalties for violations include seizure of illegal goods, injunctions, restraint of shipments that violate the law, and criminal prosecution of those responsible for the violation, with fines up to $500,000, imprisonment up to ten years, or both, for repeated offenses.

BIBLIOGRAPHY

Colford, S. W. (1991). "FDA Getting Tougher." *Advertising Age* April. [Cited in Meier, K. J., Garman, E. T., and Keiser, L. R. (1998) *Regulation and Consumer Protection: Politics, Bureaucracy and Economics.* Houston, TX: DAME Publications.

Hardy, S. B. (1990). "Assuring a Healthy Food Supply: A Case for Fundamental Reform of Regulatory Programs." *American Review of Public Administration* 20:220-243.

Versaware Technologies, Inc. "Pure Food and Drug Acts." http://www.funkandwagnalls.com/encyclopedia/low/articles/p/p020001431f.html. March 10, 1999.

PHYLLES BUNN

FORECASTING IN BUSINESS

Business leaders and economists are continually involved in the process of trying to forecast, or predict, the future of business in the economy. Business leaders engage in this process because much of what happens in businesses today de-

Procter and Gamble was the subject of an FDA investigation in 1993.

pends on what is going to happen in the future. For example, if a business is trying to make a decision about developing a revolutionary new automobile, it would be nice to know whether the economy is going to be in a recession or whether it will be booming when the automobile is released to the general public. If there is a recession, consumers will not buy the automobile unless it can save them money, and the manufacturer will have spent millions or billions of dollars on the development of a product that might not sell.

The process of attempting to forecast the future is not new. Most ancient civilizations used some method for predicting the future. Today, computers with elaborate programs are often used to develop models to forecast future economic and business activity. Contemporary models of economic and business forecasting have been developed in the last century. Today's forecasting models are considerably more statistical than they were hundreds of years ago when

the stars, and other mystical methods, were used to predict the future. Almost every large business or government agency performs some type of formalized forecasting.

Forecasting in business is closely related to understanding the business cycle. The foundations of modern forecasting were laid in 1865 by William Stanley Jevons, who argued that manufacturing had replaced agriculture as the dominant sector in English society. He studied the effects of economic fluctuations of the limiting factors of coal production on economic development.

Forecasting has become big business around the world. Forecasters try to predict what the stock markets will do, what the economy will do, what numbers to pick in the lottery, who will win sporting events, and almost anything one might name. Regardless of who does it, forecasting is done to identify what is likely to happen in the future so as to be able to benefit most from the events.

QUALITATIVE FORECASTING MODELS

Qualitative forecasting models have often proven to be most effective for short-term projections. In this method of forecasting, which works best when the scope is limited, experts in the appropriate fields are asked to agree on a common forecast. Two methods are used frequently.

Delphi Method. This method involves asking various experts what they anticipate will happen in the future relative to the subject under consideration. Experts in the automotive industry, for example, might be asked to forecast likely innovative enhancements for cars five years from now. They are not expected to be precise, but rather to provide general opinions.

Market Research Method. This method involves surveys and questionnaires about people's subjective reactions to changes. For example, a company might develop a new way to launder clothes; after people have had an opportunity to try the new method, they would be asked for feedback about how to improve the processes or how it might be made more appealing for the general public. This method is difficult because it is hard to identify an appropriate sample that is representative of the larger audience for whom the product is intended.

QUANTITATIVE FORECASTING MODELS

Three quantitative methods are in common use.

Time-Series Methods. This forecasting model uses historical data to try to predict future events. For example, assume that you are interested in knowing how long a recession will last. You might look at all past recessions and the events leading up to and surrounding them and then, from that data, try to predict how long the current recession will last.

A specific variable in the time series is identified by the series name and date. If gross domestic product (GDP) is the variable, it might be identified as GDP2000.1 for the first-quarter statistics for the year 2000. This is just one example, and different groups might use different methods to identify variables in a time period.

Many government agencies prepare and release time-series data. The Federal Reserve, for example, collects data on monetary policy and financial institutions and publishes that data in the *Federal Reserve Bulletin*. These data become the foundation for making decisions about regulating the growth of the economy.

Time-series models provide accurate forecasts when the changes that occur in the variable's environment are slow and consistent. When large-degree changes occur, the forecasts are not reliable for the long term. Since time-series forecasts are relatively easy and inexpensive to construct, they are used quite extensively.

The Indicator Approach. The U.S. government is a primary user of the indicator approach of forecasting. The government uses such indicators as the Composite Index of Leading, Lagging, and Coincident Indicators, often referred to as Composite Indexes. The indexes predict by assuming that past trends and relationships will continue into the future. The government indexes are made by averaging the behavior of the different indicator series that make up each composite series.

The timing and strength of each indicator series relationship with general business activity, reflected in the business cycle, change over time. This relationship makes forecasting changes in the business cycle difficult.

Econometric Models. Econometric models are causal models that statistically identify the relationships between variables and how changes in one or more variables cause changes in another variable. Econometric models then use the identified relationship to predict the future. Econometric models are also called regression models.

There are two types of data used in regression analysis. Economic forecasting models predominantly use time-series data, where the values of the variables change over time. Additionally, cross-section data, which capture the relationship between variables at a single point in time, are used. A lending institution, for example, might want to determine what influences the sale of homes. It might gather data on home prices, interest rates, and statistics on the homes being sold, such as size and location. This is the cross-section data that might be used with time-series data to try to determine such things as what size home will sell best in which location.

An econometric model is a way of determining the strength and statistical significance of a hypothesized relationship. These models are used extensively in economics to prove, disprove, or validate the existence of a casual relationship between two or more variables. It is obvious that this model is highly mathematical, using different statistical equations.

For the sake of simplicity, mathematical analysis is not addressed here. Just as there are these qualitative and quantitative forecasting models, there are others equally as sophisticated; however, the discussion here should provide a general sense of the nature of forecasting models.

THE FORECASTING PROCESS

When beginning the forecasting process, there are typical steps that must be followed. These steps follow an acceptable decision-making process that includes the following elements:

1. *Identification of the problem.* Forecasters must identify what is going to be forecasted, or what is of primary concern. There must be a timeline attached to the forecasting period. This will help the forecasters to determine the methods to be used later.

2. *Theoretical considerations.* It is necessary to determine what forecasting has been done in the past using the same variables and how relevant these data are to the problem that is currently under consideration. It must also be determined what economic theory has to say about the variables that might influence the forecast.

3. *Data concerns.* How easy will it be to collect the data needed to be able to make the forecasts is a significant issue.

4. *Determination of the assumption set.* The forecaster must identify the assumptions that will be made about the data and the process.

5. *Modeling methodology.* After careful examination of the problem, the types of models most appropriate for the problem must be determined.

6. *Preparation of the forecast.* This is the analysis part of the process. After the model to be used is determined, the analysis can begin and the forecast can be prepared.

7. *Forecast verification.* Once the forecasts have been made, the analyst must determine whether they are reasonable and how they can be compared against the actual behavior of the data.

Each of the seven steps has substages; however, the steps that have been presented are the major concerns to the forecaster. Those with a deep interest in forecasting might pursue more in-depth treatments.

FORECASTING CONCERNS

Forecasting does present some problems. Even though very detailed and sophisticated mathematical models might be used, they do not always predict correctly. There are some who would argue that the future cannot be predicted at all—period!

Some of the concerns about forecasting the future are that (1) predictions are made using historical data, (2) they fail to account for unique events, and (3) they ignore coevolution (developments created by our own actions). Additionally, there are psychological challenges implicit in forecasting. An example of a psychological challenge is when plans based on forecasts that use historical data become so confining as to prohibit management freedom. It is also a concern that many decision makers feel that because they have the forecasting data in hand they have control over the future.

Regardless of the opponents to forecasting, the U.S. government, investment analysts, business managers, economists, and numerous others will continue to use forecasting techniques to predict the future. It is imperative for the users of the forecasts to understand the information and use the results as they are intended.

BIBLIOGRAPHY

Fulmer, William, E. (2000). *Shaping the Adaptive Organization: Landscapes, Learning, and Leading in Volatile Times.* New York: AMACOM.

Moore, Geoffrey H. (1983). *Business Cycles, Inflation, and Forecasting.* Cambridge, MA: Ballinger.

Sherman, Howard, J., and Kolk, David X. (1996). *Business Cycles and Forecasting.* New York: HarperCollins.

Stock, James H., and Watson, Mark W., eds. (1993). *Business Cycles, Indicators, and Forecasting.* Chicago: University of Chicago Press.

ROGER L. LUFT

FOREIGN CORRUPT PRACTICES ACT OF 1977

The Foreign Corrupt Practices Act of 1977 (FCPA) evolved from investigations by the Office of the Special Prosecutor that provided evidence of illegal acts perpetrated by U.S. firms in foreign lands. More than 400 U.S. companies admitted to making questionable payments to various foreign governments and political parties as part of an amnesty program (U.S. Department of Justice http://www.usdoj.gov). Given the environment of the 1970s and the proliferation of white-collar crimes (e.g., insider trading, bribery, false financial statements, etc.), particularly the payments made to foreign officials by corporations, Congress felt obligated to introduce legislation that led to the act. Congress's objective was to restore confidence in the manner U.S. companies transacted business.

THE ACT

The FCPA is unique. Throughout history, governments have had laws making it illegal for governmental officials to *take* a bribe. One basic provision of the FCPA is that it prohibits U.S. partnerships, companies, and organizations from not only giving payments but also *offering* or authorizing payments to foreign officials or political parties with the objective of encouraging or assuring business relationships.

There are two types of bribery provisions. The first prohibits any bribes made directly by the U.S. company. The second prohibits any organization from knowingly arranging for a bribe through an intermediary. Many thought that the FCPA would place U.S. companies at a disadvantage in the international marketplace since they could no longer influence foreign governments, officials, political parties, or candidates through gifts or payments. There has been no conclusive evidence that this has actually happened.

The FCPA includes record-keeping provisions for companies not involved in criminal conduct. These provisions were an amendment to the Securities and Exchange Act of 1934. The FCPA amendment requires all firms under SEC jurisdiction to maintain an adequate system of internal control whether or not they have foreign operations. This provision of the act applies to issuers of registered securities and issuers required to file periodic reports with the SEC.

ACCOUNTING PROVISIONS

The accounting provisions require companies to "keep books and records, and accounts, which, in reasonable detail, accurately and fairly reflect the transactions and dispositions of assets". The purpose of this accounting provision is to make it difficult for organizations to "cook the books" or use slush funds to hide any corrupt payments. Representative means for transfer of corrupt payments included:

- Overpayments
- Missing records ("No receipt")
- Unrecorded transactions
- Misclassification of costs (bribes recorded as consulting fees or commissions)
- Retranscription of records

The accounting provisions include a requirement that companies design and maintain adequate systems of internal accounting controls that provide reasonable assurance that:

- Transactions are executed in accordance with management's authorization
- Transactions are recorded as necessary
- Access to assets is permitted only in accordance with management's authorization

Any internal document that misrepresents the actual nature of a financial transaction could be used as the basis for a charge that the "books and records" section of the FCPA has been violated.

ENFORCEMENT

Enforcement of the act is shared. Civil and criminal enforcement of the bribery provisions for those not required to file with the SEC rests with the Department of Justice. Responsibility for civil enforcement of the bribery provisions for those who have SEC filing requirements rests with the SEC.

In 1988 the FCPA was amended to allow for "facilitating payments" for expediting routine governmental action. These payments are distinguishable from corrupt payments in that these "grease payments" are for facilitating the performance of officials who are obligated to perform said duties. Questions regarding this amendment, affirmative defenses, or other provisions of the FCPA should be directed to counsel, or companies may wish to use the Department of Justice's Foreign Corrupt Practices Act Opinion Procedure. Under this procedure, upon receiving a question from a company or individual, the attorney general has thirty days to issue an opinion regarding the inquiry. The objective is to alleviate uncertainty regarding acts covered by the FCPA.

PENALTIES

The FCPA provides penalties for violations. Criminal penalties for bribery violations include fines of up to $2 million for firms; fines of up to $100,000 and imprisonment of up to five years for officers, directors, and stockholders; and fines of up to $100,000 for employees and agents (fines imposed on individuals cannot to be paid by companies). The SEC or attorney general may also bring actions that lead to civil penalties. Also, the act's penalties do not supersede penalties or fines levied under the provisions of other statutes. A violation of the bribery provisions of the FCPA may give rise to a private cause of action for treble damages under RICO (Racketeer Influenced and Corrupt Organizations Act).

The penalties can have long-term ramifications for companies. For example, a company found guilty of violating the FCPA may be barred from doing any business with the federal government. A company indicted for an FCPA violation may not be eligible to obtain various export licenses.

COMPLIANCE

Clearly, large multinational corporations cannot monitor every transaction of every dollar amount by every employee. However, companies do have a due-diligence obligation to implement adequate systems with sufficient internal controls. Key ways to avoid violation and liability include establishing policies and procedures that provide reasonable assurance that the business is adhering to the act's provisions. Suggested due-diligence steps for compliance with the FCPA include the following:

- Utilizing the compliance program under the Corporate Sentencing Guidelines Act (see next section)
- Performing a risk evaluation of locations known for unethical business practices
- Performing risk evaluation of employees/ agents who operate out of the home country
- Assuring that personnel who work out of the home country are knowledgeable regarding the provisions of the FCPA
- Assessing internal controls to be assured they are sufficient
- Monitoring internal controls, including reviews by auditors
- Reviewing critical transactions, such as those related to consulting services

- Establishing a procedure requiring that critical employees, vendors, and contractors provide written statements that they are in compliance with the requirements of the FCPA

SUBSEQUENT DEVELOPMENTS

On November 1, 1991, the Corporate Sentencing Guidelines Act was enacted. The guidelines appear to be a direct descendent of the FCPA. The guidelines for organizations "are designed so that the sanctions imposed upon organizations and their agents will, taken together, provide just punishment, adequate deterrence, and incentives for organizations to maintain internal mechanisms for preventing, detecting, and reporting criminal conduct" (U.S. Sentencing Guidelines, chapter 8, intro. comm., appendix p. Al).

In most corporations, accountants and auditors have responsibility to prevent, detect, and report errors and irregularities. The Corporate Sentencing Guidelines are legislation to deter white-collar crime. The guidelines' major objective is requiring organizations to monitor business activities to detect criminal conduct within their own ranks.

The guidelines allow organizations to use mitigating factors to reduce their exposure to fines. One mitigating factor is maintaining a corporate compliance program. The corporate compliance program is to be the responsibility of an officer or high-level employee. Elements of the compliance program include:

- Established standards and procedures
- Communication of the standards to employees
- Systems designed to detect criminal conduct
- A reporting system in place whereby individuals may report criminal conduct
- Disciplinary mechanisms that are consistently enforced

FURTHER GUIDANCE

Information regarding the FCPA or the Foreign Corrupt Practices Act Opinion Procedure may be obtained from the Fraud Section of the Criminal Division, U.S. Department of Justice, Room 2424, Bond Building, 1400 New York Avenue, NW, Washington, DC 20530; (202)-514-0651.

(SEE ALSO: *Securities and Exchange Commission*)

CHARLES H. CALHOUN

FOREIGN EXCHANGE

(SEE: *Currency Exchange*)

FORMALIZATION

(SEE: *Organizational Structure*)

FRANCHISING

Franchising is an arrangement whereby a supplier, or *franchiser*, grants a dealer, or *franchisee*, the right to sell products in exchange for some type of consideration. It is a business arrangement involving a contract between a manufacturer or another supplier and a dealer that specifies the methods to be used in marketing a good or service. The franchiser may receive some percentage of total sales in exchange for furnishing equipment, buildings, management know-how, and market research. The franchisee supplies labor and capital, operates the franchised business and agrees to abide by the provisions of the franchise agreement.

Historically, franchising was a grant by a king to allow a citizen an exclusive right to sell a product or render a service. For this right, the sovereign protected the exclusivity and the subject paid the government an appropriate tribute in service, food, goods, or money. Franchising in the United States started shortly after the Civil War, when the Singer Company began to set up sewing-machine franchises. The concept became increasingly popular after 1900 in the automobile industry. Because of this, other automotive franchises developed for gasoline, oil, and tires. In the 1950s, food operations made a dramatic entrance into franchising with the development of Mc-

Donald's, currently one of the world's largest franchise organizations.

In 1999, franchising accounted for $916 billion in annual sales, with 533 outlets employing more than 7 million people. A new franchise opens somewhere in the United States every six minutes. Franchising accounts for approximately 40 percent of all United States retail sales. Because of changes in the international marketplace, shifting employment options in the United States, the expanding U.S. economy, and corporate interest in more joint-venture activity, franchising will continue to increase rapidly.

Franchising represents the small entrepreneur's best chance to compete with the giant companies that dominate the marketplace. Without franchising, thousands of businesspeople would never have had the opportunity to own their own businesses.

The largest percentages of franchise operations are in the recreation, entertainment, and travel fields, followed closely by business services, nonfood retailing, and automotive products and services. In 1999, the top ten franchises in descending order were Yogen Fruz Worldwide (first place), McDonald's, Subway, Wendy's International Inc., Jackson Hewitt Tax Service, KFC, Mail Boxes Etc., TCBY Treats, Taco Bell, and Jani-King.

Retail franchise agreements fall into three general categories. In one type of arrangement, a manufacturer authorizes a number of retail stores to sell a certain-brand name item. This franchise arrangement, one of the oldest, is common in the sales of cars and trucks, farm equipment, shoes, paint, earth-moving equipment, and gasoline. About 90 percent of all gasoline is sold through franchised independent service stations, and franchised dealers handle virtually all sales of new cars and trucks.

In the second type of retail franchise, a producer licenses distributors to sell a given product to retailers. This arrangement is common in the soft drink industry. Most national manufacturers of soft drinks—Coca-Cola, Dr. Pepper, PepsiCo—grant franchises to bottlers, which then service retailers.

In the third type of retail franchise, a franchiser supplies brand names, techniques, or other services, instead of complete products. The franchiser may provide certain production and distribution services, but its primary role in the arrangement is careful development and control of marketing strategies. This approach to franchising, very common today, is used by such organizations as Holiday Inn, AAMCO, McDonald's, Dairy Queen, KFC, and H&R Block.

A good franchise system can offer the prospective franchisee a diversified array of business savvy. In most instances, the franchisee enjoys the benefit of a nationally recognized trade name, national recognition, and the instant collective goodwill of the franchise. Standard quality and uniformity of a product or service coupled with an existing—and successful—system of marketing and accounting are other benefits. In addition, expert advice on location, design, capitalization, and operational issues is provided by the franchiser. Specialization on a national level is done in order to maintain the necessary research and market analysis that will enable the franchisee to remain competitive in an ever-changing marketplace. In other words, a business framework is supplied that reduces the number of risks that may arise when starting a new business. Most often these risks are associated with the financial investment involved. However, the franchise agreement often offers a cost savings by sharing a centralized purchasing system, and in some instances, direct financial assistance.

ADVANTAGES AND DISADVANTAGES OF FRANCHISING

Franchising offers several advantages to both the franchisee and the franchiser. It enables a franchisee to start a business with limited capital and to benefit from the business experience of others. Moreover, nationally advertised franchises, such as ServiceMaster and Burger King, are often assured of customers as soon as they open. If business problems arise, the franchisee can obtain guidance and advice from the franchiser at little or not cost. Franchised outlets are generally more successful than independently owned businesses.

Less than 10 percent of franchised retail businesses fail during the first two years of operation, whereas approximately half of independent retail businesses fail during that period. The franchisee also receives material to use in local advertising and can benefit from national promotional campaigns sponsored by the franchiser. At the turn of the twenty-first century, Taco Bell franchisees profited from a national advertising campaign featuring a Chihuahua demanding "Yo quiero Taco Bell" ("I want some Taco Bell"). The ads helped boost same-store sales at Taco Bell by 3 percent in an otherwise flat industry. The talking dog was especially popular among teenagers, who spend more than $12 billion per year at fast-food restaurants.

The franchiser gains fast and selective product distribution through franchise arrangements without incurring the high cost of constructing and operating its own outlets, thus giving it more capital for expanding production and advertising. It can also ensure, through the franchise agreement, that outlets are maintained and operated according to its own standards. The franchiser benefits from the fact that the franchisee, being a sole proprietor in most cases, is likely to be very highly motivated to succeed. Success of the franchise means more sales, which translate into higher income for the franchiser.

Despite these numerous advantages, franchise arrangements also have drawbacks for both parties. The franchiser can dictate many aspects of the business: decor, design of employees' uniforms, types of signs, and numerous other details of business operations. In addition, franchisees must pay to use the franchiser's name, products, and assistance. Usually franchisees must pay a one-time franchise fee as well as continuing royalty and advertising fees, often collected as a percentage of sales. For example, Subway requires franchisees to come up with $40,000 to $80,000 in start-up costs. Franchisees often must work very hard, putting in twelve-hour days, six or seven days a week. In some cases, franchise agreements are not uniform; one franchisee may pay more than another for the same services. The franchiser also gives up a certain amount of control when entering into a franchise agreement. Consequently, individual establishments may not be operated exactly the way the franchiser would like.

When entering into a franchise agreement, franchisees must be prepared to make major commitments of both money and time. They must be prepared to invest a substantial amount of money, both in the initial franchising fee and in start-up costs and carrying funds to provide a cash flow sufficient to operate the business during the beginning months or, if necessary, years. Most franchisees average a net profit of less than $30,000 a year.

The second commitment is that of time; in the beginning, the proprietor will be obliged to devote long hours to the details of the business operation. Experience has shown that this commitment is the common denominator to many successful franchise operations. Franchisees must rely to a large extent upon their own aptitude and drive in order to learn the business. They must also rely upon the product, services, and business skills of the franchiser.

In deciding whether or not to enter into a franchise agreement, there are several key points that need to be considered. The first consideration is price and costs. What is the total cost? What are the initial fees? What are the ongoing costs? Are there any hidden extras? Are you restricted in your right to purchase other goods?

The second consideration is the location. Where will the franchise be located? What is the territory that it will serve? What are the protections and limitations? Who can compete with you?

The third issue involves control and support. What controls will be in place? What policies and regulations govern the franchise agreement? What training and ongoing support will be supplied?

Advertising is the fourth consideration. The franchisee needs to determine what national and regional advertising will be supplied, as well as what the franchisee pays for and what the franchiser finances.

The last area of concern involves profits and losses, transfer and death, and duration and termination. Potential franchisees need to determine not only what protection they will receive for their earnings if they are successful but also what obligations they will be responsible for if the franchise fails. In addition, they need to find out whether, in the event of their death, the franchise agreement can be transferred to their heirs or automoatically reverts to the franchiser. Finally, they need to determine what stipulations, penalties, and other responsibilities are involved in terminating the contract with the franchiser should they no longer wish to continue in the business.

THE FRANCHISING SECTOR

A franchise is like any other business property in that it is the buyer's responsibility to know what he or she is buying. Poorly financed or poorly managed franchise systems are no better than poorly financed or poorly managed nonfranchise businesses. It is important to remember that there are trends in franchises, just as in other types of businesses. Growth areas for franchising in the 1990s included providing home care (finding nannies for children and nurses for homebound patients), catering to children (operating educational and child-care centers), tending people's homes (maid service), servicing cars, and, as always, operating fast food establishments.

The growth of the franchised fast-food industry has been truly spectacular. These franchise operations are second only to automobile dealerships and gasoline stations in gross volume of sales. Most often located at key intersections or on busy highways, fast-food enterprises enjoy a high visibility.

In this segment of the franchise industry, the majority of franchise operators have already owned other businesses before entering into a fast-food franchise. Many successful operators are college graduates, but the significant number of successful franchisees with only a high school education suggests that education alone is not a determining factor. A fast-food franchise is the type of venture in which both husband and wife can contribute to the success of the business.

Most fast-food franchisers consider geographic location to be an important factor in the success of the operation. And, like franchisers in other fields, they cite the importance of adequate capitalization, the efficient operation of the franchise system, good customer relations, quality employees, and the contributions of the franchisees, such as their management skills and especially their hard work.

According to Cassano's Pizza and Subs, a franchiser with twelve outlets in four states, the successful franchise operator must have several traits: (1) an excellent attitude toward customer service and customer relations; (2) an entrepreneurial ability and spirit combined with good business techniques; (3) a willingness to take a hands-on attitude toward the business. Newcomers to the Cassano's franchised fast-food business must have prior retail management experience and previous food service experience. All new franchisees are trained at the home office in Dayton, Ohio, for one month. After that, the franchise provides ongoing training and managerial assistance.

GLOBAL FRANCHISING

Franchising is growing rapidly abroad, with more than 370 franchise companies operating in about 40,000 outlets overseas. Canada is the largest of these markets, followed by Japan, Europe, Australia, and the United Kingdom. In 1995, Subway signed a deal with Japanese financiers to open 1000 franchise outlets in Japan. Subway tailored its products to fit the local tastes—for example, offering the Japanese market fried pork sandwiches.

Franchising can be a workable way for small firms to enter foreign markets, especially markets where there are few competitors. For example, Automation Paper Company, a small New Jersey-based supplier of high-technology paper products, used franchising to gain exclusive representation in target markets. The franchisees receive rights to the company's trademark, as well as training for local staffs and the benefit of the firm's experience, credit lines, and advertising budget.

The problems facing franchise companies in international transactions are relatively less formidable than those facing other service sectors. Franchisers must comply with the same local requirements as other businesses, and the franchise agreements must comply with local contract law, antitrust law, and trademark and licensing laws. Aside from language and cultural differences, many of the problems of conducting business in foreign countries are the same as those involved in the United States. The success or failure of foreign franchising will depend in large measure on the soundness of the franchiser's domestic market position and on the franchiser's ability to provide the necessary expertise to others in another part of the world.

Some franchises popular in the United States actually started in another country. For example, Molly Maid started in Canada in 1980 and came to the United States four years later.

All trends indicate that franchising will continue to expand both domestically and internationally, creating great opportunities for existing and new businesses; developing new entrepreneurs, new jobs, new products, new services; and providing export opportunities. Rising personal income, stable prices, high levels of consumer optimism, and increased competition for market share are turning many companies, both small and large, to franchising. Education will play an important role in the future of franchising, as both high schools and colleges increase the number of courses that are taught in marketing, business management, and entrepreneurship. In addition, changing patterns in American demographics, coupled with the increased number of women in the work force, are influencing the number of new franchises each year. In 1998, approximately 14 percent of franchisee-owned outlets are run by women, whereas 21 percent are run by female-male partners.

Furthermore, shifting demographic patterns and the use of new technology have intensified competition among franchise companies. These factors have increased the number of mergers and acquisitions in the franchising system, and it is expected that this merger/acquisition trend will persist for several years. Creativity and imagination in the treatment of goods and services are the focus of most business ventures today. Education, computers, and the ability to work with and manage people will be profitably utilized by new emerging businesses. All these developments suggest that franchising will be one of the leading methods of doing business in the first decade of the twenty-first century, even in an environment of mixed signals in the economy.

BIBLIOGRAPHY

Conlin, Elizabeth. (1991). "Second Thoughts on Growth." *Inc.* March: 66.

Moore, Lisa. (1991). "The Flight to Franchising," *US News & World Report.* June 10: 78-81.

Pride, William, and Ferrell, O.C. (2000). *Marketing Concepts and Strategies.* Boston: Houghton Mifflin.

U.S. Bureau of the Census. (1997). *Statistical Abstract of the United States.* Washington, DC.

PATRICIA A. SPIROU

FRAUDULENT FINANCIAL REPORTING

The equity and credit markets (capital markets) in the United States are considered to be among the most efficient in the economically developed world. One reason for the efficient operation of these markets is the public availability of creditable financial statements to individuals and institutions and the confidence in these statements by those using them as a basis for their investment and credit decisions. A potential serious threat to the efficient functioning of these markets is the incidence of fraudulent financial reporting.

Fraudulent financial reporting is intentional or reckless conduct, acts, or omissions, that result in materially misleading financial statements. Confidence in the operation of capital markets is diminished when the system of public disclosure is eroded by reported instances of fraudulent reporting.

John Dingell, chairman of the Subcommittee on Oversight.

In the mid-1980s, the failure of a number of financial institutions led various groups to determine possible causes, including the extent of fraudulent reporting involved in the failures. The Subcommittee on Oversight and Investigations of the U.S. House of Representative's Committee on Energy and Commerce held hearings concerning the accounting profession. The subcommittee's intent was to determine whether the system of public disclosure and reporting needed corrective action. In opening the hearings, the chairman, Representative John Dingell, questioned whether the public disclosure and audit system then in effect was meeting public expectations. In August 1986, Congressman Dingell and other members of the committee proposed legislation to amend the Securities and Exchange Act of 1934 to require independent public accountants (auditors) to include procedures for material financial fraud detection, to require reporting on internal control systems, and to require the reporting of fraudulent activities to appropriate en-

forcement and regulatory authorities. The legislative proposals were not accepted. There persisted the belief that the profession could respond successfully to the challenges without further legal requirements.

A private-sector response to these hearings, the National Commission on Fraudulent Financial Reporting (Treadway Commission)—jointly sponsored and funded by the American Institute of Certified Public Accountants (AICPA), the American Accounting Association (AAA), the Financial Executives Institute (FEI), the Institute of Internal Auditors (IIA), and the National Association of Accountants (NAA) (now the Institute of Management Accountants)—was formed in 1985 to identify factors contributing to fraudulent financial reporting and to develop recommendations to reduce its future occurrence. The Treadway Commission issued its report in October 1987.

TREADWAY COMMISSION REPORT

The Treadway Commission concluded that the responsibility for fraudulent financial reporting was not vested in one group. While the commission conceded that financial statements are the responsibility of a company's management, it issued a series of recommendations for the public company, the independent public accountant, the Securities and Exchange Commission (SEC), and the educational community.

The report identified a number of factors that might contribute to fraudulent financial reporting, including a number of environmental, institutional, and individual personal incentives to engage in fraudulent financial reporting. Institutional incentives include falsely improving financial appearances in financial statements for the purpose of maintaining market stock prices or to meet investor expectations as well as delaying the reporting of financial difficulties in order to avoid failure to comply with covenants in debt agreements. Individual incentives include falsely reporting results in order to achieve targeted results for bonus or incentive compensation purposes, as well as to avoid penalties for poor performance in achieving targeted profit objectives.

The commission indicated that the oversight bodies that establish auditing standards and those that monitor compliance have a continuing responsibility to uphold the integrity of the public disclosure and reporting system. The Commission also concluded that many of the Securities and Exchange Commission's fraudulent financial reporting cases against auditors' alleged failure to conduct the audits in accordance with generally accepted auditing standards.

RECOMMENDATIONS FOR THE PUBLIC COMPANY

The commission made a number of recommendations affecting public companies. These included proposals that companies develop and vigilantly enforce written codes of corporate conduct because such codes foster a positive ethical climate and discourage incidences of fraudulent financial reporting by positively affecting behavior throughout the public company.

The commission noted that company audit committees (those members of a company's board of directors who have responsibility for oversight of the financial reporting process) have historically been generally successful in exercising their oversight responsibility regarding financial reporting. However, it offered a number of recommendations that would improve this system. The commission proposed that boards of directors of all public companies be required by SEC rule to be composed of independent (outside, nonemployee) directors. Other specific recommendations included proposals to expand the authority of the audit committee and to enhance communications with the company's internal auditors and independent public accountants.

RECOMMENDATIONS FOR THE INDEPENDENT PUBLIC ACCOUNTANT

The commission issued a number of specific recommendations designed to improve the auditor's ability to detect fraudulent financial reporting. One significant proposal was a recommendation that the Auditing Standards Board (ASB) of the AICPA revise standards to restate the independent public accountant's responsibility for the detection of fraudulent financial reporting. The commission recommended that the independent public accountant be required to take proactive steps to assess the potential for fraudulent financial reporting and design audit tests to provide reasonable assurance of detection. Other recommendations included suggestions for improved detection capabilities through required analytical review procedures in all audit engagements and improvements to peer review processes and other intra-accounting firm review procedures. The commission also suggested that the SEC strengthen the civil and criminal sanctions affecting registrants and the independent public accountant.

RECOMMENDATIONS FOR THE SECURITIES AND EXCHANGE COMMISSION

The commission acknowledged that strong and effective deterrence is essential in reducing the incidence of fraudulent financial reporting. The commission's recommendations to the SEC included increasing deterrence by issuance of new SEC sanctions, greater criminal prosecution, improved regulation of the public accounting profession, adequate SEC resources, improved federal regulation of financial institutions, and improved oversight by the state boards of accountancy.

RECOMMENDATIONS FOR EDUCATION

The commission concluded that education could influence present and future participants in the financial reporting system. Therefore, recommendations were made related to curricula, professional certification examinations, and continuing professional education.

The commission recommended that the business and accounting curricula should convey a deeper understanding of internal controls and the overall control environment within which financial reporting takes place. Students need to be taught the complex regulatory and law enforcement framework that government and private-sector bodies have developed to provide safeguards to protect the public interest. Students also need to develop skills that will help prevent, detect, and deter fraud in financial reporting. The ethical dimension of financial reporting should be given more emphasis in college and university programs.

The commission recommended that certification examinations and continuing education programs give greater attention to the knowledge, skills, and ethical values that would produce a better understanding of fraudulent financial reporting and possibly promote a reduction in the incidence of such fraud.

RESPONSE OF THE AUDITING STANDARDS BOARD

In response to the Treadway Commission report and to other influences, the Auditing Standards Board issued ten new auditing standards in April 1988. These Statements on Auditing Standards (SASs) include requirements affecting the auditor's responsibility to detect and report errors and irregularities, consideration of internal control structure in a financial statement audit, and communication with a company's audit committee.

SAS No. 53, "The Auditor's Responsibility to Detect and Report Errors and Irregularities," stated auditor responsibility more clearly than had the earlier statement with the same title. SAS No. 53, however, was superseded in 1997 with a new SAS, No. 82, "Consideration of Fraud in a Financial Statement Audit." This revised Statement clearly identified the responsibility of the auditor to provide reasonable assurance that the two types of misstatements are detected: those arising from fraudulent financial reporting and those arising from misappropriation of assets.

Another SAS, No. 61, "Communication with Audit Committees," was issued to enhance the role of the audit committee of the board of directors in understanding the scope and results of the audit so that the committee members would be more effective in overseeing the financial reporting and disclosure process for which the company's management is responsible. In complying with this Statement, the auditor is required to communicate to the audit committee such matters as the company's management's significant accounting policies, judgments, and accounting estimates, and disagreements with the auditors. The audit committee is to be informed of any consultation that management had with other accountants and of difficulties the auditors encountered while performing the audit.

SAS No. 55, "Consideration of Internal Control in a Financial Statement Audit," changed the responsibility of the auditor for internal control. The new Statement required the auditor to develop an understanding of internal control sufficient to plan the audit and to document the understanding. Prior to the issuance of the new Statement, the auditor was not required to develop such an understanding. SAS No. 55 was amended with the issuance of SAS No. 78 in 1997, which redefined internal control. Control environment and risk assessment, among the concerns of the Treadway Commission, were more clearly described in SAS No. 78 and the auditor's responsibility for both factors clearly specified.

CONTINUING ATTENTION TO THE PROBLEMS OF FRAUDULENT FINANCIAL REPORTING

Attempts have continued to enhance understanding of fraudulent financial reporting in the United States. In early 1999, for example, the Committee of Sponsoring Organizations of the Treadway Commission (COSO) issued the results of a study of Accounting and Auditing Enforcement Releases issued by the SEC between 1987 and 1997. This study attempted to improve ways of determining who participated in a fraud as well as the size and duration of the fraudulent behavior.

The Blue Ribbon Committee, formed at the request of the SEC chairman, the New York Stock Exchange, and the National Association of Securities Dealers, was charged with recommending ways to enhance the effectiveness of audit committees. The committee reported its recommendations in early 1999. The focus of the recommendations was related to audit committee oversight responsibilities relating to financial reporting.

The SEC, with its oversight responsibility for financial reporting, continues to provide leadership in cooperation with other groups for the reduction of fraudulent financial reporting.

(SEE ALSO: *Audit Committees*; *Auditing*)

BIBLIOGRAPHY

Mancino, June. (1997). "The Auditor and Fraud." *Journal of Accountancy* April: 32-36.

McConnell, Donald K., Jr., and Banks, George Y. (1997). "The New Fraud Auditing Standard." *CPA Journal* June:22-30.

Report of The National Commission on Fraudulent Financial Reporting. (1987).

GERARD A. LANGE

FREE ENTERPRISE

(SEE: *Economic Systems*)

FUND ACCOUNTING

(SEE: *Government Accounting*; *Not-For-Profit Accounting*)

FUTURE BUSINESS LEADERS OF AMERICA

Future Business Leaders of American (FBLA) is one of ten nationally recognized vocational student organizations in the United States (Gordon, 1999). The organization is a nonprofit educational association for students who are preparing for careers in business and business-related fields. The organization is composed of four divisions:

- FBLA for middle school students
- FBLA for high school students
- Phi Beta Lambda (PBL) for post-secondary students
- A professional division composed of business-people, educators, and other individuals who

uphold the goals of the organization ("Frequently Asked Questions," 1999).

FBLA has been in existence since 1937. Dr. Hamden I. Forkner of Teachers College of Columbia University developed the first chapter in New York City (Vaughn et al., 1990). In 1940 the National Council for Business Education recognized and sponsored FBLA. The first high school chapter was chartered in Johnson City, Tennessee, on February 3, 1942. Currently, more than 25,000 active members participate in the organization.

Students participating in FBLA have the opportunity to develop leadership skills; enter a variety of competitions at local, state, and national levels; establish occupational goals; and learn from business and professional individuals in their communities. The goals of FBLA (and PBL) are the following:

- To promote competent, aggressive business leadership
- To understand American business enterprise
- To establish career goals
- To encourage scholarship
- To promote sound financial management
- To develop character and self-confidence
- To facilitate transition from school to work ("Frequently Asked Questions," 1999)

Conferences, seminars, awards, publications, and scholarships are services provided for members of the organization. By providing practical hands-on activities for students in the business arena, FBLA continues to prepare young men and women to become successful leaders in our ever-changing society. More information is available from FBLA or PBL at FBLA/PBL Inc., 1912 Association Drive, Reston, Virginia 22091; (800)FBLA-WIN; or http://www.fbla-pbl.org/.

BIBLIOGRAPHY

"Frequently Asked Questions about FBLA-PBL." http://www.fbla-pbl.org/. 1999.

Gordon, Howard R. D. (1999). *The History and Growth of Vocational Education in America.* Needham Heights, MA: Allyn and Bacon.

Vaughn, P. R., Vaughn, R. C., and Vaughn, D. L. (1990). *Handbook for Advisors of Vocational Student Organizations.* Athens, GA: American Association for Vocational Instructional Materials.

JILL T. WHITE

G

GENERAL ACCOUNTING OFFICE

(SEE: *U.S. Government Accounting Office*)

GENERALLY ACCEPTED ACCOUNTING PRINCIPLES

Most individuals who understand the basics of financial reporting are familiar with the phrase *generally accepted accounting principles* (GAAP) and will readily identify the Financial Accounting Standards Board (FASB) as the standard-setting body in the United States currently responsible for establishing accounting principles for nongovernmental entities. However, some may not be aware that there is no single reference source for GAAP because these principles are derived from a variety of sources. For example, although the FASB is responsible for issuing FASB Statements of Financial Accounting Standards, Interpretations, and Technical Bulletins, the American Institute of Certified Public Accountants (AICPA) issues Statements of Position, Audit and Accounting Guides, and Practice Bulletins, and the FASB Emerging Issues Task Force (EITF) issues EITF Abstracts.

It may seem that accounting principles could be generally accepted because of popular vote or consensus of opinion. However, *generally accepted accounting principles* is a technical accounting phrase defined in Accounting Princi-

ples Board (APB) Statement No. 4, *Basic Concepts and Accounting Principles Underlying Financial Statement of Business Enterprises*, as "the conventions, rules, and procedures that define accepted accounting practice at a particular time." GAAP includes not only broad guidelines of general application but also detailed practices and procedures that provide a standard by which to measure financial presentations. For the most part, in financial reporting, "generally accepted" implies "substantial authoritative support."

THE GAAP HIERARCHY

Although there is no single reference source for GAAP, there is a hierarchy established by the AICPA in Statement on Auditing Standards No. 69, *The Meaning of "Present Fairly in Conformity With Generally Accepted Accounting Principles" in the Independent Auditor's Report* (SAS 69). At the foundation of that hierarchy are the principles established by the FASB and its predecessors, the APB and the AICPA Committee on Accounting Procedure. From that foundation, the hierarchy formulates a "pecking order" for all the rules and procedures that are incorporated in the preparation of financial statements and that have come to be known as GAAP.

The GAAP hierarchy includes four successive categories (A-D), each of which establishes a different level of authority. Generally speaking, if there is a conflict between accounting principles relevant to the circumstances from one or more sources in Categories A, B, C, or D, the treatment specified by the source in the higher category is then followed. In other words, Categories A through D of the hierarchy descend in authority. Therefore, Category A takes precedence over all others, Category B takes precedence over Categories C and D, and Category C takes precedence over Category D. If a situation is not covered by guidelines in Categories A through D, other accounting literature should be considered. However, that literature should be consulted only when guidelines in higher categories are not applicable.

Category A Category A consists of the following officially established accounting principles: (1) FASB Statements of Financial Accounting Standards, (2) FASB Interpretations, (3) APB Opinions, and (4) AICPA Accounting Research Bulletins. All of those accounting principles are included in Volumes I and II of *Original Pronouncements*, which is updated annually and published by the FASB. In addition, FASB Statements and Interpretations are available individually from the FASB as published.

The accounting principles included in Category A are often referred to as "Rule 203 pronouncements" because the bodies responsible for establishing those principles have been so designated by the AICPA Council, pursuant to Rule 203 of the AICPA Code of Professional Conduct. Specifically, from September 1939 to August 1959 the AICPA committees on terminology and on accounting procedure were responsible for issuing fifty-one Accounting Research Bulletins (ARBs). In 1953, the first forty-two of those were revised, restated, or withdrawn and now appear as ARB No. 43, *Restatement and Revision of Accounting Research Bulletins.* On September 1, 1959, the AICPA committees were superseded by the APB, which issued thirty-one Opinions until it ceased operations in June 1973. At that time, the FASB took over the responsibilities of standard setting from the APB and as of March 31, 2000, had issued 137 Statements of Financial Accounting Standards and 44 Interpretations.

Category B Category B consists of (1) FASB Technical Bulletins and, if cleared by the FASB, (2) AICPA Statements of Position and (3) AICPA Industry Audit and Accounting Guides. Technical Bulletins are available individually from the FASB as published and are also included collectively in Volume II of *Original Pronouncements.* Statements of Position and Audit and Accounting Guides are available individually from the AICPA as published. In addition, Statements of Position are included collectively in *AICPA Technical Practice Aids.*

FASB Technical Bulletins provide timely guidance for applying Category A accounting principles and resolving accounting issues not directly addressed in those principles. The following kinds of guidance may be provided in a Technical Bulletin:5

- Guidance that clarifies, explains, or elaborates on an underlying standard.
- Guidance for a particular situation (usually a specific industry) that differs from the general application required by the standard in an ARB, APB Opinion, or FASB Statement or Interpretation. For example, the guidance in a Bulletin may specify that the standard does not apply to enterprises in a particular industry or may provide for deferral of the effective date of a standard for that industry.
- Guidance that addresses areas not directly covered by existing standards.

The AICPA's Accounting Standards Executive Committee (AcSEC), which works closely with the FASB and its staff, is the senior technical committee of the AICPA authorized to set accounting standards and to speak for the AICPA on accounting matters. AcSEC's standard-setting activities are often industry-specific or narrow in scope, whereas the FASB's activities result in standards that are more general and broader in scope. AcSEC issues AICPA Statements of Position, which present conclusions with respect to an emerging problem or diversity in practice. In addition, AcSEC issues AICPA Audit and Accounting Guides, which either interpret GAAP as applicable to a specific industry or, in some cases, establish industry-specific GAAP. For example,

Guides have been published for agricultural producers and cooperatives, airlines, casinos, construction contractors, and health care organizations.

Category C Category C consists of (1) AcSEC Practice Bulletins that have been cleared by the FASB and (2) consensus positions of the FASB Emerging Issues Task Force (EITF). AcSEC Practice Bulletins are available individually from the AICPA as published and are also included collectively in *AICPA Technical Practice Aids*. Consensus positions of the EITF are available individually from the FASB as published and are included collectively in *EITF Abstracts*, which is published by the FASB.

The EITF was established by the FASB in 1984 to assist in the early identification of emerging issues affecting financial reporting and of problems in implementing authoritative pronouncements. Each EITF Abstract summarizes the accounting issue involved and the results of the EITF discussion, including any consensus reached on the issue. Each Abstract also reports, in its "status" section, subsequent developments on that issue, such as issuance of a relevant Securities and Exchange Commission Staff Accounting Bulletin or an FASB Technical Bulletin. If the EITF can reach consensus on an issue, usually that is taken as an indication that no action is needed by the FASB or AcSEC. Alternatively, if no consensus is possible, it may be an indication that action by one of those bodies is necessary.

AcSEC Practice Bulletins are used to disseminate AcSEC's views for the purpose of providing practitioners and preparers with guidance on narrow financial accounting and reporting issues.6 The issues covered by Practice Bulletins are limited to those that have not been and are not being considered by the FASB. Therefore, AcSEC Practice Bulletins, which are reviewed by the FASB, are only issued after the FASB has informed AcSEC that it has no current plans to consider the issue.

Category D Category D includes (1) AICPA Accounting Interpretations, (2) FASB staff implementation guides, and (3) practices that are widely recognized and prevalent either generally or in an industry.

AICPA Accounting Interpretations (not to be confused with FASB Interpretations, which are included in Category A) were issued from March 1971 through November 1973. The purpose of the interpretations was to provide timely guidance for applying APB Opinions without the formal procedures required for an APB Opinion. In addition, they were used to clarify points on which past practice may have varied and been considered generally accepted. The interpretations, prepared by AICPA staff and reviewed by members of the accounting profession, are not considered to be official pronouncements of the APB. Although most of the interpretations have been superseded by other accounting standards, Volume II of *Original Pronouncements* includes those that continue in effect as well as reference pages for those that have been superseded.

Implementation guides, which appear in a question-and-answer format, are issued as aids to understanding and implementing various FASB Statements. Typically, those guides are issued when an unusually high number of inquiries are received and the accounting required by a given FASB Statement is particularly complex. The positions and opinions expressed in those guides are those of the FASB staff and do not represent official positions of the FASB. Staff implementation guides are available individually from the FASB as published and also are included collectively in *FASB Staff Implementation Guides*.

OTHER ACCOUNTING LITERATURE

Occasionally new transactions or events for which there are no established accounting principles must be reported. In those instances, it is sometimes possible to identify an analogous transaction or event for which there is an established principle and report the new transaction or event similarly. In the absence of a pronouncement in one of the four categories above or an analogous transaction or event, other accounting literature should be considered. Examples of other literature include: FASB Concepts Statements; APB Statements; AICPA (AcSEC) Issues

Papers; pronouncements of other accounting standard-setting bodies, professional associations, or regulatory agencies; technical information service inquiries; and accounting textbooks, handbooks, and articles.

SUMMARY

Generally accepted accounting principles are not a set of specific circumscribed standards that can be easily found in one convenient set of rules. Rather, they are an amalgam arising from various sources and with an established hierarchy. Generally accepted accounting principles range from official standards established by the FASB, through literature from the AICPA, to, in some situations, articles. Yet the system seems to work reasonably well. Financial statements prepared pursuant to GAAP are highly regarded in the United States for the quality and comparability of the information they provide. Thus, investors and other users have been well served by our system of financial reporting, which results in the fair presentation of financial information prepared in conformity with generally accepted accounting principles.

(SEE ALSO: *Accounting; Financial Accounting Standards Board; Government Financial Reporting*)

BIBLIOGRAPHY

Financial Accounting Standards Board. (1999). *Accounting Standards: Vol. I. General Standards; Topical Index; Vol. II: Industry Standards; Topical Index/Appendixes.* New York: Wiley.

EDMUND L. JENKINS
CHERI REITHER

GENERIC PRODUCTS

(SEE: *Product Labeling*)

GLOBAL ECONOMY

The global economy refers to the increasing integration of fragmented national markets for goods and services into a single global market. In such a market, companies may source from one country, conduct research and development (R&D) in another country, take orders in a third country, and sell wherever there exists demand regardless of the customer's nationality. Kenichi Ohmae (1989), a Japanese consultant, calls this the *borderless world*. While nobody would argue that national borders are completely irrelevant, certain influences have caused the globe to become smaller and smaller. These include technological advances in global communication and transportation, the dilution of culture, a decrease in tariff and nontariff barriers, and a self-feeding change in the degree of global competition.

INTERNATIONAL TRADE

To comprehend the recent increase in global markets, it is important to have some understanding of the historical development of international trade. While some form of international trade existed prior to the colonial expansion of Europe in the fifteenth and sixteenth centuries, *mercantilism*, or the trading of gold and silver for goods, served as the precursor for the large flows of goods, services, and information that currently exists. This philosophy of national power postulated that those countries with large amounts of *specie* could maintain the types of armies necessary to conquer other nations. The conquered nations then provided additional sources of revenues either through goods, slave labor, or gold and silver that could be used to support additional armies, thereby creating a "virtuous" cycle.

From the demands of war, trade theory has moved through a number of stages. Adam Smith, the Scottish economist and philosopher, stated that countries traded because they had an *absolute advantage*. One nation's workers could produce a given product more efficiently than workers in other countries. Rather than produce those products that it could produce but poorly, a country could specialize and exchange those products it produced efficiently for those produced efficiently by another country and, therefore, increase its overall wealth.

David Ricardo altered this theory to suggest that a country need only have a *comparative ad-*

vantage in order to specialize and trade to increase wealth. A country having an absolute advantage in two goods might find that it would still rather specialize in that good for which it had relatively greater production expertise. It could then trade its excess for a greater quantity of the second good than it could have obtained had it split its production between the two goods.

These theories of trade were followed by Hecksher and Ohlin's *theory of factor proportions* (1933), which suggested that countries will specialize in the production and trade of either capital-intensive products or labor-intensive products, depending on whether their comparative advantage lies in capital or labor. Other theories of trade include Vernon's *product cycle theory*, which suggests that a country's comparative advantage in products changes over time as the technology to produce that product changes, and Porter's writings on the competitive advantage of nations, according to which a nation's competitive industries depend on domestic rivalry, demand conditions, factor conditions, and the strength of related and supporting industries.

CAUSES OF INCREASING GLOBALIZATION

During the time that different trade theories have risen and fallen, the world has become a smaller place. One of the primary facilitators of the global marketplace is the technological advance of the telecommunications industry.

In the days of Adam Smith, if a merchant wanted to trade a lot of wool for a case of port wine, the communication of that intent would require weeks. Sending a message to a subordinate in India took months. Such circumstances lent themselves to fragmented individualized markets with subsidiaries run by family members or close friends. These in-country managers were trusted to make decisions in the best interest of the company because no rapid means of communicating new opportunities and information existed. The opportunity to closely coordinate the activities of several foreign operations simply did not exist.

Today, communication between most parts of the world is instantaneous. A manager in Bonn can telephone a manager in Rio de Janeiro to discuss the latest news regarding the orange crop. If the Brazilian manager wants to send some contracts to the German manager, it can be done by fax; if the data demands are larger, the information can be transferred via the Internet. Should the Brazilian manager then need to travel to the middle of the Amazon rainforest to check up on the supply of a certain healing plant, that information can also be passed on to Germany through a sophisticated cellular phone.

These new capabilities allow vast amounts of business data to be transferred almost instantaneously all over the world and at ever-decreasing costs. The cost of a three-minute phone call between London and New York fell from $13.73 in 1973 to $1.78 in 1993.

These gains in communication technology closely parallel those in the transportation industry. P. Dicken (1992) indicates that between 1500 and 1840 the best average speed of horse-drawn coaches and sailing ships was about ten miles per hour. Between 1850 and 1930, steam became a dominant technology, with trains averaging sixty-five miles per hour and ships increasing their speed to thirty-six miles per hour. In the 1950s, propeller aircraft achieved speeds of three hundred to four hundred miles per hour. These speeds later increased to over six hundred miles per hour with the advent of the jet-engine technology. Again, what this means is that an executive who used to spend several weeks traveling from Lisbon to Rio de Janeiro to visit a factory could visit factories all over the world in that same amount of time.

These advances have greatly increased the potential for flows of goods and individuals across national borders. Further advances include such things as standardized shipping containers, which can be easily transferred from sea carriers to land carriers and can be packed with greater efficiency. In addition, the vast size of modern supertankers has greatly increased the amount of goods that can be shipped at one time.

In addition to advances in transportation and communication, some scholars, such as Theodore Levitt (1983), have argued that the world has become a smaller place in terms of tastes and preferences. The tastes of teenagers around the world may be as much informed by Hollywood movies and MTV as they are by cultural heritage. Levitt argues that such convergence of preferences is not limited to any one age group, since adults worldwide enjoy Chinese food, country music, pizza, and pita bread. While some convergence has certainly taken place, scholars such as Susan P. Douglas and Yoram Wind (1987) argue that this cross-border similarity of tastes and preferences is limited to certain countries and product lines.

While the extent of convergence is certainly arguable, it is clear that at least in some countries and with some product lines, the tastes and preferences of consumers seem quite similar. This reality encourages a global-market approach to business as companies attempt to reach the largest number of consumers at the lowest price possible.

Another factor leading to a more globalized marketplace is the historical decrease in tariff and nontariff barriers. In 1930 the United States raised tariffs under the Smoot-Hawley Tariff Act to an average of 53 percent. Other countries followed suit, and international trade slowed significantly. In 1947 several leading trading nations created the *General Agreement on Tariffs and Trade* (GATT) to serve as a forum for bringing down trade barriers. Between 1947 and 1994, trading countries around the world have participated in eight rounds of negotiating in an effort to reduce tariffs. The latest round, entitled the Uruguay round, boasted 117 participants and resulted in an average tariff reduction of 35 percent. As tariff barriers fell, the inducement to trade was increased as foreign-produced goods became more and more competitive with domestic goods.

In addition to the GATT agreements, several countries have participated in regional agreements encouraging even lower tariff rates among participants. An example of such an agreement is the North American Free Trade Agreement (NAFTA) implemented by Canada, Mexico, and the United States in 1994. This agreement re-

duced tariffs over a fifteen-year period, lifted many investment restrictions, allowed for easier movement of white-collar workers, opened up government procurement over a ten-year period, and created a mechanism for dispute resolution. As a result, retailers such as Wal-Mart and 7-Eleven have expanded operations into Mexico, and many Mexican and Canadian firms have been enjoying the benefits of participating in the world's largest consumer market, the United States. In the first two years of NAFTA's implementation, trade among Canada, the United States, and Mexico increased by 43 percent.

In addition to NAFTA, numerous other such agreements exist, including the European Union, the Carribean Community and Common Market (CARICOM), the Economic Community of West African States (ECOWAS), the Association of Southeast Asian Nations (ASEAN), and the Andean Common Market (ANCOM). Each of these agreements seeks to promote trade through minimizing the barriers to trade that exist in the region.

Closely related to the liberalization of trade, technological advantages, and the convergence of consumer preferences are a set of competitive factors centered around the ideas of economies of scale (larger production volumes generating lower per-unit production costs) and locational advantages. Marquise R. Cvar (1986) cites the example of Becton Dickinson, which in the 1980s was faced with new technologies in disposable syringe production that could dramatically decrease the cost of these medical devices. Unfortunately, the investment needed in technology was so high that, to be efficient, the company would have to capture 60 percent of the U.S. and Japanese markets. Further, it was believed that by doubling volume, cost would decrease by 20 percent. Becton Dickinson responded by creating standardized syringes for markets in the United States, Europe, Mexico, Brazil, Australia, the Philippines, Singapore, and Hong Kong. In so doing, they were able to reduce the cost of their product to 5 to 10 percent below those of local competitors while simultaneously providing generally higher quality. These savings led to an average market share of 45 percent in those countries.

Further, this standardization approach also allowed Becton Dickinson to shift production among various plants located in the United States, Ireland, Spain, Mexico, and Brazil. As exchanges rates fluctuated, the company was able to increase production at more cost-effective plants while decreasing it elsewhere, resulting in even greater savings. Further, companies in such situations may use profits in one country to subsidize their competitive activities in another. While anti-dumping laws prohibit selling exported goods at a price below their cost of production or at a price lower than the price in the home market, companies will sometimes seek to attack a competitor in a foreign market by engaging in dumping-like pricing in an attempt to wrest market share. If the firm under attack has operations in the foreign firm's home market, it can respond in kind. A purely domestic firm does not have such options.

In response to the competitive advantage enjoyed by global companies such as Becton Dickinson, local firms often respond by becoming more global themselves. This cycle has created a more worldwide competitive market for a large number of products and services.

CONCLUSION

Changes in communications and transportation technology, convergence of consumer tastes and preferences, trade liberalization, and the emergence of global competitors have all combined to create a much more integrated world economy. Companies like Becton Dickinson, Unilever, and Samsung profit from larger numbers of consumers and cheaper factors of production, while consumers may experience lower prices and higher quality. Of course, some might argue that the benefits of the global marketplace come at a price. Membership in trade organizations such as the World Trade Organization (WTO) may limit a country's ability to create laws regarding the conduct of business within its borders since each law must pass the scrutiny of the WTO. In addition, the interrelatedness of markets may cause a negative domino effect within a region, as happened with the Asian crisis of the 1990s. Despite these and other concerns, however, the global marketplace seems likely to continue its expansion as new technological advances continue to shrink the importance of geographic distance.

BIBLIOGRAPHY

Adonis, A. (1994). "Lines Open for the Global Village." *Financial Times* September 17: 8.

Cvar, Marquise R. (1986). "Case Studies in Global Competition: Patterns of Success and Failure." In *Competition in Global Industries*, edited by Michael E. Porter. Boston: Harvard Business School Press, pp. 483-516.

Czinkota, Michael R., Ronkainen, Ilkka A., and Moffett, Michael H. (1999). *International Business*, 5th ed. Fort Worth, TX: Dryden Press.

Daniels, John D., and Radebaugh, Lee H. (1998). *International Business: Environments and Operations*, 8th ed. Reading, MA: Addison Wesley.

Dicken, P. (1992). *Global Shift*. New York: Guilford.

Douglas, Susan P., and Wind, Yoram. (1987). "The Myth of Globalization." *Columbia Journal of World Business* Winter: 19-29.

Grubel, H. (1981). *International Economics*. Homewood, IL: Irwin, 1981.

Hill, Charles W. L. (1998). *Global Business Today*. Boston: Irwin.

Levitt, Theodore. (1983). "The Globalization of Markets." *Harvard Business Review* May-June: 91-102.

Ohlin, B. (1933). *International Trade*. Cambridge, MA: Harvard University Press.

Ohmae, Kenichi. (1989). "Managing in a Borderless World." *Harvard Business Review*, May/June: 152-161.

NORMAN S. WRIGHT

GROSS NATIONAL PRODUCT (GNP)

(SEE: *Gross Domestic Product*)

GOALS AND OBJECTIVES

(SEE: *Strategic Management*)

GOODS AND SERVICES

Goods and services are the outputs offered by businesses to satisfy the demands of consumer and industrial markets. They are differentiated on the basis of four characteristics:

1. *Tangibility:* Goods are tangible products such as cars, clothing, and machinery. They have shape and can be seen and touched. Services are intangible. Hair styling, pest control, and equipment repair, for example, do not have a physical presence.

2. *Perishability:* All goods have some degree of durability beyond the time of purchase. Services do not; they perish as they are delivered.

3. *Separability:* Goods can be stored for later use. Thus, production and consumption are typically separate. Because the production and consumption of services are simultaneous, services and the service provider cannot be separated.

4. *Standardization:* The quality of goods can be controlled through standardization and grading in the production process. The quality of services, however, is different each time they are delivered.

For the purpose of developing marketing strategies, particularly product planning and promotion, goods and services are categorized in two ways. One is to designate their position on a goods and services continuum. The second is to place them into a classification system.

The goods and services continuum enables marketers to see the relative goods/services composition of total products. A product's position on the continuum, in turn, enables marketers to spot opportunities. At the pure goods end of the continuum, goods that have no related services are positioned. At the pure services end are services that are not associated with physical products. Products that are a combination of goods and services fall between the two ends. For example, goods such as furnaces, which require accompanying services such as delivery and instal-lation, are situated toward the pure goods end. Products that involve the sale of both goods and services, such as auto repair, are near the center. And products that are primarily services but rely on physical equipment, such as taxis, are located toward the pure services end.

The second approach to categorizing products is to classify them on the basis of their uses. This organization facilitates the identification of prospective users and the design of strategies to reach them. The major distinction in this system is between consumer and industrial products. Consumer goods and services are those that are purchased for personal, family, or household use. Industrial goods and services are products that companies buy to make the products they sell.

Two major changes have affected the marketing and production of goods and services since about 1950. The first was a shift in marketing philosophy from the belief that consumers could be convinced to buy whatever was produced to the marketing concept, in which consumer expectations became the driving force in determining what was to be produced and marketed. This change in orientation has resulted in increases in both lines of products and choices within the lines.

The second change was an increased demand for services. The growth in demand for services—and resulting production—continues to increase at a faster rate than the demand for manufactured goods.

BIBLIOGRAPHY

Bearden, William O., Ingram, Thomas N., and LaForge, Raymond W. (1995). *Marketing, Principles and Perspectives.* Chicago: Irwin.

Evans, Joel R., and Berman, Barry. (1997). *Marketing,* 7th ed. Upper Saddle River, NJ: Prentice-Hall.

Jackson, Ralph W., Neidell, Lester A., and Lunsford, Dale. (1995). "An Empirical Investigation of the Differences in Goods and Services as Perceived by Organizational Buyers." *Industrial Marketing Management* March: 99-108.

EARL C. MEYER
MATTHEW F. HAZZARD

GOVERNMENT ACCOUNTING

Government accounting has been viewed historically as a key element in the movement from *absolute power*, (i.e., the government or a king or emperor) to *relative power* (i.e., a shared model of government). Under the shared model of government, government accounting was used by a parliament to limit the king's power to (1) spend public money, (2) raise taxes to cover the expenditures, and (3) determine the purpose of the expenditure. The use of governmental accounting remained unchanged during the evolution into modern democratic systems.

Thus government accounting requires the executive to (1) state the amount, nature, and purpose of the planned expenditure and the taxes needed to fund it, (2) ask for and obtain approval from the legislature, and (3) comply with the expenditure authority—that is, appropriation—granted by the legislature and demonstrate such compliance. Under government accounting, the legislature is allowed to steer and control the behavior of the government.

The basic foundation of governmental financial accounting and reporting in the United States was established by the Governmental Accounting Standards Boards (GASB) in its "Objectives of Financial Reporting," which stated that the purpose of financial reporting is to provide information to facilitate decision making by various groups (GASB, 1987). The groups were defined as (1) citizens of the governmental entity, (2) direct representatives of the citizens, such as legislatures and oversight bodies, and (3) investors, creditors, and others who are involved in the lending process. Although not specifically identified, intergovernmental agencies and other users have informational needs similar to the three primary user groups. While the three user groups have overlapping membership with corporate financial information users, citizens and legislative users are unique to governments. The use of governmental accounting information centers on political, social, and economic decisions in addition to determining the government's accountability.

Accountability (GASB, 1987, 56-58) was identified as the paramount objective of governmental financial reporting because it is based on the transfer of responsibility for resources or actions from the citizens to some other party, such as the management of the governmental entity. The assessment of accountability is fulfilled when financial reporting enables financial data users to determine to what extent current-period costs are financed by current-period revenues. Two basic types of budgets are used by governments and are the same as those used by corporate entities—an annual operating budget and a capital budget. Governmental annual operating budgets include estimated revenues and appropriations for expenditure for a specific fiscal year. Capital budgets control the expenditures for construction projects and fixed asset acquisitions. Operating or capital budgets are recorded in the accounting system as a means of control or compliance.

Many governmental entities are required by law to maintain a balanced budget in that revenues must equal or exceed appropriations; the latter situation results in a budgetary surplus. If a budgetary deficit occurs in a governmental entity with a balanced-budget requirement, additional appropriations must be enacted by the legislative process.

Governmental accounting uses a fund accounting structure as a means of controlling resources. That is, each type of financial activity is segregated into a separate set of self-balancing asset, liability, and net asset accounts. GASB codification identifies three fund groups—governmental, proprietary, and fiduciary (GASB, 1997, Sections 1100.103 and 1100.105). Governmental funds are used to account for financial resources used in the day-to-day operations of the government. Proprietary funds are those used to account for the government's business-type activities where fees are charged for the services rendered, for example, utility services. Fiduciary funds are those used to account for funds held by the government in trust for others that cannot be used to support the government's programs, for example, an employee pension fund.

State and local governments report dual-perspective financial information with both full accrual information and fund-based modified accrual information in accordance with GASB Standard No. 34, *Basic Financial Statements— and Management Discussion and Analysis—for Statement and Local Governments* (GASB, 1999).

The management's discussion and analysis (MD&A) is required supplementary information presented before the financial statements that is subjected to limited auditor review and presents an overview of the government's financial activities for the part year. This narrative description of the financial performance is much like the management discussion required of corporations by the Securities and Exchange Commission (SEC). The MD&A provides an objective and easily readable analysis of the government's financial activities based on currently known facts, decisions, or conditions. The discussion compares the government's current-year results with the previous year and may include charts, graphs, or tables to illustrate the discussion. The discussion is general rather than specific so that the most relevant information is provided. At a minimum, fourteen prescribed elements are a part of the MD&A discussion; these elements explain the relationship among the financial statements and any significant differences in the information provided in the financial statement.

The full accrual information reports the full cost of providing government services, with details on how much of the cost is borne by taxpayers and by specific users of the government's service. The full accrual reports are similar to those of profit-seeking corporations. The government's equity is displayed as net assets rather than stockholders' equity. The full accrual results of the government's financial activity are displayed in two government-wide reports—(1) the statement of net assets and (2) the statement of activities.

The statement of net assets displays information about the government as a whole, reports all financial and capital resources, and assists the financial statement user in assessing the medium- and long-term operational accountability of the

government. Separate columns are used to distinguish between the financial data for the governmental activities and the business-type activities that comprise the total primary government. As the term *statement of net assets* implies, the statement format presents the assets minus liabilities that equal the total net assets, that is, equity. Assets and liabilities are presented in their order of liquidity. That is, assets are presented in the order to their nearness to producing cash, and liabilities are presented in the order to their nearness to consuming cash. Assets and liabilities may be displayed in a classified, current, and noncurrent format if desired. The government's net assets are presented in three components: (1) capital assets net of related accumulated depreciation and debt, (2) restricted net assets with constraints imposed on their use by parties outside the government, and (3) unrestricted net assets.

The statement of activities reports the net expense over revenue of each individual function or program operated by the government. The net expense over revenue format reports the relative financial burden of each of the programs on the government's resource provides—taxpayers. The format highlights the extent to which each program directly consumes the government's revenues or is financed by fees, contributions, or other revenues.

In addition to the governmentwide full accrual information, state and local governments present financial statements on the fund-based modified accrual basis. In the modified accrual basis of accounting, revenues are recognized only when they become both measurable and available to finance expenditures for the fiscal period. Expenditures are recognized when the related liabilities are incurred, if measurable, except for unmatured interest on long-term debt, which is recognized when legally due.

Fund-based financial statements assist in assessing the government's short-term fiscal accountability. Most funds are established by governments to show restrictions on the planned use of resources or to measure, in the short-term, the revenues and expenditures of a particular activity. Fund activity displayed in the fund-based financial statements is grouped by governmental, proprietary, and fiduciary categories as identified by the GASB codification. The equity component of modified accrual fund-based financial statements is reported as fund balance rather than net assets, which is used in the full accrual statement.

A balance sheet and a statement of revenues, expenditures, and change in fund balance are required for each of the three fund groups. Because the fund financial statements are prepared using the modified accrual basis, a required reconciliation is prepared that explains the differences between the net change in fund balances and the change in net assets in the governmentwide statement of activities. The proprietary funds also present a statement of cash flows. Unlike corporate cash flow statements, the governmental cash flow statement is prepared using the direct method and has four categories—operating, noncapital financing, capital financing, and investing activities.

Although some similarities exist between accounting for state and local governments and accounting for the federal government, there are selected areas specific to each. For example, federal agencies account for quarterly apportionments to procure goods and services, a process that is generally ignored by state and local governments. The head of each agency in the executive branch of the federal government has the responsibility for establishing and maintaining accounting and control systems in conformity with principles, standards, and requirements established by the Federal Accounting Standards Advisory Board and the Federal Financial Management Improvement Act of 1996.

Federal accounting provides the information needed for financial management as well as the information needed to demonstrate compliance with budgetary and other legal requirements. Thus, federal accounting is based on a two-track system. One track is a self-balancing set of proprietary accounts intended to provide information for management. The other track is a set of self-balancing budgetary accounts that assure that available budgetary resources and authori-

ties are not overexpended or overobligated and assist in budgetary reporting requirements.

Like its state and local government counterpart, the federal financial statements include an MD&A that provides a clear and concise description of the reporting entity and its mission, activities, program and financial results, and financial condition (OMB, 1996). Federal financial statements are less prescriptive than state and local financial statements because federal agencies are permitted significant latitude on the level of aggregation presented. The six statements in the federal financial report include a (1) balance sheet, (2) statement of net cost, (3) statement of changes in net position, (4) statement of budgetary resources, (5) statement of financing, and (6) statement of custodial activity.

(SEE ALSO: *Government Accounting Standards Board*; *Government Financial Reporting*)

BIBLIOGRAPHY

Federal Financial Management Improvement Act. (1996). Public Law 104-208.

Governmental Accounting Standards Board (GASB). (1987). *Objectives of Financial Reporting.* (Concept Statement No. 1). Norwalk, CT:

Governmental Accounting Standards Board (GASB). (1997). *Codification of Government Accounting and Financial Reporting Standards.* Norwalk, CT.

Governmental Accounting Standards Board (GASB). (1999). *Basic Financial Statements—and Management's Discussion and Analysis—for State and Local Governments* (Statement of Governmental Accounting Standard No. 34). Norwalk, CT.

Office of Management and Budget (OMB). (1996). *Bulletin 97-1*, Form and Content of Agency Financial Statements. U.S. Government, Washington. DC.

MARY L. FISCHER

GOVERNMENTAL ACCOUNTING STANDARDS BOARD

The Governmental Accounting Standards Board (GASB) was organized in 1984 under the auspices of the Financial Accounting Foundation to establish financial accounting and reporting standards for state and local government entities. These standards are important because external financial reporting can demonstrate financial accountability to the public. They are the basis for many legislative and regulatory decisions, as well as investment and credit policies. The foundation is responsible for selecting the seven members of GASB and its Advisory Council, funding their activities, and exercising general oversight. Except for the chairman of GASB, all members are part time.

GASB's mission is to establish and improve standards of state and local governmental accounting and financial reporting that will (1) result in useful information for users of financial reports and (2) guide and educate the public, including issuers, auditors, and users of those financial reports. To accomplish its mission, GASB acts to:

1. Issue standards that improve the usefulness of financial reports based on (a) the needs of financial report users, (b) the primary characteristics of understandability, relevance, and reliability, and (c) the qualities of comparability and consistency.

2. Keep standards current to reflect changes in the governmental environment.

3. Provide guidance on implementation of standards.

4. Consider significant areas of accounting and financial reporting that can be improved through the standard-setting process.

5. Improve the common understanding of the nature and purposes of information contained in financial reports.

GASB formulates and uses concepts to guide them in the development of their standards. These concepts provide a frame of reference for resolving accounting and financial reporting issues. This framework helps to establish reasonable bounds for judgment in preparing and using financial reports; it also helps the public understand the nature and limitations of financial reporting. GASB actively solicits and considers the views of its various constituencies on all accounting and financial reporting issues. GASB's activities are open to public participation and observation under "due process" procedures. These procedures are designed to permit timely, thorough, and open study of accounting and financial reporting issues. Consequently, broad public participation is encouraged in the accounting standard-setting process, which permits communication of all points of view and expressions of opinion at all stages of the process. Use of these procedures recognizes that general acceptance of the GASB conclusions is enhanced by demonstrating that the comments received during due process are considered carefully.

GUIDING PRINCIPLES

In establishing concepts and standards, the GASB exercises its judgment after research, due process, and careful deliberation. Some of the principles used by GASB are as follows:

1. One of GASB's overriding principles is that it *be objective and neutral in its decision making.* This principle ensures, as much as possible, that the information resulting from its standards is a faithful representation of the effects of state and local government activities. Objective and neutral means freedom from bias, precluding GASB from placing any particular interest above the interests of the many who rely on the information contained in financial reports.

2. Another primary principle is to *weigh carefully the views of its constituents in developing concepts and standards.* This permits GASB to (a) meet the accountability and decision-making needs of the users of government financial reports and (b) gain general acceptance among state and local government preparers and auditors of financial reports.

3. A third principle is to *establish standards only when the expected benefits exceed the*

perceived costs. GASB strives to determine that proposed standards (including disclosure requirements) fill a significant need and that the costs they impose, compared with possible alternatives, are justified when compared to the overall public benefit.

4. A fourth principle is to *consider the applicability of its standards* to the separately issued general-purpose financial statements of governmentally owned special entities. GASB specifically evaluates similarities of special entities and of their activities and transactions in both the public and private sectors, and the need, in certain instances, for comparability with the private sector.

5. A fifth principle is to *bring about needed changes in ways that minimize disruption of the accounting and financial reporting processes.* Reasonable effective dates and transition provisions are established when new standards are introduced. GASB considers it desirable that change should be evolutionary to the extent that can be accommodated by the need for understandability, relevance, reliability, comparability, and consistency.

6. A final principle is to *review the effects of past decisions for appropriateness.* This permits continual interpretation, amendment, or replacement of standards, when deemed necessary.

PUBLICATIONS

As of December 31, 1998, more than thirty financial accounting and reporting standards had been issued since GASB's inception. A standard pertaining to a new financial reporting model for state and local governments has been exposed and is expected to be issued in 1999 with an effective date in 2001. Copies of these standards, along with other GASB publications, can be obtained from the GASB offices at 401 Merritt 7, P.O. Box 5116, Norwalk, Connecticut 06856-5116. Their phone number is (203) 847-0700 and

their Web site is http://www.asb.org. GASB's Web site is a subpart of the FASB (Financial Accounting Standards Board) Web site.

OTHER FINANCIAL ACCOUNTING AND REPORTING STANDARD-SETTING BODIES

Additional standard-setting bodies for the public sector are as follows:

1. The *Federal Accounting Standards Advisory Board (FASAB)* was established in 1990 by the following three U.S. government principals: the Comptroller General, the Director of the Office of Management and Budget, and the Treasurer. FASAB's primary function is to make recommendations to the principals for financial accounting and reporting standards to be adopted for the U.S. federal government. More information is available from FASAB at 441 G Street NW, Suite 3B18, Washington, D.C. 20548; (202) 512-7350; or http://www.financenet.gov/fasab.htm.

2. The Public Sector Committee of the International Federation of Accountants (IFAC-PSC) assumed responsibility in 1998 for developing a set of financial reporting standards to be adopted worldwide by public sector entities. More information is available from IFAC-PSC at 535 Fifth Ave., 26th floor, New York, NY; (212) 286-9344; or http://www.ifac.org/Committees/PublicSector/index.html.

Standard-setting bodies for the private sector are as follows:

1. The *Financial Accounting Standards Board (FASB)* also falls under the auspices of the Financial Accounting Foundation. Its responsibilities are to set the financial accounting and reporting standards to be applied by U.S. businesses. FASB is co-located with GASB in Connecticut and their Website is http://www.fasb.org.

2. Financial accounting and reporting standards recommended for use by businesses throughout the world are established by

the *International Accounting Standards Committee (IASC)*. More information is available from IASC at 166 Fleet St., London EC4A 2DY, United Kingdom; +44 (171) 353-0565; or http://www.iasc.org.uk.

BIBLIOGRAPHY

Codification of Governmental Accounting and Financial Reporting Standards as of June 30, 1998. (1998). Norwalk, CT: Governmental Accounting Standards Board.

Freeman, Robert J., and Shoulders, Craig D. (1996). *Governmental and Nonprofit Accounting: Theory and Practice.* New Jersey: Prentice-Hall.

Wilson, Earl R., Hay, Leon E., and Kattelus, Susan C. (1999). *Accounting for Governmental and Nonprofit Entities.* New York: Irwin/McGraw-Hill.

JESSE W. HUGHES

GOVERNMENT AUDITING STANDARDS

Generally accepted government auditing standards (GAGAS)—informally known as the Yellow Book—are promulgated under the leadership of the comptroller general of the United States, who heads the U.S. General Accounting Office. The responsibility includes both establishing and revising these standards. The staff of the comptroller general's office is aided by the Advisory Council on Government Auditing Standards, whose members come from units of the federal and state governments, representatives of public accounting firms, and professors of accounting.

The first set of standards was issued in 1972; the second in 1988; the third in 1994. As of mid-2000, a review of the 1994 edition continues. The guidance in the 1994 edition continues to be in effect, except for changes contained in amendments. Two amendments have been issued as of early 2000. The amendments become effective once they are completed. All changes to the Yellow Book are initially presented in exposure draft so that interested parties can comment; these comments are considered in determining the adequacy of any change being proposed.

THE AUTHORITY OF GOVERNMENT AUDITING STANDARDS

The Yellow Book includes standards to guide all audits of governmental units, irrespective of the level of the unit. The standards are considered broad statements of auditors' responsibilities. The Introduction to the Yellow Book states its purpose as providing "standards for audits of government organizations, programs, activities, and functions, and of government assistance received by contractors, nonprofit organizations, and other nongovernment organizations" (Comptroller General of the United States, 1994).

Federal legislation established the requirement that all inspectors general comply with the GAGAS. Furthermore, inspectors general are responsible for assuring that nonfederal auditors also comply with these standards when they audit federal organizations, programs, activities, and functions. The Office of Management and Budget as well as the requirements of the Chief Financial Officers Act of 1990, the Single Audit Act of 1984, and other federal policies and regulations require the use of these standards in audits where federal funds are involved. The standards are recommended for use by state and local government auditors and public accountants in audits of state and local government organizations, programs, activities, and functions even though federal funds are not involved in some instances. A number of states and local audit organizations have officially adopted these standards.

THE NATURE OF AUDITS PERFORMED

GAGAS are provided for both financial and performance audits. The comprehensive guidance applies to the following:

- *Financial statement audits.* The statements included are the statement of financial position, results of operations, and cash flows, all of which are in conformity with generally accepted accounting principles. Financial statements audits also include audits of financial statements prepared in conformity with several other bases of accounting as established by auditing standards and related statements issued by the Auditing Standards Board of the American Institute of Certified Public Accountants.

- *Financial related audits.* Among such audits are those (1) involving financial information presented in accordance with established or stated criteria, (2) related to specific financial compliance requirements, (3) related to an entity's internal control over financial reporting and/or safeguarding of assets, and (4) involving compliance with laws and regulations and allegations of fraud. Also included are segments of financial statements, statement of revenue and expenses, statement of fixed assets, budget requests, and variances between estimated and actual financial performance.

- *Performance audits.* Such audits include systematic examination of relevant evidence to provide an independent assessment of the performance of a government organization, program, activity, or function. Also, economy and efficiency and program audits are included among performance audits. Such economy and efficiency audits may, for example, determine whether the entity is following sound procurement practices; is acquiring appropriate types of resources; is properly protecting and maintaining resources; is avoiding duplication of effort by employees; is avoiding idleness and overstaffing; is using efficient operating procedures; is using optimum amounts of resources; is complying with requirements of laws and regulations that could effect acquisition, protection, and use of resources; has an adequate management control system; and has reported measures of economy and efficiency that are reliable and valid. Program audits, for example, may assess whether the objectives of a program are proper, suitable, or relevant; and determine the extent to which a program is achieving its goals; identify factors inhibiting satisfactory performance; identify ways of making programs work better; and determine whether management has reported measures of program effectiveness that are valid and reliable.

Government audits may be a combination of financial and performance audit, as, for example, when auditors conduct audits of government contracts and grants with private-sector organi-

zations as well as government and not-for-profit organizations where both financial and performance objectives must be audited.

GOVERNMENT AUDITING STANDARDS FOR FINANCIAL AUDITS

Standards are classified as general, field, and reporting. The GAGAS incorporate the generally accepted auditing standards as promulgated by the Auditing Standards Board of the American Institute of Certified Public Accountants. However, there are some additional standards that relate to the accountability of government units for compliance with laws and regulations. There are also more extensive reporting requirements related to such accountability.

General standards relate to qualifications of staff assigned to conduct an audit, to the need for the audit entity to be organizationally independent and the individual auditors to maintain independent in attitude and in appearance and to exercise due professional care in the work related to an audit, and to the need for the audit organization to have an appropriate internal quality control system that is externally reviewed at least every three years.

Field standards incorporate the three field standards as established by the Auditing Standards Board, which relate to planning, understanding internal control, and obtaining sufficient evidential matter. Additional standards relate to following up on known material findings and recommendations from previous audits; to designing the audit to provide reasonable assurance of detecting material misstatements related to irregularities and/or direct and material illegal acts; and to detecting noncompliance with provisions of contracts or grant agreements that have a direct and material effect on the financial statements. There is also a field standard related to the need to prepare adequate working papers.

Reporting standards incorporate the four reporting statements of the Auditing Standards Board. Additionally, there are standards that deal with communication with audit committee; disclosure of the fact that the audit was performed in accordance with generally accepted government auditing standards; and disclosures related to compliance with laws and regulations regarding on internal control, privileged and confidential information, and report distribution.

GOVERNMENT AUDITING STANDARDS FOR PERFORMANCE AUDITS

The general standards are the same for financial and performance audits as discussed earlier. Field and reporting standards for performance audits overlap to some extent with those for financial audits.

Field standards are related to (1) planning; (2) supervision; (3) design of the audit when laws, regulations, and other compliance requirements are significant to the audit objective; (4) understanding of management controls when relevant to the audit; and (5) sufficient, competent, relevant evidence.

Reporting standards are related to (1) preparation of written reports that communicate results; (2) appropriate issuance; (3) reporting audit objectives as well as scope and methodology; (4) the need for a complete, accurate, objective, convincing, and clear and concise report; and (5) report distribution.

AMENDMENTS TO GOVERNMENT AUDITING STANDARDS

As of mid-2000 there were two amendments to the Yellow Book. Amendment No. 1, "Documentation Requirements When Assessing Control Risk at Maximum for Controls Significantly Dependent upon Computerized Information Systems," and Amendment No. 2, "Auditor Communications."

Amendment No. 1 relates to an additional fieldwork standard requiring documentation in the planning of financial statements of the basis for assessing control risk at the maximum level for assertions related to material account balances, transaction classes, and disclosure components of financial statements when such assertions are significantly dependent on computerized information systems. The Advisory Council on Government Auditing Standards recommended this new standard as a way of

tightening the rigor applied to an audit of the financial statements when computerized information systems are used for significant accounting applications. Prior to the implementation of this standard, auditors were not required to document their assessment of control risk at maximum; only if the assessment was below maximum was support to be included in the working papers. This new standard, Amendment No. 1, became effective for financial statement audits of periods ending on or after September 30, 1999.

Amendment No. 2 adds a fieldwork standard and amends a report standard for financial statement audits. The purpose is the improvement of auditor communication concerning the auditor's work on compliance with laws and regulations and internal control over financial reporting. In the report, the auditor is to emphasize the importance of the reports on compliance with laws and regulations and internal control over financial reporting when these reports are issued separately from the report on financial statements. This amendment is effective for financial statements audits of periods ending on or after January 1, 2000.

The review of government auditing standards continued in progress as of mid-2000. The General Accounting Office staff monitors the effectiveness of the guidance provided to auditors. Review of audits that are alleged to be defective in some respects leads to an assessment of the adequacy of guidance. Furthermore, changes in standards and statements issued by the Auditing Standards Board, changes in the structure of organizations, and the need to more sharply focus auditor responsibility lead to reconsideration of audit guidance.

Audits of financial status and of programs provided by various government agencies are critical to assuring accountability and adequate management. Those audits are reported publicly. The quality of the audits as well as of the reporting is related to the adequacy of the generally accepted government auditing standards.

(SEE ALSO: *Auditing; United States General Accounting Office*)

BIBLIOGRAPHY

Comptroller General of the United States. (1999). *Auditor Communication. Government Auditing Standards. Amendment No. 2.* Washington, D.C: United States General Accounting Office.

Comptroller General of the United States. (1999). *Documentation Requirements When Assessing Control Risk at Maximum for Controls Significantly Dependent upon Computerized Information Systems. Amendment No. 1.* Washington, DC: United States General Accounting Office. May.

Comptroller General of the United States. (1994). *Government Auditing Standards (the Yellow Book).* Washington, DC: United States General Accounting Office. U.S. Government Accounting Office. http://www.gao .gov.

U.S. Government Accounting Office. www.gao.gov.

BERNARD H. NEWMAN
MARY ELLEN OLIVERIO

GOVERNMENT FINANCIAL REPORTING

Government financial reporting is the process whereby governments report their financial position and activities to the public at large. These reports are the standard that citizens, oversight bodies, and other stakeholders use to judge their government's efficiency, effectiveness, and overall financial condition. This article examines government financial reporting from a historical perspective, and today; it also looks at contemporary issues and possible future trends.

HISTORY

Government financial reporting evolved through the twentieth century. The National Committee on Municipal Accounting (NCMA) was established in 1934 by the Government Finance Officers Association (GFOA) and began to promulgate formal standards. It issued the first "blue book" in 1936, Bulletin No. Six, *Municipal Accounting Statements* (GFOA, 1988). From that point, government financial reporting, along with government accounting and auditing, began to develop into what it is today.

The National Council on Governmental Accounting (NCGA), which succeeded the NCMA, initiated the basic format of the current blue book, which was later officially titled *Governmental Accounting, Auditing and Financial Reporting* (GAAFR). In 1968, generally accepted accounting principles (GAAP) for government were established in GAAFR (GFOA, 1988). Government accountants and financial managers use the blue book to this day as a reference for current standards and practices in government financial reporting.

In the past, some confusion existed concerning who set the standards that constituted GAAP for governments. This issue became prominent when the American Institute of Certified Public Accountants (AICPA) issued an industry audit guide in 1974 that, while endorsing most, modified some principles set forth by the NCGA (GFOA, 1988). The AICPA later recognized NCGA Statement No. One, *Governmental Accounting and Financial Reporting Principles.* Even after this statement was recognized, questions still arose. Conflicts with the standards set by the NCGA generally were associated with pronouncements issued by the Financial Accounting Standards Board (FASB). These conflicts were not resolved until the Government Accounting Standards Board (GASB) was established in 1984 (GFOA, 1988). From then on, the GASB was clearly established as the primary authority for setting government standards.

The GASB was created as a five-member board under the Financial Accounting Foundation (FAF). In addition to the GASB, the FAF also established the Governmental Accounting Standards Advisory Council (GASAC) to advise the GASB of its members' views and those of the organizations they represent. The GASAC assists the FAF in approving appointments of GASB members.

FINANCIAL REPORTING TODAY

Generally, government financial reporting is the process of communicating information concerning a government's financial position and activities. Financial information is often dispersed through financial reports. Government financial

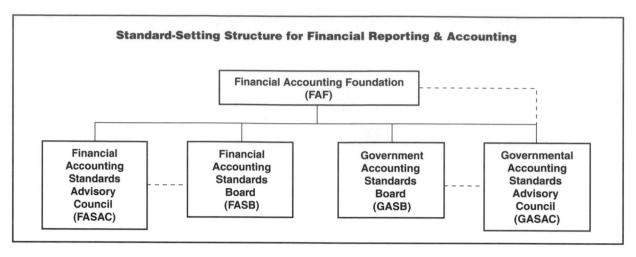

Standard-Setting Structure for Financial Reporting & Accounting

Financial Accounting Foundation
(FAF)

| Financial Accounting Standards Advisory Council (FASAC) | Financial Accounting Standards Board (FASB) | Government Accounting Standards Board (GASB) | Governmental Accounting Standards Advisory Council (GASAC) |

Table 1

reports have several uses: They can be used to compare actual financial results against the legally adopted budget; assess financial condition and results of operations; assist in determining compliance with finance-related laws, rules, and regulations; and assist in evaluating efficiency and effectiveness (GFOA, 1988). Although government financial reports cannot meet the needs of every user, they can be used in a myriad of ways to assess accountability and make effective decisions.

The GASB has the responsibility of establishing and improving financial reporting standards at the state and local government levels. Three primary user categories of government financial reports exist: citizens, legislative and oversight bodies, and investors and creditors (GFOA, 1988). The executive branch and subordinate bureaus/agencies are not identified as primary users because they have the ability to obtain this information from other sources (GFOA, 1988).

At the federal level, financial reporting wasn't required until 1996. The Chief Financial Officers (CFO) Act of 1990 was the initial legislative element requiring the federal government to provide reliable, audited financial information to taxpayers, elected officials, appointed officials, and other stakeholders. Consequently, the Federal Accounting Standards Advisory Board (FASAB) was established in October of 1990 to consider and recommend accounting principles

for the federal government. The CFP Act of 1990 was expanded in 1994 and required the federal government's twenty-four major agencies to provide annual financial statements beginning with those for fiscal year 1996.

Although various internal and supplemental financial reports exist, the most common is the comprehensive annual financial report (CAFR). The GASB's 1987 *Codification of Governmental Accounting and Financial Reporting Standards* states that "every government should prepare and publish as a matter of public record, a comprehensive annual financial report" (section 2200.101) The CAFR normally contains three distinct sections: introductory, financial, and statistical. These sections can be supplemented with other specialized sections as necessary.

Government financial reporting should assist in fulfilling government's duty to be publicly accountable by providing users of these reports with the means to evaluate the operating results of a government and assess the level of service(s) it provides. It is imperative that these reports be reliable, understandable, relevant, and timely in order to enable informed citizens, legislators, and other stakeholders to hold government fiscally accountable.

CONTEMPORARY ISSUES/THE FUTURE

There seems to be a current trend toward fiscal discipline in government that has generated a demand for better information on which to base decisions. Consequently, state and local governments must change their financial reporting from basic stewardship reports on the various government funds to a more corporate-style report that offers analysis of the long-term impact of financial management decisions (Klasney and Williams, 2000). Currently, from annual financial reports, state and local governments focus on the individual "funds" of government. These reports can be difficult for readers of financial statements to understand because the number of funds can run into the dozens or hundreds. As a result of GASB Statement No. Thirty-Four, financial reports must begin to include comprehensive information about the cost of providing government services and show all of a government's liabilities and assets, including infrastructure (Allen, 1999). This new approach calls for governmentwide reporting, enhanced fund reporting, and management's discussion and analysis (MD&A).

The concept of governmentwide reporting is the most dramatic change in the new approach. This is a significant move because, until now, government followed only the modified-accrual basis of accounting. The change is important to potential lenders and taxpayers because of the need to capitalize and depreciate general capital assets or infrastructure (Klasney and Williams, 2000). Information concerning infrastructure will include the cost and anticipated life of roads, bridges, sewer and water systems and other capital assets. Since state and local governments invest $1 out of every $10 dollars ($140 billion to $150 billion annually) in the construction, improvement, and rehabilitation of capital assets, that information should be very interesting to local taxpayers (Allen, 1999).

The elements of fund reporting have not changed much. Fund categories will continue to apply their current measurement focus and basis of accounting; however, reporting fund types (such as special revenue and capital projects) is no longer required for governmental funds in the basic financial statements. The new approach will also establish two new fund types—permanent

funds (governmental) and private-purpose trust funds (fiduciary). Governments must provide a summary reconciliation to the governmentwide financial statements at the bottom of fund financial statements or in a separate schedule. This will be an extensive undertaking for government funds because of the difference in the measurement focus and basis of accounting (Klasney and Williams, 2000). In addition to governmentwide reporting and enhanced fund reporting, each government entity's financial management will now present an MD&A as required supplementary information before the basic financial statements. In response to users' demand for a summary of a government's operations and financial situation, the GASB expanded the number of issues that the MD&A must address. They include the following:

- An objective discussion of the basic financial statements and condensed financial information comparing current and prior years
- An analysis of the overall financial position and results of operations
- An analysis of balances and transactions of individual funds
- An analysis of significant variations between the original and final budget and the final budget and actual results for the general fund
- A description of significant capital asset and long-term debt activity during the year
- Known facts, decisions or conditions expected to have a significant impact on financial position or results of operations (Klasney and Williams, 2000).

The implementation of this new approach to government financial reporting will be challenging at best. Some governments will find themselves gathering information they haven't tracked before and, in some cases, reconstructing information as far back as twenty-five years (GASB, 1999). This is precisely why the GASB established a phased implementation plan based on each government's total revenues (Klasney & Williams, 2000). Implementation will begin on June 30, 2002, for the largest governments (at least $100 million in revenues), with one additional year for medium-sized governments ($10 million to $100 million), and two additional years for smaller governments (less than $10 million) (Allen, 1999; GASB, 1999). Although implementation may be rigorous, this new method is essential for enabling decisionmakers to overcome the challenges of a new, global society.

SUMMARY

The process of government financial reporting evolved during the twentieth century. The blue book, or GAAFR, was established and continues as the primary reference for government financial reporting standards at the state and local levels. The Government Accounting Standards Board (GASB) was established in 1984 and is the authority for setting those standards. The Federal Accounting Standards Advisory Board (FASAB) was established in 1990 and prescribes financial reporting standards at the federal level. Citizens and other stakeholders use government financial reports to assess a government's performance and overall financial position in order to hold that government accountable for its actions. The most common type of government financial report is the comprehensive annual financial report (CAFR). A current trend toward fiscal discipline is the driving force behind many contemporary issues. Chief among these issues is the GASB requirement that all state and local government financial reports begin to include information concerning capital assets and debts. This changes the essence of government financial reports from basic fund stewardship to comprehensive, corporate-style reporting.

(SEE ALSO: *Government Accounting; Government Accounting Standards Board; Government Auditing Standards*)

BIBLIOGRAPHY

Allen, Tom. (1999). "GASB Issues New Reporting Rules." *American City and County*, 114 (8): 8.

Government Accounting Standards Board (GASB). (1987). *Codification of Governmental Accounting and Financial Reporting Standards.* Stanmford, CT: Author.

Government Accounting Standards Board (GASB) (1999). "GASB Overhauls Reporting Model". *Journal of Accountancy* 188 (2): 4.

Government Finance Officers Association (GFOA). (1988). *Governmental Accounting, Auditing and Financial Reporting.* Chicago: Author.

Klasney, Edward M., and Williams, James M. (2000). "Government Reporting Faces an Overhaul". *Journal of Accountancy*, 189 (1): 49.

ROBERT J. MURETTA, JR.

GOVERNMENT ROLE IN BUSINESS

Government regulation at the federal and state levels has a major impact on how businesses operate in the United States. In order to manage business activities in a complex society and to help respond to changing societal needs, governments at all levels have created numerous regulatory agencies. Although the duties and functions of each agency vary, all influence the day-to-day business activities that take place within the United States. Businesses that take a proactive stance toward understanding and complying with federal regulatory agencies will minimize their chance of fines, prosecution, or other regulatory action. Therefore, it is in the best interest of businesses to maintain healthy relationships with regulatory agencies at all levels of government. Among the business activities regulated by government are competitive practices, industry-specific activities, general issues of concern, and monetary regulations.

COMPETITIVE PRACTICES

A number of laws have been passed to protect competitive practices. Among these laws are the Sherman Antitrust Act of 1890, the Federal Trade Commission Act of 1914, and the Wheeler-Lea Act of 1938.

Sherman Antitrust Act of 1890. One of the earliest pieces of legislation that had a critical effect on the business sector was the Sherman Antitrust Act of 1890, passed by Congress in response to public outrage over a few large companies that were forcing their smaller competitors out of business and becoming monopolies. Since there was no competition, consumers were left with higher prices and usually a lower-quality product. The act had two main sections attempting to prevent the formation of monopolies. Specifically, section one maintained that forming a trust or a conspiracy resulting in the restraint of trade was illegal. Section two provided that persons monopolizing or attempting to monopolize trade were guilty of a misdemeanor. Basically, the federal government was (and is) looking for companies engaging in price fixing, in dividing up the market share among different companies to control the market, or in other business practices that may create a monopoly.

The Justice Department is the federal agency responsible for enforcing the act. By prosecuting individuals and companies violating provisions of the law, imposing fines and jail time, or calling for injunctions, the Justice Department prevents monopolies from forming. The act also allows injured parties, usually other businesses, to file suit and get relief from the federal courts for infractions of the law. The Justice Department also reviews almost every large merger or acquisition that affects the U.S. marketplace. If the Justice Department opposes a proposed merger, companies involved in the transaction can try to work out an agreement to allay the government's concerns or oppose the Justice Department in federal court, asking a judge to rule on the merits of the case. Most companies planning a merger or takeover normally have their legal departments conduct exhaustive research in order to answer potential questions from the Justice Department. The primary reason for this research is to avoid a long legal fight with the government that is expensive and can cause significant delays in the proposed merger or takeover.

Federal Trade Commission Act of 1914. The Federal Trade Commission Act of 1914 created the Federal Trade Commission (FTC), which consists of five members with staggered terms of seven years each. Board members are nominated by the president and confirmed or rejected by the Senate. One person serves as the chairperson of the commission and guides the agency's daily operations. The FTC was originally created to enforce the provisions of the Sherman Antitrust and Clayton Acts. The FTC has the power to investigate unfair competitive practices on its own. Firms may also petition the FTC to investigate alleged unfair competitive practices of which it might otherwise be unaware. The agency can hold public hearings to investigate the alleged infractions, and it may also issue cease-and-desist orders when it believes unfair competitive business practices are being used. Since the enforcement powers of the FTC and Justice Department overlap, the two agencies often work together to solve problems.

Wheeler-Lea Act of 1938. Congress responded to public complaints about improper and deceptive advertising by passing the Wheeler-Lea Act of 1938, which empowered the FTC to investigate businesses that engage in deceptive business activities or companies that use misleading or less than truthful advertising to entice consumers into their stores. A common deceptive practice that some companies have used in the past is called "bait and switch." This practice refers to advertising a product at an extremely low price to draw customers into a store but in reality having very little or none of the product available. Store employees then attempt to sell customers a more expensive product. This is but one example of what the FTC may investigate.

INDUSTRY-SPECIFIC FEDERAL AGENCIES

Federal legislation has created agencies to monitor and regulate particular industries because of concern over industry-specific practices, among them the Interstate Commerce Commission, the Federal Communications Commission, and the Food and Drug Administration.

Interstate Commerce Commission (ICC). In 1887, Congress passed legislation creating the Interstate Commerce Commission. Originally, only railroads were regulated, but as modern transportation methods developed, other transportation modes were added to its list of responsibilities. The primary purpose of the ICC was to monitor railroad companies (prices charged) that may have had a monopoly in some parts of the country. The commission could take corrective action, such as price modification, if it found that a railroad or other interstate business was engaging in monopolistic business activities and charging high prices for its services. Since this act applied to a limited number of industries, Congress later passed the Sherman Antitrust Act of 1890 (discussed earlier) to provide a much broader coverage of monopolies regardless of industry.

Federal Communications Commission (FCC). The FCC monitors and regulates CB radio, radio, telegraph, telephone, and television operations. It has broad powers to set acceptable standards for television regarding language, nudity, violence, or other material that may be perceived as inappropriate by the general public. For example, television shows that are adult-oriented or contain violence are typically on late in the evening so that children are less likely to see them. In addition, television shows often warn viewers about their content through a rating system; since the rating is displayed on the screen, viewers can make an informed decision before watching a particular program.

The FCC also has the power to fine broadcast companies that use inappropriate language in their programming. Since most television and radio stations know what are considered acceptable standards, fines are rarely issued. When fines are issued, however, a television or radio station may take the FTC to federal court to appeal the decision. Broadcast companies that fight the FCC over a show's content normally argue that the First Amendment gives them the right to broadcast the contested material.

Food and Drug Administration (FDA). The FDA is responsible for ensuring the safety of cosmetics, drugs, and food. One of the most important functions of the agency is new drug approval. The FDA requires pharmaceutical companies to provide detailed scientific data regarding new drugs prior to approval. Specifically, the FDA will review the potential benefits and negative side effects of all proposed drugs. The agency reviews the information submitted by the pharmaceutical company and may also conduct its own tests if additional study is deemed needed. The FDA is extremely important to the business community because if it rejects a new drug, the pharmaceutical company developing it cannot sell it. FDA regulators must balance the interests of the general public with those of the pharmaceutical company. The FDA does not endorse new drugs; rather, it approves them, stating that they are thought to be safe.

GENERAL FEDERAL REGULATORY AGENCIES

Federal legislation has also created agencies addressing a broad range of issues, including the Equal Employment Opportunity Commission, the Occupational Safety and Health Administration, the Environmental Protection Agency, and the Consumer Product Safety Commission.

Equal Employment Opportunity Commission (EEOC). The Civil Rights Act of 1964 prohibits discrimination on the basis of race, color, creed, sex, or national origin. This law applies to almost every private company, nonprofit organization, and government employer, although some exceptions were granted to religious corporations, Indian tribes, and private-membership clubs. The Civil Rights Act also created the Equal Employment Opportunity Commission.

The original purpose of the EEOC was to monitor and enforce the provisions of the Civil Rights Act. Its powers were enhanced in 1972 with passage of the Equal Employment Act, which gave the EEOC the power to file civil lawsuits in federal court and to represent a person filing a grievance. Prior to filing the suit in federal court, the EEOC must first try to settle the case out of court with the alleged offending company—an attempt to promote a more conciliatory approach to solving discrimination problems and to reduce the number of court cases. The company could agree, for example, to settle the complaint by paying a fine, ordering remedial steps to prevent further discrimination, and/or working out the problem for the original complainant. In large cases, the EEOC may work with the Civil Rights Division of the Justice Department in order to settle the problem.

Occupational Safety and Health Administration (OSHA). Enacted in 1970, the Occupational Safety and Health Administration, was designed to ensure safe and healthy working conditions in nearly every environment. OSHA's basic premise is that employers must provide a work environment that is safe and free from hazards that may cause harm or death to their employees. In addition, employers are obligated to follow occupational safety and health standards that are ordered by the secretary of labor (OSHA falls under this department). Employers are given written guidelines so they know specific OSHA rules and regulations.

In order to verify that organizations are complying with these regulations, OSHA can conduct surprise inspections. Technically, employers can ask OSHA to show a search warrant before the search is executed, but this is not normally done because OSHA can get a warrant relatively quickly. OSHA investigators may inspect the building, but an employer has the right to have a representative accompany the regulators during the tour. The investigators review accident records and other documents to verify that compliance has been maintained. OSHA investigators also observe employees to verify that guidelines set by the agency are followed (e.g., wearing eye protection). If OSHA investigators believe that violations have occurred, they can issue citations against the employer. If the employer agrees to pay a fine, OSHA will normally inspect the building at a later date to ensure compliance. If an employer believes that the fine or other sanction is inappropriate, a court order can be sought seeking relief from the fine or sanction. In rare instances, the secretary of labor may ask for an injunction against an employer. Injunctions are only sought in the most serious cases, such as those in which there is imminent danger to employees.

Environmental Protection Agency (EPA). One of the most pressing issues in the United States is protecting the environment. A combination of pressure from consumer groups, news media, and voters encouraged Congress to pass legislation creating the Environmental Protection Agency in 1972. Prior to the creation of the EPA, no single federal agency had control over environmental issues, resulting in fragmented enforcement and confusing or conflicting codes. The EPA was created to act as the focal point regarding all pollution issues (air, noise, water, etc.).

In recent years, Congress has passed several laws addressing a host of environmental issues (e.g., noise, pesticide, radiation, and water pollution). When Congress passes a new law regarding the environment, it is the EPA's job to enforce its provisions with the powers contained in the legislation. One example of the EPA's power is that it can set acceptable air-quality standards for a state. If air-quality standards are not met within a specified frame of time, fines or other punitive measures may be imposed on the offending state.

Consumer Product Safety Commission (CPSC). Another powerful federal agency was created in 1972 under the Consumer Product Safety Act. The law created the Consumer Product Safety Commission, which was intended to protect consumers from defective and dangerous products. In addition, Congress also wanted to unify the majority of laws regarding product safety (except food, automobiles, and other products already regulated by federal agencies) so that they would be effective and clear. The CPSC is very powerful; it can ban products without a court hearing if they are deemed dangerous and can order recalls, product redesigns, and the inspection of production plants. In more severe cases, the CPSC may also charge officers, managers, and/or supervisors with criminal offenses.

FEDERAL MONETARY REGULATORY AGENCIES

Several federal agencies have been established to monitor monetary practices in the United States, including the Securities and Exchange Commission, the Federal Reserve Board, and the Federal Deposit Insurance Corporation.

Securities and Exchange Commission (SEC). The SEC was established to regulate the securities industries in the United States. A quasi-regulatory and judicial agency, the SEC regulates publicly traded stock-offering companies by requiring them to issue annual and other financial reports. In addition, the SEC regulates the stock market, brokers who sell securities, and large investment firms. The SEC also looks for insider trading, such as trading on secret knowledge about a company, other white-collar crime that may affect a company's stock price, and securities fraud by stockbrokers. The agency can initiate civil or criminal action against the individual or firms charged with securities violations. Depending on the circumstances, the penalties levied by the SEC can be severe, with large fines and long jail terms being the norm. The SEC normally works closely with the Justice Department when criminal prosecution is involved. As always, the SEC's actions can be appealed to the federal courts if the individual or firm believes the charges are inaccurate or unjust.

Federal Reserve Board As the United States grew, the nation's banking system became more complex and subject to greater fluctuations without government regulation. The United States experienced an acute money panic in 1907 that put a severe strain on the banking system. As a result of the financial panic, a National Monetary Commission was established by Congress to study how the United States could protect the banking system and, in turn, the money supply. National Monetary Commission recommendations were implemented by Congress in 1913 when the Federal Reserve Act was passed and the Federal Reserve Board was established. The primary purpose of the Federal Reserve Board is to function as a semi-independent board designed to protect the banking system in the United States.

Federal Reserve Board activities are guided by a board of governors. The board has seven members, all of whom are nominated by the president and confirmed or rejected by the Senate. Each member is appointed to a fourteen-year term, with vacancies occurring about every two years. To be nominated to the Federal Reserve Board, an individual must possess excellent academic credentials, be an established leader in the financial world, and have achieved an impeccable business reputation. In order to separate the Board from political influences and to ensure that all decisions are based on economic rather than political issues, Board members are appointed and will likely serve through several presidential administrations. The Board is headed by the chairperson, who is considered to be the most powerful banker in the world. As such, the chairperson directs the overall mission of the Board and consults regularly with the president, secretary of the treasury, banking executives, stock market representatives, and top banking regulators from other countries to coordinate financial policy.

Federal Deposit Insurance Corporation (FDIC). Created after the Great Depression of the 1930s, the FDIC insures each account up to $100,000 in the event of a bank failure. In return for this protection, participating banks, credit unions, and other financial institutions must pay premiums, which the FDIC uses to build up funds for any future bailouts.

SUMMARY

Government regulations and agencies at all levels of government have had a major impact on how businesses operate. In order to manage business activities in a complex, ever-changing society, governments at all levels have created numerous regulatory agencies through the legislative process. Although the duties and function of agencies vary, all influence day-to-day business practices. Frequently regulated business activities include competitive practices, industry specific activities, general issues of concern, and monetary regulations.

BIBLIOGRAPHY

Boone, L. E., and Kurtz, D. L. (1992). *Contemporary Marketing*, 7th ed. New York: Dryden/Harcourt Brace.

Brue, S., and McConnell, C. (1999). *Economics*, 14th ed. New York: McGraw-Hill.

Churchill, G., and Peter, J. P. (1998). *Marketing: Creating Value for Customers*, 2d ed. Boston: Irwin/McGraw Hill.

Dickson, P. R. (1994). *Marketing Management*. New York: Dryden/Harcourt Brace.

Kotler, P., and Armstrong, G. (1991). *Principles of Marketing*, 8thd ed. Englewood Cliffs, NJ: Prentice-Hall.

ALLEN D. TRUELL
MICHAEL MILBIER

GROSS DOMESTIC PRODUCT (GDP)

Led by the auto industry, the United States economy grew rapidly in the 1920s, generating more jobs, more income, and more free time that the American consumer had in order to spend. As long as people were employed, paying for goods and services, there was really no need to measure how the economy was doing. However, in the 1930s, the American economy went bust and a frustrated Congress asked if there was any way to measure the depth of the Great Depression.

On January 4, 1934, economist Simon Kuznets, professor at the University of Pennsylvania, sent to the Senate a report entitled "National Income: 1929-1932," the first accounting of U.S. productivity, essentially the gross national product (GNP). More than 4500 copies of this report were sold in just eight months. The basic concept that Kuznet had was to limit this accounting measurement to the marketplace, and thus to the amount that consumers paid for goods and services. Until 1992, the term *GNP* was used to refer to the total dollar value of all finished goods and services produced for consumption in society during a particular period of time (usually one year). In 1992 the Commerce Department began to compute gross domestic product (GDP) instead of GNP. The differences between the two are slight and involve how to count earning of assets owned by foreigners.

GNP counts the earnings in the homeland of the owner of the asset, while GDP counts the earnings of a manufacturer in the country in which the assets exists. For the United States, there is virtually no difference between the two measures.

There are three basic components that determine the U.S. GDP:

1. Consumption, the amount that consumers pay for goods (durable and non-durable).

2. Investment, the amount of money spent on new production facilities, that is, plants and facilities.

3. Services, the amount that consumers pay for the services they use.

Several things were not included in GNP and subsequently in GDP:

- Work that is provided in an economy by nonmarket transactions such as homemakers and military personnel. These factors were too difficult for Kuznets and his team to measure.

- Illegal activities such as gambling and drug trafficking. These factors are also difficult to estimate; in addition Kuznets excluded them from GNP because he deemed them a "disservice" to the economy.

- Goods and services that are bartered. These were excluded because they cannot be measured.

- Sale of intermediate goods (raw materials).

- Sale of used goods (used cars, furniture, etc.).

- Purely financial transactions such as sale of stocks and bonds.

- Imports (goods made outside the United States).

The GDP is the ultimate benchmark that measures the expansion and contraction of the U.S. multitrillion dollar national economy. It covers everything that is produced and sold in the marketplace. Bankers, investment brokers, and government officials use the GDP to determine such things as interest rates, investment opportunities, and tax rates. The GDP is not the only measure of output, however; economists use GDP because it is the most comprehensive of

Product and Prices

Goods	Year 1		Year 2	
	Output	Prices	Output	Prices
Balls	10 balls	$50 per ball	10 balls	$55 per ball
Bats	10 bats	$25 per bat	12 bats	$25 per bat
Gloves	10 gloves	$25 per glove	9 gloves	$30 per glove

Table 1

output measures. This measure is important because it helps societies understand both inflation and employment.

In the flow of payments in the economy, *where* does one measure? Consider, for example, an automobile. The mining operator receives an income from the sale of iron ore, the mill owner receives income from the sale of finished steel, and the automobile manufacturer receives income from the sale of the finished car. In order to avoid the inaccuracy of counting the same money three times, Kuznets decided to use only final sales; thus the amount paid to the dealer for the car is the only amount used in calculating GDP. The labor cost of the workers at all three locations is added to GDP. In essence, the price of the automobile includes the cost of the materials purchased from suppliers. The value added to manufacture the automobile can be found by deducting the cost of one product from the total cost of the automobile.

The more goods and services a country produces, the healthier that country's economy becomes. There is a major flaw in measuring economic success, however, in that when GDP (production) increases, negative externalities (air and water pollution) also increase. The environment becomes degraded and negatively affects the quality of life. GDP measures goods and services traded, but the negative externalities are not included in this counting; however, these negative externalities increase GDP. For example, when the automobile industry wants to produce more cars, the smoke that is emitted from the smokestacks includes carcinogens that may make people in the area sick. A person who gets sick

from the emitted smoke may go to the doctor. The doctor may prescribe medication. The cost of the visit to the doctor and the cost of the medication are added to the total value of GDP.

Table 1 contains output and price statistics for a simple economy that produces only three goods. In the first year, the value of output, or GDP, is $1000; in the second year, the GDP is $1120. These numbers are obtained by multiplying quantities by prices and then summing the resulting values. They give us current dollar or nominal GDP, that is, the value of output measured in prices that existed when the output was produced.

GDP has risen by 12 percent from the first year to the second, but this increase is only partially due to additional output ($1120 − $1000 = $120). Part of the increase is due to changes in prices. To get a measure that contains only the increase in output, we can multiply the outputs of the second year by the prices of the first year. When we add up these values, they total $1025. This number implies that if only the quantities of output had changed and not the prices, GDP would have increased only from $1000 to $1025, a rise of only 2.5 percent. This $1025 is real GDP.

BIBLIOGRAPHY

Eggert, James. (1997). *What is Economics*, 4th ed. Mountain View, CA: Mayfield Publishing Company.

"GDP: Gross Domestic Product." http://www.dismal.com/toolbox/dict_gdp.stm. (1999).

"Gross Domestic Product." http://131.93.13.212/econ/Measuring/GNP1.html. (1999).

Mansfield, Edwin, and Behravesh, Nariman. (1992). *Economics USA*, 3rd ed. New York: Norton.

Mings, Turley, and Marlin, Matthew. (2000). *The Study of Economics: Principles, Concepts, and Applications*, 6th ed. Dushkin/McGraw-Hill.

"Narrative." http://www.subjectmatters.com/indicators/HTMLSrc/Trainging/Indicators/GNP.html. (1999).

"PP Presentation: Gross Domestic Product." http://sorell.humboldt.edu/~economic/econ104/macto/ppt/tsld002.html. (1999).

Wilson, J. Holton, and Clark, J. R. (1997). *Economics.* Cincinnati, OH: International Thomson Publishing.

GREGORY P. VALENTINE

H

HARDWARE

The concept of inventing hardware to assist in commercial productivity is not new. For example, thousands of years ago the Chinese sought greater efficiency in calculating numbers, leading to the invention of the abacus, a hand-held mechanical device. Another hardware milestone was reached when Charles Babbage, in 1822, proposed a machine that would calculate mathematical tables; much of his design was used in later computers (Long and Long, 1999). Herman Hollerith designed a method to store numbers onto punched cards in order to calculate the 1890 census, and the company he founded eventually became IBM Corporation (Long and Long, 1999).

THE COMPUTER ERA BEGINS

The first electronic computer, the ENIAC, was developed at the University of Pennsylvania in 1946. It used vacuum tubes and weighed thirty tons. Remington Rand Corporation produced the first commercial computer, the Univac, in 1951, which also used transistors (Long and Long, 1999). Transistors replaced vacuum tubes, were far smaller, and used less power than tubes. Transistors were shortly thereafter replaced by integrated circuits, which further minimized size and lessened power requirements. The availability of integrated circuits made the first personal computer possible in 1977 when Stephen Jobs and Steve Wozniak introduced the "Apple II"

(Long and Long, 1999). IBM offered their first microcomputer in 1981, and Apple's Macintosh was introduced in 1984. The Macintosh was the first popular computer with a graphical user interface (GUI), and it also had a laser printer that could combine text and pictures (Long and Long, 1999). A GUI operating system receives input from both the keyboard and a pointing device (mouse). This type of system was a boon to computer users who were not proficient or comfortable with keyboarding, and today most personal computers require the use of a mouse.

CLASSIFICATIONS AND DEFINITIONS OF COMPUTERS

There are three main classifications of computers: mainframe, minicomputer, and microcomputer. The major categories can only be used as general guidelines because of the huge variety in product lines. Computer "servers" have also been included in this discussion because of their important role in networking and Internet applications.

A mainframe computer is any large computer system, such as that used by the Internal Revenue Service. Another typical use of a mainframe computer would be for an airline ticketing system, which can have thousands of users connected to one computer. The next smaller-sized computer is termed a minicomputer. It is of medium scale and can serve up to several hundred users. The microcomputer is the smallest in size

Steve Jobs (left) and Steve Wozniak (right).

[The CPU is] the computing part of the computer. Also called the processor, it is made up of the control unit and ALU. Today, the CPUs of almost all computers are contained on a single chip. The CPU, clock and main memory make up a computer. A complete computer system requires the addition of control units, input, output and storage devices and an operating system.

Micro, or personal, computers use microprocessors that run at approximately 500 megahertz per second. Mainframe computers measure their speed in millions of instructions per second.

Random Access Memory Random access memory (RAM) consists of microchips that allow for the temporary storage of data. RAM functions as the workspace for the CPU. The "workspace" temporarily holds the program and the active calculation before deriving an outcome. One example would be using a word processor's spelling check tool on a document. The words being checked and the program would be temporarily stored in RAM.

Input Devices Computers receive information from a variety of sources. The most common input device is a keyboard, but the pointing device (mouse or trackball) is equally important with today's GUI interface. Other input devices include video cameras, scanners, microphones, digital cameras, CD-ROMs, and voice commands that operate the computer.

Output Devices The computer monitor is an output device that is changing rapidly. For several decades computer screens only displayed letters or numbers onto a green or amber screen. As computers began using GUIs, the display device took on greater significance. The success of Apple's Macintosh computer with the graphical user interface caused Microsoft to come out with their GUI, called the Windows Operating System. Thus, all current operating systems use GUI and color for both print and images.

The standard monitor for many years has been a cathode-ray tube (CRT). CRT monitors are still very common, and they are capable of high-quality pictures. However, they are inherently bulky and relatively heavy. Portable compu-

and power, and the term is "generally synonymous with personal computer, such as a Windows PC or Macintosh, but it can refer to any kind of small computer" (CMP Net Online Encyclopedia). Microcomputers can also be portable, and some have Pentium processors, fourteen-inch color screens, and multi-gigabyte hard drives. Very small computers include hand-held units and pen computers that store information the user enters with a stylus rather than a keyboard (Hutchinson and Sawyer, 1998).

A "server" computer is one that is used to connect a cluster of personal computers through using a local area network (LAN). World Wide Web pages are also stored on a "Webserver," which is typically a dedicated personal computer.

COMPUTER COMPONENTS

Central Processing Unit (CPU) The CPU is at the heart of all computers. All data passes through it. According to the *CMP Net Online Encyclopedia:*

ters became possible only when smaller and lighter-weight and display units became available. Current portable or laptop computers use LCD (liquid crystal display) panels, which are flat. LCD panels are now also being used for desktop monitors. LCD units cost about three times what comparable CRT units do, but they occupy far less space and have a very bright picture.

Computer projectors are commonly used to display data or information onto a large screen. This setup can be used to demonstrate programs, provide visuals for training, or show Web sites to large groups of people. Many businesspeople travel with both a portable computer and a computer projector to visually display information for training or to aid in sales.

The GUI and the general popularity of computers have caused significant changes in the hardware available for printing. The earliest printers were essentially automatic typewriters and had little flexibility. Today, there are a wide variety of printers currently available that are capable of nearly professional-quality output.

Laser printers, which first became available in the early 1980s, had an inherent advantage over earlier computer printers; that is, the laser beam could place tiny ink dots anywhere on the page. In practice, this means that laser printers can print fonts of any size or typeface. Further, they can print text in any direction and also print pictures. Current laser printers print at a very crisp 1200 dots per square inch and are considered to be very reliable. Color laser printers are also available, though they are much slower and also more expensive than black-and-white printers.

Ink-jet printers essentially spray ink onto the paper. They are normally very quiet, are relatively inexpensive, and have high-quality output. Further, all the newest ink-jet printers offer reasonably high-quality color printing. Both the increased use of the Internet to download color pictures and the prevalence of digital cameras have significantly increased the popularity of color ink-jet printers.

Connection Devices Partially because of the popularity of the Internet, more and more computers of all kinds have some means of connecting to other computers. For desktop computers in schools and businesses, a network interface card (NIC) is frequently used. Portable computers and home desktop units typically use a modem as a connection device. Modems connect a personal or portable computer to dial-up networks through a regular telephone line. This connectivity has served as a boon to telecommuting and changed the way work is performed in organizations. Modems and NICs can serve as both input and output devices, depending on whether the computer is receiving or sending information.

Sound Cards and Speakers Today, any multimedia computer contains a device to reproduce sound. Typically this means that computers have a sound card that contains a mini-amplifier and connects to speakers. Sounds can also come from programs, from the Internet, and from participants in desktop teleconferences. A sound card can also function as an input device when it utilizes a microphone.

Storage Devices The number and size of storage devices are increasing. Floppy disks are portable, but they can store only a relatively small amount of information compared to the newest storage units, Zip® disks, which are also portable and small. A Zip® disk has about a hundred times the storage capacity of a floppy disk. Hard drives are internal storage devices that hold the computer's operating system, the application software, and other files.

A LOOK TO THE FUTURE

Computers have become a critical component of the workplace, home, and school. As we look toward the future, some trends are emerging based on the past few decades of hardware development. It is highly probable that computer hardware will become even smaller, lighter in weight, more portable, and less expensive. Keyboards may even become obsolete as voice-activation equipment becomes more sophisticated. It is also likely that there will be a greater degree of connectivity within and between systems on a global basis, as well as between home to work.

There is an increasing emphasis in elementary and secondary schools on the use of technology to access information and change the way students learn. We will see new generations of students entering the work force with surprisingly sophisticated computer skills and, perhaps, less fear of new hardware and change in general. The foreseeable future holds the promise of more and more integration of work and home by means of computers.

BIBLIOGRAPHY

CMP Net Online Encyclopedia. (1999). http://www.techweb .com/encyclopedia/.

Forcier, R. (1996). The Computer as a Productivity Tool in Education. Boston: Merrill.

Hutchinson, S., and Sawyer, S. (1998). Computers, Communications, and Information. Boston: Irwin/McGraw-Hill.

Long, L., and Long, N. (1999). Computers. Upper Saddle River, NJ: Prentice-Hall.

ARMAND SEGUIN
CYNTHIA SHELTON SEGUIN

HAWTHORNE STUDIES

(SEE: Motivation)

HEALTH ISSUES IN BUSINESS

Health issues in business are as critical today as they were in the mid-twentieth century. Many of the injuries and illnesses have changed but their impact is no less dramatic. The increased use of computers and job specialization have contributed to a new generation of occupational hazards, especially repetitive motion injuries, also known as cumulative trauma disorders. These are injuries caused by repetitive hand, arm, or finger motions that cause tendons to swell and become progressively more painful. In advanced cases, workers lose the strength in their thumb and fingers and eventually become unable to com- plete simple tasks, such as lifting a baby or tying their shoes. Cumulative trauma disorders were the most common type of illness reported in 1997, accounting for 64 percent of the 430,000 cases of illness reported (Herington and Morse, 1995).

Every five seconds a worker is injured on the job, and every ten seconds a worker is temporarily or permanently disabled. The estimated cost for injuries alone is $121 billion annually (Herington and Morse, 1995). This cost includes lost productivity and wages, administrative expenses, and health care. In reality, these costs may be much higher. It is virtually impossible to pinpoint exact costs due to the lack of accurate statistics on workplace injury and illness. There is no comprehensive, integrated national system for collecting data on occupational injury, illness, and fatalities. Another factor contributing to inconsistent data is the reluctance of many companies to report incidents for fear of being targeted by the Occupational Safety and Health Administration for on-site inspections.

FEDERAL AGENCIES

There are two federal agencies designed to operate in the occupational health and safety arena: the Occupational Safety and Health Administration (OSHA) and the National Institute for Occupational Safety and Health (NIOSH). Both were created by the same act in Congress in 1970; however, each has a very distinct purpose. OSHA, which is part of the Department of Labor, is responsible for developing and enforcing rules and regulations in regards to workplace health and safety. NIOSH, which is part of the Department of Health and Human Services, is a research agency, identifying the causes of work-related disability and injury as well as potential hazards of new technology and practices.

During the 1990s, OSHA was criticized for being an agency of red tape that had lost sight of its original mission "to assure as far as possible every working man and woman in the nation safe and healthful working conditions." Historically, OSHA agents have been compensated for the number of violations they have found at job sites.

This has created an environment in which citations are given for all violations regardless of how small, causing employers to fear OSHA rather than seek its help with health and safety issues. Until recently, OSHA has not promoted partnerships with companies to solve health- and safety-related issues in the workplace. This did begin to change under the Clinton administration. OSHA now offers companies a choice between a partnership or a traditional enforcement relationship. The companies who choose to go into partnership with OSHA work with the agency to develop health and safety programs. OSHA recognizes the companies that truly commit to the new partnership by reducing or eliminating workplace hazards through a more lenient inspection policy, priority assistance, and reductions in penalties up to 100 percent. By involving both the companies and the workers, a more collaborative relationship has developed that has initiated better workplace practices and solutions to health and safety issues. OSHA has also committed to focus on the greatest hazards and most dangerous workplaces and to update confusing rules and regulations.

The National Institute of Occupational Health and Safety, whose primary role is research, has developed the National Occupational Research Agenda (NORA), which identifies the top twenty-one health and safety research areas on which to focus its work through 2009 (see Table 1). The agenda was developed in collaboration with numerous stakeholders, including employers, employees, and labor organizations. Research areas were chosen based on the greatest needs and the areas most likely to produce the greatest overall gains to workers and industry as a whole. NIOSH is not able to tackle all of these alone. It must be a collaborative effort with the entire health and safety community.

LEGISLATION

Two acts passed in recent years have had a significant impact on people who have experienced an occupational illness or sickness. The first is the Americans with Disability Act, passed in July 1990. This act, which applies to employers with more than fifteen employees, prohibits discrimination against people with disabilities. Under this act, an employee is entitled to certain rights regarding employment upon returning from disability leave and proving the ability to perform the essential functions of the job. The employer is required to provide "reasonable accommodation" when necessary, that is, to change work schedules, adjust equipment, or modify tasks to enable the employee to continue to perform the job held prior to taking the disability leave. Reasonable accommodation is required except when the employer can prove that it would cause undue hardship on its part. Another option is to transfer the worker to another position within the company.

The second act is the Family Medical Leave Act (FMLA), which was enacted in August 1993 and applies to employers with fifty or more employees. Employees who have worked for employers in this category longer than one year are entitled to take up to twelve weeks of unpaid leave annually for certain medical or family situations, including suffering from a serious health condition themselves. The FMLA requires employers to guarantee employees who take a leave the right to return to an equivalent job, that is, the pay, benefits, and other terms and conditions of employment must be equivalent. This provides employees who are temporarily disabled with job security.

THE ROLE OF WORKERS' COMPENSATION LAWS

The original purpose of workers' compensation laws was to protect employers as well as employees in cases of occupational injury or illness. Employers were protected from lawsuits initiated by employees seeking restitution for workplace illness or injury, and employees were compensated for the cost of medical care in addition to lost wages. Today, most private employers are required to have workers' compensation insurance, with the exception of employers in New Jersey, South Carolina, and Texas.

Workers' compensation insurance is no-fault. In other words, regardless of who is at fault (the

The National Occupational Research Agenda

Category	Priority Research Areas
Disease and Injury	Allergic and Irritant Dermatitis Asthma and Chronic Obstructive Pulmonary Disease Fertility and Pregnancy Abnormalities Hearing Loss Infectious Diseases Low Back Disorders Musculoskeletal disorders of the Upper Extremities Traumatic Injuries
Work Environment and Workforce	Emerging Technologies Indoor Environment Mixed Exposures Organization of Work Special Populations at Risk
Research Tools and Approaches	Cancer Research Methods Control Technology and Personal Protective Equipment Exposure Assessment Methods Health Services Research Intervention Effectiveness Research Risk Assessment Methods Social and Economic Consequences of Workplace Illness and Injury Surveillance Research Methods

Table 1

worker, employer, or neither), the employer is responsible for compensating the worker for health care and lost wages. The employee's responsibility is to notify the employer as soon as an injury or illness occurs. Today, workers' compensation issues have become extremely complex because what is considered a compensable illness or injury (warranting restitution by the employer) varies considerably from state to state. The most liberal state is California, where any disease alleged to be aggravated by work-related stress could be compensable. This liberal approach can distort statistical data and also discourage employers from reducing workplace hazards. It also makes it extremely difficult to control the costs of workers' compensation insurance.

PREVENTION

Employers play a vital role in the prevention of workplace injuries and illnesses. They are responsible for evaluating workplace injuries to discover possible causes and for developing prevention strategies for those injuries. Other employer responsibilities include safety and hazard training, drug testing, workstation evaluations, and enforcement of the use of protective equipment. Employers have an array of resources from which to draw when analyzing workplace hazards and developing health and safety programs. These include industrial hygienists, certified safety professionals, federal and state OSHA programs, and NIOSH.

Ergonomics also plays a significant role in the prevention of workplace injuries and illness. Ergonomics is the science of designing and arranging tools and equipment to fit workers. The overall goal is to prevent workplace illness and injuries that result from poor workstation design or improperly designed equipment. Workstation evaluations are an example of an ergonomic program that many large companies employ. During this evaluation, a health and safety professional evaluates a worker performing daily tasks at his or her workstation. The health and safety professional observes the worker in order to evaluate the "fit" of the workspace, furniture, and equipment to the worker. In the case of a worker who spends the majority of the day at a computer, the professional would look at several factors to determine the degree to which the workstation fits. These factors include the height and position of the computer screen and keyboard in reference to the worker's body posture, the height and position of the worker's chair, and the types of movements the worker makes while performing tasks. From this evaluation, changes may be made to alleviate discomfort and prevent harmful injuries. Early intervention is the key to preventing potentially disabling injuries. In addition to the evaluation, the health and safety professional gives the worker advice on how to sit, how to position hands on the keyboard, and how often to take breaks.

There are no comprehensive ergonomic standards in force in the United States today. In February 1999, OSHA proposed its first draft of ergonomics standards. Proponents believe it will help control the large numbers of musculoskeletal disorders (disorders involving both muscle and skeleton, such as back pain and neck strain). These disorders account for 34 percent of all lost workday injuries and illnesses and cost $15 billion to $20 billion dollars annually in workers' compensation costs, according to the Bureau of Labor Statistics. Business groups object to the federally imposed standards, saying that the standards will be a "blank check" for OSHA inspectors and will require all American businesses to become full-time experts in ergonomics. In addition, the U.S. Chamber of Commerce points out that there are presently (1) no scientifically established standards for what is "overuse" and (2) no existing studies that demonstrate the connection between ergonomic adjustments and injury prevention. While the connection does seem to make sense, it must be admitted that more studies need to be done before meaningful standards can be established.

A final critical element in the prevention of workplace injuries and illnesses is the development of health and safety programs designed to train and educate workers on workplace hazards. OSHA recommends the following elements for a comprehensive health and safety program:

- Management leadership and commitment
- Meaningful employee participation
- Systematic hazard identification and control
- Employee and supervisor training
- Medical management and program evaluation

In conclusion, the prevention of occupational injuries and illnesses is a collaborative effort involving employers, employees, federal and state agencies and health and safety professionals. The field of occupational safety and health is extremely broad and complex.

BIBLIOGRAPHY

Bureau of Labor Statistics. http://stats.bls.gov/.

Herington, Thomas N., and Linda H. Morse, eds. (1995). *Occupational Injuries*. St. Louis, MO.

National Occupational Research Agenda (NORA) http://www.cdc.gov/niosh/images/table1.gif.

Rosenstock, Linda, and Cullen, Mark R. (1994). *Textbook of Clinical Occupational and Environmental Medicine*. Philadelphia, Pa.: Saunders.

U.S. Department of Health and Human Services, National Institute for Occupational Safety and Health. http://www.cdc.gov/niosh/.

U.S. Department of Labor, Occupational Safety and Health Administration. http://www.osha.gov.

BRENDA J. REINSBOROUGH

HUMAN RELATIONS

Owners and managers of profit and nonprofit organizations define human relations as fitting people into work situations so as to motivate them to work together harmoniously. The process of fitting together should achieve higher levels of productivity for the organization, while also bringing employees economic, psychological, and social satisfaction. Human relations covers all types of interactions among people—their conflicts, cooperative efforts, and group relationships. It is the study of why our beliefs, attitudes and behaviors sometimes cause interpersonal conflict in our personal lives and in work-related situations.

One of the most significant developments in recent years has been the increased importance of interpersonal skills in almost every type of work setting. For many employers, interpersonal skills represent an important category of transferable skills a worker is expected to bring to the job. Technical ability only is usually not enough to achieve career success. Studies indicate that many people who have difficulty in obtaining or holding a job possess the needed technical competence but lack interpersonal competence.

HUMAN RELATIONS MOVEMENT

Problems in human relations are not new—cooperative efforts carry the potential for conflicts among people. It is only within the past few decades that management has recognized that human relations can have considerable impact on organizational productivity. During this period, the human relations movement has matured into a distinct and important field of study.

Although it is difficult to pinpoint exactly when the human relations movement began, most researchers agree that the earliest developments emerged in the mid-1800s. In the beginning, the focus was mainly on improving efficiency, motivation, and productivity. But over time, this research became more involved with redefining the nature of work and perceiving workers as complex human beings.

Prior to the Industrial Revolution, most work was performed by individual craftworkers. Generally, each worker saw a project through from start to finish. Skills such as tailoring, carpentry, or shoemaking took a long time to perfect and were often a source of pride to an individual. Under this system, however, output was limited.

The Industrial Revolution had a profound impact on the nature of work and the role of the worker. Previously, an individual tailor could make only a few items of clothing in a certain time period; factories could make hundreds. Employers began to think of labor as another item in the manufacturing equation, along with raw materials and capital.

Employers at that time did not realize how workers' needs affected productivity. As a result, few owners or managers gave much thought to working conditions, safety precautions, or worker motivation. Hours were long and pay was low.

Around the turn of the century, Frederick Taylor and other researchers interested in industrial problems introduced the concept of scientific management. They believed that productivity could be improved by breaking down a job into isolated, specialized tasks and assigning each of those tasks to specific workers. The development of scientific management coincided with the revolutionary concept of mass production. Eventually it paved the way for the assembly line.

Taylor's work was sharply criticized by those who believed it exploited workers. Employees were treated as a commodity, as interchangeable as the parts they produced. Taylor thought that by increasing production, the company would end up with a larger financial pie for everyone to share. Management would earn higher bonuses; workers would take home more pay. He did not foresee that his theories would be applied in ways that dehumanized the workplace.

In the late 1920s, Elton Mayo and other researchers from Harvard University initiated what have become known as the Hawthorne Studies at the Hawthorne plant of Western Electric Company near Chicago. The purpose of the investigation was to explore the relationship between changes in physical working conditions and employee productivity. Specifically, Mayo was interested in the effect of different intensities of light on employee output. In one experiment, ample light was provided to a group of six female workers. Later, the amount of light was significantly reduced; but instead of productivity decreasing, as was expected, it actually increased.

The researchers attributed the phenomenon to what has since become known as the Hawthorne effect—employees who participate in scientific studies may become more productive because of the attention they receive from the researchers. This discovery became important in the human relations movement because it has been interpreted to mean that when employees feel important and recognized, they exhibit greater motivation to excel in their work activities.

HUMAN RELATIONS AS A FIELD OF STUDY

Human relations is an interdisciplinary field because the study of human behavior in organizational settings draws on the fields of communications, management, psychology, and sociology. It is an important field of study because all workers engage in human relations activities. Several trends have given new importance to human relations due to the changing workplace.

The labor market has become a place of constant change due to the heavy volume of mergers, buyouts, a labor shortage, closings, and changing markets. These changes have been accompanied by layoffs and the elimination of product lines. Even those industries noted for job security have recently engaged in layoffs. As the United States attempts to cope with rapid technological change and new competition from international companies, there is every reason to believe that we will see more volatility in the labor force. Interpersonal skills will be even more critical in the future.

Organizations are developing an increasing orientation toward service to clients. Relationships are becoming more important than physical products. Restaurants, hospitals, banks, public utilities, colleges, airlines, and retail stores all must now gain and retain patronage. In any service firm, there are thousands of critical incidents in which customers come into contact with the organization and form their impressions of its quality and service. Employees must not only be able to get along with customers; they must also project a favorable image of the organization they represent.

Most organizations recognize improved quality is the key to survival. The notion of quality as a competitive tool has been around for many years, but today it is receiving much more attention. In a period of fierce competition, a consumer may not tolerate poor quality. Human beings are at the heart of the quality movement because workers are given the power and responsibility to improve quality.

Companies are organizing their workers into teams in which each employee plays an important role. If team members cannot work together, the goals of the organization will suffer. In some cases, workers are cross-trained so they can do the work of others, if necessary.

The demographics of the workplace are also changing. Diversity is more and more typical. In the years ahead, a large majority of those entering the work force will be women and minorities. Passage of the American with Disabilities Act in 1990 opened the employment door to more people with physical or mental impairments. And in the future, we will see increased employment of the population over age sixty-five. Within this heterogeneous work force, we will find a variety of values and work habits. Supervisors will need to become skilled at managing diversity.

The leaders in today's work force need different skills to be successful. The current generation of workers is better educated and better informed, and it also has higher expectations. They seek jobs that give not only a sense of accomplishment but also a sense of purpose. They want jobs that provide meaningful work. Today's managers must therefore shift from manager as order-giver to manager as facilitator. They must also learn how to assume the roles of teacher, mentor, and resource person.

Few lines of work will be immune from these trends. Today's employee must be flexible and adaptable in order to achieve success within a climate of change. It is important for everyone to develop those interpersonal skills that are valued by all employers.

UNDERSTANDING HUMAN BEHAVIOR

Mental perceptions are influenced by everything that has passed through an individual's mind. That includes all of a person's experiences, knowledge, biases, emotions, values, and attitudes. No two people have identical perceptions because no two people have precisely the same experiences.

Mental perceptions may sometimes lead to conflict. Each person has formed mental perceptions relating to a number of controversial issues. For example, most workers have an opinion on abortion and capital punishment, among other issues. When proponents and opponents clash in voicing mental perceptions of controversial issues, conflict occurs. If the issue is one pertinent to the workplace, such as affirmative action, human values have the potential to lead to problems.

Ethics also play a role in interpersonal conflict. Ethics refer to moral rules or values governing the conduct of a person or group. Perhaps more than anything else, an individual's adherence to values related to what is morally right determines the respect that others hold for that person. Lack of respect for one individual by another is likely to lead to poor human relations between the two.

The social dimension of behavior is determined by a person's personality, attitudes, needs, and wants. An individual's personality is the totality of complex characteristics, including behavior and emotional tendencies, personal and social traits, self-concept, and social skills. The objective of many training sessions for employees and supervisors is to improve a person's ability to get along with others. A person's personality has a major impact on human relations skills.

People reveal their attitudes through their personality. An attitude is a mental position one possesses with regard to a fact, issue, or belief. Attitudes that often present problems in the workplace are those that concern biased and prejudiced viewpoints. Generally, employees who possess positive attitudes and who are open-minded are judged to have more desirable personalities than those with negative attitudes who hold biased viewpoints.

COMMUNICATION

Perhaps the single most important aspect of designing any work environment is the plan that links all workers and supervisors with multiple channels of communication. Good communication may be cited as the most important component of sound human relations. Despite the recognition of the importance of communication, it presents one of the most difficult and perplexing problems faced in modern organizations.

Even in small organizations, where only a few people are involved, sound communication is difficult to establish. When an organization expands in numbers, as well as in diversity among its members, the establishment of communication channels becomes even more difficult. Good communication is essential for the smooth functioning of any organization. Managers need clear lines of communication to transmit orders and policies, build cooperation, and unify groups. Employees must be able to convey their concerns or suggestions and feel that management has heard them. Clear communication among coworkers is vital to good teamwork, problem solving, and conflict management. In short, effective human relations is founded on good communication.

When people in organizations want to send messages, conduct meetings, or communicate person to person, they have many options. With increased use of voice mail, e-mail, fax machines, and videoconferencing, it is a wonder people have time to read all the incoming information, let alone interpret and respond to it.

Costly communication breakdowns are a prime factor in organizational problems ranging from high employee turnover to low productivity. Poor communication also takes a toll in employee injuries and deaths, particularly in industries where workers operate heavy equipment or handle hazardous materials.

Although some communication breakdowns are inevitable, many can be avoided. Employees who are treated with respect, are empowered to think for themselves, and feel a sense of loyalty are more apt to communicate openly with other workers and leaders throughout the organization.

TYPES OF RELATIONSHIPS

Human relations occurs on several levels. Individuals interact in a variety of settings—as peers, subordinates, and supervisors. No matter what the setting, relationships are built. All types of groups exist in an organization. Formal groups are officially designated, while informal groups are formed unofficially by the members themselves. Some would argue the informal groups have more power. In either situation, important human relationships are taking place.

Employees relate to their work group, other formal groups, and informal groups. The norms set by a group can greatly influence a person's behavior. Dress and language are two examples. Considering the number of groups in today's complex organizations, the influence is unlimited.

The organization provides an opportunity for individual satisfaction. To achieve such satisfaction, and to continue as a successful member in the organization, the individual must comply with organizational policies, procedures, and rules. The organization requires certain behaviors from its employees. The rewards for such behaviors are demonstrated in the form of raises, promotions, and continued employment. When the organization promotes an employee, it is relating to the individual.

Today's complex organizations depend on dividing the work among many formalized groups. Informal groups will also emerge, either positively or negatively affecting organizational outcomes. The relationship between organizations and groups must also be considered when quotas or standards are established. The acceptance or rejection of such standards illustrates the interaction between the organization and the group.

One also has a relationship to one's self. Are you happy with yourself? Are you happy with your relationships with others? With the organization? With your future? If not, perhaps you should analyze your relationship with yourself.

Managers and supervisors achieve results through people. Therefore, today's complex organizations require managers and supervisors to display a concern for people. The successful leader creates an effective balance between people and productivity, and recognizes human relations as the key ingredient transforming organizational plans into organizational results. Although it is often misunderstood, effective human relations will lead to success.

Human relations is not limited to supervisors—it applies to every employee in an organization. Statistics indicate that successful people competently practice interpersonal skills, while the incompetent are left behind. Fortunately, these skills can be developed.

Good relationships must be built among individuals and within groups of an organization. Although this is not an easy task, success without good human relations in not possible. Every individual must be prepared to meet the challenge.

BIBLIOGRAPHY

Wray, Ralph, Luft, Roger, and Highland, Patrick. (1996). "*Fundamentals of Human Relations: Applications for Life and Work*". Cincinnati, OH: Southwestern Publishing.

PATRICK J. HIGHLAND

HUMAN RESOURCE MANAGEMENT

Humans are an organization's greatest assets; without them, everyday business functions such as managing cash flow, making business transactions, communicating through all forms of media, and dealing with customers could not be completed. Humans and the potential they possess drive an organization. Today's organizations are continuously changing. Organizational change impacts not only the business but also its employees. In order to maximize organizational effectiveness, human potential—individuals' capabilities, time, and talents—must be managed. Human resource management works to ensure that employees are able to meet the organization's goals.

"Human resource management is responsible for how people are treated in organizations. It is responsible for bringing people into the organization, helping them perform their work, compensating them for their labors, and solving problems that arise" (Cherrington, 1995, p. 5). There are seven management functions of a human resources (HR) department that will be specifically addressed: staffing, performance appraisals, compensation and benefits, training and development, employee and labor relations, safety and health, and human resource research.

Generally, in small organizations—those with fewer than a hundred employees—there may not be an HR department, and so a line manager will be responsible for the functions of HRM. In large organizations—those with a hundred employees or more—a human resource manager will coordinate the HRM duties and report directly to the chief executive officer (CEO). HRM staff in larger organizations may include *human resource generalists* and *human resource specialists*. As the name implies, an HR generalist is routinely involved with all seven HRM functions, while the HR specialist focuses attention on only one of the seven responsibilities.

Prior to discussing the seven functions, it is necessary to understand the job analysis. An essential component of any HR unit, no matter the size, is the *job analysis*, which is completed to determine activities, skills, and knowledge required of an employee for a specific job. Job analyses are "performed on three occasions: (1) when the organization is first started, (2) when a new job is created, and (3) when a job is changed as a result of new methods, new procedures, or new technology" (Cherrington, 1995).

Jobs can be analyzed through the use of questionnaires, observations, interviews, employee recordings, or a combination of any of these methods. Two important tools used in defining the job are (1) a *job description*, which identifies the job, provides a listing of responsibilities and duties unique to the job, gives performance standards, and specifies necessary machines and equipment; and (2) the *job specification*, which states the minimum amount of education and experience needed for performing the job (Mondy and Noe, 1996).

STAFFING

Both the job description and the job specification are useful tools for the staffing process, the first of the seven HR functions to be discussed. Someone (e.g., a department manager) or some event (e.g., an employee's leaving) within the organization usually determines a need to hire a new employee. In large organizations, an *employee requisition* must be submitted to the HR department that specifies the job title, the department, and the date the employee is needed. From there, the job description can be referenced for specific job-related qualifications to provide more detail when advertising the position—either internally, externally, or both (Mondy and Noe, 1996).

Not only must the HR department attract qualified applicants through job postings or other forms of advertising, but it also assists in screening candidates' resumes and bringing those with the proper qualifications in for an interview. The final say in selecting the candidate will probably be the line manager's, assuming all Equal Employment Opportunity Commission (EEOC) requirements are met. Other ongoing staffing responsibilities involve planning for new or changing positions and reviewing current job analyses and job descriptions to make sure they accurately reflect the current position.

PERFORMANCE APPRAISALS

Once a talented individual is brought into an organization, another function of HRM comes into play—creating an environment that will motivate and reward exemplary performance. One way to assess performance is through a formal review on a periodic basis, generally annually, known as a *performance appraisal* or *performance evaluation*. Because line managers are in daily contact with the employees and can best measure performance, they are usually the ones who conduct the appraisals. Other evaluators of the employee's performance can include subordinates, peers, group, and self, or a combination of one or more (Mondy and Noe, 1996).

Just as there can be different performance evaluators, depending on the job, several appraisal systems can be used. Some of the popular appraisal methods include (1) ranking of all employees in a group; (2) using rating scales to define above-average, average, and below-average performance; (3) recording favorable and unfavorable performance, known as critical incidents; and (4) managing by objectives, or MBO (Mondy and Noe, 1996).

Cherrington (1995) illustrates how performance appraisals serve several purposes, including: (1) guiding human resource actions such as hiring, firing, and promoting; (2) rewarding employees through bonuses, promotions, and so on; (3) providing feedback and noting areas of improvement; (4) identifying training and development needs in order to improve the individual's performance on the job; and (5) providing job-related data useful in human resource planning.

COMPENSATION AND BENEFITS

Compensation (payment in the form of hourly wages or annual salaries) and *benefits* (insurance, pensions, vacation, modified workweek, sick days, stock options, etc.) can be a catch-22 because an employee's performance can be influenced by compensation and benefits, and vice versa. In the ideal situation, employees feel they are paid what they are worth, are rewarded with sufficient benefits, and receive some intrinsic satisfaction (good work environment, interesting work, etc.). Compensation should be legal and ethical, adequate, motivating, fair and equitable, cost-effective, and able to provide employment security (Cherrington, 1995).

TRAINING AND DEVELOPMENT

Performance appraisals not only assist in determining compensation and benefits, but they are also instrumental in identifying ways to help individuals improve their current positions and prepare for future opportunities. As the structure of organizations continues to change—through downsizing or expansion—the need for training and development programs continues to grow. Improving or obtaining new skills is part of another area of HRM, known as training and development.

"*Training* focuses on learning the skills, knowledge, and attitudes required to initially perform a job or task or to improve upon the performance of a current job or task, while *development* activities are not job related, but concentrate on broadening the employee's hori-

zons" (Nadler and Wiggs, 1986, p. 5). *Education,* which focuses on learning new skills, knowledge, and attitudes to be used in future work, also deserves mention (Nadler and Wiggs, 1986).

Because the focus is on the current job, only training and development will be discussed. Training can be used in a variety of ways, including (1) orienting and informing employees, (2) developing desired skills, (3) preventing accidents through safety training, (4) supplying professional and technical education, and (5) providing supervisory training and executive education (Cherrington, 1995).

Each of the training methods mentioned has benefits to the individual as well as to the organization. Some of the benefits are reducing the learning time for new hires, teaching employees how to use new or updated technology, decreasing the number and cost of accidents because employees know how to operate a machine properly, providing better customer service, improving quality and quantity of productivity, and obtaining management involvement in the training process (Cherrington, 1995). When managers go through the training, they are showing others that they are taking the goals of training seriously and are committed to the importance of human resource development.

The type of training depends on the material to be learned, the length of time learners have, and the financial resources available. One type is instructor-led training, which generally allows participants to see a demonstration and to work with the product first-hand. On-the-job training and apprenticeships let participants acquire new skills as they continue to perform various aspects of the job. Computer-based training (CBT) provides learners at various geographic locations access to material to be learned at convenient times and locations. Simulation exercises give participants a chance to learn outcomes of choices in a nonthreatening environment before applying the concept to real situations.

Training focuses on the current job, while development concentrates on providing activities to help employees expand their current knowledge and to allow for growth. Types of development opportunities include mentoring, career counseling, management and supervisory development, and job training (Cherrington, 1995).

EMPLOYEE AND LABOR RELATIONS

Just as human resource developers make sure employees have proper training, there are groups of employees organized as unions to address and resolve employment-related issues. Unions have been around since the time of the American Revolution (Mondy and Noe, 1996). Those who join unions usually do so for one or both of two reasons— to increase wages and/or to eliminate unfair conditions. Some of the outcomes of union involvement include better medical plans, extended vacation time, and increased wages (Cherrington, 1995).

Today, unions remain a controversial topic. Under the provisions of the Taft-Hartley Act, the *closed-shop arrangement* states employees (outside the construction industry) are not required to join a union when they are hired. *Union-shop* arrangements permit employers to hire non-union workers contingent upon their joining the union once they are hired. The Taft-Hartley Act gives employers the right to file unfair labor practice complaints against the union and to express their views concerning unions (Cherrington, 1995).

Not only do HR managers deal with union organizations, but they are also responsible for resolving collective bargaining issues—namely, the contract. The contract defines employment-related issues such as compensation and benefits, working conditions, job security, discipline procedures, individuals' rights, management's rights, and contract length. Collective bargaining involves management and the union trying to resolve any issues peacefully—before the union finds it necessary to strike or picket and/or management decides to institute a lockout (Cherrington, 1995).

SAFETY AND HEALTH

Not only must an organization see to it that employees' rights are not violated, but it must also provide a safe and healthy working environment. Mondy and Noe (1996) define *safety* as "protecting employees from injuries caused by work-related accidents" and *health* as keeping "employees free from physical or emotional illness" (p. 432). In order to prevent injury or illness, the Occupational Safety and Health Administration (OSHA) was created in 1970. Through workplace inspections, citations and penalties, and on-site consultations, OSHA seeks to enhance safety and health and to decrease accidents, which lead to decreased productivity and increased operating costs (Cherrington, 1995).

Health problems recognized in the workplace can include the effects of smoking, alcohol and drug/substance abuse, AIDS, stress, and burnout. Through employee assistance programs (EAPs), employees with emotional difficulties are given "the same consideration and assistance" as those employees with physical illnesses (Mondy and Noe, 1996, p. 455).

HUMAN RESOURCE RESEARCH

In addition to recognizing workplace hazards, organizations are responsible for tracking safety- and health-related issues and reporting those statistics to the appropriate sources. The human resources department seems to be the storehouse for maintaining the history of the organization— everything from studying a department's high turnover or knowing the number of people presently employed, to generating statistics on the percentages of women, minorities, and other demographic characteristics. Data for the research can be gathered from a number of sources, including surveys/questionnaires, observations, interviews, and case studies (Cherrington, 1995). This research better enables organizations to predict cyclical trends and to properly recruit and select employees.

CONCLUSION

Research is part of all the other six functions of human resource management. With the number of organizations participating in some form of international business, the need for HRM research will only continue to grow. Therefore, it is important for human resource professionals to be up to date on the latest trends in staffing, performance appraisals, compensation and benefits, training and development, employee and labor relations, and safety and health issues—both in the United States and in the global market.

One professional organization that provides statistics to human resource managers is the Society for Human Resource Management (SHRM), the largest professional organization for human resource management professionals. Much of the research conducted within organizations is sent to SHRM to be used for compiling international statistics.

BIBLIOGRAPHY

Cherrington, David J. (1995). *The Management of Human Resources.* Englewood Cliffs, NJ: Prentice-Hall.

Mondy, R. Wayne, and Noe, Robert M. (1996). *Human Resource Management.* Upper Saddle River, NJ: Prentice-Hall.

Nadler, Leonard, and Wiggs, Garland D. (1986). *Managing Human Resource Development.* San Francisco: Jossey-Bass.

CHRISTINE JAHN